DAY CARE: SCIENTIFIC
AND SOCIAL POLICY ISSUES

DAY CARE

Scientific and Social Policy Issues

Edited by

EDWARD F. ZIGLER
Yale University

EDMUND W. GORDON
Yale University

Under the auspices of
The American Orthopsychiatric Association

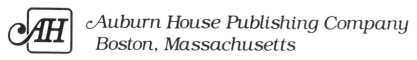

Auburn House Publishing Company
Boston, Massachusetts

Preparation of this book was made possible by a grant from the Bush Foundation, St. Paul, Minnesota. The editors would like to note with thanks the help they received from Winnie Berman, Carol Buell, Robyn Carey, Ernest Herman and Susan Muenchow. The contribution by Michael Rutter is reprinted, with permission, from the *American Journal of Orthopsychiatry*, copyright 1981 by the American Orthopsychiatric Association, Inc.

Library of Congress Cataloging in Publication Data

Main entry under title:

Day care.

    Includes index.
    1. Day care centers—United States—Addresses, essays, lectures. 2. Day care centers—Government policy—United States—Addresses, essays, lectuers. I. Zigler, Edward Frank, 1930–   II. Gordon, Edmund W. III. American Orthopsychiatric Association.
HV854.D39   362.7′12′0973   81–12838
ISBN 0–86569–098–7 (Hardbound)   AACR2
ISBN 0–86569–109–6 (Paperbound)

Printed in the United States of America

PREFACE

The rationale for a collection of articles on day care is clear: Today over 50 percent of mothers in the United States work outside the home, and this figure is expected to rise to 75 percent by 1990. Still more striking, the fastest-growing segment of working mothers is among those with children under two. Whether one sees this trend as good or bad, potentially reversible or here to stay, it is a demographic reality of tremendous import. For the question is not only who will care for these children while their parents work, but also who will pay for the care, and will it help or harm children?

This book is an attempt to combine recent research on the effects of day care with policy analyses on the delivery of day care. The authors come from a variety of disciplines—experimental psychology, early childhood education, psychoanalytic training, economics, pediatrics, and public health. Aware that theoretical analysis is often too far removed from the political arena, we have also included contributions by two United States senators.

The first section of the book focuses on theoretical and social science issues related to day care, with special emphasis on infant care. On the positive side, we now have a sufficient research base on day care to eliminate some of our worst fears: as Michael Rutter points out in his review, there is no evidence that good quality day care undermines parent-child attachment, or that it commonly results in substantial emotional or social problems. There is even some evidence that good quality day care—as described by Rescorla, Provence, and Naylor in the chapter on the Yale Child Welfare Program —can further the development of infants from disadvantaged families. Conducted by Trickett, Apfel, Rosenbaum, and Zigler, a five-year follow-up of participants in that program showed benefits, not only for the children but also for their parents.

There is also evidence that the quality of care matters. The chapters by Sally Provence and Ava Siegler both demonstrate the practical applications of psychoanalytic principles to the construction of quality day care programs. Social science research is also beginning to provide some clues about the components of quality care. As Brian Egeland and Ellen Farber found in their study, inconsistent caregivers in the early years of life may contribute to anxious attachments. Another important component of quality care is a high degree of verbal interaction between caregiver and child. According to the study we have included by McCartney, Scarr, Phillips, and Grajek, the amount of verbal interaction in day care not only affects the child's acquisition of verbal skills, but also influences the child's overall emotional adjustment.

In some cases, social science research is even beginning to modify some traditional assumptions as to what constitutes quality child care. While child advocates have long assumed that a staff-child ratio was the key to quality care, Richard Ruopp and Jeffrey Travers remind us in their chapter that the National Day Care Study found that small groups are more important than more caregivers. The study also found that specialized training led to a high degree of social interaction, whereas formal education *per se* made little difference.

Despite the gains made in research on day care in the last decade, however, there are still many gaps in our knowledge base on day care. First, at the most basic level, we still do not know how many children actually need extrafamilial day care. Estimates of the need for preschool day care are undercut by many factors, including parental unwillingness to admit that a child currently lacks satisfactory care. As James Levine points out in his chapter on school-age day care, estimates of the need for after-school care currently fail to adequately reflect the number of kindergarten children in need of care. Second, we still do not know as much as we should about the effects of infant day care. Part of the problem is that most studies have been conducted in high quality, university-based centers, not the kind most young children really experience. In addition, as Douglas Frye argues in his chapter, the reliability of many studies on infant day care has been hindered by the difficulties in finding a proper control group. And, as the response by Victoria Seitz suggests, this is a problem unlikely to disappear. For unless we are willing to randomly assign (or consign) children to poor quality care, rejecting all quasi-experimental research would lead us to abandon one of the most urgent topics of research—namely, the study of the effects of bad versus good care.

Beyond these methodological problems, we do not know what we need to know about day care because, as a society, we have so far failed to commit ourselves to the kind of longitudinal studies required. Soon it may be too late. Perhaps the most relevant parallel is to research on the effects of television. How could we have allowed such a major influence as television to develop without better research on its effects on children? We certainly would not allow a new drug to be introduced without more adequate inquiry into its likely effects. But now, 30 years after television's introduction, it would be difficult to find a control group of children who do not watch television. Research on the effects of day care also bears another parallel to research on the effects of television: just as television researchers have tended to dwell on the single issue of how television affects aggression, day care researchers have too long limited their inquiry to whether children in day care like their mothers more than strangers.

Despite the overall "passing grade" which Frye gives to infant day care, several chapters in this book indicate potential trouble spots. Anne Robertson, in her study on "Day Care and Children's Responsiveness to Adults," suggests that day care may be more problematic for boys than girls, with teachers rating younger boys in day care more "troublesome" than those reared exclusively at home. Rutter also warns that the impact of day care may be influenced by the age of the child, the child's temperament and prior experience, and other family characteristics.

Still more troubling, the study by Edward Zigler and Polly Turner offers little encouragement for champions of the view that parents and caregivers should work closely together. In this study, parents spent an average of 7.4 minutes per day in the day care center, and 10 percent of the parents did not even enter the center with their children in the morning.

By far the thorniest issue in day care, however, is the fundamental issue of quality versus cost. While research indicates that quality makes a difference, most parents can neither afford to stay home to deliver this care themselves nor can they earn enough to purchase quality care if they work. As Ruopp and Travers point out, "after a decade of research, quality day care can to some degree be both defined and delivered. . . . The question is: Who will pay the piper and how will he be paid?"

The quality versus cost debate is highlighted in the chapters by Senators Hatch and Kennedy. Both senators underline the importance of *quality* child care. Kennedy begins with the premise that child care is a right, not a privilege. He adds that the federal government has a responsibility to help parents pay the cost of quality care. Senator Hatch, however, not only opposes "a massive, federally funded network of child care facilities" but also does not voice support for other, more indirect subsidies such as child care tax credits. The ultimate responsibility for ensuring that children get quality care—and for paying for that care—should, he says, rest with parents.

Senators Kennedy and Hatch may represent two extremes of the political spectrum on day care. But they also help illustrate two peculiarly American traditions which have long complicated the provision of day care for children of working parents in this country. First, while European nations routinely accept the notion that society shares in the responsibility for child care, Americans have usually wanted to restrict this responsibility to parents. Thus, day care is bound to be controversial because it challenges this deeply entrenched tradition of family autonomy in the area of child care. Second, support for day care in the United States is complicated by the fact that the nation seems to vacillate between universal concern for the welfare of its citizens and the tradition of individual responsibility for one's own welfare.

Given research findings on the importance of quality care and the current political unwillingness to help many families afford quality care, what social policy options remain? In the third section of this book, Rochelle Beck sums up various options for breaking what she calls the day care stalemate. These options include (1) doing nothing more; (2) taking an incremental approach, which involves increasing Title XX and tax credits; (3) setting up community networks for child care; (4) child care insurance; and (5) reintroducing major child care legislation.

Neither Beck nor any of the authors seems very optimistic about the chances of reviving comprehensive national day care legislation. Instead, the major direction for the 1980s seems to be, as Levine suggests, measures aimed at "making the system work better." There are two main thrusts to this better management approach—tax credits, and information and referral centers. W. Gary Winget recommends a properly "sliding" tax credit, supplemented by the existing Title XX social services program. Perhaps the major argument in favor of both child care tax credits and information and referral centers (I & R) is that they seem politically feasible. As Levine points out, at a time when support is waxing for a national child care system, and when the emphasis is on the diversity of child care forms and maximizing consumer choice, these measures make sense.

Yet, while child care tax credits and information and referral centers may be our best hope for breaking the current day care stalemate, neither measure addresses one of the foremost issues identified by research—namely, the importance of quality care. To be sure, efforts to deal directly with the quality issue have been less than successful. For 13 years, as John Nelson recites the history, there have been federal day care regulations, but they have never been enforced. The most recent attempt to revise and implement federal standards floundered against the antiregulatory spirit in Congress, aided, as Kagan and Glennon point out, by the increasingly powerful proprietary child care lobby. Similarly, as Millie Almy explains in her chapter, efforts to professionalize day care teachers have been hindered by the general economic downturn. As long as other jobs are not plentiful, says Almy, there will probably be an endless supply of young people—many with training in child development and early childhood education—willing to work at minimum wage.

Nevertheless, leaving child care entirely to the private market is unlikely to improve quality. As Julius Richmond and Juel Janis report, the health of children in day care is already endangered by a laissez-faire approach. Not only do many centers fail to require basic immunizations and fire safety provisions, but they sometimes lack proper sanitation. Twenty percent of all series viral A hepatitis can be linked to day care centers, according to Richmond and Janis. In addition, few day care facilities provide the dental or nutrition education programs which have proven to benefit children from low-income families especially.

The federal retreat from regulating day care and from categorical programs targeted at the poor especially troubles Evelyn Moore, who offers "a Black perspective" on day care. "As a service which combines early education programs for children with relieving parents for employment," she says, "child care holds a particularly important promise for Black families, especially those living on the margin of economic self-sufficiency." Black children, who comprise a disproportionate share (44 percent) of the total enrollment of non-profit, federally funded centers, are also apt to suffer disproportionately from cutbacks in public services. These same children and their families are also the least likely to benefit from child care tax credits, which are much more apt to benefit middle- and upper-income families. Far from seeing targeted programs and federal day care regulations as intrusive, Moore therefore sees a strong federal role "as both desirable and unavoidable." Far from construing child care tax credits as a measure to maximize family choice, Moore fears a child care policy based on tax credits is likely to deny low-income Black families any place in the child care market.

We are left, then, not with one day-care stalemate, but with several. Measures which might help some families afford child care may not help other families, and measures to make child care "affordable" by no means guarantee that the quality will be acceptable.

While keenly aware that this volume offers no simple or single solution to the nation's day care problems, we hope that it will clarify the complexity of the problems. We also think the book suggests a series of policies which, taken together, would begin to promote the provision of quality child care at an affordable price.

EDWARD F. ZIGLER
EDMUND W. GORDON

CONTENTS

THE EDITORS

EDWARD F. ZIGLER, PH.D.   Sterling Professor of Psychology and Director of the Bush Center in Child Development and Social Policy, Yale University. Dr. Zigler was the first Director of the Office of Child Development and Chief of the U.S. Children's Bureau. He was a member of the Head Start national planning and steering committee and serves on Presidential and Congressional committees.

EDMUND W. GORDON, ED.D.   Professor of Psychology, Yale University. Dr. Gordon is Editor of the *American Journal of Orthopsychiatry*.

THE CONTRIBUTORS

MILLIE ALMY, PH.D.   Professor (Emeritus), University of California, Berkeley.

NANCY H. APFEL, ED.M.   Associate in Research, Yale University.

ROCHELLE BECK, ED.D.   Director of Public Affairs and Policy Analyst, Children's Defense Fund, Washington, D.C.

BYRON EGELAND, PH.D.   Professor of Psychoeducational Studies and Director of Mother-Child Interaction Project, University of Minnesota.

ELLEN A. FARBER   Research Fellow, Mother-Child Interaction Project, University of Minnesota.

DOUGLAS A. FRYE, PH.D.   Professor of Psychology, University of Cambridge, England.

THERESA GLENNON   Research Assistant, Bush Center, Yale University.

JODY GOODMAN   Research Assistant, Department of Psychology, Yale University.

SUSAN GRAJEK, M.A.   Pre-Doctoral Fellow, Bush Center, Yale University.

ORRIN G. HATCH   Senior Senator from Utah, Chairman of the Senate Committee on Labor and Human Resources.

JUEL M. JANIS, PH.D.   Assistant Dean, School of Public Health, University of California, Los Angeles.

SHARON L. KAGAN   Associate Director, Bush Center, Yale University.

EDWARD M. KENNEDY   Senior Senator from Massachusetts, Ranking Member of the Senate Committee on Labor and Human Resources.

JAMES A. LEVINE   Professor, Bank Street College of Education, New York.

KATHLEEN McCARTNEY, M.S.   Doctoral Candidate, Yale University.

EVELYN MOORE   Executive Director, National Black Child Development Institute, Washington, D.C.

AUDREY NAYLOR, M.S.W.   Assistant Clinical Professor, Yale Child Study Center.

JOHN R. NELSON, Jr., PH.D.   Research Associate, University of Chicago, National Opinion Research Center, Washington, D.C.

DEBORAH PHILLIPS   Research Assistant, Yale University.

SALLY PROVENCE, M.D.   Professor of Pediatrics, Yale Child Study Center.

LESLIE A. RESCORLA, PH.D.   Lecturer, Department of Psychology, University of Pennsylvania.

JULIUS B. RICHMOND, M.D.   Professor of Health Policy, Harvard Medical School and Children's Hospital, Boston.

ANNE ROBERTSON, PH.D.   Assistant Professor, Department of Psychology, University of Wisconsin, Milwaukee.

LAURIE K. ROSENBAUM, M.A.   Associate in Research, Psychology Department, Yale University.

RICHARD R. RUOPP, ED.D.   President, Bank Street School of Education, New York.

MICHAEL RUTTER, M.D. Professor of Child and Adolescent Psychiatry, Institute of Psychiatry, London.

SANDRA SCARR, PH.D. Professor of Psychology, Yale University.

J. CONRAD SCHWARZ Professor of Psychology, University of Connecticut, Storrs.

VICTORIA SEITZ, PH.D. Associate Professor, Child Study Center and Department of Psychology, Yale University.

AVA L. SIEGLER, PH.D. Director, Child and Adolescent Clinic, Child and Adolescent Training Program, Post Graduate Center for Mental Health, New York.

JEFFREY TRAVERS, PH.D. Former Associate Director, National Day Care Study, Abt Associates, Cambridge, Massachusetts.

PENELOPE K. TRICKETT, PH.D. Senior Staff Fellow, Laboratory of Developmental Psychology, National Institute of Mental Health, Rockville, Maryland.

PAULINE TURNER, PH.D. Assistant Professor, University of New Mexico, and Director, Manzanita Day Care, Albuquerque.

W. GARY WINGET, B.S. Mid-Career Fellow, Bush Center, Yale University.

DAY CARE: SCIENTIFIC
AND SOCIAL POLICY ISSUES

Part One

THEORETICAL AND SOCIAL SCIENCE ISSUES

Chapter 1

SOCIAL-EMOTIONAL CONSEQUENCES OF DAY CARE FOR PRESCHOOL CHILDREN

by Michael Rutter

During the 30 years since Bowlby's World Health Organization monograph on maternal care and mental health,[7] there has been a tremendous growth in knowledge of children's psychosocial development[8,9,44,75,76] and the experiences during the preschool years that may facilitate or impede normal emotional and social development.[14,54,71,73] Moreover, the last decade or so has been marked by an outpouring of empirical studies looking at the effects on young children of various forms of day care and of their mothers' working outside the home. The research findings have been well reviewed in several substantial books and papers,[3,39,54] and it is clear that early claims that proper mothering was only possible if the mother did not go out to work[2] and that the use of day nurseries and crèches had a particularly serious and permanent deleterious effect on mental health[91] were not only premature but wrong. Nevertheless, the issues are still far from closed, both as judged by the continuing contradictory arguments on whether day care should be greatly extended[85] or severely curtailed,[28] and by the recognition of the inconclusive nature of the research findings on a number of issues that are critical to both theoretical formulations and policy decisions.[3] This chapter will review these issues and the empirical research findings that bear on them.

Concerns About Day Care

Before doing so, however, it may be helpful to summarize the main
reasons why many people have supposed that group day care is
likely to be damaging to very young children. In essence, the arguments involve several separate steps. Firstly, the first three years of
life constitute the period when children ordinarily begin to develop
selective bonds or attachments. Usually, these bonds are made with
the child's mother (or, sometimes, father) and it seems that attachments are most likely to develop to the individuals who *actively*
interact with the baby and who are sensitive and responsive to the
baby's cues. While there is still some dispute over the details of the
process by which infants develop attachments, there is a broad measure of agreement on the main findings and conclusions.[1,75] The
concerns about day care stem from the fear that if the child has prolonged daily separations from his parents, and if caretaking is divided
among a large number of different adults, then either the bonding
process may be impaired or the attachments formed will be in some
way less secure or less effective in bringing comfort and security.

Secondly, these fears have seemed to be borne out by the evidence
that an institutional upbringing which involves multiple changing
caretakers *has* been shown to lead to important social deficits and
problems in interpersonal relationships.[22,84,90] Of course, there is a
world of difference between institutional care without any parental
involvement and day care in which the mother remains a key figure
who continues to participate actively in looking after the child. For
these reasons, little weight can be attached to the results of *residential* group care as a basis for assessing the probable sequelae of group
day care. Nevertheless, some links have seemed to be evident in the
observations that children who experience "pillar to post" day care
arrangements which lack both stability and continuity do appear to
suffer an increased risk of emotional and social difficulties.[49,50] Unfortunately, the strength of this argument is much weakened by the
fact that the day care arrangements that lack continuity also tend to
be of poor quality in many other respects.

Lastly, although the findings are contradictory and inconclusive,
as will be demonstrated later in this chapter, a few empirical studies
have appeared to demonstrate that group day care does lead to
insecurity and anxiety or aggression in some children. Writers who
argue that day care for very young children is often damaging tend
to dismiss the research findings which show that day care children
are not more often maladjusted than other children; they point out
that most of the evidence applies to children *over* the age of three
years, whereas developmental considerations arising out of attachment
theory suggest that it is those under three years who are most at

risk.[63] Moreover, the range of psychological outcome variables in most investigations has been so narrow and so limited that it would be misleading to conclude that their negative findings rule out the presence of damage. These various strands of argument, then, provide a reasonable basis both for assuming that social experiences during the first three years might well have an important influence on psychosocial development and also that there are aspects of group day care that might constitute adverse circumstances for the optimal social development of very young children. But it is not enough to conclude on *a priori* grounds that day nurseries and child-minding centers *might* be harmful to toddlers. We need to go on to ask whether the empirical evidence suggests that group day care does in fact have the disadvantageous features that the critics allege— and, if it does, the extent to which these features produce the ill effects attributed to them.

Social-Emotional Sequelae of Day Care

These matters are most conveniently examined by discussing first the overall findings on the different aspects of the psychosocial sequelae of day care, and then by proceeding to consider both the possible mechanisms involved and the possible modifying variables.

Attachment

Initially, the concerns were that group day care might prevent the development of primary selective attachments or cause the bonds to be made with the day care staff rather than with the child's own parents (possibly impairing family cohesion), or that it would result in anxious, insecure attachments. The first two of these concerns have been consistently negated by the empirical findings. Not only do day care children develop emotional bonds in much the same way and at much the same time as children reared at home, the main bonds are usually with the parents rather than with the child care staff.[13,21,25,27,39,58,60,61,68] There can be reasonable confidence in this finding in that the results are so consistent across a variety of different ways of assessing attachment in both naturalistic and laboratory settings. Thus, children generally show more distress when separated from their mothers than from their day center caretakers, they are more likely to go to mothers for comfort when upset, and they seem more responsive to reunion with their mothers. Furthermore, as shown by Kagan *et al.*,[39] the developmental course of separation anxiety seems very similar for day care and home-reared children. These findings apply not only to children who experience day care for the first time at age two or three years (when it might be assumed that parent-child bonds are already well established), but also to children who attend day care centers from the first 12 months of life, when primary attachments are still forming. For example, Fox's[27] kibbutzim children were born on the kibbutz and reared by *metaplot* in a group situation from four days onwards; Cummings's[21] children first attended day care centers at a mean age of 10.5 months; and in Kagan *et al.'s* study,[39] the children were enrolled at the center between 3.5 and 5.5 months of age. The only serious caveats regarding the conclusion that day care children ordinarily develop their primary bonds with parents rather than with day center staff is that most of the research has been undertaken with stable, nondeprived families and at centers that almost certainly are of well above average quality.

The further question of whether day care might lead to anxious, insecure attachments was raised by Blehar's finding[5] that, compared with home-reared children, day care children cried more, showed more oral behavior, and showed more avoidance of the stranger during Ainsworth's experimental strange-person situation procedure; furthermore they exhibited more avoidance and resistant behavior upon reunion with the mother. It should be noted that the children in this study had entered day care only at two or three years of age and had been reared at home during the period when selective attachments are usually first formed.

Blehar's study[5] has several methodological limitations,[3,39] including the fact that the day care group included more first-born children who in other studies have been found to be more liable to show adverse responses to separation.[27] However, more importantly, other research has tended to produce rather different findings. Thus, Moskowitz *et al.*[51] used a basically similar research design with children entering day care at about age three. Few differences were found between the day care and home care children but such differences as there were suggested that, contrary to Blehar's findings, the day care children were *less* upset by the strange-person situation. Cornelius and Denney[19] also found that children entering day care at about three years were no more anxious and insecure than home-reared children (although it did seem that day care altered sex differences in the response to separation). Portnoy and Simmons[55] looked at the responses of children who started day care at about one year of age and also at those starting at three years; neither showed differences from the home care children.

It is clear that most studies have failed to confirm Blehar's findings. In considering why her results were different, various explanations may be suggested. Thus, it could be that Blehar's findings were an artifact of limitations in the design of the study. Alternatively, it might be that her results reflected transient short-term effects (she obtained measures some four to five months after the children started at the day center, whereas other investigators have tended to make their assessments rather later than that). Some support for this suggestion is provided by Blanchard and Main's[4] finding (based on cross-sectional data) with younger (one-to-two-year-old) children that both parental avoidance on reunion and social-emotional maladjustment *diminished* the longer a child was in day care.

However, it is also possible that the differences between the day care and home care children reflected patterns of parent-child interaction which *antedated* the day care experience and which were not due to this experience at all. It is relevant, in this connection, that none of the studies discussed thus far had any measures of the children's behavior before starting day care. The one exception is the investigation by Roopnarine and Lamb,[64] which used the same Ainsworth "strange situation" procedure. Their findings suggested that the day care children were *more* anxious and insecure than the home care children when assessed during the week *preceding* their enrollment in day care but that they became *less* distressed and more friendly while in day care, so that three months later there were no day care–home care group differences. The preadmission findings are curious; it is unclear whether they represent differences in the prior characteristics of families and children using day centers, or whether they represent the children's anticipatory anxiety about a new experience. It should be noted that this study, like most others, suffers from uncertainties about the comparability of groups (this uncertainty is increased by the information that 40% of eligible families declined to participate—a possibly important source of bias, as shown by Cox *et al*.[20]). Nevertheless, it is clear that the balance of the evidence from the research taken as a whole is that, at least with three-year-olds, insecure and anxious attachments are certainly not the *usual* result of day care.

Other researchers have examined the same issues with children entering day care during infancy or as toddlers. It is important to consider these separately, as the effects of day care at a time when selective attachments are first developing could well be different from the effects at a later age when parent-child bonds are well established. Cummings[21] studied 30 children, all of whom had begun group care before two years of age (mean age of 10.5 months) and who had experienced day care for at least two months (mean of 10.4 months). Fourteen children from the day center waiting lists constituted the home care comparison group (the use of waiting list children has the major advantage of going a long way toward ensuring reasonable comparability prior to day care). Eight trials, using the Cohen and Campos[18] stranger procedure, were planned. Although the day care and home care children did not differ in their behavior during the first trial, far more day care children became upset during subsequent trials; only nine of the 30 completed all conditions, compared with 13 of the 14 home care children. On the other hand, although more of the day care children became distressed in the strange situation of the laboratory, few showed distress in the familiar setting of the day care center.

Cochran[16] studied 120 children aged 12 to 18 months, comparing those reared in their own home, those in a family setting being looked after by a "day mother" together with one or two other children, and those in a group day center with a 1:4 caretaker-to-child staff ratio. The first two groups were obtained from the day center waiting lists, thus providing reasonable control for family characteristics. Observations were made in a semistructured separation situation in the child's own home (rather than the more commonly used laboratory setting). No differences between groups were found in the children's responses to separation (however, few details are given and it seems that the measures may not have been either very detailed or very subtle). Ragozin[58] found no differences between day care and home care children, aged 17 to 38 months, in the degree of distress in the strange-person situation. After the mothers' departure from the day center, the children tended to increase their rate of play and also their attention to the caregiver, but few showed distress or called for their mothers. Doyle[23] studied 24 five-to-thirty month day care children with a matched home care control group, using the Ainsworth "strange situation" procedure in the laboratory and a modification of the same procedure in the child's own home. Not unexpectedly the laboratory setting produced more clinging behavior in both groups. While no overall significant differences between the home-reared and day care infants were evident in either setting, there was a significant group-by-sex-by-location interaction in which day care boys showed less contact with the stranger in the lab than home care boys, whereas the reverse applied to girls.

It is obvious that too few data are available for firm conclusions to be drawn. The Cochran, Doyle, Ragozin, and Brookhart and Hock findings are generally reassuring about the infrequency of adverse effects on the quality of attachment, as are the Cummings observations in the day center. On the other hand, the day center children in the Cummings[21] study were much more likely to become insecure and anxious in the stressful circumstances of repeated separation procedures under unusual conditions in the laboratory. This was not the case in the Brookhart and Hock[11] study, but it may be relevant that the experimental procedures were not identical. Although Blanchard and Main[4] found that the pattern of parent reunion was generally similar in a day care center and in a laboratory, Brookhart and Hock[11] found the latter to be more stressful. It seems likely that curious procedures involving mother, caretakers, and strangers not only going in and out of rooms every minute for reasons quite obscure to the child but also not initiating interactions in the way they usually do, could well bring latent anxieties to the surface. The findings are not consistent and it is not evident why the Brookhart and Hock[11] and Cummings[21] results disagree. However, questions must remain about the effects of day care on the security of toddlers' attachments. The evidence is inconclusive but it seems that, although most young children do not become overtly insecure and anxious as a result of day care, it is possible nevertheless that more subtle ill effects occur in some children. The matter warrants further study.

Social-Emotional Adjustment and Behavior

Up to this point, research findings have been considered solely in relation to attachment, which constitutes just one specific aspect of psychosocial development. It is necessary now to examine other indices of outcome, once more differentiating findings according to the age of the child. Schwarz *et al.*[78] studied affect, tension, and social interaction on the first day and fifth week after 3½-year-old children started attending a new day care center. Children who had experienced day care from before 22 months of age (the mean age of starting was 9.5 months) were compared with those attending a day center for the first time (although several of these had experienced other forms of substitute care). Few statistically significant differences were found, but the early day care children tended to show more positive affect, less tension, and more social interaction—especially immediately after starting at the new center. The findings are particularly difficult to interpret because the early day care group not only differed in having experienced day care from infancy but also in their starting at the new center as part of a preexisting group of children who already knew one another well. The same children were rated by their day center teachers four months after starting at the center.[79] The children who experienced day care from infancy were rated as significantly less cooperative with adults, more physically and verbally aggressive with peers and adults, and more active; there was also a tendency ($p < .10$) for them to be less tolerant of frustration. Putting the results of the two studies together, we may tentatively conclude that early day care had probably resulted in some differences in style of social interactions (although this did not amount to maladjustment and the differences could be a consequence of characteristics of the families rather than of the day care as such) but that the presence of familiar peers had made starting at a new center a less strange, and probably less stressful, experience.

Macrae and Herbert-Jackson[46] compared two-year-olds at a day center according to whether they had experienced day care for less than six or more than 13 months. They found that the more prolonged day care experience was associated with better peer relationships but nonsignificant tendencies toward a lower level of frustration tolerance, a higher level of activity, and more aggression—as assessed from ratings made by caregivers. The authors commented on the differences from the Schwarz study but the similarities appear rather greater. Nevertheless, detailed comparisons are not warranted, since the age groups in the two studies were different.

Ragozin[58] and Moskowitz *et al.*[51] both found that, in the strange-person situation in the laboratory, day care children tend to interact less with a stranger than do home care children. Apparently, at least in that somewhat stressful setting, day care results in some social inhibition with adults rather than social facilitation as might have been expected. Other studies, too, have tended to show both that most (but not all) infants and toddlers adapt fairly rapidly to a day care setting and also that early day care experiences lead to slight differences in social behavior, although there is no particular tendency for any increase (or decrease) in maladjustment or psychosocial disorder as such. However, many of the changes in social interaction that take place during the preschool years seem to be largely a function of maturation and of peer group experiences, rather than specifically home care or day care. For example, in one of the most detailed and systematic studies undertaken, with all the advantages of a longitudinal design, Kagan *et al.*[39] showed systematic growth functions across age for interactions with other children. Apprehension in the presence of an unfamiliar child tended to peak at about 20 months, with a gradual lessening of social inhibition thereafter associated with a concomitant increase in reciprocal play during the subsequent months. However, in group-reared children the apprehension tended to diminish more quickly (in a comparison of kibbutz and family-reared Israeli children) or to wax and wane at an earlier age (as in the study of day care and home-reared children in the U.S.A.). American children who had experienced day care from infancy played more than home-reared children in an unfamiliar day care center, suggesting that they may have been less apprehensive. The finding is not unexpected as, of course, the situation would be a less novel one for them. While day care did not seem substantially to alter children's basic social behavior, the mothers of day care children regarded them as more patient and less shy with adults, compared with home care children.

It also seems that day care experiences may alter patterns of parent-child interaction at home. Vandell[86] compared six play group and six home care families with 16-month-old boys, using observations in a semistructured laboratory setting furnished as a living room. Measures were taken before the beginning of the play group, and three and six months later. The changes over time indicated that the play group experience was associated with an increase in proximity-seeking and in object-related social acts (*i.e.*, showing, offering, or demonstrating objects) together with a decrease in the extent to which the toddlers terminated parent-child interactions. As Vandell[86] pointed out, it is uncertain whether the changes reflect an increase in insecurity or a rise in social skills.

McCutcheon and Calhoun[45] observed five-to-thirty-month-old infants one week and again one month after entering a day care program. During that first month at the center, crying decreased in frequency (from 9.5% to 4.3% of observations) and interactions with other children increased. Finkelstein *et al.*[26] observed two groups of day center children, infants in the seven-to-fourteen-month age range and toddlers in the 15-to-31-month age range. The toddlers showed more peer interaction and greater social responsiveness. The implication that peers are likely to play a greater role in the socialization of older preschool children is also borne out by other research.[68] Raph *et al.*[59] observed children in their first year at school comparing those who had extensive nursery school and kindergarten experiences with those who had not; prior observations had also been made at nursery school for the latter group. Social interactions increased with age irrespective of nursery school experience. Negative interactions with other children *decreased* and negative interactions with teachers *increased* between three and five years; this tendency was marginally greater in those with the greatest nursery group experience prior to starting school.

The only study of the long-term effects of day care is that by Moore.[50] As part of a longitudinal study of London children, he compared those who had experienced full-time home care by the mother ("exclusive mothering") and those who had had some form of substitute day care ("diffused mothering"), usually beginning just before age three. Interview and questionnaire measures were taken at six-to-eight years and at 15 years. For boys, the findings from the mothers' inventory indicated that exclusive mothering tended to result in "sensitive fastidious conformity" to adult rather than peer group standards, self-control, timidity, and academic interests. In contrast, diffused mothering tended to result in "fearless aggressive non-conformity" to parental requirements with outgoing, active, social interests which showed a peer-group orientation. The group differences for girls were fewer, smaller, and less consistent. However, the exclusive and diffused mothering groups (especially for boys) also differed in terms of maternal personality measures, so that the differences in the children might well reflect family features as much as the experience or nonexperience of day care. It should be added that there was substantial overlap between the groups, and that the findings generally reflected personality variations within the normal range rather than maladjustment. However, there was a tendency for the exclusively mothered boys to have more fears at four to five years; the observation that this difference only emerged after day care began implies that day care in the older preschool child may actually somewhat *diminish* fearfulness. On the other hand, day care that began before age two was associated with an *increase* in fearfulness. Because early day care tended to involve unstable changing patterns of child care, it remains uncertain whether the findings reflect the age of the child when group day care commenced or rather the consequences of frequent changes of substitute care and generally unstable family circumstances.

Thus, the results suggest that group day care may well incline children to be somewhat more assertive and peer-oriented but that it does not usually result in any increase or decrease in psychosocial disorder as such. However, Moore's findings[50] emphasize that the consequences may well depend on the quality, consistency, and overall pattern of substitute care provided. So far the research findings have been discussed simply in terms of whether children had or had not experienced group day care. While most studies have been reported in this way, the implicit assumption that "day care" encompasses a homogeneous set of experiences is obviously untenable. The other implicit assumption—that the parents who utilize day care are similar to those who do not—is equally questionable. Accordingly, we need to turn now to those investigations that provide data on either point.

Characteristics of Day Care

Not only does day care take several different forms, day care also differs from home care on a variety of dimensions, including multiplicity of caretakers, continuity in caretaking, upbringing as part of a same-age peer group, and the experience of new environments. In addition, of course, it might also vary in the characteristics of adult-child interaction.

Caregiver-Child Interactions

That possibility has been examined in several different studies of rather different types of day care. Rubenstein *et al.*[69] observed the interactions with 38 mother-reared and 27 substitute-reared black infants aged five to six months. Fifteen of the latter group had been looked after by relatives and 12 by nonrelated baby-sitters, some of whom provided care in their own and some in the infants' homes. It was found that the mothers provided a more stimulating and responsive environment than did the substitute caretakers—as shown by more positive affect, more playful interactions, and a greater variety of experiences. However, the substitute caretakers who had had the infants for a longer period of time acted more like the mothers, suggesting that some of the differences were a function of the short duration of the caretaker-infant relationship.

Rubenstein and Howes[68] also compared caretaker-infant interaction with 18-month-old Caucasian children attending day care centers and comparable children being reared at home. In many respects the interactions in the two settings were very similar, but there were some differences. For example, adults in the day care centers patted the children more frequently and held them longer; were more likely to intervene physically to help infants with objects, and were more likely to enter into a game with the infant. On the other hand, mothers were more verbally directive and were more restrictive of infant exploration and play. Positive affective exchanges between infant and caretaker (such as reciprocal smiling, hugging, and mutual play) were more frequent in day care; and more negative affect was expressed at home by both infants and caretakers—as shown by more crying and more reprimanding. Obviously, peer interactions were more frequent in the day centers just because in many instances there were no peers in the home. However, a comparison of the eight home-reared infants who had a peer with whom they played regularly and 12 day care infants matched for ordinal position, showed that peer interactions were generally similar in the two settings. It appeared, too, that the presence of peers influenced caretaker-infant interaction; maternal reprimands were reduced in the home-reared sample when peers came to visit.[67]

Cochran[16] also compared interactions with 12-to-18-month-old children in day centers and in the infants' own homes; in addition, he studied day care in which the infant was with a substitute caretaker in her own home with just one or two other children. Like Rubenstein and Howes,[68] he found that interactions were similar in many respects but mothers were more controlling (as shown by a higher frequency of "do's" and "dont's"), with the family home caretakers more like mothers than day center caretakers. Verbal interactions were also more frequent in both types of family home than in the day centers.

From these findings, it appears that the social context is likely to influence caretaker-child interaction. Family homes must function

as living quarters for parents as well as children while day centers
are designed exclusively for child care. As a consequence, mothers
may need to exercise more control than do center caretakers simply
because there are more objects about that are not suitable for infant
play. It may also be that the isolated setting of the home makes more
demands on the mother; the infant's needs compete with the need to
undertake household chores and to have social contact with other
adults.[68] The presence of another child with whom the infant may
play may also reduce the intensity of pressure on the caretaker. The
amount and quality of adult-child interaction in day centers is also
likely to be influenced by the staff-child ratio. Center staff have the
advantage over mothers of not having many other competing activities, so that they are able to devote all their time to child care. On
the other hand, this advantage may be reversed if the center caretaker has many children to look after, so that there is inadequate
opportunity for individual play and interaction with any one child.

This issue was examined systematically by Stallings and Porter[81]
in a study of 303 family day care homes (*i.e.*, substitute care in private homes rather than in day centers). In general it was found that
caregivers provided a positive and supportive environment for the
children, with positive affect much more frequent than negative. The
caregivers spent about half their time interacting with the children
and the other half in different activities. Caregivers in officially sponsored or regulated homes tended to be more actively involved with
the children and talked with them more; such homes also tended to
provide a safer physical environment. In homes with several infants
and toddlers, individual children received less caretaker attention
and it appeared that toddlers were likely to fare best in homes with
only a few children. The findings suggested that children become a
little more unruly when there are several toddlers together and the
caregiver spends more time controlling their behavior and less time
engaged in developmental activities. In short, it seems that the presence of another child of similar age is an advantage for toddlers but
that homes with several toddlers all together may place undue strains
on caretakers.

The family day care provided in the homes studied by Stallings
and Porter[81] was of a generally satisfactory standard but this is not
universally so. In Mayall and Petrie's[48] study of British child minders, the quality of care proved to be very variable. In some cases it
was fine, in others it was not. Many children looked after by child
minders spent a low-level, understimulated day in cramped surroundings; some did not get the love and attention they needed, and some
experienced frequent unsettling changes of caretaker. It is clear that
day care, like home care, cannot be regarded as a homogeneous set
of experiences. Both vary greatly in style and quality of child-rearing.

Polymatric vs. Monomatric Upbringing

Quite apart from the quality of caregiver-child interactions provided, day care differs from home care in terms of the number of adults who look after the child. A traditional home upbringing is usually described as monomatric, as if there were only one adult who provided parenting for the child. Of course, this is misleading. There may be only one mother, but fathers often take an active role in looking after and playing with the children.[40] In addition, grandparents, older brothers and sisters, and other relatives or neighbors may also play a role. Nevertheless, it certainly is the case that day care usually involves a greater dispersion of child care among a larger number of adults than is usual with infants reared solely at home. Patterns of polymatric infant care take may forms, ranging from the Israeli kibbutzim,[27] where the caretaking is provided in a setting designed specifically for the purpose; to the more informal, less structured arrangements of shared care in the East African Highlands;[43] to the rather varied arrangements associated with day care in Western societies. While it seems evident that the development of attachments* follows much the same course when there are several stable caretakers rather than just one,[27,60] questions remain about the consequence of having *many* different caretakers and especially of having a roster of changing caretakers. It has been shown that the latter situation is associated with anomalous psychosocial development if it constitutes the *only* care arrangement, as it does in residential care.[22,84] However, the circumstances of day care are different in that stability is provided in the form of the child's own parents, who share the care with the day center staff. The issue, then, is what are the effects of consistency or inconsistency of individualized caretaking in the day center when there is consistency in parenting at home? The matter has been little studied so far, but there are a few relevant investigations.

Cummings[21] compared attachment behavior in 12-to-28-month-old infants in relation to "stable" caretakers (*i.e.*, those who had worked at the center a long time) and "unstable" caretakers (*i.e.*, those who had been there only a brief time). In the day care environment, the infants showed a preference for "stable" caretakers; but the trend was less marked and short of statistical significance in the more strange and stressful laboratory situation. The findings were not particularly clear cut, but they suggested that children formed a

---

* Nevertheless, it should be noted that "attachment" is not a unitary concept and that different measures of "attachment" may not agree in their findings.[75] Accordingly, it may well be misleading either to rely on just one measure or to pool all together as if they all meant the same thing, as in many studies up to now.

sort of intermediate attachment to caretakers, greater than that to strangers but substantially less than that to mothers—with the attachment to "stable" caretakers greater than that to "unstable" caretakers. While the findings show that attachments to caretakers tend to be greater when the children have known them some time, they do not deal with the crucial comparison between day care in which there is consistency in individualized caregiving and day care in which there is not.

That comparison was made, however, by Wilcox et al.[88] in a study in which 12-to-24-month-old infants were assigned in a quasi-random fashion to two otherwise identical nurseries: in one there were five caregivers and 20 infants, with care so arranged that each caregiver was assigned to four specific infants; in the other nursery there was multiple caretaking so that the five adults shared responsibility for all 20 children. Most of the infants came from socially disadvantaged black families. Observations were made of social contacts at the day center and of separations from and reunions with the mother. No differences in mother-attachment (as judged from the child's observed behavior during separations from and reunions with the mother) were found between the infants in the individual and in the multiple caregiver assignment settings. However, there was a rather limited range of outcome variables and, perhaps more importantly, it was found that in the supposedly individually assigned caregiver setting, nearly half of the child's adult contacts were with someone other than the assigned caregiver—a proportion no different from that in the multiple assignment setting. It appears that, in a group day care setting with as many as 20 children in one room, practicalities mean that very little individualized caregiving is possible. As a result, this investigation failed to provide an adequate test of individualized versus multiple caregiving.

Mention has already been made of Moore's study,[49,50] which showed that unstable, frequently changing day care arrangements seemed to lead to insecurity and emotional upset. However, not only is it uncertain how far the ill effects stemmed from the pattern of day care itself (rather than the family difficulties that led to it), it is also unclear how far the insecurity was a result of multiplicity of caregivers and how far a consequence of the repeated major changes in caregiving arrangements.

It is all too obvious that we have insufficient data for any firm conclusions on this important issue. Nevertheless, it may be useful to look at the described characteristics of the day centers concerned in the reports suggesting possibly adverse effects of day care. In the Blehar[5] study, the staff-child ratio ranged from 1:6 to 1:8; from the statement that "two caregivers were assigned to each group," it may be inferred that the children were probably in groups of 12 to 16; nothing is said about individualized assignment of caregivers. In the

Schwarz *et al.*[19] study, the staff-pupil ratio was similar (1:7) and there was no individualized assignment. In the Cummings[21] study, the staffing ratio was better (1:4) but again there was no individualized assignment and the group size was 15 to 20. The Moore[50] report involved a variety of day centers and settings but the adverse effects were found in children with an early experience of care with changing caregivers and settings. Of course, all of these characteristics also applied to centers where studies have *not* shown adverse effects and neither the numbers nor the nature of the data allow systematic comparisons. However, certain tentative suggestions may be made. Firstly, it seems highly likely that effects of multiple nonindividualized caregiving in an institution that lacks any primary caregiver will be quite different from the effects of multiple caregiving that is supplemental to an ordinary upbringing by the child's parent in the child's home—the former is often damaging whereas the latter may not be. Secondly, however, truly individualized caregiving during day care is more likely than multiple caregiving to foster attachments that will bring the child comfort and security at times of stress. We do not know how important this difference is in practice, and it may well vary according to the quality and security of the child's relationships at home. Thirdly, both because it will involve adaptation to new environments and because it may involve loss of attachment-figures, it seems likely that multiple changes of day care arrangements will prove unsettling for many children.

One further issue in this connection is whether there are advantages in polymatric child-rearing just because it allows the child to develop multiple attachments and hence a greater range of sources of security and a less precarious reliance on a single relationship. Once again, the crucial data are lacking. However, it may be that the key question is how far the pattern of care *actually* leads to multiple attachments of any strength and utility. In this connection, the kibbutzim findings[27] and the East African findings[43,60] both suggest that these forms of polymatric care *do* lead to multiple functional attachments, although the attachments to the substitute caretakers are generally less strong than those to the mothers. On the other hand, Cummings's data[21] suggest that group day care with multiple shared caregiving leads to such weak attachments (for example, 40% of the children failed to approach the caregiver in any of the test conditions) that the attachments are of little use to the child.

Employed and Unemployed Mothers

A further issue concerns the differences between employed and unemployed mothers. Actually, this involves several rather different questions including the differences between families that use and families that do not use day care; the effect of having a job outside the home on the mother's self-esteem, satisfaction, and mental health; the effects of the use of day care on parent-child interaction; and the consequences for the child of having two working parents.

The issues were well reviewed by Hoffman,[36] who has recently updated her appraisal of maternal employment.[37] The main findings may be summarized as follows: Firstly, there are differences between families using and not using day care. These involve social and ethnic features (as illustrated in the study by Winnett *et al.*[89]) and they involve marital circumstances (for example, Cohen[17] found that employed mothers were more likely to be without a cohabiting husband). In addition, however, working mothers may differ in their attitudes in ways that could influence their infant's response to day care. Thus, Hock[35] found that, as well as being more career-oriented, working mothers perceived less infant distress at separation, were less anxious about separation, and were generally less apprehensive about other caregivers. Of course, these findings could mean both that the mothers' lack of anxiety may make it easier for their children to adapt positively to day care, and also that the mothers may be less perceptive of insecurities when and if they arise. Thus, Cohen[17] found a tendency for employed mothers to show less "reciprocal positive attentiveness" than nonworking mothers.

Secondly, a variety of studies have shown that when the mother has a job outside the home, fathers tend to take a more active role in family life (although this is likely to be influenced by the father's attitude to his wife's return to work[41]), children tend to take on more household responsibilities, and it is more likely that someone outside the home will be involved in child care.[30,31,36,89] Not surprisingly, the fact that there tends to be less differentiation between the parents in both work and parenting roles has meant a similar tendency for the children to have a less differentiated or otherwise modified perception of sex roles.[30,31,47,87] On the other hand, the evidence is consistent in showing that this is not associated with any increase in rates of psychosocial disorder.[36,77]

Thirdly, it has been found that the experience of having a paid job outside the home may have beneficial effects on the mother's sense of well-being. Most studies have found that, compared with housewives, employed women have a greater sense of self-esteem and personal satisfaction in their role.[30,31,52,57] The findings with respect to mental health are more contradictory, with some finding no differences between employed women and housewives, whereas others have found that employment serves as a factor protecting working-class women from depression.[12,66] Many (but by no means all) full-time housewives are dissatisfied with their situation;[29,53] Yarrow *et al.*[92] found that child rearing posed most difficulties for women who wanted to work but who remained at home out of a sense of duty. Clearly, what remaining at home or having a job does for the mother's mental state is likely to make a big difference to the children.[36] It may well be more important to have a satisfied, happy mother than to have a mother at home all day.[77] Whether maternal employment is or is not a good thing for the family is likely to depend very much on whether the mother wants to work. Presumably, too, it matters whether the job proves to be a satisfying one and not so tiring as to lead to role strain or conflict. Many mothers of young children prefer part-time work; stress and fatigue may result if full-time work is the only available alternative.

Fourthly, there are scattered rather contradictory findings that employed women may differ from housewives in their styles of interaction with their children, either as a result of preexisting differences or as a result of their having been away from their child all day.[3,17,86,89] It is not self-evident that day care will necessarily reduce the amount of exclusive, intensive parent-child interaction. It could mean that, on return from work, parents are more likely to arrange uninterrupted time to play and talk with their children—or it could mean that the involvement in a job outside the home reduces interest in the children. The data to decide between these and other alternatives are not yet available, but there is a need to consider both maternal employment and day care in terms of their impact on the broader ecological systems within which children develop.[3]

Modifying Factors in Children's Responses

Finally, it is important to consider possible modifying factors that may influence how children respond to day care. Necessarily, this section of the paper is short, but numerous studies attest to the importance of individual difference in other circumstances[24,72] and it is highly likely that they will prove to be similarly crucial in relation to day care. The few research findings available to date suggest that the relevant variables may include the child's age, sex, ordinal position, temperament, prior experiences, and relationship with parents.

Age of the Child

It is well established that children's responses to hospital admission are much influenced by their age at the time,[71] and it seems that developmental maturity similarly influences responses to other separation experiences.[62] On these grounds and on what is known about course of the development of selective attachments[39,60,75] it would be expected that reactions to day care would also vary according to the age at which commenced. Actually, there are surprisingly few direct examinations of age differences. However, it is known that children's responses to peers change with increasing age,[39] and that peer interactions and reciprocal social behavior are more frequent among toddlers than among infants,[26] and still more common among three-to-five-year-olds than among toddlers.[81] The importance of peers in influencing young children's play, interaction with adults, and response to separation has been suggested by Rubenstein and Howes's data,[67,68] and it may be that older preschool children are better able to take advantage of the peer group opportunities, although even toddlers do so to some extent. Findings on age trends in separation-protest would suggest that day care might be more stressful for infants under the age of 2.5 or three years than for older preschool children, but empirical evidence to indicate whether or not this is in fact the case is lacking. (Moore's results[50] are consistent with the suggestion, but there are too many confounding variables to have confidence in the finding; moreover, other studies suggest the converse[5] or no differences,[55] so the matter must remain open.)

Sex

Several studies have shown that the effects of day care on boys are more marked, more consistent, and somewhat different than is the case with girls.[11,19,50,51,55] The sex differences in these various studies are not identical, so that no coherent set of conclusions is yet possible. Cornelius and Denney[19] found that day care boys were more independent and interacted more with the strange male adult; Brookhart and Hock[11] found that, with respect to contact-maintaining behavior, boys and girls responded in the opposite fashion to day care; Moskowitz et al[51] found that day care boys functioned more independently in the mother's presence but were responsive to her return from a separation (note that all these results refer to a group-by-sex interaction effect); Portnoy and Simmons[55] found that boys cried more and showed more resistance and avoidance of the stranger than did girls; Moore[50] found that the personality differences that followed day care were more marked and more consistent in boys. While the sex difference findings remain rather inconclusive so far, it is highly probable that ultimately they will prove to be valid and meaningful in view of the evidence of sex differences in children's responses to other forms of stress.[70]

Ordinal Position

Fox[27] found that first-born children were more anxious than later-born children during an experimental separation procedure. The matter has been little investigated otherwise but there is a substantial body of evidence indicating that parents tend to interact differently with their first-born than with their later-born children.[15,33,38,42,65,83] Thus, it would seem plausible that ordinal position might influence responses to day care. The matter warrants study.

Temperament

Although there is a growing body of evidence indicating the importance of temperamental differences in relation to various aspects of psychosocial development and of responses to stress,[24,72] little is known regarding its importance with respect to day care. However, it may be relevant that Kagan *et al*.[39] found quite marked differences between Chinese and Caucasian babies in their responses to separation. These differences seemed to reflect temperamental variations that may have resulted from either constitutional or experiential factors. Once more, the variable requires investigation.

Prior Experiences

It would be expected that children's prior experiences of happy and of unhappy separation, as well as of interaction with peers, might well influence their responses to day care. There are suggestive findings that this may be the case for children's responses to hospital admission[80] and there is some indication that this also applies to day care[78] but the data so far provide no more than tentative leads.

Family Characteristics

Lastly, it is necessary to consider family characteristics and the nature of children's relationships with their own parents. The whole notion of "insecure" attachments[82] implies that the quality of bonding will influence the child's response to separation-experiences; hence one might infer that children with "insecure" attachments (whether as a result of their own temperament or the quality of their upbringing) might be more vulnerable to the adverse effects of day care. Circumstantial support is provided by the animal data[34] which showed that the infant monkeys who exhibited most distress after separation were those whose relationship with their mothers had shown most tension *before* the separation. Also, it appears that human infants from discordant or otherwise troubled homes are more likely to show disorder following repeated hospital admission.[56] However, both situations are rather remote from that of day care and it would be unwise to do more than conclude that the issue merits further examination.

It is evident that children vary in their responses to day care and that, in considering the possible effects of day care on social and emotional development, these individual differences must be given adequate consideration. However, it is also clear from the few scattered data so far available that we still have much to learn on the nature and sources of such differences and that very little is known as yet on the mechanisms by which they affect children's responses to day care.

Conclusions

In most Western countries there has been a steady increase over recent years in the proportion of women with dependent children obtaining a job outside the home.[10,74] The most recent and most rapid increase has applied to the mothers of young children and, not suprisingly, there has been a corresponding increase both in the use of and demand for some form of day care for preschool children. In Britain today, a majority of mothers of children aged two years desire day provision, although only a fifth currently use it.[6] Play groups, followed by child caretakers, remain the most frequently used facilities for the under-threes—but group day centers have been much more often the subject of research. While it is clear from this review and from its predecessors[3,39,54] that some of the more alarming stereotypes about day care can be rejected, it is equally obvious that we have some way to go before we are in a position to make well-based policy decisions on what type of care is most suitable for which children in which circumstances. Heinicke *et al.*[32] Pilling and Pringle,[54] Belsky and Steinberg[3] and Kagan *et al.*[39] have all made valuable suggestions on some of the key issues to be considered; other considerations have been introduced in the present paper. We know that good quality day care does not disrupt children's emotional bonds with their parents; moreover children continue to prefer their parents over alternative caregivers. Furthermore, even day care for very young children does not *usually* result in serious emotional disturbance. On the other hand, there are indications that day care influences to some extent the form of children's social behavior (in ways that may be either helpful or deleterious). Further, there are indications that the ways in which it does so may be determined by the specific characteristics of the day care (and by its quality; it is important to note that most research has concerned day centers of above average quality), by the age and other characteristics of the child, and by the characteristics of the family (including the meaning of maternal employment and the meaning of day care for the parents). It would be wrong to conclude that day care, any more than home care, is without effects, and it would be misleading to assume that it carries no risks (even though these have been greatly exaggerated in the past). What is now needed is research that moves beyond the crude day care versus home care comparison in order to determine the specific effects of the various aspects of care in specific circumstances.

Postscript on Practice and Policy

The review of empirical research in the main body of this paper concluded that strong assertions on what form of care would be best for young children would not be warranted in view of the lack of firm evidence on some of the most crucial issues. Research must continue if we are to be in a better position to develop optimal services for children in the future. Nevertheless, the question of what should be done *now* with respect to day care remains and we have an obligation to act as best we can on the basis of what we do know (which is considerable). Accordingly, this chapter is brought to an end with some more speculative suggestions regarding practice and policy— suggestions that are based on the research findings reviewed above but that, necessarily, have to move beyond what is known with certainty.

Perhaps the first issue is whether day care of any quality is so harmful that steps should be taken to ensure that all mothers of young children remain home in order to provide full-time care. In this connection, of course, it is relevant that children have two parents and it should not necessarily be presupposed that it has to be the mother who gives up employment outside the home. Although it is likely that there is some sex difference in nurturance,[44] most men, like most women, are able to provide the necessary parenting qualities. The question, therefore, is better posed in terms of whether it is essential for one parent to remain at home during the children's early years. In that the research findings fail to show that day care commonly results in substantial emotional or social problems, the answer must be that it is *not* essential.

Whether it is usually *desirable* is less easy to answer. Probably no general statement would be sensible in view of the many variations associated with individual circumstances. Certainly, it is not good if economic or other pressures *force* both parents to go out to work when one would rather stay at home to care for the children. Equally, it is evident that poor conditions of work and poor quality day care (especially for the under-threes) sometimes make employment outside the home an unsatisfactory arrangement for both mother and child. On the other hand, it seems that many mothers are happier and more contented when parenting and outside work can be combined (see references cited above). When this is the case, it may benefit the child as well as the parent for the mother to hold a job, on the grounds that (other things being equal) a happy mother is likely to be a better mother. In short, it appears that it is best all round for mothers to be able to *choose* whether or not they wish to work outside the home while their children are very young. Not all women will make the same choice, and there should be available a range of socially acceptable alternatives.

However, for day care to have a good outcome, several rather different conditions must be met (obviously, a closely parallel set of conditions apply to home care). These include the effects of employment on parenting, the implications for the mother of holding a job outside the home, the meeting of individual needs, and the quality of care provided for the child while both parents are away. Quite apart from what happens during day care, it is desirable that outside work enhance parenting and improve parent-child relationships while the parents and child are together. This means that there should be *time* to be together during the child's waking hours and that neither the child nor the parent be so worn out at the end of the day that their interactions are less than pleasurable. Particularly with infants and toddlers, this may mean that part-time work is preferable to full-time. In addition, it may well be that children adapt more easily if they can adjust to half-day care before moving to a full day care program.[32] It is also likely to require that *both* parents share the housekeeping chores to enable both to enjoy their children as well as maintaining a job. In addition, it is necessary that the working hours and work commitments of both parents be sufficiently flexible for one or the other to be able to take time off when the child is sick, or to be available when needed for other reasons. Clearly, these requirements should apply to the employment of fathers and mothers.

If the work experience is to be rewarding and satisfying for the mothers of young children, however, other needs must also be met. The combination of earlier childbearing, smaller families, and increased life expectancy[74] means that most parents are likely to have a prolonged period of employment after their children have grown up. Accordingly, women (and men) need to be able to prepare themselves adequately for this period of their life. Traditionally, many of the less rewarding or less well-paid jobs have been regarded as "female." What is required is a greater opening up of job opportunities to women and also a more equitable distribution of remuneration between traditionally "male" and traditionally "female" jobs. As implicit in the first set of conditions, it is also necessary that part-time employment be available without loss of training opportunities, status, or promotion prospects. These qualifications are particularly necessary with respect to the professions requiring prolonged training which tends to be concentrated during the childbearing years.

It is clear from the research findings reviewed above that children vary in their responses to day care and that these individual differences need to be taken into account in deciding what is the best set of arrangements. While the empirical data do not as yet indicate which personal qualities or which environmental circumstances are most crucial in this respect, various tentative suggestions may be made. In general, there is most concern regarding the under-threes in view of the greater likelihood of responding adversely to separation experiences at this age. Although there is a paucity of adequate data on age differences in response to day care, it is likely that under-threes find it less easy to cope with a long day of care away from home; further, the type and quality of care provided may be more crucial at this age. Temperamental factors may also mean that some children are less likely than others to respond well to day care. First-born children, who are not used to sharing their mother with other children, may find adaptation to group day care more difficult—and there is some suggestion, too, that boys may be more affected than girls. Those from an unhappy, unsettled, or discordant home may be more liable to suffer from separations from their family. This consideration poses a problem, of course, in that it might be thought that it is just those children who are most likely to need positive experiences away from the stresses of home. Particular care is also needed in the placement of children with markedly insecure attachments or with previous unhappy separation experiences. In addition, it is probably wise not to start day care at a time when the child is having to cope with other stresses or when there are major changes in family routines. Kagan *et al*.[39] felt that it is probably better, too, to initiate day care either before attachments are beginning to be formed or after they are well-established, rather than during the seven-to-eighteen-month-old age period. These various considerations do not necessarily mean that the child should not have day care, but that parents need to be particularly concerned with the adequacy of the arrangements and that in all cases parents should be guided by the actual manner in which the individual child responds.

While there is general agreement that the overall "quality" of day care is crucial, it is less certain which features are essential in determining quality—especially with the under-threes. With the three-to-five-year group, it seems that most children respond positively to a fairly wide range of settings—provided that the care is warm and concerned, that the atmosphere is happy and friendly, that there are enough toys and activities, that there is a staff-child ratio adequate to provide proper supervision, and that the caregivers interact with the children in play and conversation. At this age, children gain much from their peers and there is less exclusive reliance on adults for meeting their needs. Reasonable stability and continuity in staffing is certainly desirable but most youngsters can cope with interactions with several different caregivers provided that these always include people familiar to them.

The situation is less straightforward with the under-threes. Obviously, they show the same requirements with respect to a warm, happy atmosphere with ample provision for play and for conversational interchange with caregivers. However, there are at least two respects in which their needs are somewhat different from those of three-to-five-year-olds. Firstly, they are less able to make use of interactions with peers and are more reliant on adults for play and conversation. As a consequence, it is probably necessary to have a higher staff-child ratio with one-to-three-year-old children than with the older preschoolers who are better able to organize their own activities. Kagan *et al.*[39] recommended that no caretaker should be responsible for more than three infants. Stallings and Porter[81] suggested that it is better not to mix toddlers with either babies or older preschoolers, both because their needs differ but more particularly because, in a mixed-age group, toddlers tend to lose out on caregiver attention. Secondly, under-threes not only are at an age when parent-child attachments are forming, strengthening, and becoming more secure, it is also normal for children of this age to be more clinging and dependent on their parents than are older preschool children. It is these considerations that have led the Robertsons[63] and others to argue that group day care is unsuitable for under-threes although it may well provide a useful and worthwhile experience for older preschool children. Certainly, as already noted,[88] it has proved difficult in practice to provide really individualized caregiving in a group care setting and sometimes multiple shared caregiving is distributed so widely that children fail to form strong or secure attachments with any of the day care staff.[21] A likely consequence of this circumstance is that the staff will be less able than parents to provide adequate comfort if and when the children become distressed or frightened at the center. On the other hand, the empirical findings suggest that this has far fewer adverse consequences than one might at first sight suppose. Just as the Robertsons[62] some years ago pointed to the fallacy of treating all forms of residential care as synonymous, so it is also wrong to equate day care with *residential* care. Children *do* need individualized caregiving by someone who is present sufficiently consistently for secure attachments to develop. However, it is possible that if this is available at home, it may be somewhat less crucial for it to be available during day care as well. There are too few data for any firm conclusions. Common sense, as well as extrapolations from the evidence applicable to other situations, suggests that the under-threes are likely to be happier and more contented when they receive day care in a familiar setting with individualized caregiving by someone they know. But equally, what little evidence there is indicates that the dangers of day care that does not have these optimal characteristics have been exaggerated in the past.

Finally, given that day care should be available for those children whose family circumstances make it desirable, the question is what form it should take—child care by a relative, friend, or neighbor either in that person's home or the home of the child; group child care by a paid caretaker who looks after many children in her own home; play groups with or without parental involvement; crèches at the parents' place of work; or day nurseries. Once again, these issues are most critical for the under-threes. Although sound comparative studies are lacking, it would seem highly likely that toddlers would be better off cared for by someone they know in a familiar setting in the company of not more than one or two other children of similar age. For those families fortunate enough to have that option open to them, it would seem to provide the best solution. However, for most people, other alternatives need to be considered. While a family setting in a private home might seem more "natural" than a purpose-designed group day care center, it is by no means self-evident that it is generally preferable.[48,81] The caretaker may well have other competing responsibilities that interfere with her ability to give individual time to the children in her care, the setting and facilities may be less adequate, and (because child care tends to be a poorly paid, low-status job) some caretakers take on more children than they can look after adequately. In addition, for the same reasons, caretakers may turn to more lucrative occupations when they are able to do so, necessitating unsettling changes in child care arrangements. On the other hand, day centers are likely to find it more difficult to provide individualized care, and staff turnover may be greater. Crèches at the parents' place of work should allow the parent to see the child at the lunch break and should reduce the overall hours of day care (because there is no need to build in time for the parents to travel to and from their jobs). However, so far, they have been little studied, and not much is known of their *actual* advantages and disadvantages.

Probably, at this stage of our knowledge, it would be unwise to opt for any one type of care as generally superior to all others. Indeed, a flexible variety of different arrangements is more likely to meet the varying needs of different families. However, with all types of care it is important to individualize care as far as possible; to keep staff changes to a minimum; to provide suitable training for those serving as caregivers; to ensure adequate staffing, space, and play facilities; and, by suitable recruitment and adequate remuneration, to ensure that care is provided by people with the necessary qualities. The term "child care" itself carries the danger of understating what is required of the caretaker. The "care" needed must include play, conversation, and emotional comfort as well as the meeting of the child's physical needs and the avoidance of dangers. Given these qualities, and given stable arrangements with someone the child likes and is fond of, day care can be a positive and helpful experience all round for many children. However, it has to be emphasized that much child care today falls far short of these relatively low-level ideals, and strenuous efforts are needed to improve both the quality of what is already provided and to increase the availability of suitable services for those families who so far lack them. This constitutes a sizable task. Nevertheless, as indicated above, the improvement of day care services would not be sufficient in itself. The goal must also include changes in the patterns of employment for parents, which are equally necessary if the needs of young children are to be met.

References

1. Ainsworth, M. 1973. "The development of infant-mother attachment." In *Review of Child Development Research*, Vol. 3, B. Caldwell and H. Ricciuti, eds. University of Chicago Press, Chicago.
2. Baers, M. 1954. "Women workers and home responsibilities." *Inter. Labor Rev.* 69:338–355.
3. Belsky, J. and Steinberg, L. 1978. "The effects of day care: a critical review." *Child Devlpm.* 49:929–949.
4. Blanchard, M. and Main, M. 1979. "Avoidance of the attachment figure and social-emotional adjustment in day care infants." *Devlpm. Psychol.* 15:445–446.
5. Blehar, M. 1974. "Anxious attachment and defensive reactions associated with day care." *Child Devlpm.* 45:683–692.
6. Bone, M. 1977. "Pre-School Children and the Need for Day Care." *HMSO*, London.
7. Bowlby, J. 1951. *Maternal Care and Mental Health*. World Health Organization, Geneva.
8. Bowlby, J. 1969. *Attachment and Loss: I. Attachment*. Hogarth, London.
9. Bowlby, J. 1973. *Attachment and Loss: II. Separation, Anxiety and Anger*. Hogarth, London.
10. Bronfenbrenner, U. 1976. "Who cares for America's children?" In *The Family—Can It Be Saved?*, V. Vaughan and T. Brazelton, eds. Year Book Medical Publications, Chicago.
11. Brookhart, J. and Hock, E. 1976. "The effects of experimental context and experiential background on infants' behavior toward their mothers and a stranger." *Child Devlpm.* 47:333–340.
12. Brown, G. and Harris, T. 1978. *Social Origins of Depression: A Study of Psychiatric Disorders in Women*. Tavistock, London.
13. Caldwell, B. et al. 1970. "Infant day care and attachment." *Amer. J. Orthopsychiat.* 40:397–412.

14. Clarke, A.M. and Clarke, A.D.B. 1976. *Early Experience: Myth and Evidence*. Open Books, London.
15. Clausen, J. 1966. "Family structure, socialization and personality." In *Review of Child Development Research*, Vol. 2, L. Hoffman and M. Hoffman, eds. Russell Sage, New York.
16. Cochran, M. 1977. "A comparison of group day care and family child-rearing patterns in Sweden." *Child Devlpm.* 48:702–707.
17. Cohen, S. 1978. "Maternal employment and mother-child interaction." *Merrill-Palmer Quart.* 24:189–197.
18. Cohen, L. and Campos, J. 1974. "Father, mother and stranger as elicitors of attachment behaviors in infancy." *Devlpm. Psychol.* 10:146–154.
19. Cornelius, S. and Denney, N. 1975. "Dependency in day care and home care children." *Devlpm. Psychol.* 11:575–582.
20. Cox, A. et al. 1977. "Bias resulting from missing information: some epidemiological findings." *Brit J. Prevent. Soc. Med.* 31:131–136.
21. Cummings, F. 1980. "Caretaker stability and day care." *Devlpm. Psychol.* 16:31–37.
22. Dixon, P. 1980. Paper in preparation.
23. Doyle, A. 1975. "Infant development in day care." *Devlpm. Psychol.* 4:655–656.
24. Dunn, J. 1980. "Individual difference in temperament." In *Scientific Foundations of Developmental Psychiatry*, M. Rutter, ed. Heinemann Medical, London.
25. Farran, D. and Ramey, C. 1977. "Infant day care and attachment behaviors toward mothers and teachers." *Child Devlpm.* 48:1112–1116.
26. Finkelstein, N. et al. 1978. "Social behavior of infants and toddlers in a day-care environment." *Devlpm. Psychol.* 14:257–262.
27. Fox, N. 1977. "Attachment of kibbutz infants to mother and metapelet." *Child Devlpm.* 48:1228–1239.
28. Fraiberg, S. 1977. *Every Child's Birthright: In Defense of Mothering*. Basic Books, New York.
29. Gavron, H. 1966. *The Captive Wife*. Routledge and Kegan Paul, London.
30. Gold, D. and Andres, D. 1978. "Relations between maternal employment and development of nursery school children." *Canad. J. Behav. Sci.* 10:116–129.
31. Gold, D. and Andres, D. 1978. "Comparisons of adolescent children with employed and nonemployed mothers." *Merrill-Palmer Quart.* 24:243–254.
32. Heinicke, C. et al. 1973. "The organization of day care: considerations relating to the mental health of child and family." *Amer. J. Orthopsychiat.* 43:8–22.
33. Hilton, I. 1967. "Differences in the behavior of mothers to first-born and later-born children." *J. Pers. Soc. Psychol.* 7:282–290.
34. Hinde, R. and Spencer-Booth, Y. 1970. "Individual differences in the responses of rhesus monkeys to a period of separation from their mothers." *J. Child Psychol. Psychiat.* 11:159–176.
35. Hock, E. 1978. "Working and nonworking mothers with infants: perceptions of their careers, their infants' needs, and satisfaction with mothering." *Devlpm. Psychol.* 14:37–43.

36. Hoffman, L. 1974. "Effects of maternal employment on the child—a review of the research." *Devlpm. Psychol.* 10:204–228.

37. Hoffman, L. 1979. "Maternal employment: 1979." *Amer. Psychol.* 34:859–865.

38. Jacobs, B. and Moss, H. 1976. "Birth order and sex of sibling as determinants of mother-infant interaction." *Child Devlpm.* 47:315–322.

39. Kagan, J., Kearsley, R. and Zelazo, P. 1978. *Infancy: Its Place in Human Development.* Harvard University Press, Cambridge, Mass.

40. Lamb, M. ed. 1976. *The Role of the Father in Child Development.* John Wiley, New York.

41. Lamb, M. 1979. "The changing American family and its implications for infant social development: the sample case of maternal employment." In *The Social Network of the Developing Infant*, M. Lewis and L. Rosenblum, eds. Plenum, New York.

42. Lasko, J. 1954. "Parent behavior toward first and second children." *Genet. Psychol. Mongr.* 49:96–137.

43. Leiderman, P. and Leiderman, G. 1974. "Affective and cognitive consequences of polymatric infant care in the East African highlands." In *Minnesota Symposium in Psychology*, Vol. 8, A. Pick, ed. University of Minnesota Press, Minneapolis.

44. Maccoby, E. 1980. *Social Development: Psychological Growth and the Parent-Infant Relationship.* Harcourt Brace Jovanovich, New York.

45. McCutcheon, B. and Calhoun, K. 1976. "Social and emotional adjustment of infants and toddlers to a day care setting." *Amer. J. Orthopsychiat.* 46:104–108.

46. Macrae, J. and Herbert-Jackson, E. 1976. "Are behavioral effects of infant day care program specific?" *Devlpm. Psychol.* 12:269–270.

47. Marantz, S. and Mansfield, A. 1977. "Maternal employment and the development of sex-role stereotyping in five-to-eleven-year-old girls." *Child Devlpm.* 48:668–673.

48. Mayall, B. and Petrie, P. 1977. *Minder, Mother and Child.* University of London Institute of Education, London.

49. Moore, T. 1963. "Effects on the children." In *Working Mothers and Their Children*, S. Yudkin and A. Holme, eds. Michael Joseph, London.

50. Moore, T. 1975. "Exclusive early mothering and its alternatives: the outcome to adolescence." *Scand. J. Psychol.* 16:255–272.

51. Moskowitz, D., Schwarz, J. and Corsini, D. 1977. "Initiating day care at three years of age: effects on attachment." *Child Devlpm.* 48:1271–1276.

52. Newberry, P., Weissman, M. and Myers, J. 1979. "Working wives and housewives: do they differ in mental status and social adjustment?" *Amer. J. Orthopsychiat.* 49:282–291.

53. Oakley, A. 1974. *Housewife.* Allen Lane, London.

54. Pilling, D. and Pringle, M. 1978. *Controversial Issues in Child Development.* Paul Elek, London.

55. Portnoy, F. and Simmons, C. 1978. "Day care and attachment." *Child Devlpm.* 49:239–242.

56. Quinton, D. and Rutter, M. 1976. "Early hospital admissions and later disturbances of behavior: an attempted replication of Douglas' findings." *Devlpm. Med. Child Neurol.* 18:447–459.

57. Radloff, L. 1975. "Sex differences in depression: the effects of occupation and marital status." *Sex Roles* 1:249–265.
58. Ragozin, A. 1980. "Attachment behavior of day-care children: naturalistic and laboratory observations." *Child Devlpm.* 51:409–415.
59. Raph, J. et al. 1968. "The influence of nursery school on social interactions." *Amer. J. Orthopsychiat.* 38:144–152.
60. Reed, G. and Leiderman, P. 1981. "Age related changes in attachment behavior in polymatrically reared infants: the Kenyan Gusii." In *Culture and Infant Interaction*, T. Field et al, eds. Lawrence Erlbaum, Hillsdale, N.J. (in press).
61. Ricciuti, H. 1974. "Fear and development of social attachments in the first year of life." In *The Origins of Human Behavior: Fear.* M. Lewis and L. Rosenblum, eds. John Wiley, New York.
62. Robertson, J. and Robertson, J. 1971. "Young children in brief separation: a fresh look." *Psychoanal. Study of the Child* 26:264–315.
63. Robertson, J. and Robertson, J. 1977. "Taking the side of the under-threes." *Austral. Women's Weekly* (July 20).
64. Roopnarine, J. and Lamb, M. 1979. "The effects of day care on attachment and exploratory behavior in a strange situation." *Merrill-Palmer Quart.* 24:85–95.
65. Rothbart, M. 1971. "Birth order and mother-child interaction in an achievement situation." *J. Pers. Soc. Psychol.* 17:113–120.
66. Roy, A. 1978. "Vulnerability factors and depression in women." *Brit. J. Psychiat.* 133:106–110.
67. Rubenstein, J. and Howes, C. 1976. "The effect of peers on toddler interaction with mother and toys." *Child Devlpm.* 47:597–605.
68. Rubenstein, J. and Howes, C. 1979. "Caregiving and infant behavior in day care and in homes." *Devlpm. Psychol.* 15:1–24.
69. Rubenstein, J., Pedersen, F. and Yarrow, L. 1977. "What happens when mother is away: a comparison of mothers and substitute caregivers." *Devlpm. Psychol.* 13:529–530.
70. Rutter, M. 1970. "Sex differences in children's responses to family stress." In *The Child in the Family*, E. Anthony and C. Koupernik, eds. John Wiley, New York.
71. Rutter, M. 1972. *Maternal Deprivation Reassessed.* Penguin, Harmondsworth, Middx.
72. Rutter, M. 1977. "Individual differences." In *Child Psychiatry: Modern Approaches*, M. Rutter and L. Hersov, eds. Blackwell, Oxford.
73. Rutter, M. 1979. "Maternal deprivation, 1972–1978: new findings, new concepts, new approaches." *Child Devlpm.* 50:283–305.
74. Rutter, M. 1980. *Changing Youth in a Changing Society: Patterns of Adolescent Development and Disorder.* Harvard University Press, Cambridge, Mass.
75. Rutter, M. 1980. "Attachment and the development of social relationships." In *Scientific Foundations of Developmental Psychiatry*, M. Rutter, ed. Heinemann Medical, London.
76. Rutter, M. 1980. "Emotional development." In *Scientific Foundations of Developmental Psychiatry*, M. Rutter, ed. Heinemann Medical, London.

77. Rutter, M. 1980. "Separation experiences: a new look at an old topic." *J. Pediat.* 95:147–154.
78. Schwarz, J., Krolick, G. and Strickland, R. 1973. "Effects of early day care experience on adjustment to a new environment." *Amer. J. Orthopsychiat.* 43:340–346.
79. Schwarz, J., Strickland, R. and Krolick, G. 1974. "Infant day care: behavioral effects at preschool age." *Devlpm. Psychol.* 10:502–506.
80. Stacey, M. et al. 1970. *Hospitals, Children and Their Families: The Report of a Pilot Study.* Routledge and Kegan Paul, London.
81. Stallings, J. and Porter, A. 1980. *National Day Care Home Study: Observation Component.* (Final Report, Volume III to Department of Health and Human Services, Washington, D.C.) S.R.I. International, Stanford, Calif.
82. Stayton, D. and Ainsworth, M. 1973. "Individual differences in infant response to brief, everyday separations as related to other infant and maternal behaviors." *Devlpm. Psychol.* 9:213–225.
83. Thoman, E. et al. 1970. "Neonate-mother interaction: effects of parity on feeding behavior." *Child Devlpm.* 41:1103–1111.
84. Tizard, B. and Hodges, J. 1978. "The effect of early institutional rearing on the development of eight-year-old children." *J. Child Psychol. Psychiat.* 19:99–118.
85. Tizard, J., Moss, P. and Perry, J. 1976. *All Our Children: Preschool Services in a Changing Society.* Temple Smith, London.
86. Vandell, D. 1979. "Effects of a playgroup experience on mother-son and father-son interactions." *Devlpm. Psychol.* 15:379–385.
87. Vogel, S. et al. 1970. "Maternal employment and perception of sex roles among college students." *Devlpm. Psychol.* 3:384–391.
88. Wilcox, B., Staff, P. and Romaine, M. 1980. "A comparison of individual and multiple assignment of caregivers to infants in day care." *Merrill-Palmer Quart.* 26:53–62.
89. Winett, R. et al. 1977. "A cross-sectional study of children and their families in different child care environments: some data and conclusions." *J. Comm. Psychol.* 5:149–159.
90. Wolkind, S. 1974. "The components of 'affectionless psychopathy' in institutionalized children." *J. Child Psychol. Psychiat.* 15:215–220.
91. W.H.O. (Expert Committee on Mental Health). 1951. *Report of the Second Session, 1951.* World Health Organization, Geneva.
92. Yarrow, M. et al. 1962. "Child rearing in families of working and non-working mothers." *Sociometry* 25:122–140.

Chapter 2

INFANT DAY CARE: RELATIONSHIPS BETWEEN THEORY AND PRACTICE

by Sally Provence

In 1970 an effort was begun to develop a series of handbooks that would provide guidelines for day care of America's children. One of the goals of this project was to formulate and communicate recommendations for child care anchored in knowledge about the developmental needs of children. The developmental approach to services was emphasized and the term "developmental day care" was introduced to indicate the necessity of going beyond custodial care in order to enhance the growth and development of children. This period was one when, it will be recalled, there was much energy and funding at the federal level directed at improving the quality of life for disadvantaged parents and children. The OCD series on day care thus became one of the key sources of information for day care planners and providers. As Professor Zigler wrote in the foreword to the handbook *Serving Infants*,[28] "They [this and the other handbooks] do not attempt to provide all the answers or to lay down an inflexible set of rules; however, I regard them as excellent statements of our current knowledge about developmental day care."

This project, conceived by Dr. Edward Zigler, Mr. Jule Sugarman, and Dr. Ronald K. Parker, the project director, involved more than 200 individuals—a broad-based and representative group of parents, nongovernmental child development experts, and practitioners. The author was a member of a work group convened by Edward Zigler, the first director of the Office of Child Development, which is now part of the Agency for Children, Youth and Family of the U.S. Department of Health and Human Services.

In the more than 10 years since that time, child day care has continued to be a subject of public and private concern and study. There
has also been a steadily increasing interest in infant day care for a
variety of reasons, among them the growing number of one-parent
families, more mothers whose economic need or personal preference
entails a return to work outside the home during their children's
infancies, and the fact that the grandparent generation is less available to provide child care assistance because of distance or because
it, too, is in the work force. Moreover, for many two-parent families,
the income from two jobs is, in these days, necessary for economic
survival. There are also attitudinal changes that tend to devalue the
emotional satisfactions and the importance of the time and effort
spent by mothers in the daily care of infants. Etaugh's[14] survey of
attitudes toward nonmaternal care of children is instructive in this
context.

The body of knowledge about the development of children and
what is likely to facilitate or impede it is derived from many sources,
especially from the accumulated wisdom of generations of living
with children, from a variety of research studies of children in traditional families, from clinical practice and studies of vulnerable, ill,
developmentally disturbed and handicapped children, and from research and practice with children in atypical situations.

It is important, in my view, that those who define experiences of
good quality for children, those who evaluate them, and those who
translate the ideas about meeting developmental needs into programs
operate from a well-articulated set of propositions. One of the interests of child development experts in recent years has been the effort
to provide a conceptual framework for planning for children that
takes advantage of knowledge of child development and of parent-
child relationships. Such an effort is essential, even though many of
the direct providers of good care act according to assumptions and
beliefs they cannot easily define. Terms such as "common sense,"
"intuitive behavior" and "doing what comes naturally" are often
used to suggest that little knowledge is involved in child rearing or
that one learns all one needs to know about child care in the school
of life. The informal learning of child care through one's own family
relationships and cultural traditions has been the major instruction
in child care and has often, of course, worked out very well for the
child. But there are important differences between the care of one's
own child, with the personal interest and abiding relationships involved, and the provision of care to the children of others. In the
latter, one does not have the safeguards of the close relationships
over time that not only support learning and social-emotional development with positive experiences, but also provide many opportunities for the resolution of conflicts and other difficulties—the long

term affectionate care that, in spite of difficulties and stresses, is the environment that facilitates development. Thus it is of great importance that day care programs expect of themselves that they will provide experiences that optimize development, and that these be based on the best knowledge available. To do less is to court danger for child and family.

Given the need for adopting sound, clearly articulated approaches to infant day care, there are pitfalls to be avoided. The translation of theory and research findings into practice is beset by several hazards, among them the tendency to overvalue the significance of a particular practice or method without paying sufficient attention to the larger context that acknowledges the complexity of development. The fact that a specific method of child care or education affects one child differently from another is one example. As early childhood specialists, we usually make best use of child development knowledge when we deal with individual children and families or with small groups in familiar contexts. We are less skillful in translating that knowledge into nationwide programs and social policy. Nevertheless, translation is very important. (A promising, organized effort in regard to social policy is that of the Bush Center's program.[30])

The task I have set for myself, then, is to lay out the major assumptions that provide a basis for planning day care for infants and toddlers and to illustrate some of the ways in which these tenets are translated into action. In contrast with the OCD series in which recommendations reflected consensus views of the work group for each handbook, this chapter can claim only local consensus, and perhaps not even that. Nonetheless, much of what is said is congenial with the views of other child development specialists. The way in which the ideas have been combined obviously is shaped by my experience and theoretical preferences.

It is with apology that some of the constructs to follow are included since they may seem too basic and well accepted to warrant discussion. However, it is the combination and interrelatedness of the constructs that require emphasis. My special plea is for the delineation of a coherent approach to meeting the needs of infants, one that provides a rationale for planning, that defines a conceptual base to return to both for adjustments in planning and for examination of what has gone on, and one that allows for the flexibility and individualization that is known to be necessary in addressing the needs of the unique individual each child is. The selection of empirical data and theoretical formulations will, no doubt, differ from that of other persons as intensely interested and concerned as I am for infants. It is well known, for example, that those of us who observe infants and parents may relate the same behavioral data to quite different developmental theories. Moreover, those who work with children sensitively and with effectiveness may differ widely in their explanatory formulations. Such is the state of the art. We have not yet arrived at a unitary child development theory, nor does it appear that we shall, since the complexity of development and the multiple factors that influence it are such as to defy, or perhaps make inappropriate, such efforts.

Yet it seems to me that it is possible to specify certain premises and ideas about development that provide explanatory constructs and guidelines—ideas that when translated into attitudes and action are likely to favorably influence the development of children. My defense of the propositions to be put forward is that over a period of years they have provided basic principles and guides for clinical work with young children and parents in the Yale Child Study Center that seem sensible, practical, and useful. They also guided the planning and carrying out of a comprehensive program of services (including day care) in a research and demonstration project for disadvantaged young children and parents reported in *The Challenge of Daycare*.[49]

The approach leans heavily on psychoanalytic developmental psychology, especially constructs regarding the role of parent-child relationships in the child's emotional and cognitive development, encompassing also propositions related to developmental conflicts and conflict resolution, the importance of innate factors, and the adaptive ego processes. Biological dimensions of the approach include concern for physical health, as well as ideas regarding endowment, maturation, phase or stage specificity, and adaptation. The role of learning in adaptation processes is emphasized, as is the philosophy that the growth of cognitive functions cannot be separated from the growth of emotional and interpersonal processes. An awareness of the importance of family relationships and of the societal system that influences children and parents is also central to the approach.

The focus in this chapter will be on the relevance of these views for infant day care.

Maturation, Endowment, and Experience

One begins with the proposition that the development of the child is a complex, dynamic, interactional process in which inborn characteristics and the many experiences that comprise the child's environment continuously influence one another. Maturation of inborn somatic and psychic systems takes place in established sequences according to a time table specific for the human child and in constant interaction with environmental influences. Cohen[9] has summarized the usefulness of conceptualizing the organization of behavior as an interaction of biological and psychosocial forces and has pointed out the general acceptance of the multivariate, interactional model as a way of approaching issues regarding the complexity of development and the ways in which physiology and experience interact. The child's endowment at birth is a function not only of genetics but also of the intra-uterine and neonatal environments and the events surrounding birth. Cohen points out that from the match or fitting together of the child's endowment and the environment there are early adaptations and patterns of response and perception:

"In basic and still unclear ways, congenital endowment and congenital organization of behavior are patterned by complex biochemical interactions. In turn the early experiences of a child—including nutrition, infection, drugs, and trauma of delivery—lead to enduring patterns of behavior encoded in central nervous system metabolism. These persistent early adaptations . . . shape the child's later adaptations and style of approach to new developmental tasks. Behavioral patterns and hierarchies of action patterns in this way assume a type of autonomy which may become crystallized characteristics of behavior through social reinforcement," (pp. 386–387)

Normal newborns, while resembling one another in many ways, also differ in various ways. While the significance of these differences is only partially understood, there is evidence that they are factors influencing the variations in characteristics we refer to as individuality. Many writers, among them Peiper,[41] Fries and Woolf,[22] Escalona,[12,13] Kagan and Lewis,[29] Fantz,[15] Brazelton,[7] Korner and Grobstein,[32] Kessen,[31] Wolff,[63] Lustman,[35] Sander,[53] Sander et al,[54] Thomas, Chess and Birch,[59] Thomas and Chess,[58] Richmond and Lustman,[52] have studied differences in newborns and have speculated about their significance for development. These studies include observations on sensory reactivity in various modalities, motility, state and state regulation, autonomic reactivity, and biological rhythms. The importance of endowment factors in development has also been emphasized in psychoanalysis: Hartmann[26] extended and expanded Freud's emphasis on biological factors, proposing the idea of autonomous ego functions based on inborn somatic apparatuses—an ego constitution. Functions such as motility, perception, memory, intelligence, speech, the capacity for delay, and the organizing functions of the mind are among the ego functions thus identified that broadened the theoretical views of psychoanalytic investigators and clinicians. From psychoanalysis, too, came propositions regarding drive endowment and in respect to both drives and ego, the idea of progressive development and differentiation out of an undifferentiated state. (See, for example, Hartmann, Kris and Loewenstein,[27] A. Freud,[20] Alpert, Neubauer and Weil.[1])

When the biological equipment is impaired for any reason, future development may be jeopardized, not only by the somatic impairment but because biologically immature or impaired children are more vulnerable than entirely healthy ones to adverse psychosocial factors, as shown, for example, in Parmelee's[40] longitudinal studies of premature infants, Fraiberg's studies of the blind,[17,18,19] and Zigler's[65] studies of retarded children in institutions.

One might question why it is important for infant day care that constructs such as congenital characteristics, biological vulnerability, maturation, and endowment be considered, since they are not at first glance a concern of the day care planner or provider. However, acknowledging the relevance of these ideas is useful because they explain, in part, the necessity to individualize care and thus make caregivers more tolerant of the varying needs of normal infants. For example, a baby who is very sensitive to stimulation and reacts with disorganization and crying often needs quite different handling than one who is more adaptable or less sensitive. The fact that every experienced caregiver knows this at some level does not change the fact that explanation and sanction are important, since those who plan programs and routines of child care, especially for groups of children, do not usually allow time for individualizing care. One common danger in the practice of infant day care relates to the human infant's substantial capacities for adapting to his environment, even to an environment far from optimal. The observed resilience of some infants is often invoked in defense of rigidities in caregivers and programs in which there are too few adults or too little child care talent to permit each infant's needs to be met even reasonably well. Children with recognized developmental handicaps are usually identified as having special needs requiring special consideration. In many instances, however, day care programs are asked to provide services to very needy children without the support necessary to do so.

The designation *experience* in considering a child's development is a useful term, as Escalona[12] suggests, since while it includes much of what is called environmental, it is subjective and implies a definite influence on the child. For example, when one sets about to describe the characteristics of an environment that facilitates development, the way in which infants in general or a specific infant might *experience* it is a necessary component of examining the merits of a particular program. Experience also involves a consideration of the child's characteristics as codeterminants of the effect of a specific event or stimulus. In planning child care and programs for infants there are two general levels at which the concept experience requires reflection: (1) what general plans would one make based upon knowledge of what infants of a particular age are likely to need to facilitate development, and (2) within that general framework how would one individualize plans for a particular child in accordance with his current needs? Determinants of the influence of a particular factor or event include the child's congenital characteristics, his developmental phase with its vulnerabilities and competencies, and antecedent experiences, especially with respect to similar situations. Another set of determinants is related to the immediate situation of the event and its context; for example, its intensity, duration, and timing in relation to the child's physiological and psychological state at a given time on a specific day. What one will choose to do or ask of an infant will be influenced by his mood, state of comfort or discomfort, fatigue, readiness for interaction, coping abilities, and a host of other things best discerned by an adult who knows him well.

Escalona's paper referred to above, entitled "Patterns of Infantile Experience and the Developmental Process," is an especially clear statement about the importance of experience. In spelling out aspects of this concept she says: "What infants experience as they are fed, clothed, bathed, the nature of their perceptual and motor encounters with the world, about and with their own bodies and most importantly their transactions with the mother and with other people—the nature of these events is influenced by the baby's established reaction tendencies (which may be biologically given or acquired) and by the mother and outer circumstance . . . the actual reality to which they must adapt." (p. 197) Her data support the notion that very different actions on the part of mothers (or other environmental variations) may have similar consequences in terms of their impact upon the child's experience and, conversely, that similar or identical external stimulation may have varying and opposite consequences as reflected in behavior.

A central task of infant day care is to provide experience addressed to the developmental needs of children, to take into account current developmental characteristics, and to be aware of those trends and incipient behaviors that are likely to emerge in the near future. Much of the day care literature is addressed to the task of providing growth-promoting experiences—physical, cognitive, social, and emotional. Planners and providers vary in the priorities they set in these general areas and their views of what it takes to carry them out. But there is at least general agreement—based on humanitarian attitudes as well as developmental theory—that some definition of what constitutes good infant care is necessary and that experiences that facilitate learning and social relationships are part of good care.

The Phase or Stage Concept

Another aspect of developmental theory of special relevance in planning for children in day care is the phase or stage concept. In the broad sense this means that there are developmental trends that, on the average, converge at a given time and in characteristic ways. The stages of psychosexual development as outlined in psychoanalytic theory and the well-delineated causes of anxiety related to them are examples (Freud,[21] A. Freud,[20] Kris,[33] Spitz,[56] Benjamin[3]) that apply to work with young children and parents. The concept includes characteristic dynamic constellation and dominant central regulatory mechanisms as well as behavioral norms. Erikson's[10] psychosocial theory outlines a sequence of epigenetic phases and relates them to psychosexual development. In describing phases or stages in the life cycle and phase-specific developmental tasks which must be solved in each, he points out also that the solutions are prepared in previous phases and further worked out in later ones. The stages of sensory-motor intelligence as defined by Piaget[42] provide another example—this in relation to the development of intelligence.

In respect to applications of the phase concept, traditional psychoanalytic theory as well as Erikson's psychosocial theory emphasize that there are optimal periods for every step in learning, integration, and overcoming conflicts. It follows that child-rearing practices, education, socialization, and training of all kinds, and aspects of medical care, in order to be most supportive of the child's development, must take into account what is known about phase- or developmental-stage specificity. Counseling of parents, provision of child care and education in a positive sense, and protection of the child from experiences judged to be excessively depriving or stressful, traumatic, or frankly noxious are among the aspects of infant day care programs influenced by the phase concept. This concept also affects views about the parent-child relationship and the development of parenthood: specific phase characteristics in the child interact with parental attitudes, nurturing talents, coping capacities, and unresolved conflicts in ways that can have a profound influence on the immediate behavior of each and the relationship between them.

Parenthood as a Developmental Process

Propositions regarding parenthood as a developmental process, too, provide important guidelines relevant for infant day care. Becoming a parent has been called one of the normal developmental crises of life (Bibring[5]). New tasks are associated with becoming a parent, and new stresses as well as new sources of strength, pleasure, and satisfaction (Benedek,[2] Erikson,[11] Naylor[39]). Earlier experiences, particularly experiences with their own parents and important others, are powerful influences in the way young parents adapt to, cope with, and feel about parenthood. All young parents need certain psychological and tangible supports, including those parents who have been well nurtured as children and whose current life situation is favorable. Child rearing is not easy in our complex society, even for parents who are competent, reasonably healthy in mind and body, desirous of children, and able to earn a decent living. Erikson describes very well what happens in a favorable child care situation. "While far removed from any mastery over the physical world, newborn man is endowed with an appearance and with responses which appeal to the tending adults' tenderness and make them wish to attend to his needs; which arouse concern in those who are concerned with his well-being; and which, in making adults care, stimulate their active caretaking . . . . Defenseless as babies are, they have mothers at their command, families to protect the mothers, societies to support the structure of families, and traditions to give a cultural continuity to systems of tending and training." In large segments of our society today one or another part of Erikson's structure of wholeness and continuity is missing or impaired. Many babies do not have nurturing mothers at their command, many mothers suffer and decompensate from not having families to support them, no stable societal institutions and cultural traditions to provide the continuity and the guidelines of which Erikson writes. These realities explain in part why child day care is in greater demand, and why it is often difficult to do well.

But to return to parenthood: many new skills are involved simply in the techniques of infant care. Feeding, bathing, dressing, diapering, holding, and comforting the baby require learning and practice. Even those who have handled infants before find things somehow different and more intense when caring for their own babies. "Getting to know the baby" stands for a large array of perceptions and interpretations of the baby's rhythms and responses which are, fortunately I believe, usually cast in terms of how the baby feels—what he want or needs, likes or dislikes, is attracted to or rejects. Putting it this way emphasizes the needs of the infant at a time when he is most defenseless and dependent on others. Moreover, it is the social context, the interaction between infant and caregiver that provides the experiences essential for development and learning in infancy.

On the parents' side, then, there are big adjustments to be made; the new role of each parent and the change in the relationship between them. If the baby is not a firstborn, there will be new adjustments for siblings also. Powerful feelings accompany these events. A condensed and oversimplified statement is that some parents are better equipped than others to adapt to becoming parents and to develop as parents. Both the great satisfactions parenthood brings and the stresses encountered are noteworthy.

The idea that parenthood is a developmental process and a stage of life involving new tasks, vulnerabilities, and potentials for conflicts, as well as new opportunities and gratification helps to organize data, especially that derived from clinical experience. According to this view, how well the tasks of parenthood are carried out depends, in part, on how well the conflicts of earlier phases have been resolved. Characteristics of the baby during infancy and toddlerhood (and, of course, later as well) may reactivate in the parent unresolved problems of the same phases in her or his own development, an occurrence often accounting for acute parent-child conflict. But, as Benedek[2] suggests, the parent is also provided with opportunities to work on the unresolved problems, and the result is often a new level of personality integration characterized by greater maturity and feelings of well-being.

Again, one might ask what this has to do with the work of day care providers. Parents using day care are often under greater stress than those who have or exercise the option not to do so. Some of this stress may be related to economic need, pressures on the job, and other situational realities. Much of the time it is internal, psychological reality that determines what is experienced as stressful and how one copes with stress. Many mothers who use infant day care are especially vulnerable to feelings of guilt, self-criticism, and criticism —real or implied—by others. If infant day care is to be done in a way that is as supportive as possible for infants, there must also be empathic concern and psychological support for the parent. Providing good care for infants is a necessary but not sufficient condition for infant day care programs. There must also be staff members who are able to respond sensitively and helpfully to parents.

The Central Role of Human Relationships

We share with others the view that the child's experiences with other persons—first with parent figures and later with others—are basic and vitally influential factors in determining the course of development. Such a view inevitably influences conceptions of the needs of infants in day care. Constructs regarding the importance of human relationships influence day care programs in two additional ways: (1) in the consideration given to the importance of establishing good working relationships between parents and day care providers, which can have both short- and long-range benefits for the child, and (2) in the development of good working relationships among staff members of day care centers because these relationships strongly influence the quality of the program.

The close and abiding relationships so influential in the child's behavior and successive phases of development have their beginnings in the interactions between mother and child in the early days and weeks; these relationships gradually grow and are differentiated, becoming increasingly complex. There are, fortunately, many opportunities in the lives of infant and parent for the relationship to deepen and develop. Only a selective, highly condensed summary of major propositions, derived from theory, practice, and research can be included here. The major theoretical source of the viewpoint expressed is psychoanalytic developmental psychology.[27,33,51,20,57,36]

Through his human relationships from early on, the infant receives not only the necessary physical nurturance, but also the protection, stimulation, training, and the organizing influences that enhance cognitive, social, and emotional development. His perception and approaches to the social and material world, his capacity to cope with the tasks of development, his ability to feel and deal with pleasure and pain, his becoming a thinking, feeling, and communicating person—all are anchored in his experiences with others, mainly the adults who nurture him. The society into which he is born transmits its values and attitudes, exerts its influence, makes him its member primarily through his social relationships. A few more specific examples of the influence of the parent-child relationship have been summarized (Provence[46]) as follows: such mental functions as discrimination between things and persons in the environment, the distinction between the self and the other and between inner and outer stimuli, and the psychological investment in sensory-motor experiences depend in important ways on the child's human object relationships. "Such ego functions as motility, perception, speech, and intelligence may be enhanced or impeded according to the adequacy of the young child's object relations; attitudes toward reality are deeply influenced [by them]; and trouble in object relations often interferes with another important function of the ego, the formation of stable defenses." (p. 210–211) Object relations also codetermine instinctual drive development, its organization and behavioral expression. The infant's relationships, especially with parent figures, also influence his relations to toys and other inanimate objects during the early years. This latter has been perhaps most dramatically demonstrated in studies of severely deprived infants (see, for example, Provence and Ritvo[50]).

The interaction between infant and parent is an important source of interest in toys, and the parents' pleasure in the baby's activity with the toy further promotes his own pleasure and investment in it. Those who work with infants are familiar with how an adult's enthusiasm makes a toy or activity attractive to the child. Such knowledge is widely used in infant day care with healthy babies and in therapeutic situations with apathetic, excessively passive, indifferent, or developmentally impaired children whom one wants to help with learning, with play, with affective expression.

A belief in the central importance of human relationships can be translated in a variety of ways into practices in infant day care. In particular it determines how many persons one has on the staff and the personal qualities and competencies looked for. It determines also the choice of experiences for infants the program will provide and how these experiences are to be individualized. Day care staff, as substitutes for the parents, must provide many of the experiences outlined earlier as important for infants. They do this primarily through the way in which they interact with each infant, through their affectionate interest, through the infants coming to know and trust them, and through their personal warmth, child care skills and knowledge of developmental needs. In the project at Yale reported in *The Challenge of Daycare*[49] a belief in the importance of the human relationships was also the source of a commitment to work with parents, and of our expectation—repeatedly confirmed—that any young child away from parents for long hours a day would undergo some degree of stress, with which he would need our assistance. We believed also that the influence of the day care experience for the child would depend in part on the relationship between parents and staff members, and that responsibility for developing a partnership with parents on behalf of the child lay initially with us. We thought it of great importance, as we said, that, "the staff recognize the basic importance of the parent to the child, respect the parents' feelings, recognize that turning the child over to others involves stress for parents, and that most parents try to do the best they can for their children even when they fail them in some way." (p. 7) Thus, supporting the relationship between infant and parents through appropriate responses to both of them defines an important goal. The quality of the relationships among staff members is known to be another determinant of the quality of the day care experience for infant and parent. A frequent consequence of staff dissension, for example, is a negative impact on children, because caregivers function less well and the affective atmosphere is less conducive than it should be to learning and to feelings of security. What follows from this is that the leadership of the program must be able to recognize signs of such very human conflict and dissension, develop methods of resolving them, freeing the staff to devote their energy and creativity to making the experience for infant and parent a positive one.

Benefits of the Care of the Body

The provision of good physical care in infant day care is important in several ways. Healthful surroundings, attention to nutrition, early recognition of illness or other health problems, and safeguards against accidents are obvious and are generally recognized as necessary for good day care. But the care of the child's body is important for other reasons too. A great many affective communications, cognitive cues and reciprocal response patterns are apparent in these physical care activities. Psycho-social development is also affected by the nature of the care. Feeding, bathing, cleaning, diapering, and dressing are events around which many communications come to the child from the caregiver. He hears her voice, sees her face, feels her touch. Very early, her concern for his comfort, her pleasure in being with him begin to be transmitted in these ordinary caring situations. Her handling may be gentle or rough, intrusive or adaptive to the child, it may reflect the mutuality of the relationship or its opposite. His body and its boundaries, its feelings and sensations, and the person and actions of the caregiver are the most constant and influential sources of his earliest learning. The first stages in the sense of self, of a personal identity, involve awareness of the body self. The care the child receives and the attitudes of caregivers toward his body strongly influence his later sense of identity and feelings of self worth. As he enters the second year, his development is influenced either favorably or unfavorably by adults' attitudes and behavior in regard to such developmental tasks as self-feeding and sphincter control. When he begins to walk, run and climb, to move out toward his environment, he at first has little judgement about realistic dangers and he may protest the adult's limiting and protecting him. But, so protected, he learns eventually to distinguish between what is safe and what is dangerous. The expectation that the important adults will keep him from harm is characteristic of the well cared for young child and is one important aspect of his feeling valued. Protecting the child's body from the aggression of others and preventing him from aggressing too strongly against others conveys interest in him. It also conveys an attitude that favorably influences his development toward control of his own impulses.*

It was also amply documented in our project that the staff's attention to the infants' physical well-being had great meaning for parents. It went far toward alleviating their anxiety about the long hours they were separated from their infants and toddlers. Such things as

---

* Much of the foregoing material is paraphrased from Provence, Naylor, and Patterson, *The Challenge of Daycare* (1977), and is used with the permission of The Yale University Press, New Haven.

letting a parent know what the child had eaten or discussing any signs of illness or minor injuries the child had received, and the staff's obvious pleasure in dressing the children in fresh clothing and getting them ready for their parents in the afternoon communicated, perhaps more effectively than words, a degree of interest in the children that comforted parents and helped them to trust us.

Learning and Play as Factors in Adaptation

It is through learning, during infancy and later, too, that the human child acquires many of his adaptation processes. This has been recognized in developmental psychology especially since the publication of Hartmann's *Ego and The Problem of Adaptation.*[26] Hartmann's adaptation theory opened the way for the coordination and examination of various experiences of clinicians and educators concerned with the learning process. His propositions included the concept of the ego as man's means of adaptation and adjustment to his environment. Influential, too, in Hartmann's theory were propositions regarding the ego constitution (roots of the ego)—the somatic and mental apparatuses with which an infant is born that underlie the ego's autonomous functions, among them motility, perception, intelligence, memory, speech, and mechanisms of modulation and regulation of impulse. He formulated the view that through the maturation, differentiation, and functioning of these apparatuses and the coordinations they effect, the human not only adapts to an average expectable environment but also, through his action, helps to create that environment. Hartmann, Kris and Loewenstein[27] contributed further hypotheses regarding adaptive ego processes, and those related to early learning are of greatest relevance in this context.

The child, in his prolonged helplessness, is dependent upon a social structure (the family) which provides the setting in which early learning takes place. As far as the infant's learning experiences are concerned, psychoanalytic hypotheses, Hartmann, Kris and Loewenstein[27] note, "take mainly four factors into account: first, the stage of maturation of the apparatuses; second, the reaction of the environment; third, the tolerance [of the child] for deprivation; and, fourth, the various types of gratification afforded by processes of learning and the satisfaction that can be obtained as a consequence of mastery." (p. 26)

The beneficial role of experiences of mastery in the child's development has been especially emphasized by R.W. White[62] who noted that effectance motivation (competence) has high adaptive value and that it involves satisfactions in transactions in which behavior has an exploratory, varying, experimental character and produces changes in the stimulus field. In regard to infants, White says, "crawling and walking, attention and perception, language and thinking, exploring novel objects and places, manipulating the surroundings and producing effective changes in the environment . . . they all form part of the process whereby the child learns to interact effectively with the environment." (pp. 297–333) The studies of Harter,[24] Harter and Zigler,[25] L. Yarrow and his colleagues[64] and Burton L. White[61] have examined and contributed further to views on the origins of competence, of mastery motivation and to relationships between cognition and motivation in infancy and early childhood.

Lois Murphy's studies of coping have brought another dimension to the understanding of the infant's adaptation. Murphy[38] notes that coping begins at birth and there are individual differences in coping resources. The concept of coping focuses on what the child is *trying* to do and does not necessarily imply success—but successful coping contributes increments to competence. Coping strategies are learned, in part, directly from others, but for Murphy, as for White, coping involves original, imaginative, and innovative behavior. From her studies of infants, Escalona[12] brought together aspects of ego psychology and Piaget's work on cognition in a hypothesis regarding development that has been very useful to me in planning experiences for infants. She said: "my data suggest the possibility that what Piaget proposes for cognition is true of all adaptive aspects of mental functioning: namely, that the emergence of such functions as communication, modulation of affect, control over excitation, delay, and aspects of object relation, and hence indentification, all are the result of a developmental sequence in sensory motor terms, before they can emerge as ego functions in a narrower sense." (p. 198) Escalona's hypothesis underscores the importance of the infant's acting, imitating and practicing. It is also congenial with empirical data on the effectiveness of therapeutic methods involving activation of infants with developmental delays, especially those suffering from deficits in the environment. (See, for example, Provence and Lipton,[48] Brazelton *et al.*,[8] Provence,[45,47] Ferholt and Provence,[16] Fraiberg *et al.*[19])

These constructs regarding adaptive processes, experiences of mastery, and coping efforts have direct applicability to the selection of the array of experiences that should be provided in infant day care. While these can be subsumed under the definition of developmental needs, it is worthwhile to formulate how these specific ideas about development can be translated into aspects of the infant's experiences in day care. It is well known that infants who are experientially deprived or are subjected to great discontinuity and inconsistency in care do not learn normally. They also suffer in respect to the development of modes of coping, adaptation, and defense. Pleasure in mastery and motivation to mastery are often severely impaired. Prevention of such dysfunction through the provision of positive, supportive experiences is one of the specific tasks of infant day care.

Play and playful activity are characteristic of the human child and, indeed, of the young of many other species. Play activities and playful interchanges between adults and infants quite naturally occur to those involved in planning infants' days. The following ideas about play in the child's life are representative views on its role in the child's life and how it promotes development. Waelder[60] stressed the importance of play for the child in reducing anxiety by its role in overcoming and mastering those situations that cause anxiety. Greenacre[23] has pointed out that, "play, being under the child's direction, can represent fragments and bits of reality according to his needs and wishes. Thus he can dose himself with larger or smaller bits and need not bring the whole overwhelming situation down on himself at one time, even in played-out form." Waelder and Greenacre also accept the existence of functional pleasure in play (a term introduced by Karl Bühler). This refers to the sense of pleasure in performance without regard to the success of a specific activity.

Piaget[43,44] has had much to say about play and particularly about the importance of symbolic play. Symbolic play fulfills an essential role in the young child's life. It is, in Piaget's[44] view, indispensable to affective and intellectual equilibrium that the child "have available to him an area of activity whose motivation is not adaptation to reality but, on the contrary, assimilation of the reality to the self without coercion or sanctions. Such an area is play. . . ." (p. 58) The systems of symbols characteristic of play, Piaget continues, provide a means of self-expression constructed by the child and capable of being bent to his wishes. Piaget emphasizes, as do Erikson and Murphy, the creative nature of play and its role in the resolution of conflicts, compensation of unsatisfied needs, reversals of roles, problem solving, and so on.

Erikson[11] says, "Play is to the child what thinking, planning, and blueprinting are to the adult, a trial universe in which conditions are simplified and methods exploratory, so that past failures can be thought through, expectations tested. . . . In the toy world, the child plays out the past, often in disguised form, in the manner of dreams, and he begins to master the future by anticipating it in countless variations and repetitive themes." (p. 120) Erikson further speaks of the evolutionary necessity for representational play in order that the child can "learn to bind together an inner and outer world, a remembered past and an anticipated future, before he can learn to master the tools used in cooperation, the roles distributed in the community, and the purposes pursued in a given technology." (p. 121)

Lois Murphy[37] says, "It seems that play is most fun, and most playful, when it is spontaneous, evolving from an integration of impulse and ideas in providing expression, release, sometimes climax, often mastery, with a degree of acceleration and refreshment. . . . The patterns of play seen in children are individually shaped by wishes, angers, fears, conflicts, worries, but they also reveal puzzlements, questions, the need to clarify experience, to make a cognitive map or to improve on nature." (p. 120) Learning through play has been one of the philosophies of early childhood education for many years. It has also been defined as the child's work. Those who are closely associated with infants and toddlers at play (as well as older preschoolers) cannot fail to note its many faces. Seriousness, effort, anxiety, joy, pleasure, sadness, anger, tenderness, and excitement are only a few of them. Play as one of the windows into the child's mind, as well as its function in his development, is well known. While the characteristics of play in the first two years have not been as extensively documented as the play of 2-to-5-year-olds, enough is known to emphasize its importance as an experience to be facilitated for infants in day care.

Playful behavior, social play, and play with toys characterize the infant who is developing well. It is known that a young child who does not or cannot play is a child in trouble. As my colleagues and I have written elsewhere[49] and here paraphrase: Playful interaction with adults is initiated by well cared for infants beginning at around four months when spontaneous social smiling and vocalization are actively used to engage the adult. If adults respond, this social play becomes progressively varied and complex. Mutual imitation is an important factor in its development. Throughout the first year at least, much of the baby's play goes on in relation to the care of his body, i.e., while he is being fed, bathed, changed, cuddled, and put to sleep. It begins in interaction with the adult and is gradually extended to include the child's use of toys and his own body in spontaneous, self-initiated activity as well as in activities the adult makes attractive to him. Adults are important as arrangers of an environment that encourages play; they also provide the protection and social atmosphere in which the child is secure enough and stimulated enough to play. They are comforters, organizers and sources of renewed energy. They are also play partners, and this partnership ranges widely from, for example, a game of peek-a-boo to helping the toddler make sand pies, work a puzzle, manage a rocking horse, feed a baby doll, negotiate with another toddler, etc. Infant day care providers need to appreciate the value of their personal involvement as facilitators of play and to be aware that planning a program of playtimes for infants and toddlers is more fluid and informal than is true for older children. While working with young children of every age, good teachers are alert to what captures a child's interest and how to use these observations to facilitate development through play, nowhere is this more important than in the earliest years.

Finally, some recognition must be given to the contributions of the field of early childhood education to the issues of optimizing development and, especially, learning during infancy. There is a very large literature and no possibility of recognizing its many contributors. One approach has been chosen for description that has been an important influence on the work with young children in the Child Study Center. The philosophy of education that is built on the inseparability of cognitive and affective development has been especially well articulated in the developmental-interaction approach associated with the Bank Street College of Education (see Biber,[4] Shapiro and Biber[55]). This philosophy has been evolving for about six decades and its premises have been derived from continuous study of advancing knowledge in the field of child development. Biber's[4] summary noted that basic assumptions about learning as the foundation of educational practices were derived from psychodynamic theory, especially those aspects having to do with autonomous ego processes and the understanding of motivation, and from the work of the Gestalt and developmental theorists, especially Wertheimer, K. Lewin, Piaget, and Werner. The Bank Street approach to education has influenced our own, both in the educational philosophy and in the systematic observation of how children learn and develop. It includes emphasis, as Biber says, on the existence of autonomous ego processes propelled by motivations independent of instinctual drives, but dependent in important measure on the qualities of support, restraint, and stimulation in the environment; on the importance of action as a mode of learning, including the role of exercising skills and the regeneration of motivation to activity through pleasure in mastery; the normal occurrence of moments of equilibrium and instability; "mixed" rather than "fixed" levels in regard to functional patterns; the concept of the self as both image and instrument, i.e., not only the process of differentiation of the self from the other, but the child's internalized view of his own skills; the concept that growth and maturing involve conflict—conflicts within the self and between the self and outer reality—and that conflict resolution bears the imprint of the interaction with the salient figures and the demands of the culture. The Bank Street developmental-interaction approach to education provides a fine example of the development of teaching strategies and program activities based on a progressive refinement of a philosophy in which basic assumptions and systematic observations of children continuously influence one another. Such continuing study of the relationships between theory and practice are important for the years of infancy as well, since it is difficult to imagine how one can provide adequate programs of day care without thoughtful attention both to planning and evaluation of the day care experience. Indeed the term developmental day care implies the responsibility of adults to provide experiences that facilitate learning, coping and adaptation.

It is crucial that learning in day care be understood in its broad context—not restricted to an emphasis mainly on speech and cognitive development in targeted curricula. The inseparability and interdependence of the cognitive and affective life, of drive and ego development, of all of these with the child's human relationships and the nature of his interaction with the environment argue strongly against simplistic conceptual approaches to infant day care.

To recapitulate, the foregoing series of statements defining my choices of theoretical propositions and clinically tested practices were translated into a set of guidelines for day care of infants and preschool children in the project referred to earlier and reported in *The Challenge of Daycare.*[49] In summary, perhaps, it is sufficient to note that providing a nurturing environment included such major headings as (1) physical care, (2) a supportive physical environment, (3) responsiveness to individual needs, (4) opportunities for the child to act upon his environment, (5) an enriching affective atmosphere, (6) a speaking social partner, (7) experiences of consistency and repetition, variety, and contrast, (8) toys and other playthings, (9) quiet moments and (10) limits, prohibitions, and expectations for conformity. It is but a step from the statement of those developmental needs to the attitudes and child care and educational activities that elaborate them.

The purpose here is not to try to persuade nor to argue that ours is the correct approach and that others are less valid. Rather, as I said in the beginning, the discussion is an effort to describe a particular approach to facilitating the development of infants.

Finally, in respect to infant day care programs specifically, three important and interrelated questions should be asked: (1) does the program meet the developmental needs of infants reasonably well? (2) does the day care experience promote and support the parent-child relationship? (3) does the day care experience protect and support the development of a specific child and his relationship with his parent? If the answer to any one of these is *no*, day care for the infants in that program is at least highly questionable and probably harmful, in spite of good intentions.

References

1. Alpert, A., Neubauer, P.B. and Weil, A. 1956. "Unusual variations in drive endowment." *Psychoanal. Study of the Child.* 11:125–163.
2. Benedek, T. 1959. "Parenthood as a developmental phase." *J. Amer. Psychoanal. Assoc.* 7:389.

3. Benjamin, J.B. 1963. "Further comments on some developmental aspects of anxiety." In H. Gaskill, ed. *Counterpoint.* International Universities Press, New York.

4. Biber, B. 1977. "A developmental-interaction approach: Bank Street College of Education." In M.C. Day and R.K. Parker, eds. *The Preschool in Action,* 2nd edition. Allyn and Bacon, Inc., Boston.

5. Bibring, G.L. 1959. "Some considerations of the psychological process in pregnancy." *Psychoanal. Study of the Child.* 14:113–121.

6. Bibring, G.L., Dywer, T.F., Huntington, D.S. and Valenstein, A.F. 1961. "A study of psychological processes in pregnancy and of the earliest mother-child relationships." *Psychoanal. Study of the Child.* 16:9–72.

7. Brazelton, T.B., Young, G.G. and Bullowa, M. 1971. "Inception and resolution of early pathology." *J. Amer. Acad. Child Psychiat.* 10:124–136.

8. Brazelton, T.B. 1973. *Neonatal Behavioral Assessment Scale.* Spastics International Medical Publishers, London and Philadelphia.

9. Cohen, D.J. 1974. "Competence and biology: methodology in studies of infants, twins, psychosomatic disease and psychosis." In *The Child and His Family: Children at Psychiatric Risk,* Vol. 3. E.J. Anthony and C. Koupernik, eds. John Wiley & Sons, New York.

10. Erikson, E.H. 1959. "Identity and the Life Cycle." *Psychol. Issues,* Vol. 1, No. 1, Monograph 1. International Universities Press, New York.

11. Erikson, E.H. 1964. "Human strength and the cycle of generations." In *Insight and Responsibility: Lectures on the Ethical Implications of Psychoanalytic Insight.* W.W. Norton, New York.

12. Escalona, S.K. 1963. "Patterns of infantile experience and the developmental process." *Psychoanal. Study of the Child.* 18:197–244.

13. Escalona, S.K. 1968. *The Roots of Individuality.* Aldine Publishing Company, Chicago.

14. Etaugh, C. 1980. "Effects of non-maternal care in children: research evidence and popular views." *Amer. Psychol.* 35(April): 4, 309–319.

15. Fantz, R.L. 1966. "Pattern discrimination and selective attention as determinants of perceptual development from birth." In A.H. Kidd and J.L. Rivoire, eds. *Perceptual Development in Children.* International Universities Press, New York.

16. Ferholt, J.F. and Provence, S. 1976. "Diagnosis and treatment of an infant with psychophysiological vomiting." *Psychoanal. Study of the Child.* 31: 439–459.

17. Fraiberg, S. 1968. "Parallel and divergent patterns in blind and sighted infants." *Psychoanal. Study of the Child.* 23:264–300.

18. Fraiberg, S. 1969. "Libidinal object constancy and mental representation." *Psychoanal. Study of the Child.* 24:9–47.

19. Fraiberg, S., Smith, M. and Adelson, E. 1969. "An educational program for blind infants." *J. of Spec. Ed.* 3(2):121–139.

20. Freud, A. 1965. *Normality and Pathology in Childhood.* International Universities Press, New York.

21. Freud, S. 1926. "Inhibitions, symptoms and anxiety." *The Standard Edition of the Complete Psychological Works of Sigmund Freud.* Vol. 20.

22. Fries, M.E. and Woolf, P.J. 1953. "Some hypotheses on the role of the congenital activity type in personality development." *The Psychoanal. Study of the Child.* International Universities Press, New York.

23. Greenacre, P. 1959. "Play in relation to creative imagination." *The Psychoanal. Study of the Child.* 14:61–80.

24. Harter, S. 1978. "Effectance motivation reconsidered: toward a developmental model." *Human Development.* 21:34–64.

25. Harter, S. and Zigler, E. 1974. "The assessment of effectance motivation in normal and retarded children." *Developm. Psychol.* 10:169–180.

26. Hartmann, H. 1939, 1958. *Ego Psychology and The Problem of Adaptation.* International Universities Press, New York.

27. Hartmann, H., Kris, E. and Loewenstein, R.M. 1946. "Comments on the formation of psychic structure." *Psychoanal. Study of the Child.* 2:11–38.

28. Huntington, D., Provence, S. and Parker, R., eds. 1972. *Day Care 2: Serving Infants,* Pub. No. (OCD) 73–14. U.S. Government Printing Office, Washington, D.C.

29. Kagan, J. and Lewis, M. 1965. "Studies of attention in the human infant." *Merrill-Palmer Quarterly,* 11:2.

30. Kagan, L. and Shiff, T. "The Bush Center in Child Development and Social Policy: agents for change." pp. 1–3. In S. Provence, ed. *Zero to Three: Bulletin of the National Center for Clinical Infant Programs.* Vol. 1, No. 2. (December 1980)

31. Kessen, W. 1961. "Selection and test of response measures in the study of the human newborn." *Child Developm.* 32:7–24.

32. Korner, A.F. and Grobstein, R. 1967. "Individual differences at birth: implications for the mother-infant relationship and later development." *J. Amer. Acad. Child Psychiat.* 6:676–690.

33. Kris, E. 1950. "Notes on the development and on some current problems in psychoanalytic child psychology." *Psychoanal. Study of the Child.* 5:24–46.

34. Kris, E. 1951. "Opening remarks on psychoanalytic child psychology." *Psychoanal. Study of the Child.* 6:9–17.

35. Lustman, S. 1956. "Rudiments of the ego." *The Psychoanal. Study of the Child.* 11:89–98.

36. Mahler, M., Pine, F. and Bergmann, A. 1975. *The Psychological Birth of the Human Infant.* Basic Books, New York.

37. Murphy, L.B. 1972. "Infants' play and cognitive development." In M.W. Piers, ed. *Play and Development.* W.W. Norton, New York.

38. Murphy, L.B. 1974. "Coping, vulnerability and resilience in childhood." In G.V. Coehlo, D.A. Hamburg, and J.E. Adams, eds. *Coping and Adaptation.* Basic Books, New York.

39. Naylor, A.K. 1970. "Some determinants of parent-infant relationships." In *What We Can Learn from Infants.* Laura Dittman, ed. National Association for the Education of Young Children, Washington, D.C. (pp. 25–47)

40. Parmelee, A.H., Jr. 1981. "Social influences on infants at medical risk for behavioral difficulties." In J. Call and E. Galenson, eds. *Proceedings of The First World Congress on Infant Psychiatry.* Basic Books, New York (in press).

41. Peiper, A. 1949. *Cerebral Function in Infancy and Childhood*. Translation of the third revised German edition. Nagler and Nagler, New York. Consultants Bureau. (1963)
42. Piaget, J. 1937. *The Origins of Intelligence in Children*. International Universities Press, New York. (1952)
43. Piaget, J. 1951. *Play, Dreams and Imitation in Childhood*. W.W. Norton, New York.
44. Piaget J. and Inhelder, B. 1969. *The Psychology of the Child*. Basic Books, New York.
45. Provence, S. 1972. "Psychoanalysis and the treatment of psychological disorders of infancy" in B.B. Wolman, ed. *Handbook of Child Psychoanalysis*. Van Nostrand Reinhold Co., New York.
46. Provence, S. 1977. "Some clinical applications of research on parent-child relationships" in M. McMillan and S. Henao, eds. *Child Psychiatry: Treatment and Research*. Brunner/Mazel, New York.
47. Provence, S. 1979. "A clinician's view of affect development in infancy." In M. Lewis and L.A. Rosenblum, eds. *The Development of Affect*. Plenum Press, New York.
48. Provence, S. and Lipton, R. 1962. *Infants in Institutions*. International Universities Press, New York.
49. Provence, S., Naylor, A. and Patterson, J. 1977. *The Challenge of Daycare*. The Yale Press, New Haven, Conn.
50. Provence, S. and Ritvo, S. 1961. "Effects of deprivation on institutionalized infants: disturbances in development of relationship to inanimate objects." *Psychoanal. Study of the Child*. 16:189–205.
51. Rapaport, D. 1959. "A historical survey of psychoanalytic ego psychology." In Erikson, E.H. *Identity and the Life Cycle*. *Psychol. Issues*. Vol. 1, No. 1, Monograph 2, International Universities Press, New York.
52. Richmond, J. and Lustman, S. 1955. "Autonomic function in the neonate: implications for psychoanalytic theory." *Psychosom. Med.* 17:269–275.
53. Sander, L. 1969. "Regulation and organization in the early infant caretaker system." In R.J. Robinson, ed. *Brain and Early Behavior*. Academic Press, New York and London.
54. Sander, L.W., Stechler, G., Burns, P., and Lee, A. 1978. "Change in infant and caregiver variables over the first two months of life: integration of action in early development." In E. Thomas, ed. *Origins of the Infant's Social Responsiveness*. Lawrence Erlbaum Association, Hillsdale, New Jersey.
55. Shapiro, E. and Biber, B. 1972. "The education of young children: a developmental interaction approach." *Teachers College Record* (1)74: 55–79.
56. Spitz, R. 1950. "Anxiety in infancy: a study of its manifestations in the first year of life." *Inter. J. of Psychoanal.* 31:138–143.
57. Spitz, R.A. 1951. "The psychogenic disease in infancy: an attempt at their etiologic classification." *Psychoanal. Study of the Child.* 6:255–275.
58. Chess, S. 1973. "Temperament in the normal infant." In S. Sapir and A. Nitzburg, eds. *Children with Learning Problems*. Brunner/Mazel, New York. (pp. 291–307)

59. Thomas, A., Chess, S. and Birch, H.G. 1968. *Temperament and Behavior Disorders in Children.* New York University Press, New York.
60. Waelder, R. 1932. "The psychoanalytic theory of play." *Psychoanal. Quart.* 2:208–224.
61. White, B. 1975. "Critical influences in the origins of competence." *Merrill-Palmer Quarterly.* 21:243–266.
62. White, R.W. 1959. "Motivation reconsidered: the concept of competence." *Psychol. Review.* 66:297–333.
63. Wolff, P. 1966. "The Causes, Controls and Organization of Behavior in the Neonate." *Psychol. Issues*, Vol. V, No. 1, Monograph 17. International Universities Press, Inc., New York.
64. Yarrow, L.J., Rubenstein, J.L. and Pederson, F.A. 1975. *Infant and Environment: Early Cognitive and Motivational Development.* Halsted Division, John Wiley & Sons, New York.
65. Zigler, E. 1963. "Rigidity and social reinforcement effects in the performance of institutionalized and non-institutionalized normal and retarded children." *J. of Personal.*, Vol. 31, No. 2 (June)

Chapter 3

CHANGING ASPECTS OF THE FAMILY: A PSYCHOANALYTIC PERSPECTIVE ON EARLY INTERVENTION

by Ava L. Siegler

The purpose of this chapter is to identify and describe a substantial population of day care children and their mothers who are both "at risk" and "vulnerable," to use certain psychoanalytic formulations to increase our understanding of the factors that contribute to this psychological outcome, and to outline a delivery-of-services intervention model which has been developed to meet the needs of this particular population.

Changing Aspects of the Family: An Emergent Population in Day Care

The most striking post-war demographic change in this country has been the increase in the labor force of women with preschool children. In New York City alone, more than 100,000 single, working mothers are raising children under six years of age. These are not women who choose to work, or who return to work after a divorce,

This project was privately supported through funds raised by the Board of Directors of Prescott House Day Care Center, New York City (Rose Presti, Director), under the leadership of James Amster. Five thousand dollars per year was allocated for the project, which has been in existence for six years.

bolstered by household help, an "interesting" job, child-support payments, and the father's week-end visits with the children. These are women who must work since they are the sole support of their families. They are witness to the fact that economic, social, and political contingencies in this country have made maternal employment the rule rather than the exception it was a generation ago.[44] Clearly, fewer and fewer American women are *able* to be full-time mothers, though the question of whether they are *willing* to be is still unanswered.

The *nature* of these families has changed as well as the *number* of them.[5,9,26,38,44,48] These women are likely to be younger than they used to be, with younger and fewer children (reflecting the national decline in birth rates). Many have only one child. They are also more likely to be divorced, separated, abandoned, or never married—rather than widowed—and they face the complex responsibilities of parenthood alone. The father of this woman's child is unlikely to be available to her as an emotional, social, or economic partner, and financial insecurity is a constant burden. Living alone in an inner-city neighborhood, the single mother is constantly apprehensive about her own safety, as well as the safety of her child. Accidents, illness or surgery, addiction, sexual or physical abuse, and the observation of a crime or other violence (suicide, fires, etc.) are events which place an unusual burden upon maturing mental and emotional structures in children. Yet poor urban children are most likely to be subjected to several of the above events before the age of six. In fact, a frequently voiced fear is that these children "see too much," are "street-wise" too early and cannot be properly protected from exposure to the violence of city life.[26,29]

In addition, the single, working mother must make arrangements for the care of her child while she works. Children from these families constitute a special and substantial proportion of the children in preschool day care centers throughout the city.[20,24,26]

A Clinical Profile

By the time these children enter the day care center at the age of three, they have already sustained serious psychological blows. They have lost the presence of their father in the home. (Further, many of these children have little or no contact with their fathers after this separation.) They have lost their mothers to full-time employment. The break-up of the family has meant a drop in income with a marked change in living conditions, usually a change in apartments and/or neighborhoods. In addition, the frenetic tempo of commuting and the urgencies of job and school schedules interrupt the daily rhythms of attachment and separation between mother and child. Finally, the mother's need to build a new life for herself can easily place her desires and the developmental needs of her child in direct conflict.

For many of these children, the day care center may represent the first stable alternative to a series of transient baby-sitters or unreliable family arrangements. Yet initial entry into the center may appear to exacerbate the child's stress, as he is suddenly thrust into a new complex social setting for most of his waking day. A young child is bound to experience uneasiness in unfamiliar surroundings. This uneasiness can only be dispelled when he begins to establish trust in the adults who are available to him. In the case of many of these children, important developmental lags due to the disruptions and deficiencies of their early history will make it difficult for them to trust, to communicate, to listen, to learn, to play—in short, to function in the group setting.

The Impact of Cumulative Stress: "At Risk"

While single-stress situations may create no appreciable risk in psychological development, when children or adults must deal with either chronic stress or multiple, concurrent stresses, pathological consequences may be anticipated. [9,21,35,37,38,41,45]

We are suggesting that these mothers and their children have been exposed to such a series of accumulated stresses, each of which, in and of itself, may have proven manageable, but which together prove overwhelming. With these observations in mind, it is hard to remain sanguine about the particular social and emotional consequences of the cultural changes we are describing. Bereft of so many of its supports, can such an "altered" family still serve its vital socializing function? What are the effects of the absence of the father upon the child's subsequent cognitive and emotional development? Of maternal employment in the early years of childhood? Of separation or divorce upon the mother and child? Of home care arrangements vs. day care facilities? What resources can children and their mothers bring to these special circumstances?

There is, of course, an enormous literature which has addressed itself to each of these factors.[1,2,4,6,9,13,20,21,22,24,26,27,33,35,37,38,42,45,48] But the questions raised and the conclusions drawn cannot address the clinical experience of this particular population. This is because, as we have tried to describe, in our population it is rare that any one of these factors is found by itself: a child without a father is also likely to be a child with a working mother. He is also more likely to be an only child. Sometimes he is a child with very little access to extended family members. (Here, racial and ethnic factors do make a difference, as certain groups have access to more extended kinship networks.) This child often lives in a poor neighborhood in a large city and is usually enrolled in a day care center. Disentangling the influence of any one of these conditions upon the child's psychological development becomes an intricate and frustrating task.

The Special Demands of the Oedipal Phase of Development

By the time we see these children in day care, there is yet another strand which must be woven into the tangled web of stress that they share with their mothers. They face, in the years which coincide with the child's enrollment in day care (3–6 years), the unique developmental demands of the oedipal phase. This phase is one in which major cognitive and affective structures will become crystallized for the child, but many analytic writers have emphasized that oedipal struggles and attainments are potentiated in the context of an intact family structure, one with three points of exchange for the oedipal triangle.[11,14,16,25,27,31,33] Neubauer, in his important contribution to this question twenty years ago, stated:[33]

> The lack of oedipal stimulation, normally found in the continuous day-to-day interplay between the child and the parent, and especially as evidenced by the relationship of the parents to each other, imposes a primary imbalance. (p. 305)

Additionally, there are special developmental claims which are placed upon adults when they become parents.[7,25] Each new phase in the child's development ideally dictates a corresponding modification in parental handling. But to accomplish this, the parent must be sensitive and attuned to issues in child development as well as to the individual temperament of the child.

How do the single mother and her child negotiate this developmental hurdle in the absence of the father's participation? How do the stresses and limitations of their special life circumstances affect the outcome of mother-child reciprocities during these crucial years? Addressing these complex influences left us with the conviction that this particular population of children and their mothers were both "at risk" in the environment, and "vulnerable" in the psychosocial realm.

The Early Intervention Project: Rationale

The following Early Intervention Project was developed to meet the needs of the special population of day care families that we have described. The project functioned within the Prescott House Day

Care Center that served an inner-city multiracial, multiethnic group of parents who either lived or worked in the "catchment" area. The majority of these families were single-parent families. (During the six years that the project has been in existence, single mothers constituted from 67 to 79% of the day care population.)

Roughly sixty-five 3-to-6-year-old children were enrolled in the nursery and kindergarten classes, each of which was staffed by a qualified group teacher and assistant teacher. The center was open from 8:00 a.m. to 6:00 p.m., and in all other respects complied with the standards for city day care services as maintained through the Agency for Child Development.

While these children do not ordinarily attract the attention of any specific child advocacy group—they are neither psychotic, nor orphaned, nor retarded, nor physically handicapped—an initial clinical exploration revealed that they were suffering from a wide range of cognitive and emotional difficulties.

When clinical problems arose, children and their mothers were previously referred to two main community resources: mental health agencies, and therapeutic nursery schools. Referral to mental health agencies proved unsatisfactory for several reasons:

1. Fees were too high for our families, particularly when double fees were involved for the treatment of both mother and child.
2. Clinic hours conflicted with the job schedules of working mothers, evening hours were not feasible for such young children, and few clinics were open on Saturdays.
3. Very few agencies were prepared to treat preschool children and their families; those that were (mainly hospital centers) frequently changed their staff because of training requirements.
4. Very few agencies were prepared to coordinate psychological and educational goals, a particular necessity for our population of children, where impairment was often expressed in the cognitive realm. (The assumption that cognitive and affective functioning are inextricably intertwined, and that they must be approached simultaneously has been supported by abundant research evidence.[10,23,30,49])

Referrals to therapeutic nursery schools for moderately disturbed children were unsuccessful as well, since they rarely provided the full-time day care required by our working mothers. The full-time facilities primarily served seriously disturbed, dysfunctional youngsters, and were therefore unsuitable for most of our children.

Thus, while our clinical observations indicated that these families were *most likely* to need psychological intervention, their circumstances dictated that these families were *least likely* to take advantage of existing mental health facilities. This population was "falling between the cracks."

An On-Site Delivery-of-Services Model

Clearly, one solution to this clinical problem was to provide on-site psychological services directly within the day care center, since this is where the children spent most of their waking day, and where the mothers could be easily contacted. In this approach, we were in accord with the 1978 Report of the President's Commission on Mental Health, which emphasized: " . . . focusing upon children who are presently underserved . . . as well as searching for new delivery-of-service models leading to effective delivery."[34]

Our wish to intervene was based upon the belief that receptivity to change is characteristic of the young child.[3,11,14,19,23] By virtue of this plasticity, the child's years in day care can provide a crucial preventive and promotive setting in which social, emotional, and cognitive potentials can be activated and earlier developmental damage can be repaired.

We also assumed that the mother's active participation was essential to any intervention that we might try to make in the life of a young child. We were alerted to the fact that mothers who feel overwhelmed, irritable, and depleted are more likely to act abusively toward their children, and the day care center provided us with an unusual opportunity to observe mother-child interactions and to intervene immediately.[24,42]

The project also emphasized the mutuality of parent-child exchange, that is, that the child both responds to and shapes the mother's parental handling. Mothers under stress are often totally unaware of the inner psychic experiences of their child, and totally unaware of their contribution to that experience. Young mothers of only children are also bewildered and confused by behaviors which may be simply age-appropriate developmental patterns. Single mothers are particularly in need of an opportunity to share child-rearing experiences with other women in order to extend their exposure to both child development and parenting. In single-parent families, the mother is a uniquely powerful mediator of her child's experiences of life.

Finally, for children in day care, the teacher easily becomes an important attachment. A child in day care spends the better part of his waking day with his teacher. He eats with her, sleeps in her presence, is toileted, plays, learns, is disciplined, etc. Vital physical, social, emotional, and cognitive tasks are performed with and for the teacher. This circumstance affords the teacher an unusual opportunity for intervention as well.

But teachers must be alerted to the special characteristics of these children. Initially, for example, teachers would report how "friendly" many of these children were. They were impressed with the fact that they didn't fuss or cry during the initial "adjustment period" upon entry. They commented that these children hardly noticed when their mothers came or went. With more psychological awareness of the tasks of early development, teachers were able to have a more informed appreciation of the meaning of the previously perceived "friendliness," and to understand that it might signify unresolved separation issues—a developmental impairment rather than a developmental attainment.

Teachers must also be alerted to the needs of this special group of mothers. They may initially perceive a single, working mother as irresponsible, abandoning, or even cruel in her handling of her child. It was difficult, for instance, for a teacher to cope with her hostility toward a mother who would bring her child into the day care center with a racking cough and a fever. She did not understand that the mother might be fearful of losing her job without warning if she missed a day of work, or that an inexperienced mother might feel that the staff at the center could provide a safer and more competent environment for a sick child than she herself could provide at home.

A Triadic Model for Intervention

It follows from these assumptions about the mediating power of the mother and teacher, and the special vulnerabilities of the children, that the psychological services in the project were organized around three areas of intervention:

Psychological Services for Children:
1. observation and evaluation of children in order to detect early dysfunction
2. individual psychotherapy for selected children (play therapy)
3. educational planning for the remediation of cognitive deficiencies

Psychological Services for Mothers:
1. didactic discussion groups on child development
2. mothers' therapy groups for selected mothers (Group work was selected as an intervention method which had particular potential for single mothers. In the *group circle* we hoped to create a substitute for the *family circle* which seemed strikingly absent in their lives.)
3. individual psychotherapy for selected mothers
4. weekly "emergency hours" were available to mothers in crisis for psychological consultation

Consultant Services for Teachers:
1. ongoing weekly case conferences to provide in-service training and support for teachers

2. individual conferences focusing on the special psycho-educational needs of disturbed children and techniques for dealing with them in the classroom

All psychological services were provided by the project director and doctoral students in clinical and school psychology programs who worked under her supervision, through a liaison established with a large city university.

Since the intervention project began in 1974, over 200 families have participated. Hundreds of hours of community consultation have been given in clinical observation, parent education, individual psychological consultation, group therapy, and individual treatment.

I would like to turn now to the formulations of psychoanalytic developmental theory in order to clarify our understanding of the vulnerabilities and resources of this particular population of mothers and children.

Preoedipal Issues

The Children

Many of our single, working mothers were unable to make the necessary adjustments in their lives to accommodate the infant, and they characterized their early exchanges with the baby as tense and sporadic. Understandably, many of the subsequent problems revealed in our population of children reflected incomplete resolutions and distortions of those ego processes which characteristically emerge in the first three years of life. That is, by the time the children entered the day care center, the course of their development was already obscured and obstructed in specific ways. The management of impulses, self-control, concentration, frustration tolerance, ego autonomy, were all impaired. (Many psychoanalytic writers have particularly stressed the father's role in the acquisition of ego autonomy.[1,2,31,32]) Both the form and the content of the oedipal tasks these children now faced were, of course, shaped by these preoedipal conflicts.

In many of our children, age-appropriate curiosity was suppressed, there were significant attention-deficit disorders, night terrors and phobias dominated their fantasy life, and unmodulated rage, language deficits, and accident-proneness revealed the presence of considerable intrapsychic dysfunction.

Interestingly, this range of psychosocial dysfunction was not confined to "poor" or "disadvantaged" youngsters. While the mothers of these children had to earn an income which enabled them to qualify for day care,* the designation "low-income" or "working-class," or "lower socio-economic group" does not adequately describe them. Many mothers, for example, are poor due to current circumstances in their lives, but may themselves have been raised in middle-class or even wealthy homes (as was the case with political refugees from Cuba, South America, or the Orient). Dysfunctional children, then, were drawn from a wide variety of ethnic, racial, and social backgrounds. What they shared was a set of situational or environmental circumstances which produced a "shared psychic reality" that had developmental consequences for the family.

The Mothers

Most of the mothers we saw reported that the early years of infant care were difficult. They were usually young when the baby was born, and the birth itself was often an unexpected and/or unwelcome event in their lives, interrupting their late-adolescent search for identity and intimacy.[5]

Still, despite these early difficulties, most mothers had felt that they were *necessary* and indeed, *sufficient* to the tasks of preoedipal development. They felt that they had been unable to be reliable mothers because of the responsibilities that they had had to assume in the absence of the father, but they perceived this absence as the loss of a social, sexual, and financial partner. They did not feel that the father's presence was essential to the *child's own development*, but rather to their own ability to adequately mother their child.

Prugh's Functional Approach

In our clinical understanding upon which these observations are based, we were guided by Prugh's functional approach to mental phenomena. Briefly described, this approach involves articulating criteria for psychosocial dysfunction in terms which lend themselves easily to evaluation. (For example, classification of a preschool child as suffering from *incipient dysfunction* might be based upon such criteria as lack of interest in learning, frequent nightmares, determined resistance to controls, or persistent regressive behavior.) Prugh's approach combines an appreciation of normative concepts of psychosocial functioning and of the entire family matrix in which

---

* A single mother with one child making approximately $4,000 per year would pay no fee. The same mother making a maximum of approximately $15,000 per year would pay $40 weekly. A mother whose income exceeds that figure, with no other children, would be ineligible for day care.

the child develops. This produces a descriptive schema that is particularly attractive and accessible to teachers and student-clinicians.

The classification of psychosocial function/dysfunction is based upon five categories ranging along the following continuum: optimal functioning, functioning but vulnerable, incipient dysfunction, moderate dysfunction, and severe dysfunction. Seventy-eight percent of the children treated in the project suffered from either *incipient* or *moderate dysfunction*, the others fell into the *functioning but vulnerable* category.

Oedipal Issues

With the onset of the oedipal phase in development, which coincided with the child's entry into the day care center, single mothers began to experience greater qualms about raising their child alone, and reported greater anxiety about what we would theoretically describe as *oedipal outcomes*. They worried on behalf of the child, about the meaning of the child's loss of the father, particularly the mothers of boy children, and their worries clustered around the following issues:

1. *Sexual Differentiation and the Crystallizing of Sexual Identity*: "Will my son grow up to be homosexual with no man around?"
2. *Superego Formation*: "I really worry that with no man around, he won't learn respect. I try to be tough on him so he'll learn not to take advantage."
3. *The Emergence of Ego-Ideals and the Sense of Self*: "I don't know what to tell her about her father. I mean when she was little, it didn't matter, but now she asks me all the time, Was he a bad man, Am I a bad girl?"

Oedipal Mother-Child Reciprocities in Absence of Father

The Oedipal Frustrator

One of the most crucial tasks facing the parent of any oedipal child, is, of course, the gradual disengagement from the child's seductive attempts to include the parent in the fulfillment of erotic desires. The oedipal phase marks the first time in the child's life that the parent stands in such an obstructive role.

In a single-parent family, there is no "good-cop"/"bad-cop" alternation between the mother and the father. The mother must therefore assume the entire role of "oedipal frustrator" without recourse to a partner in the father who will either initiate the constraints upon the child, or at least, support her efforts.

Many single mothers, for example, permit their young children to sleep with them. While this arrangement is often encouraged by financial limitations which preclude separate bedrooms, its meaning extends beyond these considerations. Sleeping with the child is the mother's way of soothing her own fears during the night and meeting her own needs for intimacy. Because of this, the single mother may delay assuming the restrictive oedipal role which this phase of development requires. They either lock the child into preoedipal modes of relating (keeping them babies) or encourage and precipitate erotic promises which they cannot keep. Both attitudes can produce rage and despair in the child.

The Missing Point in the Triangle

Single parents face another critical difficulty at this developmental juncture. It is in the oedipal phase of development that the child ordinarily becomes aware of his parents as a *couple* in a new way, that is, as two people that have something to do with each other that has nothing to do with him. This perception represents a significant developmental attainment.[1,2] The child's sense of himself as *singular* is heightened by this perception. The emergence of the self, then, is, in a way, both synchronized with and dependent upon this perception of the parents as a couple.

The child moving into the oedipal phase of development, in a single-parent family, with a working mother, spending his entire day in a group setting, does not have the perception of "coupling" available to him in either a continuous or a reliable manner. He and his mother must therefore compensate for the blind spot in their vision of the oedipal drama, and indeed, this is exactly what they attempt to do.

We were constantly impressed by the mother's attempts to create what we called a "makeshift" oedipal triangle, by calling upon male figures in the environment who were available to her even in the most transitory ways (priests, janitors, storekeepers, dentists, etc.), and weaving them into the fabric of her life with her child.

The Use of Fantasy

Both mother and child may turn to another resource as well: the capacity for fantasy. They will use fantasy to conjure up what is missing in reality, so that at least the shadow of the father will still fall upon the developmental path that the child is negotiating.

Despite the loss, the child struggles valiantly to maintain an image of the father. The absence of the father does not mean that the child has no thoughts or feelings about him. "Out of sight" does not mean "out of mind." It means, rather, that the child has little or no opportunity to test out his fantasies against the real experience of the father. Therefore the fantasies will remain in an unmodulated and inflexible state, and the growth of certain ego processes, particularly those which bear upon the development of the superego, and ego-ideals, may be hampered.[33]

Some researchers have suggested that mourning for the father and fantasies of reconciliation are particularly intense and prolonged in preschool children.[21,45] I would suggest that the special demands of the oedipal phase contribute to the intensity of these processes and represent the child's attempts to use the image of the father to achieve certain oedipal resolutions when the actual presence of the father cannot be experienced. We still know very little about how the child accomplishes this, or how successful these attempts are.

The Maternal Narrative

In our clinical investigations we were also struck by the ways in which the effects of events in the child's life could be shaped by the manner in which the mother *defined these events for the child,* as well as by the child's own capacity to invest these events with psychic meaning. Mothers can keep the image of the father alive for the child, in both positive and negative ways, by constructing a *narrative* about the father's absence. This family tale organizes the child's thoughts and feelings. However, in cases of abandonment, this narrative may not be able to have a satisfactory beginning, middle, and end. For one thing, it is extremely difficult for a mother to construct a narrative out of events that she herself does not understand. As one mother stated, "I know he's out there somewhere, but I don't know when or if he'll ever show up. He's not alive and he's not dead; it's a living death."

A Clinical Spectrum

On the basis of our clinical data, we were able to identify certain reciprocities between the single working mother and her child, in response to the demands of oedipal development. These reciprocities can best be described as a tendency on the part of mother and child to form certain kinds of "pairings." It is important to keep in mind, though, that these "pairings" are presented as points on a clinical continuum, for descriptive purposes. In between these extremes we can observe many gradations of these interactions. The gradations reflect individual differences in character structure and result in the wide variation in oedipal outcome which can be accommodated in human development, without recourse to pathology.

The Erotic Pair

In this response, the single mother permits and encourages the child's oedipal overtures toward her, without representing the taboos and restrictions appropriate to this phase. Exchanges between the mother and the boy-child ranged from the mild eroticism expressed in the proud description, "He's Mommy's little man," to actual incestuous behavior.

The Hostile Pair

In these instances, the emerging desires of the oedipal child are warded off by hostility on the part of each partner. The mother might displace hostility from the boy's absent father onto the child, or see in a girl child all she dislikes in herself, or victimize the child as she herself had felt victimized by the child's father. Exchanges between mother and child are suffused with anger. The boy child, left with no paternal obstruction against his emerging desires for the mother, may mobilize anger in order to create and maintain a safe distance from her. The girl child, on the other hand, without a father to turn to in her own attempt to move away from the power of the mother, experiences rage toward the "mean" Mommy who "got rid of Daddy." Both boy and girl children are frightened of their anger toward the mother, as she is the only parent remaining for them.

The Fearful Pair

In this interaction, the mother feels overwhelmed by her own impulses and the child is closely identified with her. Her perception of her fate is informed by dread, fear, and hopelessness. She sees herself and the child set adrift, without direction, helpless and surrounded by danger. This perception of danger from without mirrors the perception of danger from within. Sometimes, the child, experiencing the mother's fragility, will attempt to take over the role of parent to his own parent, a position of precocious mastery. More often, the child shares the mother's agitation and loss of functioning and retreats from the oedipal challenges.

Summary

Everything that we have been emphasizing in our clinical explorations of these mother-child exchanges supports our initial assumption that these particular day care children and their mothers are experiencing and have experienced accumulated stresses in the environment which have intrapsychic consequences that are of considerable importance for human development. The use of psychoanalytic formulations about the special demands of the oedipal phase upon both mother and child provides us with a model of the way in which environmental actualities may unite with maturational potentials and psychic realities to produce developmental distortions and handicaps.

The role of the mother as a powerful mediator of these events is emphasized, as is the substantial developmental potential inherent in the day care center, as a setting in which these families can be reached and disturbances in the psychosocial realm prevented or ameliorated.

The rationale and method of the early intervention project converge with its ultimate goal: to create and maintain a setting in which mothers and children can be helped to reveal and analyze their conflicts, and to internalize stronger, more resilient, more effective ego structures—with more curiosity, more self-reflection, more energy, and more understanding than would have been possible without clinical intervention. With this model, and through this project, we hope to enlarge the vocabulary of possibility in these families' lives.

References

1. Abelin, E.L. 1975. "Some further observations and comments on the earliest role of the father." *Inter. J. Psychoanal.* 56:293–302.
2. Abelin, E.L. 1971. "The role of the father in the separation-individuation process." In *Separation-individuation*, J.B. McDevitt and C.F. Settlage, eds. International Universities Press, New York.
3. Ainsworth, M.D.S. 1969. "Object relations, dependency and attachment." *Child Development.* 40:969–1026.
4. Aries, P. 1962. *Centuries of Childhood: A Social History of Family Life.* Knopf, New York.
5. Baldwin, W.H. 1977. "Adolescent pregnancy and childbearing: Growing concern for Americans." *Population Bulletin.* 31:(2).
6. Belsky, J. and Steinberg, L.D. 1978. "The effects of day care: A critical review." *Child Development.* 49:929–949.
7. Benedek, T. 1959. "Parenthood as a Developmental Phase." *J. Amer. Psychoanal. Assoc.* 7.
8. Beres, D. 1958. "Vicissitudes of superego functions and superego precursors in childhood." *Psychoanal. Study of the Child.* 13:324–351.
9. Bloom, B.L., Asher, S.J. and White, S.W. 1978. "Marital disruption as a stressor: A review and analysis." *Psych. Bulletin.* 85:867–894.
10. Coopersmith, S. 1967. *The Antecedents of Self-Esteem.* W.H. Freeman, San Francisco.

11. Erikson, E.H. 1964. *Insight and Responsibility.* W.W. Norton & Co., New York.
12. Erikson, E.H. 1959. "Growth and Crises of the Healthy Personality." In *Identity and the Life Cycle. Psych. Issues,* No. 1. International Universities Press, New York.
13. Fraiberg, S. 1977. *Every Child's Birthright: In Defense of Mothering.* Basic Books, New York.
14. Freud, A. 1965. *Normality and Pathology in Childhood.* International Universities Press, New York.
15. Freud, S. 1925. "The Ego and the Id." In *The Standard Edition,* Vol. 19. Hogarth Press, London.
16. Freud, S. 1924. The dissolution of the Oedipus Complex. In *The Standard Edition,* Vol. 19. Hogarth Press, London.
17. Freud, S. 1924. "Some psychical consequences of the anatomical distinction between the sexes." In *The Standard Edition,* Vol. 19. Hogarth Press, London.
18. Glasscote, R. and Rishman, M.E. 1974. *Mental Health Programs for Preschool Children: A Field Study.* National Assoc. for Ment. Health Public., Washington, D.C.
19. Hartmann, H., Kris, E. and Lowenstein, R. 1946. "Comments on the formation of psychic structure." *Psychoanal. Study of the Child,* Vol. 2:11–38.
20. Heinicke, C. *et al.* 1973. "The organization of day care: considerations relating to the mental health of child and family." *Amer. J. Orthopsychiat.* 43:8–22.
21. Hetherington, E.J., Cox, M. and Cox, R. 1979. "Family interaction and the social, emotional, and cognitive development of children following divorce." In *The Family: Setting Priorities.* V. Waughan III and T. Brazelton, eds. Science and Medicine, New York.
22. Hoffman, K.W. 1974. "Effects of maternal employment on the child: A review of the research." *Devlpm. Psych.* 10:204–228.
23. Kagan, J. and Moss, H.A. 1962. *Birth to Maturity.* Wiley, New York.
24. Kempe, C.H. 1976. "Approaches to preventing child abuse." *Amer. J. Diseases Child.* 130:941–947.
25. Kestenberg, J. 1975. *Children and Parents.* Jason Aronson, New York.
26. Kriesberg, L. 1970. *Mothers in Poverty: A Study of Fatherless Families.* Aldine, Chicago.
27. Lamb, M.E. 1976. *The Role of the Father in Child Development.* Wiley, New York.
28. Lampl-de Groot, J. 1962. "Ego ideal and superego." *Psychoanal. Study of the Child.* 17:94–106.
29. Lasch, E. 1977. *Haven in a Heartless World: The Family Besieged.* Basic Books, New York.
30. Loevinger, J. 1976. *Ego Development.* Jossey-Bass, San Francisco.
31. Loewald, H. 1951. "Ego and reality." *Inter. J. Psychoanal.* 32:10–17.
32. Mahler, M., Bergman, A., and Pine, F., 1977. *The Psychological Birth of the Human Infant.* Basic Books, New York.
33. Neubauer, P.B. 1960. "The one-parent child and his oedipal development." *Psychoanal. Study of the Child.* 15:286–309.

34. President's Commission Report on Mental Health. 1978 U.S. Govt. Print. Off., Washington, D.C.

35. Prugh, E.G. 1973. "Psychosocial Disorders in Childhood and Adolescence: Theoretical Considerations and an Attempt at Classification." In *The Mental Health of Children: Services Research and Manpower.* Report of the Joint Commission on Mental Health of Children. Harper & Row, New York.

36. Ritvo, S. and Solnit, A.J. 1958. "Influences of early mother-child inter-action on identification processes." *Psychoanal. Study of the Child.* 13:64–91.

37. Rutter, M. 1974. *The Qualities of Mothering: Maternal Deprivation Reassessed.* Jason Aronson, New York.

38. Rutter, M. 1979. "Maternal deprivation, 1972–1978: New findings, new concepts, new approaches." *Child Devlpm.* 50:283–305.

39. Sandler, J., Holder, A., and Meers, D. 1963. "The ego ideal and the ideal self." *Psychoanal. Study of the Child.* 18:139–158.

40. Spitz, R. 1959. *A Genetic Field Theory of Ego Formation.* International Universities Press, New York.

41. Sroufe, L.A. 1979. "Socioemotional Development." In *Handbook of Infant Psychology.* J. Osofsky, ed. Wiley, New York.

42. Terr, L. 1970. "A family study of child abuse." *Amer. J. Psychiat.* 127:125–131.

43. Turkel, R.A. 1960. *Study of N.Y.C. Clinics for Children.* Amer. Psychiat. Assoc. N.Y.S. District Branch Bulletin.

44. U.S. Department of Labor, Women's Bureau. 1977. *Working Mothers and their Children.* U.S. Govt. Print. Off., Washington, D.C.

45. Wallerstein, J.S. and Kelly, J.B. 1975. "The effects of parental divorce: Experiences of the preschool child." *J. Amer. Acad. Child Psychiat.* 14:600–616.

46. Webb, R.A. 1977. *Social Development in Childhood: Day Care Programs and Research.* Johns Hopkins University Press, Baltimore.

47. White, R. 1959. "Motivation reconsidered: The concept of competence." *Psych. Rev.,* 66.

48. Yarrow, M. *et al.* 1962. "Child rearing in families of working and non-working mothers." *Sociometry* 25:122–140.

49. Zigler, E. 1970. "The Nature-Nurture Issue Reconsidered." In *Socio-cultural Aspects of Mental Retardation.* H.C. Haywood, ed. Appleton-Century-Crofts, New York.

50. Zigler, E. 1978. "America's Head Start Program: An agenda for its second decade." *Young Children.* 33:4–11.

Chapter 4

JANUS FACES DAY CARE: PERSPECTIVES ON QUALITY AND COST

by Richard R. Ruopp and Jeffrey Travers

[Janus was the Roman god of beginnings. The first hour of the day, first day of the month, first month of the year—which bears his name—were sacred to him. He was the guardian of gates and doors, and was well suited to the post since he had two faces that looked in opposite directions. Thus he could maintain two opposed perspectives at the same time: the past and future, the homely and the worldly. Janus is also well suited to viewing the contemporary child day care scene.* That scene is best understood from multiple perspectives—the homely perspective of the child, parent and provider, as well as the worldly perspective of the policymaker. It confronts concerned citizens with a series of stark dilemmas that pull in two directions at once, dilemmas centering around the fundamental issue of quality and cost—the subject of this paper.]

---

* The National Campaign for Child Daycare for Working Parents adopted the nomenclature "child daycare" in response to a longstanding semantic dispute. For many professionals, "child care" includes foster, adoptive, and abused-child services. For others, "day care" has included services to handicapped and elderly adults. The campaign defines "child daycare" as "care provided to a child by a person or persons outside the child's immediate family, in centers, family day care homes, or in the child's own home at any time of any day or night of the week."[22] Here we use the Campaign's nomenclature and definition. We do not use its spelling (as one word) in order to conform to usage in the other chapters of this book.

Discussions of quality in child rearing by psychologists and early childhood educators have, understandably, been developmental in orientation and, until the recent past, have implicitly or explicitly favored care by the mother in the home. For those who could afford them, part-day nursery schools have been seen as an educational supplement to parental care. Quality has generally been viewed from the microperspective of the individual child: "What is the very best way we can ensure Joshua's or Jessica's healthy growth?" From this perspective the child is clearly central—all other persons and environmental factors are arrayed around the child.

The developmental perspective has given rise to useful research on quality and its determinants. However, any realistic discussion of quality in child day care must take account of current economic realities. Many families cannot choose whether or not to use day care —they are forced to do so by financial necessity. And while parents would almost always choose the best possible care for their children, they are constrained by three facts—day care costs a lot of money, good care costs more than mediocre care and there isn't enough good day care available. The gap between what is needed and what individuals, especially at the low end of the income spectrum, can afford has inexorably drawn government into the child care market. Thus the policymaker, from his or her macro perspective, is also confronted with issues of quality and cost in child care—with an additional variable to complicate the picture; namely, the *quantity* of care provided or subsidized by public monies.

We address ourselves to both micro- and macroperspectives on the quality/cost issue here. First, we set the stage by selectively surveying the current day care scene, with emphasis on the role of government and on patterns of usage in full time day care. Next, we turn to the developmental issues affecting children in group care settings, summarizing what has been learned about quality and about some of the factors that influence it. (We also take a brief look at some neglected aspects of quality—those having to do with the interface among day care, the family, and community institutions.) We then examine in detail a series of cost-quality tradeoffs, beginning with those facing parents and providers and proceeding to the public policy issues of quality vs. quantity of care in the face of scarce public resources vs. private resources. Finally, we offer some suggestions about possible policy directions for the eighties.

Day Care Today: The Government's Role and Patterns of Use

Child rearing has traditionally been seen as a private, not public, responsibility. In the past, government, primarily local and state, became involved in cases of abuse, neglect, and custody disputes.

Only when two crises, the Depression and the Second World War, precipitated a pressing need for women in the labor force did the federal government intervene. In the late 1930s, the Works Projects Administration (WPA) created 1900 programs that provided jobs for the unemployed and care for 40,000 children. During the Second World War, the Lanham Act funded day care centers so women could work in defense industries. After the war it was assumed that the need for subsidized day care was past, and federal support ceased for almost two decades.*

In the early 1960s, two events rekindled government interest in early childhood. First, there was the marked increase in the poverty status of single mothers with young children. Second, there was a growing belief that education at all levels could ameliorate, if not end, poverty. By 1965 the government had created a nursery-school-like early education program, Head Start. At the same time policy-makers concluded that day care was a necessary ancillary support if low-income parents were to get off and/or stay off the welfare rolls. (To a much lesser degree, day care was seen as a legitimate public service for relief from personal and familial stress.)

This new federal day care intervention continued and expanded through the late 1960s, 1970s and into the 1980s. It has taken three major forms. First, through Title IV-A of the Social Security Act (SSA), child day care is treated as a work-related expense for working families on welfare rolls. Its cost can be deducted from a parent's income before determining the size of an Aid to Families of Dependent Children (AFDC) grant. Second, through Title XX of the SSA, funds are allocated for the direct purchase of day care services for low- and moderate-income families. Third, tax relief has been made available to working families. In 1954, a small (but over the years increasing) annual deduction was allowed. More recently, in 1976, the deduction was shifted to a modest child-and-dependent care tax credit: the maximum for day care has been $400 for one child, $800 for two or more. Under the Economic Recovery Act of 1981, the maximum child care credit will rise (starting with the 1982 tax year) to $720 for one child and $1440 for two or more children for families with an income under $10,000. The maximum credit decreases, on a sliding scale, to $480 and $960, respectively, for families with an income above $30,000.

Total federal expenditures for these three day care support programs reached $1,393 million in 1977. If the costs of related activities such as the Work Incentive Program, the Child Care Food Program,

---

* Unless otherwise noted, data appearing in this introduction are taken or derived from the first chapter of *Children at the Center*, Volume 1 of the final report of the National Day Care Study.[26]

Table 4-1   Children in All Forms of Nonrelative Care, 30 or More Hours Each Week (1975)[a] (000)

Age of Child	Family Day Care	Center Care	In-Home Care	Total
0–2	365 (54%)	180 (27%)	130 (19%)	675 (100%)
	(31%)	(17%)	(21%)	(24%)
3–5	394 (32%)	709 (57%)	139 (11%)	1,242 (100%)
	(33%)	(66%)	(23%)	(43%)
6–9	314 (44%)	173 (25%)	218 (31%)	705 (100%)
	(27%)	(16%)	(35%)	(24%)
10–13	111 (45%)	5 (2%)	132 (53%)	248 (100%)
	(9%)	(<1%)	(21%)	(9%)
	1,184 (41%)	1,067 (37%)	619 (22%)	2,870 (100%)
	(100%)	(100%)	(100%)	(100%)

[a] Derived from the National Child Care Consumer Study.[25]

and a handful of other direct programs are added to this cost, then the federal support for day care in 1977 reached $1.67 billion. Taken in perspective, this amount is less than one-half percent (.41%) of all federal expenditures, less than one-tenth percent (.091%) of the Gross National Product for the same year. Since 1977, use of the tax credit by low-middle and middle-income families has doubled from $500 million to an estimated $1 billion (some 5 million claims at an average of $200 per claim). In contrast, Title IV-A/Title XX support for some 1 million children from low-income families has risen only fractionally.

During the decade of the 1970s, the continuing rise in the incidence of single-parent families, rampant inflation, and the influence of feminism have all contributed to a large increase in the number of mothers with young children entering and reentering the labor force. In 1978 almost 52 percent of the country's 24.4 million families with children under 13 had either two working parents or a single working parent. At that time, more than 5 million children under 13 were cared for by someone other than a parent for 30 hours or more each week—most (56%) of this care was provided by nonrelatives and most (69%) of it took place away from children's homes. (Full-time care by nonrelatives represents the typical situation that people conjure up when they hear "day care" and is the primary focus of this article.)

Table 4-1 shows the distribution of some 2.9 million children receiving full-time care from nonrelatives, by age of child and type of care—centers, family day care homes, and in-home care. As can be seen from this table, preschool children aged three to five are the major users of full-time day care. Preschool children also predominate in center and family day care. Over half of the infants and toddlers in day care are found in family day care homes, while school age children are in both family day care and in-home care in roughly equal numbers. (There are an estimated 670,000 family day care homes.) Another 6 million children under 13 spend 10 to 30 hours each week in part-time care. As might be expected, these are predominately school age children.

Licensed day care facilities—centers and family day care homes—currently provide only 17 percent of all out-of-home care for children in care 10 hours or more each week. The remainder of the children are in unlicensed family day care homes. Licensed family day care providers are generally permitted to care for one to six children. Unpublished data gathered in late 1976 indicate that there are slightly more than 100,000 licensed day care homes serving an estimated 300,000 children. There are approximately 18,300 licensed day care centers in the United States serving some 900,000 children on either a part-time or full-time basis.[5]

Who are the families who use day care? As a group, they can be distinguished from the general population on several dimensions. Although the majority of the children enrolled in centers are white, minorities—especially Blacks—are disproportionately represented. Twenty-eight percent of the children are Black, and 9 percent are of other minority groups. In contrast, minorities account for only 17% of the U.S. population under 15 years of age. Single-parent families and low-income two-parent families are also disproportionately represented among families using center-based day care. In 1977 less than 20 percent of all U.S. families with children under 18 years of age were single-parent families, and about half had incomes below $15,000 per year. Of U.S. families with one or more children enrolled in day care centers, however, 33 percent were single-parent families and 73 percent had incomes below $15,000 per year.

The figures cited above point to a simple fact that must be taken into account in any discussion of quality and cost in day care: many families who use day care, and virtually all who receive public subsidy, are either low-income single parents struggling to stay off welfare and to remain self-sufficient, or two-parent families in which the second income keeps the family above the poverty line. The U.S. Department of Labor reports that 25% of all working families with single parents would have no earned income if they did not work; 49% of all working families with two parents in the labor force would have annual incomes below $15,000 [1978] if the mother did not work. Fathers of two-parent families with children under six have average incomes of $13,800, 29% below the median for all married couples.[15] Thus, millions of American parents have essentially no choice but to share the rearing of their children with others for extended periods of time each week.

This situation will continue at least for the next decade and data indicate that it may well be a permanent and irreversible feature of American life.[19] Reasonable demographic projections indicate that by 1990 there will be as many as 6 million *more* children under 6 years of age. This would bring the total number of children under six to 24 million. Projections also show that half to two-thirds of these children will have a working parent or parents and thus will need care in an out-of-home setting 10 or more hours each week. The projections are consistent with data from the recent past, which show that the increase in labor force participation has been particularly rapid among mothers of young children. For example, the labor force participation of mothers of children under six years old more than tripled (from 14% to 47%) from 1950 to 1980.[28] For families with children under three, labor force participation of mothers increased from 26% to 38% during the past decade alone.[6]

It is highly significant that the most rapid growth in labor force participation has taken place among mothers of younger children, since these are the children for whom developmental concerns are greatest. The authors' response to these concerns is as follows: It may be true that the best arrangement for most, if not all, young children is to live in a loving and safe environment with one or two siblings and their parents—according to the traditional pattern of a mother who stays at home, supported by an extended family and neighbors, and a father who works. But this is not the life a majority of parents are able to lead, especially those struggling to provide food, shelter, clothing, and medical care for their children. What might be best for children cannot become the enemy of what can realistically be good for children. Fortunately, current research, discussed in the next section, indicates that high-quality day care does not threaten the child's well-being and that certain concrete characteristics of day care facilities can serve as benchmarks by which parents, providers, and policymakers can predict and control the quality of care.

Perspectives on Quality

How one views quality in day care depends on one's view of day care's goals and functions. Day care can be seen as a *service to children*, designed, ideally, to improve their daily lives and promote their development. It can be seen as a *service to parents*, designed to free them for work or for other pursuits. It can be viewed as a *source of support for families*, helping them to carry out their dual economic and childrearing functions. It can be seen as a *vehicle for delivering services*, such as health care, supplemental nutrition, parent counseling, and other social services to low-income families.

Finally, it can be viewed as a *social policy* tool, designed to stimulate employment, reduce the welfare rolls, and increase the tax base. These views are not mutually exclusive, but they entail differing emphases in deciding whether a particular day care facility or day care delivery system is "good."

Parents, providers and policymakers share an interest in the quality of care but have different kinds of concern and different ways of influencing quality. The concern of the parent is finding care that is convenient, affordable, and appropriate to the perceived needs of the child. Parents influence the quality of care received by their children primarily by their choice of a facility, and secondarily by direct and indirect participation in the operation of the facility (e.g., serving on governing boards, working as volunteers, exchanging information and suggestions with caregivers). The concern of the provider is to offer services that meet the (varying) needs of client children and families on an economically viable basis (i.e., at a cost that can be covered by parent fees and/or government subsidies). The provider can influence quality of care in many ways: by personal interaction with children and parents; by choice of program or "curriculum," equipment, and staff; by seeking government support for special services, such as food and health subsidies; or by training staff.

The policymaker at the local, state, or federal level is concerned with the quantity and mix of child care services available to families within his or her purview, as well as with setting a lower bound on quality of care, below which facilities may not operate. The policymaker cannot directly influence the match between individual needs and services provided, nor can he or she guarantee that children will be protected from physical and psychological harm, or that human interaction in the day care setting will be warm and stimulating. Rather, the policymaker must attempt to create an efficient "market" in which parents are able to find providers who meet their own needs and those of their children. To accomplish this goal, policymakers must rely on relatively crude devices, primarily funding mechanisms, licensure, and regulation, supplemented by the provision of training programs, information and referral programs, and special services such as food subsidies and health programs.

There exists a substantial amount of research on day care that speaks to issues of quality. However, given the multiplicity of functions and kinds of concern outlined above, it is not surprising that this research addresses quality in fragmentary fashion. Certain issues have been studied in great detail, others have been only partially addressed, while still others have been neglected. In particular, developmental psychologists have devoted much attention to the effects of day care per se—as opposed to home rearing—on aspects of the development of the individual child. Relatively few studies, all of them recent, have examined variations in quality within day care. Effects on parents, families, and communities have likewise received only limited attention. Economists and policy researchers have conducted a few large-scale studies of the supply and demand for day care. These have addressed some of the policymaker's broad concerns about the mix of services and their match to existing needs. However, only one or two studies have attempted to link the kinds of variations in day care facilities that are subject to control through regulation or funding formulae to their subsequent effects on children or families.

Quality from the Perspective of the Individual Child

A strong case can be made that the most fundamental aspect of quality in day care is its effects on the immediate experience and long-term development of the individual child. And it is this aspect of quality that has been most thoroughly studied to date. Until the mid-1970s most studies of the psychological effects of day care focused on comparisons with home rearing. There was great concern, aroused in part by studies of institutionalized children, that prolonged absence from the mother would damage the bond of attachment between mother and child, with deleterious consequences for the child's social and emotional development. There were related concerns that —at least in some group care settings—children would lack the verbal and intellectual stimulation normally received through one-to-one interaction with adults, and that the children's cognitive development would suffer as a result. Studies addressing these issues led to rather consistent findings, which have been ably summarized by several authors.[2,3,8] In brief, the findings were as follows:

(1) With a few exceptions, studies have not found major differences in mother-child attachment between young children reared in their own homes and children reared in day care for substantial periods. (Attachment has typically been measured by naturalistic observations and/or variants of Ainsworth's "strange situation,"[1] involving the child's responses to separation from and reunion with the mother, responses to unfamiliar adults and exploration of an unfamiliar environment in the mother's presence.)

(2) For children from middle-class backgrounds, studies have found no differences in intellectual development, as measured by standardized tests, between children reared entirely at home and those who spent substantial periods in day care. For children from low-income families, day care appears to offset some of the decline in test scores that such children usually show as they grow older.

(3) Measures of social behavior in the day care setting or in kindergarten or early elementary school, as well as measures of cognitive style and skill other than standardized tests, have produced a mixed picture. In most cases there were no differences between home-reared and day care children; in other cases, one or the other group showed an advantage, but there were no clearcut overall advantages for either setting.

These findings must, however, be qualified in several ways. Most significantly, as pointed out by authors of the original studies and by the cited reviewers, almost all of the studies examined children reared in "high-quality" center care, i.e., in well-equipped facilities with favorable ratios of children to staff. Center care of "average" or questionable quality was not usually studied, nor were other forms of substitute care, such as family day care and paid care in the child's own home. (As we have seen, in the United States the latter forms of care together affect far larger numbers of children than does center care. In particular, children under age three—the group for whom the greatest concern about substitute care exists—are much more likely to be found in family day care than in centers.)

In the late seventies these imbalances began to be redressed. While comparisons between center care and home rearing continued to appear, they were joined by studies that included family day care.[4,12] A major policy study of the determinants of quality in center care (to be discussed below) appeared in 1979.[26] A large-scale descriptive study of family day care has also been recently published.[10] In short, current research shows an increasing appreciation both of the diversity of environments in which children receive care and of the practical concerns of parents, providers, and policymakers.

The National Day Care Study (NDCS), in which the authors of this article took part, illustrates this generalization.[26] One of its major objectives was to determine whether and to what degree the experiences and development of children in center care are affected by the characteristics of centers that are susceptible to federal regulation, particularly staff/child ratios, group size, and the education, experience, and training of staff. The study was also concerned with the costs associated with these center characteristics (an issue to be treated in this paper in some detail). The NDCS focused on preschool children in urban centers—the largest single group receiving federal subsidy. The research was conducted over a period of several years in a total of 67 centers in three cities (Atlanta, Detroit, and Seattle). Sites and centers were chosen to maximize diversity of the sample; centers varied widely in staff characteristics, staff/child ratios and group sizes, per-child expenditures and in the ethnic and socioeconomic composition of client populations.

The NDCS incorporated several different approaches to design and analysis. A quasi experiment was conducted in 49 centers at all three sites. Fourteen centers, normally operating at low staff/child ratios (many children per caregiver) received subsidies to improve their ratios. These centers were compared (a) to 14 matched centers that received no subsidies and therefore continued to operate at low ratios, and (b) to 21 centers that normally operated at high ratios. In addition, a randomized experiment was conducted in 30 classrooms in a set of centers operated by the Atlanta Public School System. The design was a factorial, with two levels of ratio crossed by three levels of education of the lead caregiver. Children were randomly assigned, within centers, to classrooms with various configurations of ratio and level of staff education. Finally, the study investigated other regulatable center characteristics, such as group size, the prior day care work experience of the staff, and their education or training in fields specifically related to young children (as opposed to the general level of staff education). These center characteristics were not manipulated in either the quasi experiment or randomized study; however, the studies were arranged so that these characteristics would vary almost independently of ratio and staff education, so that their correlates could be examined through multiple regression analysis.

Dependent variables were of two kinds. First, the daily behavior of children and caregivers was examined through systematic naturalistic observation using detailed coding systems. The observations were used to describe variations in the social environment that were associated with different configurations of regulatable characteristics. Approximately 200 caregivers and 1400 children were observed during the experimental phase of the study.

Second, standardized tests of cognitive and linguistic development —the Preschool Inventory and the Peabody Vocabulary Test—were administered to children in the fall and spring of the study's experimental year. Fall-to-spring change scores, adjusted to take account of well-known technical difficulties with simple pre-post difference scores, were used as growth measures. Approximately 1000 children were tested at these two time points.

Results were relatively clearcut and consistent across components of the study and across sites. In groups where the absolute number of children was small, children were more cooperative and responsive to initiatives by adults and other children, more likely to engage in spontaneous verbalization and creative/intellectual activity, and less likely to wander aimlessly or to be uninvolved in activities than were children in larger groups. Children in small groups also made more rapid gains on standardized tests than their peers in larger groups.

These findings held true even when favorable staff/child ratios prevailed in the larger groups; more caregivers did not appear to off-set the negative effects of grouping large numbers of children to-gether. Favorable ratios, however, were related to some aspects of caregiver behavior. Higher ratios (fewer children per caregiver) seemed to make management of children easier; caregivers spent relatively little time commanding and correcting children. They also spent more time interacting with other adults and carrying out neces-sary routine chores such as cleanup, arranging materials, etc. The latter findings suggest that high ratios provide benefits to caregivers, in the form of relief from the pressures of constant interaction with children. By the same token, the findings also suggest that high ratios may not always translate into benefits for children, in the form of one-to-one interaction with adults. Significantly, however, an NDCS subsidiary study of center care for infants and toddlers suggested that ratios were as important as group size for this age group; high ratios were associated with less overt distress and apathy on the part of children, less exposure to potential physical danger, and less man-agement on the part of caregivers.[26]

The preschool study also found that caregivers with specialized training in early childhood education, child development, day care, and the like, showed a relatively high degree of social interaction with children—praising, comforting, responding, questioning, and instructing—and that children in their care made relatively large gains on standardized tests. Formal education per se—years of school-ing or diplomas and degrees achieved—showed no consistent rela-tionship to the behavior of caregivers or children, or to children's test scores.

Taken in tandem with findings on cost, these results have signifi-cant implications for public policy (to be discussed later). What is important to note here is that the National Day Care Study, as well as other recent work, has begun to identify some important factors influencing quality in day care. Thus it complements earlier work that suggested that high-quality care need not have deleterious ef-fects relative to home rearing. Moreover, the study indicates that some of the determinants of quality are subject to fairly direct con-trol both by the individual practitioner and by public policy. The study in no way minimizes the importance of less easily controllable determinants of the quality of the child's day care experience and consequent development, such as the personal style of the caregiver or the interpersonal chemistry of the peer group. But it does give practical guidance about tangible matters such as recruitment, train-ing, and grouping arrangements.

A recent study of family day care suggests that policy can poten-tially affect the experiences of children even in that extremely heter-ogeneous and largely unregulated environment.[10] Paralleling the results of the National Day Care (center) Study, this investigation suggested that both group size and caregiver training relate in important ways to the behavior of caregivers in family day care homes. In addition, the study found major differences in group structure, services provided, and behavior patterns among unlicensed, licensed, and sponsored family day care homes. (Sponsored homes participate in formal systems for purposes of purchasing, training, sharing equipment, recruiting staff and clients, and other functions.) Sponsored homes had better trained caregivers and provided a broader range of services than either unaffiliated licensed homes or unlicensed homes. For groups of any given size, caregivers in sponsored homes engaged in more teaching and more direct interaction with children than their counterparts in other family day care settings. Groups in sponsored homes were, however, generally larger than those in other family day care homes, though still small by center standards. Thus, while it is not possible to make global quality judgments about the three types of family day care, it is significant that predictable differences do exist and that the quality of the child's experience is likely to be related to licensure and sponsorship as well as group size and training.

Quality from the Perspective of Parents, Families, and Community

The state of knowledge about the effects of day care on families and communities contrasts sharply with the state of knowledge about effects on children. As indicated above, substantial strides have been made in the latter area, while empirical knowledge in the former area remains scattered. Effects of the *availability* of day care on maternal employment and family income have been examined fairly extensively in various "income maintenance experiments" and other studies. Results from these studies indicate rather modest effects: women's labor force participation increases only about 10 percent when day care is readily available.[7,16,17,27] However, relatively little research attention has been devoted to other effects on parents or families, and almost none has been devoted to the community. Moreover, the research that does exist—like the early work on the effects of day care on the child—focuses mainly on effects of day care per se, and not on variations *within* day care that might affect quality as experienced by families or communities.

From the perspective of the family as a unit, day care might be expected to have an impact that transcends both benefits to the child and an influence on employment and income. To the degree that day care helps to relieve economic stress, to facilitate fulfillment of the career aspirations of women, and to diminish anxieties about the effects of maternal employment on the child, it might be expected to contribute to family stability and harmony. To the authors' knowledge, however, there have been no studies relating availability of day care to concrete indices of these family characteristics, such as lowered divorce rates, increased remarriage rates, reduced rates of foster care placement, reduced rates of child abuse, and the like. There have been several studies that attempted (with mixed results) to relate participation in day care to parent-child interaction,[4,24] to measures of family functioning[12] and to the quality of the home environment.[11] However, for purposes of understanding variations in quality among day care settings, it would be useful to know how these family effects relate to the configuration of services provided in day care. For example, effects on the family may be conditioned by provision of services such as parent education and family counseling, but such relationships, if they exist, have not been demonstrated. Similarly, effects on the family may also be conditioned by the amount and type of communication between parents and providers; while parent-provider communication itself has been investigated in at least two provocative studies,[14,23] the broader effects on the family remain open to further study.

Another new and important area of investigation has to do with the impact on family life of the coordination (or lack of coordination) between day care and other institutions, notably schools and employers.[18,20,21] Problems of scheduling and logistics can be severe for working parents, especially when their children are in different day care facilities (perhaps because the day care center that serves their preschooler cannot accommodate their school-aged children in the afternoon). Various approaches have been tried in order to alleviate these problems—among them day care at the workplace, "flexitime" work schedules, after-school care, and day care for preschoolers in the school. Though case studies describing some of these experiments have appeared, further systematic investigation of their effectiveness at relieving scheduling problems and their ancillary effect on family life (e.g., quantity and quality of time that parents spend with each other and/or with their children) need to be conducted.

From the perspective of the local community as a whole, the availability of quality day care might have both tangible and intangible consequences. To the degree that it is viewed as a benefit for children—like good schools—it may make communities more attractive to families. "Attractiveness" might be measured by such concrete indices as rates of in- and out-migration, or even real estate values. Less concretely, but no less importantly, good day care may contribute to a sense that a community is a good place for families and that its social services are accessible and geared to significant human needs. Again, the authors know of no research that has addressed questions of quality in day care at the community level.

In short, there are important aspects of quality in day care that have not yet been measured successfully or studied extensively. Nevertheless, enough is known about quality from the perspective of the individual child, and about the concrete features of care that help create a quality experience, so that we can begin to pose questions of practical importance to parents and providers, as well as policymakers—namely, questions about the price tag attached to good care. These questions are the subject of the next part of this article.

Perspectives on Cost

In an environment of unconstrained resources there would be no quality-cost issue. High quality care could be provided to as many families as needed and wanted it at a price those families could afford. Some, indeed, would argue that children are so important that high quality nurturing and education in the early years is worth whatever price has to be paid. However, it is undeniable that such voices would be crying in the contemporary wilderness defined by massive and competing needs for services and the clear insufficiency of resources to go around.

The moment that money for day care is in short supply, a series of difficult tradeoffs emerges. The first set of tradeoffs takes place at the micro level of child, parent and provider. It is reasonable to assume that both parents and providers want what have been identified as the key ingredients of quality care. Well-composed classrooms (small groups with favorable staff/child ratios) make a difference. So do staff trained in child development and/or early childhood education —staff who are stable in their employment patterns, who value children and themselves. However, variations in classroom composition (especially ratio) and in caregiver wages are the two factors most decisively related to major variations in the cost of care. A favorable classroom composition and a more highly paid trained and stable caregiver increases cost. All care is costly—average annual center care costs nationally were about $2000 per child in 1980. When parents pay the cost of care themselves, they must also consider the tradeoffs with other important family "goods"—food, shelter, clothing, medical care.

The second set of tradeoffs—at the macro level—is of most interest to policymakers. Here the issues include not only those of quality, cost of care and wages—policymakers must also grapple with the questions of quantity of care. We do not propose to tell parents or providers how to weigh quality against cost, nor to give pat answers to the policymaker's difficult questions. Rather, in this section we attempt only to pose the micro- and macro-tradeoffs clearly, illustrating with numerical examples and indicating where alternative policies might play a role.

Quality-Cost Tradeoffs for Parents and Providers

From the perspective of parents and providers there are three clear points of stress when quality-cost tradeoffs must be made:

1. Parents and caregivers want to give each child care of the highest possible quality;
2. Parents want to purchase care at a price that does not compete excessively with other "goods" needed for the family's market basket; and
3. Caregivers want to receive a wage that will promote stable employment and be commensurate with their training, experience, and with the value of the service they provide.

These three dynamics enter the day care quality-cost equation in decisive ways. There is no more graphic way to illustrate this than the following real-life interchange:

Maryanne, a mother in a two-parent, two-child family, has an opportunity to work and lift family income from its near poverty level of $9,200 per year to $17,000, about 75% of the median income for families of four. In order to accept the job, she needs to find full day care for her three-year-old daughter, Joanne, from 8:30 to 5:30 (9 hours). Her seven-year-old son, Steven, will be cared for after school by a neighbor in exchange for some weekend work by Maryanne's husband.

Maryanne and her husband John are both caring parents. They want the best for Joanne. Maryanne is interested in more than just a babysitting arrangement; she would like her daughter to have an educational experience like her neighbor's four-year-old who is in a local nursery school. A friend at church tells her that a day care research specialist who knows about day care quality and cost is coming to town to speak. She goes to hear him and afterward asks him how much she should plan on spending for good care.

"Tell me," he says, "how many other children do you think should be in your child's class? How big a group of kids would be best for her?"

Maryanne thinks a minute and says, "I'd prefer a smaller rather than a bigger group; maybe five or six kids. My daughter is shy, and three-year-olds can be pretty hard on each other."

"O.K.," says the specialist, "now tell me what you think your child's teacher should earn?"

"Well, I want Joanne's teacher to know how to teach Joanne so she'll be ready for school and so she can learn how to get along with other kids and feel good about herself. And I want Joanne to know about art materials and that sort of thing. So I suppose her teacher should have some college training." Maryanne pauses for a moment thinking. "I guess she should get about $6.00 an hour—that's $240 a

week. I'll only get $150 a week, but I'll be a forms clerk and I only have a high school education."

"Fine. Let's see what we've got. A rough rule of thumb is that day care classroom teachers' wages are about fifty percent of the total center costs. The other half is made up of fringe benefits, wages of other staff—like the director and the cook—meals, space and utilities and so forth. So the classroom you want for your child will cost the center $12 an hour. And you said you wanted a small group, about six children. That's $12 an hour divided by six, or $2 per child an hour." The specialist could see a dismayed look on the mother's face.

He continued, "At nine hours a day, five days a week and fifty weeks a year—that would bring the total cost to $4500 a year."

"But that's over half my yearly wages—before taxes!" gasped Maryanne. "In fact, John and I just figured out that I will be paying almost $1400 of my income in income tax, which after social security will leave me $5900 to take home. So if I had to pay $4500 for child care, what would I bring home each week?"

The specialist had taken out a pocket calculator. "You'd be eligible for the full day care tax credit of $400, so you would bring home a net of $35 each week. Another way of saying it is that you would be spending two dollars and fifty cents for child care for every one dollar of spendable income you brought home."

"Well, what's the least I could spend on day care and still have it be all right for Joanne?" Maryanne asked.

"Let's take the question I asked you earlier and turn it around. What's the largest number of three-year-olds you think one adult can handle and still have time for each child?"

"No more than ten," said Maryanne, somewhat grimly.

"And what is the minimum you think the teacher should be paid?" the child care specialist asked.

"No less, and I guess no more, than I'm going to make!"

"All right," said the specialist calculating, "That means three dollars and seventy-five cents an hour times two, divided by ten kids . . . " He paused, punching in more numbers, "which will bring your take-home pay to about $88 a week. Your investment in day care is now thirty cents to bring home a dollar of spendable income."

"I don't think I have any choice," said Maryanne sadly. "We aren't making it now. Can I find good day care center at that price?"

"You might be able to. Thirty-four dollars a week is somewhat under the average cost of care nationally. You might also find a family day care mother at that price whom you'd feel good about."

This true story lays out the dilemma. The two day care ingredients commonly identified as crucial to quality have significant cost implications. Fewer children in the care of an adult mean higher costs for the center and thus more expensive care. Higher wages for caregivers also mean higher costs and more expensive care. And to the extent that private and public resources are scarce, variations in the

Table 4-2   **Illustrative Tradeoff Analysis**[a]

Center Day Care: Ratio vs. Wages vs. Price of Care

	Staff/Child Ratio[b]	Caregiver Wage	Price of Care/Year	Result
A.	1:6	$3.60	$2,400	Baseline
B.	1:10	3.60	1,800	Lower Ratios Same Wages Lower Price
C.	1:10	5.77	2,400	Lower Ratio Higher Wages Same Price
D.	1:6	5.77	3,140	Same Ratio Higher Wages Higher Price
E.	1:8	4.50	2,250	Lower Ratio Higher Wages Lower Price

[a] Data from National Day Care Study extrapolated to 1981 and used only to illustrate critical tradeoffs.
[b] Enrolled ratios adjusted for absenteeism.

cost may not only be associated with variations in quality, but also will heavily affect the number of children who can be served.

Maryanne's story is not uncommon. Table 4-2 makes the same point graphically. The table illustrates the tradeoffs among variations in staff/child ratios, caregiver wages, and the price of care to parents. Row A (baseline) represents the estimated average ratio, current wages, and costs of care in day care centers serving preschool children. Lowering the baseline ratio by 67 percent in B, and holding caregiver wage constant, produces a 33 percent decrease in price. In C, holding the baseline price constant, the decrease in ratio permits a 60 percent increase in caregiver wage, to $5.77 (the hourly equivalent of the Department of Labor's "Low Income" budget of $12,000 per year). In D, holding constant both the more favorable baseline ratio and the higher wage increases the price to parents by 31 percent. In the final example, E, the effect of lowering the ratio by a smaller amount, 33 percent, is divided more evenly. Caregiver wages increase 25 percent, and the price to parents goes down 7 percent.

This situation in Table 4-2 is as provocative from the point of view of the caregiver as from that of the parent. Sixty-three percent of all center caregivers earn less than the $3.75 per hour that Maryanne was prepared to pay. The actual average wage in day care centers (estimated to be $3.60 per hour) is lower than the Department of Labor designated poverty line. However, the average educational attainment of caregivers is close to 14 years. Caregivers are above the 50th percentile in years of education and in the bottom five percent wage bracket for all workers. Head teachers in day care centers earn about half the income of their counterparts in the public schools.

Wage levels not only have a direct bearing on the well-being of caregivers but may also relate indirectly to quality of care from the child's perspective. Not surprisingly, evidence suggests that lower wages are predictors of higher staff turnover rates. In addition, available evidence also suggests a weak relationship between education/training in a child-related area and slightly higher wages.[26]

Table 4-2, in short, depicts a serious conflict of interest between providers on the one hand and parents and (perhaps) children on the other.

Women—working mothers—are the overwhelming majority of the purchasers of day care. Few are wealthy. Women—many of whom are mothers themselves—also work as the providers of day care. Their incomes from this activity hover near the poverty line. Meeting the needs of one set of mothers (by lowering prices or increasing wages) creates economic pressure on the other set. This dilemma is not going to be resolved until the infusion of additional resources rationalizes and stabilizes the current chaotic day care marketplace. (Later we will offer some thoughts as to how this may be accomplished in a time of government fiscal austerity.)

Quality-Cost Tradeoffs for Policymakers

While quality-cost tradeoffs for parents and providers are at the concrete, intimate, and human level, policymakers must grapple with more abstract issues as they consider the impact of these tradeoffs on large numbers of children, parents and providers.

They must strike an acceptable balance among cost of care, quality of care and wages paid to caregivers. They must also consider the impact of alternative policies on the total number of children who can be served at any given level of resource outlay.

Table 4-3 illustrates the tradeoffs facing the policymaker; it incorporates those tradeoffs shown in Table 4-2 with the addition of a column showing the number of children who could be served per $100 million of public expenditure for any given configuration of staff/child ratio and caregiver wages. Once again, the implications of alternative choices about ratio and wages are striking. At the ex-

Table 4-3 Illustrative Tradeoff Analysis[a]

Center Day Care: Ratio vs. Wages vs. Price of Care vs. Number of Children
Served for each $100 million expended (estimated in 1981 dollars)

	Staff/ Child Ratio[b]	Caregiver Wage	Price of Care/Year	Number of Children Served	Result
A.	1:6	$3.60	$2,400	41,670	Baseline
B.	1:10	3.60	1,800	55,560	Lower Ratios Same Wages Lower Price More Children
C.	1:10	5.77	2,400	41,670	Lower Ratio Higher Wages Same Price Same Children
D.	1:6	5.77	3,140	31,850	Same Ratio Higher Wages Higher Price Fewer Children
E.	1:8	4.50	2,250	44,440	Lower Ratio Higher Wages Lower Price More Children

[a] Data from National Day Care Study extrapolated to 1981 and used only to illustrate
critical tradeoffs.
[b] Enrolled ratios adjusted for absenteeism.

tremes of the table, the number of children served for $100 million
could be increased by 74 percent (from 31,850 to 55,560) if the
policymaker were willing to hold wages at present levels and allow
ratios of 1:10 rather than 1:6. In the final example, E, a higher wage,
a lower price, *and* a 7 percent increase in the number of children
served can be achieved by lowering the ratio from 1:6 to 1:8.

The tradeoffs illustrated in this and the previous section make it
clear why the major policy issues of the 1980s will be centered on
resources. After a decade of research, quality day care can to some
degree be both defined and delivered. Given adequate resources,
competent caregivers can be found or developed, facilities made
stimulating and safe, and smaller rather than larger groups formed
and maintained. The question is: Who will pay the piper and how
will he be paid? In the next section we offer some opinions about
the public responsibility for financing day care, and some suggestions
about how this might be accomplished.

Policy Directions for the 1980s

This section briefly reviews the case supporting a legitimate public interest in day care, summarizes some of the potential economic and social policy objectives served by day care, and then specifies five interconnected policy initiatives needed to address the national day care dilemma which, left unattended, may well reach crisis proportions in this decade.

Viewed from a policy perspective, the government's role in day care raises questions that have less to do with facts known and unknown, research done or not yet done, than with basic premises about the role and responsibility of government. It is still argued that child care is a private family concern and that, therefore, government should not interfere. The historical fact is, however, that the responsibility for caring for children has been shared in the United States. Families have been the primary caregivers, particularly in the early years, but government has always responded unilaterally to children in distress. The courts have intervened to protect abandoned, abused or neglected children and children of divorce and separation. Public agencies have responded to malnourished and hungry children and children who are sick and emotionally disturbed. Some would argue that these interventions in clearly pathological situations are as far as government should go. Quality from this perspective, is of limited concern, so long as children are protected from harm.

There is an alternate view of the government's role with respect to the family—one that the authors find persuasive: The duties of government are more than merely protective. According to this opinion, government has a positive responsibility to promote twin goals: full employment for parents and the sound development of the young. Self-sufficient families contribute to the near-term economic well-being of the country; healthy children are the critical long-term resource for a strong and stable nation. Good day care, it is argued, is necessary if these important goals are to be achieved. In this formulation, day care is somewhat analogous to public education, which is not merely provided as an optional service but is mandatory, except where parents choose to purchase a private substitute. As Norton Grubb has pointed out, day care, like schooling, is a service that, at its best, supports normal families by joining with them to raise sound children.[13]

What must the concerned policymaker consider if he or she accepts the premise of some public responsibility, both economic and social, for the family? In the economic sphere the issues are relatively clear. To the extent that market day care is in fact necessary to full family employment, it should be fostered as a means to family self-sufficiency and general economic growth. The more self-sufficient families there are, the greater the general *family* contribution to the Gross National Product, to increasing capital investments, and to annual tax revenues. Conversely, nonproductive families contribute to greater costs for unemployment, welfare, and other social programs.

To the degree that day care makes a difference to family productivity, it becomes vitally important in domestic policy equations. Many lower-middle and even middle-income families can't afford to purchase care at full market prices. The current small day care tax credit is of only marginal assistance to these families for three reasons. First, the credit has been a fixed 20 percent of costs. Therefore, low-income families have received proportionately less help than higher-income families because they cannot afford to pay as much for day care. Second, unless special arrangements are made to reduce withholding tax deductions, the credit is not available when it is needed—at the time of a day care expenditure. Finally, there is a whole segment of the population for whom no government day care assistance is available. Since the current tax credit is not refundable, the working poor who make too little to pay taxes get no benefit from it. At the same time they may well have too much income to be eligible for Title IV-A or Title XX subsidies.

It is not surprising, therefore, that the day care marketplace is in serious disarray. In many states there are two (barely) overlapping tiers: a subsidized tier primarily serving low-income families at a higher cost of care, and a lower-cost parent-fee tier serving lower-middle and middle-income families. Analysis of the demographics of this situation shows that *de facto* segregation results.[5]

The economic benefits of government interventions in the day care marketplace have yet to be determined. It is in the best interest of government to stimulate the development of an orderly and durable day care market if day care subsidies are: (a) less than welfare costs, or (b) a work-related expense that produces a net gain in tax revenues. Among the principal policy questions to be addressed here are: Who should receive subsidies? By what mechanism? Through income transfers (via consumers)? Through categorical programs (via providers) or some mix of both? How many public dollars is it reasonable to spend per child? What proportion and amount should be spent from parents' pockets as opposed to or in addition to the local/state/federal purse?

In the social sphere, the issues facing the policymaker are more complex. The relationship of labor force participation of working mothers and the availability of good care has not been addressed *from the perspective of the long-term impacts on children.* It has been widely assumed that there is no excess demand for day care, that parents can and will find some kind of care, and therefore that additional subsidy is not needed to stimulate the supply.[29] The more salient policy question, from the child-as-national-resource viewpoint is, "What happens to children's long-term development under different day care demand-and-supply conditions?" As stated earlier, quality day care is not only not harmful, it can provide positive benefits. But no one would be likely to contest the fact that inadequate arrangements are likely to have serious long-term consequences leading to costly school failure, delinquency, unemployability, and ill-health. While data on inadequate arrangements are sparse, they include uninterested or ignorant caregivers, patchwork arrangements with neighbors and older siblings, and up to 1.5 million latchkey or left-home-alone children. It is precisely because many working parents don't feel they have choices about day care that they often settle, unhappily, for whatever care they can find. They feel forced to accept an expedient day care arrangement, however poor or short-term, so that their family can survive.

If government does assume some responsibility over the quality of day care for social as well as economic reasons, as in fact it has, then further questions arise. Does its responsibility extend to all children, or only to those whose parents are too poor to purchase adequate care? Who will decide what services children receive and what programs they experience? Who will carry out these programs? What balance should be struck between the quality of programs for those who receive them and equity for those who pay? Between quality and breadth of access? And how will quality be assured? By regulation? By consumer education? In short, considering quality from a national perspective confronts the policymaker with an additional series of tough and unresolved policy questions.

Thus the policymaker has inadequate answers to questions arising from both spheres of interest. He or she doesn't know fully the extent to which subsidized day care leads to the economic benefits of increased self-sufficiency and reduced welfare costs. At the same time, the policymaker cannot be clear about the long-term social benefits of good versus inadequate child care arrangements. He or she is even less able to determine the qualitative meaning of variations in day care classroom staff/child ratios or teacher wages. The policymaker is most likely to be concerned with increasing the quantity of less costly care, since lower costs mean that parents are more likely to purchase care without large subsidies, and public budgets will thus stretch further to meet the 1980s expanding need for day care.

What options exist for those policymakers who are not prepared to wait until all the questions are answered about the role of day care in supporting family productivity or the healthy development of children? What can they do when they sense—the authors believe correctly—the urgent need to stimulate the rapid growth of an adequate supply of acceptable day care at a price that working parents can afford?

First, there must be a decision as to the shape the day care marketplace should take. It is the authors' judgment that the defining characteristics of that market should be:

- *A consumer orientation.* While a certain amount of support needs to be given to providers to help them start up and sustain successful day care enterprises, the orientation of policymakers should be focused on parents and their need both for information that can inform their choice of day care and for some financial support so they can afford what they have chosen.
- *A concern with both the child's welfare and development.* The distinction made a decade ago between custodial and developmental care is no longer meaningful. Head Start has adequately demonstrated that nurturing and education can and must go hand in hand.
- *A diverse supply of providers.* Rather than a single form of care, the growth of all kinds of care should be supported—center-based and home-based; nonprofit and for profit; freestanding or sponsored by other institutions such as schools, churches, hospitals, unions, industry, and business.

In order to achieve the policy goal of an increased supply of quality day care at a price parents can afford, the authors propose that five interconnected policy initiatives be undertaken: (1) maintain the current day care support programs for low- and moderate-income families; (2) expand tax relief; (3) integrate support programs and tax relief; (4) develop more adequate day care information and information distribution systems; and (5) create a short-term day care economic development authority.

(1) *Maintain current day care support programs for low- and moderate-income families.* As of this writing it is not clear what will happen to the major current day care support programs for poverty families—Titles XX and IV-A of the Social Security Act (SSA). Some cuts appear to be a certainty. The question is, how much?

Title XX funds are distributed to the states in the form of a social service block grant on a matching basis (75 percent federal, 25 percent state, local, or privately donated funds). These funds are expended for a wide variety of social service programs, generally through a purchase-of-service agreement with providers. Title XX day care serves children whose parents work but earn less than 80% of their state's median income. In some states, partial subsidies are provided to families with incomes up to 115% of their state's median income. Title XX day care is also used to support low- and moderate-income families while a parent is in training or seeking employment. It also serves parents with a child's daytime care because of a handicapping condition or a parent's chronic ill health. The quality of Title XX day care has been regulated by both state licensing and federal purchasing standards. As of 1977, some 30 percent of the $2.7 billion Title XX funds allotted to states was being spent to provide day care for a reported 800,000 children.[6]

Title IV-A (AFDC) allows the state to "disregard" the work-related expense of day care when it calculates the monthly AFDC benefit for a parent, while he or she is seeking work, or is employed at an income below established levels. Parents have some control over the quality of care they purchase under the disregard provision of Title IV-A. They make the selection of both the form of care and the specific provider; there are no licensing or other regulatory restrictions on parental choices. Title IV-A serves fewer children than Title XX. Again, as of 1977, the government reported spending $84 million to provide day care services for some 145,000 children.

It may be true, as some allege, that there is a general mood to abandon the poor altogether. However, it is imperative that these day care support programs be maintained. Many low-income families are in the process of moving, or have moved, toward increasing self-sufficiency. Title XX and Title IV-A support assists these families in maintaining some level of independence. Certainly, an analysis of the potential cost of reducing or eliminating day care funds would be advisable *before* drastic action is taken. It would be ironic, indeed, for the new administration to find itself in the position of having to increase safety-net spending in greater amounts than those currently being spent on day care support through the Social Security Act.

(2) *Expand tax relief.* In addition to maintaining current day care support programs, there should be an expansion of day care tax relief for those who are stably employed. The Congress made important progress on this front in the Economic Recovery Act of 1981. Effective in 1982, the Act increases the current day care tax credit and makes it "slide." The maximum rate will now be 30% of the cost of care at an adjusted gross family income of $10,000 or below. The rate will drop one percent for each additional $2000 in income until it reaches $30,000, when it will level out at 20%. The amount of day care cost on which the credit applies also is increased from $2,000 to $2,400 for one child and twice that amount for two or more children. These changes are summarized in Table 4-4.

Perhaps the most important feature missing from the 1981 tax reform package is a refundability provision. Under the current law, for example, a single-parent family with two children in which the parent earned $5,300 or less in 1980 would not receive any assistance

Table 4-4 Effect of the Child and Dependent Care Provision of the 1981 Economic Recovery Act

Taxable Income	Percent Credit	Maximum 1 Child	$ Credit 2 or More	% Increase Over Current Credit
$10,000 or below	30%	$720	$1,440	80%
12,000	29	696	1,392	74
14,000	28	672	1,344	68
16,000	27	648	1,296	62
18,000	26	624	1,248	56
20,000	25	600	1,200	50
22,000	24	576	1,152	44
24,000	23	552	1,104	38
26,000	22	528	1,056	32
28,000	21	504	1,008	26
30,000 or above	20	480	960	20

from the credit because it has no tax liability. The same situation prevails for a family of four at an income level of $7,400. Under a refundable provision, these families would get back 30% of their day care expenditures even though they paid no taxes. This feature would be similar to the current earned income credit of up to $500 which is available to families (with children) that have incomes less than $10,000.

The bill has two other features specifically related to day care. First, payments to day care centers are eligible for the credit only if the center is in compliance with all applicable state and local laws and regulations. Secondly, in general, employer subsidies for the care of an employee's dependent need not be included in the employee's gross income, providing that the employer has a written nondiscriminatory plan.

In summary, the new sliding credit is an important step in addressing the problem facing the "working poor." Some will argue that the credit should continue to increase, perhaps even accelerate, to 80 or 90 percent of the cost of care at $6,000 or $7,000. Others will argue that 20 percent credit is too high at the upper income end. Perhaps the most serious problem with the tax credit is timeliness, that is, delivering day care dollars when they're needed. This the bill does not explicitly address. While it is true currently that a reduction can be made in amount of taxes withheld by refiling the W-4 employee's withholding allowance certificate, this requires a fairly sophisticated knowledge of the tax system and appears not to be widely used or publicized. (Probably many people are not aware that this change was made in the W-4 in October of 1979.) It would be better if the W-4 form contained even more specific and clear instructions to employees using day care. A two-page addition to "Circular E: Employer's Tax Guide" could provide the table necessary to estimate the annual credit and divide it by the number of pay periods, so that a dollar reduction could be entered on the W-4. Such a system could address refundability as well, since an employer's quarterly withholding tax and FICA liabilities are more than sufficient to cover refunds to employees not paying any withholding tax.

(3) *Integrate support programs and tax relief.* At the present time, the three major federal programs—Titles XX and IV-A of the SSA, and the tax credit—operate independently of one another. There is virtually no way an individual parent can move among these systems without suffering some break in day care services, or worse, a severe income "notch" effect. (A "notch" occurs when, for example, benefits are lost that are of greater value than the increase in income which produced ineligibility for the benefit.) A truly effective system of day care support will bring the three major sources of funds into harmony with one another. Positive and increasing incentives for family self-sufficiency should be the major design premise underlying the development of an integrated system.

(4) *Develop more adequate day care information and information distribution systems.* There exists a great deal of useful information about day care, what it is, how to find it, and how to assess its quality. All around the country, day care information and referral activities and organizations are being started. Some specialize only in day care information. Others are part of broader efforts to improve the flow of information about human services. (A national study of day care information and referral, Project Connections, is due to be completed next fall. It is being conducted by the Administration of Children, Youth, and Families, with joint funding by the Ford Foundation.) However, most of this information is available only at the local level. Virtually no day care consumer or provider information has been developed at the national level. What little there has been has not been effectively distributed.

A major effort should be made to establish a national day care clearinghouse. The function of the clearinghouse would be to gather, evaluate, organize, and disseminate information for the many interested constituencies—parents, researchers, and policymakers at the local, state, and federal levels.

(5) *Create a short-term day care economic development authority.* In addition to stimulating the demand-side through selective subsidies, there needs to be a corresponding stimulation of the supply-side. The model which makes sense would be a relatively short-term—five-to-ten year—national day care economic development initiative. While it could be part of an existing agency, it would

probably work best if it were set up as an independent national authority, operating at the state level. Its major functions would be:

- To provide information about the alternative ways to become a day care provider—center or family day care homes, profit or nonprofit, corporation or proprietorship. It would provide guidance about the kind of market research that needs to be done in order to make a sound going-into-business decision. It would also provide operating information about day care programs, administration, personnel management, staff development, costs, financing, cash-flow management, accounting, and so forth.
- To provide start-up, facility, and operating loan guarantees. Such financial supports would materially increase the prospects of a period of stable growth for the day care marketplace.

These five initiatives, undertaken together, would constitute a comprehensive and rational means of addressing the rising need for more and better day care at an affordable price.

Summary and Conclusions

The message of this article is an easy one to summarize but also a rather harsh one, for it confronts those of us who care about quality in child care with some simple and apparently inescapable economic realities. Eight points tell the story:

1. Day care is an economic necessity for increasing numbers of American families. Day care will constitute a significant part of the early experience of large and growing numbers of children for the forseeable future.
2. For families at the lower end of the income scale, and increasingly for middle-income families, the costs of care represent a burden that cannot comfortably be carried—if it can be carried at all—without government assistance. Through tax credits and various direct and indirect subsidies, government currently plays a major role in the day care market. Despite pressures to trim public budgets, some form of continued or expanded government presence appears to be necessary if adequate care is to be available to low- and middle-income families.
3. Care of high quality does not appear to be harmful for young children and may even be beneficial for some children from low-income families.
4. Some of the determinants of quality in child care are known and are subject to control by parents, providers, and policymakers. Among the best established benchmarks of quality are

smaller groups, higher staff/child ratios, and caregivers trained to work with young children.

5. Good care costs more than less good care. Higher staff/child ratios in particular have major cost implications. Trained staff also tend to command slightly higher wages than untrained staff. Consequently, individual parents are faced with a trade-off between the quality of care experienced by their children and the amount of money left to purchase other necessities.

6. When the perspective of the provider is taken into account, the cost-quality tradeoff acquires another element. Relative to other workers, caregivers are well educated but poorly paid. Any significant increase in caregiver wages, however, will confront parents with a less desirable tradeoff than currently exists. Care of a given quality will cost much more or, alternatively, a given outlay of funds will buy care of significantly lower quality.

7. When the perspective of the policymaker is taken into account, still another element is added to the equation. For any given configuration of wages and quality/cost choices, a given number of children can be served within current government outlays. An increase in either wages or quality entails a decrease in the number of children served; conversely, expansion of services (within current budgets) entails either sacrifices of quality or (less likely) a reduction in caregiver compensation.

8. The one escape from the vise of these simple realities is to find ways to increase both public and private funding for day care. Increased funding will allow an increase either in the quality of care, the number of children served, or both. Increased funding can be achieved by five policy initiatives: maintaining existing day care support programs for low-income families; providing additional tax relief; integrating support programs and tax relief into a single system; developing and disseminating more day care information; and creating a supply-side economic development authority.

While such an increase may at first blush seem like mere wishful thinking, there is some room for optimism. In particular, proposals for even further expansion of the tax credit mechanism rather than increased direct subsidies, appear to be in tune with the temper of the current administration. Of particular importance is the pressing need for the addition of a refundability provision that will benefit the working family that pays no taxes. Such proposals are a form of tax cut, espoused in principle by the administration; they place discretion in the hands of parents, and minimize bureaucratic control. Of course, they also place a burden on parents to educate themselves about the determinants of quality and to seek out good care. But belief in the intelligence of parents and in their willingness to make efforts on behalf of their children is a faith that liberals and conservatives alike can share.

References

1. Ainsworth, M. and Wittig, B. 1969. "Attachment and exploratory behavior of one-year-olds in a strange situation." In *Determinants of Infant Behavior*, Vol. 4, B. Foss, ed. Methuen, London.
2. Belsky, J. and Steinberg, L. 1978. "The effects of day care: a critical review." *Child Development* 49:929–947.
3. Belsky, J., Steinberg, L. and Walker, A. 1981. "The ecology of day care." In *Childrearing in Nontraditional Families*, M. Lamb, ed. Lawrence Erlbaum, Hillsdale, N.J.
4. Clarke-Stewart, A. 1979. "Assessing social development." Presented to the Society for Research in Child Development, San Francisco.
5. Coelen, C. *et al.* 1979. *Day Care Centers in the U.S. Final Report of the National Day Care Study*, Vol. III. Abt Books, Cambridge, Ma.
6. Congressional Budget Office. 1978. *Child care and preschool: options for federal support*. U.S. Government Printing Office, Washington, D.C.
7. Ditmore, J. and Prosser, W. 1978. *A study of day care's effect on the labor force participation of low-income mothers*. Office of Economic Opportunity, Washington, D.C.
8. Etaugh, C. 1980. "Effects of nonmaternal care on children." *American Psychologist* 35:309–319.
9. Farran, D. and Ramey, C. 1980. "Social class differences in dyadic involvement during infancy." *Child Development* 51:254–257.
10. Fosburg, S. and Hawkins, P. 1981. *Final Report of the National Day Care Home Study*, Vol. I. Abt Books, Cambridge, Ma.
11. Fowler, W. and Khan, N. 1975. "The development of a prototype infant and child day care center in metropolitan Toronto." *Progress Reports,* year IV. Ontario Institute for Studies in Education, Toronto.
12. Golden, M. *et al.* 1977. *"The New York City infant day care study: a comparative study of licensed group and family day care programs and the effects of those programs on children and their families.* Medical and Health Research Association of New York City, Inc., New York.
13. Grubb, N. 1977. "Alternative futures for child care." In *Broken Promises: the State, Children and Families in Postwar America*. Forthcoming in 1982, Basic Books, New York.
14. Joffe, C. 1977. *Friendly intruders: child care professionals and family life*. University of California Press, Berkeley.
15. Johnson, B. 1981. *Marital and family characteristics of the labor force, March 1979*. Special Labor Force Report #237, USDOL, Washington, D.C.
16. Jusenius, C. and Shortlidge, R. 1975. *Dual careers: a longitudinal study of the labor market experience of women*. Ohio State University Center for Human Resource Research, Columbus.

17. Kurz, M., Robins, R. and Spiegelman, R. 1975. *A study of the demand for child care by working mothers.* Stanford Research Institute, Menlo Park, Ca.
18. Martensson, S. 1977. "Childhood interaction and temporal organization." *Economic geography* 53:99–125.
19. Masnick, G. and Bane, M.J. 1980. *The nation's families 1960–1990.* Joint Center for Urban Studies of MIT and Harvard University, Cambridge.
20. Michelson, W. 1980. "Spatial and temporal dimensions of child care." *Signs: Journal of Women in Culture and Society* 5:242–247.
21. National Research Council, Committee on Child Development Research and Public Policy. 1980. *Work, family and community: summary proceedings of an ad hoc meeting.* National Academy of Sciences, Washington, D.C.
22. National Campaign for Child Day Care for Working Families. June, 1980. Platform statement. P.O. Box 28607, Washington, D.C. 20005.
23. Powell, D. 1978. "The interpersonal relationship between parents and caregivers in day care settings." *American Journal of Orthopsychiatry* 48: 680–689.
24. Ramey, C., Farran, D. and Campbell, F. 1979. "Predicting IQ from mother-infant interactions." *Child Development* 50:804–814.
25. Rodes, T. and Moore, J. 1976. *National childcare consumer study: 1975.* USHHS, Administration for Children Youth and Families, Washington, D.C.
26. Ruopp, R. et al. 1979. *Children at the center.* Final Report of the National Day Care Study, Vol. I. Abt Books, Cambridge.
27. Shaw, L. 1974. *The utilization of subsidized child care in the Gary income maintenance experiment: a preliminary report.* Office of Economic Opportunity, Washington, D.C.
28. U.S. Department of Labor—Women's Bureau, Pamphlet 23. January 1981. "Employers and Child Care: Establishing Service Through the Work Place."
29. Woolsey, S. 1977. "Pied piper politics and the child-care debate." In *Daedalus*, a special spring issue on the family: 127–145.

Chapter 5

DEVELOPMENTAL CONSEQUENCES OF OUT-OF-HOME CARE FOR INFANTS IN A LOW-INCOME POPULATION

by Ellen A. Farber and Byron Egeland

Rising rates of maternal employment have resulted in a dramatic increase in the use of out-of-home care for infants and young children. In 1979 Hoffman[31] cited statistics compiled by the Department of Commerce reporting that more than one-third of the mothers with children under three years were employed. The need for out-of-home care has generated much research and fueled a heated debate over the potential impacts of nonparental care on developmental outcomes for children.

One particularly acrimonious debate concerns the impact of alternative care on the infant-mother attachment bond.[29] Partly as a result of the intensity of the arguments presented both for and against the use of out-of-home care, research relevant to day care and infant-mother attachment has increased dramatically over the past decade. For example, Rutter[44] cited 92 articles in a review of the social and emotional consequences of day care for preschool children; nearly

Our study was supported in part by a grant from the Maternal and Child Health Service of the Department of Health, Education, and Welfare (MC-R-270416-01-0). We thank Brian E. Vaughn for comments on an early draft of this article.

90% were published during the 1970s. Unfortunately, even the current wealth of research data leaves many important issues concerning infant-mother attachment and day care unresolved.[8,44]

In this chapter, we first present the individual differences perspective of attachment articulated by Ainsworth[3] and by Sroufe and associates.[48,49] With this framework for understanding why it is important to study attachment as well as subsequent developmental tasks, we discuss two of the issues involved in the day care–attachment debate. Third, we explore some of the problems and limitations of the research relating the experience of out-of-home care to individual differences in the quality of attachment. Fourth, we present the rationale and results of our own previous study of infants and mothers in a low-income population; and, finally, the data from the current investigation, for which the previous study served as a basis.

Individual Differences Perspective of Attachment

The development of an affective bond, an attachment, between the infant and its mother is a major developmental task in the first year of life. According to the ethological-evolutionary theory of attachment,[12] it is the natural course of events for an infant to become attached to a mother figure. This enduring affectional tie arises from interaction and continues to develop and change in response to the behavior of either partner.

Ainsworth and her associates have developed and validated a procedure, the Strange Situation, for assessing individual differences in the organization of attachment behaviors.[3,4] The Strange Situation was designed to assess the balance of attachment and exploration behaviors in increasingly stressful circumstances. It consists of a series of episodes in which the infant's exploration of a novel environment in the presence of the mother, reaction to separation from the mother, and reunion with the mother are observed. In addition, the baby's reaction to a stranger with and without the mother present is observed. Based primarily on behaviors seen upon reunion with the mother after the separations, infants are assigned to a classification group reflecting both the patterning and the quality of observed attachment behaviors.

Infants are classified in three main groups. Infants are classified as "secure" in their attachment (Group B, Secure) if the presence of the mother supports exploration of the room and the toys prior to separation *and* if the presence of the mother reduces distress and facilitates a return to play and exploration after a separation. Infants not identified as secure in the Strange Situation are said to be "anxiously" attached. "Anxious" attachments are manifested in two different patterns. Infants may avoid contact with the mother after separation or ignore her attempts to initiate interaction (Group A, Anxious-Avoidant), or they may resist contact and interaction with the mother during the reunion episodes of the Strange Situation and/or fail to be comforted by the presence of the mother after the separations (Group C, Anxious-Resistant). In the former (Group A) infants, exploration appears to be ascendant over attachment, even when the infant is distressed, while in the latter (Group C) infants, exploration is often impoverished even prior to separations.

The Empirical Status of the Strange Situation

Waters[54] has shown that these individual differences in patterns of attachment are highly stable between 12 and 18 months of age for middle-class families. Frequencies and durations of particular behaviors were not stable. This is consistent with the view that attachment is a construct reflecting the organization of behavior rather than any particular behavior.[49] In other words, how much or how little contact an infant seeks, how much or how little it cries, will vary across time and is only meaningful within the overall pattern of behavior. In our less stable, economically disadvantaged sample, patterns of attachment behavior observed in the Strange Situation were also significantly stable, although more changes occurred than for middle-class samples.[53]

In addition to the demonstrated reliability of the Strange Situation procedure, numerous studies support the validity and importance of the attachment construct. It has been possible to identify antecedent factors, maternal and infant behaviors in the first year of life, which predict the quality of attachment relationships.[3,27] Furthermore, individual differences in attachment relationships have been related to various aspects of functioning at later ages. These include effectiveness in a problem-solving situation at two years of age,[37] initial peer sociability,[40] peer competence and ego strength during the preschool years,[56] and teacher-rated competence and ego resiliency at age five.[5]

Attachment and Day Care: The Two Major Issues

In his recent review of the literature, Rutter[44] identified two major areas of interest with respect to the relationships between out-of-home care experiences and infant-mother attachment. First, do infants experiencing out-of-home care during the period when primary attachments are being established and consolidated actually form their first selective attachments to their substitute caregivers rather than their mothers? This issue was first raised after publication of Bowlby's monograph on maternal care and mental health.[11] This monograph led to speculation[6] that mothers who went back to work could not provide proper care for their infants. Subsequent research has shown this early conclusion to be mistaken. Both across cultures[28] and within the broader culture in American society[33] children experiencing early day care form their primary bonds with their parents, just as home-reared children do. Further, there is no evidence that day care "dilutes" or "weakens" attachment bonds which have been previously established.[15] The second question suggested by Rutter concerns possible relationships between the experience of out-of-home care and individual differences in the *quality* of infant-mother attachments. The research evidence on this issue has been more ambiguous and there is presently no consensus among investigators about the implications to be drawn from the data.

The question of whether day care experience was related to individual differences in the quality of infant-mother attachments was raised by Blehar.[10] She reported that two- and three-year-old children in day care were found to exhibit different behavior towards their mothers (as compared to home-care controls) when they were seen in the Strange Situation. The day care children were more likely than the home-reared children to exhibit behaviors (avoiding mother at reunion or showing anger or resistance to contact with the mother during the reunion episodes) that Ainsworth and associates[3] have shown to be indicative of difficulties in the infant-mother attachment relationship for one-year-old children. Blehar suggested that the experience of day care led to anxiously toned attachments for the children in her study. She further suggested that the younger children (two-year-olds) were more seriously affected than were the older children (three years of age). Not surprisingly, Blehar's study was controversial and several recent reports have substantially qualified her initial interpretations.

Blehar's study has been criticized for several methodological flaws.[8] Among other problems, the raters for the Strange Situations may not have been blind to the rearing status of the children, and the time lapse between day care entry and the attachment assessments may have over-emphasized transient effects of day care on child behavior. Blanchard and Main[9] have reported that avoidance of the mother is heightened upon entry into day care but declines over time. Attempts to replicate Blehar's findings have basically not been successful.[14,23,39,42] Though many of these studies have reported minor differences between day care and home care children, none have found meaningful, significant differences with respect to infant-mother attachment between the comparison groups.

Even though the bulk of the research evidence to date has failed to demonstrate a clear-cut relationship between the experience of out-of-home care and individual differences in attachment, there are several limitations in the data which caution against a hasty acceptance that no effects of day care on attachment will be found. In the majority of the studies cited above, subjects have been children who are likely to have established and consolidated initial attachments well before they entered day care. Two recent studies[46,51] assessed the quality of attachment at 12 and 18 months for infants who had started day care before one year of age, during the period of "attachment in the making."[12] In both of these studies, more infants in the out-of-home care groups were avoidant of the mother after a brief separation than were home care controls. In addition to the discrepant conclusions drawn from these two studies, there were methodological and theoretical differences which distinguish the Schwartz[46] and the Vaughn *et al.*[51] studies from previous research on this topic. These distinctions form the basis of the discussion in the following section.

Empirical and Conceptual Problems in Attachment-Day Care Research

As we have noted above, research on individual differences in attachment as related to the experience of out-of-home care has not afforded a straightforward resolution of the issue. There are several reasons for these difficulties. We suggested above that the age at which children enter day care may influence whether or not effects are observed. Another possible problem arising from the previous research is that the bulk of the studies have been carried out in high-quality day care centers with well-trained day care providers (and most of the children have come from middle-class families). There has been little systematic effort to study the possible effects of out-of-home care in other situations (though see Hock[30]). Belsky and Steinberg[8] felt that this was a major limitation of previous research. A further problem with earlier research is that there are usually no assessments made prior to entry into day care. This means that possible *pre-day-care* differences in the children, their families, or the infant-mother attachments are not taken into account. In addition, when assessments take place only after the entry into day care, it is not possible to assess whether *changes* in the quality of attachment are related to the onset of out-of-home care. Finally, the particular measures used as indices of attachment often vary from study to study and the validity of these measures is largely unknown. Therefore, it is not possible to know whether or not differences observed (or not observed) have any relevance to infant-mother attachment relationships. For example, the majority of the day care–attachment studies have used frequencies of discrete behaviors, proportions of time in which discrete behaviors were observed, or differential responsiveness to the mother as dependent measures to assess between group differences. As discussed above, these assessments are neither reliable nor stable and are not valid measures of infant-mother attachments.[36]

In some of the day care—attachment studies[10,14,30] attempts were made to use ratings of the children's responses to reunions with the mother based on the coding system devised by Ainsworth and associates.[3] However, to date, only the studies by Schwartz[46] and Vaughn et al.[51] have used the classification scheme suggested by Ainsworth to identify individual differences in infant-mother attachments. This procedure and classification system is, to our knowledge, the only extensively validated, reliable assessment of infant-mother attachment available at this time.

The predictive validity of the Strange Situation has been demonstrated only for attachment relationships assessed between 12 and 18 months of age. There is no evidence that behavior observed in this procedure beyond the age of 18 months validly assesses the quality of the infant's attachment relationship. The available data concerning behavior of children over 18 months of age in the Strange Situation[34,35] suggest that older children are less distressed than infant/toddlers in the 12–18 month age range. Since attachment theory suggests that proximity-seeking (attachment) behavior should be heightened by stress,[1,55] it is not clear that the behavior of children older than 18 months in the Strange Situation is related to the quality of their attachment relationship with their mothers. Unfortunately, most of the studies which have used the response to separation and reunion as the assessment of attachment have observed children older than 18 months. Since many of the day care–attachment studies have either used frequency measures and/or distorted the circumstances/sequence of the Strange Situation procedure, or have used as subjects children beyond the age ranges for which the validity of the procedure is known, we believe that the results of the previous studies can be interpreted only with particular caution.

Background for this Investigation

In an earlier study[51] with this sample, some of the questions raised by the limitations of the previous research efforts were investigated. Data were available from a large, ongoing, longitudinal study of parent-infant interaction and the development of competence.[25] The sample was drawn from a local maternal and child care clinic which serves families of lower socioeconomic backgrounds. The majority of the mothers were single and receiving some form of public assistance at the time their babies were born. Most of the pregnancies were not planned. This sample clearly differs from those used in most of the day care–attachment research, as do their out-of-home care arrangements in both consistency and the quality of the settings.

Thirty-four mothers had returned to work or school by the time their infants were 12 months of age and had placed them in routine out-of-home care; 18 mothers returned to work/school between 12 and 18 months of infant age. These two groups were designated the Early and Late Work groups, respectively. A control group of women (No Work group) who did not utilize out-of-home care was chosen from the larger sample. We had a wide variety of test and observational data on these mother-infant pairs as well as assessments of attachment at 12 and 18 months.

In the earlier study we were concerned about pre-day-care differences between groups of mothers who placed their infants in out-of-home care and those who did not. There were almost no differences between the Early, Late, and No Work groups on a variety of factors derived from maternal personality tests, observations of mother-infant interactions at 3 and 6 months, observations of infants in the neonatal nursery, Brazelton exams, Bayley tests, and mothers' perceptions of infant temperament. One difference suggested that mothers who returned to work were more able to cope with their ambivalence concerning child rearing than were mothers who did not eventually return to work. Since there were no pre-day-care differences between the groups, it was then possible to attribute any outcome differences (i.e., differences in the quality of attachment) to out-of-home care experiences. It was hypothesized that since attachments arise from interaction, and working mothers have limited physical and possibly psychological availability, more of their infants might be anxiously attached than infants of mothers not using out-of-home care. As predicted, infants whose mothers returned to work prior to their first birthday were overrepresented in the group identified by Ainsworth[3] as Anxious-Avoidant when assessed in the Strange Situation. Ainsworth has suggested that infants who avoid their mothers when stressed are likely to have had a history of rejection by the mother. We interpreted our data to imply that physical unavailability, occasioned by out-of-home care, was also related to the development of avoidance.

Another variable which proved to be of interest in that study was the presence of an adult male partner in the home. Fewer of the women in the work groups (particularly the Late Work group) were living with an adult male than the women in the No Work group. Furthermore, by 18 months of age, anxious attachments were significantly related to whether or not a man was living in the home. Thus, there is a higher proportion of anxiously attached infants in the working mother groups, and for single working mothers the proportion of anxiously attached infants is even higher.

Based on these earlier findings, the current investigation has several purposes. We identified an additional group of working women —those who returned to work/school between 18 and 24 months of infant age—in order to determine whether these women differed from those who returned to work earlier, and whether this disruption had any immediate impact on their children. Besides analyzing the same factors previously used to assess between group differences, we decided to do more extensive comparisons. The factor scores used in the earlier report provide global measures, perhaps shielding more specific differences. In this report, we present additional between-group analyses using individual test scores to be certain that there are no pre-day-care differences. It is only if there are no pre-day-care differences that we can assume post-day-care differences are attributable to the out-of-home care experience. For example, it is known that mothers who are disinterested in their children tend to have anxiously attached infants. If it is disinterest in their children that causes mothers to return to work, then this factor and not the out-of-home care experience could account for anxious attachments.

Secondly, we present data reflecting the continued effects of out-of-home care. At 24 months the child's style and approach in a problem-solving situation were assessed. Just as attachment is considered to be a salient developmental issue at 12 and 18 months, for the toddler, emerging autonomy, independent environmental engagement, and resources to cope with a frustrating situation reflect the salient developmental task for this age.[48]

Though we did not find many between-group differences among the mothers who placed their children in out-of-home care during the first 18 months of life and those who did not, we did not examine our data to determine whether or not there were differences within the day care groups that might have led to anxious or secure attachments. Although anxious attachments were clearly overrepresented in the Early Work group, one half of those infants did form secure attachments. Are the factors which typically account for secure and anxious attachments[27] exerting a similar influence within the out-of-home care groups?

Thus, following Rutter's advice,[44] a major focus of this report is the examination of within-group data. Rutter noted that many factors may modify a child's response to day care. He suggested that age, gender, temperament, and prior relationships with the parents could be particularly important in determining whether or not day care experience would (or would not) have an effect on individual differences in the quality of attachments with parents.

Some of the previous research[14,20,38] have shown more marked effects of day care on boys. Especially pertinent to our interests are the findings of Moore,[38] who reported that personality differences following day care were more marked and persistent for boys than for girls. We have presented data elsewhere[41] suggesting that boys in this sample are more likely to show deleterious effects of father absence. It seems important to determine whether or not similar effects are to be found within day care families.

Another point underscored in Rutter's review[44] is that no examinations of relationships between temperament and day care experience have been made. Data from the present sample included a rating of the mother's impressions of temperament made at six months of age. While we do not believe that this rating is necessarily related to infant behavior,[52] maternal perceptions may well be predictive of later outcomes for children. In the present paper, we will examine the potential relationships between temperaments and individual differences in attachment quality within groups of both home care and out-of-home care infants.

To summarize, we will identify an additional group of working women, analyze our data more extensively for possible pre-daycare differences, assess the outcomes of out-of-home care experience at 24 months, and explore factors (including sex and temperament) which may account for secure and in insecure attachments within work groups.

Method

Sample

The subjects for this investigation were 110 mothers and their infants who were participating in the larger longitudinal study.[25] The total sample was composed of 267 primiparous women receiving prenatal care through public assistance. At the time of the babies births, the mothers ranged in age from 12 to 37 years ($M = 20.52$, $SD = 3.65$). Sixty-two percent of the mothers were single and 86% of the pregnancies were not planned. Educational level ranged from junior high school to post-college-graduate level. Sixty percent of the mothers had graduated from high school by the time their infants were born.

A group of mothers ($N = 34$) was identified who had returned to work/school prior to their infant's first birthday and who had placed their infants in out-of-home care at that time (Early Work). A second group of mothers ($N = 18$) was identified who had returned to work/school and started routine out-of-home care between 12 and 18 months (Late Work). A third group of mothers ($N = 11$) returned to work/school and started routine out-of-home care between 18 and 24 months (Later Work). A fourth group of mothers ($N = 47$) who had not used routine out-of-home care during the first 24 months was made up from the remainder of the sample. (Five of the mothers in the No Work group of the Vaughn *et al.*[51] study were deleted because they returned to work.)

Since not all of the mothers started work/school at the same time and since changes in work status were common (e.g., changing jobs, being promoted, fired, etc.), mothers had to meet one of the following criteria to be assigned to one of the work groups: (1) she must have returned to full-time work/school at least one month prior to the infant's 12-, 18-, or 24-month anniversary date. Because there is evidence that the onset of out-of-home care may temporarily heighten avoidance of the caregiver,[9] mothers who started routine out-of-home care for their infants within one month of the Strange Situation assessments were not included in either of the first two work groups.* These three groups of working women include all of the mothers from this sample who met these criteria.

The subjects were assigned to work status groups on the basis of their responses to interview questions at 12, 18 and 24 months. The interviews were not specifically designed to assess types of out-of-home care, but only whether such care had been initiated. Therefore, it was impossible to make quantifiable estimates of the quality of care provided, nor was it possible to retrieve exact data concerning the number of changes in caregivers, group size, etc.

Infant care for the working groups was most frequently provided by an adult female, often a relative or friend of the infant's mother, in the alternate caretaker's home. Some of these women also provided care for other infants and/or young children. A few of the infants received their care in licensed day care centers. Changes in the day care arrangements were common (at least 80% of the infants experienced a change in the substitute caregiver during the period they were receiving out-of-home care). In sum, out-of-home care arrangements were quite varied and changes in these arrangements were routine. While this makes comparisons of different types of day care settings impossible for this sample, it is representative of the types of alternative child care arrangements used by this population and, thus, deserves research attention.[51]

---

* When, however, a woman began work/school within one month of her infant's 12-month birthday and subsequently met the criteria for inclusion in the Late-Work group, she was so included ($N = 2$).

Measures

Maternal assessments. At approximately 36 weeks of pregnancy and three months postdelivery, a battery of tests were given to assess personality characteristics: intellectual level;[47] aggression, dependence, impulsivity, succorance, and social desirability (Personality Research Form);[32] anxiety (IPAT Anxiety Scale);[19] locus of control;[26,43] and parents' feelings and perceptions of pregnancy, delivery, and their expected child (Maternal Attitude Scale;[22] Pregnancy Research Questionnaire[45]).

Life events inventory. At both 12 and 18 months the mothers completed an inventory of life events[24] adapted from the list reported by Cochrane and Robertson.[21] In this report, weighted scores were used. Each item checked was assigned a 0 to 3 weight depending on the degree of disruption involved and readjustment required.

Infant assessments. Naturalistic observation ratings were provided by having the nurses in the newborn nursery rate each newborn in the study on 15 items. They included such behaviors as activity level, alertness, and soothability of the newborn, as well as the mother's skill with and interest in the new baby. The infants were rated throughout their stay in the neonatal nursery.

The Neonatal Behavioral Assessment Scale (NBAS)[13] was administered to each infant at home on two separate occasions. The NBAS consists of 26 behavioral items and 21 reflex items. The behavioral items examine habituation to repeated stimuli, orientation to inanimate and animate stimuli, motor maturity, state control, and physiological regulation. The first administration of the NBAS was on the infant's seventh day of life. The second administration was usually on the infant's tenth day of life.

At six months, each mother completed the Carey Infant Temperament Questionnaire (ITQ).[16,17] The responses to the ITQ were coded, scores were assigned to each infant on each of the nine temperament dimensions, and a diagnosis of "easy," "intermediate low," "intermediate high," or "difficult" was made, using Carey's algorithm.

The Bayley Scales of Infant Development (mental and motor)[7] were administered at nine and 24 months.

Mother-infant interaction. At three and six months postnatal age, observers visited the home to watch a feeding situation. At six months, feeding was observed on two separate occasions. For each feeding, the mothers and infants were rated on 33 variables, which included such items as frequency and quality of verbalizations, timing and synchronization of feeding, quality of handling the baby, facility in caretaking, and expression of positive and negative regard. Scales of Sensitivity and Cooperation[3] were also used to rate the mothers at six months.

Attachment assessments. All of the infants were seen at both 12 and 18 months in the Strange Situation procedure.[4] At each time, infants were assigned to one of the groups previously described: A (anxious/avoidant), B (secure), or C (anxious/resistant).

All of the Strange Situation procedures were videotaped. Two coders independently classified the infants at 12 months (rater agreement = 89%), and two additional coders classified the infants at 18 months (rater agreement = 94%). All disagreements for the Strange Situation classifications were resolved by the more experienced coders after conferencing the tapes in question. All of the Strange Situation data were collected and coded without knowledge of the hypothesis being tested here.

Problem-solving assessments. At 24 months each child's style and approach in a problem-solving situation was assessed. The tool-use situation is a laboratory procedure developed by Matas, Arend, and Sroufe[37] consisting of four tool-using, problem-solving tasks. Mother is present in the room with the toddler and is told to let the child first work on the problem independently and then to "give any help you think he or she needs." The first two problems were simple and were not included in the scoring. The third and fourth problems were increasingly difficult: putting two sticks together, end to end, in order to get a lure from a long tube, and weighting down the end of a lever with a block to raise candy through a hole in a plexiglass box. This problem cannot be solved without the help of an adult. The procedure was videotaped, and a set of observers recorded the frequency of the following discrete behaviors: whining, aggressive behaviors, frustration, positive and negative affect, and noncompliance. The mean scores for the third and fourth tools were used. At a more molar level, the following behaviors were rated by another set of observers on a 5 to 7 point scale: enthusiasm, dependency, noncompliance, anger, frustration toward the mother, coping, and persistence.

Results

Pre-Day-Care Differences Between Work Groups

The first set of analyses involved a series of one-way ANOVAs computed to test whether the four groups (Early, Late, Later, and No Work) constituted by our selection procedures were in some way different prior to the onset of out-of-home care. The Student-Newman-Keuls was used for post hoc comparisons. For these analyses we used the wide variety of maternal and infant test and observational data gathered during the first nine months of life. Individual rating and test scores as well as factor scores were used.

In all of the analyses conducted, the Later Work group appeared essentially the same as the No Work group. The only differences were a higher external locus of control as assessed prenatally and a higher life stress score at 12 months for the Later Work group compared to the other groups. Events in these mothers' lives (Later Work group) may have forced them back to work. However, they appear to have been providing quality care and, except for locus of control they did not differ from the other Work and the No Work groups on the different personality, anxiety, and parental expectation and understanding measures. For the Later Work group, placing their children in out-of-home care between 18 and 24 months did not prove to be disruptive as assessed in the 24-month problem-solving situation. Given the small sample size of the Later Work group and their similarity to the No Work group on the maternal and infant measures, including attachment and two-year problem solving, we decided to omit this group in our presentation of the results. It is possible, of course, that longer-term follow-up may indicate deleterious effects, and this group should be investigated in the future.

Having eliminated the Later Work group, we analyzed the pre-day-care differences between the Early, Late, and No Work groups. None of the demographic data—age, education, pregnancy complications, etc.—discriminated those mothers who returned to work/school from those who did not.

Of the 20 maternal personality variables assessed, only 2 were significant. The Early Work group had a higher mean score than the No Work group on the Maternal Attitude Scale—acceptance vs. denial of emotional complexity in child care, $F(2,95) = 3.02$, $p = .03$. This variable loads highly on the Psychological Complexity factor found to be significant in the previous paper.[51] This finding suggests that mothers who return to work may have a more mature adaptive attitude; they recognize the ambivalent feelings that of necessity accompany the childrearing role. The only other significant finding was that the No Work group had a higher external locus of control than the Late Work group. This suggests that mothers who eventually return to work may feel more in control of their lives than those who stay at home.

It is important to note that there were almost no differences between mothers who returned to work at varying times and those who stayed at home. There were also no meaningful pre-day-care differences between the infants or in the quality of mother-infant interaction in each of those groups. Due to the number of analyses conducted, the differences that were found could be significant purely by chance. We are confident in concluding that there were no basic differences in maternal characteristics and caretaking skills among the Work groups or between the Work and No Work groups.

The life events data were included to assess whether the return to work/school was associated with, or even preceded by, increased levels of life stress for this sample. High levels of life stress may be the precipitating factor in a mother's decision to go to work and place her child in out-of-home care. Stress may also reduce a mother's emotional availability to her child. A comparison between the Early, Late, and No Work groups on this measure administered at 12 months was significant, $F(2,92) = 3.27$, $p < .05$. Post hoc comparisons indicated that mothers in the No Work group reported experiencing significantly less life stress than mothers in the Early Work group. Because several of the items on the checklist referred specifically to work-related items, a second analysis was conducted deleting those items. This did not reach the conventional level for significance although it approached significance, $F(2,92) = 2.39$, $p < .10$. Thus, while mothers in the Early Work group had higher life stress scores than the No Work group at 12 months, these stresses were primarily associated with the return to work/school and not to other events. For the 18-months life stress data, the analyses were not significant; for the whole inventory, $F(2,93) = .59$, $p = .5$ and, deleting work-related items, $F(2,93) = .08$, $p = .9$. Even with their change in work status between 12 and 18 months, the Late Work group was not experiencing more life stress than the other groups. It appears that the decision to return to work within the first 12 months of infant life is more likely to occur when there are other stressful life events; mothers who return to work at later intervals may do so more out of choice. (These findings are essentially identical to those found in the previous report using scores which treat each item as equivalent rather than the weighted score which considers the amount of disruption.)

The fact that we have found so few differences between the Early, Late, and No Work groups after an extensive number of analyses makes us more confident that any differences found on our outcome measures may be tied to the out-of-home care experience rather than to differences on mother characteristics.

Attachment Data

Table 5-1 presents the distribution of attachment classifications for each work group at 12 and 18 months. These findings were mentioned in the introduction; the important findings from the previous article will be presented here. The relationship between work status and attachment classification was significant at 12 ($\chi^2(4) = 15.96$, $p = .003$) and 18 months ($\chi^2(4) = 13.07$, $p = .01$). At 12 months, the 47% of the infants in the Early Work group who were *not* securely attached were all in the anxious-avoidant group. At 18 months, the

Table 5-1 Attachment Classifications for Infants in Each Work Status Group

Work Status Group		12-Month Attachment Classification			18-Month Attachment Classification		
		Anxious-Avoidant(A)	Secure(B)	Anxious-Resistant(C)	Anxious-Avoidant(A)	Secure(B)	Anxious-Resistant(C)
Early Work	Boys	7(41%)	10(59%)	0	7(41%)	8(47%)	2(11.8%)
	Girls	9(52%)	8(47%)	0	7(41%)	9(53%)	1(6%)
	Total	16(47%)	18(52.9%)	0	14(41%)	17(50%)	3(8.8%)
Late Work	Boys	3(30%)	2(20%)	5(50%)	2(20%)	4(40%)	4(40%)
	Girls	2(25%)	5(62.5%)	1(12.5%)	1(12.5%)	5(62.5%)	2(25%)
	Total	5(28%)	7(39%)	6(33%)	3(16.7%)	9(50%)	6(33.3%)
No Work	Boys	6(21.4%)	17(60.7%)	5(17.9%)	2(7%)	20(71%)	6(21%)
	Girls	3(15.8%)	12(63.2%)	4(21.1%)	4(21%)	13(68%)	2(10.5%)
	Total	9(19%)	29(62%)	9(19%)	6(13%)	33(70%)	8(17%)

NOTE: Numbers in parentheses indicate percentage of cases so classified within each respective work status group for each sex and for the total work group.

Early, Late, and No Work groups had 50%, 50% and 70% securely attached infants, respectively; however, the Early Work group still contained a disproportionately large number of anxious-avoidant babies (41% vs. 16.7% and 13% for the Late Work and No Work groups, respectively).

Moderator variables: Sex and temperament. To determine whether day care might have more marked effects on one sex than the other, the attachment classification data are presented for girls and boys within each work group (see Table 1). None of the chi-square analyses (sex x attachment x work group) were significant. In the Early Work group, the distribution of attachment classifications for males and females is quite similar at 12 and again at 18 months. In the Late Work group, although the chi-square did not reach significance ($\chi^2(2) = 3.98$, $p = .14$), many more of the males than females were anxiously attached prior to the onset of out-of-home care (80% vs. 37.5%, boys and girls, respectively). This was still true at 18 months, although the differences were not as great. Thus, it does not appear that out-of-home care differentially affects boys and girls.

Our next set of analyses was conducted to determine if infant temperament had an influence on out-of-home care experience. The easy-to-difficult rating from the six-month Carey Infant Temperament Questionnaire was used. None of the chi-square analyses (temperament rating x attachment classification x work group; or temperament rating x attachment classification x sex for each work group) were significant. Thus, within the work groups infants judged as "easy to care for" were not any more likely to be securely attached than infants judged by their mothers as "difficult." In this sample, then, temperament rated by the mother at 6 months was not particularly useful for predicting individual differences in the quality of attachment following out-of-home care experiences.

In sum, a large proportion of the mothers who returned to work/school before their infant's first birthday had infants who were later classified as having anxious-avoidant attachments. Knowledge of sex and temperament did not serve any function in explaining anxious and secure attachments within the out-of-home care or home care groups.

Two-Year Data

The problem-solving situation provided a second outcome measure for assessing the effects of work status and out-of-home care. One of the molar ratings, enthusiasm, and none of the discrete variables differentiated the children from the three work groups at the conventional level of significance. Toddlers in the Early Work group displayed less enthusiasm than those in the No Work group, $F(2,84)$ = 3.93, $p = .02$. Two of the ratings approached significance. Toddlers in the Early Work group tended to be less compliant ($p = .09$) and less persistent ($p = .13$) than toddlers in the other groups. Display of negative affect also approached significance, $F(2,84) = 2.35$, $p = .10$. Both the Early and Late Work groups had higher mean frequencies of negative affect than the No Work group. Repeating these analyses for each sex revealed enthusiasm to be significant only for males; that is, boys from the Early Work group showed significantly less enthusiasm than boys in the No Work group, $F(2,46) = 4.8$, $p = .01$. For the girls, work status was significantly related to frustration directed toward the mother, $F(2,35) = 3.36$, $p < .05$. Girls in the Late Work group tended to show the most frustration, and girls in the No Work group exhibited the least.

Mean developmental quotient as measured by the Bayley at 24 months did not differ among the work groups. Thus, findings from the two-year assessments suggest that toddlers of mothers who returned to work during the first year are at an equivalent developmental level yet may have less adequate coping skills to deal with a frustrating problem-solving situation than children reared at home. These findings are far from conclusive.

Within-Work-Group Comparisons: Secure vs. Anxious Attachments

Although there was a disproportionate number of anxiously attached infants in the Early Work group, 50% of that group did form secure attachments. In the next set of analyses we sought to determine if there were differences between mothers or infants within each of the work groups which may have accounted for the anxious and secure attachments. In a previous investigation using the whole longitudinal sample, we found several of the maternal personality, infant, and interactive variables predictive of later quality of attachment.[27] For the total sample, mothers of infants who later became securely attached were more mature in their understanding of childrearing and presented themselves in a more desirable fashion than mothers of anxiously attached infants. Mothers of infants who developed anxious attachments had more negative reactions to pregnancy, were more tense and irritable, and had significantly more life stress than those women whose infants developed secure attachments. During the feedings, mothers of securely attached infants showed greater facility in caretaking, were more sensitive to their infants' needs and responsive to the infants' behavior, and expressed more positive regard toward the infant.

The within-work-group comparisons between securely and anxiously attached groups were computed for each work group (i.e., Early and Late) as a whole and then again for each sex. Results are presented for each work group as a whole since analyses by sex did not result in any additional significant findings. Due to group sizes, the two anxious groups (As and Cs) were combined.

Early Work Group. Of all the variables analyzed, there were few significant differences between the secure and anxiously attached groups. The mothers of anxiously attached infants at 12 months had a higher external locus of control and a lower desire for motherhood prenatally ($F(1,31) = 6.5$, $p = .01$; $F(1,31) = 5.01$, $p < .03$, respectively) than mothers of securely attached infants. The mothers of securely attached babies had significantly higher scores on the postnatal anxiety measure ($F(1,31) = 4.62$, $p < .04$). Although this is contrary to previous findings on the antecedents of attachment,[27] within this group the increased anxiety may represent a greater concern about returning to or having returned to work, thus being an adaptive response. Beyond these few potentially meaningful differences, neither infant temperament nor mother-infant interaction observed during feeding was related to the later quality of attachment. This is somewhat surprising since for the total sample a number of feeding interaction variables were related to quality of attachment.

Late Work Group. There were no significant relationships between maternal personality assessed prenatally and 12-month attachment classification. Nonsignificant trends suggest that mothers of anxiously attached infants were more anxious ($p = .11$), less dependent ($p = .07$), and had a more internal locus of control ($p = .08$) than mothers of securely attached babies. As assessed postnatally, mothers of securely attached infants had a higher desire for pregnancy ($F(1,14) = 7.9$, $p = .01$) but were more irritable ($F(1, 13) = 6.7$, $p < .02$) and had less understanding of the need for reciprocity between mother and infant (Maternal Attitude Scale, $F(1,15) = 6.8$, $p < .02$) than mothers of anxious infants. Mothers who displayed more positive affect during the 6-month feeding had securely attached infants at 12 months ($F(1,15) = 5.3$, $p = .03$). There were no significant relationships between maternal personality and 18-month attachment classifications.

We found few factors which predict the secure and anxious attachments within the work groups. This is surprising, particularly in light of the numerous variables mentioned above, which are known to differentiate among securely and anxiously attached groups. It appears that the out-of-home care or some unassessed factor particular to each of those groups is accounting for the quality of attachment.

Discussion

Using data gathered during a prospective longitudinal study, we have explored several issues pertaining to the use and effects of out-of-home care in a low-income population. First, we assessed the quality of mother-infant attachment at 12 and 18 months and problem-solving behavior at 24 months to determine the effects of out-of-home care. Second, we examined possible pre-day-care differences between the children and their parents who utilize out-of-home care and those who do not. Our third major question was whether or not there were differences on factors such as maternal personality and life stress that might have explained the differential outcomes (i.e., secure or anxious attachments) *within* the work groups. This set of analyses also included exploring sex and temperament as variables which might relate to the outcomes of day care experience.

The results indicate that out-of-home care initiated in the first year of life greatly increases the likelihood of anxious-avoidant attachments. This is a potentially important finding in light of the implications of anxious attachments for future development.[48] However, at two years of age the effects of out-of-home care were no longer striking. The differences, mostly borderline, tended to be on affect and compliance. During the problem-solving situation, children from the working groups tended to display more negative affect and less enthusiasm and comply less with their mothers than children cared for at home. For this sample, then, it appears that the cumulative adverse effects of out-of-home care were minimal. The negative effects of out-of-home care demonstrated by the anxious quality of attachments at 12 and 18 months seem relatively temporary. However, a long-term follow-up is necessary before reaching any definite conclusions about the outcomes of day care experiences.

It should be noted that boys and girls are similarly affected by day care experiences. For the children placed in out-of-home care prior to their first birthday, approximately half of the boys and half of the girls developed anxious attachments. The one striking finding with respect to sex is that many more boys than girls were anxiously attached prior to the onset of out-of-home care. By two years of age, we also did not find more marked effects of day care on boys as has been suggested by previous studies.[14,20,38] Boys of working mothers showed less enthusiasm than boys of nonworking mothers, whereas girls of working mothers became more frustrated in the problem-solving situation than girls of nonworking mothers.

Rutter[44] suggested that differences between the day care and home care children, in previous studies, may have reflected patterns of parent-child interaction which antedated the day care experience and were not due to that experience at all. He states that few studies have measured the children's behavior before starting day care; equally lacking is measurement of maternal behavior before starting work. On a wide variety of measures, we found no differences between the women who returned to work and those who did not; nor were there differences between their infants prior to out-of-home care. Although the samples were relatively small, the fact that there were no significant trends or patterns among the different personality, attitude, and knowledge measures makes us confident that the mothers in the Work and No Work groups were not different from each other. Therefore, we are confident in concluding that it was the out-of-home care that caused the anxious attachments and not some characteristics of the mother.

Two environmental variables did differ among the Work and No Work groups and may have been related to the decision to return to work. For mothers who returned to work prior to the infant's first birthday, life stresses may have precipitated the return. For a mother returning to work during the six-month interval following the infant's first birthday, a precipitating factor may have been single parenthood. As discussed in the introduction, most of the mothers in the Late Work group were not living with or involved in any stable relationship with an adult male during the infant's first year of life. This fact may account for the unexpected finding that a large number of boys were anxiously attached prior to starting out-of-home care. Father absence is known to have a greater adverse effect for boys than girls with respect to attachment.[40] A nonintact family may have influenced boys to develop anxious attachments and influenced their mothers to return to work.

Other than life stress and intactness, the fact that we found almost no differences between the Work and control groups on a number of maternal personality and caretaking measures suggests that the overabundance of anxious attachments in the Early Work group was the result of placement in out-of-home care during the time the attachment bond was developing. However, even though there were more anxiously attached infants in the work group, it should be noted that half of the infants placed in out-of-home care did form secure attachments. Thus, out-of-home care does not of necessity lead to anxious attachments. We then wondered if there were differences between the mothers *within* the work groups which may have explained the secure and anxious attachments. In other words, were there certain parental or child factors that made the child less vulnerable to the effects of out-of-home care? Variables which have been shown to predict individual differences in attachments within the total sample were of no value in explaining secure and anxious attachments within the Early Work group. We conclude that the *type* of out-of-home care experienced may be the significant predictor of individual differences in the quality of attachment for low-income families.

As previously discussed, the majority of day care–attachment studies have used stable, intact middle-class families who place their children in high-quality day care centers for an extended period of time. In our sample this was clearly not the case. The care was frequently of low quality and inconsistent. Several of our infants experienced as many as five different sitters within their first two years of life. Care arrangements were more often chosen for the mother's convenience rather than the infant's needs. While these varied alternative care arrangements make it more difficult to study the effects of out-of-home care, these arrangements reflect a reality for many children. As Belsky and Steinberg[8] state, the findings from existing research on day care may not be generalizable to the kind and quality of care available to most of the nation's families. Children of economically disadvantaged single mothers are known to be at greater risk for adverse developmental outcomes,[25] yet it is precisely that group for whom the least adequate care is available if and when their mothers decide to return to work. Whether or not mothers of infants and toddlers should work is a moot question. What types of out-of-home care arrangements are best for fostering development and are feasible, particularly for low-income families, is the relevant question both for policymakers and researchers.

References

1. Ainsworth, M. 1979. "Infant-mother attachment." *American Psychologist* 34(10):932–937.
2. Ainsworth, M. and Bell, S. 1970. "Attachment, exploration, and separation: illustrated by the behavior of one-year-olds in a strange situation." *Child Development* 41:49–68.
3. Ainsworth, M. *et al.* 1978. *Patterns of Attachment.* Lawrence Erlbaum Associates, Hillside, New Jersey.
4. Ainsworth, M. and Wittig, B. 1969. "Attachment and exploratory behavior of one-year-olds in a strange situation." In *Determinants of Infant Behavior* (4) B.M. Foss (ed.). Methuen, London.
5. Arend, R., Gove, F. and Sroufe, L.A. 1979. "Continuity of early adaptation: from attachment in infancy to resiliency and curiosity at age five." *Child Development* 50:950–959.
6. Baers, M. 1954. "Women workers and home responsibilities." *International Labor Review* 69:338–355.
7. Bayley, N. 1969. *The Bayley Scales of Infant Development.* The Psychological Corporation, New York.
8. Belsky, J. and Steinberg, L.D. 1978. "The effects of day care: a critical review." *Child Development* 49:929–949.

9. Blanchard, M. and Main, M. 1979. "Avoidance of the attachment figure and social-emotional adjustment in day care infants." *Developmental Psychology* 15:445–446.
10. Blehar, M.C. 1974. "Anxious attachment and defensive reactions associated with day care." *Child Development* 45:683–692.
11. Bowlby, J. 1951. *Maternal care and mental health.* World Health Organization, Geneva.
12. Bowlby, J. 1969. *Attachment and Loss: Volume 1, Attachment.* Basic Books, New York.
13. Brazelton, T.B. 1973. *Neonatal Behavioral Assessment Scale.* J.B. Lippincott, Philadelphia.
14. Brookhart, J. and Hock, E. 1976. "The effects of experimental context and experiential background on infants' behavior toward their mother and a stranger." *Child Development* 47:333–340.
15. Caldwell, B.M. *et al.* 1970. "Infant day care and attachment." *American Journal of Orthopsychiatry* 40:397–412.
16. Carey, W.B. 1970. "A simplified method for measuring infant temperament." *Journal of Pediatrics* 70:188–194.
17. Carey, W.B. 1973. "Measuring infant temperament in pediatric practice." In *Individual Differences in Children,* J.C. Westman (ed). John Wiley & Sons, New York.
18. Carey, W.B. and McDevitt, S.D. 1978. "Revision of the infant temperament questionnaire." *Pediatrics* 61:735–739.
19. Cattel, R.B. and Scheier, I.H. 1963. *Handbook for the IPAT Anxiety Scale.* Institute for Personality and Ability Testing, Champaign, Illinois.
20. Cornelius, S. and Denney, N. 1975. "Dependency in day care and home care children." *Developmental Psychology* 11:575–582.
21. Cochrane, R. and Robertson, A. 1973. "The life events inventory: a measure of the relative severity of psycho-social stressors." *Journal of Psychosomatic Research* 17:135–139.
22. Cohler, B., Weiss, J. and Grunebaum, H. 1970. "Child care attitudes and emotional disturbance among mothers of young children." *Genetic Psychology Monograph* 82:3–47.
23. Doyle, A.B. 1975. "Infant development in day care." *Developmental Psychology* 4:655–656.
24. Egeland, B., Breitenbucher, M. and Rosenberg, D. 1980. "A prospective study of the significance of stress in the etiology of child abuse." *Journal of Consulting and Clinical Psychology* 48(2):195–205.
25. Egeland, B., Deinard, A. and Sroufe, L.A. 1977. "Early maladaptation: a prospective transactional study." Project Proposal Submitted to the Office of Maternal and Child Health.
26. Egeland, B., Hunt, D. and Hardt, R. 1970. "College enrollment of upward-bound students as a function of attitude and motivation." *Journal of Educational Psychology* 61:375–379.
27. Farber, E.A. and Egeland, B. 1980. "Maternal, neonatal, and mother-infant antecedents of attachment in urban poor." Paper presented at the American Psychological Association, Montreal.

28. Fox, N. 1977. "Attachment of kibbutz infants to mothers and metapelet." *Child Development* 48:1228–1239.
29. Fraiberg, S. 1977. *Every Child's Birthright: In Defense of Mothering.* Basic Books, New York.
30. Hock, E. 1980. "Working and nonworking mothers and their infants: a comparative study of maternal caregiving characteristics and infant's social behavior." *Merrill-Palmer Quarterly* 46:79–101.
31. Hoffman, L.W. 1979. "Maternal employment: 1979." *American Psychologist* 34:859–865.
32. Jackson, D.H. 1967. *Personality Research Form Manual.* Research Psychologists Press, New York.
33. Kagan, J., Kearsley, R.B. and Zelazo, P.R. 1978. *Infancy: Its Place in Human Development.* Harvard University Press, Cambridge, Mass.
34. Maccoby, E. and Feldman, S.S. 1972. "Mother attachment and stranger reactions in the third year of life." *Monographs of the Society for Research in Child Development* 37.
35. Marvin, R.S. 1972. "Attachment and cooperative behavior in two-, three-, and four-year-olds." Unpublished Doctoral Dissertation, University of Chicago.
36. Masters, J.D. and Wellman, H. 1974. "Human infant attachment: a procedural critique." *Psychological Bulletin* 81:218–237.
37. Matas, L., Arend, R. and Sroufe, L.A. 1978. "Continuity in adaptation: quality of attachment and later competence." *Child Development* 49:547–556.
38. Moore, T.W. 1975. "Exclusive early mothering and its alternatives: the outcome to adolescence." *Scandinavian Journal of Psychology* 16:255–272.
39. Moskowitz, D.S., Schwarz, J.C. and Corsini, D.A. 1977. "Initiating day care at three years of age: effects on attachment." *Child Development* 48:1271–1276.
40. Pastor, D.L. "The quality of mother-infant attachment and its relationship to toddler's initial sociability with peers." *Developmental Psychology,* in press.
41. Pastor, D.L. *et al.* 1981. "The effects of different family patterns on the quality of the mother-infant attachment." Paper presented at the Society for Research in Child Development, Boston, Mass.
42. Portnoy, F.C. and Simmons, C.H. 1978. "Day care and attachment." *Child Development* 49:239–242.
43. Rotter, J.B. 1966. "Generalized expectancies for internal versus external control of reinforcement." *Psychological Monographs* 80.
44. Rutter, M. 1981, "Social-emotional consequences of day care for preschool children." *American Journal of Orthopsychiatry* 51:4–28.
45. Schaefer, M.S. and Manheimer, H. 1960. "Dimensions of parental adjustment." Paper presented to Eastern Psychological Association, New York.
46. Schwartz, P.M. 1980. "Length of daily separations due to child care and attachment behaviors of 18-month-old infants." Manuscript submitted for publication.
47. Shipley, W.C. 1946. *The Shipley-Hartford Vocabulary Test.* Shipley Institute for Living Scale.

48. Sroufe, L.A. 1979. "The coherence of individual development: early care, attachment, and subsequent developmental issues." *American Psychologist* 34:834–841.

49. Sroufe, L.A. and Waters, E. 1977. "Attachment as an organizational construct." *Child Development* 48:1184–1199.

50. Tracy, R., Lamb, M. and Ainsworth, M.D.S. 1976. "Infant approach behavior as related to attachment." *Child Development* 47:571–578.

51. Vaughn, B.E., Gove, F.L. and Egeland, B. 1980. "The relationship between out-of-home care and the quality of infant-mother attachment in an economically disadvantaged population." *Child Development* 51:1203–1214.

52. Vaughn, B. *et al.* "The assessment of infant temperament: a critique of the Carey infant temperament questionnaire." *Infant Behavior and Development*, in press.

53. Vaughn, B.E. *et al.* 1979. "Individual differences in infant-mother attachment at 12 and 18 months: stability and change in families under stress." *Child Development* 50:971–975.

54. Waters, E. 1978. "The reliability and stability of individual differences in infant-mother attachment." *Child Development* 49:483–494.

55. Waters, E. 1980. "Traits, relationships and behavioral systems: the attachment construct and the organization of behavior and development." In *Proceedings of the Bielefeld Interdisciplinary Conference: Development of Behavior*, G. Barlow, K. Immelman, M. Main and L. Petrinovich (eds). Cambridge University Press, Cambridge.

56. Waters, E., Wippman, J. and Sroufe, L.A. 1979. Attachment, positive affect, and competence in the peer group: two studies in construct validation." *Child Development* 50:821–829.

Chapter 6

ENVIRONMENTAL DIFFERENCES AMONG DAY CARE CENTERS AND THEIR EFFECTS ON CHILDREN'S DEVELOPMENT

by Kathleen McCartney, Sandra Scarr, Deborah Phillips, Susan Grajek, and J. Conrad Schwarz

Increasing rates of maternal employment have necessitated alternative child care arrangements. More and more infants and young children are being placed in nonmaternal substitute care that varies widely in cost and quality. Though policymakers and parents have turned to psychologists to assess the effects of day care, there has been little relevant information. Belsky and Steinberg,[2] in their review of the effects of day care, attribute this ignorance to many factors, primarily methodological constraints in day care research to date. Among the constraints cited are the restriction of research to

This research was supported by a grant to Sandra Scarr from the William T. Grant Foundation and by the generosity of the Department of Education, Bermuda Government, which provided interviewers, test results for the older children, and help in gaining the cooperation of teachers and parents. We are particularly grateful to Sinclair Richards, Mansfield H. Brock, Jr., Conchita Ming, Ruth Thomas, and David Critchley, all of the Bermuda Government, and Michael West of the Bermuda College, who provided additional interviewers. We also wish to thank the directors and caregivers of the day care centers, the Primary 3 teachers and the parents of all of the children.

126

high-quality, center-based care; the confounding of differences in family background among children in various forms and qualities of day care; and the reliance on standardized tests of intellectual and social development as outcome measures.

No general conclusions can be reached about the effects of various forms and qualities of day care experiences for the vast majority of children in nonmaternal care. Research is largely limited to comparisons of children in high-quality, university-based programs with home-reared children. Although few differences among day care and home-reared children have been consistently reported, it is not clear whether the qualities of the centers simulate the qualities of the homes or whether other background factors of the children in the two kinds of care confound the effects of the day care experience. For example, children in day care may come from more disadvantaged homes than those whose mothers do not work, but the enriched day care environments may compensate for the disadvantaged homes.[8]

Selection of children into day care environments is the most serious limitation to the generalizability of the results from studies that compare children in day care with home-reared children. In the United States, a small minority of children are cared for in centers, even in the later preschool years. The children who are in the centers are certainly not a random sample of children. Therefore, any differences that could be found between children in day care and those who are home-reared are necessarily confounded with genetic and environmental differences in their home background.

The reliance on standardized measures of intellectual development, in particular, can severely limit the sensitivity of studies of the effects of day care environments. As we have discovered from studies of other forms of intervention, traditional IQ tests are not good measures of program effects, because they sample too broadly from the child's life experiences and not from the curriculum of the program. Similarly, it is unreasonable to expect a day care environment to affect profoundly all that a child knows and knows how to do. Rather, measures of those aspects of development that are most likely to be affected by the group experience with nonparental adults and nonsibling peers should be preferred.

Indices of day care environments that are frequently used to measure the quality of those environments include child/staff ratio, staff training, group size, and various measures of the physical facilities. It is possible that important aspects of children's everyday experiences are not fully captured by the index variables and would be better measured by observations and ratings based on observations. The nonresults of much of the research on day care versus home care environments may result from reliance on index variables that are too broad to capture important differences in children's experiences.

A quick review of the research literature, with all of the limitations noted earlier, suggests that high quality day care does not have deleterious effects on children's development. Day care per se does not reduce the parent-child bond; children in day care show the same degree of preference for their parents as those who are home reared.[14,19] Regarding social development, the most consistent finding is that day care increases the degree to which children interact, both positively and negatively, with peers.[2,10] Contrary to original hypotheses, children who attend day care programs are not more independent[5,13] than children reared at home. Regarding cognitive development, day care seems to have neither positive nor negative effects on the average; although disadvantaged children can profit from an enriched day care experience,[12,17] middle class children may be disadvantaged by group care in comparison to home care.

There are suggestions in the research literature that differences in language development might be associated with differences in substitute care. For example, comparing children in center care with two matched samples, one consisting of children in home care and the other of children in family day care, Cochran[4] found that adults in family day care and in home care engage in more teaching and supervised small talk with children than adults in day care centers. As such, it is perhaps not surprising that the children in both home settings engaged in more verbal and play behavior than did center children. For example, center children initiated fewer social interactions with adults than children reared at home.[6] Similarly, Parmenter[15] found that home care children experienced more than twice as much verbal interaction with adults as center children. Thus, it seemed advisable to look more closely at language skills than at more global measures of intelligence.

The goal of this research was to address the concerns outlined by Belsky and Steinberg by investigating day care centers varying in quality, using a variety of standardized and observational measures, and controlling for family background variables. More specifically, the goal was to investigate the immediate and long-term consequences of differences in day care environments on children's social, emotional, intellectual, and language development.

Method

Setting

Bermuda was chosen as the site for this research effort for three major reasons: 1) 90% of Bermudian children are in some form of substitute care by their second year of life, thereby reducing the selective biases that naturally occur in studies of U.S. children in day care; 2) day care programs on the island have existed for many years and are stable, so that children who are now in primary school have experienced day care environments similar to those currently in operation; and 3) day care environments in Bermuda represent a wide range of quality along dimensions such as curriculum, staff training, facilities, staff-child interaction, and educational philosophy.

In the first year of life only about 25% of Bermudian children are in the group care centers, about 50% in day care homes or with sitters, and about 25% with their mothers. In the second year of life, only 10% have mothers as primary caretakers, and about half are in group care. By 36 months, more than 90% of Bermudian children are in group care for least half of the day, most for all day. Primary school begins at age 5.

Nearly all Bermudians work, including the parents of young children. Day care for these children comes in many forms and qualities. The most organized day care is in the centers, all of which are privately-owned or church-run except one government center for low income, multiproblem families. Fees for day care services ranged from $25 to $35 per week per child in 1980. Parents tend to select centers that are near their homes or their work places and report surprisingly little information about the qualities of their children's day care environments. We quickly discovered that most parents do not know how many children or caretakers are in their children's groups or how the children spend their days. Their lack of information may provide the explanation for the lack of correlation between family SES and day care centers in Bermuda.

Among the many day care centers on the island, we chose those that provide infant care as well as care for older preschoolers, so that children in the centers could have experienced those day care environments from early infancy or have entered as late as 36 months of age. According to the records of Bermuda's Ministry of Education, Health, and Social Services, there were ten such centers that had been in operation for five or more years. The directors of all ten centers agreed to participate in the study. Their participation involved completing caregiver rating forms regarding students' social, emotional, intellectual, and language development, and allowing the investigators to assess the quality of the environment and the children's intellectual and language skills.

Subjects

Children, age 3 years and older, who attended a target center for 6 months or more, and their parents were asked to participate in the study. The children ranged in age from 36 to 60 months. Children were tested in the day care centers, and parents were interviewed in their homes. No parent refused to allow his or her child to participate in the study; a few parents failed to keep interview appointments, however. In total, 156 families with children in day care centers participated; the sample is almost the entire population of Bermudian preschoolers attending the centers with infant care.

In addition, 189 children in Primary 3 (fourth graders), who had been in some form of substitute care as preschoolers, and their parents participated as subjects in a retrospective study on the long-term consequences of differences in day care environments. These data have not yet been analyzed, so that the measures and results of the retrospective part of the study will not be reported here.

Procedures

The day care centers were contacted and observations began in March, 1980. Permission slips were sent out to all parents of children 36 months of age and older, and all parents of children in Primary 3, to seek their consent to participate in the study. During the summer the authors collected data in the schools and day care centers and trained 10 Bermudian college students (mostly educated in the United States and Canada) to interview the 350 families of children currently in day care and those in primary school who were in day care. Four Bermudian college students tested many of the day care children and administered the communication task. Because not all of the interviews were completed by the end of summer, additional students at the Bermuda College were trained by Kathleen McCartney, the first author, who remained on the island for the year. Data collection on the families of children currently in day care was completed in February, 1981. Some additional data are still being collected on the primary school children.

Measures of Children Currently in Day Care

Assessments were made of the day care environments, children's emotional and social development, intellectual and language skills, and family background. The assessment of the day care environments included several hours of investigator observations, and both investigator and staff ratings. The assessment of children's development included standardized and experimental tests, as well as caregiver and parent ratings. The assessment of family background included several interview questionnaires that have not been analyzed, and demographic variables that are included in this report. Table 6-1 shows the specific measures employed. Since the data collection has only recently been completed, it was not possible to include all measures in the first stage analyses that will be reported here.

Table 6-1   Measures Employed with the Preschool Sample

Content Area	Measure
I. Day Care Environment	
Descriptive	Prescott: Day Care Environment Inventory (adapted)
Quality	Harms-Clifford: Early Childhood Environment Rating Scale
Language Stimulation	Observational Coding System
II. Child Development Measures	
Cognitive Competence	PPVT—revised
Language Competence	Blank: Preschool Language Assessment Instrument
	Feagans & Farran: Adaptive Language Inventory
	Communications Task
Social Competence	Schaeffer, Aaronson & Edgerton: Classroom Behavior Inventory—Preschool form
	Behar & Stringfield: Preschool Behavior Questionnaire
	Peer v. Adult Orientation
III. Family Background and Home Environment	
Family Demographies	Questionnaire
Child Substitute Care Experience	History of Child Care
Attitudes Toward Day Care	Steinberg & Green: Maternal Attitudes Toward Day Care Questionnaire
Home Environment	Schaeffer & Edgerton: Parent as Educator Interview
Mother's Cognitive Competence	PPVT—revised

Day Care Environments. Sections from Prescott's *Day Care Environment Inventory*[16] were used to assess qualitative aspects of the day care programs; for example, child/staff ratio, caregiver training, quantity of varying materials, and so on. In addition, directors responded to questions about program goals and philosophy. Harms and Clifford's *Early Childhood Environment Rating Scale*[11] was used as an index of center quality. The scale consists of 37 items that are scored on 7-point scales, anchored by definitions of each point. The items comprise 7 dimensions of quality, such as personal care routines, language stimulation and creative activities. Because the subscores were so highly correlated in this study, a total quality score was computed.

An observational coding system, based on one developed by Wells,[23] was used to measure the amount of language stimulation in the centers. Four boys and four girls, 36 months and older, were randomly selected at each of the 10 centers. Each child was observed for six 10-minute segments, three by each of two observers. Adult and peer utterances to the target children were coded for function and frequency. Thus, the language environments of *centers* were assessed for a total of eight hours, distributed across eight children, several days, and several times of the day.

Child Measures. Several measures of the children's intellectual, language, emotional, and social development were administered to the children, or rated by caregivers and parents. The newly revised *Peabody Picture Vocabularly Test*[7] was used to assess general level of intellectual development. The revised version includes more comtemporary pictures that are more representative of varied ethnic groups and gender roles than the older version of the test. Children's intellectual levels were also rated by caregivers and parents on the intelligence and task orientation factors of the *Classroom Behavior Inventory*, Preschool Form.[21]

Blank's *Preschool Language Assessment Instrument*[3] was used as one measure of language development. The PLAI is a standardized test consisting of items that vary in level of abstraction. Feagans' and Farran's Adaptive Language Inventory[9] was also used to assess language competence. The Inventory is an 18-item questionnaire designed for teachers or caregivers to rate children's verbal skills as evidenced in the classroom. The items are scored on five-point scales and comprise six dimensions, such as comprehension, production, and fluency. A total language score was used with a random subset of children from each center. Subjects participating in this task were audiotaped as they retold a story they had previously been read, talked on the telephone to a Sesame Street character, and invented a story about a magic truck on a farm. The tapes were rated along dimensions from the ALI.

Social development was measured by the *Classroom Behavior Inventory* (Preschool Form)[21] and by four items concerning peer versus adult orientation composed by one of the investigators (DP). All items were rated by a caregiver and by one or both parents. The 43-item *Classroom Behavior Inventory* yields five factors: intelligence, task orientation, dependency, consideration, and extraversion, here called sociability. The last three factors were considered measures of social development.

Emotional adjustment was measured by the *Preschool Behavior Questionnaire*,[1] which consists of 30 items on three scales of maladjustment: hyperactive-distractible, aggressive-hostile, and anxious. This measure is a downward extension of Rutter's *Child Behavior*

Questionnaire.[20] A caregiver and one or both parents rated each child.

Family Background. During a visit to the home, parents were asked to report their educational levels, occupational statuses (scored on the expanded NORC scale[18]), and family income. Mothers were given the revised PPVT to estimate their intellectual levels. The ethnicities of the parents were also recorded. In Bermuda there are three major groups: Black Bermudians, who are about 50 percent of the population, Portuguese, who are about 10 percent; and whites, who are about 40 percent. In another study in Bermuda, we found that we could scale ethnicity in a linear fashion with respect to child development variables. The scale confounds ethnicity and social class, needless to say, but is a useful measure of cultural and social differences among Bermuda's residents. The scale is $0 =$ Black, $1 =$ Portuguese, and $2 =$ white.

The background variables, mother's education, ethnicity, and PPVT IQ, were found to correlate more highly with child behaviors than father's education, either parent's occupational status, or family income. Therefore, mother's education, ethnicity, and PPVT IQ were chosen to represent controls for family background. Because all of the background variables were moderately intercorrelated, the inclusion of others would have created problems of multicollinearity in the predictors and would not have added to the prediction of child measures.

Data Analyses

The major goal of the study was to estimate the effects of differences in day care experiences on children's intellectual, language and social and emotional development, with differences in family background controlled. Although the focus of the study was on the qualities of the day care environments, we were also interested in the age at which children began group care and the amount of time spent in the centers. Because families who differ in socioeconomic and ethnic background may select different day care centers, and may enroll their children in center care at earlier or later ages, it was crucial to control for possible genetic, social class, and cultural differences in the children's developmental levels, so that day care effects, if any, could be evaluated.

Therefore, a hierarchical, multiple regression model was chosen. Measures of the children's development were regressed first on age and family background variables. In a second step, age at entry into group care and length of time in group care were added to the equation to estimate the effects of day care experience per se when family background variables were controlled. Finally, measures of the qualities of day care environments were added to the equation to estimate the effects of quality, controlling for family background and the effects of group care per se.

Results

Because this can be only a very preliminary report of only *some* of the results of the study of children currently in day care centers, we chose the caregiver ratings and the tests administered to the children as the first measures to examine. Table 6-2 gives the means and standard deviations of the measures of child behaviors, family background, and day care environments.

Table 6-2   Means and Standard Deviations of Measures of Child Behaviors, Background, Group Care Experience, and Qualities of Group Care Environment

	Means	SD	Range
Child Behaviors			
PPVT IQ	82.8	16.7	40–123
PLAI Score	1.3	0.5	0.2–2.9
Adaptive Language Inventory Score	3.1	0.7	1.3–5.0
Teacher Rating of:			
Intelligence	3.1	0.9	1.2–5.0
Task Orientation	3.1	0.9	1.3–5.0
Sociability	2.9	0.5	1.4–3.6
Consideration	3.0	0.4	1.9–3.8
Dependency	2.5	0.7	1.0–5.0
Adult Orientation	3.0	0.6	1.5–4.8
Total Maladjustment	1.7	0.4	1.1–2.5
Hyperactivity	2.0	0.5	1.0–3.0
Aggressiveness	1.7	0.5	1.0–2.8
Anxiety	1.4	0.2	1.0–2.7
Background			
Child's Age (months)	46.6	6.5	36–65
Mother's PPVT IQ	85.0	20.8	42–160
Mother's Education (years)	12.2	2.2	5–22
Mother's Ethnicity (0 = Black, 2 = White)	0.3	0.7	
Day Care Experience			
Age at Entry into Group Care (months)	19.2	11.8	3–42
Total Hours in Group Care	1104.5	514.4	108–2700
Quality of Group Care Environment			
Total Quality Rating	123.2	35.3	66.5–91.0
Adult Talk to Children, 10-min. segment			
Number of utterances to child alone	3.6	1.8	1.7–10.2
Number of utterances to child in group	11.2	7.6	2.4–23.8

The measures of children's verbal IQ's and language scores suggest that the children in group care are functioning in the low average range. The standardization of the revised PPVT gave surprisingly low average scores of 83 for these children, who were scoring well below comparable children in another Bermudian sample who are also in group care. On the Stanford-Binet, the group care children in the other sample scored 94 on the average. There may be some problems in the standardization of the revised PPVT. The children in the present sample scored in the average range of the PLAI and Adaptive Language Inventory for their ages.

On the five-point scales of social development and the three-point scales of emotional adjustment, the teachers rated the children, on the average, near the middle of each scale. There is reasonable variance on all of the scales with the possible exception of anxiety.

Of the background variables, mother's PPVT IQ was suspiciously low, given twelve years of education on the average. Most of the children were Black, and their ages averaged nearly four years. The ethnic distribution of the sample was 130 black, 7 Portuguese, and 21 white.

The average age of entry into group care at the center in which the children are now in care was 19 months. Because a few of the children had been at other centers earlier, the average age of beginning any group care was 18 months, but the total number of hours of care in the current center was 95 percent of their total group care experience.

The qualities of group care were measured on the Harms-Clifford Scale with 37 items rated by the investigators on seven-point scales. Of a possible 259 points, the mean score was 123, or in the middle range, and the standard deviation of 35 suggests that there was a great deal of variation in quality among the centers. The language measures were simply the number of adult utterances addressed to the average of the eight children during the average 10-minute segment at each center. The number of utterances to the child in a group includes instructional utterances, as well as other functions, such as directions and reprimands. There is considerable variability among centers in the amount of adult speech addressed to children in groups and alone. Other measures of the center environment were so highly correlated with these that we could not include them in the regression analyses.

Correlations Among Measures

Correlations among measures of child behaviors, family background, group care experience, and quality of group care environments are shown in Table 6-3.

Table 6-3a   Correlations among Measures of Child Behaviors, Family Background, Group Care Experience, and Qualities of Group Care Environment (N ≅ 150)

	A1	A2	A3	A4	A5	A6	A7	A8	A9	A10	A11	A12	A13
A. Child Behaviors													
1. PPVT IQ	1.00	.42	.35	.37	.28	.19	.30	.07	.14	.03	−.13	.00	.00
2. PLAI		1.00	.53	.50	.43	.28	.36	−.12	.23	−.19	.04	.13	.13
3. ALI			1.00	.85	.79	.42	.52	.36	.34	.05	−.09	−.03	−.03
Caregiver rating of:													
4. Intelligence				1.00	.88	.56	.69	.40	.18	−.02	−.10	−.12	−.12
5. Task Orientation					1.00	.42	.65	.51	.23	−.23	−.29	−.22	−.22
6. Sociability						1.00	.70	−.32	.06	.32	.33	.25	.28
7. Consideration							1.00	.00	−.06	.00	−.08	.02	.02
8. Dependency								1.00	−.19	.58	.48	.66	.66
9. Adult Orientation									1.00	−.09	−.33	−.16	.07
10. Total Maladjustment										1.00	.73	.88	.72
11. Hyperactivity											1.00	.70	.28
12. Aggressiveness												1.00	.38
13. Anxiety													1.00

r ≧ .17, p < .05

Table 6-3b   Correlations among Measures of Child Behaviors, Family Background, Group Care Experience, and Qualities of Group Care Environment ($N \cong 150$)

	B1	B2	B3	B4	C1	C2	D1	D2	D3
A. *Child Behaviors*									
1. PPVT IQ	-.16	-.22	.32	.15	-.05	.00	.21	.12	.21
2. PLAI	.50	-.25	.17	-.21	-.02	.08	-.03	.26	.21
3. ALI	.42	-.01	.16	.06	-.11	.25	.18	.47	.33
Caregiver rating of:									
4. Intelligence	.32	.01	.18	.14	-.04	.17	.30	.50	.45
5. Task Orientation	.32	-.03	.17	.10	-.04	.14	.29	.55	.37
6. Sociability	.07	-.01	.10	.15	.02	.04	.27	.46	.67
7. Consideration	.16	.04	.13	.11	.01	-.01	.24	.59	.58
8. Dependency	.22	-.11	-.05	-.01	-.00	.08	.07	.14	-.13
9. Adult Orientation	.14	-.06	.03	-.14	.00	.16	.50	.21	.26
10. Total Maladjustment	-.05	-.03	.04	-.06	-.20	.16	-.03	-.01	.11
11. Hyperactivity	-.14	-.08	-.11	-.01	-.11	.00	-.07	.01	.11
12. Aggressiveness	.06	.13	-.01	.00	-.13	.15	-.05	-.05	.03
13. Anxiety	.06	.13	.15	-.08	-.13	.13	-.06	-.05	.17

$r \geqq .17, p < .05$

Theoretical and Social Science Issues

Table 6-3c Correlations among Measures of Child Behaviors, Family Background, Group Care Experience, and Qualities of Group Care Environment

	B1	B2	B3	B4	C1	C2	D1	D2	D3
B. Background									
1. Child's age (months)	1.00	.04	.02	.06	.05	.23	−.20	.25	−.03
2. Mother's PPVT IQ		1.00	.30	.33	.00	−.08	−.06	−.10	.02
3. Mother's education			1.00	−.01	−.01	.05	.08	.13	.06
4. Mother's ethnicity				1.00	.27	−.30	.00	−.21	.03
C. Day Care Experience									
1. Age at entry into group care					1.00	−.65	.10	.21	−.01
2. Total hours in group care						1.00	.12	−.07	.10
D. Quality of Group Care Environment									
Adult talk to children									
1. Number of utterances to child alone							1.00	.21	.57
2. Number of utterances to child as group member								1.00	.67
3. Total quality rating									1.00

$r \geqq .17, p < .05$

The three measures of child IQ and language skills were moderately correlated. Although the correlation between the two language measures was slightly higher than the correlations of the language measures with the PPVT, the language measures were less well standardized to control for age than the PPVT; as will be shown, all three measures were confounded with age in the sample. The test measures of IQ and language skills, the PPVT and the PLAI, are also moderately correlated with the caregiver's ratings of intelligence, task orientation, and the social behaviors, sociability, consideration, dependency, and adult orientation. The *Adaptive Language Inventory*, completed by the caregivers, was highly correlated with their ratings of intelligence and task orientation, but moderately correlated with the other, social ratings. It seems that the caregivers' ratings of intelligence and task orientation were highly influenced by the children's effectiveness in communication, following instructions, and similar abilities that are sampled on the ALI. The other notable correlations are the positive relationships among ratings of intelligence, sociability, and consideration, and between hyperactivity and aggressiveness. It seems reasonable that caregivers may find intelligent, socially mature children both more positively sociable and more considerate of others and very active children more aggressive.

Correlations among the background variables showed the expected positive relationship between mothers' PPVT scores and their educational levels. Ethnicity was not related to educational differences among the mothers, but was correlated with PPVT scores. White mothers scored higher on the PPVT. Neither mothers' educational levels nor PPVT scores were related to differences in children's day care experiences or the quality of the centers in which their children were enrolled. It is reassuring that intellectual differences among the mothers were not confounded with differences in the quality of the care these children receive at the centers. Ethnicity, on the other hand, was related to the age at entry and number of hours in group care: Black mothers entered their children into day care centers at earlier ages, so that the children have had more hours of group care as well.

On the other hand, Black children were also more likely to be in centers where there is more adult talk to children in groups. Much of the adult speech to groups of children was instruction in the preschool, nursery fashion—teaching colors, numbers, reading stories, and the like.

Children who were younger at the time of the study were, of course, likely to have had fewer hours of group care in their lives, but the two variables, age at entry and total hours, were not so highly

correlated ($-.65$) that they could not both be used to predict differences among the children.

Finally, the two verbal measures of the center environments were
not highly correlated. Adult speech to children alone and in groups
were virtually independent. The language measures were moderately
correlated with the overall quality of the center environment, as
rated on the Harms-Clifford Scale, however. Centers with higher degrees of adult-child language interaction were scored as more adequate on other aspects of the physical environment, play materials
and opportunities, and the scale of language interaction.

Reliabilities of the Environmental Measures

Eleven aspects of the verbal environment were coded by two independent observers. The reliabilities ranged from .92 to .99. The Early
Childhood Environment Scale was also rated by two observers, and
the reliability of the total score was .88.

Regression Analyses

Tables 6-4, 6-5, and 6-6 present the hierarchical regression models
for the effects of family background, group care experience, and
quality of group care on the children's intellectual and language
development, social development, and emotional adjustment, respectively. The results will be reported in that order.

Intellectual and Language Development.   In the first set of equations to predict differences in the children's general level of intellectual functioning, the PPVT was regressed on the differences in
background, group care experience, and quality of the day care
environment the children experienced. As predicted, the PPVT was
not sensitive to differences among day care environments. Only
differences in family background were significant predictors of general levels of intellectual development. The higher the mother's
education and the more likely the mother was to be white rather
than black, the higher the child's PPVT IQ. Although the final equation with all of the variables is statistically significant, the three sets
of predictors accounted for only 13 percent of the variance (adjusted
R^2). Age at entry into group care and number of hours spent in
group care in the first three to four years of life had no significant
effect of PPVT scores, nor did differences in the qualities of the day
care environments.

The standardized measure of language development was more
sensitive than the global PPVT IQ to differences in the overall
qualities of the day care environments. The total score from the

Table 6-4a Regression of Children's Intellectual and Language Development on Family Background, Group Care Experience, and Qualities of Group Care

	Child's PPVT IQ (N = 137)		
	B	B	B
Background			
Child's age (months)	−.19[a]	−.19[a]	−.16
Mother's PPVT IQ	.08	.07	.07
Mother's education	.25[b]	.25[b]	.24[b]
Mother's ethnicity	.16	.19[a]	.19[a]
Group Care Experience			
Age at entry (months)		−.08	−.13
Number of hours in group care		−.01	−.06
Quality of Group Care			
Adult talk to children:			
Number of utterances to child alone			.12
Number of utterances to child as group member			.05
Total quality score			.07
$R^2 =$	.143	.151	.186
$\tilde{R}^2 =$	.117	.112	.128
$p <$	.001	.002	.002

[a] $p < .05$
[b] $p < .01$

Harms-Clifford Scale accounted for about five percent of the variance in the children's PLAI scores, after age was controlled. The effects of family background and group care experience were trivial. Like the PPVT, the PLAI is a global measure of language-intellectual functioning that samples far more of the child's learning than can be reasonably affected by a high- or low-quality day environment. There was evidence, however, for a greater effect of differences in day environments on PLAI than even more global PPVT scores.

By contrast, the *Adaptive Language Inventory* and two ratings of intelligence and task orientation by the caregivers were strongly affected by the differences in quality among the centers. Scores on the *Adaptive Language Inventory* were not affected by differences in family background or group care experience per se. The child's age predictably accounted for about 16 percent of the variance in ALI scores in a group of children that vary in age from 36 to 60 months. The addition of the day care environmental variables accounted for nearly 20 percent additional variance in the scores. Children in higher quality centers where adults talk more to children, particularly in groups, scored higher on the ALI. Mother's ethnicity made a small contribution to this prediction.

Table 6-4b   Regression of Children's Intellectual and Language Development on Family Background, Group Care Experience, and Qualities of Group Care

	Child's PLAI Score (N = 136)			Adaptive Language Inventory (N = 130)		
	B	B	B	B	B	B
Background.						
Child's age (months)	.50[c]	.51[c]	.54[c]	.40[c]	.37[c]	.34[c]
Mother's PPVT IQ	.17[a]	.16	.15	−.11	−.11	−.09
Mother's education	.08	.09	.07	.12	.12	.05
Mother's ethnicity	.12	.15	.14	.10	.15	.21[a]
Group Care Experience						
Age at entry (months)		−.10	−.12		−.07	−.16
Number of hours in group care		.01	−.07		.13	−.01
Quality of Group Care						
Adult talk to children:						
Number of utterances to child alone			−.00			.13
Number of utterances to child as group member			−.01			.34[b]
Total quality score			.25[a]			.10
R^2 =	.347	.355	.411	.184	.213	.406
$\tilde{R}^2$ =	.327	.325	.369	.158	.175	.361
$p <$	.001	.001	.001	.001	.001	.001

[a] $p < .05$
[b] $p < .01$
[c] $p < .001$

Similarly, caregivers' ratings of the children's intelligence, as they observe it in the day care setting, and their ratings of the children's task orientation were strongly affected by the language environment of the center. The items that make up the *Classroom Behavior Inventory* are behaviorally anchored statements about children that are summed to the factors reported. It is clear that caregivers at centers with more favorable language environments report higher levels of intelligent behavior and task orientation for their children. Among the background variables, age and ethnicity had some predictive power, with older and white children rated by caregivers as more intelligent and task oriented than younger and black children. The background variables accounted for only 12 percent of the variance in the ratings. Age at entry and number of hours in group care per se had no predictive power. The qualities of the language environments, however, accounted for an additional 26 percent of the variance in rated intelligence and 31 percent in task orientation.

Table 6-4c   Regression of Children's Intellectual and Language Development on Family Background, Group Care Experience, and Qualities of Group Care

	CBI: Ratings of Intelligence (N = 130)			CBI: Ratings of Task Orientation (N = 130)		
	B	B	B	B	B	B
Background						
Child's age (months)	.32^c	.28^c	.28^c	.31^c	.28^b	.25^b
Mother's PPVT IQ	−.11	−.10	−.08	−.13	−.12	−.08
Mother's education	.15	.14	.07	.20^a	.19^a	.10
Mother's ethnicity	.16	.20^a	.25^b	.11	.14	.24^b
Group Care Experience						
Age at entry (months)		.02	−.11		.03	−.13
Number of hours in group care		.18	−.01		.14	−.08
Quality of Group Care						
Adult talk to children:						
Number of utterances to child alone			.24^a			.36^c
Number of utterances to child as group member			.36^c			.59^c
Total quality score			.09			−.18
$R^2 =$	.145	.170	.437	.146	.158	.474
$\tilde{R}^2 =$	.118	.130	.395	.119	.117	.435
$p \lessdot$	.001	.001	.001	.001	.002	.001

^{a} $p < .05$
^{b} $p < .01$
^{c} $p < .001$

Social Development. Caregivers' ratings of the children's levels of sociability, consideration, dependency, and peer vs. adult orientation are given in Table 6-5. Neither family background nor group care experience per se predicted sociability, but higher quality day environments predicted higher levels of social behavior by the children in them. Nearly half of the variance in ratings of sociability was accounted for by the total quality scores for the centers. Similarly, showing consideration for others was predicted by the qualities of the language environment and the overall quality of the center. Higher quality centers have children who are rated as more considerate of others.

Dependency and peer vs. adult orientation were less well predicted by the quality of the center than sociability and consideration. The adjusted R^2's were about .25. The children who were rated as high in dependency tended to be in centers with lower overall quality but a lot of adult talk to children alone and in groups. It may be

Table 6-5a   Regression of Children's Social Development on Family Background, Group Care Experience, and Qualities of Group Care

	CBI: Sociability (N = 130)			CBI: Consideration (N = 130)		
	B	B	B	B	B	B
Background						
Child's age (months)	.04	.02	.02	.13	.12	.07
Mother's PPVT IQ	−.11	−.10	−.12	−.05	−.05	−.03
Mother's education	.15	.14	.07	.20[a]	.20[a]	.11
Mother's ethnicity	.18	.21[a]	.19[a]	.07	.08	.14
Group Care Experience						
Age at entry (months)		−.02	−.05		.00	−.07
Number of hours in group care		.08	−.05		.04	−.12
Quality of Group Care						
Adult talk to children:						
Number of utterances to child alone			−.17			.00
Number of utterances to child as group member			.03			.37[c]
Total quality score			.74[c]			.35[b]
$R^2=$	.045	.053	.497	.060	.061	.454
$\tilde{R}^2 =$	.014	.007	.459	.030	.015	.413
$p <$	n.s.	n.s.	.001	n.s.	n.s.	.001

[a] $p < .05$
[b] $p < .01$
[c] $p < .001$

that much of the talk in the lower quality centers is control, but we cannot be sure of that until the functions of the utterances are analyzed. Or, more likely, it may be that high verbal interaction with adults in centers whose programs are not well organized fosters the development of dependency. Children who are adult- rather than peer-oriented were likely to be in centers with a lot of adult talk to children alone, regardless of overall quality.

Emotional Adjustment.   Poor emotional adjustment, as rated by the caregivers, was related both to the age at entry into group care and to the qualities of the day care environments. These results are shown in Table 6-6. The total maladjustment score is predicted by early entry into group care at centers that were rated high in overall quality but low in verbal interaction. In centers where the physical facilities and play materials are good but where there is less than the average amount of adult verbal interaction with children, chil-

Table 6-5b   Regression of Children's Social Development on Family Background, Group Care Experience, and Qualities of Group Care

	CBI: Dependency (N = 130)			Adult Orientation (N = 130)		
	B	B	B	B	B	B
Background						
Child's age (months)	.30[b]	.26[b]	.23[a]	.15	.11	.24[c]
Mother's PPVT IQ	−.10	−.08	−.03	−.03	−.01	.00
Mother's education	.00	−.01	−.03	.02	.01	−.03
Mother's ethnicity	−.03	−.02	.08	−.12	−.10	−.11
Group Care Experience						
Age at entry (months)		.13	.02		.18	−.12
Number of hours in group care		.17	.08		.12	−.11
Quality of Group Care						
Adult talk to children:						
Number of utterances to child alone			.43[c]			.56[c]
Number of utterances to child as group member			.47[c]			.04
Total quality score			−.68[c]			.01
$R^2 =$	.102	.117	.295	.040	.055	.313
$\tilde{R}^2 =$	.073	.074	.242	.009	.009	.261
$p <$	.01	.02	.001	.23	.25	.001

[a] $p < .05$
[b] $p < .01$
[c] $p < .001$

dren who entered in early infancy are more emotionally maladjusted than children who entered the same centers later or who were enrolled in more verbally interactive centers. Although only 19 percent of the variance in maladjustment scores was predicted by the combination of group care experience and quality variables, the results have important implications for the evaluation of infant day care environments.

The three scales that make up the total maladjustment score are hyperactive-distractible, aggressive-hostile, and anxious. Hyperactivity and aggressiveness were poorly predicted by any of the variables. Only four to eight percent of the variance was predicted by age at entry into group care and the qualities of the environment. The pattern of results was the same as for the total maladjustment score: hyperactive and aggressive children were more likely to have entered day care at an early age and to be in centers with higher overall

Table 6-6a Regression of Children's Emotional Adjustment on Family Background, Group Care Experience, and Qualities of Group Care

	PBQ: Total Score—Emotional Maladjustment (N = 130)			PBQ: Hyperactive-Distractible (N = 130)		
	B	B	B	B	B	B
Background						
Child's age (months)	−.13	−.09	−.06	−.19[a]	−.15	−.19
Mother's PPVT IQ	−.05	−.10	−.13	−.04	−.08	−.09
Mother's education	−.08	−.06	−.06	−.09	−.07	−.08
Mother's ethnicity	−.04	.12	.04	.02	.06	.05
Group Care Experience						
Age at entry (months)		−.38[b]	−.31[b]		−.25[a]	−.19
Number of hours in group care		−.15	−.11		−.15	−.10
Quality of Group Care						
Adult talk to children:						
Number of utterances to child alone			−.31[b]			−.25[a]
Number of utterances to child as group member			−.33[b]			−.07
Total quality score			.60[c]			.30[a]
$R^2 =$	.029	.115	.243	.049	.082	.130
$\tilde{R}^2 =$	−.002	.072	.186	.019	.037	.065
$p <$	n.s.	.02	.001	n.s.	n.s.	.05

[a] $p < .05$
[b] $p < .01$

quality but less adult verbal interaction with the children in the center.

By contrast, more than a quarter of the variance in ratings of anxiety was predicted by differences in the qualities of the day care environments. Children in high-quality, low-verbal day care centers were rated as more anxious than children in more verbally interactive environments that are lower on other aspects of quality, such as the physical facilities. Again, children who entered the lower-quality but more verbally rich environments at an early age tended to be less anxious than children who were enrolled later in their preschool years and children in less verbally interactive centers. Verbal interaction with adults had positive effects on emotional adjustment as well as on language skills. This suggests that measuring adult verbal interactions with children captures qualities of emotional as well as language stimulation.

Table 6-6b Regression of Children's Emotional Adjustment on Family Background, Group Care Experience; and Qualities of Group Care

	PBQ: Aggressive-Hostile (N = 130)			PBQ: Anxious (N = 130)		
	B	B	B	B	B	B
Background						
Child's age (months)	−.07	−.05	−.04	−.02	.03	.08
Mother's PPVT IQ	−.12	−.16	−.18	.13	.08	.04
Mother's education	−.09	−.08	−.08	−.01	.01	.01
Mother's ethnicity	.10	.18	.14	−.05	−.01	−.12
Group Care Experience						
Age at entry (months)		−.33[b]	−.28[a]		−.30[a]	.21
Number of hours in group care		−.07	−.04		−.20	−.16
Quality of Group Care						
Adult talk to children:						
Number of utterances to child alone			−.19			−.42[c]
Number of utterances to child as group member			−.19			−.48[c]
Total quality score			.31[a]			.87[c]
$R^2 =$	.037	.112	.147	.014	.060	.324
$\tilde{R}^2 =$	.006	.069	.083	−.018	.030	.273
$p <$	n.s.	.05	.05	n.s.	n.s.	.001

[a] $p < .05$
[b] $p < .01$
[c] $p < .001$

Discussion

The major results of this study so far are that many aspects of children's development are moderately to highly related to differences in their day care environments. Children at the better quality centers score higher on measures of language development, the PLAI and the Adaptive Language Inventory. Caregivers at higher quality centers rate their children as more sociable and considerate than do caregivers at centers with less adult-child verbal interaction and poorer overall quality. These results support the hypotheses that qualities of day care environments affect the developmental levels of language and social behaviors of children in them.

Good overall quality but low adult-child verbal interaction was associated with maladjustment in the children. Children in such centers were reported by their caregivers to be more anxious, hyperactive and aggressive. The total maladjustment scores of children in centers with little adult-child interaction but good facilities were higher than those in centers with poorer overall quality but good language environments. These results point to more specific aspects of the day care environments that affect the emotional adjustment of children in them.

The age at which the children entered group care affected their emotional adjustment, even when the quality of that care was controlled. Children who began group care in infancy were rated as more maladjusted than those who were cared for by sitters or in day care homes for the early years and who began center care at later ages. One should recall that nearly all Bermudian children are in nonmaternal care by the second year of life, so that these results are not based primarily on a comparison of home-reared and day care children. Regardless of the quality of the center environment, infant care in centers may be less desirable for emotional adjustment than early substitute care in homes.

Early entry into day care centers had no significant effect on intellectual, language or social development. The trends, however, are that children who entered *early* into the good quality centers, with high adult-child verbal interaction, have *higher* scores on intellectual and language measures. The inclusion of quality controls in the prediction equation raised all of the coefficients for early age at entry, predicting better intellectual and language development. Given that many of these children come from, and were cared for in, homes where verbal interaction is not a primary form of communication with very young children, the high quality day care centers may well provide more stimulation for intellectual and language development than many of the homes.

The results reported in this chapter are based on tests administered to the children and on caregivers' ratings. It is interesting to note that caregivers in the day care centers that *we* rated as having higher overall quality and better language environments rate their children as having better skills. This means that caregivers were using a normative view of child development rather than a relative one, comparing only the children in that center. When parents' ratings of their children's development are analyzed, it will be important to question the basis of their ratings, as we have discovered in another study of Bermudian children that our investigators' ratings of children's social development are better predictors of even mother's views of her child's competence than are her own ratings of social behavior. Alas, parents may have intimate knowledge of their children but little normative basis for comparison. The caregivers in the day care centers seemed to have adopted suitable normative standards, however.

One could argue that the caregivers' ratings have limited generality to the children's behaviors and adjustment outside of the day care center, because the samples of child behavior that caregivers have are limited to that setting. The fact that the language test we administered was also related to differences in the day care environments suggests that the children's behaviors rated by the caregivers are not just specific to the day care center. The magnitude of the measured effects of day care environments was certainly greater for most (but not all) behaviors rated by the caregivers than for our tests. Whether these differences in magnitude of effects for tests versus caregiver ratings reflect situational specificity in caregiver ratings or real differences in the effects of day care environments on language versus social and emotional development cannot be determined without the parents' ratings.

The family background variables that we chose for these analyses were those with the highest zero-order correlations with the child behavior variables. We have not yet analyzed the interviews and parents' ratings of their satisfactions with their children's day care. Nor have we scored the Parent-as-Educator form, which may well control for more family background differences among the children than the SES variables we have here included. It seems unlikely, however, that the powerful effects of day care differences among the center environments will be accounted for by family differences, because the background variables are largely uncorrelated with center differences.

If the results continue on further analysis to show that differences in the quality of day care environments have important effects on children's language, social, and emotional development, the social policy implications for child care are obvious. It will be important to train child caregivers to provide stimulation and language environments that promote both language and emotional development. A closer look at the effects of infant care in group centers will be necessary, especially in those centers that do not have high degrees of adult-child interaction. Ultimately, one would hope that policy makers will care enough to assure high quality day care for all children who need it. Once we know more about the specific qualities of the day care environments that matter, it will be possible to plan those environments in more detail. This study will provide detailed information about the qualities of day care environments that affect various aspects of children's development, not only in the short run for those currently in day care, but also for children who are currently nine years old and who experienced the same variations in day care during their preschool years. We feel that this study will have much to say about the standards that ought to be set to promote children's development in group care settings.

As we evaluate the implications of our findings for child care policy in the United States, it will be incumbent on us to consider the feasibility of recommendations. For example, although staff/child ratios and staff training are amenable to governmental regulation and monitoring, the director's philosophy and relationships with parents are not. Asserting the value of assuring high-quality care must be accompanied by a relevant set of recommendations that speak to the concerns of policymakers in terms they can use.

References

1. Behar, L. and Stringfield, S.A. 1974. "A behavior rating scale for the preschool child." *Developmental Psychology* 10:601–610.
2. Belsky, J. and Steinberg, L.D. 1978. "The effects of day care: critical review." *Child Development* 49:929–949.
3. Blank, M., Rose, S.A. and Berlin, L.J. 1978. *Preschool Language Assessment Instrument: The Language of Learning in Practice.* Grune and Stratton, New York.
4. Cochran, M.M. 1977. "A comparison of group, day and family child-rearing patterns in Sweden." *Child Development* 48:702–707.
5. Cornelius, S.W. and Denny, N.W. 1975. "Dependency in day care and home care children." *Developmental Psychology* 11:575–582.
6. Doyle, A. 1975. "Infant development in day care." *Developmental Psychology* 11:655–656.
7. Dunn, L.M. 1979. *Peabody Picture Vocabulary Test*—revised. American Guidance Service, Circle Pines, Minnesota.
8. Etaugh, C. 1980. "Effects of nonmaternal care on children: Research evidence and popular views." *American Psychologist* 35:309–319.
9. Feagans, L. and Farran, D. "Adaptive language inventory." Unpublished.
10. Finkelstein, N.W. *et al.* 1978. "Social behavior of infants and toddlers in a day care environment." *Developmental Psychology* 14:275–262.
11. Harms, T. and Clifford, R.M. 1980. *Early Childhood Environment Rating Scale.* Teachers College Press, New York.
12. Kagan, J., Kearsley, R.B. and Zelazo, P.R. 1978. *Infancy.* Harvard University Press, Cambridge, Massachusetts.
13. McCrae, J. and Herbert-Jackson, E. 1976. "Are behavioral effects of infant day care programs specific?" *Developmental Psychology* 12:269–270.
14. Moskowitz, D.S., Schwarz, J.C. and Corsini, D.A. 1977. "Initiating day care at three years of age: Effects of attachment." *Child Development* 48:1271–1276.
15. Parmenter, G.R. 1976. "Environmental factors influencing the use of language." Unpublished dissertation, University of Melbourne.
16. Prescott, E. *et al.* 1972. *The Day Care Environment Inventory.* Department of Health, Education and Welfare.
17. Ramey, C. and Campbell, F. 1977. "The prevention of developmental retardation in high-risk children." In *Research to Practice in Mental Retardation*, P. Mittler (ed.). University Park Press, Baltimore.

18. Reiss, A.J., Jr. 1961. *Occupations and Social Status.* Free Press, New York.
19. Rubenstein, J.L. and Howes, C. 1979. "Caregiving and infant behavior in day care and in homes." *Developmental Psychology* 15:1–24.
20. Rutter, M. 1967. "A children's behavior questionnaire for the completion by teachers: Preliminary findings." *Journal of Child Psychology and Psychiatry* 8:1–11.
21. Schaeffer, E.S., Aaronson, M. and Edgerton, M. 1976. "Classroom Behavior Inventory." Unpublished.
22. Schaeffer, E.S. and Edgerton, M. 1976. "Parent as educator interview." Unpublished.
23. Wells, G. 1975. "The context of children's early language experiences." *Educational Review* 27:114–125.

Chapter 7

DAY CARE AND CHILDREN'S RESPONSIVENESS TO ADULTS

by Anne Robertson

As greater numbers of preschool children are cared for at day care centers, the need is increased for studies of the impact of day care attendance on child development. However, as recent reviews of the day care literature point out,[4,34] the day care research available is limited primarily to studies of the impact of attendance at high-quality centers on measures of children's interactions with their mothers.[9,13,20] This study was an attempt to look at the influence of day care on children's behavior outside their families and to determine if that influence interacted with their socioeconomic status and sex. This study investigated the impact of full-time attendance at preschool day care centers on boys and girls who were of elementary school age (5–6 years and 8–9 years) when assessed and who were from middle and lower socioeconomic status groups. Dependent measures included assessments through individual testing and elementary-school teacher ratings of children's interactions with nonparental adults, interactions with peers, and competence motivation. Subjects who had attended day care centers as preschoolers (N = 57) were compared with those who had been cared for at home (N = 64).

The research for this chapter was based on a doctoral dissertation submitted to the Psychology Department of Yale University. It was supported in part by the Bush Foundation. A portion of this chapter was presented at the biennial meeting of the Society for Research in Child Development, Boston, 1981.

The author wishes to express appreciation to Edward Zigler for his support and advice; to Thomas Berndt, Victoria Seitz, and Sandra Scarr for their comments on an earlier draft of this work; and to the school systems of New Haven, Hamden, Bridgeport, and Ansonia, Connecticut, for their participation in the study.

This study provides evidence generalizable to the experience of the majority of children currently attending day care centers in the United States. Most day care studies include day care subjects from one, or at most two, different day care centers, thereby creating the possibility that the findings reported are specific to the centers involved. In contrast, day care subjects in this study represented attendance at over 30 different day care centers, thereby substantially increasing the generalizability of the findings. By including subjects from so many different centers, any care effects found would have to be attributed to those variables common to nearly all day care centers (daily parent-child separations, multiple caretakers, the presence of large numbers of peers, and the increase in structure and routine that this usually necessitates), rather than to characteristics of particular centers such as adult-child ratios and educational philosophies.

Furthermore, most day care center children attend centers of average quality for approximately 40 hours per week, beginning at age three. However, previous research has not focused on the impact of this modal day care experience, but rather has examined the impact of high-quality programs on children who began care in infancy[9,20] or assessed the "effect" of day care after attendance periods as short as 4 months.[6,25] The subjects in this study attended day care centers of varying quality and, most typically, attended 30 to 40 hours per week for two years.

This study differed from many other day care studies in that it did not assess the impact of day care on children's interactions with their mothers. The vast majority of day care studies have focused on how day care attendance might influence child-mother attachment. With the exception of Blehar's study,[6] findings of day care studies are quite consistent in reporting no difference between day care and home care children in the preferential attachments they exhibit towards their mothers.[9,12,13,14,20,25,29,31,36]

This study considered the impact of day care attendance on children's interactions with nonfamily members in settings outside the family. Children's interactions with nonparental adults were assessed in terms of attention-seeking, responsiveness to social reinforcement, and imitation. Teacher rating scales and individual assessments were used to determine day care's influence on school-related variables, such as interactions with teachers and peers, feelings of competence, academic achievement, and IQ.

The rationale for choosing the dependent measures was twofold. First, previous research has shown these measures to be sensitive to major differences in children's social histories (differences due to factors such as educational interventions, institutionalization, short- and long-term deprivation, and social class).[17,37,41,44] It seemed possible that these measures might also discriminate between day care and home care subjects.

Second, they were measures which previous day care research would predict should be most likely to be influenced by the day care/home care difference. Although day care does not seem to influence children's interactions with their mothers, there is considerable evidence suggesting that day care does influence children's interactions with nonfamilial adults. Several day care researchers who used Ainsworth's "strange situation"[2] report no difference in the child-mother interactions of day care and home care subjects, but did find differences in children's interactions with the "stranger."[6,12,25,31] Day care children were consistently more avoidant and less interactive with the stranger than home care children.

A number of other studies have suggested that day care children are more aggressive, less cooperative, and show more negative reactions toward adults and adult standards than home care children.[7,22,32,35] However, it may be that the negative aspects of substitute and group care are true only for male subjects.[24] These findings generated the prediction that in this study teachers would rate day care subjects as less cooperative and more aggressive toward adults and peers than home care children, with the possibility that this might be found true only for boys.

Nearly all day care studies have used children currently in day care as subjects, so very little data has accumulated concerning potential long-term effects of day care attendance. This study included two groups of elementary school-aged children (5–6 and 8–9), and so assessed potential longer-term effects of day care. A study by Moore[24] is one of the very few studies to provide any evidence concerning the longer-term effects of substitute care. His findings under score the importance of using subjects older than preschool age and of doing follow-up studies, because he reports that the proportion of interview and test items which discriminated between care groups was greater at age 15 than at younger ages, even though the selection criterion was "type-of-care-before-age-five." Moore compared boys and girls who had experienced either exclusive mothering or some form of daily substitute care for at least 12 months before the age of five, and he followed his subjects up to age 15.

This study was designed to analyze for interactions between type of care and subjects' SES and sex. It is important that the findings of day care studies be analyzed with regard to SES because any impact day care may have would depend upon how day care compared with the child's home care, and SES constitutes a gross indicator of the nature of the child's home care. However, with the exception of Kagan, et al.,[20] who failed to find important SES effects, previous day care studies have either precluded finding Care × SES interactions by including subjects from a single SES group[6,9,35] or have not analyzed for SES effects when subjects were selected from a broad range of SES groups.[24,25]

While there are almost no Care × SES interactions reported in day care literature, a few studies do report Care × Sex interactions.[11,24,25] These interactions indicate that type of care appears to affect boys' behavior more than girls', with day-care or substitute-care males appearing more active, more independent and less oriented toward adults than home care males. By including boys and girls of two ages and from two SES groups, this study provided more specific data than most previous studies about how day care might affect particular groups of children.

This study was exploratory in the sense that few specific predictions regarding the impact of group day care on the dependent measures were made. Conflicting hypotheses regarding the effects of typical day care could be proposed. For example, regarding attention-seeking and desire for social reinforcement, it might be that day care provided a child with numerous positive experiences with adults and so decreased the child's desire to seek attention from or interact with an unfamiliar adult. On the other hand, if day care involved some degree of deprivation of adult attention (and with child-adult ratios of 4:1 to 8:1 this is not unlikely), then the child's attention-seeking and desire for social reinforcement might be expected to increase as a result of day care attendance. Gewirtz and Baer,[15,16] using experimental manipulations, and Zigler and his colleagues,[8,19,43,44,45] using real-life situations, have proposed such a satiation-deprivation formulation with regard to responsiveness to social reinforcement.

Day care might also have two different effects on performance on effectance motivation measures. In some cases the greater independence required by day care might encourage a strong sense of competence in some children, thereby increasing their effectance motivation. For others, though, the reduced opportunity for self-initiated behavior in day care[30] might reduce children's confidence in their own efforts, and so reduce their effectance motivation.

In sum, this study examined the influence of preschool group day care on the performance of school-aged boys and girls from two age and two SES groups on measures of social, motivational, and cognitive development.

Method

Subjects

The subjects were 121 Caucasian (N = 68) and Black (N = 53) school-aged children. The children were nearly evenly divided with regard to age, sex, SES, and group day care experience. The younger children were 5 or 6 years old (N = 62, $\overline{X}$ = 70.6 months, SD = 4.4), and the older were 8 or 9 years old ($N = 59$, $\overline{X} = 107.1$ months, $SD = 4.1$). Of the subjects, 60 were boys and 61 were girls.

The children were divided into two SES groups on the basis of their parents' educations and occupations, following the method presented in the Hollingshead Index of Social Position.[18] The 58 children designated middle-SES came from professional and semiprofessional families (Hollingshead I-III). The parents of the 63 lower-SES children were either unskilled or semiskilled workers or were on public assistance (Hollingshead IV-V). The ages and SES ratings of day care and home care children for each age group were comparable.

The variable of primary interest was group day care experience prior to first grade. Children were included in the day care group if they had attended a day care center for at least 20 hours per week for at least two years. In fact, the day care subjects' day care experience considerably exceeded this minimum. Of the children, 82.6% had attended day care for 30 or more hours per week for at least two years, usually beginning day care at age three or four. The no-day-care, or home-care, children had been cared for at home by their parents, primarily by their mothers.

The day care subjects reflected experience in a wide range of day care centers; the 57 day care subjects attended 32 different private or publicly funded centers. However, the continuity of the children's day care arrangements was high; 76.5% of the day care subjects had attended only one day care setting.

The day care centers involved served from 15 to 60 children, in groups averaging 15 children. The child-adult ratio ranged from 5:1 to 8:1, and centers typically provided traditional nursery school programs, although three of the children attended a setting in which an academic Montessori curriculum was followed in the mornings.

Although the home-care subjects were all cared for at home primarily by their mothers, many of them (62.5%) had had some form of group care before kindergarten. This was especially true of the middle-SES group. Of these children, 87.5% had attended nursery schools and play groups, most commonly for 5 hours per week at age 3, and for 7.5 hours per week at age 4. On the other hand, only 34% of the lower-SES home care children had had any prekindergarten group experience. This was typically a Head Start program at age 4, for from 10 to no more than 12.5 hours per week. All the home care children also went to kindergarten for 12.5 hours per week at age 5.

Subject Selection

Subjects were selected from 8 elementary schools in south-central Connecticut, 4 of which were predominantly lower-SES and 4 of which were predominantly middle-SES. Children were excluded from the study who: (1) did not speak English at home, (2) had either skipped or repeated a grade, and/or (3) had foreign-born parents. Parents were asked to describe their children's preschool care, and on the basis of this information, children were classified as either day care or home care. (The information was always verified in a telephone interview with a parent of each child.) An attempt was made to select an equal number of day care and home care children of each age from each school in order to achieve some degree of matching with regard to school and neighborhood. The permission return rate ranged from 25% in a lower-SES, inner-city school to 90% in an affluent suburban school. In order to assess the possible impact of different permission return rates, the mean scores of children attending two lower-SES schools (one with a low permission return rate—25%—and the other with a moderately high permission return rate—78%) were compared. The only significant difference found was on the PPVT-IQ measure on which children from the lower-return-rate school scored lower. (This school was also located in the more disadvantaged neighborhood.)

Seven of the original day care subjects were excluded from the study because their day care experiences were atypical in that they had not attended day care centers staffed by paid child-care workers. Rather, six had attended parent-cooperative centers staffed primarily by rotating parent volunteers, and one child's day care experience had been entirely in family day care homes. No more than two subjects were lost from any single cell of the design.

Procedure

Each child had two individual testing sessions with one of four experimenters who were all Caucasian women in their mid-twenties to mid-thirties and had been trained to administer the experimental tasks in a standardized manner. Sessions were held in a private area of the school during school hours and each lasted between 30 and 40 minutes. Sessions were usually held a week apart, but the intersession time period ranged from 2 to 10 days.

The order of experimental tasks was constant for all children, with the order determined so as to reduce possible contamination of one measure on another. The order of experimental tasks was as follows: Session 1—Marble-in-the-Hole and Preference for Challenging Problems Task; Session 2—Sticker Game Imitation Task, Peabody Picture Vocabulary Test, and Pictorial Curiosity Task. Verbal attention-seeking was scored only while the child played the Sticker Game, because it was the only measure during which child-tester interaction was minimal and recording feasible.

Child Measures

Intelligence (IQ). IQ was assessed by the Peabody Picture Vocabulary Test (PPVT-Form B).

Preference for challenging problems. The measure of preference for challenging problems used was a puzzle preference task taken from the Harter and Zigler[17] battery of effectance motivation measures. The child is shown a set of four identical 12-piece wooden puzzles which vary only in the number of pieces which have been removed (3, 6, 9, or 12). The child is asked to choose one puzzle to complete. Two sets of four puzzles each are used with each child, and the dependent measure is the sum of the two difficulty levels chosen (scores could thus range from 2, when the child selects the easiest puzzle on each trial, to 8, when the child selects the most difficult on each trial).

Pictorial curiosity. The curiosity measure was also selected from the Harter and Zigler[17] effectance motivation battery. Children are shown a series of 15 cardboard "houses." The front of each house has two doors, one with a picture drawn on it and one blank. It is explained to the child that behind the door with the picture is an identical picture, but that behind the blank door is a "new picture, one you haven't seen before." Following three practice trials to ensure that the child understands the task, the child is shown each of the 15 houses and permitted to open only one door of each. The extent to which a child chooses to open the blank door to see a novel picture is taken as measure of the child's curiosity. The dependent measure is the number of blank doors the child selects, a maximum of 15.

Imitation: Sticker Game. A child's tendency to imitate an adult was measured by an adaptation of the Sticker Game Imitation Task.[1,38,41,42] The task involves the child's making pictures on construction paper with gummed paper of different colors, shapes, and sizes. The tester begins by making a sticker picture and giving it a name (Kitty Cat, Rocket Ship, and Go-Cart were the three pictures used in this study). Then, with the tester's picture in the child's view, the child is asked to make a picture and name it also. The order of model pictures was random.

The tester and the child each make three pictures. The child's imitation score is based on the degree to which his or her pictures are similar to the models made by the tester with regard to: (1) picture's name, (2) picture's form, and (3) color of background paper used.

Responsiveness to social reinforcement. A child's desire for and responsiveness to social reinforcement from an unfamiliar adult were assessed by the Marble-in-the-Hole task.[40,3] The measure involves a simple, repetitive game, which was designed to reduce quickly the child's desire to "play the game" for its own sake, so that the primary motive for continuing to play could be assumed to be the desire to interact with the tester.

The child's task is to put marbles of one color into one hole of an enclosed wooden box and marbles of another color into a second hole while the tester provides verbal reinforcement. The child plays until he or she wants to stop or until 10 minutes have passed. The game is played in two parts, the second part differing from the first only in that the appropriate holes for each color marble are reversed. The dependent measure is the length of time spent playing the game (maximum of 20 minutes for sum of Part I and Part II).

Marble-in-the-Hole has been used for 20 years in studies which demonstrate its sensitivity to differences in many aspects of children's social experiences. In a review criticizing much of the methodology of the social reinforcement literature, Parton and Ross[27] concluded that the time spent playing Marble-in-the-Hole was one of the few valid measures of the effectiveness of reinforcement for a child.

Verbal attention-seeking. The verbal attention-seeking score was obtained by recording verbatim all that a child said while playing the Sticker Game Imitation Task. During this task the tester initiates no conversation and responds only minimally to the child's responses. The child's verbalizations are scored by a method used by Kohlberg and Zigler:[21] a score of 3 is given to a verbal request for something other than information, of 2 to a simple question, of 1 to a declarative statement not requiring a response, and of $\frac{1}{2}$ to an egocentric comment. In this study, the dependent measure used was the attention-seeking score per minute spent playing the Sticker Game.

Teacher Evaluations of the Children

Achievement ratings. Teachers were asked to rate each child's academic performance in reading and arithmetic on a 4-point scale. The four points indicated the following levels of achievement: 1—below average, 2—average, 3—above average, and 4—excellent, well above average. Teachers were asked to rate children relative to other children in the same school.

Teacher rating scale. Teachers also completed a 31-item Teacher Rating Scale for each child. Items dealt with a child's relations with teachers and peers, work habits, and feelings of competence. The items were selected from the 50-item Operation Headstart Behavior Inventory.[26] The scale consists of statements worded either positively or negatively and expressing either positive or negative attributes.

Each item is rated in an assumed positive direction on a 4-point scale from "very much like" to "not at all like." The items of the scale can be factor analyzed and factor scores computed for each child.

Results

The results of this study suggest that group day care does affect children's social and motivational development, but that the nature of the effect is nearly always interactive and complex. On none of the 11 dependent measures was care a significant main effect, but on seven measures it interacted significantly with one or more of the other factors, most commonly with SES. The care factor did not contribute significantly in any way to scores on the following four measures: PPVT-IQ, Pictorial Curiosity and two factors derived from the Teacher Rating Scale (Sociability and Self-Confidence).

The design of the study was a Sex $\times$ Age (5–6, 8–9) $\times$ Care (day care, home care) $\times$ SES (lower, middle) factorial design. Of the eleven dependent measures, six were taken from children's behavior in testing sessions and five were taken from teacher ratings. These two sets of variables were analyzed separately.

Since there were no systematic differences due to testers or schools, these factors were ignored in the analyses to be reported. The possible influence of race and number of parents was assessed by t-tests comparing Black and Caucasian lower-SES subjects and lower-SES subjects from single- and two-parent homes. No significant differences were found on measures affected by care.

Since the focus of the study was on the effects of type of care, only significant care findings are presented in detail. Results concerning the impact of SES, sex, and age are briefly summarized below (for complete results, see Reference 33).

Child Measures

The six child measures were analyzed by means of both univariate analyses of variance (ANOVA) and multivariate analyses of variance (MANOVA). The significant results of these analyses are presented in Table 7-1. The decision was made to interpret those significant univariate findings for which the MANOVA results were at least marginally significant ($p < .15$). This seemed reasonable given the low statistical power of the study (with 6–8 subjects per cell), the small magnitude of the significant correlations among the measures, and the possibility that these results could suggest areas of concern for future day care research.

Table 7-1 Summary of ANOVA Findings (for Which MANOVA Findings Were $p < .15$)

Effect	Child Variables (p values)						Teacher Variables (p values)				
	PPVT-IQ	Pref. for Challeng. Probs.	Pic. Cur.	Imit.	Response to Social Reinf.	Att.-Seek.	Factor 1	Factor 2	Factor 3	Read. Ach.	Arith. Ach.
Sex (S)	.002				.001			.01			
Age (A)		.003	.007	.045	.001						
Care (C)				(.08)							
SES (E)			.002	.003	.001		.003		.001	.001	.002
S × A											
S × C											
S × E			.003		.02						
A × C											
A × E									.01		
C × E		.03			.025					.03	.02
S × A × C											
S × A × E								.006			
S × C × E				.04		.03					
A × C × E					.004						
S × A × C × E											

NOTE: Blank spaces indicate that univariate results did not attain statistical significance.

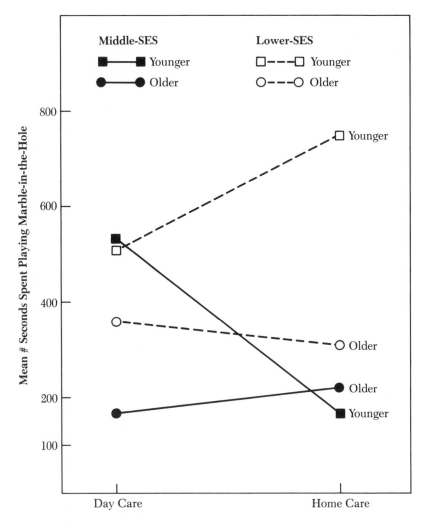

Figure 7-1   Age × Care × SES Interaction for Responsiveness to Social
Reinforcement Measure.

Responsiveness to social reinforcement.   Two significant interactions involving care were found, Care × SES, $F(1,105) = 5.24$, $p <$
.025, and Age × Care × SES, $F(1,105) = 9.03$, $p < .004$. The Age
× Care × SES interaction is shown in Figure 7-1. Although the overall Care × SES interaction reached significance, separate analyses of
each age group indicated that the interaction was significant only in
the case of the younger subjects, $F(1,54) = 11.44$, $p < .001$. Using
the Newman-Keuls method of comparing means, neither significant
care nor SES effects were found for older children, while both factors

significantly influenced younger children's behavior. Younger middle-SES children showed significantly greater ($p < .05$) responsiveness to social reinforcement if they had attended day care than if they had had home care ($\overline{X} = 534.04$, $SD = 350.12$ and $\overline{X} = 182.06$, $SD = 137.32$, respectively). The opposite effect was true for younger lower-SES children, with home care children displaying greater responsiveness than day care children ($\overline{X} = 762.50$, $SD = 474.34$ and $\overline{X} = 521.38$, $SD = 297.38$, respectively, a nonsignificant difference). Briefly, among younger children, day care was associated with an increase in the desire for social reinforcement from an unfamiliar adult for the middle-SES group, but with a decrease for the lower-SES group.

Imitation: Sticker Game. A significant second-order Sex × Care × SES interaction resulted, $F(1,105) = 4.33$, $p < .04$. Separate analyses of each SES group showed a Sex × Care interaction to be significant only in the lower-SES analysis, $F(1,55) = 3.9$, $p < .05$. Comparisons of means by the Newman-Keuls method indicated that the effect of care was significant ($p < .05$) only in the case of lower-SES girls, for whom day care was associated with higher levels of imitation than was home care ($\overline{X} = 8.28$, $SD = 4.54$ and $\overline{X} = 4.80$, $SD = 4.56$).

Attention-seeking. The analysis of verbal attention-seeking yielded a significant Sex × Care × SES interaction, $F(1,105) = 4.82$, $p < .03$. Newman-Keuls comparisons were nonsignificant. Day care was associated with slightly higher levels of attention-seeking for all groups except middle-SES girls. Among middle-SES girls, though, day care was associated with a much lower level of attention-seeking than was home care. Middle-SES home care girls were the most verbal of all subjects, but middle-SES day care girls were nearly the least verbal.

Preference for challenging problem. The analysis yielded a significant Care × SES interaction, $F(1,105) = 4.68$, $p < .03$. Greater preference for challenging problems was associated with home care for lower-SES children, but with day care for middle-SES children. Comparisons of the means by the Newman-Keuls method were nonsignificant, as were separate analyses of the main effect of care for each SES group.

Teacher Measures

Achievement ratings. Analyses of teacher ratings of subjects' achievement in both reading and arithmetic produced significant Care × SES interactions which reflected the superior ratings given middle-SES home care children (for reading, $F(1,105) = 4.77$, $p < .03$; and for arithmetic, $F(1,105) = 5.52$, $p < .02$). For both aca-

demic subjects middle-SES home care children were rated significantly higher than the other three groups which did not differ
significantly among themselves.

Factor analysis of teacher rating scale.   A principal components
factor analysis was performed on the scores of the scale's 31 items,
and the factors were submitted to an orthogonal varimax rotation.
Three factors, accounting for 59.6% of the variance, were interpreted. Factor 1 was the largest, accounting for 39.9% of the variance; followed by Factor 2, accounting for 12.3%; and Factor 3,
accounting for 7.4%. The factors are described below.

Factor 1: Sociability, talkativeness.   Items with high loadings on
this factor concern children's socializing with teachers and other
children. Children with high factor scores for Factor 1 would be
talkative, sociable children who ask many questions and especially
enjoy talking with adults.

Factor 2: Obedience and cooperativeness.   Items with high loadings on Factor 2 deal with children's ability to get along with their
teachers and peers. Children with high positive factor scores for
Factor 2 would give a teacher very little trouble in the classroom,
would be respectful of the rights of other children, and would be well
liked by their peers. On the other hand, children with low factor
scores would most likely be viewed by their teachers as demanding,
disobedient, quarrelsome, and jealous of attention paid to other
children.

Factor 3: Self-confidence.   Items with high loadings on Factor 3
concern children's ability to work independently, to show persever-
ance, and to show confidence in their own abilities and ideas. Children with low factor scores on Factor 3 would be timid, dependent
children who give up quickly when faced with difficult tasks.

As with the child measures, a MANOVA and univariate ANOVA's
were performed on the teacher measures, with the ANOVA results
interpreted when the MANOVA findings were $p < .15$. The results
of these analyses are summarized in Table 7-1.

No significant effects of care were found for Factors 1 and 3. However, significant interactions of care with other factors were found
on Factor 2. The analysis of Factor 2 scores yielded a significant
Sex × Age × Care interaction, $F(1,105) = 8.15$, $p < .006$. As can be
seen in Figure 7-2, and as was confirmed by separate analyses of each
sex group, the Age × Care interaction was significant only in the case
of boy subjects, $F(1,52) = 13.75$, $p < .001$. The care factor had no
impact on girls' ability to get along with teachers and peers, but it
did make a difference in the ability of boys. However, the day care/
home care difference was significant ($p < .01$, by the Newman-Keuls
method) only in the case of younger boys. Teachers regarded those

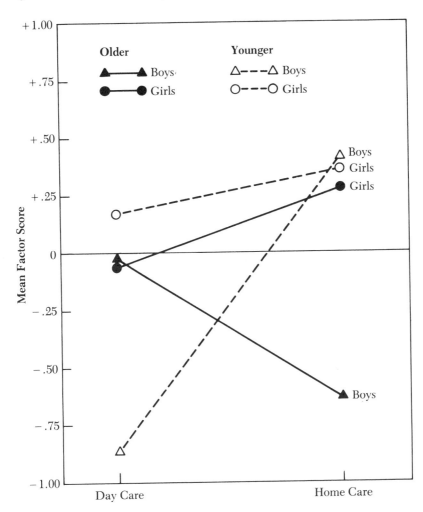

Figure 7-2 Sex × Age × Care Interaction for Factor 2 (Cooperativeness-Obedience Factor).

younger boys who had attended day care as significantly more troublesome in the classroom than their home care peers ($\overline{X} = -.85$, $SD = 1.04$ and $\overline{X} = +.42$, $SD = .55$, respectively).

SES, Sex, and Age Results

Significant findings involving the factors SES, sex, and age were generally consistent with previous studies of the impact of these variables on the dependent measures (see Table 7-1). SES was a main effect on five of the 11 dependent measures. Middle-SES children performed significantly better than lower-SES children on the cognitive measures (PPVT-IQ and Reading and Arithmetic Achievement Ratings) as well as on measures tapping social and motivational characteristics. Specifically, middle-SES subjects imitated less than lower-SES subjects on the Sticker Game imitation task and were rated as more sociable and talkative by their teachers (Factor 1).

Significant main effects of SES were also found on the Pictorial Curiosity task, Marble-in-the-Hole, and the self-confidence factor of the Teacher Rating Scale. However, first-order interactions with SES were also significant for each of these measures, with the SES effect appearing within only one sex or age group. On the Pictorial Curiosity measure, SES did not affect the performance of boys, but middle-SES girls showed significantly greater interest in seeing novel pictures than did lower-SES girls. On Marble-in-the-Hole, lower-SES boys were much more responsive to the social reinforcement than middle-SES boys, while the SES effect was small and nonsignificant for the girls. On the self-confidence factor of the Teacher Rating Scale, middle-SES subjects were rated as significantly more at ease and more confident in the predominantly middle-class world of teachers and school. This SES difference was most pronounced among the younger subjects.

Sex was a main effect on only two measures, Marble-in-the-Hole and the cooperativeness-obedience factor (Factor 2). (Interactions of the sex factor with SES and care have already been reported.) Boys showed more responsiveness to social reinforcement by playing Marble-in-the-Hole for longer periods of time. Teachers rated girls as significantly more cooperative and obedient than boys.

Significant main effects of age were found on both measures of effectance motivation. Older children demonstrated greater effectance motivation by choosing to see a greater number of novel pictures on the Pictorial Curiosity task and by choosing to complete more difficult puzzles on the Preference for Challenging Problems measure. Consistent with previous findings, the older children also imitated less than the younger children and played Marble-in-the-Hole for shorter periods of time.

Discussion

The results of this study indicate that type of preschool care, interacting with other factors, significantly influenced children's behavior in three ways: (1) it influenced children's responsiveness to adults as measured by responsiveness to social reinforcement, imitation, and attention-seeking, with the specific effect depending on SES and sex;

(2) it influenced the cooperativeness and obedience of boys in school, but not of girls, and (3) it affected the academic achievement ratings given middle-SES subjects, but not lower-SES. Each of these three effects will be discussed separately.

1. Responsiveness to Adults

Type of care influenced children's responsiveness to nonfamilial adults as measured by responsiveness to social reinforcement, imitation, and attention-seeking. This finding is consistent with those of other researchers who found that type of care affected interactions with nonfamilial adults even when it did not affect children's interactions with their mothers.[6,12,25,31]

A significant Age × Care × SES interaction was found on the responsiveness to social reinforcement measure, and significant Sex × Care × SES interactions were found on the measures of imitation and attention-seeking.

On the measure of responsiveness to social reinforcement, a Care × SES interaction was significant only among the younger subjects. Type of care had almost no effect on the responsiveness of older children (among whom it was uniformly low), most probably because Marble-in-the-Hole is particularly suited to younger children. Among the younger children, day care increased the responsiveness of middle-SES children, but reduced the responsiveness of lower-SES children.

Increased responsiveness to social reinforcement has most often been interpreted as reflecting some degree of social deprivation.[3,19,40,45] Within this formulation, day care is more socially depriving than home care for middle-SES children, but home care is more socially depriving than day care for lower-SES children. The deprivation involved in day care is most likely that of one-to-one contact with adults.

Since nearly all the children in this study did not begin day care until age three, the degree to which they experienced day care as socially depriving would depend upon how it contrasted with the amount of adult attention they had been used to receiving at home. For this reason, these results might not be generalizable to children who began attending day care in early infancy. Middle-SES children in this study may well have experienced day care as socially depriving since it probably provided them with much less one-to-one, individualized, adult attention than home care did. On the other hand, a good day care center may have provided lower-SES children with more predictable and supportive adult attention than their families were able to, families which in many cases had single parents and several children, and which in all cases were struggling with the multiple problems of poverty. A similar interaction is reported by Zigler, Butterfield, and Capobianco,[44] who used Marble-in-the-Hole in a study of institutionalized retarded children. They found that the experience of institutionalization was more socially depriving for children from relatively good homes than from relatively poor homes.

Type of care also affected whether children chose to imitate the behavior of an adult model (the tester) or not. A significant Sex × Care × SES interaction on the Sticker Game imitation task reflected a Sex × Care interaction among only the lower-SES subjects. Since the Sticker Game is an easy task for school-aged children, higher imitation scores in this case should be interpreted as indicating greater outerdirectedness and reduced self-confidence. Day care substantially and significantly increased lower-SES girls' imitation, but slightly and nonsignificantly decreased lower-SES boys'. The children who imitated most of all were lower-SES day care girls and lower-SES home care boys. It may be that a lower-SES home environment is more supportive of girls' developing autonomy and self-confidence than of boys'. Consistent with this possibility are the research findings which suggest that boys suffer greater social deprivation than girls in economically disadvantaged families.[37,41] The decrease in lower-SES day care boys' imitation scores may reflect the benefit that they in particular may have received from day care.

On the verbal attention-seeking measure, day care was associated with slightly increased verbal interaction for all Sex × SES groups except middle-SES girls. Middle-SES girls were moderately talkative if they had had home care, but were very quiet if they had attended day care. Moore's findings[23] suggest an interpretation of this result. He found that home care girls showed closer identification with their mothers than substitute care girls. It may be that the middle-SES home care girls in this study were especially talkative because they also identified more closely with the middle-SES female experimenters. This does not, however, explain the low level of verbal interaction among middle-SES day care girls.

2. Cooperativeness and Obedience

Several previous studies[22,32,36] have reported an association between group care and increased negative behavior towards adults and peers. In this study, however, such an association was found only with regard to boys. A significant Sex × Care × Age interaction was found on the cooperativeness-obedience factor (Factor 2) of the Teacher Rating Scale. Among the boys, the effect of type of care was dependent on their ages. Older day care boys were rated as slightly and nonsignificantly less troublesome in school than older home care boys, but younger day care boys were rated as substantially and significantly more troublesome than younger boys reared at home. While this opposite effect of care for the two age groups of boys may indicate a reversal of effect at the older ages, a more likely interpretation is that the nonsignificant day care/home care effect among the older boys is due to the items of the Teacher Rating Scale discriminating best among behaviors most typical of younger children.

The findings for the younger boys are consistent with those reported by Moore.[24] In his longitudinal study of children who were either "exclusively mothered" or had had some form of daily substitute care in the first five years, he found that the two groups of boys became increasingly dissimilar. Substitute care boys were less concerned with adult approval and became increasingly active, aggressive, independent, and relatively fearless. The younger day care boys in this study were described by their teachers in some of the following ways: "shows little respect for the rights of other children"; "is quarrelsome, disobedient, and excessive in seeking teacher's attention." The younger home care boys, though, were rated as highly cooperative and obedient (as highly as the home care girls).

It is worth noting that the sexes were differentially affected by type of care on a measure of what might generally be called "aggressive behavior." Maccoby and Jacklin,[23] in their extensive review of the psychological literature pertaining to sex differences, conclude that one of the four sex differences they believe is fairly well established (and the only noncognitive one) is that males are more aggressive than females. If this is so, then boys, but not girls, must learn to inhibit their aggressive tendencies in order to learn to behave appropriately in school. Psychoanalytic theory suggests that children learn to inhibit aggressive tendencies by identifying with and hoping to please a loved parent. If day care dilutes the intensity of children's identifications with their parents, then the motivation for boys to inhibit their aggressive feelings and actions might be considerably reduced.

Another possible explanation of this Care × Sex interaction is that boys' naturally more aggressive behavior is reinforced in group care settings by the attention it receives from other children.[28,5] Additional research will be necessary to determine if either of these interpretations is accurate regarding Care × Sex interactions on measures of aggressive behavior. However, these findings do underline the importance of considering sex differences in future day care studies.

3. Achievement Ratings

Type of care did not affect PPVT-IQ scores, but significant Care × SES interactions were found on teacher ratings of Reading and Arithmetic Achievement. Middle-SES home care subjects were given higher ratings than middle-SES day care subjects, while type of care did not influence the ratings given lower-SES subjects. Other investigators[18,24,35] have likewise found no effects of care on measures of intelligence, but Moore[24] found that his "exclusively mothered" subjects scored higher on achievement measures than his substitute care subjects.

Why are the achievement ratings of middle-SES home care subjects higher than those of middle-SES day care subjects? Moore would argue that the superior achievement of the home care children was at least partially due to their greater identification with adult standards and parental expectations. Prescott[30] and Cochran,[10] though, investigated differences in the social environments of day care and home care, and both concluded that the experience and interactions with adults provided by home care were generally more cognitively stimulating than those provided by day care centers. It should be remembered, though, that the achievement measure used in this study was a 4-point teacher rating scale. More conclusive evidence concerning the effects of day care on school children's academic achievement might be provided by including standardized tests in future day care studies.

While in this study day care appears to have influenced children's behavior, it must be pointed out that because the subjects were neither randomly assigned to care conditions nor assessed and equated prior to day care attendance, the effects observed cannot be attributed for certain to the experience of day care. Since one group of parents chose to care for their children at home and the other group chose to send their children to day care centers, it is possible that these two groups of families also differed in potentially influential ways such as the parents' personalities and their child-rearing styles and methods. This qualification also applies to most other day care research.

Another aspect of the study to consider is the confounding of race and type of care among the lower-SES subjects. Middle-SES day care and home care subjects appeared highly comparable demographically. However, in the lower-SES group, 97% of the day care subjects were Black, compared to only 35% of the home care subjects. Although analyses of race effects within the lower-SES group yielded no significant differences on measures affected by type of care, the confounding may still be a reason for interpreting the day care/home care effects within the lower-SES group more cautiously than those within the middle-SES group.

The findings of this study underscore a number of issues to be considered in future research on day care: (1) The importance of investigating day care's impact on behaviors other than those related to attachment, (2) the need to consider children's SES and sex in making predictions about the impact of day care, and (3) the need to include subjects of older than day care age. While the study examined the impact of day care irrespective of the differences among the individual day care centers involved, research is also needed regarding the influence of specific differences among centers (such as adult-child ratios, staff-turnover ratios, and curricula) and among day care arrangements (such as half- or full-time, small or large group, family or center setting).

References

1. Achenbach, T. and Zigler, E. 1968. "Cue-learning and problem-learning strategies in normal and retarded children." *Child Development* 39: 827–848.
2. Ainsworth, M.D.S. and Wittig, B.A. 1969. "Attachment and exploratory behavior of one-year-olds in a strange situation." In B.M. Foss (ed.), *Determinants of infant behaviour.* Vol. 4. Methuen, London.
3. Balla, D. and Zigler, E. 1975. "Preinstitutional social deprivation, responsiveness to social reinforcement, and IQ change in institutionalized retarded individuals." *American Journal of Mental Deficiency* 80:228–230.
4. Belsky, J. and Steinberg, L. 1978. "The effects of day care: a critical review." *Child Development* 49:929–949.
5. Berndt, T.J. April 1978. Personal communication.
6. Blehar, M.C. 1974. "Anxious attachment and defensive reactions associated with day care." *Child Development* 45:683–692.
7. Bronfenbrenner, U. 1975. "Research on the effects of day care." Unpublished manuscript, Cornell University.
8. Butterfield, E.C. and Zigler, E. 1965. "The influence of differing institutional social climates on the effectiveness of social reinforcement in the mentally retarded." *American Journal of Mental Deficiency* 70:48–56.
9. Caldwell, B.M., Wright, C.M., Honig, A.S. and Tannenbaum, J. 1970. "Infant day care and attachment." *American Journal of Orthopsychiatry* 40: 397–412.
10. Cochran, M.M. 1977. "A comparison of group day care and family childrearing patterns in Sweden." *Child Development* 48:702–707.
11. Cornelius, S. and Denney, N. 1975. "Dependency in day care and home care children." *Developmental Psychology* 11:575–582.
12. Doyle, A. 1975. "Infant development in day care." *Developmental Psychology* 11:541–545.
13. Farran, D.C. and Ramey, C.T. 1977. "Infant day care and attachment behaviors toward mothers and teachers." *Child Development* 48:1112–1116.
14. Feldman, S. "The impact of day care on one aspect of children's social-emotional behavior." Paper presented at meeting of American Association for the Advancement of Science, San Francisco, February, 1974.
15. Gewirtz, J. and Baer, D.M. 1958. "The effects of brief social deprivation on

behaviors for a social reinforcer." *Journal of Abnormal and Social Psychology* 56:49–56.

16. Gewirtz, J. and Baer, D.M. 1958. "Deprivation and satiation of social reinforcers as drive conditions." *Journal of Abnormal and Social Psychology* 57:165–172.

17. Harter, S. and Zigler, E. 1974. "The assessment of effectance motivation in normal and retarded children." *Developmental Psychology* 10:169–180.

18. Hollingshead, A.B. 1957. "Two-factor index of social position." Box 1965 Yale Station, Yale University, New Haven, Connecticut.

19. Irons, N.M. and Zigler, E. 1969. "Children's responsiveness to social reinforcement as a function of short-term preliminary social interaction and long-term social deprivation." *Developmental Psychology* 1:402–409.

20. Kagan, J., Kearsley, R. and Zelazo, P. 1978. *Infancy: Its place in human development.* Harvard University Press, Cambridge, Mass.

21. Kohlberg, L. and Zigler, E. 1967. "The impact of cognitive maturity on the development of sex-role attitudes in the years 4 to 8." *Genetic Psychology Monographs* 75:89–165.

22. Lippman, M. and Grote, B.H. 1974. *Social-emotional effects of day care: Final project report.* Office of Child Development, Washington, D.C.

23. Maccoby, E. and Jacklin, C. 1974. *The psychology of sex differences.* Stanford University Press, Stanford, Calif.

24. Moore, T.W. 1975. "Exclusive early mothering and its alternatives: The outcome to adolescence." *Scandinavian Journal of Psychology* 16:225–272.

25. Moskowitz, D.S., Schwarz, J.C. and Corsini, D.A. 1977. "Initiating day care at three years of age: Effects on attachment." *Child Development* 48:1271–1276.

26. *Operation Headstart Behavior Inventory.* 1966. Yale University.

27. Parton, D.A. and Ross, A.O. 1965. "Social reinforcement of children's motor behavior: A review." *Psychological Bulletin* 64:65–73.

28. Patterson, G.R., Littman, R.A. and Bricker, W. 1967. "Assertive behavior in children. A step toward a theory of aggression." *Monographs of the Society for Research in Child Development* 32(5), (serial no. 113), 1–43.

29. Portnoy, F.C. and Simmons, C.H. 1978. "Day care and attachment." *Child Development* 49:239–242.

30. Prescott, E.A. 1973. "A comparison of three types of day care and nursery school-home care." Paper presented at the meeting of the Society for Research in Child Development, Philadelphia.

31. Ragozin, A.S. 1980. "Attachment behavior of day-care children: naturalistic and laboratory observations." *Child Development* 51:409–415.

32. Raph, J.B., Thomas, A., Chess, S. and Korn, S.J. 1968. "The influence of nursery school on social interactions." *American Journal of Orthopsychiatry* 38:144–152.

33. Robertson, A. 1979. "Day care and children's responsiveness to adults." (Doctoral dissertation, Yale University, 1978). *Dissertation Abstracts International* 40:476B–477B. (University Microfilms No. 7916480)

34. Rutter, M. 1981. "Social-emotional consequences of day care for preschool children." *American Journal of Orthopsychiatry* 51:4–28.

35. Schwarz, J.C., Krolick, G. and Strickland, R.G. 1973. "Effects of early day

day experience on adjustment to a new environment." *American Journal of Orthopsychiatry* 43:340–346.

36. Schwarz, J.C., Strickland, R. and Krolick, R.G. 1974. "Infant day care: Behavioral effects at preschool age." *Developmental Psychology* 10:502–506.

37. Silverstein, B. and Krate, R. 1975. *Children of the dark ghetto.* Praeger, New York.

38. Turnure, J. and Zigler, E. 1964. "Outerdirectedness in the problem-solving of normal and retarded children." *Journal of Abnormal and Social Psychology* 69:427–436.

39. Unruh, S.G., Grosse, M.G. and Zigler, E. 1971. "Birth order, number of siblings, and social reinforcer effectiveness in children." *Child Development* 42:1153–1163.

40. Zigler, E. 1961. "Social deprivation and rigidity in the performance of feebleminded children." *Journal of Abnormal and Social Psychology* 62:413–421.

41. Zigler, E. and Abelson, W. 1976. "Is an intervention program necessary in order to improve economically disadvantaged children's IQ scores?" Unpublished manuscript, Yale University.

42. Zigler, E., Abelson, W.D. and Seitz, V. 1973. "Motivational factors in the performance of economically disadvantaged children on the Peabody Picture Vocabulary Test." *Child Development* 44:294–303.

43. Zigler, E. and Balla, D. 1972. "The developmental course of responsiveness to social reinforcement in normal children and institutionalized retarded children." *Developmental Psychology* 6:66–73.

44. Zigler, E., Butterfield, E.C. and Capobianco, F. 1970. "Institutionalization and the effectiveness of social reinforcement: A five- and eight-year follow-up study." *Developmental Psychology* 3:225–263.

45. Zigler, E. and Williams, J. 1963. "Institutionalization and the effectiveness of social reinforcement: A three-year follow-up study." *Journal of Abnormal and Social Psychology* 66:197–205.

Chapter 8

PARENTS AND DAY CARE WORKERS: A FAILED PARTNERSHIP?

by Edward F. Zigler and Pauline Turner

During the past two decades, we have witnessed a marked change in the nature of America's families.[4] The primary precipitant of this change is the ever-growing number of mothers in the work force. Today, over 50% of mothers work outside the home; this figure is expected to rise to 75% by the end of this decade. While parents, both of whom are wage-earners, continue to raise their children, they almost invariably do so with the assistance of a variety of day care arrangements. Children as young as a few weeks of age are now being routinely placed into day care settings. While the practice of infant day care has been the subject of debate,[22] this practice may only be a symptom of a more serious problem in our society's current rearing of its young. Given the contemporary social scene, we must entertain the possibility that we are witnessing a general weakening of the attachment bond between parents and their children. Just how are children viewed by the cohort of parents commonly referred to as the "me-generation"? The self-centeredness, self-actualization, and narcissism of the adult members of our society have been noted frequently by astute observers of the current social scene.[11,3,15] Evidence that the most basic relations between parents and children are undergoing a marked change was presented in a recent large national survey.[21] In addition to families labeled as "traditional," Yankelovich

The authors would like to thank Winnie Berman for her help on this chapter.

174

described a large number of families which he labeled "the new breed." The attitude of these new breed parents toward their children can be summarized by the statement that "parents owe their children nothing and in turn children owe their parents nothing." Yankelovich's distinction between traditional and new breed families is reminiscent of Novak's distinction between "family people" and "individual people."[15] Further evidence that there has been a marked weakening in the bond between parents and children can be seen in the current epidemic of child abuse in our society, in which the number of reported cases each year now numbers over one million.[9] The most striking indicator of what may be a declining parental attachment toward children is the growing number of parents who decide either to have no children or to have but a single child.

However one views the nature of the bond between parents and children, the realities are that women *will* continue to work outside the home in ever-growing numbers and that children in our society will be socialized by some combination of efforts by parents and nonparental child caretakers in our nation's informal day care system. In the face of these realities our society's child-development experts have developed a conventional wisdom which asserts that it is in the interest of the child for parents and nonparental caretakers to form a close relation so that a true partnership will develop in the rearing of the child.[8,13,24] A corollary of this assertion is that any sociopsychological discontinuities that are created between home and day care center operate to the detriment of the child. There does appear to be some disagreement as to the importance of the sheer amount of time that parents spend with their children. A frequently heard current phrase is that it is not the amount of time spent with children by parents that is important but rather the quality of these interactions. In opposition to such a view Robert Coles has forcefully argued that some minimum amount of time must be spent by parents with their children if normal child-parent attachment is to develop with resulting optimal development of the child.[7]

However the quantity versus quality argument is resolved, some evidence exists[1,10,12,24] that the more parents are involved in the activities of the child care center and are more involved in the shaping of their children's lives, the more children benefit from such involvement. Thus both the conventional wisdom of experts and empirical evidence converge in generating the conclusion that it is in the child's interest for parents and nonparental child caretakers to form a close and synergistic relationship. Child care centers, of course, vary in the degree to which they welcome parental involvement. The reactions to the parental involvement policy of even a program heavily committed to parental involvement, such as Head Start, make clear that in many

Table 8-1

| AGE | N | GENDER | | ETHNIC GROUP | | | |
		Male	Female	Anglo	Black	Mexican-American	Other
under 1	8	4	4	5	0	1	2
1–3	19	9	10	11	5	2	1
4–5	23	12	11	10	8	4	1

child care centers parental involvement continues to be viewed as parental intrusion.

The central question addressed in the present study is how much time is spent by parents in a day care center that is heavily committed to the principle of parental involvement, and thus one extremely hospitable to the parents' presence. The authors were particularly interested in whether or not the conventional wisdom of experts concerning a partnership between parents and nonparental child caretakers has filtered down to parents to a sufficient degree to impact such a fundamental behavior as the sheer amount of time parents spend in the day care center where their children are housed for a large segment of their daily lives. It is clear that a variety of factors (e.g., the demands and conditions of the parents' jobs) in addition to the parents' concern for their children influence the amount of time parents spend in their children's day care center. The second goal of the present study, therefore, was to conduct an exploratory investigation of how a variety of often-used demographic variables (e.g., family income) influence the amount of time parents spend in a day care center.

Method

Families Investigated

Central to this study was a heterogeneous group of 50 children, 25 girls and 25 boys enrolled in a laboratory day care program at a southwestern university and their parents. The children ranged in age from six weeks to five years and represented ethnic groups including Anglo, Black, Mexican-American, and mixed. The age and ethnic distributions of the 50 children are presented in Table 8-1.

Both two-parent and single-parent families were represented in the study. Parents' employment status included unemployed, manual workers, and professional employees; gross monthly income ranged from $80 to $2500, with a mean of $518. The tuition of 38 of the children—16 whose parents were students and 22 whose parents were unemployed or received sufficiently low incomes—was covered by Title XX funds.

The Day Care Center

The day care center was a university setting open every week-day from 7:30 a.m. to 5:30 p.m. The primary staff consisted of one director, one parent educator, five teachers (all of whom had degrees in child-related fields), and five paraprofessional teacher aides. The center was one which strongly encouraged, but did not require, parent participation, visitation, and observation. There was a consistent "open door" policy. In addition, the center offered monthly evening meetings for parents on a variety of topics of interest, and teachers were available after hours for conferences.

Demographic Variables and Their Categorization

Gender: boys or girls.

Ethnic group membership: see Table 8-1.

Age of child: see Table 8-1.

Family size: total number of family members, including mother and father.

Marital status of parents: married (legal or common-law, $N = 28$); separated ($N = 21$); divorced ($N = 14$); other (father unknown, $N = 6$).

Gross monthly income: absolute amount.

Employment status: full-time (mothers, $N = 26$; fathers, $N = 23$); part-time (mothers, $N = 10$; fathers, $N = 3$); unemployed (mothers, $N = 14$; fathers, $N = 14$).

Nonworking students ($N = 13$) were classified as part-time and working students ($N = 8$) were classified as full-time.

Both mothers' and fathers' employment statuses were analyzed.

Length of time target child enrolled in the program: Range $= 2$–24 months. Mean $= 10.5$ months.

Procedure

For a period of 70 consecutive days the total amount of time that each parent (of the 50 target children) was present in the day care center was recorded. Time recorded included time parents spent when dropping off or picking up their children, in conferences with center staff, in observation of their children, and in participation in group meetings. Analyses of time scores were based on the total amount of time spent by parents over the course of the study.

Results

Absolute Amount of Time Spent

The average amount of time that the parents spent in the day care center in all types of involvement was 7.4 minutes per day. There was a tendency for parents to spend somewhat more time when picking up their children in the afternoon than when leaving them in the morning. The distribution of time scores was extremely skewed. One mother (of a nursing infant) spent from 25 minutes to one hour at lunch time with her child on more than half of the 70 days examined. At the other end of the distribution, approximately 10% of the parents did not even enter the center with their children in the morning, even though an unenforced regulation stipulated that a parent must remain until his child received a health check. Another approximately 10% of the children were typically brought to the center by someone other than a family member. On only three occasions did any parent have a conference with a teacher that lasted longer than 10 minutes. On the more positive side, approximately half of the parents spent at least one hour on one or more occasions observing their child and his activities at the center, with such observations being noticeably more common for younger children (infants and toddlers) than for older children. Further, 40% of the parents of infants and toddlers "dropped in" during the day on one or more occasions to visit and/ or play with their child, while only 8% of parents of older children did so.

Of the total amount of time spent, 86% was by mothers, 6% by fathers, and 8% by someone other than a parent (relative or friend). The mean amount of time spent at the center by nonworking students was greater than that for all other parents taken together ($\overline{X} =$ 584.48 minutes vs. 480.6 minutes respectively, $t[48] = 4.47$, $p <$ .001). No significant differences in mean time spent at the center were found for students receiving Title XX funds as compared with nonstudents receiving Title XX funds and with all other parents. Analyses between mean times spent by nonworking students, other nonworking parents, and working parents also failed to show significant differences.

Regression Analysis

The demographic variables were entered into a stepwise regression.[5] Three variables were found to be significantly (all p's $< .05$) related to the time scores. In the order of the amount of variance they predicted the variables were family size, age of child, and income level. Taken together these three variables accounted for only 16% of the total variance of the time scores. It thus appears that variation in time scores was due primarily to variables other than those examined in the present study.

In regard to directionality, the findings of the present study indicated that the amount of time spent in the day care center goes up (1) the smaller the family, (2) the younger the child, and (3) the lower the income.

Discussion

The significance of the present study lay as much in what was not found as in the few significant relations disclosed. While there has been a suggestion[15,16] that familial ties vary with ethnicity, across the ethnic groups examined in this study no relation was found between ethnic membership and amount of time spent in the day care center. The findings are consistent with the conclusion of Yando, Seitz, and Zigler[20] that ethnicity *per se* is a relatively weak predictor of human behavior. Analogously, neither the parents' marital status nor the length of time the children had been in day care was found to be related to the time measure. Thus the present study provides no replication of Powell's[17] findings that marital status and length of day care usage were related to degree of parental involvement.

Champions of the view that parents and nonparental child caretakers should work closely together cannot help but be discouraged by the miniscule amount of participation in the day care center found in this study. The conclusion cannot be escaped that the parents involved in this very hospitable day care center chose to spend an extremely limited amount of time there. This finding of a very small investment of time in the children's day care center is quite consistent with earlier findings.[2,17] These consistent findings underline the validity of a conclusion of *The National Child Care Consumer Study*[14] that child caregivers see a real need for parents to show more interest in how their children are faring in their daily activities in the centers.

As to the variation in this time measure, it is not particularly surprising to discover that time spent in the day care center goes up as the number of children for which the parent is responsible goes down. This finding thus supports the commonsensical view that any parent has a finite store of warmth, concern, and time that must be allocated among the children for whom that parent is responsible. The finding of greater participation with fewer children does cause the authors to call into question those who deplore the tendency in our society for families to have an ever-decreasing number of children. If smaller families result in more care and concern for each child, then children should benefit from such a state of affairs. Unfortunately, we do not yet know whether smaller family size in our society has in fact been accompanied by greater concern and involvement of parents with their children. The issue is an empirical one and, given the striking changes in this demographic of family life, an issue extremely worthy of investigation in its own right. The findings that parents spend more time in the day care center if their children are under three is also not particularly surprising if one assumes that parents believe that infants and toddlers are more in need of parental concern and attention than are four- and five-year olds. Such a view can be found in the work of one of our authorities,[19] who has expended a considerable amount of energy in attempting to convince laymen that the first three years of life represents a particularly critical period of development. Arrayed against such a view is the position of equally eminent authorities[5] that developmentalists have overemphasized the psychological significance of the early years (also see Kagan on this point). The authors shall continue to support the view that all periods in development, from conception through adolescence, are critical periods in which the child requires the care and attention of loving adults as well as other environmental nutrients in order to ensure optimal development.[23] With regard to the ages examined in this study, it would certainly be a sad commentary if, as appears, children as young as four or five are not capable of extracting from their parents the same amount of concern and involvement that is found for younger children. The finding that nonworking students spend more time at the day care center than do all other parents, however, suggests that parents' actual concern may not be the only issue involved here. Rather, parents may be prevented from manifesting their concern for their children by factors such as work demands. Perhaps if other parents had as much time available as do students, they too would spend more time at their children's day care centers.

The finding of a negative relation between income and time spent at the center is surprising. One interpretation of this finding might be that parents who qualified for day care services under Title XX guidelines, and therefore did not pay for the care their children received, spent longer at the center, perhaps because they felt more obliged to participate in the program than those parents who paid for the service. This explanation, however, was not supported by the data, which failed to show a significant difference in time spent between Title XX parents and other parents. Two types of families proved to be income-eligible under Title XX: young adults who were students and thus in a close proximity to the center; and older parents who, though not students, also had relatively low income. Since Title XX students spent somewhat more time at the center than did other Title XX parents, it may again be that the difference in time available to working parents and to those who are students contributed to the time spent by each at the center. That being poor *per se* doesn't guarantee participation in a child care center is indicated in a study by Bauch et al.[2] which found minimal visitation by parents in free Head Start programs.

A final caveat is in order. The variables found to be related to the amount of visitation accounted for but a small portion of the variation in the time scores. The bulk of the variation remains unaccounted for, and explaining this variation would appear to be an inviting area of research for those interested in the issue of just how the parent-nonparental child caretaker partnership concept is faring.

References

1. Auerbach, A. 1975. "Parent's role in day care." *Child Care Quarterly* 4(3), Fall: 180–187.
2. Bauch, J., Vietze, P. and Morris, V. 1973. "What makes the difference in parent participation?" *Childhood Education*, October: 47–52.
3. Bronfenbrenner, U. 1967. "The split-level American family." *Saturday Review*, October: 60–63.
4. Calhoun, J., Grotberg, E. and Rackley, W. Ray. 1980. *The status of children, youth and families 1979*. U.S. Department of Health & Human Services, August.
5. Clarke, A.M. and Clarke, A.D.B. 1976. *Early Experience: Myth and Evidence*. Open Books, London.
6. Cohen, S. and Cohen, P. 1975. *Applied Multiple Regressive/Correlation Analysis for the Behavioral Sciences*. Lawrence Erlbaum Associates, Publishers, Hillsdale, N.J.
7. Coles, R. 1980. Paper presented to League of Women Voters Conference.
8. Deutsch, M. 1964. "Facilitating development in the preschool child: social and psychological perspectives." *Merrill-Palmer Quarterly* 10:249–263.
9. Gerbner, G., Ross, C. and Zigler, E., eds. 1980. *Child Abuse: An Agenda for Action*. Oxford University Press, New York.
10. Gray, S. and Klaus, R. 1970. "The early training project: a seventh year report." *Child Development* 4:909–924.
11. Lasch, C. 1979. *Culture of Narcissism: American Life in an Age of Diminishing Expectations*. Norton, New York.
12. Levenstein, P. 1971. *Verbal interaction project: aiding cognitive growth in disadvantaged mother-child home program*. Final report. Family Service Association of Nassau County, Inc., February.
13. Lippitt, R. 1968. "Improving the socialization process." In *Socialization and Society*, J.A. Clausen, ed. Little, Brown & Co. Boston, 321–374.
14. National Child Care Consumer Study. 1978. U.S. Department of Health, Education and Welfare, Office of Human Development, Office of Child Development, Head Start Bureau.
15. Novak, M. 1976. "The family out of favor." *Harper's Magazine*, April: 37–46.

16. Novak, M. 1972. *The Rise of the Unmeltable Ethnics.* Macmillan, New York.
17. Powell, D. 1977. "The coordination of preschool socialization: parent caregiver relationships in day care settings." Presented to the Society for Research in Child Development, New Orleans, La, March.
18. U.S. Department of Labor. 1976. *Handbook of labor statistics.* Bureau of Labor Statistics, Washington, D.C.
19. White, B. 1975. *The First Three Years of Life.* Prentice-Hall, Englewood Cliffs, N.J.
20. Yando, R., Seitz, V. and Zigler, E. 1979. *Intellectual and Personality Characteristics of Children: Social-Class and Ethnic-Group Differences.* Lawrence Erlbaum Associates, Hillsdale, N.J.
21. Yankelovich, D. 1977. "Raising children in a changing society." *The General Mills American Family Report 1976–1977.* General Mills, Minneapolis.
22. Zigler, E. and Finn, M. 1981. "A vision of childcare in the 1980s." In *Facilitating Infant and Early Child Development,* L.A. Bond and J.M. Jaffe, eds. University Press of New England, Hanover, N.H.
23. Zigler, E. and Seitz, V. In press. "Social policy implications of research on intelligence." In *Handbook of Human Intelligence,* R. Sternberg, ed. Cambridge University Press, New York.
24. Zigler, E. and Valentine, J. 1979. *Project Head Start: A Legacy of the War on Poverty.* The Free Press, New York.

Chapter 9

THE YALE CHILD WELFARE
RESEARCH PROGRAM:
DESCRIPTION AND RESULTS

by Leslie A. Rescorla, Sally Provence, and Audrey Naylor

This chapter presents some of the results of a comprehensive intervention project for low-income families and their children: the Yale
Child Welfare Research Program, carried out at the Yale Child Study
Center from 1967 to 1972. The project has been described in detail
in *The Challenge of Day Care*, by Provence, Naylor, and Patterson.[14]
The data reported here were collected during the intervention program, as well as five years after the project ended when the families
were seen for follow-up.

There were a large number of comprehensive intervention projects
undertaken in the late sixties to help disadvantaged families and
children.[1,5,6,8,9,10,11,12,13,15,16,17,18] Some of these were center-based
programs, others were home-based, and still others combined home-
based and center-based components. Projects varied widely in philosophical orientation, from Montessori to Piaget, from Bank Street

The Yale Child Welfare Research Program received its financial support from
the United States Children's Bureau, Office of Child Development, Department
of Health, Education and Welfare (#PR900). A grant from the Ford Foundation, New York, supported the work on data organization and analysis. Sally
Provence, M.D. and Audrey Naylor, M.S.W., served as project director and
assistant project director. Data analysis and reporting were performed by Leslie
Rescorla, Ph.D., recruited several years after the project ended.

The authors wish to thank the many dedicated people who served as staff
members for the Yale Child Welfare Research Program and the children and
parents who shared their lives with us.

to Bereiter-Engelmann. Many studies used random assignment to experimental and control conditions, but others used matched comparison group designs, with sample size varying widely. In some studies, blind evaluation of experimental and control children was done, but in other projects this was not feasible. Duration of the intervention program and age of the children participating also differed across projects. Project staff varied from professionals such as teachers, social workers, and psychologists to paraprofessionals drawn from the community. In sum, there were a large number of projects varying in research design, methodological adequacy, intervention philosophy, and program style. The common denominator of these projects was the hope and assumption that intervening early in the lives of disadvantaged children would help them make a more successful adjustment to school and hence to later adult life.

The effectiveness of early intervention programs has long been a controversial research issue. Initial evaluations, such as the Westinghouse/Ohio University report,[20] concluded that preschool intervention did not yield lasting gains in intellectual development. In his review of a large number of projects, Bronfenbrenner[2] concluded that projects which involved parents were more effective than center-based programs and that the best period for intervention was in the first three years of life.

Recent studies have provided empirical support for optimism regarding early intervention. The Consortium for Longitudinal Studies has reported long-term follow-up data from eight major preschool projects, indicating that intervention children were retained in grade or placed in special education significantly less often than control children throughout their school years.[4] Weikart[17] has recently reported a long-term follow-up of the Perry Preschool Program, which also showed a highly significant effect of intervention on later school adjustment and performance.

A recurrent dissatisfaction in the early intervention field has been the reliance on IQ as the main index of program effectiveness. While the majority of early intervention programs showed significant IQ gains relative to the performance of control children, most studies have reported a fading out of IQ gains as the children advance through grade school.[2,4] In recent years, there has been widespread advocacy of better and more meaningful criteria to assess intervention programs. For example, Zigler and Trickett have proposed gains in social competence as a more appropriate index of program effectiveness.[21]

Much early intervention research concentrated on children, both in terms of the services provided and the outcomes measured. However, it has become increasingly clear in recent years that intervention programs can have a profound effect on parents as well. Some intervention projects have reported positive changes in mothers, such as educational and occupational advancement or increased vocational aspirations for their children.[4,6,8,10] It is becoming increasingly acknowledged that interventions are successful to the degree that they make a significant impact on families' aspirations, expectations, lifestyle, and modes of interaction.[15] Recently, Gray and Wandersman[7] have stressed the value of home-based intervention because of its capacity to adapt to the needs and strengths of individual families and to create meaningful changes in parent-child interaction patterns.

While many of the short-term and long-term effects of early intervention programs have been documented in the literature, important issues remain. The degree to which different types of intervention produce different outcomes is one such issue. It is not yet known which factors or variables in the preschool period are the best predictors of intervention outcome. Finally, a crucial issue concerns the capacity of different types of families and children to utilize the intervention provided. Gray and Wandersman[7] have summarized these issues thusly: "What characteristics of home-based interventions are effective in facilitating which areas of competence for which members of the families in which social contexts?"

The Yale Child Welfare Research Program reported here was a broad-scope intervention project involving both home-based and center-based components. Because of its small sample size and its methodology, it is different from most of the intervention programs cited in the literature. However, its intensive, clinically oriented case approach may serve to illuminate some of these important and subtle issues associated with program impact.

Method

Project Goals and Theoretical Approach

The goals of the Yale Child Welfare Research Program were to provide services to a group of disadvantaged families, in order to help them improve their quality of life and foster the healthy development of their children, and to develop effective intervention methods which could be disseminated to other providers of human services. The intervention can best be described as a service-centered investigation with a clinical-developmental approach. Clinical assessment provided the basis for individualizing services to child and family, and clinical methods and constructs were used in collecting and organizing the research data. The approach was developmental in its view of the child's physical, mental, social, and emotional growth, with development seen as resulting from both interaction and transaction effects between innate and experiential factors. Concepts from psychoanalytic child psychology were central to the project, particularly propositions about the influence of the parent-child relationship on the child's emotional and cognitive development, his view of himself, and his relationships with others. The project shared with the Bank Street educational approach the assumption that the growth of cognitive functions is inextricably intertwined with the growth of emotional and interpersonal processes. Lastly, the project was shaped by an awareness of the importance of the societal systems which influence children and their families, particularly health services, social services, and schools.

Subject Selection

The subjects of the study were 18 children from 17 low-income families who participated in the intervention project from birth to 30 months of age. All children were firstborn, with the exception of one younger sibling born during the project. Mothers were chosen during pregnancy from the obstetrical records of the Yale–New Haven Hospital Women's Clinic. Criteria for selection were: (1) residence in the inner city; (2) income below the federal poverty guideline; (3) no serious complications of pregnancy; (4) and no presence of marked retardation or psychosis. Using these criteria, 25 women were selected and interviewed and 20 agreed to participate in the project; the factors contributing to this self-selection are unknown, but they must be considered in evaluating the project's outcome. From these 20 families, one child was stillborn, one family withdrew from the project, and one child was born with a biological handicap; the remaining 17 families constituted the project group.

Of the 18 research children, 12 were Black, two were white, two were mixed (white mothers and Black fathers), and two were siblings from a Puerto Rican family. There were 11 boys and seven girls. There were eight intact and nine one-parent families. In seven of the latter, either the child's father or another man was a more or less regular member of the household. At the beginning of the project, six of the eight intact families were self-supporting and two were on public welfare. Of the single young women, one was entirely self-supporting, one was supported by her parents, and seven were supported by public welfare. The age range of mothers was 18–24, with a mean age of 20. Eleven of the mothers had completed high school, six had not.

Project Staff and Services

The project was located in a remodeled old residence called Children's House in one of the inner city slums of New Haven. The project staff consisted of experienced clinicians in social work, psychology, nursing, pediatrics, and psychoanalysis, as well as early childhood educators and research psychologists. There were four components to the intervention: home visitor program, pediatric care, developmental evaluation, and day care and/or toddler school.

Home visitor program.   The home visitor was the staff member most closely identified with the parents' needs, interests, and goals. Five social workers, two psychologists, and one nurse served as home visitors. The home visitor met with each mother at least twice a month during the first year and monthly thereafter, with more frequent contacts if the parents wished. The goal was to form a relationship with the parents, with help taking the form of assistance with social service agencies, psychological and emotional support, child care advice, or therapeutic counseling; the services were geared to the needs and wishes of the parent.

Pediatric care.   Pediatricians were responsible for care when children were sick and for well-child examinations, given monthly during the first year and every three months after that. Psychological support and protection of the health of the child were important functions, as well as treatment of illness, with special emphasis on helping parents become more confident of their ability to use medical care effectively.

Developmental evaluation component.   Developmental examinations using the Yale Developmental Schedules were administered at 2, 3, 6, 9, 12, 18, and 24 months, and for the final time at 30 months of age. This is a composite test scale including items from the Gesell, Viennese, Merrill-Palmer and Binet tests. Total developmental age (DA) and developmental quotient (DQ) can be computed, as well as DA and DQ in component areas of the test, with all DQs having a mean of 100. One or both parents attended each developmental examination and discussed the results with the staff, helping parents to become interested in their child's interests, his problem solving skills, and his sensitivities.

Day care and toddler school.   The program of child care and education was committed to planning for children in accordance with their developmental needs, that is to arrange experiences which would enhance physical, intellectual, and emotional development. Twelve children used the day care component of the project: five had 20 or more months in the day care program; five had from 10–19 months in day care; two spent 5 months or less. Five of the six children who did not need day care attended a "toddler school" twice a week for one and one-half hours with their mothers present, from 16 to 30 months of age.

Comparison Group Study

About one year after the intervention project ended, a decision was made to collect data on a comparable group of disadvantaged children who had not received any intervention. Thus, a comparison sample of 18 children of 30 months of age was selected from records in the same hospital clinic used to select the research mothers. Families were matched on income, marital status of mother, and race of parents, with the matching based on family status at the time of pregnancy in both sets of mothers; children were matched on sex and ordinal position. All comparison children were full term and free from congenital defect or illness at birth, as were the research children. This use of a post hoc comparison group makes it more difficult to interpret the results of the intervention program than if random assignment to intervention and control groups had been employed.

Each comparison mother was seen for a single in-depth interview by a psychiatric nurse who was part of the project staff. The interview covered family history, demographic characteristics of the family, child's birth and health history, and child's general development. Each child in the comparison group was seen once for developmental evaluation at age 30 months, using the Yale Developmental Schedules; the testing was done by a psychologist who had not been involved in the intervention project. That it was not possible to conduct blind evaluations of the two groups of children and mothers is recognized as a methodological limitation of the research.

Follow-Up Study

In order to assess the long-term effects of the Yale Child Welfare Research Program, two follow-up studies were carried out five years after the program terminated, when the children were 7 to 8 years old. One of these was an independent follow-up conducted by Trickett and her colleagues, reported elsewhere in this volume.[19] The other follow-up was conducted by the Yale Child Study Center staff. The 16 research families still resident in New England were contacted, and all but one family agreed to participate. Each research mother was seen for an interview of about one hour's duration by her home visitor from the project or by another familiar project staff member. The interview covered changes in family unit, residence, education, occupation, and health, as well as the child's general development and school experience since the project's close. Each child was seen for one testing session using the Revised Wechsler Intelligence Scale for Children by a child psychologist who did not know the families. The results of this Child Development Unit follow-up will be reported in a later section of this paper. It was regrettably not feasible to follow up the comparison group children at this same time, because they were roughly 18 months younger. These children have subsequently been located and the follow-up will be reported in a future paper.

Results

Data Reduction

The analysis of the results of the project was carried out by the first author. She had not participated in the design or execution of any aspect of the intervention project, but she was of necessity informed as to the group status of the subjects when conducting the data analysis. Because there were so little data available on the comparison group, relative to the enormous volume of material on the research group, a decision was made to restrict the two-group analysis to the data sources which were roughly comparable for the two groups: the 30-month test report for each child, the comparison group mother interviews, and the concluding home visitor summaries for the research mothers.

To convert the narrative data into analyzable form, four rating instruments were developed. The Child Assessment Scale was a 17-item rating instrument covering such qualitative characteristics of the child as attention span, anxiety, coping skills, and presence of emotional problems. Ratings were done by the first author and another rater skilled in developmental assessment from the 30-month developmental test report of each child. All disagreements were settled by consensus. The overall rate of perfect agreement across items and subjects was 79%. Using the weighted Kappa[3] statistic to take partial agreement into account, the percentage obtained agreement ranged from 83% to 94% across items, with 16 of the 17 Kappa values significant at the .001 level and one item significant at the .01 level.

The Mother Interview Scale covered demographic information, aspects of parental history, assessments of current parental functioning, child's health history, and child-rearing practices. Ratings were done independently by Rescorla and a clinical social worker from the mother interview summaries, with all disagreements settled by consensus. Agreement was 90 to 100% on factual items and 60 to 75% on qualitative judgments. Using weighted Kappa[3] on the qualitative judgment items, the obtained agreement ranged from 81% to 96%, with all items significant at the .001 level.

The Project Utilization Scale summarized each research family's use of the four project components. Ratings were done by Rescorla in collaboration with the staff members who best knew each of the families. The Follow-Up Interview Scale summarized research family and child characteristics at follow-up. Topics included family history since follow-up and the mother's assessment of her child's development. Ratings were done by Rescorla in collaboration with the author of the interview summary. Because it was most feasible to do the rat-

Table 9-1 Developmental Quotients at 30 Months

Sex	N	Group	
		Research	Comparison
Total developmental quotient			
Boys	11	102.0	93.6
Girls	7	110.4	105.1
Total	18	105.3	98.1
Adaptive developmental quotients			
Boys	11	103.6	98.3
Girls	7	110.1	106.7
Total	18	106.2	101.5
Language developmental quotients			
Boys	11	97.5	79.6
Girls	7	102.3	94.7
Total	18	99.4	85.5

ings on these latter two instruments collaboratively, no reliability statistics were obtained.

Two-Group Comparison at 30 Months

The research and comparison groups were compared on their performance on the Yale Revised Developmental Schedules at 30 months of age. Two-way analysis of variance was used to examine group and sex differences on Total Developmental Quotient (TDQ), the Adaptive Developmental Quotient (ADQ), and Language Developmental Quotient (LDQ), each with a norm of 100. Because the groups were matched, Group was treated as within-subjects factor using a repeated measures analysis of variance.

As can be seen from Table 9-1, there was a small but nonsignificant superiority of the research group over the comparison group and of girls over boys for both TDQ and ADQ. However, there was a highly significant difference on Language DQ favoring the research group, $F(1, 16) = 14.04$, $p < .01$. None of the Group X Sex interactions was significant, although there was a tendency for the intervention effect in language to be stronger in boys than in girls. In contrast to the research children, the comparison group children were already delayed in language development relative to their adaptive performance (85 vs. 101). An item analysis of the children's developmental test performance revealed that the research group superiority in language function was manifest in both vocabulary and syntactic development.

Using a Group X Sex analysis of variance, there were no significant differences for total Child Assessment Scale score or for any of the component item scores. It is not clear to what degree the failure to find reliable differences on these qualitative variables is attributable to limitations in treatment effectiveness, as opposed to reflecting measurement error resulting from the limitations imposed by the research methodology.

Group differences on the 38 items from the Mother Interview Scale were explored using χ^2 analyses. This analysis pertains to the two groups at the time the children in each group were 30 months old. While there were no significant differences between the research and comparison families on demographic factors, several non-significant differences suggested that the comparison families may have been a group with slightly better functioning; this occurrence is one of the common pitfalls of a matched-group design. In this study research fathers tended to be more underemployed or intermittently unemployed than comparison fathers. Thirteen comparison families were self-supporting, as opposed to eight research families supported without welfare or supplementary benefits. More research children lived alone with their mothers than did comparison children (nine vs. five). Finally, more comparison children had a significant nonfather male figure in contact with the family than did research children (eight vs. four). It is worth noting that despite the availability of free day care in the intervention project, the same number of research and comparison mothers worked, namely, eight mothers.

One of the three psychological-experiential variables which significantly differentiated the two groups also points to some superiority favoring the comparison group. Eight comparison group mothers were rated as having good psychological adjustment and coping, as opposed to only three research mothers, $\chi y^2 (1) = 4.33$, $p < .05$. While this finding may reflect genuine group differences, it is also possible, even probable, that it reflects the superficial acquaintance the project staff had with the comparison group.

There was a highly significant difference between the two groups of mothers on their expectations for their children. Nine research mothers were rated as expecting their children to be more mature than their age in behavior, habit training, or development. No comparison mothers were seen as setting this type of overly high standards ($\chi^2 (3) = 12.86$, $p < .005$). Furthermore, ten research mothers felt that their children had some or many problems in development, but only two comparison mothers expressed such concerns ($\chi y^2 (1) = 6.12, p < .01$).

These two findings suggest that research mothers set higher standards for their children and were more critical and/or observant about their children's problems than comparison mothers. It is not clear whether this was an inadvertent program effect or a result of the self-selection factor in subject recruitment. It is important to stress here that while a main project goal was to foster parental aspirations for school achievement and social advancement, an equally important goal was to help parents be realistic with regard to habit training, behavior, and developmental accomplishments and to not demand overly mature behavior in these areas.

Interrelationships Among Child and Family Variables

Correlational analysis was used to explore relationships between child Total DQ, family variables, and project utilization. When the data for the combined research and comparison groups were examined, only two variables were significantly related to Total DQ at 30 months: amount of cognitive stimulation (r $(34) = .66$, $p < .01$) and provision of play materials (r $(34) = .58$, $p < .01$). These two variables were also significantly correlated with each other (r $(34) = .63$, $p < .01$). Similar significant correlations were found between these childrearing variables and both Adaptive DQ and Language DQ.

The findings on Total DQ, Adaptive DQ, and Language DQ described above were also obtained when the research group data were analyzed separately. Additionally, it appeared that language development in the research children was related in some measure to the enrichment provided by the day care program, as measured by months enrolled in day care. It must be noted, however, that the positive correlation (r $(16) = .47$, $p < .05$) was only significant when one child was credited for months spent in another day care center when the family moved out of town temporarily.

Total DQ in the research children was significantly related to three items on the Project Utilization Scale: parental involvement and interest in child developmental exam performance (r $(16) = .62$, $p < .01$), parental involvement and interest in the day care program (r $(10) = .76$, $p < .01$), and parental positive relation to the day care staff (r $(10) = .67$, $p < .05$). The families who were most involved and interested in the day care program tended to be those in which fathers made an economic contribution, mothers were employed, mothers had been married, and the family was self-supporting (correlations of .79, .71, .77, .62 respectively, $df = 10$, $p < .05$). Similarly, families with a strong positive relation to the day care staff had mothers with a more skilled level of employment and more education (correlations of .74 and .65, $df = 10$, $p < .05$); these families also had better day care attendance, used pediatric care more appropriately, and complied more with pediatric recommendations (correlations of .75, .86, .63, $df = 10$, $p < .05$). While this pattern of findings is complex, there is an implication in the data that families with better economic, educational, and social functioning tended to be more involved in the intervention program and to utilize services more effectively than less well-functioning families.

The Project Utilization Scale also dealt with the home visitor aspect of the project. Mother's relationship to the home visitor, use of the home visitor for services, mother's sharing of concerns, and mother's seeking advice from the home visitor were all significantly intercorrelated with each other (correlations of .57 to .79, $df = 16$, $p < .05$). It is interesting to note that mother's use of home visitor's recommendations was not closely related to these other home visitor variables. However, use of home visitor recommendations was significantly correlated with the rating of mother's psychological adjustment and coping, r (16) $= .72$, $p < .01$. This finding supports the experience of clinicians that disturbed or poorly adjusted clients often have difficulty utilizing advice. Alternatively, the finding might be interpreted as showing that mental health professionals tend to regard clients who have difficulty using advice as poorly adjusted and present them as such in their records.

Follow-Up Findings

Data suggesting some sustained, long-term impact of the intervention program were obtained in both the Child Development Unit follow-up and the independent follow-up, reported elsewhere in this volume.[19] Intelligence test data from the Child Development Unit follow-up suggested that the research children continued to function somewhat above the norm for inner-city, disadvantaged children.[4] The average score for the 15 research children tested on the WISC-R was 91.8, with only a negligible 5 point superiority of Performance IQ over Verbal IQ. This VIQ-PIQ pattern suggests that some strength in language function continued to characterize the research children, relative to what is often found in disadvantaged samples.

The correlation of WISC-R FIQ at follow-up and Total DQ at 30 months was .58 ($df = 13$, $p < .05$). Mature, cooperative, and persistent behavior at 30 months, as indicated by total score on the Child Assessment Scale, was an even better predictor of follow-up WISC-R FIQ, r (13) $= .75$, $p < .01$. The correlation between Adaptive DQ at 30 months and Performance IQ at follow-up was .73, ($df = 13$, $p < .01$), in contrast to a correlation of only .44 (N.S.) between Language DQ at 30 months and Verbal IQ at follow-up. Mother's view of the child's development at follow-up was highly correlated with her view of the child at 30 months, r (13) $= .80$, $p < .01$. It appears the mothers were basing their appraisal of their children's development to some degree on verbal skills, as shown by a correlation of .55 ($df = 13, p < .05$) between mother's view of development at follow-up and WISC-R VIQ. The mother's perception of her child's behavior in school also seemed to contribute to her overall view of the child's development, r (13) $= .53, p < .05$.

The strongest findings obtained from the follow-up pertain to general upward mobility of the research families. Some follow-up information relevant to this issue was obtained from all 17 research families. As can be seen in Table 9-2, the families showed striking gains by several indices of upward mobility, relative to their position at the beginning of the project. In the area of educational advancement, 10 out of 17 research mothers obtained some further education during the project. At the time of follow-up, eight mothers had continued to advance educationally. A parallel pattern was evident in terms of progress toward economic self-sufficiency. At the end of the project, the number of families on welfare had declined from nine to five, at the time of follow-up, there were only three families still on welfare. Additionally, the project appears to have had a striking effect on birth rate in the research families. At the end of the project 14 families had only one child, and at follow-up there were still 10 such families. While these findings are only tentative, due to the absence of comparable comparison group data, they suggest important life-style changes in the research families relative to disadvantaged families in the general population.

Finally, a qualitative assessment was made of general improvement in quality of life for the research families. The criterion for improvement was positive change in one or more of the following areas: housing, medical care, socioeconomic status, educational or training status, social life, or engagement in community life. By the end of the project, 12 families had improved in quality of life using these criteria. At the time of follow-up, 14 families showed clear evidence of tangible improvements in quality of life. Two others were not materially better off but seemed happier in their personal life and more positive in outlook. Only one mother had deteriorated in quality of life and general functioning.

Discussion

The Yale Child Welfare Research Program was designed as an intensive clinically-oriented service-centered longitudinal study with a small sample of families. Because the project was of this character and because an experimental design was not employed, the study

Table 9-2   Changes in Education, Economic Support, and Birth Rate in Research Families over Time

Area of Change	Time of Assessment		
	Project Start	Project End	Five Year Follow-Up
Mothers' Education	11 high school graduates 6 partial high school	10 with more education: 2 finished high school 6 took training courses 2 took college courses 7 education unchanged	8 with more education: 4 took training courses 4 working toward B.A. 9 education unchanged
Economic Support	7 self-supporting 1 supported by parents 9 on welfare	8 self-supporting 4 partially self-supporting 5 on welfare	11 self-supporting 1 partially self-supporting 2 on college grants 3 on welfare
Birth Rate	17 families with one child	14 families with 1 child 2 families with 2 children 1 family with 3 children	10 families with 1 child 4 families with 2 children 3 families with 3 or more children

is not directly comparable to the larger, more well-known projects in the field of early intervention research.[2,4,10] The nature of the project's design must be taken into account in considering the study's methods and findings.

The findings from the Yale Child Welfare Research Program constitute a modest but interesting addition to the literature documenting the effectiveness of early interventions for disadvantaged families. The research described here documents that a broad scope, clinically oriented intervention program can be effective in fostering child development for disadvantaged infants and their families. A finding of particular interest is that without the intervention program's having a curriculum targeted specifically on speech development, there was a highly significant effect on the children's language development at 30 months of age relative to comparison subjects. The follow-up data suggest that the program impact on cognitive and language functioning did not appear to "fade out" after the project ended.

The long-term project impact on family patterns appears to be the most striking outcome of the research. The follow-up data revealed impressive changes in the families in terms of improvements in residence, educational advancement, economic self-sufficiency, and quality of life. The low birth rate in the research families at follow-up is a further suggestion of a change toward more autonomous control of important life decisions and a striving for improved social circumstances. These demographic and socioeconomic effects of the Yale Child Welfare Research Program highlight the importance of using a multiplicity of outcome variables as an index of project effectiveness, such as advocated by Zigler and Trickett.[21]

In addition to these specific outcomes, the project has implications of a more general nature. The project data suggest that the intervention's primary effect was its impact on families—on their aspirations, life choices, and patterns of functioning. While the program served an educational role, it was not designed to teach parents how to educate or interact with their children, in the manner of some other projects.[11,16] The fact that significant project effects have been achieved in such a variety of programs suggests that the crucial mediating factors of many interventions may be interpersonal and motivational ones—that the recipient of the intervention comes to believe that the service providers value him as a person and consider his or her development and achievement as an important goal worth striving for.

Thus, the results of the Yale Child Welfare Research Program are consistent with Bronfenbrenner's[2] view that a project must significantly impact family patterns and attitudes in order to have long-standing effect. The project was highly similar to Bronfenbrenner's proposal for a mother-child interaction program during infancy, followed by a preschool enrichment program. Furthermore, the project underscores the importance of *early* intervention by showing that a difference between intervention and comparison children in language development can be detected as young as 30 months of age.

The project results are directly relevant to many of the issues raised by Gray and Wandersman,[7] particularly a concern with the ecological factors promoting the development of competence in parents and children and influencing their capacity to utilize intervention. That is, an important aspect of the Yale Child Welfare Research Program was that effective utilization of the project services varied considerably. As reported, the data suggest that the better-functioning families made best use of the services. However, examination of the individual research families reveals striking exceptions to this general pattern which illuminate the issue of why some were better able than others to utilize the program for helping themselves. Despite some similarities in members of this disadvantaged group, there were large variations in them, as in other groups, with respect to general adaptive abilities, personality characteristics, and capacity for relating, trusting others, and developing as parents. They also varied widely in their childhood experiences, including the strengths in their families of origin and the quality of their nurturance, conditions which influenced their capacities as adults. This study suggests that once good services are made available by qualified personnel who respect their clients and understand human complexity, what will be utilized depends upon the participants, what they bring to the situation, and, hence, what each can use. One implication of this study for social policy is that intervention programs for disadvantaged families should provide a spectrum of quality services, offering options which are responsive to the needs of individual participants.

References

1. Beller, E.K. 1974. "Impact of early education on disadvantaged children." In *A Report on Longitudinal Evaluations of Preschool Programs*, Vol. 1, S. Ryan, ed. DHEW Publication No. (OHD) 74–24, Washington, D.C.
2. Bronfenbrenner, U. 1975. "Is early intervention effective?" In *Handbook of Evaluation Research*, Vol. 2, M. Guttentag and E. Streuning, eds. Sage Publications, Beverly Hills, Calif.
3. Cohen, J. 1968. "Weighted Kappa: nominal scale agreement with provision for scaled disagreement or partial credit." *Psychological Bulletin* 70: 213–220.
4. Darlington, R.B. et al. 1980. "Preschool programs and later school competence of children from low-income families." *Science* 208:202–204.
5. Deutsch, M., Taleporos, E. and Victor, J. 1974. "A brief synopsis of an

initial enrichment program in early childhood." In *A Report on Longitudinal Evaluations of Preschool Programs*, Vol. 1., S. Ryan, ed. DHEW Publication No. (OHD) 74–24, Washington, D.C.

6. Gordon, I.J., Guinagh, B. and Jester, R.E. 1977. "The Florida Parent Education Infant and Toddler Programs." In *The Preschool in Action: Exploring Early Childhood Education Programs*, 2nd Ed., M.C. Day and R.K. Parker, eds. Allyn and Bacon, Boston, Mass.

7. Gray, S.W. and Wandersman, L.P. 1980. "The methodology of home-based intervention studies: problems and promising strategies." *Child Development* 51:993–1009.

8. Karnes, M.B., Zehrback, R.R. and Teska, J.A. 1974. "The Karnes preschool program: rationale, curricula offerings and follow-up data." In *A Report on Longitudinal Evaluations of Preschool Programs*, Vol. 1, S. Ryan, ed. DHEW Publication No. (OHD) 74–24, Washington, D.C.

9. Klaus, R. and Gray, S. 1968. "The Early Training Project for disadvantaged children: a report after five years." *Monographs of the Society for Research in Child Development* 33 (Whole No. 120).

10. Lally, J.R. and Honig, A. 1977. "The Family Development Research Program." In *The Preschool in Action: Exploring Early Childhood Education Programs*, 2nd ed., M.C. Day and R.K. Parker, eds. Allyn and Bacon, Boston, Mass.

11. Levenstein, P. 1977. "The Mother-Child Home Program." In *The Preschool in Action: Exploring Early Childhood Education Programs*, 2nd ed., M.C. Day and R.K. Parker, eds. Allyn and Bacon, Boston, Mass.

12. Miller, L.B. and Dyer, J.L. 1975. "Four preschool programs: their dimensions and effects." *Monographs of the Society for Research in Child Development* 40 (5–6, Serial No. 162).

13. Palmer, F.H. and Siegel, R.J. 1977. "Minimal intervention at ages two and three and subsequent intellective changes." In *The Preschool in Action: Exploring Early Childhood Education Programs*, 2nd ed., M.C. Day and R.K. Parker, eds. Allyn and Bacon, Boston, Mass.

14. Provence, S., Naylor, A. and Patterson, J. 1977. *The Challenge of Day Care*. Yale University Press, New Haven, Conn.

15. Ramey, C.T. et al. 1976. "The Carolina Abecedarian Project: a longitudinal and multidisciplinary approach to the prevention of developmental retardation." In *Intervention Strategies for High-Risk Infants and Young Children*, T. Tjossem, ed. University Park Press, Baltimore, Md.

16. Schaefer, E. and Aaronson, M. 1977. "Infant Education Research Project: implementation and implications of the home-tutoring program." In *The Preschool in Action: Exploring Early Childhood Education Programs*, 2nd ed., M.C. Day and R.K. Parker, eds. Allyn and Bacon, Boston, Mass.

17. Schweinhart, L.J. and Weikart, D.P. 1980. *Young Children Grow Up: the Effects of the Perry Preschool Program on Youths Through Age 15*. High/Scope Press, Ypsilanti, Mich.

18. Seitz, V., Apfel, N. and Efron, C. 1978. "Long-term effects of early intervention: the New Haven project." In *Found: Long-term gains for early intervention*, B. Brown, ed., Westview Press, Boulder, Colo.

19. Trickett, P. et al. "A five-year follow-up of participants in the Yale Child Welfare Research Program." (This volume)
20. Westinghouse Learning Corporation and Ohio University. 1969. *The impact of Head Start experience on children's cognitive and affective development.* U.S. Department of Commerce Clearinghouse, Springfield, Va.
21. Zigler, E. and Trickett, P. 1978. "I.Q., social competence, and evaluations of early childhood intervention programs." *American Psychologist* 33 (9): 789–798.

Chapter 10

A FIVE-YEAR FOLLOW-UP OF PARTICIPANTS IN THE YALE CHILD WELFARE RESEARCH PROGRAM

by Penelope K. Trickett, Nancy H. Apfel, Laurie K. Rosenbaum, and Edward F. Zigler

A few years after the introduction of Project Head Start and other "compensatory" preschool programs during the 1960s, many researchers became interested in expanding the scope of intervention programs to include children younger than preschool age. One reason for this interest was the interpretation of early evaluation efforts as showing a fade-out of positive effects of preschool programs a year or two after completion of the program. Bolstered by the writings of Hunt,[18] Bloom,[4] and other advocates of the critical importance of early experience for later development (e.g., White[42]), many people came to believe that preschool intervention programs were "too little–too late" and that, to minimize the negative effects of a poverty-stricken home environment and to make a lasting and meaningful

This study was supported by Grant PHS-90-C-912 from the Administration for Children, Youth, and Families and Research Grant HD-03008-13 from the National Institute of Child Health and Human Development. The authors wish to thank the families who participated in the study and the staff of the New Haven Public Schools for their cooperation and assistance. We are also indebted to Judy Feldman, Kate Wexler, and Karen Anderson, who assisted with the data collection, and to Lisa Rosenberg for editorial assistance. We are especially grateful to Victoria Seitz and Edison J. Trickett for many constructive criticisms of this manuscript.

difference in the lives of low-income children, one should intervene as early as possible. Hand-in-hand with this notion was the view that the inclusion of the parents, and particularly the mother, of the children in the program was a necessary ingredient for success.[5,47]

Many infant/toddler intervention programs were initiated at that time. They varied widely in such dimensions as the ages of the children served, whether the program was center- or home-based, whether the staff consisted of professionals or paraprofessionals, and how narrowly the program was focused on the cognitive development of the children. The results of many of these programs have been evaluated, and in general, positive immediate effects have been found. The adequacy of these studies, however, has been criticized on two important grounds: they tell us little about the long-term effects of such programs, and they define program success very narrowly in terms of IQ gains by the children.[5,6,14]

An important recent study which has addressed these issues is reported by Darlington and his colleagues,[8] who analyzed data from a collaborative long-term follow-up of 12 early intervention projects initiated in the 1960s. These follow-up studies were conducted from 4 to 13 years after the programs terminated. The investigators found long-term effects, including reduced likelihood of grade retention or placement in special education classes, improved school achievement and attitudes, and IQ gains during the primary school years for the children who had received early intervention. Of the 12 programs investigated, however, only three had served children below the age of 3 and only one had served children younger than 2. The long-term effects of programs aimed at infants and toddlers still need to be examined.

The present study is an evaluation of the long-range effects of the Yale Child Welfare Research Program, an infant/toddler intervention program developed by Sally Provence and her colleagues at Yale University's Child Study Center.[24,25,28] Several factors distinguish this program from most other intervention programs. First, it involved the very young child: families were accepted prior to the birth of their first child and were served by the program until the child was 30 months of age. Second, it dealt with the family as a whole, rather than focusing on the infant, the mother, or the infant-mother interaction. Third, it was a comprehensive and intensive intervention with four main components: (1) free medical care for the infants; (2) regular developmental checkups; (3) a professional social worker assigned to each family, who visited the home regularly and provided the family with varied types of assistance according to its needs; and (4) full-day day care for those families who wanted it and a toddler school, a more traditional nursery school, for those families who did not want day care.

While intensive and comprehensive, this intervention was flexible and oriented toward individual needs. The role of the home visitor varied considerably in different homes, as did the use of day care services.[28] The flexibility of this intervention distinguished it from such infant projects as the Milwaukee Project[12,16] and the Abecedarian Project,[26] in which all infants were enrolled in full-day, five-day-a-week day care at which a specific prescribed curriculum was taught.

At the time the Yale Child Welfare Research Program ended, when the children were 30 months old, the performance of each on the Yale Developmental Schedules was evaluated and compared with the performance of children in a matched control group. The major finding was that, while the two groups did not differ significantly in overall score, the project children did score significantly higher than the controls on the language scales.[28]

The current study is a follow-up of the intervention children at approximately eight years of age, about five years after the end of the program. Two new control groups of children were developed and their performance on a variety of academic and motivational measures was compared with that of the program children. Comparisons were also made on family characteristics as determined by interviews of program and control group mothers.

Method

Subjects

Intervention group. All of the 17 families who had participated in the intervention were located and asked to participate in the follow-up. All but one family agreed, resulting in a total of 17 children (two children from one family) in the Intervention Group. Table 10-1 presents information on the characteristics of these children and their families.

Control group. No attempt was made to locate the children in the matched control group who were seen in the 30-month evaluation reported by Rescorla and her colleagues.[28] Because the children in this control group were 18 months younger than the intervention children, testing these groups simultaneously would have limited the number of dependent measures which would be appropriate. For example, some of the control children would have been just under or barely 6 years of age, most certainly nonreaders, and unable to respond to the achievement measures in the study.

The strategy chosen instead was to develop a control group by sampling peers of the intervention children who attended public

Table 10-1   Characteristics of the Three Groups of Children and Their Families at the Time of Follow-Up

Characteristic	Intervention Group	Control I (Wilton)	Control II (Highpoint)
Children's Characteristics	($N = 17$)	($N = 33$)	($N = 31$)
Mean Age in Months	94.9	94.8	93.2
Sex:			
Boys (N)	11	17	15
Girls (N)	6	16	16
Grade Placement:			
First (N)	6	7	15
Second (N)	7	21	16
Third (N)	4	5	0
Ethnic Group:			
Black (N)	13	31	20
Hispanic (N)	2	0	10
White (N)	2	2	1
Preschool Experience:			
Head Start (N)	5	15	12
Other Preschool Exp.[a] (N)	9	6	1
No Preschool Exp. (N)	3	12	18
Family Characteristics	($N = 17$)	($N = 10$[b])	($N = 11$[b])
Father or Stepfather Present (%)	54	60	46
Total Number of Siblings in the Home	.94	1.70	2.27
Families with Only 1 Child (%)	53	10	0
Family SES[c]	5.69	6.10	6.82
Mother's Education (Median)	12	12	10
Mothers Employed (%)	52	20	9

[a] This category includes nursery school, day care, or a combination of both.
[b] These Ns refer to the subsample of control families who were interviewed.
[c] Based on a Hollingshead Occupational Scale[17] rating of Head of Household (with a range of 1 [highest] to 7 [lowest]).

schools in neighborhoods comparable to those where the project families lived. The difficult question, though, was "which neighborhoods?" Prior to the intervention, the modal residence for the intervention group was in a very impoverished neighborhood, "Highpoint," and the second largest proportion lived in a somewhat less impoverished neighborhood, "Wilton." (These names are pseudonyms.) By the time of the follow-up, the families had moved in an upwardly mobile direction. Two families had moved out of the New Haven area, a few lived in working-class towns neighboring New

Haven, and the remainder lived in New Haven. None still lived in Highpoint. The modal neighborhood now seemed to be Wilton.

Since it was impossible to know whether this upwardly mobile change was an outcome of the intervention, two control groups were developed. Based on the assumption that the project families might have "moved up" regardless of participating in the intervention, the first control group was taken from children attending neighborhood schools in the Wilton area. (This could be considered a "conservative-contrast" control group.) On the opposite assumption that the project families would still be as impoverished without the intervention, the second, "liberal-contrast," control group was selected from children attending neighborhood schools in Highpoint.

Upon the advice of public school administrators familiar with the schools and neighborhoods, schools were selected from the control neighborhoods for having school populations representative of the neighborhood as a whole and for being receptive to research. Census tract data were examined to determine how the socioeconomic makeup of these two control neighborhoods compared with that of the neighborhoods in which the project families resided. As reported by Trickett and her colleagues,[39] this comparison confirmed that, on the average, the intervention families now lived in circumstances that were less depressed than at the beginning of the intervention. These comparisons also confirmed that the conservative-contrast neighborhood described above provided a good match to the neighborhoods in which the intervention families were residing at the time of the follow-up.

The conservative-contrast control group selected from the Wilton schools was designated "Control Group I" and the liberal-contrast control group from Highpoint schools, "Control Group II." The sampling procedure was as follows: For each school selected from the two neighborhoods, a list was compiled of all enrolled children whose birthdates, like those of the intervention children, fell between December, 1968 and March, 1970. The prekindergarten experience of the age-eligible group was determined from school records. The list from each school was then subdivided into four cells, by sex and Head Start participation. (Because results of comparisons of intervention children with control children who had had Head Start essentially paralleled the results based on the entire control samples,[39] the Head Start factor is not considered further in the present report.)

A random selection of children in each cell received permission letters to carry home. When an insufficient number of acceptances were received, follow-up procedures were used, usually a visit to the home by the school community worker. When more positive responses were returned than were needed, random choice within cells determined which children would participate. Overall, 66% of those parents who received letters were willing to have their children participate. However, due primarily to the energetic efforts of one school community worker, the acceptance rate for families of Control Group II children (82%) was considerably higher than for those of Control Group I children (57%). The comparison sample resulting from these selection procedures consisted of 33 children in Control Group I and 31 in Control Group II. See Table 10-1 for demographic information on these groups.

The permission letters that the children carried home contained an additional request for permission to interview the parents. A small cash remuneration was offered for their time and cooperation. Of those families willing to have their children in the study, 54% indicated that one parent was willing to be interviewed (the acceptance rates of families in the two neighborhoods did not differ). Since our resources did not allow us to interview all the assenting control parents, we selected 60% of those parents to derive a sample balanced with respect to the stratified sampling procedure used with the children. Thus, we interviewed 10 parents of Control Group I children (6 girls and 4 boys) and 11 parents of Control Group II children (5 girls and 6 boys).

Measures

The dependent measures selected for this study were chosen to correspond with the general child development goals of the project. The measures also reflect a belief that the most appropriate goal of early childhood interventions is to increase the overall social competence of the child and/or the parents.[50]

Individually administered academic measures.   The Peabody Picture Vocabulary Test (PPVT) is a standardized measure of receptive vocabulary from which a verbal IQ score is derived. Information on the reliability, validity, and standardization procedures can be found in the manual.[9]

The Peabody Individual Achievement Test (PIAT) is a standardized academic achievement test that measures the child's progress in math, reading recognition and comprehension, spelling, and general information. This test requires about 30 minutes to complete, resulting in five subtest scores and a total score. Information about standardization procedures and reliability can be found in the manual.[10]

Motivational measures.   The Box Maze was used to determine if children prefer to seek out variation when confronted with a repetitive task, or whether they confine themselves to a single, acceptable solution. The child is presented with the same maze on five successive trials, and is instructed to draw a path so that the boy at one end of the maze can get to the store at the other end. Numerous pathways are possible. The measure is scored by comparing each path the child draws with the one drawn on the preceding trial. Scores can range from 0 (no variation) to 200 (maximum variation). This measure has been found to discriminate between institutionalized and noninstitutionalized retarded children,[15] with institutionalized children showing less variation in their responses. A social class factor has also been found for this measure, with middle class children showing greater variation than lower class.[32] A detailed description of the measure with verbatim instructions and information on test-retest reliability can be found in Harter and Zigler.[15]

The Sticker Game was designed by Achenbach and Zigler to assess the child's tendency to use his or her internal resources rather than to rely on external cues in problem solving.[2] It has been found to discriminate between normal and retarded children[2] and economically disadvantaged and nondisadvantaged children.[48] In each of three trials, the examiner makes a picture using sticker cutouts on a piece of colored paper, names the picture, and then gives the child a turn (verbatim instructions can be found in Achenbach and Zigler). The child's pictures are scored according to their degree of resemblance to the examiner's picture. Scores for each design are summed to obtain a total score which can range from 0 (low imitation) to 21 (high imitation). This measure has been found to have high interscorer reliability and to discriminate between normal and retarded children.[2] In the present study interscorer agreement, based on a subsample of 21 protocols, was $r = .99$.

The Locus of Control scale was developed by Shipman and her colleagues[11] to measure the child's feelings of control over what happens to him or her. The tester shows the child a series of 20 cartoonlike drawings of a child and a teacher or another child. In each picture a person is shown asking a child the reason for the child's success or failure in a situation that might occur in school. The child is asked to choose one of two responses to this question, one of which attributes the responsibility for success or failure to an external cause, the other to the child (internal response). The child's score is the sum of internal responses chosen and may range from 0 to 20. Reliability coefficients from previous research with this measure are low, with Kuder-Richardson coefficients ranging from .32 to .58.[40] These values, however, are comparable to those from other locus of control measures that have been used with children of this age.[38] Using the present measure, Stipek found that middle class children entered first grade with higher internal locus of control than low SES children. She also reported validity information that children's performance on this locus of control measure was positively related to later academic achievement.[38]

Tester ratings. These ratings were developed by Shipman[36] to provide an overall picture of the testing sessions for each child. Eight one-item scales rate various aspects of the child's reaction to the testing situation (e.g., attentiveness, response speed, talkativeness). There are no published data on the reliability of these ratings.

School record information. School record information was collected at the end of the school year on each child's grades, school attendance figures, and whether the child was in the correct grade for his or her age. Because grading systems varied from school to school, each child's overall grades were categorized as either below average, or average or above. These ratings were then combined with information about grade placement to obtain a School Performance Index. Below-average school performance on the Index meant either that the child earned below-average grades in the correct grade for age, or was a grade behind, regardless of grades. Average or above-average school performance in the Index was defined as being in the correct grade for age (or above) and obtaining average or above-average grades.

Parent interview. The interview developed for this study contained questions on family size, presence or absence of parents in the home, and parental education and employment history.

Procedure

All but three of the children were tested in their schools, by one of three white women who were experienced testers. Each tester saw approximately the same number of boys and girls from each of the two control groups and from the intervention group. The three children remaining were intervention children who were no longer living in New Haven. One child returned from a nearby state and was tested in university facilities. The other two children (from a single family) were tested in their home in Puerto Rico. The motivational measures were translated into Spanish and administered, along with the Spanish language version of the PPVT, by a bilingual examiner. (No Spanish language PIAT was available.)

The testing was divided into two sessions, usually on consecutive days. The tester escorted the child from his or her classroom to the testing place, usually an unused classroom. In each session motivational measures were administered first, because they are gamelike and give the child a chance to warm up. These measures were then followed by one of the achievement measures. The first session lasted about 45 minutes and consisted of the Box Maze and the PIAT; in the second session, which lasted 20 to 30 minutes, the Sticker Game and Locus of Control were completed before administering the

PPVT. At the end of the second session, the tester filled out the Tester Ratings form for each child.

Parent interviews were conducted by two women. Both were white, college graduates, experienced interviewers, and familiar with the research design. Each interviewed the same number of intervention parents. Similarly, the interviews of the control parents were balanced across the two neighborhoods between the two interviewers. For intervention parents, interviews were conducted in the home. Control parents were interviewed at school, except for those parents who requested home interviews. For two Spanish-speaking mothers, a translator from the school assisted the interviewer.

Results

Family Characteristics

Information about certain family characteristics of the three groups was obtained from the interview of the mothers. This information is presented in Table 10-1. Group differences were determined by Fisher's Exact Test or, when appropriate, one-way analysis of variance. These analyses revealed that the groups did not differ significantly in the percentage in which the father or father surrogate was present in the home. The groups did differ in the number of siblings currently living in the home ($F[2,32] = 3.179, p < .05$). Intervention children had significantly fewer siblings than did Control Group II children. Control Group I children were not significantly different from the other two groups. An analysis of the proportion of children who were only children yielded comparable findings.

A significant difference was found in family SES rating ($F[2,34] = 3.738, p < .05$). The Intervention Group had a higher average rating than did Control Group II. Control Group I was intermediate and not significantly different from either group. Median educational level of the mothers was not significantly different for the three groups, but a significant difference was found in the proportion of mothers currently employed in the three groups. Significantly more ($p < .05$) Intervention Group mothers were working than Control Group II mothers. Again, Control Group I mothers were intermediate and not significantly different from the other two groups.

In sum, the three groups did not differ in the proportion with fathers or father substitutes living in the home or in the mother's educational level. They differed in the size of families (the intervention families were smaller than Control Group II families); in family SES (the intervention families had a higher average rating than Control Group II families); and in the proportion with working mothers (more intervention group mothers were currently employed than Control Group II mothers). In each of these cases Control Group I families were intermediate and not significantly different from the other two groups.

Children's Performance Measures

Preliminary analyses revealed no significant effects associated with testers. Because all but one of the intervention children were first-borns, other preliminary analyses were conducted to determine whether any group differences could be attributed to that fact. The birth order of control children was known only for those 21 children whose parents were interviewed; 11 of these children were first-borns. The results of *t*-tests comparing the performance of the Intervention Group and first-born controls were comparable to results of analyses with all control children combined.

The means and standard deviations on all the performance measures for all subjects are reported separately for boys and girls in Tables 10-2 and 10-3. For each dependent measure, a Group (Intervention, Control I, and Control II) by Sex analysis of variance was performed on the data for all children. Post hoc comparisons were performed by the Newman-Keuls method.

Peabody Picture Vocabulary Test (PPVT). The analysis of variance on the PPVT IQ scores yielded a significant main effect for group ($F[2,73] = 11.028$, $p < .001$). Because the Group by Sex interaction was also significant ($F[2,73] = 3.290$, $p < .05$), results are reported separately by sex. As may be seen in Table 10-2, the mean for the Intervention Group girls was significantly greater ($p < .01$) than that of both Control Group I and Control Group II, which did not differ from one another. As shown in Table 10-3, for the boys, the means for the Intervention Group and Control Group I did not differ from one another, but the mean for Control II was significantly lower than that of the Intervention Group ($p < .01$) and Control Group I ($p < .05$). (Since the comparability of the Spanish-language version of the PPVT is uncertain, the PPVT scores were also analyzed excluding the two Spanish scores. The same significant effects emerged.)

Peabody Individual Achievement Test (PIAT). Univariate analyses of variance parallel to those performed on the IQ scores were conducted on the five subtest scores and on the total score of the PIAT. (A multivariate analysis of variance yielded comparable results.) The analyses revealed significant group effects on two subtests, Spelling ($F[2,73] = 5.41$, $p < .01$) and General Information ($F[2,73] = 5.55$, $p < .01$), and on the PIAT Total Score ($F[2,73] = 3.51$, $p < .05$). In all cases, the means for the Intervention Group

Table 10-2   Means and Standard Deviations on Performance Measures for Girls in the Intervention Group, Control Group I, and Control Group II

Measure	Intervention Group (N = 6)			Control Group I (N = 16)			Control Group II (N = 16)		
	X	SD	Grade Equiv.	X	SD	Grade Equiv.	X	SD	Grade Equiv.
Peabody Picture Vocabulary Test IQ	111.8	11.8		88.1	9.5		81.2	13.3	
Peabody Individual Achievement Tests:									
Mathematics	28.8	5.8	2-7	25.9	5.8	2-4	25.8	8.6	2-4
Reading Recognition	36.2	6.8	3-9	30.6	5.6	3-3	27.2	7.1	2-6
Reading Comprehension	32.9	4.6	3-5	28.3	6.1	2-9	25.5	5.8	2-7
Spelling	40.2	6.6	3-9	32.3	8.3	3-2	26.9	8.0	2-5
General Information	21.6	4.5	3-2	14.8	3.6	1-6	12.8	6.4	1-0
Total Score	159.6	21.4	3-4	131.9	22.5	2-6	117.6	32.9	2-2
Sticker Game	5.8	.8		8.8	3.2		8.6	4.7	
Locus of Control	14.0	1.4		14.2	2.2		12.2	2.9	
Box Mazes	110.8	62.7		94.6	57.4		73.1	67.1	
Tester Ratings:									
Factor I	.33	1.23		.62	.88		-.52	1.02	
Factor II	.56	.33		-.22	1.3		-.03	1.05	
School Attendance (days present)	169.8	5.4		163.0	16.7		161.4	20.7	
School Performance Index:									
Below Average	0%			18.8%			31.3%		
Average or Above	100%			81.3%			68.8%		

and Control Group I did not differ significantly, while the mean for Control Group II was significantly lower than either of the first two groups.

Significant sex differences emerged on two of the PIAT subtests, Reading Comprehension ($F[1,73] = 4.22$, $p < .05$) and Spelling ($F[1,73] = 10.60$, $p < .005$), and on the PIAT Total Score ($F[1,73] = 5.53$, $p < .05$), with girls scoring higher than boys in all three cases. For the Spelling subtest the Group by Sex interaction was also significant ($F[2,73] = 3.19$, $p < .05$). As Table 10-2 shows, for girls, the mean of the Intervention Group was higher than the means for Control Group I ($p < .05$) and Control Group II ($p < .01$); the two control group means did not differ from one another. For boys, as shown in Table 10-3, the mean of Control Group I was significantly higher than that of Control Group II ($p < .05$). The mean for the Intervention Group was intermediate and not significantly different from either of the control groups.*

Comparison of the PIAT scores obtained by the children in this study with the norms published in the PIAT manual[10] reveals that, on the average, the children in the Intervention Group performed at the second grade–sixth month level, Control Group I at the second grade–seventh month level, and the Control Group II children at the second grade–zero month level. Since the testing took place during the eighth month of most of the children's second grade year, this indicated that on average the children in the Intervention Group and Control Group I were functioning quite close to grade level. The sex differences, however, were substantial. The average performance of the girls in the Intervention Group was at the third grade–fourth month level, for Control Group I at the second grade–sixth month level, and for Control Group II at the second grade–second month level. For the boys, the average performance of the Intervention Group was at the second grade–second month level; for Control

---

* Comparisons with random samples from the same control schools resulted in stronger evidence of the intervention children's advantage. (The random samples were obtained from a study conducted two years earlier.[35] The intervention girls significantly exceeded both random control groups of girls on the PPVT ($X = 111.8$, 90.1, and 77.8 for Intervention, Wilton, and Highpoint, $p < .001$ for each comparison) and on Total PIAT ($X = 159.6$ [3–4], 132.0 [2–6], and 109.5 [1–9], respectively, $p < .05$ for the comparison with Wilton, $p < .01$ for the comparison with Highpoint). The intervention boys significantly exceeded both random control groups of boys on the PPVT ($X = 99.8$, 83.8, and 85.0, respectively, $p < .01$ for each comparison). On the Total PIAT, intervention and Wilton boys were comparable and both performed significantly better ($p < .05$) than did the Highpoint boys ($X = 119.2$ [2–2], 118.9 [2–2], and 104.1 [1–7], respectively). The samples in the present study thus appear to provide a conservative test of the effects of the intervention.

Table 10-3　Means and Standard Deviations on Performance Measures for Boys in the Intervention Group, Control Group I, and Control Group II

Measure	Intervention Group (N = 11)			Control Group I (N = 17)			Control Group II (N = 15)		
	X	SD	Grade Equiv.	X	SD	Grade Equiv.	X	SD	Grade Equiv.
Peabody Picture Vocabulary Test IQ	99.8	9.9		96.1	11.9		81.1	15.5	
Peabody Individual Achievement Tests:									
Mathematics	24.4	8.4	2–2	30.4	9.8	2–9	20.9	7.6	1–9
Reading Recognition	27.2	8.0	2–6	32.8	10.3	3–5	25.5	11.0	2–2
Reading Comprehension	25.1	4.9	2–6	29.6	8.4	3–2	22.3	8.1	2–2
Spelling	25.7	7.5	2–4	31.1	9.6	3–0	22.5	6.9	1–8
General Information	16.7	3.7	2–2	16.6	6.1	2–2	12.6	5.0	1–0
Total Score	119.2	27.0	2–2	140.4	40.0	2–8	103.8	32.5	1–7
Sticker Game	8.8	3.0		8.7	4.0		12.1	6.1	
Locus of Control	14.4	2.9		13.5	1.9		13.5	2.8	
Box Mazes	109.1	53.7		121.1	57.5		106.4	60.2	
Tester Ratings:									
Factor I	.49	.94		−.03	.81		−.48	.74	
Factor II	−.16	1.15		.33	.39		−.27	.97	
School Attendance (days present)	172.2	5.8		161.6	24.6		157.5	20.0	
School Performance Index:									
Below Average	40.0%			17.6%			40.0%		
Average or Above	60.0%			82.4%			60.0%		

Group I at the second grade–eighth month level; and for Control Group II at the first grade–seventh month level.

Motivational measures. Analysis of variance of Box Maze scores revealed no significant main effects or interactions. For the Sticker Game, because of tester error, data were unscorable for 15 children (3 Intervention, 4 Control Group I, and 8 Control Group II children). Analyses were performed only for those subjects with complete data. Because of a correlation between means and variances, a square root transformation was performed on the scores and the analysis of variances performed on the transformed scores. This analysis yielded no significant main effects or interactions.

For the Locus of Control measure, the main effect for group approached significance ($F[2,75] = 2.84$, $p = .06$). Mean scores for the three groups on this measure were 14.29 for the Intervention Group, 13.85 for Control Group I, and 12.87 for Control Group II. No sex differences or interactions were found.

Tester ratings. The eight one-item scales pertaining to the child's approach to the testing situation were factor-analyzed using a principal components method. Two factors with eigenvalues greater than 1 were found, accounting for 63.3% of the variance. These factors were rotated using a Varimax criterion. Factor I was defined primarily by the items labeled Talkativeness (which loaded .847), Response Speed (which loaded .769), and Initial Reaction (with a loading of .677). It seemed to characterize an outgoing, enthusiastic, quick-to-warm-up approach to the testing situation. The negative pole of this factor was very similar to the construct "wariness of adults," which has been posited by Zigler and his colleagues to be a characteristic of institutionalized and economically deprived children.[41,49] Factor II was defined primarily by Attentiveness (with a loading of .923), Speech Comprehensibility (−.596), and Emotionality (.535). It seemed to characterize a general involvement and attentiveness to tasks.

Means and standard deviations of the factor scores from this factor analysis are reported in Tables 10-2 and 10-3. Analyses of variance performed on Factor I scores yielded a significant group effect ($F[2,72] = 6.18$, $p < .005$). No significant sex differences or interactions were found. Post hoc comparisons showed that the mean for Control Group II (−.50) differed significantly ($p < .01$) from both the Intervention Group (with a mean of .44) and Control Group I (with a mean of .28). The latter two groups did not differ from one another. The direction of this difference was that the children in Control Group II were rated as less enthusiastic, or more wary, than were children in the other two groups. Analyses of Factor II scores yielded no significant main effects or interactions.

School record information. Fisher's Exact Tests were performed on the School Performance Index data for all possible 2×2 frequency tables for both sexes combined and for boys and girls separately. No significant effects emerged.

The means and standard deviations of school attendance (number of days attended out of a possible 180) are reported in Tables 10-2 and 10-3. As may be seen in these tables, the variances of the three groups were very different. A Bartlett's Test of the homogeneity of variances performed on these data yielded a significant χ^2 ($\chi^2 = 39.93$, $p < .005$). Because of this, t-tests were done between each pair of means using Darlington's formula to test the significance of the difference between means when the variances differ significantly.[7] These t-tests showed a significant difference ($p < .05$) between the mean school attendance of the Intervention Group (171.70) and that of both Control Group I (162.25) and Control Group II (159.52). The latter two groups did not differ from one another.

Interrelationship of the Dependent Measures

Table 10-4 presents the correlation matrix of the dependent measures for all the children, boys and girls combined. The correlation obtained for boys differed significantly from that obtained for girls in only two instances, a number not exceeding that expected by chance.

Predicting Performance Within the Intervention Group

Stepwise multiple regressions were used to predict PPVT IQ and PIAT Total Scores for the Intervention Group only. Eight predictor variables were entered into the regression. The first four variables described the intervention child's family at the time the child was born and the intervention began: the number of years of school the mother had completed; mother's marital status; whether the mother had been employed prior to the birth of the child; and a neighborhood poverty index consisting of a 1970 census variable, "percentage of families in census tract below poverty level." The next three variables were related to the use of the project's services by the intervention families: the number of months in which the child had been enrolled in the day care program, a rating of the mother's relationship to the home visitor, and a rating of the mother's interest in the developmental exams. (The latter two ratings were made previously by Rescorla[28] and were selected from a number of project utilization ratings because factor analysis had shown them to be independent of one another and of the "months in day care" variable.) The final

Table 10-4 Correlation Matrix of Dependent Measures for All Children in the Follow-Up Study

	PPVT IQ	PIAT Total	Sticker Game	Mazes	Locus of Control	Tester Rating (1)	Tester Rating (2)	School Attendance
PPVT IQ								
PIAT Total Score	.46**							
Sticker Game	.39***	-.48***						
Mazes	.16[a]	.31**	-.12					
Locus of Control	.34**	.29**	-.23	.15				
Tester Rating— Factor I	.22	.17	-.07	.02	.17			
Tester Rating— Factor II	.22	.27*	-.09	.22	.05	.00		
School Attendance	.12	.23*	-.20	.03	-.07	.00	.11	
School Performance Index	.30**	.49***	-.39**	.23*	.29**	.03	-.10	.11[b]

* $p < .05$
** $p < .01$
*** $p < .001$

[a] There was a significant difference ($p < .05$) between the correlations for Mazes and the PPVT IQ obtained for boys ($-.06$, n.s.) and girls (.39, $p < .05$).

[b] There was a significant difference ($p < .05$) between the correlations for school performance with school attendance obtained for boys (.35, $p < .05$) and girls ($-.27$, n.s.).

Table 10-5 Best Regression Equation[a] for PPVT-IQ and PIAT Total Score, Regression Coefficient, R^2 and F Value for Each Term

	Beta Weight Coefficient	Cumulative R^2	F
PPVT-IQ			
Sex	−.497	.25	8.823
Neighborhood Poverty Index	−.495	.48	8.753
Mother's Interest in Developmental Exams	.396	.64	5.607
PIAT Total Score			
Sex	−.627	.39	8.439

[a] The "best regression equation" was defined as all steps of the regression up to and including the last step which produced a significant increment in R^2.

predictor variable entered into the regression was the sex of the child.

Table 10-5 presents the results of both multiple regression analyses. As Table 10-5 shows, for both the PPVT IQ and PIAT Total Score the sex of the child was the best predictor, accounting for 25% of the variance on the PPVT IQ and 39% of the variance on the PIAT Total Score. None of the remaining seven variables entered into the regression contributed significantly to the variance on the PIAT; but for the PPVT IQ, the Neighborhood Poverty Index added significantly and accounted for almost as much of the variance as sex did (23%). The third variable which added significantly to the equation for PPVT IQ was the rating of the mother's interest in the developmental exams (16%).

Discussion

In comparison with children from their original neighborhood (Control Group II), the Intervention Group children scored higher on measures of IQ, school performance, locus of control, reaction to the testing situation, and school attendance. They surpassed the children from the less impoverished neighborhood (Control Group I) on school attendance and IQ (although only the Intervention Group girls had significantly higher IQs than Control Group I girls).

Given the absence of random selection procedures in recruitment, there is reason for concern that the mothers of the Intervention Group were a select group of highly motivated individuals. There are indications, however, that this was not the case. Early comparisons of the intervention mothers with a matched control group showed the control mothers functioning better in overall psychological adjustment and coping.[28] As described by Provence and her colleagues,[25] some intervention mothers had lengthy periods of depression, and many required substantial assistance to find more adequate living quarters and to solve other pressing problems. In short, the case records do not give the impression of a highly select group of mothers, although they were not the most severely deprived women in their inner-city neighborhood.

The results of this study would have been easier to interpret if the researchers who mounted this intervention had employed random assignment of subjects to experimental and control conditions, but for ethical and practical reasons this was impossible to do. Nevertheless, the consistency of the present results with those of evaluations of other extensive early childhood programs[26,27] and of certain adoption studies[30,31] are provocative. The overall picture from these studies makes it plausible that the differences in groups found in the present study reflect long-term effects of the Yale Child Welfare Research Program. Although other interventions also seem to have helped disadvantaged children to obtain IQ scores in the normal range[26,27,30,31] and to improve their school performance,[30,31] the present project is different in having focused on providing family support rather than on replacing parents for all or most of the children's waking hours. This implies not only that early intervention can be lastingly effective in improving the quality of life and educational prospects of disadvantaged children, but also that effective intervention can be more flexible and oriented toward individual needs than other successful projects have been.

The findings of the present study refute the current, popularly held view that children's immediate gains from early intervention efforts tend to fade out in a year or two after the children leave the program. They also contradict the arguments of theoretical neomaturationists that variations in early childhood experience are unimportant in determining behavior later in life.[19,29,37]

A number of differences were found between the two control groups employed in the present study. The performance of the control children living in a somewhat better environment was superior to the children in the second control group, although by current criteria both control groups of children would be classified as economically disadvantaged. These findings support the argument that economically disadvantaged children are not psychologically homogeneous, but rather are a diverse group with great interindividual variation.[22,43]

The children's gender proved to be a moderator variable on a number of dependent measures examined, a finding consistent with other evidence gathered by our research group.[33,34,49] Gender effects were seen most clearly in the regression analyses where gender was found to be significantly related to both IQ and achievement scores, with the performance of girls being higher than that of boys. Evidence appears to be accumulating that the deleterious consequences of growing up in impoverished circumstances may be greater (or less remediable) for boys than they are for girls.[3,13,20]

Generally more differences between groups were obtained on the cognitive and achievement measures than on the motivational measures. This pattern of findings may be due to the psychometric superiority of the cognitive as compared to the motivational measures employed.[21,46] However, the authors continue to believe that motivational factors are important determinants of the behavior of economically disadvantaged children.[50] Some support for this stance was obtained in the present study in the intercorrelation matrix of dependent measures, where motivational measures were found to be related not only to individual cognitive measures but to the overall School Performance Index as well.

The findings of the present study are relevant to the current controversy over the optimal curriculum to be employed with children, specifically, whether disadvantaged children can be helped most by employing a structured program with an explicit cognitive development orientation.[1,23] Zigler has argued that the development of economically disadvantaged children, including their cognitive growth, would be more enhanced by directing intervention toward the general social and personality development of these children.[44,49] As Zigler[49] has pointed out, this was the original rationale for the Head Start program. It was also the philosophy on which the intervention assessed in the present study was based.

The findings of the present study indicate the long-term value of programs that adopt this "whole-child" approach,[45] including the medical care of children and the close involvement of the parents. Unfortunately, the diverse facets of the Yale Child Welfare Research Program make it difficult to interpret its effects, as we cannot determine how particular aspects of the intervention affected the children's performance on specific tasks five years after leaving the program. Is their superior performance due to experiences in the day care program or due indirectly to their parents' involvement in the intervention? Would similar results be obtained with economically disadvantaged children who received only the medical benefits of this intervention?

In the face of this ambiguity, the authors would offer the hypothesis that the key element in this intervention was the work done with the parents. It was the parents, far more than the day care or toddler program personnel, who determined the nature of the developmental terrain through which these children traveled from infancy through midchildhood. The parents changed dramatically as a result of their involvement in this program: In addition to having moved to somewhat better neighborhoods, the intervention mothers, as compared to the controls, had smaller families, were more frequently employed, and had a higher socioeconomic status. Given this pattern, it seems probable that these mothers provided their children with socialization experiences different from those provided by control mothers.

Our reasoning that the causal chain for the child effects discovered in the study runs from program to parent and from parent to child is consistent with the analysis advanced by Bronfenbrenner.[5] The regression analyses revealed that the parents' interest in their children's developmental progress during the intervention program was related to the children's IQ five years later. Two factors may mediate this finding. First, the parents may have become aware that there is a continuum of child development on which their children could do well or poorly. Secondly, the parents may have recognized that their own behaviors were important in influencing the course of this development. Those who mounted the Yale Child Welfare Research Program explicitly attempted to influence both factors. They attempted to teach parents that there is a course to child development, and to help parents develop enough of a sense of control over their lives so that they might view their own behavior as an important influence on their children's growth.

Given the appeal of the hypothesis that the parent is the causal agent of the long-term effects of intervention programs, it is surprising that so much of the evaluation of such programs is directed at the child's behavior and so little at changes induced in the parent. Perhaps the results of the present study will provide encouragement for greater use of this strategy.

References

1. Abt Associates. 1979. "Final Report of the National Day Care Study: Children at the Center." Contract No. 105–74–1100 (March).
2. Achenbach, T. and Zigler, E. 1968. "Cue-learning and problem learning strategies in normal and retarded children." *Child Development* 39: 827–848.
3. Apgar, V. and Hames, L.S. 1962. "Further observations on the newborn scoring system." *American Journal of Diseases of Children* 104:419–428.
4. Bloom, B. 1964. *Stability and Change in Human Characteristics.* Wiley, New York.
5. Bronfenbrenner, U. 1974. *A Report on Longitudinal Evaluations of Preschool Programs, Vol. 2: Is Early Intervention Effective?* Department of Health, Education and Welfare, Publication No. (OHS) 74–25, Washington, D.C.

6. Clarke-Stewart, K.A. with Apfel, N.H. 1978. "Evaluating parental effects on child development." *Review of Research in Education*, Vol. 6, L. Shulman, ed. F.E. Peacock Publishers, Itasca, Ill.

7. Darlington, R.B. 1975. *Radicals and Squares: Statistical Methods for the Behavioral Sciences*. Logan Hill Press, Ithaca, N.Y.

8. Darlington, R.B. et al. 1980. "Preschool programs and later school competence of children from low-income families." *Science* 208:202–204.

9. Dunn, L. 1965. *Expanded Manual for the Peabody Picture Vocabulary Test*. American Guidance Service, Circle Pines, Minn.

10. Dunn, L. and Markwardt, F.C. 1970. *Peabody Individual Achievement Test Manual*. American Guidance Service, Circle Pines, Minn.

11. Educational Testing Service. 1968. *Disadvantaged Children and Their First School Experience: Theoretical Considerations and Measurement Strategies* (Report to Office of Economic Opportunity under Contract #4206 and Grant #C6-82-56). Princeton, N.J.

12. Garber, H. and Heber, F.R. 1977. "The Milwaukee Project: indications of the effectiveness of early intervention in preventing mental retardation." In *Research to Practice in Mental Retardation, Vol. 1: Care and Intervention*, P. Mittler, ed. University Park Press, Baltimore, Md.

13. Garcie, J.E. and Scheinfeld, A. 1968. "Sex differences in mental and behavioral traits." *Genetic Psychology Monographs* 77:169–299.

14. Goodson, B.D. and Hess, R.D. 1976. "The effects of parent training programs on child performance and parent behavior." Unpublished manuscript, Stanford University, Stanford, Cal.

15. Harter, S. and Zigler, E. 1974. "The assessment of effectance motivation in normal and retarded children." *Developmental Psychology* 10:169–180.

16. Heber, F.R. 1978. "Sociocultural mental retardation: a longitudinal study." In *Primary Prevention of Psychopathology, Vol. II: Environmental Influences*, D.G. Forgays, ed. University Press of New England, Hanover, N.H.

17. Hollingshead, A.B. 1957. "Two-factor index of social position." Unpublished manuscript, New Haven, Conn.

18. Hunt, J. McV. 1961. *Intelligence and Experience*. Ronald Press, New York.

19. Kagan, J., Kearsley, R.B. and Zelazo, P.R. 1978. *Infancy: Its Place in Human Development*. Harvard University Press, Cambridge, Mass.

20. Kessler, J.W. 1966. *Psychopathology of Children*. Prentice-Hall, Englewood Cliffs, N.J.

21. Mediax Associates, Inc. 1979. "Accept My Profile! Perspectives for Head Start Profiles of Program Effects on Children." (An options paper prepared for the Administration for Children, Youth and Families, Office of Human Development.) Department of Health, Education and Welfare, Contract No. 105–77–1006 (May), Washington, D.C.

22. Pavenstedt, E., ed. 1967. *The Drifters: Children of Disorganized Lower Class Families*. Little, Brown, Boston, Mass.

23. Pines, M. 1967. *Revolution in Learning: The Years from Birth to Six*. Harper and Row, New York.

24. Provence, S. 1968. "The Yale Child Study Center Project." In *Early Child Care: The New Perspectives*, L.A. Chandler, R.S. Lourie and A.D. Peters, eds. Atherton Press, New York.

25. Provence, S., Naylor, A. and Patterson, J. 1977. *The Challenge of Day Care.* Yale University Press, New Haven, Conn.
26. Ramey, C.T. et al. 1976. "The Carolina Abecedarian Project: a longitudinal and multidisciplinary approach to the prevention of developmental retardation." In *Intervention Strategies for High-Risk Infants and Young Children*, T. Tjossem, ed. University Park Press, Baltimore, Md.
27. Ramey, C.T. and Haskins, R. In press. "The causes and treatment of school failure: insights from the Carolina Abecedarian Project." In *Prevention of Retarded Development in Psychosocially Disadvantaged Children*, M.J. Begab, H. Garber and H.C. Haywood, eds. University Park Press, Baltimore, Md.
28. Rescorla, L.A., Provence, S. and Naylor, A. 1981. "The Yale Child Welfare Research Program: description and results." In *Day Care: Scientific and Social Policy Issues.* Auburn House Publishing Company, Boston, Mass.
29. Rosenfeld, A. 1978. "The 'elastic mind' movement: rationalizing child neglect?" *Saturday Review* (April 1) 5:26–28.
30. Scarr, S. and Weinberg, R.A. 1976. "IQ test performance of Black children adopted by White families." *American Psychologist* 31:726–739.
31. Schiff, M. et al. 1978. "Intellectual status of working-class children adopted early into upper-middle-class families." *Science* 200:1503–1504.
32. Seitz, V. 1974. "Long-term motivational-cognitive effects of day care." Final Report for Grant No. OCD–CB–292 from the Child Welfare Research and Demonstration Grants Program, Office of Child Development. Department of Health, Education and Welfare, Washington, D.C.
33. Seitz, V., Apfel, N.H. and Efron, C. 1978. "Long-term effects of early intervention: the New Haven Project." In *Found: Long-Term Gains from Early Intervention*, AAAS 1977 Selected Symposium 8, B. Brown, ed. Westview Press, Colo.
34. Seitz, V., Apfel, N.H. and Rosenbaum, L.K. In press. "Projects Head Start and Follow Through: a longitudinal evaluation of adolescents." In *Prevention of Retarded Development in Psychosocially Disadvantaged Children*, M.J. Begab, H. Garber and H.C. Haywood, eds. University Park Press, Baltimore, Md.
35. Seitz, V. and Efron, C. 1977. "Follow Through in inner city schools: a comparison of five school programs." Unpublished manuscript, Yale University, New Haven, Conn.
36. Shipman, V.C. 1972. *Disadvantaged Children and Their First School Experiences, ETS-Head Start Longitudinal Study.* Educational Testing Service, Princeton, N.J.
37. Skolnik, A. 1978. "The myth of the Vulnerable Child." *Psychology Today* (February) 11:56–65.
38. Stipek, D.J. 1977. "Changes during first grade in children's social motivational development." Unpublished manuscript, Yale University, New Haven, Conn.
39. Trickett, P.K., Apfel, N.H., Rosenbaum, L.K. and Zigler, E.F. 1979. "Yale Child Welfare Research Program: an independent follow-up five years later." Unpublished manuscript, Yale University, New Haven, Conn.
40. Walker, D.K. 1973. *Socioemotional Measures for Preschool and Kindergarten Children.* Jossey-Bass, San Francisco, Cal.

41. Weaver, J., Balla, D. and Zigler, E. 1971. "Social approach and avoidance tendencies of institutionalized retarded and noninstitutionalized retarded and normal children." *Journal of Experimental Research in Personality* 5:98–110.
42. White, B.L. 1975. *The First Three Years of Life.* Prentice-Hall, Englewood Cliffs, N.J.
43. Yando, R., Seitz, V. and Zigler, E. 1979. *Intellectual and Personality Characteristics of Children: Social Class and Ethnic Group Differences.* Lawrence Erlbaum Associates, Hillsdale, N.J.
44. Zigler, E. 1970. "The environmental mystique: training the intellect versus development of the child." *Childhood Education* 46:402–412.
45. Zigler, E. 1971. "The retarded child as a whole person." In *Advances in Experimental Clinical Psychology*, Vol. 1, H.E. Adams and W.K. Boardman, III, eds. Pergamon Press, New York.
46. Zigler, E. 1973. "Project Head Start: success or failure?" *Learning* 1:43–47.
47. Zigler, E. 1976. "Head Start: not a program but an evolving concept." In *Early Childhood Education: It's an Art! It's a Science!*, J.D. Andrews, ed. National Association for the Education of Young Children, Washington, D.C.
48. Zigler, E., Abelson, W.D. and Seitz, V. 1973. "Motivational factors in the performance of economically disadvantaged children on the Peabody Picture Vocabulary Test." *Child Development* 44:294–303.
49. Zigler, E., Abelson, W.D., Trickett, P.K. and Seitz, V. 1980. "Is an intervention program really necessary to raise disadvantaged children's IQ scores?" Unpublished manuscript, Yale University, New Haven, Conn.
50. Zigler, E. and Trickett, P.K. 1978. "IQ, social competence, and evaluation of early childhood intervention programs." *American Psychologist* 33:789–798.

Chapter 11

THE PROBLEM OF INFANT DAY CARE

by Douglas Frye

The problem of infant day care can be separated into two parts. The first, of course, is: what are the effects of this child-rearing alternative? The popularity of infant day care in American culture is quite recent. It comes at a time when we know that some forms of infant care—prolonged residence in institutions, for example—are likely to influence development adversely.[40,44] We do not have nearly enough information, however, to state definitively whether or not infant day care belongs in this category. Yet parents who are considering day care for their child deserve to know what the probable consequences of the experience will be.

The second part of the problem is that, on the whole, our expert attempts to evaluate infant day care have been inadequate. There are many reasons for this shortcoming. Significant among these are changes in accepted research procedures and the intractability of the problem itself. All of these factors combined amount to a body of research which must be carefully weighed for what it truly shows about infant day care. If it is worth worrying about the effects of infant day care, it is also worth worrying about the research used to discover those effects. Our knowledge of one will only be as good as our practice of the other.

This paper was written while the author was a predoctoral fellow in the Bush Foundation Training Program in Child Development and Social Policy, Yale University.

The Limitations of the Research

Each of the four reviews[2,5,34,39] of the infant day care literature has discussed the limitations of the research in this field. The drawbacks of the various studies fall into all three of the possible domains of independent variables, dependent variables, and design. Typically, infant day care studies have restricted independent variables to care in high quality or university-based centers serving children of particular socioeconomic classes. Dependent variables have usually been limited to measures of intelligence and attachment. Experimental designs have almost invariably not followed random assignment of subjects to conditions. Although the reviews have highlighted all of these constraints, none has given the last its proper due, which is unfortunate, since of the three it is the most important.

When infant day care began to be studied ten years ago, social science was under the sway of works like Campbell and Stanley's influential *Experimental and Quasi-experimental Designs for Research*. The approved wisdom of that time favored experimental designs for evaluating programs like infant day care—designs which randomly assigned children to treatment and control groups—but also accepted the legitimacy of quasi-experimental designs, those which relied on prematching or later adjustment by analysis of covariance to replace random assignment. Though preferred, other considerations made random assignment much the less popular research alternative. In studies of "real world" outcomes, it is often very difficult to find parents who would like their child to be in infant day care and have the treatment, but are also willing to have the child act as a control if so assigned by the draw. Furthermore, there is always the associated ethical question of the defensibility of willfully depriving some children of a treatment which may indeed be beneficial. Given these considerations, it is not surprising that the majority of studies of infant day care have used quasi-experimental designs.

In recent years, quasi-experimental designs have been reexamined. The accepted and convincing wisdom now is that these designs are not viable. It has been found that without randomization neither matching nor the analysis of covariance is sufficient to control for the artifactual differences which may be present in self-selected groups.[8,13] Indeed, these practices may actually produce confoundings through regression effects. This flaw of quasi-experimental designs is not slight, for it does not merely produce experimental results that are limited, but results that are uninterpretable. If it is not possible to exclude artifacts, then it will not be possible to assign the results found in a quasi-experimental study to the treatment tested, whether the results were good, bad, or indifferent. The early matched-sample evaluations[11] which mistakenly found Head Start to be ineffective or even harmful made precisely this error.[8] Accepting the results of infant day care studies done without random assignment of subjects is as mistaken as accepting the results of the early evaluations of Head Start.

Since the design flaw of many infant day care studies undermines the results of those studies, it presents a more serious fault than the limitations in independent and dependent variables which only restrict the generalizability of results. Stated another way, the design flaw threatens the internal validity of the experiments, while the external validity is determined by the independent and dependent measures. Not all of the research on infant day care is compromised by threats to internal validity. There are several studies which have either incorporated a random control or, more recently, have found fair and practicable ways around the problem. The results of these studies are reviewed in the next section. The results reported can be accepted, although they have clear restrictions in independent and dependent measures. As a consequence, what has been found cannot be assumed to apply to all types of infant day care and all aspects of infant development. Questions on these latter two points are taken up later in this paper.

Outcome Studies

Subjects Randomly Assigned

The Carolina Abecedarian Project at the University of North Carolina may be the only infant day research program to use a fully experimental design. The pilot study[35] for this project tested matched home controls to determine the effect of day care on cognitive development, but with the start of the project itself in 1972 infants of willing parents were randomly assigned to home or day care groups. The sample is now made up of close to sixty children from high-risk, i.e., poverty-level, homes.[10,31] Approximately half of the children have been enrolled in high-quality, academic-based infant day care since they were three months old. The child-caretaker ratio at the center is 1:3 for infants under a year and 1:4 for those over a year.[31] Children in both the day care and home groups are provided with medical care, nutritional supplements, and social work services for their families. Since the groups were formed by random assignment, the sample is of unique value for evaluating infant day care.

Research on the Abecedarian children is reported in a series of studies[10,30,31,32] by Ramey and his colleagues. The research has principally tested the effect of day care on infant cognitive development and on infant-mother interaction. Since new infants are enrolled in the project annually, some of the studies are based on a smaller sample than others. Many include an appropriate, stratified, general population control group to furnish a kind of scale to which to compare the two high-risk groups.

The cognitive development of the children was measured at 6, 12, and 18 months using the Bayley scales and at 24 and 36 months with the Stanford-Binet. Testing was done at the day care center, which may have initially favored the day care children, but both groups were tested the same number of times and eventually the testing session should have also become familiar to the home group. No differences were found between groups at 6 and 12 months, and scores were within the normal range of the general population. Between 12 and 18 months a difference favoring the day care group appeared. Closer analysis revealed that the day care group was staying within the normal range while the controls dropped off. This same pattern of results persisted at 24 and 36 months on the Stanford-Binet. Ratings showed that during the earlier tests the day care children were more cooperative and at ease. A detailed analysis of the tests themselves indicated that the groups seemed to be differing primarily on language and perceptual-motor as opposed to problem-solving or imitation tasks.

Two measures of social interaction between infant and mother were used in the project. One was Caldwell's HOME inventory scale, and the other was an unstructured laboratory observation session lasting 25 minutes. The observations were done when the children were 6 and 21 months of age in a place novel to both groups. The observation sessions revealed the strongest differences between the groups. In general, the day care infants spent significantly more time vocalizing and interacting with their mothers, while the home controls fed, slept, and fussed more. These differences seemed to be due to both the mothers and children in the two groups. There were no differences on the HOME scale administered at 6 and 18 months except that at the older age, day care mothers were rated as being significantly more responsive to their child. Since the children were randomly assigned to groups, this difference would seem to be a consequence of the day care experience on the mother, the child or both.

The Ramey studies demonstrate a basic ameliorative effect for infant day care. Cognitive development and infant-mother interaction were improved or kept within normal bounds by the child's participation in a day care program. Of course, the breadth of these results is restricted in several ways. All of the children in the project were from economically impoverished homes, and the day care center attended may have been of unusually high quality. Furthermore, the dependent measures used—standardized intelligence tests, the HOME scale and observation of infant-mother interaction—by no means exhaust the appropriate measures of cognitive and social development during infancy. Nonetheless, for the independent and dependent variables tested here, it is reasonably certain that this program and others like it will have a beneficial, rather than harmful effect.

Waiting-List Controls

In a study of center day care, home day care and home-rearing in Sweden, Cochran[12] employed a method of subject selection which both avoided bias and was practical to carry out. Subjects were not randomly assigned to the three conditions, but the home day care and home with natural mother groups were constituted from families who were on the waiting list for a place in a day care center. Consequently, it would not be expected that there would be confounding differences between the sixty families who made up the day care center group and the sixty families who combined made up the home day care and home groups.

The twelve day care centers in this study were located in one city in Sweden. The centers were not university-based or exceptional in any apparent way, although staff-child ratios were 1:2 for 12-month-olds and below, and 1:4 for 1- to 3-year-olds. The personnel in the centers were usually college trained. In the family day care, there were always only two or three children in each family setting.

Measures of attachment and cognitive development were taken at 12, 15, and 18 months of age. Attachment to mother was probed through a semistructured separation episode conducted in the child's home. The Griffiths Mental Development Scale was administered on a subsequent visit to the home. The results were consistent and simple. The three groups did not differ.

Cummings[14] recently used a design similar to Cochran's to test maternal attachment in a small sample of American infants. Children from two centers serving the University of California at Los Angeles were compared with controls from the waiting lists of those centers. A laboratory test situation unfamiliar to both groups assessed attachment using measures of infant proximity-seeking to mother and response to stranger. No difference between the groups was detected.

The design of the Cochran and Cummings studies, like that of Ramey's, provides the internal validity necessary for the unambiguous interpretation of the studies' results. Cochran and Cummings, like Ramey, did not find harmful effects of day care on infant development. Cochran's results enlarge on those of the Abecedarian project in that family as well as center day care was assessed, the children were not from high-risk homes, a measure of attachment and a different instrument for determining cognitive development were included, and all testing was done in the home to reduce bias. Cummings shows that Cochran's results for attachment may be extended to an American sample in university-based care. Of course, the dependent variables measured in all three studies are still somewhat circumscribed, and the quality of the day care tested was probably quite high, even though Cochran's used what is "average" for Sweden. There may also be effects of day care which only emerge after long periods. These effects, if present, may have gone undetected, but do have a chance of being uncovered since both Cochran and Ramey are continuing to follow their samples.

Studies Lacking Internal Validity

Aside from the work reviewed above, the remainder of the outcome studies testing infant day care are of problematical design. Indeed, these studies stand in the majority. Given the particular quasi-experimental designs that have been used, our present scientific expertise is not sufficient to credit, dispute or even evaluate the results of this research. It may be of use, however, to examine briefly some of the research to understand the problems it presents. The studies can be divided, on the basis of their own emphases, into those testing cognitive development and those concerned with socio-emotional development or attachment.

Cognitive development. The recently published study[18] of infant day care in New York City is an excellent example of the research in this category. In many ways, this study is one of the best that has been done on infant day care. Over 400 children and 31 day care centers were involved. Homes, family day care arrangements and day care centers were all represented. Obviously, though, the study could not control which children entered which type of care. Consequently, the evaluation confounds the effect of the care experience on the different children with possible differences in parental attitudes towards day care and child rearing (see, for example, Reference 20) and observed differences in the three groups' initial levels of ability. The researchers tried to correct this deficiency of the quasi-experimental design with analyses of covariance. Most of the other studies of the effects of infant day care on cognitive development[17,20,21,22,23,35] have used matching of subjects for the same purpose. Neither tactic, as has been noted,[8] is satisfactory.

In the New York City study, IQ was tested in the family and center day care samples when the children entered care and when they were

18 and 36 months old. In addition to these longitudinal samples, two separate cross-sectional treatment samples were drawn, again at 18 and 36 months. Children in the cross-sectional samples were just then entering day care. They served as home-reared controls. The Bayley was administered at the earlier ages, the Stanford-Binet and the Peabody Picture Vocabulary Test at 36 months. The results of the study showed that at 18 months both the day care groups had IQ scores in the normal range, while the home-reared controls scored significantly lower. At 36 months, the day care center group had not changed, but the family day care group had fallen to the level of the home controls.

The three groups in the New York City evaluation were different in several important ways. For example, although all of the groups were made up primarily of Black and Hispanic children, the representation of each in each group was not constant. Family income level varied and the two day care groups differed in measured cognitive ability at the time of enrollment. In the two cross-sectional comparisons, at 18 and 36 months, these confounding differences could not, for the most part, be "adjusted for," so it is perfectly possible that the observed differences among the groups were due to factors besides rearing experience. In the longitudinal comparisons between the two day care conditions, the problem of earlier differences confounding later ones was attacked with analyses of covariance. These analyses were responsible for revealing that IQ scores declined in the family day care group relative to the center sample. Without knowing more about the underlying differences between the groups, i.e., knowing how representative of real differences the observed initial differences were, it is impossible to judge if analysis of covariance provides a trustworthy correction for interpreting the later scores. Indeed, it would probably be possible to find a family day care sample in New York City which compared to this sample would, even after using analysis of covariance, make the effect of the center experience look deleterious.[8]

Several other points about the New York City study should be mentioned. During the study, there seemed to be a differential attrition of children with low birth weight or birth complications from the center group. This difference would be likely to inflate the later scores of the center group. There were also two important negative findings: (1) length of time in day care did not relate to test performance, and (2) structured observations did not reveal any differences in the cognitive-language stimulation given the two day care groups. It might have been expected, although it would not have to be so, that these findings would not have been negative if day care experience was responsible for the difference between the center and family groups.

It should be noted as an incidental point that studies which have explicitly tried to examine variables like age of entry and length of time in day care often carry the same design flaw as the New York City project (see References 24, 37, 41 although 4 is on better ground since age was not fixed). Schwarz, Strickland and Krolick and Macrae and Herbert-Jackson searched for differential effects of home versus day care by observing day care children who had either been enrolled a short or a long time. Schwarz et al. found that children who had been in day care since infancy were rated as less co-operative, more aggressive, and more active motorically than children who had only entered day care several months ago. Macrae and Herbert-Jackson made the same sort of test at a different day care center and found the infant day care group was *better* at getting along with peers, problem solving, ability to abstract, and planning. The direct conflict in results prompted Macrae and Herbert-Jackson to speculate that the effects of infant day care may be program-specific. Both groups of researchers acknowledge, however, that their use of *ex post facto* designs makes it impossible to be certain that the effects of day care, rather than covarying differences in the children, were being measured. If there were important covarying differences, then it is logically possible that the two studies could reach conflict-ing conclusions even if the effect of day care had been the same in each.

The New York City study was selected as a representative of the research that has used matching of subjects or the analysis of co-variance to assess the effects of infant day care on cognitive devel-opment. The results of all of these studies present the same difficulties of interpretation as in the New York City case. In properly controlled experiments, Ramey and Cochran did not find adverse effects of in-fant day care on cognitive development. Fortunately, with one ex-ception,[17] the quasi-experimental results do not contradict this conclusion, so there is no necessity to argue for the dismissal of a large portion of the reported work. The one study out of line with the rest is Fowler's, which seems to show that infant day care, com-pared to home rearing, boosts IQ scores above average levels, at least for a couple of years. The design of Fowler's study hampers an evaluation of this result.

Attachment. The results of the studies of day care and attach-ment to mother are not consistent, although the research designs followed are. Excepting Cochran's and Cummings's studies, all of the others[3,6,7,15,16,20,21,26,27,28,41] have matched subjects from different rearing conditions. Cochran found no differences in attachment for infants in home, family, or center care. Cummings similarly did not find a difference between home and day care. Some of the quasi-experimental studies have found differences. In particular, Blehar found, in contradistinction to Caldwell et al., that day care children's attachment to their mothers was of a poorer quality than home-reared controls. Among the quasi-experimental studies, Blehar's stands in the minority, except for a new study which offers partial support. Vaughn et al. found that there were more infants who showed anxious-avoidant attachment in a group which entered day care before 12 months compared to a group starting after 12 months and a group in home care. Besides these findings, two studies[6,26] have reported sex by rearing-condition interactions.

There is certainly no lack of possibilities to account for the variance in the quasi-experimental results. Some of the candidates that have been mentioned include differences in time in care, in quality of care given, in socioeconomic status of the infants tested, and in measures of attachment used. To this list must always be added the possibility of preexisting group differences which may confound the effect-of-care comparison and the possibility that those differences take different forms in different studies.[5] As Ramey and Mills note, these last two concerns arise directly from the absence of the random assignment of subjects to conditions. Until these possibilities are removed, moreover, it will be impossible to tell whether any or all of the others are implicated. As the literature now stands, Cochran and Cummings are the only tests of the effects of infant day care on attachment to mother which can be accepted with equanimity.

Summary of the outcome research. The three outcome studies with experimental control sufficient to insure the interpretability of results do not show detrimental effects of infant day care on standardized IQ test performance and several measures of the mother-infant relationship. Cochran found no differences in IQ or attachment among the home, family day care and day care center groups in his Swedish sample. Cummings did not find attachment differences between home and center day care in his American sample. The work of Ramey and his colleagues found beneficial effects of center day care compared to home rearing for IQ scores and mother-infant interaction in the laboratory for a sample of infants from low socioeconomic households. Needless to say, the results of these studies are restricted. Day care of good quality was tested on a limited number of measures over the first couple of years of life. Nonetheless, within these constraints these results are significant.

Independent Variables and Care Given

The outcome studies show very clearly the need for experimental or very special kinds of quasi-experimental investigations of the effects of infant day care. Also needed, as has been almost universally remarked, are studies which add to the list of independent variables considered. To make a judgement about infant day care, it is imperative to know the consequences of this care alternative as it exists and is used every day. We must know about the effects of the full range of quality of care, know what effects different types of day care are likely to have, know the effects on different sorts of children, and know the importance of time of entry and length of time in day care (see, for example, Reference 1). It will not be enough just to expand the research, however. These new questions need to be asked, as we have seen, in ways which will provide meaningful answers.

Effects of Different Regimes

Besides the studies of family versus center care mentioned previously, there have been extremely few well-designed investigations which explore the effects of different aspects of the day care experience. Without research of this sort, there are no empirical guidelines for deciding how day care programs should be planned and run. A paradigmatic instance of how this research might be conducted is to be found in a study[42] of the effects of different caregiver configurations in day care. Wilcox et al. instituted two different caregiver arrangements in two separate rooms of an infant day care center. In both, the caregiver-infant ratio was 1:4, but in one each caregiver was responsible for 4 particular infants while in the other the 5 caregivers shared responsibility for all 20 infants. Teachers and children were randomly assigned to the two rooms. In the high quality center in which this study was conducted, there were no differences over two years between the two arrangements for the infants' scores on the Bayley or in their reaction to separations and reunions with their mothers.

One of the reasons Wilcox et al. may not have found differences between the two arrangements is that the two did not differ radically in practice. The amount of contact with other children and the amount of time each child spent with a single "primary" caregiver was the same for both groups. The Wilcox et al. study is thorough in including these last two measures. To test the effects of different aspects of day care, evidence is necessary that those aspects are present. One of the growing areas in infant day care research is aimed at finding differences in care *per se*. So far, much of this work has concentrated on discovering the differences inherent in home, family day, and center care, but any of the other relevant independent variables could be the object of study.

In assessing the care actually given to infants in different situations, random assignment of the infants to the different settings may be of slightly diminished importance. Of course, in the properly controlled experiments, the occasion for worry will not have to arise. There also may not be the need to worry about variables which are fairly securely under outside control. For example, the infant's physical environment in different types of care may not be contaminated by subtle differences in the types of infants who are placed in various types of care. For other domains the problem is more acute. One of the hard-won lessons of the last ten years of infancy research is that infants have effects on their caregivers as well as the reverse. For measures of infant-caregiver interaction and the like, it may very well be that care differences are caused in part by uncontrolled-for differences in the infants being studied.

Care Given

The New York City study made a variety of comparisons of the care provided in representative settings. As has been noted, the children attending the two types of day care in this study showed preexisting familial and ability differences. It is possible, however, these differences would not contaminate all of the differences uncovered by naturalistic observation of the settings. The study found that day care centers had fewer physical safety hazards than family day settings, although the safety practices in the two did not differ. It was found, in addition, that day care centers provided more play possibilities, materials, equipment, and space, but the family settings enjoyed a more favorable staff-to-child ratio. The day care centers furnished a better diet and health care (e.g., immunizations) although the authors suggest that these two differences may stem from differences in the City's administration of the two types of programs. Finally, some differences emerged favoring family day care for individual social interaction, especially during the noonday meal.

Cochran looked at two aspects of the care given his Swedish sample. The home, family day, and center settings were rated for caregiver-infant interaction and for the range of possible experiences they offered the child. Both rating scales revealed that there were more commonalities than differences among the three settings. Children explored more, and were carried more in the two home situations, while they played more in center day care. There were also more interactions with caregivers in home and family day care. Interactions with caregivers there tended to be cognitive-verbal and involve more exploration and play. At the same time, compared to the day care centers, caregivers were more likely to be instructive and restrictive in the home settings. In this study, it is possible to conclude that the differences observed were due to setting, although Cochran raises the possibility that caregiver behavior may have differed in part because mothers more than teachers made adjustments in response to the presence of the observer.

Rubenstein and Howes compared the experiences of 18 month olds in home rearing and in non-university-based day care centers. The group membership followed was not the product of anything except parents' choice and matching. Infants were observed and rated on affect and on the nature and duration of interactions with caregivers, peers and toys. Again, there were strong similarities between the care given. The overall time spent in positive interaction with caregivers was almost exactly the same in both situations. The cognitive and linguistic stimulation offered the child was also the same. Number of playthings in the two settings agreed, although they were of different types, with the centers having more toys *per se* and the homes having other objects that served as toys.

The differences Rubenstein and Howes found overlapped with the ones Cochran discovered. Rubenstein and Howes did not measure exploration, but they did find, like Cochran, that there was more play in day care. The day care play was also of a higher developmental level than that found at home. Mothers were again strongly found to be more restrictive and directive than day care teachers who tended more to praise. Even though Rubenstein and Howes did not find differences, as Cochran did, in the occurrence of cognitive-linguistic interactions in the two settings, they did find that home infants were slightly more responsive linguistically. Finally, Rubenstein and Howes's measures detected more positive affect, mutual regard, reciprocal smiling, and less crying in day care.

A further scrutiny of their results led Rubenstein and Howes to two important discoveries. An analysis of the play data showed that the increase *and* higher developmental level of play in day care was a consequence of the presence of peers in that setting. In addition to showing the importance of peers for children of this age, this finding may help explain why Cochran found more play overall in day care, but more play with caregivers in homes—the presence of peers could account for the difference. Rubenstein and Howes also found a preponderant importance for the role of the head teacher in day care. Although head and assistant teachers were found to be equally available, the infants were much more likely to touch, talk to and smile at the head teacher.

Summary of Setting Differences

Comparisons of the care given infants in the various settings tested show, by everyone's report, more similarities than differences. The differences occurred in several domains. Centers seemed to differ from home and family day care in the types of toys available and in the nature of the physical surroundings. Centers may also provide better nutrition and health care than family day arrangements, at least in a city like New York. On more psychological dimensions, the three settings appear remarkably alike. Differences in the behavior of caregivers were not numerous. Cochran found some advantage in home care for a number of cognitive-linguistic interactions. This result was not found in the other studies, but since Cochran's was the best designed, his finding should probably be respected. It was a consistent finding that mothers were more directive and restrictive than day care teachers. Children appear to explore more at home, while there is more play in day care centers. Play with peers is responsible for this difference and for a positive effect on the level of infant play. Except in Cochran's and the Wilcox et al. study, initial differences in the children may influence caregivers and thereby produce or obscure setting and regime differences. It cannot be assumed that *any* child entering these types of care would be treated in the ways these other studies have found—care might change on the basis of the child's characteristics, and certain children might not "match" certain settings. It must also be remembered that since the outcome studies have not in general shown differential effects, there is no evidence that the differences observed in settings produce striking differences in development although, of course, it is altogether possible that the appropriate measures have not been used, or the differences only emerge over time.

Dependent Variables

Dependent variables need to be considered in relation to two areas of infant day care research. They are relevant to the outcome and setting comparisons already reviewed and to another type of study.

Studies of Day Care Alone

The outcome and setting studies of infant day care depend on making comparisons among various aspects and alternatives of care. Another type of study which only tests the status of day care children is possible for certain dependent variables. Attachment has been the most common dependent variable in infant day care studies of this kind (see References 33, 43). Cummings, for instance, investigated the adequacy of day care infants' attachments, not by comparing them to home controls, but by testing the day care children's reactions to various possible attachment figures. Cummings replicated the established finding that day care infants show attachment to their mothers and their teachers, but given the choice, direct many more behaviors to mother. Attachment shown to strangers, as would be expected, was virtually nil. Cummings also added a new comparison of stable versus nonstable caregivers where stability was defined by the amount of time the caregivers were regularly in the day care center. In a laboratory test, differences in attachment to the two types of caregivers were not seen, but when a test was carried out in the day care center a preference for the stable caregivers was observed.

Several other dependent variables besides attachment have been given attention with day care infants. Johnson and Ricciuti in all-day observations over the course of a year found that levels of fussing and crying in infant day care were low and that what instances there were generally brought response from the staff in less than 10 seconds. McCurcheon and Calhoun and Schwarz, Krolick and Strickland measured indicators—smiling, crying, playing, etc.—of infants' social and emotional adjustment to day care for the first month after entry into the center. The results show better adjustment after the month and a change in social interaction which consisted of a decrease in interactions with caregivers and an increase in interactions with peers.

Outcome and Setting Studies

The question of choice of dependent variables is of importance for studies of infant day care alone and for studies which use a comparison group or groups. The reviews of the infant day care literature all criticize the selection of dependent variables that has been tested. Without a wider range of measures, it is conceivable that infant day care has any number of consequences, either positive or negative, which remain undetected. The effects that are known, the ones derived from the properly controlled experiments, are trustworthy but limited, since they do cover so few variables.

Belsky and Steinberg and Bronfenbrenner, Belsky and Steinberg strongly argue that the research on infant day care has lacked ecological validity. The wide implications have not been sought. Infant day care affects not only the infant, but, to some degree, siblings, parents, the community, and society as a whole. To evaluate infant day care as a policy alternative, all of these factors need to be considered. At present, the research has concentrated entirely on the infant.

The conclusion that research on infant day care has lacked ecological validity is just. There almost certainly are effects of this rearing scheme which extend beyond the child. It is not implausible to expect, for example, that inexpensive infant day care might improve the economic status of some families by freeing the parent or parents to join the work force (see Reference 18). At the same time, it must be acknowledged that even though the research efforts need to consider these questions, the main concern must still rest with the infant. The direct and lasting consequences of day care focus on the infant first and so must the research.

Another point in the Bronfenbrenner, Belsky and Steinberg critique, one which appears in the other reviews as well, is that infant measures in day care research are narrow and many times artificial. The research cannot continue to rely overwhelmingly on standardized IQ tests and the Ainsworth strange situation. Both may lack the ecological validity necessary to detect real differences in cognitive development or attachment. Silverstein urges that Piaget's scales be used to assess infant cognitive development. Investigations into attachment need to be done, as they are beginning to be, in the infant's natural environments of the day care setting and at home, as well as being carried out in the laboratory. On all counts, studies of infant day care need to be developmental.[39] Experiences which have no impact at 3 months may very well have a powerful influence at 12 months or vice versa. Sensitivity to the developmental changes that are occurring at a head-over-heels pace in infancy has not yet figured adequately in the research on infant day care.

Just as development is accelerated during infancy, the pace of the study of infant development has similarly quickened. New areas of research open every year. These areas typically have not been represented in studies of infant day care, yet they are of obvious importance. Language development is a primary example. Much work has been devoted in the last fifteen years to determining how the infant acquires language. The latest chapters in these investigations suggest that language acquisition may depend on subtle and complex games infants play with their caregivers many months before they learn to talk. It would be crucial to know whether these same games are played between infants and their day care teachers. Are these sorts of subtle, very attention-consuming activities possible in infant day care? If not, it is likely that there are differences in language development between infants in home and day care. Since most of the tests which have been used to consider this question were developed long before the new findings on language acquisition, the question remains unanswered. There is an analogous need to incorporate into the day care research assessments of infant functioning based on new work on cognitive and social development. As yet, very little along these lines has been done, even though the new work represents our best efforts to understand infant development.

Summary on the Question of Dependent Variables

Several studies have tested children in infant day care on particular dependent measures, especially on measures of attachment. This research shows that infants in day care appear to be attached to both their mothers and day care teachers, while still showing a strong preference for mother. In the day care setting stable caregivers are favored and adjustment to day care seems to improve over the first month. These papers are restricted in that only high quality centers have been studied and, of course, the studies tested children whose parents chose for them to be in day care. In addition to these day care-alone studies, the question of dependent measures is relevant to the outcome and setting studies already reviewed. An adequate evaluation of the effects of infant day care will not be in place until a broader range of dependent variables is commonly used. Assessments need to be followed which admit ecological validity—test the infant in natural settings and test implications of care which go beyond the infant—and take advantage of the substantive advances made in the study of infant development in the past two decades.

Conclusion

As a new and moderately different child care alternative, infant day care presents a problem to parents and social scientists alike. Each has a compelling interest in knowing the probable effects of this sort of care. Parents especially deserve the best information available on the subject, since they bear a responsibility to and for their children. In spite of this strong need to know, the research on infant day care has to a large extent compounded, rather than solved the original problem. The majority of studies have followed experimental designs which are now known to be inadequate. In short, although these studies have produced results, the results cannot in good conscience be relied on. The only interpretable evaluations available on infant day care are a very small number of studies which have used properly selected control groups.

The results of this small collection of studies seem to show that good quality infant day care does not disrupt the development of intelligence or maternal attachment. For children from low-income homes in our society, high-quality center care may further intellectual development, though it is not known if this benefit persists. Besides these findings on the effects on the child, some more tentative conclusions can be drawn from investigations of the care actually given in day settings versus home settings. Day care centers, quite naturally, present slightly different physical environments than homes do. Day care teachers seem to be slightly less restrictive and more praising than parents. Children reared at home may have more cognitive-linguistic interactions with their caregivers, although infants in day care seem to benefit from the opportunity of playing with their peers. All in all, the different settings have been found to be more similar than different, and at the moment it is not obvious that any of the differences has a strong influence on development.

The current data meeting the test of modern research standards give a good passing grade to infant day care. Of course, it must immediately be noted that there is not a great deal of data available and much of what is available is problematical. The research is restricted in independent variables. We do not know even a minimum about different sorts of day care, day care of differing quality and the effects of day care on different sorts of children. The dependent measures which have been used are also much too constrained. Performance on standardized intelligence tests and tests of attachment have been studied to the exclusion of assessments which might be more sensitive to development in these domains, to infant development in other areas, and to the recent developments in the study of infancy itself. In attacking these new questions, the research needs to incorporate adequate comparison groups to insure the interpretability of results.

To some degree, then, infant day care remains a problem. It is possible that there are effects, harmful or beneficial, of this care alternative which have not been measured or measured adequately. Certainly it can be said that it is likely more signs would have been seen by now if infant day care were disastrously harmful. The signs that can be seen show the problems of doing research on this topic; these are problems that are difficult but ones within our power to correct and ones which must be corrected before we can give the competent evaluation of infant day care which parents expect and deserve.

References

1. Anderson, C. 1980. "Attachment in daily separations: reconceptualizing day care and maternal employment issues." *Child Development* 51:242–245.
2. Belsky, J. and Steinberg, L. 1978. "The effects of day care: a critical review." *Child Development* 49:929–949.
3. Blehar, M. 1974. "Anxious attachment and defensive reactions associated with day care." *Child Development* 45:683–692.
4. Blanchard, M. and Main, M. "Avoidance of attachment figure and socio-emotional adjustment in day-care infants." *Developmental Psychology* 15(4):445–446.

5. Bronfenbrenner, U., Belsky, J. and Steinberg, L. 1976. "Day care in context: an ecological perspective on research and public policy." Paper prepared for the Office of the Assistant Secretary for Planning and Evaluation, Department of Health, Education and Welfare.
6. Brookhart, J. and Hock, E. 1976. "The effects of experimental context and experimental background on infants' behavior toward their mothers and a stranger." *Child Development* 47:333–340.
7. Caldwell, B., Wright, C., Honig, A. and Tannenbaum, J. 1970. "Infant day care and attachment." *American Journal of Orthopsychiatry* 40:397–412.
8. Campbell, D. and Erlebacher, A. 1970. "How regression artifacts in quasi-experimental evaluations can mistakenly make compensatory education look harmful." In *Compensatory Education: A National Debate, Volume 3, Disadvantaged Child,* J. Hellmuth, ed. Brunner/Mazel, New York.
9. Campbell, D. and Stanley, J. 1966. *Experimental and Quasi-experimental Designs for Research.* Rand-McNally, Chicago.
10. Campbell, F. and Ramey, C. 1977. "The effects of early intervention on intellectual development." Presented to the Society for Research in Child Development, New Orleans.
11. Cicirelli, V. et al. 1969. "The Impact of Head Start: An Evaluation of the Effects of Head Start on Children's Cognitive and Affective Development." A report presented to the Office of Economic Opportunity.
12. Cochran, M. 1977. "A comparison of group day and family child-rearing patterns in Sweden." *Child Development* 48:702–707.
13. Cook, T. and Campbell, D. 1979. *Quasi-experimentation: Design and Analysis Issues for Field Settings.* Rand-McNally, Chicago.
14. Cummings, E. 1980. "Caregiver stability and day care." *Developmental Psychology* 16(1):31–37.
15. Doyle, A. 1975. "Infant development in day care." *Developmental Psychology* 11:655–656.
16. Doyle, A. and Somers, K. 1978. "The effects of group and family day care on infant attachment." *Canadian Journal of Behavioral Science* 10:38–45.
17. Fowler, W. 1978. *Day Care and Its Effects on Early Development.* Ontario Institute for Studies in Education, Toronto.
18. Golden, M., Rosenbluth, L., Grossi, M., Policare, H., Freeman, H. and Brownlee, E. 1978. *The New York City Infant Day Care Study.* Medical and Health Research Association of New York, New York.
19. Johnson, J. and Ricciuti, H. 1974. *Crying and the relief of distress in an infant day nursery.* Technical Report, Cornell Research Program in Early Development and Education, Ithaca, New York.
20. Hock, E. 1980. "Working and nonworking mothers and their infants: a comparative study of maternal caregiving characteristics and infant social behavior." *Merrill-Palmer Quarterly* 26(2):79–101.
21. Kagan, J., Kearsley, R. and Kelazo, P. 1976. "The effects of infant day care on psychological development." Presented to the American Association for the Advancement of Science, Boston.
22. Keister, M. 1970. "A demonstration project: group care for infants and toddlers." Mimeographed final report.

23. Kohen-Raz, R. 1968. "Mental and motor development of kibbutz, institutionalized and home-reared infants in Israel." *Child Development* 39: 489–504.

24. Macrae, J. and Herbert-Jackson, E. 1976. "Are the behavioral effects of infant day care program specific?" *Developmental Psychology*, 12:269–270.

25. McCurcheon, B. and Calhoun, K. 1976. "Social and emotional adjustments of infants and toddlers to a day care setting." *American Journal of Orthopsychiatry* 46:104–108.

26. Moskowitz, D., Schwarz, C. and Corsini, D. 1977. "Initiating day care at three years of age: effects on attachment." *Child Development* 48:1271–1276.

27. Portnoy, F. and Simmons, C. 1978. "Day care and attachment." *Child Development* 49:239–242.

28. Ragozin, A. 1980. "Attachment behavior of day care children: naturalistic and laboratory observations." *Child Development* 51:409–415.

29. Ramey, C. and Farran, D. 1975. "Infant day care and attachment behaviors toward mother and teachers." Presented to the American Psychological Association, Chicago.

30. Ramey, C. and Mills, J. 1975. "Mother-infant interaction patterns as a function of rearing conditions." Presented to the Society for Research in Child Development, Denver.

31. Ramey, C. and Mills, J. 1977. "Social and intellectual consequences of day care for high risk infants." In *Social Development: Family and Group Experience*, R. Webb, ed. Johns Hopkins Press, Baltimore.

32. Ramey, C., O'Brien, C. and Finkelstein, N. 1975. "The influence on mother-infant interaction patterns." Presented to the Southeastern Psychological Association, Atlanta.

33. Ricciuti, H. 1974. "Fear and the development of social attachments in the first year of life." In *The Origins of Human Behavior: Fear*, M. Lewis and L. Rosenblum, eds. John Wiley and Sons, New York.

34. Ricciuti, H. 1976. "Effects of infant day care experience on behavior and development: research and implications for social policy." Paper prepared for the Office of the Assistant Secretary for Planning and Evaluation, Department of Health, Education and Welfare.

35. Robinson, H. and Robinson, N. 1971. "Longitudinal development of young children in a comprehensive day care program: the first two years." *Child Development* 42:1673–1683.

36. Rubenstein, J. and Howes, C. 1979. "Caregiving and infant behavior in day care and in homes." *Developmental Psychology* 15:1–24.

37. Schwarz, J., Krolick, G. and Strickland, R. 1973. "Effects of early day care on adjustment to a new environment." *American Journal of Orthopsychiatry* 43:340–346.

38. Schwarz, J., Strickland, R. and Krolick, G. 1974. "Infant day care: behavioral effects at school age." *Developmental Psychology* 10:502–506.

39. Silverstein, L. 1977. "A critical review of current research on infant day care." Paper prepared as part of the U.S. report on Alternative Policies for Caring for Children Under Three.

40. Spitz, R. 1945. "Hospitalism: an inquiry into the genesis of psychiatric

conditions in early childhood." *Psychoanalytic Study of the Child* 1:53–74.
41. Vaughn, B., Gove, F. and Egeland, B. 1980. "The relationship between out-of-home care and the quality of infant-mother attachment in an economically disadvantaged population." *Child Development* 51:1203–1214.
42. Wilcox, B., Staff, P. and Romaine, M. 1980. "A comparison of individual with multiple assignment of caregivers to infants in day care." *Merrill-Palmer Quarterly* 26:53–62.
43. Willis, A. and Ricciuti, H. 1974. "Longitudinal observations of infant's daily arrivals at a day care center." Technical Report, Cornell Research Program in Early Development and Education, Ithaca, New York.
44. Yarrow, L. 1964. "Separation from parents during early childhood." In *Review of Child Development Research*, M. Hoffman and T. Hoffman, eds. Russell Sage, New York.

Chapter 12

A METHODOLOGICAL COMMENT ON "THE PROBLEM OF INFANT DAY CARE"

by Victoria Seitz

Frye has provided an impressive critique of research on infant day care, and I agree with many of his conclusions. I am concerned, however, that he has overstated the objections to quasi-experimental designs. In arguing for the value of classical experiments, with random assignment of subjects to treatments, Frye implies that other methods have been shown to be unacceptable. Specifically, he states: "In recent years, quasi-experimental designs have been reexamined. The accepted and convincing wisdom now is that these designs are not viable."

I agree with Frye that the particular research designs used in many studies of infant day care have tended to muddy rather than clarify our understanding of the effects of day care. But any implication that quasi-experimental designs in general must necessarily yield uninterpretable results would be unwarranted. A too-sweeping rejection of such designs might have effects on research as negative as those Frye seeks to remedy.

Despite his statement, Frye is not in fact rejecting all quasi experimentation, that is, studies in which experimental and control groups are formed by means other than random assignment. Rather, he objects to two particular kinds of such studies, those using matching

Preparation of this paper was supported by Research Grant HD-03008-12 from the National Institute of Mental Health and Grant PHS-90-C-912 from the Administration for Children, Youth and Families.

and those using analysis of covariance to attempt to "equalize" experimental and control groups. He rightly praises another form of quasi-experimental design, in which control groups are formed from persons on waiting lists for the treatment being studied. I thus have no quarrel with Frye on anything but terminology: he has unfortunately chosen to criticize quasi-experimental designs in general, while he objects to only some of them.

But, in a wider sense, Frye's review highlights a dilemma faced by a growing number of researchers. As psychologists have become interested in extrafamilial socialization factors and have begun to study the impact of such programs and policies as infant day care, flexible work schedules for parents, or compensatory preschool education, they have also become increasingly concerned with the problem of how to conduct scientifically adequate research in nonlaboratory settings. Despite a growing body of knowledge about quasi-experimental designs,[4] it is widely held that, regardless of subject matter, population, or context, true experimentation is always to be preferred to quasi experimentation. Sometimes this advice is forcefully phrased.[5,22,26] It is actually in response to this rather purist philosophy that I wish to address my comments, not to Frye alone. I believe that quasi experimentation has a very important role to play in psychological research in nonlaboratory situations.

Before leaping to my defense of certain quasi-experimental designs, I would first like to restate the key problem that random assignment is designed to solve, as it is a serious one. The problem of selection-treatment confounding is the patron devil of evaluation research in general, whether the variable of interest is infant day care or any other service or program. As Frye points out, and as Sibbison[21] and Hock[7] have confirmed, parents who choose to enroll their children in infant day care programs may be presumed to differ in many ways from parents who do not. Something about these differences could easily be more important than the day care itself in producing any differences later observed between children who receive day care and those who do not.

This kind of problem is even more readily apparent in a related area, the comparison of private versus public education. Not only do different kinds of parents seek out different kinds of schools, but also private schools can reject applications of unwanted students, whereas public schools cannot. Thus, although students in private schools often outperform those in public ones, the conclusion that private schools have the superior educational programs is questionable. As Albert Shanker pointed out in a recent editorial,[20] we might equally logically argue that YMCAs have better health programs than do hospitals, since people attending the local Y's are so much healthier than are people in hospitals. Obviously, we do not wish to draw equally specious conclusions in day care research.

As is well known, randomization offers the best theoretical solution to this serious, persistent problem of selection-treatment confounding. Where random assignment to conditions can be undertaken, effects of selection can be cleanly disentangled from effects of treatment.[4,9] Theoretically, therefore, if we could only persuade parents to accept the choice of day care versus no day care on the basis of a lottery, the interests of science would be better served. But the fact that parents do not prefer to behave this way is not only an ethical concern, but a scientific matter as well. Because randomization is not an inert procedure, but can affect subjects in many ways, its use may solve one problem only to raise others. (I will elaborate on this point later.) Randomization also provides no solution to other, equally serious, problems. And, while it is the strongest procedure for ruling out selection-treatment confounding, it is not the only available tool for doing so. In short, desirable as it often is, randomization is neither a necessary nor a sufficient condition for a good study.

Consider, first, its nonsufficiency. Even though most researchers, if asked, would agree that random assignment to conditions does not guarantee that a study will be unambiguously interpretable, in practice they tend to place undue weight on this single factor. Perhaps it is because randomization is so very difficult to achieve in real-life settings that appreciative fellow scientists tend to overlook the many other threats to interpretability in assessing the outcome of the few true experiments. One of the most serious such threats is the problem of subjects' and experimenters' expectations.[12,15,16] For the subjects, there are social demands in participating in an experiment. Especially in intervention research, people may change simply because participating in a special program makes them feel important.

In medical research, the dangers of expectations concerning the outcome of research are so deeply respected as to have made double-blind procedures the norm. In psychological research, we cannot use such simple means as gelatin capsules to disguise our treatments, and it is less easy to achieve the double-blind standard of objective distance from procedures. We could, however, strive more creatively to develop unobtrusive measures whenever possible.[23] And, at the very least, we should recognize that it is dangerous for the person who designs or implements a treatment also to attempt to evaluate it.

To consider the area of infant intervention programs, for example, most researchers have both created the experimental conditions they wish to study and also mounted the evaluations.[6] With such factors as professional advancement and continuation of research funds at stake, even the most conscientious of researchers may be swayed to affect the outcome of an evaluation in ways he or she cannot objectively assess. I am not arguing that, like the medical community, psychologists should adopt the standard of double-blind procedures as an essential prerequisite for publishability of findings. Rather, I am arguing that we should not single out any one characteristic of ideal research, whether it be experimental objectivity or random assignment to groups, and make it the yardstick by which we accept or reject results of any given study.

Just as randomization does not guarantee a scientifically valid study, neither does a scientific study require randomization. Frye himself clearly recognizes this fact, endorsing "very special kinds of quasi-experimental studies of the effects of infant day care." I would like to underscore this argument and to elaborate upon it.

Quasi-experimental designs vary greatly in quality. (For an extensive discussion of this topic, see Cook and Campbell.[4]) One of the best such designs involves using as control subjects persons who are on waiting lists for the program to be studied. While waiting-list subjects may differ in some way from persons actually receiving the service (e.g., perhaps they are more transient, since long-time residents of a community tend to have earlier information about scarce resources; perhaps they are procrastinators), they are certainly comparable in such critical ways as being a self-selected group of persons explicitly desiring the program. Frye cites the example of Cochran's study of infant day care in Sweden;[3] another example is Peters's study.[13] This kind of high quality quasi-experimental design has also been effectively used in studies of Project Head Start.[25] Another strong quasi-experimental design is the multiple-time-series—a longitudinal study in which the rate of change of each of two or more groups is established on several occasions before the differential treatment begins.[2] (See also the forbiddingly named "Interrupted time series with a nonequivalent no-treatment control group" described by Cook and Campbell.[4])

At the opposite end of the spectrum, designs involving a posttest only with nonequivalent control groups are poor designs, and I agree with Frye's attempt to discourage their use. One of the potentially most serious errors involves the injudicious use of matching to form control groups. When matching variables are not actually differently represented in the treatment and control groups, the procedure may not be problematic. In studying day care, matching on sex or ethnicity, for example, might not be misleading. When two populations actually differ on some important variable, however, the attempt to "equate" samples through matching distorts the sampling process in a manner so biasing that it is almost invariably misleading.[1,10,11,17,24] This situation might arise, for example, in studies of certain kinds of day care where the income of those families using the service differs from that of those who do not.

In my opinion, the strongest defense of the better quasi-experimental methods is that they may sometimes be more scientifically appropriate for a given subject matter and population than is a true experiment. I recognize that this is heresy, when the orthodox view is that true experiments constitute the loftiest ideal of the psychological enterprise. But successful methodology has always had to be tailored to the problem and populations in question. As social psychologists have repeatedly demonstrated, humans are intelligent social animals whose attitudes and attributions play critical roles in directing their behavior. Thus, a central problem with which psychological research must deal is the fact that the subjects' feelings can so strongly affect the research outcome.

The role of subjective expectations is particularly evident in medicine, where the placebo effect often provides a surprisingly strong rival to such intrusive treatments as drugs, surgery, or radiation. Once regarded as artifactual and a nuisance, the placebo is increasingly viewed as an alternative treatment, reflecting the action of some not-yet-well-understood mechanism by which people's feelings affect their physical well-being. Even more so than in medicine, psychologists must consider the weight of the subjects' attitudes and beliefs relative to that of the treatment they are attempting to evaluate. In psychological research, such attitudes could easily have consequences far more profound than those of any treatment we might choose to administer.

It is for this reason that we need to use randomization very carefully and sometimes to use other strategies instead. Resentment at being denied a desired service can lead to a subject's refusal to participate or to an early withdrawal from a study. Changes in control groups, such as demoralization or compensatory rivalry (the John Henry effect) may arise from having been denied the treatment rather than reflecting its simple absence. In short, random assignment may actually create conditions that threaten the internal validity of an experiment. This may particularly be true in the realm of social intervention projects, such as the provision of day care services to poor, working families.

It might seem that one way to have a true experiment and to avoid potentially negative effects of randomization would be to use treatment partitioning. That is, one could design several forms of a treatment, each of which is attractive, and randomly assign subjects to the different versions. The Abecedarian project Frye discusses represents an example of such an approach, as a number of special services were provided both to experimental and control families.[14] The latter

were thus receiving at least a partial treatment. The drawback, however, is that comparing various forms of treatment is not a very
powerful way to detect effects, since all forms of a treatment may
have similar consequences. For example, if the psychoanalytic view
were correct that any form of extended absence from the mother
produced changes in the child's attachment, then comparing family
day care with center-based day care would not reveal this fact.
Treatment partitioning may sometimes be a good strategy, but only
if the different versions of the treatment can be expected to have
different effects. When a service or treatment is of limited duration,
another viable approach might be to offer it in a randomly determined order. All persons would thereby eventually receive the service, but those who received it later would serve as controls during
the early portion of the study.

The principal weakness of all quasi-experimental designs is that
their use results in a more laborious task of interpretation than would
have been true had an experiment been possible.[4] While it might
appear that quasi experimentation represents taking the easy way
out, *successfully* employing quasi experimentation actually places
greater demands on the researcher to rule out competing alternative
explanations for the outcome than does employing an experiment.
The situation can be likened to the problem of starting a fire—it is
easier with matches, but a skilled person can accomplish it by rub-
bing two sticks together.

Sometimes a researcher can conduct supplementary studies which
help rule out competing explanations for the outcome of a quasi
experiment. As a supplement to a longitudinal study evaluating the
effects of Project Follow Through, for example, my colleagues and
I were able to compare schools in which parents had selected the
Follow Through program with similar schools in which the same
curriculum had been imposed by the central school district.[19] The
absence of differences between self-selected and nonselected groups
made it more reasonable to believe that differences found in the
original study between Follow Through and non-Follow Through
children were the result of the treatment rather than being due to
self-selection. Sometimes the outcome of a quasi-experimental study
contributes to its interpretability. In the Follow Through study I
have been describing, the pattern of results that was found would
have been difficult to explain on the basis of selection factors, since
the Follow Through children were not generally superior perform-
ers. Rather, they excelled in only a few areas more easily explained
by the specific treatment they had received.[18]

As the examples just given suggest, the use of quasi-experimental
designs can represent a gamble. The waiting-list control group study
can be interpreted regardless of outcome; certain other designs may

be interpretable only for certain patterns of results. But the extent of the gamble is related to the nature of the problem being investigated. Even a crude design could detect such unsubtle changes as the bed-wetting and nightmares of the English children sent to rural areas to live with strangers during the wartime bombing of London.

Since most day care is not high quality, but rather has been rated as only poor to fair,[8] a pressing area of needed research is to ascertain whether children receiving such undistinguished care are suffering from it. Much existing day-care research is analogous to studying the effects of nutrition by comparing children who eat steak with those who eat chicken and finding that the kind of food we give children doesn't affect their growth. We should also be looking at children who, having no steak, are eating candy and potato chips. No researcher could ethically assign a child to receive poor quality services in order to study its effects. But a good quasi-experimental study might well reveal the existence of presently unrecognized negative outcomes of poor quality day care on health, cognition, or personality development that do not occur to a child who receives high quality care. It is in cases such as these that any insistence upon the necessity of performing only true experiments could have particularly detrimental consequences in reducing the likelihood that valuable, needed research will be performed.

I would like to end by commenting on the continuous, rather than dichotomous, nature of methodology. Faced with a given problem, an investigator can draw from a variety of methods, differing greatly in purpose and potential. Frye and other reviewers have demonstrated how the thoughtful scientist typically considers the entire matrix of available data, weighing results from a variety of sources: experiments, quasi experiments, cross-cultural studies, "natural" field studies, historical data, case studies, and, generally, whatever seems capable of shedding light on the questions of interest. In evaluating such matrices of information, true experiments are usually given greater weight. If the results of true experiments refute those of quasi-experimental methods, and if the experiments are not flawed in some manner, their results are considered valid and those of the quasi experiments discredited. But quasi-experimental studies and experiments may also yield comparable findings, and in such cases the existence of the experiments give added weight to the results of the quasi experiments. When the phenomenon one is investigating is relatively straightforward and robust, one is likely to be able to find it with a variety of investigatory techniques. In the area of day care research, as Frye notes, many studies, though methodologically weak, have yielded results that are consonant with results from a true experimental study (the Abecedarian project) and a strong quasi-experimental one (Cochran's).

Quasi experimentation has often been badly employed and the results deservedly viewed with disfavor. But, as the existence of the recent, nearly 400-page Cook and Campbell book testifies,[4] interest in such designs and knowledge of how to use them are hardly relics of the past. For ethical or financial reasons, quasi-experimental designs may sometimes offer the only feasible means of studying certain problems; sometimes their use may prevent experimentally induced changes that threaten the validity of a study. In our society, freedom of choice and a belief in merit rather than chance as determinants of one's fate continue to be cherished social values. Because our subjects are thinking human beings whose interpretations may easily be more powerful determinants of their behavior than any given condition we choose to administer, quasi experiments may sometimes be the method of choice. The situation is not at all that we should seek to reject quasi experiments, but rather that we should become more expert in their use.

References

1. Campbell, D.T. and Erlebacher, A. 1970. "How regression artifacts in quasi-experimental evaluations can mistakenly make compensatory education look harmful." In *Compensatory Education: A National Debate, Vol. 3: Disadvantaged Child*, J. Hellmuth, ed. Brunner/Mazel, New York.
2. Campbell, D. T. and Stanley, J.C. 1966. *Experimental and Quasi-Experimental Designs for Research*. Rand McNally, Chicago.
3. Cochran, M. 1977. "A comparison of group day and family child-rearing patterns in Sweden." *Child Development* 48:702–707.
4. Cook, T.D. and Campbell, D.T. 1979. *Quasi-Experimentation: Design and Analysis Issues for Field Settings*. Rand McNally College Publishing Company, Chicago.
5. Gilbert, J.P., McPeek, B. and Mosteller, F. 1977. "Statistics and ethics in surgery and anaesthetics." *Science* 198:684–689.
6. Gray, S.W. and Wandersman, L.P. 1980. "The methodology of home-based intervention studies: problems and promising strategies." *Child Development* 51:993–1009.
7. Hock, E. 1980. "Working and nonworking mothers and their infants: a comparative study of maternal caregiving characteristics and infant social behavior." *Merrill-Palmer Quarterly* 26:79–101.
8. Keyserling, M.D. 1972. *Windows on Day Care*. National Council of Jewish Women, New York.
9. Kirk, R.E. 1968. *Experimental Design: Procedures for the Behavioral Sciences*. Brooks/Cole, Belmont, Cal.
10. Meehl, P.E. 1970. "Nuisance variables and the ex post facto design." In *Minnesota Studies in the Philosophy of Science*, Vol. 4, M. Radner and S. Winokur, eds. University of Minnesota Press, Minneapolis.

11. Meehl, P.E. 1971. "High school yearbooks: a reply to Schwartz." *Journal of Abnormal Psychology* 77:143–148.
12. Orne, M. 1962. "On the social psychology of the psychological experiment." *American Psychologist* 17:776–783.
13. Peters, D. 1973. *A Summary of the Pennsylvania Day Care Study.* Pennsylvania State University, University Park, Penn.
14. Ramey, C. and Mills, J. 1977. "Social and intellectual consequences of day care for high risk infants." In *Social Development: Family and Group Experience*, R. Webb, ed. Johns Hopkins Press, Baltimore, Md.
15. Rosenthal, R. 1976. *Experimenter Effects in Behavioral Research*, 2nd ed. Irvington, New York.
16. Rosenthal, R. and Rosnow, R.L. 1975. *The Volunteer Subject.* Wiley-Interscience, New York.
17. Seitz, V. 1980. "Statistical issues and comparative methods." In *Comparative Methods in Psychology*, M.H. Bornstein, ed. Lawrence Erlbaum Associates, Hillsdale, N.J.
18. Seitz, V., Apfel, N.H. and Rosenbaum, L.K. In press. "Projects Head Start and Follow Through: A longitudinal evaluation of adolescents." In *Prevention of Retarded Development in Psychosocially Disadvantaged Children*, M.J. Begab, H. Garber and H.C. Haywood, eds. University Park Press, Baltimore, Md.
19. Seitz, V. and Efron, C. 1975. "A comparison of self-selected and non-self-selected recipients of Project Follow Through and non-Follow Through children in comparable neighborhoods." Unpublished manuscript, Yale University, New Haven, Conn.
20. Shanker, A. 1981. "Where we stand. Tax credits: the myth of parental choice. Despite propaganda, schools do the picking." *The New York Times*, Sunday, January 25, E9.
21. Sibbison, V.H. 1973. "The influence of maternal role perceptions on attitudes toward and utilization of early child care services." In *A Summary of the Pennsylvania Day Care Study*, D. Peters, ed. Pennsylvania State University, University Park, Penn.
22. Tukey, J. 1977. "Some thoughts on clinical trials, especially problems of multiplicity." *Science* 198:679–684.
23. Webb, E.J., Campbell, D.T., Schwartz, D. and Sechrest, L. 1966. *Unobtrusive Measures: Nonreactive Research in the Social Sciences.* Rand McNally, Chicago.
24. Yando, R.M., Seitz, V. and Zigler, E. 1979. *Intellectual and Personality Characteristics of Children: Social Class and Ethnic Group Differences.* Lawrence Erlbaum Associates, Hillsdale, N.J.
25. Zigler, E. and Butterfield, E.C. 1968. "Motivational aspects of changes in IQ test performance of culturally deprived nursery school children." *Child Development* 39:1–14.
26. Zimring, F.E. 1976. "Field experiments in general deterrence: preferring the tortoise to the hare." *Evaluation* 3:132–135.

Part Two

LEGISLATORS' PERSPECTIVES

Chapter 13

FAMILIES, CHILDREN, AND CHILD CARE

by Orrin G. Hatch

Those of us who are directly involved with decisions about policy are constantly in need of the best, most up to date, and most accurate information available. Knowledge is a crucial and nonpartisan commodity which is essential in guiding the policy-making process. We have developed a long tradition in this country of supporting the pursuit of new knowledge, both in our extensive system of public education and in nationally-sponsored institutes and organizations such as the National Institutes of Health. I am convinced that our commitment to expanding our understanding of human development will continue to be a national need. I am equally convinced that we will want to develop public policies that will promote optimal human development. In order to develop such policies, we will need new knowledge about development, careful evaluations of present programs and practices, and—because new policies usually need to jump beyond the known into the unknown—we will continue to need common sense.

Unfortunately many of the decisions currently being made regarding children are motivated by circumstances outside the parent-child relationship. Because of increasing economic pressure on the family, many couples are deciding that both husband and wife must work outside the home. Because of rising divorce rates, increasing numbers of children are raised in single-parent households and in reconstituted families. Because of current social trends regarding the roles of women in society, many women are considering mutiple roles that include marriage, children, and a career. Each of these circumstances can have an impact on the parent-child relationship. As parents seek to divide their time between family and other workplace or community demands, questions about caring for children in the parents' absence will continue to press upon us.

I believe there are several guiding principles which should be considered by each couple, and by program directors and policy makers, when examining the issue of child care.

1. *Children are delightful and desirable.* Of course, raising children is also a challenge. It requires sacrifice. Children are demanding. But, rather than seeing childrearing as a burden to be avoided, or to be put off onto someone else, we should welcome the opportunity of parenthood as a chance to participate in what is probably life's greatest enterprise. There will be couples who choose not to raise children, and, of course, their right to do that should be respected. In the past, and currently, the overwhelming majority of couples choose to raise children. That should be considered as a joyful and positive decision. We have too much gloom-and-doom philosophy unnecessarily burdening today's parents. I feel we have gone too far in painting parenthood as a terrible responsibility, which distracts from life's better goals. As a father of six children myself, I have had my share of sleepless nights, frayed nerves, and self-doubts about the quality of my parenting. I am increasingly aware, however, that as I come to evaluate my life in the broad perspective, the joys, the satisfactions, the opportunities for personal growth, and moments of pride I have felt as a parent will be among the most positive and significant of my life's experiences.

2. *The responsibility for raising children rests with parents.* Day care centers cannot do a better job; schools cannot do a better job; community organizations cannot do a better job. Optimal child development means raising children who can thrive in their society. They should be able to adapt to society's values and laws. They should reflect the cultural and social heritage of their family. They should be able to succeed and achieve. They should be as healthy as possible, physically and mentally. To raise such children requires direction, help, support, appropriate role models, love and appreciation. Parents are best equipped and motivated to provide this needed child-rearing environment.

3. *Approaches to child care should be family centered.* When some child-rearing tasks are delegated from parents to others, as we see in the school system, care should be taken to reinforce and promote the concerns of the parents within the support system. This is particularly true for young children. Child-care approaches that are sensitive to a continuity between the parents' perspectives, values, and needs are desirable. Continuity between the child's experience at home and his experience in other settings should be maximized. One of the best aspects of the Head Start programs over the years

has been their involvement of parents both in the planning and the actual running of the programs.

What are the next steps we need to take in considering child care alternatives? Here I am sure that other contributors to this volume, who have devoted much of their professional life to the substantive details related to child care programs, will have more specifics to furnish in terms of program planning and execution than I. It will probably not come as a surprise to many that I disagree with one of the other contributors, Senator Kennedy of Massachusetts, in a few areas. I suspect that our approaches to child care would reflect some of those differences. I know that we would agree—and in this I know we would be joined by all our colleagues in the Congress—that we must do all we can to promote the quality of family life in America. We all value our nation's children. They are our national treasure. And we realize that the experiences they have as they grow up will determine in some measure the future of our country. I do have some concerns and some questions which I would like to raise here. If there are answers or approaches which focus on these concerns, I would like to learn more about them.

First, I am concerned that the forces which are driving the desire for child care are too frequently centered in the social changes, or unfortunate economic circumstances, which we currently face. Since we value family life, and are concerned with the well-being of our children as a priority issue, we need to place these values and concerns at the top of our agenda as we plan for child care approaches. Ensuring a high quality of care—regardless of the setting—should be a primary objective. This may mean working with parents to help them make the most of their time with their children, in addition to continued efforts in improving the quality of extrafamily care. Individuals, couples, employers, care providers, and governments all need to proceed by asking first: How can we improve and strengthen families and be sensitive to child needs within the family context? If approaches are begun in that framework, more positive results seem likely.

Second, we need to monitor and evaluate our approaches to child care very carefully. There are many different forms of child care, each with different goals: parents care for their children at home; grandparents tend their grandchildren; neighbors tend neighborhood children; Head Start centers aim at improving school performance; some preschools focus on social and emotional development; some day care centers provide barely adequate custodial care. What are the effects of each of these on the child? What are the immediate effects, and the long-range influences? What influences do alternate forms of care have on the parents, and the broader family relationships between parent and child, and/or between siblings? How can the specific needs of the parents be matched with the most appropriate care alternatives? For example, a mother who works for two mornings a week is likely to have different needs than a mother employed full time. Are some caregiving approaches better suited to specific needs than others?

The answers to these questions seem crucial in developing a policy, or policies, regarding child care. We need to have answers which are reasonably firm before the federal government becomes further involved. I do not see the development of a massive, federally-funded network of child care facilities for very young children as either inevitable or even desirable. The approaches that we do develop should be sensitive to local needs and concerns, and controlled by the states, local communities, and neighborhoods. Even then, parents still have the ultimate responsibility for ensuring that the best approaches are found. Whenever possible extrafamily child care should also be self-supporting. Support might also come from local governments and businesses. We have seen too frequently in the past that federal support usually leads to federal control and federal inefficiency, neither of which is desirable, nor tolerable, in the child-rearing enterprise.

Finally, we need to revitalize our interest in children and child development as a national priority. Children should be seen as desirable, but I think we need to go far beyond this perception. We need to think of our children and youth as national assets. Increased efforts from both the public and the private sectors need to be made to incorporate our children into society as valued contributors. I am troubled by the number of youth who are unemployed, particularly in our large cities. I am deeply troubled by the young people who are barely able to make it through our public school system, and who drop out or graduate only to feel completely alienated from and disenfranchised by their own society. Rates of drug addiction, alcoholism, and suicide continue to rise alarmingly among our youth. I am concerned by the increasing numbers of latch-key children who are left home alone, while parents pursue careers. I am troubled by the burgeoning demand for day care centers which too frequently is not accompanied by an equal demand for accountability and quality control in the care system. Unfortunately, I do not see a unified national commitment to working out the solution to these problems on an individual-by-individual, family-by-family, neighborhood-by-neighborhood basis.

Other countries with whom we have substantial differences are not as casual about their children as we sometimes seem to be. The U.S.S.R. is very careful and attentive about child-rearing practices. From the orderly classrooms and polite children I have seen in the People's Republic of China, I wonder if they may be more effective in some ways than we in developing discipline and attitudes of community involvement. Of course, I am acutely aware that we are ideologically very different from the Communist countries—and I pray we always will be—but I am concerned that our real commitment to our nation's children and youth is less than it should be. We are very distressed to learn that we may be falling behind other countries in technology and defense; are we also interested in preventing the problems which may result from too little concern being given to our nation's families and children?

If I have learned one thing in Washington, it is that expressing national commitment by developing large federal programs is a futile approach. Since we are a pluralistic society, we cannot develop a single national child care organization, run by a "Secretary of Child Care." We must work on helping our children on an individual, family, and community basis. Looking passively to Washington for the solution to our problems will only lead to further frustration. We must continue to work to understand children and their development. We must continue to develop family-centered perspectives and approaches to our economic, social, and child care needs. I feel we will need to examine many alternatives, and develop flexible solutions.

In closing, let me say that I will probably take greater interest in reading what the professionals in this field have to say here than they may take in what I have said. I hope we will be able to continue this dialogue. I also hope that parents, educators, researchers, and all who have a vital interest in children will continue to try to communicate ideas, findings, successes—and even failures—to those of us who are trying to make some difficult decisions about policy. Our future demands that we do the best we can for our children, and I hope we will all continue to work together in that cause.

Chapter 14

CHILD CARE—A COMMITMENT TO BE HONORED

by Edward M. Kennedy

In supporting the cause of day care and child development, we are working for the only minority that includes all Americans at some time in their lives. We are working for the rights of children, who have no right to vote and no influence to peddle. We are working to meet the needs of the family, the most important and the most pressured institution in our society today.

The special cause of child care is a cause that is central to all our other concerns about the family. As the Day Care and Child Development Council of America told the Senate Human Resources Committee in testimony in 1978,

> *Only in the context of a firm policy in support of families and a national commitment to the maximum development of every child, will we begin to find solutions to the problems that overwhelm the family today.*

In our national policy on children and families, nostalgia is no substitute for rational decisions. It is not only morally right, but also far less expensive, for government to assist children in growing up whole and strong and able, than to pay the bill later for children and adults who grow up with health, social, and educational problems.

During the past three decades, America has split the atom of the nuclear family. In 1980, more than half of all married women worked outside the home. By 1990, three-quarters will do so. And we have nearly nine million families today headed by a single parent.

We cannot afford a reactionary policy based on a family structure that often no longer exists—a father on the job, a mother at home all

260

day taking care of the children. On this issue, the danger is not from those who seek to deal with reality in sensitive and human ways; the danger comes from those who wishfully think that yesterday's preconceptions can be fitted to today's reality, if only government will keep out.

National decisions inevitably affect the state of the family. Governmental policies on jobs, prices, taxes, education, medical care, and child care can burden the family further and contribute to the continuing deterioration of family life. Or, government can establish policies to strengthen family life—to assure that every public program is designed to sustain families instead of subverting them.

An appropriate family policy calls for many new measures. For example, it is unconscionable that the welfare system in state after state still creates broken families as the price of bare subsistence. A top priority of family policy must be to reform our medieval welfare system in ways that provide reasonable benefits for all families, and fiscal relief for states and cities.

Another urgent task is to assure adequate child care for every family that needs it. Today, established child care centers serve only a fraction of the 28 million children of working mothers. At least two million school children between 7 and 18 are left at home each day without any supervision. And 20,000 preschool children who have no classes to attend are left alone because their parents have to work.

Beyond the statistics, there is a tragedy that must be seen and felt in human terms. In its Senate testimony, the Day Care Council spoke of this tragedy in vivid words.

> *It is not the numbers on computer cards and in neat columns in reports that really describe the dilemma. It is the voice of the mother frantically searching for adequate arrangements, and the vacant look in the eyes of the child who suffers from the lack of developmental care, that give definition to the problem.*
>
> *It is tragic but not unusual that a ten-year-old is kept home from school to stay with the baby; that a first grader with a key around his neck returns home from school to an empty house; that a well-meaning but untrained neighbor crowds a group of infants and preschoolers into her house for an uneventful and fretful day.*

Child care in modern American life is not just a bonus for the poor, but a necessity for families of all types and conditions—intact families, single parent families, families at every step on the income ladder.

We cannot permit mistrust and misinformation to deny adequate care for children—or to block access to child care for every parent who needs it. We cannot accept a neglect which means that too many families cannot stay together, that too many children are forced into institutions and foster care, and that too many other children end up in trouble—and in the juvenile justice system.

We must also reject a policy that makes the well-being of children a pawn to be sacrificed in the battle of the budget. For example, funds for day care under Title 20 of the Social Security Act have fallen far behind inflation; yet few have resisted efforts to slash the program.

We must stand for a federal budget that cuts subsidies for the oil companies before lunches for school children. And if cutbacks are necessary in a food stamp program, we should spare the hungry and act instead to reduce the billion dollar subsidies for business meals —which are food stamps for the rich.

Some have opposed increased support for child care and auxiliary services on the ground that federal aid is already substantial and that no additional efforts to provide child care are warranted at this time.

Those who take that view ought to visit the Newark Neighborhood Child Care Center, where the waiting list is three times the capacity of the center. They ought to visit Colorado, where only single-parent families are eligible for child care and yet 24,000 children are competing for 8,000 places. They ought to visit Chinatown in San Francisco, where only a tenth of the children who need day care actually receive it.

It is fashionable now to be against government. It is easy to denounce spending and programs as ineffective and inefficient. But in the field of day care, to be antigovernment is to be antichildren.

The proper role of government is not to mandate a single system, but to make available a variety of options. The public responsibility is not to dictate to parents, but to support their efforts. The proper role of government must be to set standards for the quality of services and the training of personnel. And it must assist a wide range of services—from day care center to in-home care, extended family care, community networks, and day care in cooperation with other structures, such as nursery schools. Above all, we must renounce a stratified system of child care, separate and unequal, with government child care for the poor, private child care for the wealthy, and no child care for middle-income families.

The agenda for child care includes both immediate and long range steps:

First, government must be sensitive to child care in shaping all its policies and programs. Child care is not exclusively a matter of tax credits or titles of the Social Security Act. It must also be an important factor in determining federal policies on housing, transportation, education, employment, and health.

Second, Title 20 of the Social Security Act should be strengthened to insure that funds set aside for improving child care will actually be spent for that purpose.

Third, the Head Start program should be expanded. Today, Head Start reaches only 25 percent of the eligible children. Yet, even this modest effort is in danger. If the budget is cut, thousands of children will be eliminated from the program. For them, the hopeful promise of Head Start will become the dismal reality of a false start. By any standard, Head Start is one of America's most successful programs, and millions more deserve this benefit that serves them all their lives.

Fourth, the federal government should increase support for child welfare services, and allocate more of it to preventive care. For many children and families, this could ultimately make the difference between self-sufficiency and dependency.

Fifth, we should move ahead on a child health assurance program. Each year we delay, one hundred thousand pregnant women, and one-and-a-half million children in families at the poverty level, are denied the right to better health.

Sixth, we must establish demonstration projects to help families whose special needs are often totally neglected. These needs include sick child care, care for children who are handicapped, and care before and after school hours.

Seventh, we must offer incentives for the private sector to create flexible work schedules, to extend maternity and paternity leaves, to apply a child's illness to a parent's sick leave, and to expand part-time employment, shared jobs, and on-site day care.

As we pursue these separate goals, our long range purpose must be clear and unequivocal—child care as a right, not a privilege or a pittance measured by a fading federal commitment.

In all this, we must be guided by a coherent national vision that coordinates efforts both inside and outside the government. And we must put our resources where our ideals are, so that never again will child care be treated as a principle not worth paying for.

Our goal is the maximum development of every child. Economic circumstance should never force children to be less than their talents and their determination can make them. If economic opportunity and social justice mean anything, they mean that all children must have a fair chance in life. Only then can we strengthen the structure of both the family and our democracy.

The goal is worth all the years of struggle, of setbacks and success. As Aeschylus wrote, "In the rearing of our children, we are handing on life like a torch from one generation to another." If we remain true to our commitment, we can have confidence that our cause will prevail.

Part Three

SOCIAL POLICY ISSUES

Chapter 15

THE POLITICS OF FEDERAL DAY CARE REGULATION

by John R. Nelson, Jr.

For thirteen years there have been federal regulations to govern federally funded day care. Yet, for all intents and purposes, these regulations—the Federal Interagency Day Care Requirements, or FIDCR—have never been enforced. While they have played a role in the policy debates over AFDC-WIN, the Family Assistance Plan and Title XX, the regulations have had virtually no effective role in regulating child care. This anomalous situation is a product of the complex political and social forces which have surrounded the issue of child care regulation throughout its history. It is the purpose of this chapter to relate, if not explain, that history and the political milieu that confronts any future efforts to make policy in this area. It chronicles the history of federal child care regulation in five sections: the prologue to the 1968 Federal Interagency Day Care Requirements (FIDCR), the 1968 FIDCR, the 1972 revision of the FIDCR, the Title XX controversy, and the debate over federal regulation of child care since Title XX.

Regulation of Out-of-Home Child Care

The late nineteenth and early twentieth centuries marked the first government attempts at regulating out-of-home child care. Their

---

This chapter is based in part upon a case study by the author written at the National Academy of Sciences. The views expressed are solely his own. See "The Federal Interagency Day Care Requirements," in *Final Report: Panel for the Study of the Policy Formation Process*, Cheryl D. Hayes, editor (Washington: National Research Council-National Academy of Sciences, 1981).

central purpose was to stem the appalling infant and child mortality rates in orphanages and other 24-hour institutions. At issue were basic health measures, sanitation, nutrition, and disease prevention. As national child advocacy organizations and state licensing agencies arose at the turn of the century, their overriding concern was disease and its transmission among institutionalized children. Similarly, state and local licensing codes sought to protect children from primal dangers: epidemics, fire, severe neglect, and starvation. At the federal level, the Children's Bureau suggested provisions for state codes and offered goals for better child care.

Licensing laws were by no means comprehensive. Linked to general fire safety and health codes of cities and counties, they allowed little room for the nuances of day care. States were reticent to enforce their laws against church-sponsored institutions. Funds were always limited and often lowest in times of greatest demand for facilities. It was difficult to suspend licenses because the alternative to poor facilities was frequently no facilities. Finally, the enforcers were drawn from the ranks of social workers. They lacked experience in administration, and found themselves regulating their colleagues. Thus, over the first half of the twentieth century effective regulation suffered from poor administration and the general inadequacy of the regulations themselves.

During the Second World War the Children's Bureau and Office of Education received powers to approve local and state day care plans for federal funding. The Office of Education had jurisdiction over school district plans, the Children's Bureau over nonschool plans. Since 95 percent of the facilities were school-related, the Office of Education predominated. For the first time the government did issue a set of standards for day care. Under the aegis of the Children's Bureau, a Conference on Day Care of Children of Working Mothers met in July, 1941, to confront the problem war mobilization posed for women and children. Its February, 1942, report proposed a set of day care standards based upon the experience and expertise of the participants. These standards preceded the Bureau's power to approve state plans, granted in August, 1942, and did not have the force of law. As were all the standards of the Children's Bureau, they were merely recommendations to state and local authorities.

The standards assumed school age children received adequate education in school and required only supervision and a safe play area until the end of the workday. They recommended that children under three stay with their mothers and those women be discouraged from working. Those children between two and five received the greatest attention. The standards suggested a maximum group size of 30 children with a minimum ratio of 10 children to one adult.

They discussed the child's need for "warmth and affection" and opportunities "for music, conversation, poetry, stories, work with materials, group play, etc." The needs of the family were also to be considered. Staff directors were to be trained in a broad range of children's needs, including education, psychology, family relations, health, nutrition, and child development. Ideally, a facility should provide proper nutrition and health training as well as conforming to safety codes. Since they were conceived only as goals, these standards were never enforced as a precondition of federal funding. Federal regulatory authority extended only to state and local plans, not their operation. As goals, however, they no doubt exerted some pressure for better day care facilities than otherwise would have developed.[1]

The expiration of direct federal aid to day care did not halt Children's Bureau activities in this area. In 1953, the Bureau, in conjunction with the Women's Bureau of the Department of Labor, held a National Conference on Planning Services for Children of Employed Mothers. The Conference stressed the growing number of women with children entering the labor force. They noted that two million working women had children under six, and over five million had children under eighteen. In an effort to promote more state and local aid to day care the conferees pointed to industry's need for labor and the working woman's need for supplemental family income. Forty percent of those women working were the sole supporters of their families. To touch all bases, the conferees explained the growth of kindergartens and nursery schools as a result of parents "eager to profit from the new scientific knowledge of child development . . . ." Their central plea, however, remained the expansion of day care to abet the entry of women into the workforce. No federal programs were enacted, but the year following the conference Congress passed the child care tax deduction.[2]

The issue of day care and its regulation persisted throughout the fifties. The Children's Bureau conducted a major study of day care in 1958. In October, 1960, the Child Welfare League published *Standards for Day Care Service*. "These standards," Director Joseph H. Reid stressed, "are intended to be *goals* for continuous improvement of services to children." In many respects the standards recapitulated the earlier ones of the Children's Bureau: health supervision, family counseling, educational experiences, and physical/emotional security. They suggested group sizes according to age: three years old, 12–15 children per group; four to six years old, 15–20 children per group; and over six, 20–25 children per group. Each group "should have a full-time teacher and assistant." As in the earlier Children's Bureau standards, children under three were not recommended for day care. The effective staff ratios were roughly equal, but recommended group size was one-third smaller in the Child Welfare League standards.[3]

Soon after the publication of these standards the Children's Bureau and Women's Bureau sponsored a day care conference, which stressed, among other things, the continued influx of women into the labor force and their purported demand for day care services. Again the conferees raised the issue of child care in terms of dependency. Day care was touted as a means to escape welfare. President-elect John Kennedy wrote approvingly of the conference's recommendations. Once inaugurated, he had his new HEW secretary, Abraham Ribicoff, draft a welfare reform package for Congress—a package which included a $10 million day care program for welfare clients.

In several respects the legislation was similar to a 1958 day care bill Senator Jacob Javits had proposed to Congress. His bill had gone nowhere, but now packaged with the first of a long line of welfare reforms, it became law in 1962. The rationale for the reform measures would become a familiar litany throughout the next two decades. Welfare costs were rising. The present system was an administrative nightmare and a failure. Only by breaking the cycle of dependency could the welfare burden be lessened. Employment and training were necessary means to break that cycle and day care was a requisite support service.

Enacted as Public Law 87-543, the bill authorized $5 million for fiscal 1963 and $10 million for each ensuing year. Although the House report on the bill recounted the latest figures on the numbers of working women with children in its explanation of the day care provision, the promise of lower welfare costs appears more relevant to its passage. After all, women with children had been entering the labor force in significant numbers for well over a decade—a fact of which the Women's Bureau consistently reminded Congress. Even under the welfare reform rubric, the day care program managed only to extract $800,000 of its $5 million authorization from the conservative appropriations committees.

From its inception within HEW the welfare reform legislation contained one specific regulatory provision regarding day care. Federal funding was made conditional upon a facility obtaining a state license. This provision left primary regulatory responsibility in the states, where it had traditionally resided. The promise of federal money encouraged states to modernize their licensing procedures and some 40 percent of that money went in the first years of programs to fund this modernization. The results, however, were less than heartening. Still plagued by the social worker-enforcer, state licensing authorities suffered also from a lack of technical knowledge and funds. The regulators were often confronted by the choice of closing substandard centers with no prospect of a replacement or allowing them to continue. They usually chose the latter. To compensate for this bending of the code, they intensified their scrutiny of new applications. Thus, expansion of day care facilities was curtailed, while older, less satisfactory centers continued to operate. This problem was compounded by the succession of new antipoverty programs which provided funds for day care to allow mothers on welfare to receive vocational education or other training. The proliferation of federal programs operated by various agencies and departments precluded any easy centralization of day care regulation, even if one were attempted. By default, the states retained regulatory power over the expanding day care industry.

The developmentalist approach to out-of-home child care was not to be denied its heyday also. In 1964 Congress passed the mainstay of the War on Poverty, the Economic Opportunity Act. Although touching practically every aspect of poverty, the showpiece of the act and of its creator, the Office of Economic Opportunity (OEO), became Head Start. In the tradition of middle-class nursery schools, Head Start was designed to enhance the psychological development of poor children. The recent research of psychologists J. McVicker Hunt and Benjamin Bloom and various local preschool education projects in universities had indicated the positive impact of instruction and a salutary environment upon a child's cognitive development. Head Start was more firmly rooted in empirical psychology than its antecedent nursery schools. Although its stated purpose, social uplift, was very similar to the moral uplift the reformers of the early twentieth century sought, there was a significant difference. The poor generally welcomed Head Start; it was not the kind of hegemonic imposition that the infant schools of an earlier era were. It was also more of an effort to reach the rural than the urban poor. Yet, there remained a common motif of getting the ghetto out of the child. The prospect of derailing multigenerational poverty had great political appeal. Sargent Shriver, OEO's director, wisely chose to capitalize upon it.

Although Head Start was planned as a pilot project involving 100,000 children, Shriver allowed over half a million to enroll. The OEO found Congress very willing to increase its budget to fund such a potentially revolutionary approach to poverty. Since employment and the cost of care were less relevant to Head Start's purpose, smaller groups, more attention to education, health care, and nutrition became paramount. Head Start's stress upon direct community participation circumvented the traditional federal-state-local funding chain and escaped the extant licensing morass. It had different priorities than the employment-oriented day care. This difference in priorities was no better reflected than in their child-to-staff ratios of four-and-five-to-one for preschool children. Based upon their own experience with preschool education and consultations with outside experts, Head Start's organizers reduced the traditional day care ratios by one-half to two-thirds. Costs, of course, were tripled.

As the federal government expanded its day care funding, a schism in purpose surfaced and slowly widened. In the developmental area, comprehensive child care grew with OEO's increase of Head Start. In the employment area, every new program or proposal to replace welfare with "workfare" carried a day care provision. Such provisions became more integral as the welfare explosion was recognized to be among unmarried mothers. Work, many believed, would take these young women off the dole and occupy their time with pursuits other than procreation. Meanwhile, the children required care so that their mothers could find jobs. Ultimately, both kinds of day care shared the common purpose of reducing poverty and welfare dependency. Nonetheless, their means were in most respects antithetical. Where minimum costs were essential to making employment practical, comprehensive services and education were integral to breaking the poverty cycle. There would obviously be a crisis if the two were ever compelled to integrate their programs. In 1967 that integration was mandated by law.

Nineteen hundred and sixty-seven was a watershed year for day care. OEO was coming under heavy criticism from conservatives. Accused of waste and mismanagement, its programs ran into the backlash against the urban riots and the economic pressures of the war in Vietnam. It being basically a creation of Johnson's administration, few in Congress felt responsible to defend it. The task fell to Shriver. To defuse his critics Shriver formulated a revision to the Equal Opportunity Act which promised tighter administrative procedures, expanded OEO's support services for welfare recipients seeking work, and proposed employing welfare mothers in child care centers. His revisions first encountered opposition within the administration. The Bureau of the Budget (BOB) feared the administrative provisions were too constraining and probably unworkable. Their very complexity insured that they would not be followed and would merely invite more congressional criticism. HEW resented the further erosion of its policy purview. Particularly, they fought OEO's proposal to administer the day care program. At HEW behest, the language was broadened to include them. The change was portentous since Congress expanded the day care subsection to include the FIDCR mandate.

The legislation encountered more problems in the Ninetieth Congress. Republicans worked to divest OEO of its established programs, such as Head Start, and to restore program control to the traditional departments. Budget authorizations were cut and appropriations reduced. Finally, the Senate Labor and Public Works Committee sought to bring some administrative order to the plethora of social welfare initiatives by mandating a set of interagency regulations to govern the numerous federal day care programs. From the perspective of many in OEO, HEW, and BOB, however, day care regulation was not the issue. They worried about the potential cost of the greatly expanded day care programs mandated by the OEO legislation and the new Work Incentives Program. They estimated that over one billion dollars would be needed to care for all children under six of the working poor affected by these programs.[4]

The new employment thrust in OEO's legislation did not reduce Head Start's funds nor did it eliminate the smaller Follow Through Program designed to preserve the child's early gains. But OEO's suggestion for employment of welfare mothers echoed loudly in the House Ways and Means Committee. Confronted by an unanticipated and politically frightening expansion in the nation's welfare rolls, the committee and the Congress enacted the AFDC-Work Incentives Program (WIN). The incentive for working was simplified: get a job or lose all benefits. For the first time Congress imposed this requirement on women with young children. Day care became a necessary support service and was included in the WIN program. This legislation and the OEO revision complicated the day care program further; they required the use of welfare recipients to staff centers. Obviously, employment-oriented care was overwhelming developmental care in congressional enactments. They only catch was that those who would write the regulations governing these day care programs were developmentalist in orientation.

Writing the Requirements

Although some staff members within the Children's Bureau and OEO pondered the day care requirement mandate in the early months of 1968, such interagency coordination could be achieved only by someone on high. In April HEW Secretary Wilbur Cohen created the Federal Panel on Early Childhood to write the requirements. Jule Sugarman, former director of Head Start, chaired the panel. Cohen had brought Sugarman to the Children's Bureau as associate director as part of an overall strategy to insure Head Start's transfer into the Bureau. Both Cohen and Sugarman wanted to keep the program out of the Office of Education where state school administrators would dominate it. Cohen also thought it appropriate to include on the panel representatives from other departments involved in providing day care services. This inclusion created a somewhat diverse group: OEO, HEW, the Department of Agriculture, Housing and Urban Development, and Labor. Even the Defense Department participated in very early panel deliberations. Nonetheless, representatives of the Children's Bureau and Head Start predominated.

From the outset panel members divided into two groups: one favoring comprehensive developmental day care, the other advocating minimum cost day care to ease the employment of welfare mothers. The former group included the Children's Bureau, Head Start, and the Women's Bureau of the Labor Department (DOL). The employment–minimum cost group was championed by DOL's Manpower Administration and, always in the background, the Bureau of the Budget. If an agency's program were designed principally to employ the poor, then it sought day care requirements that minimized costs. If the agency were operating principally a child development and care program, it pushed for more comprehensive requirements. Two factors mitigated potential conflict. The working committee consisted of panel and staff members sympathetic to the developmental comprehensive approach, and they drafted the requirements. Secondly, the open-ended entitlement of many of the day care programs made costs of tertiary concern.

Neither group had a monopoly on the historic function of day care nor on good intentions. The employment-oriented group argued that the extent of employment programs was limited by the availability and cost of day care. Raising that cost beyond the bare minimum resulted in fewer jobs for the poor and a less effective employment program. On the other hand, the developmentalists believed day care to be the chief means of providing necessary nutrition and medical services to disadvantaged children. Staff attention and education would enhance the child's future prospects. They believed that costs should be secondary to the needs of these children. In a world of limited resources, these two positions were not easily reconciled—if they could be reconciled at all. Yet, 1968 was not a time when policymakers, at least those drafting the FIDCR, worried over such limitations.

Sugarman's position was complicated by his administrative post. Coming out of the Head Start tradition of comprehensive developmental care, he had just become deputy director of the Children's Bureau. Had he leaned against the developmentalists, he might have alienated the personnel in the Bureau. His responsibilities to the panel would end with the FIDCR draft; his relationship to Bureau personnel would continue throughout his tenure there. His solution to these problems was to draft a set of requirements which, while formally affirming comprehensive developmental child care, were sufficiently ambiguous in content and intention to subsume the interests of all panel members.

The final version of requirements specified child-to-staff ratios for center-based and family day care. They stated that the location of facilities must consider the relative need of the population for federally funded day care, travel time for users, accessibility to "other resources which enhance the day care program," and opportunities for parent and neighborhood involvement. Facilities must conform to "appropriate" safety and sanitation codes. "Educational opportunities must be provided every child . . . under the supervision and direction of a staff member trained or experienced in child growth and development." Toys, games, and daily activities for each child "must be designed to influence a positive concept of self, and motivation to enhance his social, cognitive, and communication skills." Counseling for child and family must be available to enable them to choose the best child care arrangements. Health and dental care must be provided to the child. Facilities must provide "nutritious" meals and daily checks for any indications of illness in the child.

The requirements also ordered a periodic assessment of the "physical and mental competence to care for children" of staff members. They mandated "continuous in-service training" and "career progression opportunities" for staff members. "Parents must have the opportunity to become involved themselves in the making of decisions" concerning center operations. In centers of 40 or more children, parents must be included in a "policy advisory committee" and constitute no less than 50 percent of its membership. Such a committee "must perform productive functions" in program development, funding application, selection of administrators and staff, and channeling complaints. Employment and administration policies must be written out and available to parents and employees. Finally, the facilities "must be periodically evaluated in terms of the Federal Interagency Day Care Standards." The agent for evaluation was left unstated.[5]

Despite their scope and detail, the 1968 FIDCR actually represented a series of rather subtle compromises. The development group wanted child-to-staff ratios akin to Head Start's. These ratios were lower than those suggested for day care by the Child Welfare League. The employment group objected to the costs that these ratios entailed. Sugarman's answer was to allow clerical and housekeeping personnel as well as unpaid volunteers to count as staff for the purposes of the requirement. Such volunteers could also include "older children." Moreover, the requirement specified the ratios not "normally" be exceeded. This sort of qualifier was replete throughout the 1968 FIDCR. Space must be "adequate"; safeguards must be "adequate"; ventilation "adequate"; educational material "appropriate" to the facility's "type"; and meals "adequate." What constituted adequacy or appropriateness was never specified. And this was crucial.

"The basic responsibility," the FIDCR states, "for enforcement of the requirements lies with the administering agency." By prefacing the FIDCR with this statement, Sugarman mollified disagreeing panel members. Each agency governed the compliance of its funding recipients to the requirements. The one oversight agency that might have blocked the requirements, BOB, had no authority to review agency regulations at this time. The developmental groups could enforce the FIDCR according to a strict interpretation of the requirements; the employment group could enforce a very loose interpretation. To insure this flexibility, the FIDCR preface also noted that "noncompliance may be grounds for suspension or termination of federal funds." The funding agency, then, had final determination over the only effective enforcement procedure, a funding suspension.

Consensus was achieved due to the tacit recognition among panel members that they were agreeing upon an ambiguous, nonbinding set of requirements. In other words, consensus ensued from the common premise that the 1968 FIDCR were a set of goals and, qua goals, everyone could agree that they were fine. The panel conducted no cost studies; costs were irrelevant to ideal standards. They relied upon their experience with Head Start and knowledge of child development. Moreover, soon after the promulgation of FIDCR, informal assurances were passed by the Social and Rehabilitation Service through HEW's regional offices to the states that the requirements would not be enforced.[6]

In 1968 there was a slight possibility that the Children's Bureau would enforce the FIDCR in stages. Although it had no authority over the other day care programs scattered among the bureaucracy, the Bureau did control the Title IV-A day care program. Since funding was the only effective means of enforcement, the strongest supporter of the FIDCR, the Bureau, was in a position to implement them. Moreover, at that time Title IV-A had an open-ended entitlement; money was indeed no object. The Bureau's position, however, soon changed. When the Nixon administration reorganized HEW, the Children's Bureau was divided among the Community Services Administration (CSA), the Health Services and Mental Health Administration, and the newly created Office of Child Development (OCD). OCD received the enforcement mandate for the FIDCR, but CSA received the Title IV-A program. Without control of day care funding, OCD was an unarmed policeman.

In the larger policy conflict of 1967 to 1968 the FIDCR and its legislative mandate played a symbolic role. Among the slowly shrinking Great Society supporters in Congress, the conservative push to reduce welfare costs through the WIN Program portended in the minds of many children advocates the sacrifice of the children of welfare recipients to shoddy care. On one level, the overriding stress on employment and WIN's administration by the Labor Department indicated that the children could expect the cheapest care supervised by an agency with no interest per se in the children. On another level —insofar as Sheila Rothman is correct in arguing that the WIN Program's "more fundamental purpose [than employment] was to frighten welfare recipients from applying for relief"—the poorer the day care, the more effective the deterrent.[7] Liberals on the Senate Labor and Public Welfare Committee hoped that federal interagency day care requirements might prevent a serious decline in the quality of day care. If it raised the costs of that care, then the requirements might well serve to make welfare payments to mothers at home cheaper than the day care which would allow them to work. Either contingency was more palatable than the WIN Program and its day care provisions. The committee vested the FIDCR mandate in OEO/ HEW to insure that the requirements were comprehensive and developmental in orientation. Events in 1969, however, would soon recast the political context of the FIDCR.

The Zigler Proposal for Revision

Richard Nixon's victory in November, 1968, brought the Republicans to power for the first time in eight years. As they assumed office, the now famous Westinghouse Study of Head Start appeared and questioned the long-term benefits of early intervention—a serious setback for developmentalists. In that same year, the administration advanced a sweeping proposal for welfare reform, the Family Assistance Plan (FAP). Apart from its innovative guaranteed annual income provision, FAP would entail a massive federal day care program as an adjunct to a modified WIN program. HEW estimated that the program would require 400 new day care centers each year for five years. Finally, HEW Secretary Robert Finch brought in an eminent Yale psychologist, Edward Zigler, to administer the newly created Office of Child Development. Due to their ambiguity and vague criteria for compliance, Zigler believed the FIDCR unworkable in their present form. In light of the proposed FAP day care program, which OCD would administer, he received authorization to revise them.

Above all, Zigler desired a set of day care requirements which could be enforced and which provided a minimum level of care consistent with the child's health development. Faced with more stringent limitations upon social welfare spending under the Republican administration, he worked to strike a compromise between the comprehensive developmentalists and the employment-oriented advocates. Zigler sought the best care for the most children with the fewest dollars. To commence the process of revision, he held a major day care conference at Airlie House in 1970. Over a thousand parents, child care providers, social scientists, and advocates met to discuss the requirements. The conference produced a manual to guide the revisions. In 1971, OCD began writing a new set of day care requirements.[8]

Since the FAP proposal, Congress evinced continued interest in out-of-home child care. Among the employment-oriented group, Wilbur Mills, chairman of the House Ways and Means Committee, requested a HEW report on state licensing procedures. Mills was troubled by reports that inadequate day care facilities limited the expansion of the WIN Program. Cumbersome licensing processes delayed the opening of new centers. Moreover, state codes were inconsistent and often inappropriate to child care. Russell Long, chairman of the Senate Finance Committee, also sought to deal with the problems of state licensing. He proposed minimum federal standards to supersede the states' and accelerate the expension of day care facilities. Under pressure from these committee chairmen, the Nixon administration through OCD initiated a study of state licensing codes. The administration, however, opposed federal supersedence of any state's authority in this matter. OCD did disseminate a guide for day care licensing in 1973 and encouraged states to revise their codes accordingly. Since it was only a guide, its contents reflected Zigler's position that standards must be enforceable and guarantee the minimum needs of the child. He was also sufficiently politic to seek advice during its preparation from all interested parties.[9]

In 1971, congressional advocates of comprehensive developmental child care added a two billion dollar program in this area to an OEO extension bill. Sponsored chiefly by Senator Walter Mondale and Representative John Brademas, the bill proposed comprehensive services for children in day care. Services would be free of charge for the poor and available on a graduated fee schedule for middle-income families. It also provided for new day care requirements to be developed through a complex interaction among government, caretakers, and parents. The innovation in the Mondale-Brademus bill was the extension of federal assistance to day care for nonpoor families. There was no precedent for a categorical federal program to subsidize the day care of middle-class children. The proposed program bore a large price tag while not linked directly to the employment of welfare clients or other traditional justifications. Among conservatives the program smacked of "sovietizing our (i.e., the nonpoor) children" and undermining the family. Many forgot that the tax law had for 20 years subsidized the nonparental care of middle-class children.

The OEO extension, including the Mondale-Brademus child care program, passed the Congress in December, 1971. President Nixon vetoed it and the Senate sustained the veto. From the administration's perspective, the legislation contained too many objectionable features, not the least of which was its cost. The child care program contained complex administrative procedures involving hundreds of prime sponsors working directly with federal agencies; the administration and several state governors believed these procedures to be unworkable. It impinged upon FAP's day care provision and extended day care subsidies to the nonpoor. The OEO extension included an independent governing body for its legal aid funds. Since cabinet members had complained repeatedly about OEO-funded litigation against the government, the lack of presidential discretion regarding the board controlling these funds became a significant objection to the bill. Finally, a veto helped to mitigate conservative criticism of Nixon's foreign policy. No single consideration can explain the veto.[10]

In the wake of the veto, the House Education and Labor Committee reported another OEO extension bill without the child care program. The Mondale child care program also resurfaced in a second bill which passed the Senate but died in the House. To insure that the administration, which advocates of comprehensive developmental child care now clearly perceived as antichild, did not weaken the 1968 FIDCR, the House measure included a FIDCR comparability provision which required any new day care requirements be "no less comprehensive" than the 1968 set. The legislation cost one billion dollars less than the earlier vetoed version and modified the objectionable provisions regarding legal services. There was also an expansion of Head Start, which the administration opposed, intended to offset the loss of the comprehensive child care program.

As the bill made its way through Congress in the summer of 1972, the FIDCR comparability provision raised problems for HEW's completed but unapproved revision. Secretary Richardson wrote the ranking Republican on the House Education and Labor Committee, Albert Quie, requesting a clarification of the provision. He explained the weaknesses of the 1968 FIDCR: they were vague, ambiguous, and difficult to enforce. The revised version corrected these problems. Although it increased the ostensible child-to-adult ratios, the actual number of children per caregiver was unaffected. Richardson requested a colloquy between Quie and Committee Chairman Carl Perkins to clarify that the comparability provision entailed only overall quality, not "stringent . . . quantitative measurement." The congressman performed the colloquy along the lines Richardson had requested. In September, the legislation, comparability provision included, went to the president for approval.[11]

The alignment of the executive agencies on this bill is significant to the fate of the 1972 FIDCR revisions. Both HEW and OEO recommended that Nixon sign the bill. Congress had dropped most of the objectionable provisions of the earlier extension bill. Perkins and Quie had clarified the FIDCR comparability mandate to allow HEW's revisions. Despite these changes, the other agencies' recommendations, the Office of Management and Budget (OMB) suggested a presidential veto. The bill, in general, and the comparability provision, in particular, "would limit to some extent administrative flexibility in carrying out the program." OMB had always considered the 1968 FIDCR an "unattainable level" of care. Consideration of day care standards, they argued, was relevant *only* to the still pending FAP legislation. Despite their recommendation for disapproval, Nixon signed the OEO extension under the probably correct impression that it was the best that he could expect from Congress. Nonetheless, OMB's linkage of any day care requirements to FAP's passage would become significant for Zigler's revision of FIDCR.[12]

In the spring of 1972, Zigler and his staff completed the new day care requirements. These requirements were much more specific on every aspect of a center's operation. They expanded the regulatory scope to in-home care, detailed age groupings, meals per hour of care, provider responsibilities and a minimum wage requirement for center employees. In the crucial area of child-to-staff ratios, the requirements increased the child-to-adult ratios but specified that only caregivers, not clerical or janitorial staff, could count in the ratios. Although the 1968 FIDCR mandated lower ratios, it allowed any adult volunteer or older child present in the center to count in that overall ratio. Zigler's revision counted only paid, qualified caregivers. Moreover, his revisions included ratios for children under three years old: 0 to 18 months, 3:1; and 19 to 38 months, 4:1. The 1968 FIDCR had neither any requirements for care of children under three years old nor any ratios set this low. Not only had Zigler written a rigorous set of day care requirements, but an enforceable one as well. Due to their content, they encountered OMB's opposition; due to the political context, the advocacy groups opposed them as well.

Secretary Richardson approved the new requirements by June, 1972. He proposed to hold a series of congressional and press briefings that summer to describe the administration's day care policy. The centerpiece would be the new requirements, their relationship to FAP, and the modifications in Head Start. Richardson and Zigler believed the revised FIDCR would affirm the administration's commitment to good quality day care and to children in the wake of the child care veto. OMB, however, had other plans. In a confidential "white paper" its staff assessed the HEW proposals. The OMB paper concluded that the proposed policy would: (1) commit the federal government to determine directly the nature of child care; (2) raise care in the centers to "approximately" the same quality as Head

Start's; (3) increase FAP's day care allocation from $750 million to $1.2 billion; (4) establish a prime sponsor system "similar" to the proposed system of Mondale and Brademus, but with fewer allowable sponsors; and (5) make an overall policy declaration in support of "developmental" day care. The staff assessment, in characteristic understatement, concluded that a policy statement of this sort "would be undesirable."[13]

In their analysis, OMB questioned almost every facet of Richardson's policy proposals. Not only were the staff ratios challenged, but OMB raised the very issue of "whether or not the administration wants to endorse the 'federal presence' that these standards and the accompanying enforcement effort implies (sic)." They questioned the wisdom of the requirements' application to in-home care, to volunteer participants in federal programs, and to centers serving only those persons receiving federal cash subsidies. OMB pointed out that HEW's proposed child care credit allowance would double FAP outlays and "eliminate parental incentive to get a 'good bargain,' thus resulting in an upward cost push." Presumably, the potential cost of the minimum wage requirement also bothered OMB. In sum, their central argument was that HEW's proposals "cloud the difference between child care—a federal responsibility as part of the workfare provisions of HR-1 (FAP)—and compensatory education, which is primarily a state and local function." Their alternative was to "leave quality control to parental discretion under a pure income strategy or support more limited standards . . . ."[14]

During the first half of 1972, OMB and HEW were at loggerheads over a proper day care policy for the administration. OMB wanted a minimum-cost employment policy; HEW advocated a more comprehensive developmental approach. Zigler's revision of the FIDCR was the linchpin of HEW's approach. Neither Richardson nor Undersecretary John Veneman would act without OMB's approbation. As Veneman wrote the secretary in a confidential memorandum, "I indicated to [OMB] your desire to reach an agreement on day care [and that] it would not be your intention to release our position unless it was mutually determined to be appropriate." Unable to budge OMB or induce White House intervention, such a determination never came. The revisions were quietly buried with FAP's death. Soon after, a frustrated Edward Zigler returned to New Haven.[15]

What is ironic in this is that the most vocal opponents of Zigler's revision outside the executive branch were the staunchest advocates of comprehensive day care. From the viewpoint of the Child Welfare League, Children's Defense Fund, and the others, HEW and the administration had entered into an insidious conspiracy to undermine the quality of federally funded day care. The revised FIDCR, they believed, eviscerated the impeccable standards of 1968. Caught in the middle, Zigler's revisions were soundly condemned by both sides. Politically, the administration had nothing to gain from promulgating requirements already proscribed by the very people they were designed to pacify. To the advocates of comprehensive day care, loyalty to the 1968 FIDCR had become the test of one's commitment to the proper care of children. In their minds an ambiguous, unenforceable icon was preferable to a practical, but supposedly weaker, set of Nixon administration requirements. As long as worship was voluntary, OMB, too, agreed to allow the 1968 idol to stand.[16]

A History of the Title XX Amendment

Following the failure of Zigler's revisions, there were two years of relative calm concerning day care regulations. The administration abandoned its FAP proposal and worked toward keeping down social welfare expenditures. Congress worked toward increasing them. Not until the passage of the Title XX amendment to the Social Security Act did the issue of day care standards arise. Title XX incorporated an innovation in federal social welfare aid to the states. In place of categorical programs, it broached a less rigid formula-grant approach with fewer restrictions upon state allocations of federal funds. Among the areas to be funded in this fashion was day care. The administration's move toward revenue sharing and block grants did not sit well with many members of Congress and other advocates of categorical spending. They believed that uncontrolled states and municipalities might spend the grant money in ways unintended by Congress. Day care advocates also feared the inevitable competition for funds with more powerful social service interests. A major issue was the continued assurance of adequate services to target populations. In other words, the extent to which service program grants were earmarked and regulated was central to the Title XX enactment.

In one respect the history of Title XX began in 1972. At that time federal welfare funds were distributed in categorical fashion to states under an 80 percent matching formula. Outlays had grown by 450 percent between 1968 and 1972—$350 million to $1.6 billion. To impose some degree of restraint on this rapid growth, Congress placed a ceiling of $2.5 billion on federal outlays. This ceiling, however, would still have allowed a one billion dollar increase in spending —something the administration strongly opposed. To keep spending well below the congressional ceiling, HEW issued new regulations governing federal funding in May, 1973. Their main purpose was to tighten eligibility requirements and reduce allowance for services.

Congressional opposition to these regulations resulted in a postponement of their enforcement until January 1, 1975.[17]

Congress and the administration had reached an impasse over social services spending. Organized labor, state administrators, other advocacy groups, and their congressional supporters could not agree upon the structure of any new regulations. HEW's Assistant Secretary for Planning and Evaluation, William Morrill, devised a strategy to break the impasse. In return for administration support of the $2.5 billion ceiling, Congress would enact new legislation to replace categorical specification of service programs with block grants. Federal review of the states' disposition of the founds would cease, and only an independent audit would insure that the states conform to the general parameters of the statute.

In support of this approach, OMB Director Roy Ash explained to the president that the federal government could not distinguish as well as state and local authorities the useful from the useless programs. The new approach promised to reduce federal involvement and fructify the administration's long-term policy thrust toward a "New Federalism." Ash envisioned no way of holding outlays below the $2.5 billion ceiling in the future. Congress's repeated deferrals of HEW's regulations and the various alternative bills boded only more spending in the traditional categorical vein. He believed that the administration could at least extract a block grant approach in the process.[18]

With approval from SRS, HEW's hierarchy, and OMB, Morrill commenced a prolonged series of meetings with all interested parties on the structure and content of what was to become Title XX. Through their meetings he built a consensus for Title XX. On the 1968 FIDCR, the AFL-CIO, at the request of the Child Welfare League, was particularly insistent that the requirements be retained and enforced. ASPE's draft of Title XX thus included a provision for enforcement of the FIDCR, but, at ASPE's insistence, the provision also mandated a study of the appropriateness of federal day care regulation. For in-home care they proposed to leave the decision to the states, provided each state granted "all interested individuals and organizations the opportunity to submit recommended standards." Out-of-home care would have to conform to the 1968 FIDCR except for the requirement mandating educational opportunities for children. Their draft bill gave the secretary authority to prescribe maximum permissible child-to-staff ratios for children over five provided that those ratios did not exceed 13:1 for five- to nine-year-olds and 20:1 for children over nine. The bill also included a request to the secretary to prepare a report on the overall appropriateness of the day care requirements. Regarding the requirements, OMB made one major change: the clause requiring states to consult "all interested individuals" when setting standards for in-home care became standards set "reasonably in accord with recommended standards of national standard-setting organizations concerned with the home care of children." Popular input was scotched.[19]

The House Ways and Means Committee and Senator Russell Long's Finance Committee dominated congressional action on the bill and other welfare proposals. The Ways and Means Committee concurred in the central thrust of the Title XX. They were pleased to be rid of the stalemate over social service spending. The committee lowered the overall recommended staffing ratios and imposed a two-to-one ratio for children under three. They took this latter step to raise the cost of infant center-based care in hopes of discouraging it. It was, they argued, bad for the young child. The committee also reinstated the educational requirement of the 1968 FIDCR. Finally, as a gesture to those seeking to restrain costs, their report instructed the secretary to consider the cost implications of requirements in an appropriateness report.[20]

On the Senate side, the Finance Committee retained the principal features of HEW's draft: the higher staff ratios and the waiver of the educational requirement. In place of specific staff ratios for children under three, the committee gave the secretary discretion in the matter. Walter Mondale of the Senate and Patricia Schroeder of the House opposed the relaxation of the FIDCR's staff ratios as a move toward "warehousing" children. Despite this opposition, the House conferees acceded to all the Senate's provisions regarding standards. The conference report passed both chambers by voice vote.[21]

HEW approved of the enrolled bill. Weinberger wrote Ash that the higher child-to-staff ratios were "an improvement over our proposal in this regard." Apparently, they had originally overestimated the political muscle of the comprehensive care advocates. The Treasury Department, however, objected strenuously to the parent locater provision of the bill. The IRS, they believed, would be placed in the business of enforcing child support laws. For the same reason, OMB joined the Treasury Department in recommending a presidential veto.[22] President Ford's decision was not made that easily. As a congressman, he had supported precisely such a parent locater law. The bill incorporated a very much desired revision to existing categorical programs. Since the Republicans had done very badly in the post-Watergate fall elections, the Ninety-Fourth Congress promised to be more generous than its predecessor in social welfare spending. Ford, thus, disregarded OMB's and Treasury's advice and signed the legislation on January 4, 1975.

Title XX did more than change the child-to-staff ratios: it altered enforcement procedures for FIDCR. Before 1975, enforcement rested upon a "compliance" procedure in which an administrative hearing occurred prior to any federal suspension of funds. The new method was a "federal financial participation" procedure in which the government could suspend funds at the time of the violation and require the state to reimburse any previously allocated money. Moreover, Title XX's penalty for noncompliance with the FIDCR was not the standard three percent reduction in overall funding, but a total cut-off of day care payments. This new procedure was included at the behest of the AFL-CIO and Child Welfare League as part of the price of their concurrence in Title XX. Morrill, too, thought a rigorous enforcement of the 1968 FIDCR could well clear up the question of their practicality. Indeed it would. SRS, which administered its day care programs, estimated that "well in excess of half of the child day care provided under Title XX will not meet the FIDCR." Over $300 million, one-half of all day care funds, could be withheld for noncompliance. The contrast between the old and new procedures was more striking. Neither SRS nor any other federal agency had ever held a compliance hearing to enforce the FIDCR within a state.[23]

The first rumbling of the political eruption to follow came in April, 1975. That month HEW published for public comment preliminary day care requirements based upon Title XX provisions. In the one staffing area where they had discretion, children under three, the department based the ratio upon Zigler's unenacted revision. Centers were required to have a child-to-staff ratio of 1:1 for infants under six weeks old, 3:1 for children six weeks to eighteen months, and 4:1 for children eighteen to thirty-six months. All the other ratios, including the most controversial 5:1 and 7:1 for three- to five-year-olds, were fixed by Title XX or the 1968 FIDCR. Enforcement would begin October 1, 1975. It would include Title XX and the day care authorized under Title IV. As the implications of these requirements became clearer and enforcement more likely, protests from caregivers, state administrators, and then congressmen mounted.

The reasons for the protest were obvious. A 1974 HEW audit of day care centers in nine states indicated that three-fourths of them were out of compliance with one or more health or safety requirements. The more serious cost problem was staff ratios. A center's typical child-to-staff ratio for preschool children was 8:1. To lower that ratio to 5:1 or 4:1 could increase costs by up to 50 percent. In response to this protest, HEW Secretary Casper Weinberger changed the final regulations to allow a 4:1 ratio for children between six weeks and three years old. He recognized, however, that despite these changes, the FIDCR's enforcement "would significantly reduce the availability of child care in many states." The fracas over the requirements intensified as the October deadline approached.[24]

Congressional protest against the requirements did not divide along ideological lines. Such otherwise diverse politicians as Henry Bellmon, Ronald Dellums, Carl Albert, Peter Rodino, William Brock, and George McGovern petitioned for postponement. Supporters of the requirements were more ideologically akin: Bella Abzug, Walter Mondale, Charles Rangel, John Brademas; but James Buckley also supported the requirements. Undoubtedly overwhelmed by ambivalence, Representative Joshua Eliberg signed letters of protest and of support. Opponents and supporters argued in surprisingly similar fashion. Opponents: enforcement of the requirements will price day care centers out of the market and endanger the well-being of the children. Supporters: failure to enforce the requirements will allow shoddy, inadequate day care centers to continue and endanger the well-being of the children. All were righteous; few were holy.[25]

As the deadline neared, enormous pressures came to bear on HEW. Members of Congress continued to threaten the cajole. Over 20 bills were introduced to suspend the requirements. Frantic over the possible loss of $300 million in federal aid, states warned day care operators within their jurisdiction of an impending crackdown. The AFL-CIO and Child Welfare League threatened to sue HEW if the requirements were not enforced. In the South, day care operators did bring suit against HEW to block enforcement of the requirements. Finally, on September 26, four days before they were to have taken effect, a federal district court judge issued a temporary injunction against their enforcement pending a hearing on October 20.

Within HEW, strategies for dealing with the enforcement problem abounded. No one within the department seriously considered enforcing the requirements to the extent of closing down day care centers through a wholesale suspension of federal funding. SRS, the administering agency, proposed an imaginative, though probably illegal, extension of Section 1115 of the Social Security Act, the demonstration provision. Under their plan, HEW would "allow the states to experiment with alternate requirements" and waive the FIDCR for these "experiments." That these demonstration projects might include over half of the federally funded centers throughout the nation apparently presented no difficulty for SRS. The General Counsel's office rejected their approach as unworkable and of dubious legality. An alternative, simply ignoring the law, was also rejected.[26]

The court injunction and the congressional push for suspension allowed HEW to adopt a less radical approach. On October 1, Secretary F. David Matthews sent draft legislation to the House and Senate. The legislation would amend the compliance features of Title XX. In place of total cutoff of funds, the secretary would only reduce funding by three percent—the penalty for other Title XX violations. No penalty would be imposed if the state were "making a good faith effort to upgrade day care facilities" to accord with the FIDCR. If the center were not in compliance with "licensure, health, or safety standards," the secretary could suspend all funding. HEW's proposal dealt with the crux of the issue for all concerned: the staffing requirement for children under six.[27] A "good faith" effort or, at worst, a three percent penalty would assuage the fears of the states and their day care centers. Congress, however, chose another route.

On September 29, the Ways and Means Committee reported a bill which suspended staffing requirements for six months. In deference to supporters of the lower ratios, it provided that staffing ratios must conform to state law and be no higher than those in effect prior to September 15, 1975. Overall, the bill's manager, James Corman, justified the suspension as a necessary hiatus to allow congressional review of the requirements. The measure easily passed the House and went into Senator Long's Finance Committee.[28] Long had difficulty with the House suspension. Six months, he argued, would not enlighten congressional decision making. Instead, he envisioned using the requirements to encourage operators to hire welfare mothers for their day care centers. Congress would provide additional funds to enable centers to meet staffing ratios and offer tax credits for employing welfare recipients. Long and Mondale introduced a bill containing these provisions and a $500 million authorization to defray the cost of additional staff. Centers could then meet the requirements without raising fees.

Their strategy was simple. Under the threat of FIDCR's immediate enforcement without federal assistance, they hoped to compel members of Congress into passing the aid bill with its welfare provision. Federal funding would assuage the fears of day care operators and states over added costs. The lower child-to-staff ratios would enlist support from comprehensive advocates. The welfare provisions would attract conservative votes. Finally, anticipating the administration's opposition, they were confident that these combined political forces could assure the president's acquiescence, or at worst, override his veto. The key remained the impending enforcement of the FIDCR.

With this strategy, Long, a dogged opponent of strict day care regulation, became an advocate of quick implementation provided his welfare provisions were adopted. He bottled up the House's six-month suspension in his committee. Instead, he offered a one-month suspension as an amendment to a pending tariff bill. Such a brief suspension would keep the pressure on Congress and the administration. In the first week of October, the Senate passed the amended tariff bill and entered into conference with the House. Still concerned over impending enforcement, the House conferees insisted upon a lengthier delay. Long compromised on four months. The report passed the House by a 383 to 10 vote and the Senate by voice. Since neither Congress nor the administration was prepared to enforce the staffing requirement at this time, Ford signed the suspension pending a more permanent resolution of the problem.

The hiatus allowed Long to amend the earlier House bill with the provision for aiding the states in meeting the requirements and employing welfare mothers in day care centers. By a nine-to-nine vote, the Finance Committee defeated a Republican amendment to delete the staffing requirements entirely. The committee did reduce the aid authorization from $500 million to $250 million due to a new estimate of the state's compliance costs. They waived compliance for centers with fewer than 20 percent of their children receiving federal subsidies. The bill also made the employment tax credit refundable to encourage nonprofit centers to hire welfare recipients. This credit, in conjunction with direct federal funding, would have defrayed up to $5,000 of the cost of employing a welfare recipient in a day care center. Finally, implementation of the FIDCR ratios would be delayed until July 1, 1976. Under these provisions, the employment-oriented advocates and the comprehensive developmentalists found a common cause in enforcing the FIDCR. Thus, did Mondale and Long stand the same ground.

Their bill encountered opposition from both the administration and Senate Republicans. The administration had decided that the best solution to the staffing problem was to allow each state to determine its own day care standards. This accorded with its general block-grant, defederalization approach. Moreover, it would eliminate the need to augment federal spending to enforce compliance. The administration wanted no new federal "workfare" program through the FIDCR. On the floor, the issue became one of federal versus state regulatory authority. Senate opponents lost successive amendments to delete the staffing requirements, to delay them until completion of HEW's appropriateness study, and to allow states to exempt more centers from the requirements. At the end of January, 1976, the Senate approved the bill 65 to 24. The conference committee made some minor alterations, but the Senate's provisions remained effectively intact. The final version passed the House 316 to 72 and the Senate 59 to 30.[29]

A piece of legislation more antithetical to the administration's position could not have been easily fashioned. HEW summarized the objectionable provisions to the president. First, it provided an annualized $250 million increase to Title XX funds. Secondly, it imposed the FIDCR without the appropriateness study or any other evidence that children needed the level of service mandated. Thirdly, it earmarked Title XX funds for day care—a violation of the block grant intent of the law. Finally, the welfare hiring incentives disregarded the children's interests by encouraging employment of unqualified caregivers. HEW recommended a veto and suggested the administration submit legislation simply to extend the moratorium upon FIDCR's enforcement.[30] OMB concurred for many of the same reasons, but with a significant twist.

HEW's central strategy on the FIDCR was to promote a prolonged suspension of the ratios pending the appropriateness study. In large part, HEW's hierarchy believed this approach to be the only politically viable one in light of Congress's determination to continue federal enforcement of the day care requirements. It was not that HEW opposed the administration's position that requirements were a state responsibility, but that they recognized the political difficulty of effecting that position. OMB, on the other hand, wholeheartedly, even recklessly, pursued the state regulatory approach to avoid additional appropriations. Their cudgel in this matter was enforcement of the FIDCR without federal funding to ease compliance. At the very least OMB believed that the administration could trade suspension for a further weakening of federal controls over Title XX funds.

OMB and HEW could agree to veto the Long-Mondale legislation because it would implement the FIDCR, provide compliance funds, and enact a new workfare program. Ford, in fact, vetoed the bill and in a furious lobbying effort was sustained in the Senate by three votes. The postveto situation, however, was ripe for the OMB/HEW disagreement to surface. OMB sought to use the threats of the FIDCR's enforcement as a stick to force congressional acquiescence in loosening the strings attached to Title XX money and, perhaps, returning regulatory authority over day care to the states. Long and Mondale sought to use the promise of increased federal aid as a carrot to marshal state and congressional support for federal enforcement of the FIDCR. The requirements became hostage in this contest. HEW believed OMB's approach would only push Congress into passing another bill similar to the one Ford vetoed and then overriding any subsequent veto. While Congress readied new legislation in spring of 1976, the OMB/HEW disagreement festered.

In May, Senators Mondale and Robert Packwood, the principal antagonists over the enforcement issue, worked out a compromise on the FIDCR's staff ratios. Enforcement would be suspended until October 1, 1977, when HEW should have completed the appropriateness study. The bill provided $312.5 million over a 15-month period to aid states in complying with the FIDCR's unremitted health and safety requirements. Otherwise, the bill mirrored the major features of the vetoed bill. By suspending the staff ratio for 17 months while retaining the additional day care funds, the bill allowed the states and centers to have their carrot while standing

more or less still. Although some of those opposing the vetoed legislation had done so to block additional federal spending, the rest had
done so to prevent the imposition of federally mandated requirements. In the absence of the FIDCR enforcement provision, the
three-vote margin that had sustained Ford's veto evaporated. Without a genuine veto-threat the administration's stick became a twig.[31]

As whatever remaining leverage the administration had over the
revised bill dissipated, OMB insisted on using the threat of enforcing the staff ratios to prod Congress into amendments more amenable
to its position. HEW, however, could clearly see the fatuity of such
tactics. Assistant Secretary Morrill bore the brunt of HEW's negotia-
tions with OMB and Congress. In a handwritten memo to Secretary
Matthews, Morrill explained that OMB was resisting any prolonged
moratorium on the FIDCR. "OMB [O'Neill]," he wrote, "took a
strong position that we should extend only to July 1, to keep the
pressure on the Congress about the Title XX proposals. With great
difficulty, we talked them into October 1." Morrill concluded that
OMB "is unlikely to budge."[32]

At OMB's insistence, HEW sent letters to House and Senate Republican leaders opposing the additional Title XX funds as illogical
in the face of the staff ratio suspension. The required health and
safety changes simply did not cost that much money. The letter also
objected to earmarking Title XX grants for day care. Despite these
objections, the bill passed both houses in June and went to conference. In a final attempt to salvage something from the legislation,
HEW offered to allow a $200 million increase in Title XX funds
every year for four years in return for incorporating some of the
block grant provision into the bill. Supporters, however, knew when
compromise was necessary and when it was not. This time they had
the votes to override a veto. The conference committee rejected
HEW's offer. With a reduction in funding from $312 to $240 million
and a waiver of matching requirements for some of the day care
money, the revised legislation passed the House 281 to 71 and the
Senate 72 to 15.

Congress did not enroll the measure until Ford's nomination as the
Republican presidential candidate. With Ronald Reagan's right-wing
pressure removed, they assumed a veto to be less likely. Their caution, though, was probably unnecessary; the override votes were
there. HEW recommended approval. The bill, they observed, suspended staff ratios and was backed by a veto-proof majority. OMB,
too, acquiesced in the undeniable probability of a veto override
and recommended approval. Both agencies agreed a veto would be
highly impolitic in an election year. Only the Council of Economic
Advisors suggested Ford disapprove the measure. Apparently, Chairman Alan Greenspan either had little cognizance of the situation's

political realities or had made other career plans for 1977. The President signed the bill into law on September 7, 1976.[33] Postponed until October 1977, the FIDCR would become Jimmy Carter's problem.

Analysis of the FIDCR Debate

Placing the FIDCR debate subsequent to 1976 in its political and economic context is a useful starting point for analysis. In large part, the debate over the FIDCR was a contest among different perceptions of the reality of day care. Data, statistically indisputable, were ambiguous policy-wise, while data that clearly mandated a policy course were disputed. Among the relevant data available in 1976 were the following: one-half of women with children under 18 worked; 40 percent of women with preschoolers worked; and over five million children under 13 (12 percent of the age cohort) spent 30 or more hours per week in the care of someone other than their parents or teachers. Of these 5.2 million children, 1.3 million were cared for by relatives in the relative's home, 960,000 by relatives in the child's home, 620,000 by nonrelatives in the child's home, 1.2 million by nonrelatives in "family" day care facilities, and a little over 1.1 million in centers including day care centers, nurseries, cooperatives, and Head Start.[34]

Approximately $10 billion was spent on child care annually. Individual payments accounted for roughly 60 percent; direct federal payments, 18 percent; federal tax credit, 8 percent; and state and local payments, the remaining 14 percent. The FIDCR applied to 56 percent of direct federal payments, mostly through Title XX's $800 million outlay for child care. If federally funded in-home care and family day care were discounted from the FIDCR's purview, the dollar amounts declined by 40 percent and left approximately $600 million in center-based care covering fewer than 500,000 children. The FIDCR, then, governed less than 10 percent of the nonparental out-of-school, full-time child care. Significantly, however, this total constituted nearly one half of all center-based day care. Insofar as it might affect state regulations, the FIDCR could have an impact upon all day care centers.[35]

Forty-one percent of all centers were proprietary, that is profit making. The remainder were nonprofit. Of the approximately 8,100 federal financial participation (FFP) centers, 23 percent were proprietary. Compared to the nonprofit centers, the proprietaries generally spent fewer dollars per child and had higher child-to-staff ratios. Among FFP centers, 79 percent of the nonprofit centers met the FIDCR's staffing requirements, while only 45 percent of the proprietary ones did. Among the non-FFP centers, those not governed by the FIDCR, 38 percent met the staffing requirements. The upshot was that just under one-half of all day care centers did not meet the FIDCR's staffing requirements. More importantly, one quarter of the centers subject to FFP sanctions failed to meet the requirements; whence came the protest over the FIDCR's enforcement.[36]

Day care is a labor-intensive industry. Seventy-five percent of all expenses involve staff salaries and benefits. The National Association for Child Development and Education, the trade association of the proprietary centers, estimated that lowering child-to-staff ratios to the FIDCR's level from existing state regulations would double the average staffing cost per child. For the proprietary centers, a lower staff ratio would increase costs and compel them either to lower profits, raise fees, or drop children receiving federal subsidies. A boost in fees, insofar as it was not offset by larger state and federal subsidies, would reduce demand for their services, lower center utilization rates, and, ultimately, cut their profits. If subsidies for FFP proprietary centers were increased to ease compliance to the FIDCR, fees still might rise. Centers with less than 100 percent of their children receiving federal subsidies would have to conform to the same staff ratios as would fully subsidized centers. Moreover, states might not raise their subsidy share or, worse, they might revise licensing codes to require staff ratios consistent with the FIDCR's. The latter move was a more disconcerting possibility to non-FFP proprietaries for it would increase costs without providing any offset through subsidies.[37]

The staff ratios, however, did not have the same import for non-profit centers. These centers serve a higher percentage of children completely covered by government funding. Thus, they were much more directly dependent on federal and state subsidies. Since the size of government subsidies per child were roughly based upon the staff ratios mandated in FIDCR, the nonprofit centers generally adjusted their staff sizes to conform with the requirements. Their interest lay in large staffs, not maximizing profits. Any increase in the allowable child-to-staff ratios could entail a decrease in government subsidies per child and consequently reduce staff size. Unlike their proprietary cousins, the nonprofit FFP centers generally supported low staff ratios. Although the staffing requirements of the FIDCR were very important to both proprietary and nonprofit centers, the reasons for their importance were antithetical.[38]

Among center-based providers, the proprietary centers comprised two-fifths of the total market. A multi-million dollar industry, they were expanding rapidly, particularly in the form of chain centers. As in most service industries, wages were low, $6,000 to $7,500 for caregivers. Though they pointed to a "nickel on a dollar" profit, their rate of return on equity ranged between 13 percent and 20 percent—not quite IBM's, but not quite a saving bond's either. They had a lobby in Washington and stressed their "taxpaying not tax-consuming" character. The proprietary centers were strongly opposed to any federal enforcement of child-to-staff ratios lower than current state requirements. Their central argument was that in an age of fiscal austerity, government aid could not be counted upon to pay for "absurd" staff ratios. The continued availability of day care depended upon keeping costs down. The employment-oriented advocates, as well as feminist organizations seeking to ease the entry of women into the labor force, joined them in this position.

On the other side of the staffing issue stood the many nonprofit centers, the comprehensive developmental advocates, such as the Child Welfare League and Children's Defense Fund, and the American Federation of Teachers (AFT) of the AFL-CIO. For reasons already mentioned, many nonprofit centers preferred lower child-to-staff ratios. Among many developmentalists, the 1968 FIDCR, as amended, was an article of faith. The League perceived any attempt to increase staff ratios to be an abrogation of the child's interest. Fiscal austerity and profit-making centers were the League's bêtes noires—precursors of "Kentucky Fried Children" and "Wee Willie Warehouses." The AFT had joined the advocates of comprehensive day care to press for more stringent licensing requirements as well as low child-to-staff ratios. AFT President Albert Shanker had called for "a system of universal day care (and) early childhood education" under public school sponsorship. It is no secret that the AFT has been struggling for several years to find a new market for unemployed teachers to offset declining school enrollments.[39]

On the issue of teacher certification, groups within the pro-1968 FIDCR coalition diverge. The AFT argued that education of preschool children requires professional educators, i.e., their members. Many nonprofit centers with their roots in the community action programs of the 1960s felt threatened by a legally mandated infusion of AFT members. Like the feudal baron fearing for his fiefdom if he relied too much upon the king's troops to defend his castle, the community-based providers were wary of Shanker's legions protecting their government subsidies and low staff ratios. "Perhaps they were afraid," Barry Bruce-Briggs observes, "that they could not stand up to a tough-minded operation like the AFT. . . ."[40] The defenders of the 1968 FIDCR greeted the AFT's support with one hand extended; the other they kept on their purses.

The array of the FIDCR's interest groups was matched in many respects by the differing concerns of agencies within HEW. The Office of Human Development Services (HDS) administered most day care funds within HEW. Within HDS, the Administration for

Children, Youth, and Families (ACYF) was the primary standard-setting body for children, a legacy from the Children's Bureau. As its most recent predecessor, OCD, ACYF did not administer day care funds other than Head Start's. Direct administrative responsibility for Title XX belonged to SRS's successor within HDS, the Administration for Public Services (APS). The schism between OCD's charge of enforcing the FIDCR and SRS's charge of funding day care programs persisted in their descendants, ACYF and APS.

APS's chief concern was to avoid day care requirements that exacted a level of care undesired by the states. The states were their clients and they did not want to impose punitive sanctions upon them. ACYF, on the other hand, stood in the tradition of Head Start, the Children's Bureau, and their strong concern for the child's development. They supported rigorous requirements, effectively enforced. No better example of the different perspectives of these two offices can be found than ACYF's (at this time still OCD) response to an APS-prepared "Decision Memorandum" for the undersecretary. APS had written: "the decision to modify or refine the HEW role as defined by the Title XX FIDCR is a political decision." ACYF replied that "we disagree with the statement. . . . We strongly believe it is a human value decision."[41] These were positions not easily reconciled.

In this overall context HEW began in 1976 to prepare the congressionally mandated appropriateness report and determine the fate of FIDCR. The preparation commenced in March, 1975, with formation of the FIDCR Appropriateness Committee under the Assistant Secretary for Planning and Evaluation (ASPE). Chaired by career civil servant William R. Prosser of ASPE, the committee included representatives from HDS, OCD (ACYF), and APS. Additionally, OCD and APS had commissioned several major studies of day care: three by the Abt Associates—the National Day Care Study, the Infant Day Care Study, and the Family Day Care Study—and two others, the Comparative State Licensing Study, and APS's own effort to assess compliance with the Title XX FIDCR. By far the largest, most expensive, and most significant study was Abt's National Day Care Study. It dealt with the primary issue of center-based child-to-staff ratios.

At the outset Prosser's committee faced several problems. Congress had provided little or nothing in the way of direction for the study beyond its basic mandate. The committee members had as yet no hard data from these studies on the effects of day care regulation upon children, nor did they have any criteria for evaluating appropriateness. Rather like inept explorers who knew not where they were going, nor where they were, nor where they wanted to be, ten years after first issuing the day care regulations, the regulators could judge neither the purpose, the appropriateness, or the effects of their original act. Needless to add, little progress had been made by the time the presidential election and change of administrations threw HEW's hierarchy into flux.

The Carter administration chose Joseph A. Califano to be HEW secretary. Califano chose Peter Schuck as deputy assistant secretary in ASPE and gave him oversight responsibility on the appropriateness report. Over the first year of the new administration an approach to the FIDCR's revisions and Appropriateness Report was agreed upon. In a meeting with Califano, the principals, Schuck, Prosser, and other relevant staff, briefed him on the report's format and the key issues, such as staff ratios and cost-effectiveness. Califano stressed the need for continued public involvement and a published set of regulations by January, 1979. Finally, he instructed Schuck through ASPE's assistant secretary, Henry Aaron, to keep HEW's options open in the appropriateness report.[42]

HEW contacted the appropriate congressional committees to obtain a postponement of the June 30 deadline for the report and the FIDCR's revisions. Not wanting to reenact the enforcement crisis of 1976, Congress suspended the FIDCR staffing requirement again, continued the basic Title XX provisions, and postponed to April, 1978, the submission date for the report. Their only caveat, given informally, was that the various interest groups and advocates be consulted throughout the revision process.[43]

To aid in drafting the report, Schuck recruited an advisory panel of specialists in various fields relating to child care. This move raises the larger question concerning Califano's overall "include-the-public" approach to the report and regulation-writing process. The secretary's approach was largely an effort to restrain potential critics of the final product through their inclusion at various stages in the process. A social scientist or advocate asked for advice or commissioned for a paper might be less inclined to attack the final product. The product, on the one hand, might be more akin to the advisor's point of view. On the other, a sense of loyalty, of participation, or of obligation could act to inhibit criticism. No one was bought, nor was scientific integrity compromised in any blatant manner, but the inclusion of potential critics in the process of preparation could restrain their reactions to the final outcome. The interaction between preempting the critic and incorporating his criticisms is dialectical. An ancillary effect is that criticism made of a draft is often criticism not made of a final document. Merely by acknowledging the early criticism in the final report, authors could muzzle repetition. By then, the critic is either frustrated at having had no impact or satisfied at having had the opportunity to voice his misgivings. Whatever larger political and economic considerations might mold the FIDCR, the advocates would have had their moment to protest.

Once substantially completed, the appropriateness report had five chapters and several appendices. After an introductory overview of American day care and the FIDCR, it discussed the various provisions of the requirements, their costs, and their administration. The report ended with a set of inconclusive findings and innocuous recommendations. Its attempt to include all points of view resulted in it having no point of view itself. Its recommendations expressed the FIDCR's need to "reflect current research and expert judgement" on child care, to "clarify roles and responsibilities of providers and state and local administrations," to "educate as well as regulate," to "accommodate the rich diversity in child-care needs and arrangements," and to "include participation of all interested individuals" in writing the regulations. In other words, the appropriateness report recommended that the revised FIDCR be appropriate to child care in America.[44]

In February 1978, HEW held three large public conferences on the draft report. At these conferences participants subjected it to severe criticism for its failure to make policy recommendations, to take a stand on significant issues, and to present a clear, accurate exposition of the data. Some of the criticisms were comprehended in the final document, but the report still avoided any clear policy statement. This avoidance was consonant with Califano's wishes. As his staff explained, the criticisms were "probably an inescapable cost to be incurred for the benefit of keeping all major policy choices open to debate in the course of developing the new regulations."[45]

Ill feelings toward the appropriateness report were not limited to the child care community. In Congress, Senator Daniel P. Moynihan excoriated HEW Undersecretary Hale Champion for the report's writing style. Upon reading aloud one particularly obtuse passage, Moynihan bellowed, "What illiteracy. Would you dare consign a child to the care of someone who would write something like this? . . . It is appalling. And you have a man from Brookings [Aaron] who put this out, right? . . . this junk, this disgrace. . . ."[46] Moynihan's extreme histrionics notwithstanding, the report was not without its problems. Califano's staff admitted that "given its bulky format, and technical, wordy style the FIDCR report is unlikely to have much immediate impact on its prescribed audience—Congress and congressional staff."[47]

Audience expectations, too, contributed to the report's reception. The interest groups and advocates anticipated a document that would make definitive policy statements. Califano, however, had decided against this approach; Prosser and his fellow authors were left to twist in the gales of criticism that ensued. Congress, on the other hand, looked upon the report as an instrument for postponing the enforcement of the staff ratios. Its preparation justified subsequent suspensions. Regardless of intrinsic quality, any report would have encountered harsh criticisms within this political milieu.

Once ASPE had issued the appropriateness report, the task of drafting new regulations on day care fell to HDS, the administering agency. Califano, however, had misgivings about leaving the FIDCR in the hands of HDS. It was permeated by client interests. APS was very much attuned to the states' concerns on regulations issues. ACYF was composed of many child advocates very much opposed to the custodial care for children. Strict federal regulation was their chief method of insuring a high quality of care. They were closely aligned with the advocacy groups such as the Children's Defense Fund and Child Welfare League. Regardless of which administrative unit had its way on the requirements, the whole decision-making process would be skewed. The secretary did not rely upon the senior administrators in HDS to check the predispositions of its constituent units. Neither Assistant Secretary Arabella Martinez nor her deputy, Georgian T.M. Jim Parham, were among those Califano entrusted with decision-making authority over delicate issues.

Since Califano felt that HDS could not be trusted with the policy decisions on the FIDCR, he restructured the revision-writing responsibility within HEW. In October 1978, he took overall responsibility from HDS and vested it in the Office of the General Counsel under F. Peter Libassi. Libassi was the point man for HEW's most controversial regulatory decisions and worked closely with Califano and members of the Executive Secretariat. He brought a broader political perspective to the FIDCR and, more importantly, had Califano's confidence.[48]

In the midst of the FIDCR revision process, Abt Associates completed its *National Day Care Study*. Abt's four-year study involved 1,800 preschool children, 1,100 parents, and 120 classroom groups from 57 day care centers in Atlanta, Detroit, and Seattle. The study dealt with three basic questions: how is a preschool child's development affected by variations in regulatable center characteristics; how is cost per child affected by variations in regulatable center characteristics; and how does the cost effectiveness of center day care change with regulatory variations. In essence, they studied the impact of child-to-staff ratios, group size, and caregivers' qualifications upon the preschool child and the cost of care. Abt used a combination of test scores and observations to assess the effects of different staff ratios, group sizes, and caregiver qualifications upon the child. These measurements included: reflection/innovation, co-operation, noninvolvement, aimless wandering, and performance on the Preschool Inventory and Peabody Vocabulary tests.[49]

That the Abt study was potentially relevant to the FIDCR policy debate was as much a matter of coincidence as of deliberation. The basic idea of examining these aspects of day care originated in OEO's research and planning unit years before. When the Nixon administration dismantled OEO, its research staff dispersed into OCD, ASPE, and elsewhere. One of these people, Allen N. Smith, resurfaced in OCD, and in 1974 finally contracted with a research organization, Abt Associates, to conduct this study of day care. The study was thus commissioned prior to the Title XX–FIDCR controversy and the appropriateness report. Its relevance to these matters, however, soon became evident.

By 1977 Abt had spent its entire $7 million budget gathering data for the study. They went to Smith, their project director in OCD, and asked for an additional $1 million to analyze the data and prepare their report. Smith had little choice but to agree and begin building support within OCD (now ACYF) and HEW for the additional money. There was, of course, opposition within HEW and among the research community to cutting Abt so large a share of their funding pie for what seemed like a study with an insatiable appetite. Smith needed allies and in ASPE he found one.

Prosser and his FIDCR appropriateness committee were still mired in their report when Smith came to him with an offer of help. If Prosser would support the $1 million extension of the Abt study, Smith would share Abt's early findings with him to assist in completing the report. After some hesitation, which a quick trip to Abt's headquarters in Cambridge assuaged, Prosser agreed. With his support, Abt received the additional funds. Both sides were pleased. Prosser and his associates anticipated decisive help in what increasingly became their own Vietnam, and Abt rejoiced in the hope that their study would be completed and sail in the appropriateness report to the sea of policy-relevance.

Nevertheless, Smith soon realized that the appropriateness report was headed into serious difficulties. Any strong linkage between the Abt study and the report meant only problems for his project. Already, critics at the early stages of reviewing the draft had begun to confuse Abt's study with the report. Wary of Prosser's attempts to infuse portions of Abt's preliminary findings into the text of the report, Smith prevailed upon him to publish the findings, delivered as part of the research funding arrangement, as an appendix to the report. All Prosser reaped from his early support for Abt's funding was a further delay in his report's completion and an appendix.

Abt's study did survive the appropriateness report and during 1978 and 1979 publicly disseminated its findings. Group size, Abt concluded in its briefing for HEW, was the "most powerful and pervasive factor related to NDCS (National Day Care Study) measures of quality." Children in groups of 12 with two caregivers performed in a consistently superior manner to children in groups of 24 with four caregivers. More desirable caregiver behavior was also "associated with smaller groups." Then Abt turned to the crux of the whole FIDCR controversy: "For children, staff/child ratio is ambiguously related to child behavior [and] not related to test score gains." Only infants benefited from the low child-to-staff ratios. In the social scientific stab, Abt had killed the intuitive-experiential assumption of decades of preschool education.

Low-child-to-staff ratios in themselves did not matter for the child's cognitive or social development. Staff ratios, however, were not unimportant. The Abt study concluded that they were "the most important determinant of difference in costs." In cost-benefit terms the ultimate conclusion became obvious. As long as group size was controlled, the center could reduce costs and increase the benefits of care to the child. As Keynes had once told governments, not only should they spend money they did not have, but by spending it they would receive more; now Abt was telling HEW not only could it spend less money per child on day care, but while spending less the children would benefit more.[50]

Their identification of group size as the most significant factor related to outcome was somewhat surprising. Group size had consistently been included in standards for day care, but in a manner clearly subordinate to staff ratios. Abt's researchers admit it was a "sleeper." Indeed, group size emerged in the wake of the study's earlier findings that staff ratios had no significant impact upon outcomes. Upon hearing these initial results, Smith strongly suggested that Abt's study needed to establish more than the insignificance of regulatable center characteristics. Subsequent analysis of the data revealed group size as a significant regulatable characteristic. Soon it was made a major finding of the study.

In their recommendations Abt also suggested that regulators set less stringent staff ratios than the 1968 FIDCR had required. "The staff/child ratio requirement for three-, four- and five-year-old children should be no more stringent than 1:7." That ratio was for actual attendance; the enrollment ratio, the one generally used in calculating staff ratios, should be no lower than 3:1. Abt offered three policy options ranging from 8:1 to 10:1 for enrollment, and 7:1 to 9:1 for attendance.[51] These policy options traded-off cost reduction and program quality. The minimum quality policy promised that all centers would attain current average program quality at a cost savings of 10 to 12 percent from current average expenditures. The middle policy option offered a 5 to 10 percent increase in program quality and a 6 to 8 percent savings from current costs. The high quality option offered a 10 to 20 percent improvement in program quality at a 1 to 2 percent savings from current expenditures. These three options involved enrolled child-to-staff ratios of 10:1, 9:1 and 8:1, respectively. "All three of the policy options," Abt observed, "have the potential of reducing costs." More importantly, "none of the three policy options would severely disrupt current subsidized center practices, Policy C (the minimum quality option) would require the smallest changes."[52]

Politically, Abt's policy recommendations were significant. In shifting the emphasis to group size, Abt changed the de facto compliance of FFP centers. If HEW chose the high quality option, 72 percent of FFP centers would be in compliance with staff ratios and 77 percent with group size. If HEW chose the minimum quality option, i.e., all centers reaching the average quality of current care, 83 percent would be in compliance with staff ratios and 89 percent with group size. The minimum quality option would increase centers complying with the FIDCR's staff ratios from 60 to 83 percent. Moreover, since 79 percent of the nonprofit centers were already in compliance with the current FIDCR, this increase in compliance would be almost entirely among the 55 percent of proprietary centers not in compliance.[53]

The study's results offered something for everybody involved in the FIDCR's revision. It confirmed ACYF's longstanding belief that federal regulation day care could indeed affect a child's development in measurable ways. It also sat well with APS. Since the study recommended staff ratios higher than those in the 1968 and 1972 FIDCRs, APS's clients, the states and their day care centers, would be relatively unaffected by requirements based upon these recommendations. For the cost-benefit people in ASPE, the study provided quantitative data upon which the decisions could be based. Finally, at the secretary's level, the results place a social-scientific seal of approval upon a relaxation in staffing requirements. Such approval would buttress Califano against attacks by those advocating either higher or lower staff ratios. The results might help to depoliticize an essentially political decision. Abt's study pleased most decision makers in HEW and its impact soon became apparent through the General Counsel Office.

There were some critics of the study's data gathering and the strength of the evidence supporting its conclusions. Nonetheless, Abt's careful presentations and efforts to incorporate the criticisms in their findings or the critics in their consulting staff mitigated much of the outcry that might have otherwise engulfed it. Moreover, Abt's finding of a positive correlation between center characteristics and child performance helped to preclude vehement opposition. Whatever else the study concluded about costs and staff ratios, that one finding pleased actors throughout the child advocacy establishment. Perhaps the most striking aspect to this finding, however, was that though the correlations between center characteristics and performance were real and statistically significant, they were weak. Indeed, in assessing the study, one social scientist observed that had federal regulation of day care never been attempted and had this study been the sole basis for determining whether or not to regulate, the results would not have justified the costs and the complexities of regulation. Yet, in the face of present political reality that particular policy recommendation was simply untenable.

Abt Associates' official briefing for HEW on their findings came in January, 1979. Although their final report was not released until spring, HEW's hierarchy had known of its general results for over a year. In the first public statement on the poststudy "present thinking" of HEW, General Counsel Peter Libassi spoke to a group of advocates, center operators, and state and local administrators at a "seminar" in Washington, March 2, 1979. Although carefully qualifying his pronouncements with "we are leaning," "we are inclined" and "we want to hear from all of you on this issue," Libassi indicated in unambiguous terms that HEW was taking Abt's findings and recommendations very seriously.

"The (FIDCR) task force," Libassi began, "leans toward accepting the conclusion that group composition should be used in the new regulations. . . . We believe that group composition strongly affects the benefits which children receive from day care." In the ensuing sentence he recounted Abt's recommended child-to-staff ratios. Though he made no explicit affirmation of these ratios, he clearly implied in the context of his remarks that these ratios were in the forefront of HEW's policy mind. Indeed, the *leitmotif* of Libassi's statement was that "sensible requirements are enforceable requirements." It would not be "sensible" to create a set of requirements beyond the reach of a large number of centers. Sensible, enforceable requirements were those easily attained by the centers. Regulation, like law, had to be in large part a recognition of fact—something Libassi understood.[54]

Many of the doubts he might have had concerning the Abt ratios were assuaged by the responses of participants. William Pierce of the Child Welfare League rose to condemn HEW's "inclination." Significantly, however, he was alone in this proscription. The local center operators and administrators greeted Libassi's statement with approbation. They opposed the Title XX FIDCR and "excessive" regulation of their centers. Besides Pierce, no one assailed the higher child-to-staff ratios or any further relaxation in the requirements.

Indeed, at the conclusion of his appearance, a sanguine Libassi noted the absence of any widespread acrimony over the staffing issue. Subsequent to the conference, the Abt ratios were, if anything, more firmly rooted in the FIDCR's policy soil at HEW.

The preliminary publication of the new revised FIDCR took place in June, 1979. Generally the new FIDCR proposed staff ratios recommended by the Abt study, though the requirements offered a range of options. Neither the states nor the FFP centers desired requirements which might result in punitive sanctions against them. HEW's hierarchy and, presumably, OMB also, wanted to avoid raising the costs of the child care or penalizing the states' Title XX funds. More than once the states and day care centers have demonstrated their political muscle in inducing congressional suspensions of child-to-staff ratios which they could not attain. Although the 1976 offer of additional Title XX funds for compliance did dampen state opposition, a fiscally austere Congress was unlikely to sweeten compliance with more money. Since the alternative to funding additional staff was more "sensible" requirements, most members of Congress were not inclined to oppose HEW's relaxation of staff ratios. Moreover, the Abt study provided all parties interested in less strict child-to-staff ratios with a scientific justification.

After publication of the preliminary requirements, HEW sponsored a series of meetings across the country on the requirements. Generally, participants approved the requirements, though there was some dissent over the exact child-to-staff ratios. While these meetings progressed, decision makers within HEW left to be replaced by new people. Patricia Harris replaced Califano and Joan Bernstein replaced Libassi. Such sweeping changes in senior officials meant the principals had to learn anew about the issues. Thus, the FIDCR revision process came virtually to a halt in fall, 1979.

In the face of this hiatus the advocacy groups split into three camps. In one camp were the proprietary day care centers. They believed that the changes in HEW accorded them an excellent opportunity to delay the FIDCR's promulgation and relax the staffing ratios. To this end they distributed anti-FIDCR post cards to parents who used their child care facilities. The cards went to newspapers, congressmen, and HEW. The message was simple: the new FIDCR will close the day care centers or raise costs or both and we oppose them. At the other extreme was William Pierce and the Child Welfare League. Pierce refused to accept the parameters for the staff ratios which the Abt study had recommended. He, too, wanted the new FIDCR blocked and replaced by the 1968 requirements. Pierce, however, was respectfully ignored. Somewhere in the middle was a coalition of advocacy groups lead by the Children's Defense Fund (CDF). They had accepted Abt's parameters and strove to have the new FIDCR promulgated with the strictest staff ratios within those parameters. To this end, CDF organized its own campaign to compel HEW Secretary Harris to promulgate the new FIDCR.

In response to CDF's coalition and the personal lobbying effort of CDF's leader, Marion Wright Edelman, Harris agreed to a March, 1980, deadline for the new FIDCR. Although the deadline was a small victory for CDF, the exact staff ratios remained unresolved. Here the proprietaries made some headway. Joan Bernstein, HEW's General Counsel, had somewhat of an anti-regulatory reputation from her previous stint at the Environmental Protection Agency. Bernstein and her staff produced a memorandum on the new FIDCR for Harris, which essentially argued for less stringent staffing ratios. In conjunction with the proprietary's campaign, Bernstein's memo began to sway Harris toward less strict requirements—particularly staffing ratios.

Bernstein's memo, however, was leaked to CDF and to their allies within HEW—specifically ACYF. Proponents of the stricter FIDCR realized that only a strong response could salvage their course. In desperation they turned to White House Domestic Advisor Stuart Eizenstat. Access to Eizenstat depended upon the personal relationship of one of the proponents with Eizenstat's wife. They presented their case for the stricter FIDCR to Eizenstat at his home one night and convinced him to send a memo—drafted by CDF—to Harris expressing strong White House support; proponents of the stricter FIDCR managed to overcome their opponents' objections based upon costs and promote staff ratios as strict as (or stricter than) those recommended in Abt's Policy A option.

The final regulations were issued in March, 1980. Although the staff ratios for the key preschool age cohort—three- to five-year-olds —were in the range of Abt's Policy A Option, they were still less stringent than those in the other revisions of the FIDCR. The new FIDCR could have been "enforced" because 80 percent of the day care centers were already in compliance with all or most of the new requirements. Moreover, the requirements allowed, upon application to HEW, a two year phase-in period. Thus enforcement would mean affirmation of a continuity in existing conditions, not disruption and proscription.

Notwithstanding these favorable attributes and White House support, the FIDCR were again caught in circumstances in which they assumed symbolic importance. When the inflation rate reached the 20 percent mark, the final regulations collided with an administration and a Congress facing reelection in a few months. Budget-cutting and deregulation fast became the only acceptable political posture. In this milieu a set of day care regulations, which, the Congressional Budget Office (CBO) concluded, were costly to promulgate and uncertain in result, found few supporters. Despite ASPE's attempts to scale down CBO's cost estimates, the intense lobbying effort of the proprietary centers and the symbolic value of opposing new regulations triumphed over the FIDCR. Congress once again suspended them pending further cost studies. Under the new Reagan Administration it is unlikely that the requirements will soon be imposed.

❋   ❋   ❋

Although some version of the FIDCR may someday be promulgated and enforced, federal child care regulation is creeping toward irrelevance. As Title XX appropriations—the principal source of funds for day care subject to the FIDCR—stagnate and the Child Care Tax Credit becomes the largest federal subsidy to day care, the FIDCR will govern fewer and fewer of the child care centers. Slowly, there will be a de facto retrocession of day care regulation to the states—where it probably belonged all along. The impact upon the children of this change and, indeed, of the entire history of the FIDCR remains problematic.

References

1. *Standards for the Day Care of Children of Working Mothers.* 1942. Children's Bureau Publication No. 284. Passim.
2. *Planning Services for Children of Employed Mothers.* 1953. Department of Labor. Passim.
3. Child Welfare League. 1960. *Standards for Day Care Service*, New York. Passim.
4. BOB:LRF:R1-4/67.4, RG51, NA. 1967. *Congressional Quarterly Almanac: 1967* (Washington, 1968), 1058–1086 (cited henceforth as *CQA*).
5. Federal Interagency Day Care Requirements (DHEW Publication (OHDS) 78–31081). 1978 (1968). Passim..
6. Morgan, Gwen. 1976. "Legal Aspects of Federal Day Care Standards" (DHEW), 39.
7. Rothman, Sheila. 1973. "Other People's Children: The Day Care Experience in America," *Public Interest* (Winter), 22.
8. Zigler, Edward and Cohen, David. 1976. "Federal Day Care Standards: Rationale and Recommendations" (DHEW), 6–8.
9. Zigler, Edward to Richard Nathan. April 18, 1972. File CY-1-3, HEW: Office of the Secretary (cited henceforth as OS).
10. OMB:LRF R1-4/71.2 (1971), RG51, Federal Records Center (cited hereafter as FRC). In *The Children's Cause* (Washington: Brookings Institution, 1976), Gilbert Y. Steiner apparently overstates the conservative appeasement motivation for the veto.

11. Richardson, Elliot to Albert Quie. August 31, 1972. File CY-1-3, HEW:OS.
12. OMB:LRF R1-4/7112 (1971), RG51, FRC.
13. Note for Mr. [Paul] O'Neill. June 21, 1972. OMB file A7, RG51. New Executive Office Building (cite hereafter as NEOB).
14. *Ibid.*
15. Veneman, John to Elliott Richardson. July 10, 1972. File CY-1-3, HEW:OS.
16. Zigler, Edward. "Federal Day Care Standards," 8–11; Morgan, "Legal Aspects," 39.
17. For the background to Title XX, see Martha Derthick, *Uncontrollable Spending for Social Service Grants* (Washington: Brookings Institution, 1975).
18. OMB:LFR R1-4/74.6 (1974), RG51, FRC.
19. *Ibid.*
20. House Report 93–1490.
21. Senate Report 93–1356; House Report 93–1543; *CQA:1974*, 505–508.
22. OMB:LRF R1-4/74.6 (1974, RG51, FRC).
23. Memorandum to the Secretary. September 16, 1975. File FIDCR-Title XX, HEW:ACYF.
24. Memoranda to the Secretary. August 27 and September 16, 1975. *Ibid.*
25. See the letters in File CY-1-3 (1975), HEW:OS..
26. These responses are attached to SRS's draft memorandum, September, 1975. *Ibid.*
27. Matthews, F. David to Speaker Carl Albert. October 1, 1975. *Ibid.*
28. See *CQA: 1975*, 691–692 and *CQA: 1976*, 620–625 for the details of these legislative actions.
29. *CQA: 1976*, 621–625.
30. Matthews, F. David to James Lynn. October 16, 1975. OMB:LRF 73-1(G)/75.2 (1976), RG51, NEOB.
31. *CQA: 1976*, 625–628.
32. Morrill, William to Secretary. May 6, 1976. File CY-1-3, HEW:OS.
33. OMB:LRF R3-1/76.4 (1976), RG51, NEOB.
34. These statistics are drawn from UNCO's *National Child Care Consumer Study: 1975* (DHEW-OCD, 1975) and ASPE documents.
35. Abt Associates, *National Day Care Study: Preliminary Findings . . .* (DHEW:OCD, 1978). Passim.
36. *Ibid.*, 23–25; Abt Associates, *Day Care Centers in the U.S.: A National Profile, 1976–1977* (Cambridge, 1978), 63; Abt Associates, *Children at the Center: Summary Findings and Their Implications* (Cambridge, 1979), 194–195.
37. This information is derived from statements and handouts by participants in the Day Care and Child Development Reports' Conference, Washington, D.C., March 2, 1979.
38. *Ibid.*
39. Quoted in Barry Bruce-Briggs. 1977. "Child Care: The Fiscal Time Bomb," *Public Interest* (Fall), 100.
40. *Ibid.*
41. Rosoff, Saul, OCD, to Margaret Watson, OHDS. March 22, 1977. File FIDCR, HEW:ACYF.

42. Aaron, Henry. Memorandum on his meeting with Joseph Califano on April 13, 1977. File FIDCR, HEW:ACYF.

43. Memorandum for the Record, September 28, 1977, File FIDCR, HEW: ACYF; Richard Cotton to the Secretary, September 15, 1977, File CY-13, HEW:OS, Public Laws 95–59 and 95–171.

44. *The Appropriateness of the Federal Interagency Day Care Requirements (FIDCR): Report of Findings and Recommendations* (DHEW:ASPE, 1978), XXXV.

45. Note for the Secretary (Fred Bohen), June 21, 1978, File CY-1-3, HEW: OS; note to the Secretary (Peter Schuck), March 13, 1978, *ibid.* The latter note contains handwritten comments on the report and ASPE by a staff member of the Executive Secretariat.

46. From an unedited transcript of Senator Daniel P. Moynihan's comment before the Senate Subcommittee on Welfare Reford in July 1978.

47. Note for the Secretary (Fred Bohen). June 21, 1978. File CY-1-3, HEW: OS.

48. Califano, Joseph to F. Peter Libassi. October 2, 1978. File CY-1-3, HEW: OS.

49. Abt Associates. January 19, 1979. *National Day Care Study: HEW Briefing*, 1–4. Cambridge, Mass.

50. *Ibid.*, 4–15, 21.

51. *Ibid.*, 22–25.

52. *Ibid.*, 25–30.

53. Abt Associates. 1979. *Final Report of the National Day Care Study: Children at the Center* (5 Vols.), I, 159. Cambridge, Mass.

54. Statement by F. Peter Libassi, General Counsel, DHEW. March 2, 1979.

Chapter 16

BEYOND THE STALEMATE IN CHILD CARE PUBLIC POLICY

by Rochelle Beck

As the 1980s began, the national climate for setting public policies for child care looked both much the same as and very different from a decade ago. In the early 1970s, increasing numbers of women with young children entered the labor force; public funds were insufficient to expand the number of child care slots; a patchwork of programs funded in a host of different ways served fragments of the population; there were few reliable data on need or availability; and the absence of a coherent set of national public policies permeated the child care field. All these are still true.

Yet there have been some significant changes. First of all, the growth of inflation has dramatically affected public and private child care services several distinct ways. It has severely strained existing programs' budgets, making provision of comprehensive services and maintenance of existing levels of quality extremely difficult. Unlike other commodities or services whose rates can rise to match inflation, child care is constrained by fixed public allocations or limited family incomes, neither of which stretch to keep pace with rising costs. For many programs, sheer survival is now the issue. Inflation has also made it harder to improve child care services. Recent turmoil over the revised federal day care standards was in part a replay of the timeless differences between those who want and need the government to protect adequate levels of quality versus those who abhor and reject government regulation. But the pinch

The author gratefully acknowledges support for this work from the Levi Strauss Foundation and the Children's Defense Fund.

of inflation made it more difficult to justify public expenditures for improvements, to counter the threats of some providers who promised to close care centers or turn away children if their operating costs rose or to marshal support from traditional allies, whose own financial pressures often kept them from actively lobbying on behalf of federal standards. As inflation squeezes the formal market of child care services, it is also eroding the informal market's ability to provide care. Families in the past often turned to grandmothers, aunts, trusted friends, and neighbors to watch young children. But many of those "old sources of child care are disappearing. The same women who need child care now are the ones who used to provide it. . . . [They] are increasingly unavailable or need to be paid."[1] Finally, as families' formal and informal market options to meet the growing child care need shrink due to the pressure of inflation, federal resistance to initiate a program to meet the need, or to expand eligibility or funds for existing programs, grows as well. Public spending for social programs is an area of serious cutbacks by the Reagan administration. A move similar to the one in 1971 to enact child care legislation will face different odds and need new strategies in 1981.

Second, the role and political voice of states in influencing policies for social services have grown. In the 1980s, states will probably continue to play a significant role as the national trend moves away from categorical and targeted programs (with specific purposes written into legislation) and toward block grants and federal revenue-sharing models (which leave much discretion to state-level decision-makers). Questions about delivery systems, regulations, and specific services for new and possibly for existing child care programs will have to deal with this trend.

Third, active political support for child care is more splintered and more difficult to mobilize than it was a decade ago. Then, the women's movement, child advocates, child development experts, churches, the civil rights community, and organized labor coalesced with many senators and representatives in an orchestrated demonstration of support. Together they hammered out the Comprehensive Child Development bill, whose delivery system, priority for services, and language they could publicly and strongly endorse, and they marshalled both the leadership and the national organizational strength to undergird that bill. But three repeated legislative defeats, in 1971, 1975, and 1979, cast a pall over child care as a winning legislative issue. Other more promising issues, for example, foster care or Medicaid reforms, replaced child care as a priority for legislators and private groups. And a changing Congress—more conservative and loath to spend public funds than its predecessors

—has made demonstration of political support for child care more difficult in 1981 than it was a decade ago.

Fourth, opposition to federal involvement in child care now is tough and well organized. No longer just disjointed, shrill cries heard at the fringes of policymaking, groups and individuals opposing child care have learned to use the press, the vote, and the formal channels of lobbying well. Rallying after their success in defeating the Comprehensive Child Development bill in 1971, groups such as the National Coalition for Children and the American Conservative Union have joined in "an interlocking directorate" of the New Right to maintain the pressure opposing federal support for child care. Evangelical and fundamentalist Christian groups such as the Moral Majority and the Religious Roundtable, lobbies such as the Christian Voice, think tanks such as the Heritage Foundation and the National Conservative Research and Educational Foundation, and numerous political action committees "do not work at cross purposes" but form "an institutionalized, disciplined, well-organized, and well-financed movement of loosely-knit affiliates."[2] Through their communication networks and the work of "pro-family" interest groups such as Phyllis Schlafly's Eagle Forum and the American Family Forum, effective lobbying and fundraising efforts go on to oppose federal funds for child care services. Their tactics create controversy and negative publicity, which has scared away much political support.

Fifth, there is more skepticism now about government's ability to help solve social problems, run programs efficiently, deliver services sensitively, use tax dollars well, or have models of governance that work. Proposition 13 in California, following on the heels of Watergate, reflects fiscal conservatism merging with political cynicism. The inertia fed by this "nothing works" or "curtail the federal government" mentality will make the task of mobilizing for improved publicly supported child care difficult.

Just as the economic and political picture has changed, so has the demographic portrait of need for and supply of child care. More mothers are in the labor force. More will enter it, full time and full year, when their children are younger. There are more divorces, separations, and births out of wedlock. There will be more single-parent families with young children. There are more families with one or two children close in age. This will make child care use economically more feasible and more necessary, due to fewer older siblings at home. More children are about to be born. Their post–World War II mothers will have them later in life, are more likely to be in the work force, and more likely to rejoin it very soon after the birth of their children.[3] Yet there has been no comparable recruitment and training effort to increase the number of child care-givers. Indeed, funds previously open-ended for training under Title XX were capped by Congress in 1980, seriously jeopardizing many local child care training efforts. With a few exceptions, there have been no comparable increases in local, state or federal licensing, information and referral, technical assistance, or monitoring capacities to help locate, identify, and improve publicly supported child care.[4]

Why the Stalemate?

Why do these seeming contradictions continue to exist? First, there is no clear policy or set of values to set the framework for decisions about publicly supported child care services. Throughout the history of child care in this country, its acceptance or rejection, stated goals, measured benefits, and fiscal support have been dictated by other social policy decisions. Thus, when Americanization of immigrants, women's labor in mills, job creation during the Depression, women's labor during World War II, campaigns to reduce welfare rolls, and efforts to intervene in the preschool lives of disadvantaged children were dominant, then the nation accepted and supported child care programs. When working women drove the unemployment rates up or wages down, or when postwar normalcy meant women at home solely as homemakers, then the nation rejected child care programs and withdrew public funds. Almost never debated, justified, or funded as a necessary service to children or families, child care programs were inextricably linked to other goals, constituencies, or social and economic factors. As these factors changed, child care was at their mercy. It appears as if "children, smaller than anyone else, lighter in physical weight and political clout, are easily picked up and blown wherever the winds of economic, political, and social movements are heading."[5]

In addition to having no clear child care policy, the nation has also lacked clear policies or a consensus of values about many of the social policies to which child care is intimately related. Unlike many other western industrialized countries, the United States still is not formally committed to women's equal participation in the labor force. If provision of child care is linked to women's work outside the home (as it is, for instance, in Sweden, France, Yugoslavia), then as long as there is still debate in this country about *whether* women should work, there will be reticence to support work-related programs such as child care.

Second, the stalemate continues because of the paucity of clear evidence on the subject. Even with a spate of research studies and data in the early 1970s, definitive evidence on the issues of need, supply, demand, preference, and quality remains absent. Adequate responses to questionnaires and opinion polls are undercut by working mothers' guilt and the way questions are worded. Conclusions and recommendations at worst are unsupported by evidence; at best they are only some of a wide range of possible inferences. In human services, the traditional economic models based on supply, demand, cost, and quality are inadequate. Furthermore, many of the costs (such as later necessary remedial services, family stress, lost training or employment opportunities, welfare dependency) are difficult to measure or ascribe definitely to inadequate early or preventive services such as child care.[6]

Difficult to measure, too, are happy or well-adjusted children and the precise program components that contribute to their development.[7] Even the best studies and the most carefully designed measures fail to define child care quality with much confidence above a dangerously low level or an extraordinarily enriched one. Even if researchers could isolate program characteristics that produced happy (or competent or well-adjusted) children, current developmental theories do not allow them to predict adult behavior from childhood characteristics with any certainty.[8]

In addition, the most fundamental accounting information about child care is unavailable. How many family day care homes exist? With what capacity to serve how many children? How are child care facilities distributed geographically? How many handicapped children are there needing services at age two? The list of basic data left uncollected is long. Indeed, when the largest federal program supplying funds for child care—Title XX—cannot report how many children it served, one wonders how planning and evaluation, much less policy analysis, can take place.[9]

Third, the crowded field of political players with strongly held views about child care contributes to the stalemate. Sometimes public policy is set by the sheer political strength of a particular interest. But in the case of child care, the diversity of the groups, their difficulty in reaching consensus, and the emotion with which they express their views tend to confuse or frighten policymakers instead of encouraging them to make decisions. Unlike the lobbyists for the National Rifle Association—who speak out clearly on the issues, do not disagree among themselves in public, and represent an identifiable constituency that expresses itself politically and economically— those for child care are diffuse. Ask a policymaker who it is that represents gunowners' interests and the answer is clear. Ask a policymaker who represents children's interests—or women's or families' —and the answer is murky.

Fourth, there is a vacuum of leadership at the national level—both inside and outside government—to change the dynamics, set the precedents, clarify the issues, and forge the consensus needed to formulate policy or enact legislation. Children's issues are rarely money- or vote-getters. Child care in particular has become, to some policymakers, a political liability. Major legislation has been defeated —amid fanfare—three times in the 1970s. Few leaders want to be associated with a losing issue. Just as politicians have retreated, those outside government have shifted energies to what is possible to attain. Child care, perceived as "not viable this year," waits in the wings. The stalemate persists.

Can the Stalemate Be Broken?

The contradictions and inaction have been frustrating to those seeking improved child care services, but past obstacles need not continue to spell defeat. Addressing several of the overarching causes of the stalemate could create a constructive climate in which more specific child care policy options can be analyzed.

First, useful information needs to be collected, analyzed, and reported to policymakers and the public. There are a host of immediate kinds of data that would help policymakers and citizens weigh tradeoffs, gauge risks, and make decisions about child care services. Counts of children, of families, of programs, of caregivers, of other resources are essential. There may be some methodological obstacles; some political ones (for example, "reduce red tape and paperwork," or "don't meddle in state affairs"); some philosophical ones (for example, privacy concerns); and some fiscal ones (enough funds to collect and analyze data)—but these can be overcome. Programs whose benefits are invisible will be vulnerable in an administration seeking to reduce federal spending. Until there is incontrovertible evidence of need and of ways to augment child care programs while reducing the overall levels of government intervention and expenditures, there is little chance for progress.

Second, increased political cohesion among outside child care interest groups would help break the stalemate, as would cohesion inside the government to clarify who has the responsibility for child care policy development, implementation, and evaluation. A step in this direction was taken in June, 1980, when the Office for Human Development Services (OHDS) in the Department of Health and Human Services was reorganized. Former ACYF Commissioner Calhoun hoped that the moving of several different pieces affecting child care under his jurisdiction would alter the disjointed and frustratingly fragmented way child care had been handled in the past. "Day care has been amorphously placed in OHDS," he told a panel he formed to help guide child care policy. "I want it to have more national prominence, both in terms of organizational and bureaucratic force within the government *and* to work with constituencies to develop the policies and political support necessary to make it more prominent nationally."[10]

Third, child care needs to become again a salient policy issue that attracts and holds political leadership. Political leadership in some ways is a self-fulfilling prophecy. A strong leader's commitment over the long haul can raise an issue higher on the national policy agenda. Leadership itself enhances the respect, acceptance of and eventual (although it may take a long while) movement on the issue. Child care needs such commitment.

Yet leadership can be nurtured, too. Politicians can learn the importance of an issue and adopt a strong commitment if their constituents make it politically fruitful for them to do so. They will speak out publicly if they can be assured the press will be positive as well as negative. They will propose programs and policies if given the evidence of need, of benefits, of efficiencies. They will come to see child care as important to families if they are educated about how this is so. Thus, leadership—and the public environment to support it—must come from many sources if child care policy is to advance.

Beyond the Stalemate: Principles for Child Care Policy

Proposals affecting child care services will arise in the next decade from the administration, Congress, or particular interest groups. Will these options help children? How can they be assessed? Before analyzing specific policy options that might be considered in the 1980s, below are several principles that may help professionals, policymakers, and the public to evaluate options.

Does the proposal recognize child care services as a legitimate need of different families at different times and does it define a legitimate role for public support? It is long past the time to argue about whether women should work and whether public policies should help the children of those who do. The pace of inflation, the lifestyle this country holds as available, the goals that families have for their children in terms of safe housing, health care, or higher education, and the opportunities for women to use the skills and talents they have all mean that an ever-increasing number of women will work outside their homes. Most do not see work as taking away from their families. On the contrary, as one mother who leaves her child unattended for three hours after school each day said, she cannot quit or jeopardize her job to care for that child. She works for her whole family. She works to provide them, including that latch-key child, with the resources they need to succeed in this society.[11] Like so many other families, under current policies her children are not eligible for public child care programs and she is not affluent enough to pay for one on her own.

New proposals for child care services should reflect the fact that child care is a necessary, family-strengthening service whose goal is to empower families, that is, to help them raise their children in the manner they desire. While other goals may be achieved through child care (for example, reduced welfare dependency), positive policies would recognize that the availability of child care is itself a worthwhile goal and a justified public expense.

Does the proposal increase the accessibility of child care services? As demographic trends indicate, millions of families all across the nation will increasingly need to use some form of child care at some time in their lives. Such widespread use will probably help child care gain public acceptability: use by the middle class may help remove any remaining stigma from child care as being a service only for poor or pathological families. Along with broadened use, however, must come at least two responses so that the result will not simply be heightened competition for the relatively few slots available. First, sufficient funds must be included to expand services where they are needed. Not all of the money must come from the federal government. Creative ways can be found to use federal dollars as a lever to release private, charitable, state, or local resources. But public funds and involvement to make child care more accessible will continue to be needed to ensure that important program components (such as parent choice, quality, diversity) are available. Second, ways must be devised to allow the broad spectrum of families needing care to be eligible for services and to contribute what they can. Segregation of children and separation of political strength currently are encouraged by narrow eligibility restrictions. If a policy or program could broaden eligibility to all families *and* focus the use of public funds on needy families by implementing a sliding fee scale, then the base of support for child care and its accessibility would be extended.

Does the proposal ensure that use of services is voluntary? Those opposed to public support for child care have exploited the fear that it will become compulsory, a step toward mind- and behavior-control of all children. These opponents are largely white and middle class. Yet minority and poor parents, too, have expressed opposition to private and public policies that often leave them with too few choices about which programs are available for their children. Each new proposal for child care services must clearly make its use voluntary and honor all families' rights in this matter. Scrutiny should be given to indirect coercive policies as well as to direct legislative language. For example, a workfare bill that makes the use of child care voluntary but that ends a family's AFDC eligibility if a mother with young children does not enter a training program or take a job is just as coercive as a bill mandating preschool education. Bridges between constituent groups may be built if the voluntary nature of publicly supported child care is always explicit.

Does the proposal allow funds to be targeted to protect children most in need and/or on programs that work well? It is necessary to ensure that vulnerable children and exemplary programs are not lost in decisionmaking and resource allocation processes. This is especially important in a children's program, since children are least likely to be able to stand up for their interests in the political arena. The demographic trends will likely widen the gap between the poor and the middle class and increase the middle-class's use of services.[12] What will happen to the children of the poor, of minorities, of migrants, when they can less afford to purchase services and when more families use the system? What will happen to neglected or abused, handicapped or gifted children, or to those in remote rural or deprived inner-city areas when the demand for child care services grows? These children have traditionally been helped by public scrutiny and support and will be more likely to need continued help in the next decade. At the same time, special programs to serve them —Head Start, programs for preschoolers with special needs, demonstration projects to help abusive families—must not be washed away as general reforms such as consolidation, revenue sharing, or new legislation are discussed. Each should be evaluated and its unique strengths guaranteed.

Does the proposal encourage diverse child care arrangements? Again, diversity is a value shared by all economic and racial groups. No family reliant on public programs wants to be "assigned" to a particular type of child care. No family purchasing care privately wants to have so few alternatives in an open market that choice is in theory only. It is important for policies and programs to reflect the fact that there is no one best child care arrangement at all times for all children. Methods of financing, delivering and monitoring child care services can either promote or inhibit diversity. Decisions regarding them should be made with the promotion of diversity in mind.

Does the proposal include mechanisms to protect children in care and to promote quality? There are serious flaws in the argument that says a free market will be sufficient to keep all child care services at a level of quality that safeguards children. Some kinds of services—such as those for handicapped children—never will come into being because the cost is too high or they are needed by too few. Some children will be left at risk until poor programs lose enough business to alter their practices or to close. In a seller's market, quality is sacrificed to need, price, and convenience—and, unlike products, children must be protected from the effects of that sacrifice. There are various ways to safeguard children, and combinations of them may be tried. Consumers need training, information, and real choices to make the market work as well as it can. Caregivers and providers need training, technical assistance, and support to improve their services voluntarily. Groups that can offer these support services best and most cost-effectively should be eligible and funded to do so. Agencies responsible for systems must collect comparable and useful data to feed back to parents, programs, and policymakers.

All these elements are carrots in a system of quality improvement. But some sticks are necessary, too. There must be at least a fair process for hearing and redressing complaints against facilities (on quality, racial discrimination, or other valid grounds) from parents, local residents, concerned professionals, community groups, or officials. A range of appropriate sanctions (more varied than fund cut-offs) should be available. The process should be able to extend to the federal level if necessary.

Does the proposal ensure significant parent involvement? In order for child care services to supplement and not supplant parents, there must be a close knowledge of and partnership between parents and caregivers. Given their already frenzied schedule, working parents need help in finding ways to participate. Poor parents may need help to gain confidence to join in. Fathers may need suggestions on how to share the responsibilities mothers have traditionally shouldered. Caregivers of all types may need training and advice on how to create the supports parents need and how to include parents in meaningful ways. The sharing of alternatives needs to be extended beyond the advisory councils developed more than a decade ago. The payoffs to children, families, caregivers, and support for child care programs and policies will depend on the working partnership that is established.

Policy Options for the 1980s

There are at least six distinct policy options for public support of child care that policymakers and the public can consider as the 1980s begin. This is not intended to be an exhaustive list. There are others quite different from the six models described here. But these options represent major different strategies or ways for moving toward federal support for child care services.

Policy Option 1: Do Nothing More; Preserve the Status Quo. There are currently three major forms of federal support for child care: programs providing child care services directly (for example, Title XX, Head Start, WIN); those providing auxiliary services, thereby helping to defray total child care costs (for example, the U.S.D.A. Child Care Food Program, Medicaid's Early and Periodic Screening, Diagnosis, and Treatment program (EPSDT)); and those supporting child care services indirectly by providing funds to families for meeting child care expenses (for example, the child care tax credit and AFDC Income Disregard). (See Table 16-1.)

The single largest federal expenditure for child care in fiscal year 1980—the child care tax credit—was estimated to cost $900 million in federal funds allowed to families claiming child care as a work-related expense. The next largest federal expenditure—Title XX—was an estimated $800 million spent on child care services provided directly to approximately 840,000 clients in fiscal year 1979. Third is Project Head Start, which spent $735 million in fiscal year 1980 providing comprehensive services to some 368,000 children in part- and full-day programs. Both Title XX and Head Start—unlike the tax credit—focus on the child care needs of low-income populations, as do many other federal programs (for example, Title I of the ESEA, WIN, CETA, the Community Development Block Grant Entitlement Program, AFDC Income Disregard and the Appalachian Regional Commission).

What are the relative costs of the present system? According to Congressional Budget Office estimates, total federal expenditures for child care were approximately $2.3 billion in fiscal year 1977.[13] This was about one-tenth of one percent of the Gross National Product in 1977.[14] It compared to $2.8 billion spent that year by the federal government for child nutrition; $3.2 billion federal funds for child health; and $4.8 billion in federal elementary and secondary education funds.[15] It was also approximately one-seventh of what Americans spent that year on tobacco consumption ($16.5 billion) and one-twelfth what they spent on alcoholic beverages ($28.2 billion).[16]

Who benefits from this potpourri of programs? It is impossible to get unduplicated counts of children served, but several populations can be assumed to benefit. First, a portion of poor children are served: children in full-day Head Start programs; the additional children in part-day Head Start for whom supplementary child care arrangements are made; those in Title XX-funded facilities; those whose parents are in WIN or CETA or who use the AFDC Income Disregard; those in Appalachian communities; those whose families live in low-income housing projects where HUD has made a building grant for child care facilities; those relatively few in Title I ESEA preschool programs. In addition to poor children, middle-class chil-

Table 16-1   Major Federal Programs Supporting Child Care, Expenditures and Enrollments

Program	Expenditures		Enrollment	
	Amount	*Year*	*Number Served*	*Year*
Title XX, Social Security Act	$ 653 million[a]	FY 1977	840,000[d]	FY 1979
P.L. 94–401 setaside	($200 million)	FY 1979	N.A.	
WIN	35 million	FY 1977	66,000/quarter	FY 1978
CETA	N.A.		N.A.	
CDBG	20 million[c]	FY 1978	N.A.	
CSA, CAP	N.A.		N.A.	
ARC	12.3 million[b]	FY 1977	N.A.	
P.L. 94–142, preschool	17.5 million	FY 1980	216,000	1978–79
Title I, ESEA, preschool	188.5 million	1978–79	375,000	1977–78
USDA Child Care Food Program	172 million	FY 1979	660,000/day	FY 1979
Head Start	681 million	FY 1979	368,000	FY 1979
Title IV-B	4.4 million	FY 1977	2,100/quarter	FY 1978
Child care tax credit	657 million	1978	3.4 million returns	1978
AFDC income disregard	<100 million[c]	FY 1979	145,000	FY 1977

[a] includes P.L. 94–401 monies
[b] child development programs; includes day care; states and locals also contribute $9 million (other federal monies); total $30.7 million
[c] estimate
[d] number of *clients* served, not number of children

Sources:

Title XX, expenditures—U.S. Department of Health, Education, and Welfare, Administration for Public Services, *Social Services U.S.A.*, Annual Summary, October 1976–September 1977, Table M (1979); enrollment—U.S. Department of Health, Education, and Welfare, Office of the Assistant Secretary for Planning and Evaluation, *Technical Notes: Summaries and Characteristics of States' Title XX Social Services Plans for Fiscal Year 1979*, p. 67 (June 1979).

WIN, expenditures—*Social Services U.S.A.*, Table M (1979); enrollment—U.S. Department of Health and Human Services, Administration for Public Services, *Social Services U.S.A.*, Third Quarter Report FY 1978, Table 10 (1980).

Table 16-1   Major Federal Programs Supporting Child Care, Expenditures and Enrollments (continued)

CETA—Interview with U.S. Department of Labor official by Janet Simons, June 4, 1980.

CDBG—Interview with U.S. Department of Housing and Urban Development official by Janet Simons, August 28, 1979.

CSA, CAP—Interview with Community Services Administration official by Janet Simons, August 27, 1979.

ARC—Interview with Appalachian Regional Commission official by Janet Simons, August 27, 1979.

P.L. 94-142—U.S. Department of Health, Education, and Welfare, U.S. Office of Education, *Progress Toward a Free Appropriate Public Education,* "Semiannual Update on the Implementation of Public Law 94-142: The Education for All Handicapped Children," Table 1 (August 1979).

Title I, ESEA—Interview with U.S. Office of Education official by Janet Simons, September 4, 1979.

Child Care Food Program—U.S. Department of Agriculture, Food and Nutrition Service, Budget Request FY 1981, Purpose Statement, p. 141 (1979).

Head Start, expenditures—Interview with Administration for Children, Youth, and Families official by Janet Simons, August 28, 1979; enrollment—Administration for Children, Youth, and Families, unpublished (1979).

Title IV-B, expenditures—*Social Services U.S.A.,* Table M (1979); enrollment—*Social Services U.S.A.,* Table 10 (1980).

Child care tax credit—U.S. Department of the Treasury, Internal Revenue Service. *Preliminary Statistics of Income—1978, Individual Income Tax Returns,* Table 9 (1980).

AFDC income disregard, expenditures—Interview with U.S. Department of Health and Human Services official by Janet Simons, June 3, 1980; enrollment—Congressional Budget Office, *Child Care and Preschool: Options for Federal Support,* Table 9 (1978).

dren in public school prekindergarten programs and handicapped children in the few states implementing the preschool component of the Education for All Handicapped Children Act benefit, too. Parents of middle-class children are the major beneficiaries of the child care tax credit, although, at a maximum of $400 per child per year, the benefit was small in relation to child care costs.

Who is left out? As a result of the eligibility policies and funding constraints, many poor children do not get the services for which they are eligible (for example, over 75 percent of children eligible for Head Start and 1,000 eligible communities receive no services). Other poor children are in programs of dubious quality. Audits continually find many Title XX-funded programs inadequate in a number of areas, and anecdotal reports from states using AFDC Income Disregard instead of Title XX for child care for welfare families indicate that many children now suffer temporary, changing, or less comprehensive services than they had previously received or than their parents want for them.

Many middle-class children do not benefit from publicly supported child care services even though their families can use the tax credit. The credit does not create, improve or better distribute child care services. Thus, even in relatively affluent neighborhoods, infant and after-school child care is scarce, and latch-key children as young as age 6 wait for hours in cold schoolyards until their parents come home from work.[17]

But perhaps most ignored by the current programs are the approximately 11.1 million children ages birth to 13 in families earning more than the poverty level and less than $15,000 a year.[19] They are ineligible for the vast majority of the direct service programs and they reap few of the tax credit benefits. For these families, child care is unavailable, unaffordable, unsubsidized, and, for what they can afford, usually unattractive.

What are the major advantages and disadvantages of maintaining the status quo? The advantages are clear: some children get excellent services; some get adequate services; some get services who otherwise would go without them. However, there are huge inequities in availability, scope, and quality of services. There are gaping holes in populations served. There is overlap, redundancy, and complexity in systems, with little coordination either for families or for officials. Inadequate data on need, supply, or quality are generated. There is no process or obvious agency with clout to deal with changes in policies, priorities, or funding.

Policy Option 2: The Incremental Approach.   One way to change the status quo is through a number of relatively small changes in existing programs. Many of these changes would not require new legislation, but could be accomplished by regulation, executive order, budget appropriations, or policy modifications.

One general strategy is to get increased appropriations for all or some of the existing programs: Title XX (which has current authorization levels which will not even keep pace with inflation),[19] P.L. 94-142 (incentive grants to states for preschool programs for handicapped children), U.S.D.A. Child Care Food Programs, Title IV-B child welfare services, Title XX training, and others. Enlarging each of these programs would mean more services for children and a substantial pie to fold into overarching child care legislation in the longer run.

Even relatively small increases in appropriations could improve current services' quality and availability if targeted and managed well. For instance, Title XX child care services could greatly enhance children's health by linking eligible children to Medicaid's EPSDT services. Similarly, funds to set up umbrella agencies to sponsor hundreds of family day care homes would take a modest investment, yet these agencies can then help thousands of children receive the improved nutrition offered by the U.S.D.A. Child Care Food Program.

Larger increases in funding levels could alter the current system significantly. For instance, a major expansion of Head Start would allow it to serve more children, increase its full-day programs, expand its eligibility range, demonstrate innovations such as the Parent and Child Centers, improve its services to handicapped children, and strengthen its overall capacity.[20]

In addition to expansion, existing programs could be made to work better. For example, though Title XX *can* serve families up to 115 percent of the median income, in reality states cut off eligibility at much lower income levels due to funding constraints. Sliding fee scales would augment programs' capacities. Another low-cost but important gain would be to issue new regulations governing Title XX Training programs, making child care administrators eligible to participate in training, and local, nonprofit agencies eligible to be reimbursed for providing training.

Another strategy is to increase the ways in which the tax system can help support child care. On September 15, 1980, Representative Barber Conable, then ranking minority member of the House Ways and Means Committee, introduced the Dependent Care Amendments of 1981, legislation to expand child care tax credit benefits.[21] That bill would have, among other modifications, increased the credit from 20 to 35 percent of work-related child care (up to the current maximum expense of $2,000 for one and $4,000 for two or more children); made it refundable (families would receive reimbursement from

IRS regardless of their tax liability); and expand the definition of "educational" institutions so that more child care programs could qualify for tax-exempt, 501(c)(3), status. These and other changes proposed in the bill would add $765 million in federal funds for the first full calendar year in which the amendments are in force.

Further incremental improvements could include these: (1) a graduated credit allowing families earning below $5,000 annually to get a greater proportion (say, 75 or 90 percent) of their child care expenses refunded and phasing out to the current 20 percent for families earning more than $100,000 annually; (2) a way to apply for the credit quarterly to help defray costs as they arise; (3) an increase of the maximum credit allowed for families with more than two dependents; (4) an increase of the maximum cost allowed for infant care (from $2,000 to, say, $3,000); (5) the refund made available on the short tax form; and (6) an increase of outreach efforts to inform and help families take advantage of the program.

These modifications serve to focus more public funds for child care on families who most need assistance, instead of continuing the pattern whereby 75 percent of the tax credit benefits go to families earning over $15,000 a year. The changes help the credit to make a difference in families' ability to pay for care, to choose better quality care, and to recognize the widely accepted notion that families who can afford to pay for care should do so on a sliding scale basis.

Other tax proposals generated by parents, businesses, and congressional committees with jurisdiction in this area would: (1) permit families to choose the credit or an above-the-line deduction; (2) allow charitable or volunteer activities to be treated as work, and thus make families eligible for the credit; (3) double the allowable expenses for families with severely handicapped children and permit the credit to be claimed without the work requirement; (4) allow families to reduce taxes withheld if they intend to claim the child care tax credit; and (5) allow family day care homes to use Section 188 of the tax code providing for rapid amortization of capital expenditures by prorating the hours they use their homes to provide care. These recommendations have various costs and benefits attached, and any one or several of them could be enacted in addition to action in categorical areas. Indeed, one specific recommendation has been to have the tax and program supports for child care articulate more intentionally. Title XX eligibility, for example, could be changed to assure "a sliding fee direct subsidy for those not benefiting from the tax provisions."[22]

How much would a series of incremental changes cost? Estimates would vary greatly depending on which changes were made. Proponents for Title XX appropriations lobbied for $3.1 billion for 1980 just to maintain service levels and keep pace with inflation, compared to the $2.7 billion authorized. (Let us assume that one-fourth of the difference between $3.1 and $2.7 billion, or $100 million, would have gone for child care.) Head Start requested $820 million in FY 1981 just to bring its enrollment back to 1979 levels and to allow its programs to keep pace with inflation. As stated earlier, Representative Conable's modest child care tax credit amendment would add at least $765 million a year.

Perhaps the major advantage of incremental change is that it offers a better political chance of getting more services for a larger portion of children needing child care. The major disadvantage is that the fragmentation, poor data and planning, uneven quality, and unequal distribution of services would not necessarily change.

Policy Option 3: Community Networks for Child Care. Picture a community where about half the women with children work outside their homes full time, and about half prefer and are able to be full-time homemakers. Among the half who stay home are parents who supply the care for the children of those who work (or go to school, or travel, or get sick). These caregivers are from all income strata and they work in many different settings. Some go to the homes of the children and care for one family's children. Others take another family's children into their own homes. Some take care of only one other child; others take in several children. Some form cooperatives, rent space, buy some supplies, and run informal playgroups. Others get credentials and more formal training and operate specialized services, or more elaborate daytime programs, not unlike Head Start centers.

For all these caregivers in any one community, there is a special magnet child care center staffed with professionals and others who run workshops for mothers and caregivers afternoons or evenings about a variety of topics. These topics can include cooking, arts and crafts, child health problems to watch for, good books to have around, or what to do about aggressive behavior in 3-year-olds. The center also lends toys and materials to day care home providers; has a hotline for caregivers to call if an emergency arises; and also has elaborate (and expensive) equipment that mothers can use if they bring their children to the center for a few hours. The center also provides information and referrals to health services, nutrition services, educational opportunities for caregivers, and a variety of social services that either they or parents of the children may need. The center also runs a switchboard connecting those who need child care with those who want to provide it.

All services at the center are voluntary. All are free. All are confidential. There are no eligibility, income, or other restrictions on their use—except a geographic one. They serve only those in that community. Magnet center services are funded by federal and state funds and private grants. Parents providing child care receive payments from the parents using care. For families who cannot afford the full purchase price, publicly supported subsidies are available on a sliding fee scale based on parents' incomes.

This is not a futuristic dream. Today, in fact, about half of all mothers with children under age 13 work outside the home; half do not. Currently there is a wide variety of child care arrangements, and full-time home makers provide the majority of child care for other families in which both parents work. Communities have networks or webs of information and services, although currently, except in a few places such as California, these networks are informal, fragile, and not used systematically. Some communities currently even have a hub of services resembling the magnet center. It may be a Head Start program, an excellent child care program with outreach and auxiliary services, one housed in a public school that serves as the base for the various related programs, or an information and referral system, such as the San Francisco Child Care Switchboard, which has added monitoring, research, training, and advocacy functions.

What the system described here does is to choose specific parts of several different child care programs and tie them together to form a more coherent network. The pieces are, first, a recognition that child care is not meant to force or encourage women to work, but rather is a necessary service for the children of those who do work. Community Networks for Child Care explicitly value (in fact, depend on) parents who stay at home to care for children. As such, they are a departure from other publicly-supported child care policies and programs.

Second, the services provided in these networks are extremely varied—they are not all centers, or all group homes, or all family homes, or all babysitters; not all custodial; not all enriched. Parents choose which type of care they want for their children. Special programs such as Head Start could continue to be available as one option in the community. Parents' choices are enhanced since economic constraints are reduced by the sliding scale fees and subsidies to equalize their purchasing power.

Third, in this system, the federal government would underwrite the costs of child care in ways that build on the strengths but acknowledge the weaknesses of the free market. For example, expensive equipment, services for children with special needs, information and referral, training to improve caregivers' capabilities are not services a free child-care market is likely to pick up. Federal funds directly to the magnet centers would pay for these. These services also happen to be more efficiently delivered on a community-wide rather than an individual, program-by-program basis. On the other hand, direct care services can be bought on the market fairly easily, and a minimum of federal intervention is envisioned here, allowing families to choose freely. Such a planned and varied system is probably less costly over the long run. Family child care is less expensive than center-based care and much of it would be financed by families' contributions, while the expensive items found in the center would not need to be duplicated in many individual programs in each community.

Fourth, in this model, federal guidance, standards, and quality control are present, but selective. Maintaining excellence, resources, training, and technical assistance capabilities in the centers are important tasks for the federal government. Given the relatively small number of magnet centers, the federal government could monitor them and take responsibility to upgrade their quality. The magnet centers, in turn, would serve as local, peer-oriented purveyors of quality, providing the necessary resources and services for helping to train and improve local child caregivers. In fact, there have been exciting demonstrations of centers "turning 'just babysitters' into day care professionals" and helping them cope with their demanding and often isolating job.[23]

Fifth, in these networks there is a balance between child care professionals and nonprofessionals providing care. The vast majority of services would be given by average parents, undercutting the allegations that publicly supported child care means the professionalization of childrearing or that, with federal legislation, pretty soon, "it becomes illegal to leave the baby with Grandma while Mother goes to work unless Grandma has a degree in child psychology. . . ."[24] In the networks model, enough professionals and experienced caregivers would exist to provide specific technical assistance and training. Yet costs would be kept down, since relatively few high-priced professionals would be needed to serve an entire community of children.

Sixth, the magnet centers' information and referral services link families and children to a range of services. This helps assure coordination and delivery without threatening to supplant families' responsibilities, invade their privacy, or ask child care service budgets to pay for health, nutrition, and social service items. The community nature of the center builds on the strength of families and neighborhoods, and may, in fact, enhance them over time.[25]

What would the networks cost? This depends on what pieces are implemented and to what degree. For example, subsidies to parents to purchase care could be a large expenditure if they were total for families earning $15,000 or less. They need not be, however. They could stay within the currently envisioned tax credit expenditures of $1.6 billion. The difference would be in their allocation: in the network concept, there would not be flat tax credits. Both benefits and fees would be based heavily on families' income.

Other services are less costly. For example, information and referral services—even expanded ones—are relatively inexpensive. Some 40 California systems operate at a cost to the state of $4 million per year.[26] The cost of training, too, can be reduced under the network model since so much of it is based on sharing local experiences that work and using peers to train caregivers.

The networks' major advantages are that they build on parental choice, diversity, voluntary use, direct payments with little intervening bureaucracy, direct grants to local communities to enhance magnet centers' capacities, increased and practical opportunities to train caregivers and share to expensive equipment. In the longer run, the networks could become strong community institutions, taking on advocacy and development roles that serve residents more broadly. The incremental approach described above could create Community Networks for Child Care if the pieces that were changed fit together.

The disadvantage of the networks is that they rely on the integration of several major pieces and are vulnerable if one or several are not forthcoming. For example, subsidies to families without grants to magnet centers would leave caregivers and children without special services or supports to promote quality. Similarly, establishing information and referral systems without also providing subsidies to spark increased supply of child care would, in many places, increase families' expectations without meeting their service needs. The networks' strength is coherence. In our fragmented social and political process, coherence may well be their stumbling block.

Policy Option 4: Reintroduce Major Child Care Legislation. Comprehensive child care legislation to provide major child care service expansion and to make more sense out of the fragments that now exist is still a goal of some child care advocates. At least one representative, Cardiss Collins (D-Ill.), has publicly stated she is willing to introduce child care legislation again.

What would a bill look like? There have been two models in the last decade. The first, the Comprehensive Child Development Act of 1971, was introduced by Senator Mondale and Congressman Brademas and passed both houses of Congress in 1971. The result of tough compromises by myriad organizations in the Ad Hoc Coalition on Child Development and by numerous sponsors in the House and Senate, it enjoyed the highest degree of consensus yet developed on child care legislation. Briefly, its major components were:

- Grants would be made by the Secretary of Health, Education, and Welfare to "prime sponsors" for the planning, development,

operation and maintenance (including construction and remod-
eling of facilities) of child development programs. A prime
sponsor could be any city, county, or unit of local government
with a population of 100,000, or any Indian reservation, state
or—under specific conditions—any public or private nonprofit
agency. To be eligible for grants, the prime sponsor would have
been required to (a) establish a Child Development Council to
plan, conduct, coordinate, and monitor all child development
programs in the area; (b) establish local policy councils elected
by parents of eligible children in subareas of the prime sponsor
that would assess local needs and recommend local applicants to
the Child Development Council; and (c) submit a comprehensive child development plan.

- Half of the Child Development Councils would have been composed of elected members, one from each policy council; the
other half would be appointed by the chief executive of the
prime sponsor, and be broadly representative. At least one-third
of the total members of the Child Development Council would
have been parents who were economically disadvantaged, and
at least one appointed member, a child development specialist.
- The bill would have preserved Head Start expenditures, and the
prime sponsor would have had to give priority to refunding
Head Start annually. Priority would also have been given to
migrant, Indian, and handicapped children and to the development of model programs for economically disadvantaged and
bilingual children. An additional $100 million would have been
authorized in the first year for planning programs and technical
assistance.
- Two billion dollars would have been authorized for fiscal 1973;
$4 billion for fiscal 1974; and $7 billion for fiscal 1975. Appropriations would have been allocated among the prime sponsors
based on the following formula: 50 percent for the relative
number of economically disadvantaged children under the age
of 15; 25 percent for the relative number of children under 5;
and 25 percent for the relative number of children of working
mothers and single parents. A prime sponsor would have had
to spend the first 65 percent of its allotment for poor children
("poor" was redefined to include families of four with annual
incomes below the Bureau of Labor Statistics lower living standard, or $6,960 instead of $4,540) with the remaining 35 percent available to be used for middle-class children whose
parents would pay fees on a sliding scale.[27]
- The bill also would have provided for the establishment of
minimum standards for child development programs and facilities; authorized $5 million for in-service training; provided

technical assistance and evaluation; and authorized up to $20 million for research and demonstration projects—all supervised by a Child Development Research Council. Existing child development programs would have been repeated, coordinated and consolidated with the programs authorized in the act.[28]

The second example of major child care legislation is the Child Care Act of 1979, introduced by Senator Cranston, with a companion bill sponsored by Congressman Roybal in the House.[29] There are some striking differences between the 1971 and 1979 bills. The 1979 bill, for instance, assumed that states would be prime sponsors (or would determine to which state and local agencies to delegate these responsibilities). Gone was the 1960s model of federal funds to local projects, *à la* Head Start. Although details were not written into the 1979 bill about which state agency was to assume sponsorship or how that would be decided, the clear meaning was to pass federal funds to states, which would make major policy and allocation decisions.

Another large difference was eligibility and priorities for service. The 1971 bill strove to guarantee a priority on the neediest, but with a socioeconomic mix of children through the 65/35 percent split in funds targeted for poor and middle-class children. The 1979 bill was written with poor and working women in mind. Its allocation formula used the number of children living in poverty and the number of children with working mothers as criteria for a state's share of federal dollars, and it urged states to give these children (and those of single-parent families) priority for service.

A third difference between the two bills was the scope of services provided. The vision behind the 1971 bill was based on the Head Start model, with comprehensive services to be provided by the child care program. While the 1979 bill recognized that some children and families may need related services, nowhere was "comprehensive" mentioned. Rather, the emphasis was on linking children with other systems providing health, nutrition, or social services. Burned by the "Big Brother" and "spendthrift" rhetoric applied to the 1971 and 1975 bills, Senator Cranston assiduously avoided mentioning comprehensive services in 1979.

Changed, too, was the mandated role of parents. While both bills guaranteed that all services would be voluntary and should not be seen as supplanting parents in raising their children, the 1979 bill did not establish the parent- and consumer-dominated councils with specific policymaking powers as did the 1971 bill. Parent involvement was mentioned, but its definition was vague.

The 1979 bill allowed few funds to be used for construction purposes, while the 1971 bill had included some. The change no doubt was one of perspective: in 1971, architects of the bill looked forward to a growing industry to meet the expanding child care needs and planned new facilities to match the prospective expansion. In 1979, with expansion of need already almost a decade old, sponsors saw the bill as providing funds to help existing providers fight the inroads of inflation rather than building new facilities.

Finally, the 1979 bill responded to some "new" needs that were not highlighted in 1971. Funds were included for the support of information and referral services to link families who needed care with families or facilities that wanted to provide it (as well as with other related social services); for upgrading state licensing codes to increase quality; and for technical assistance to train state agency personnel in their own training, licensing, and monitoring duties.

What are the advantages and disadvantages of new child care legislation? Depending on its language, a new bill could be a vehicle around which political action could coalesce, pressing for the creation of additional child care services, expanded eligibility, cohesion, integration, and efficiencies to the currently fragmented system. However, overcoming the conservative fiscal, political, religious, and other pressures against a piece of child care legislation will require enormous efforts by advocates and legislators. Public education about need, about the legislation and about the payoffs for families will take time, money, and coordinated efforts, as will marshalling the political support in Congress and the Administration. Groups favoring new legislation will have to face tradeoffs in their own resources and staff working on other equally important policy issues to ensure that time, money, and political energy will be forthcoming.

Policy Option 5: Child Care Insurance. Given the problems inherent in establishing and delivering social services directly through government programs, another policy option is to enable all families to buy child care (or other needed services) on the open market. After all, wealthy families buy child care all the time, but the service is called a babysitter, live-in maid, or *au pair*, and it does not connote family pathology, a threat to the family's survival, harm to the children, shirking of parental obligations, or unnecessary expenditures. Nor is it debated as a fundamental American value. It simply is what families do to cope with normal career, household, and childrearing demands. Therefore, some have argued that public policies should help all families purchase the services they need.

Vouchers for child care could purchase services, but vouchers would be publicly financed, and many of the same debates would be reopened. Children's allowances, once proposed by David Stockman, the current director of the Office for Management and Budget in the White House, would increase families' ability to purchase services such as child care. But they, too, raise thorny policy issues.

Some policy analysts have proposed an insurance model similar to Social Security or health insurance; one that forces savings, spreads risks, and, therefore, could make funds for child care available. One such proposal—childhood disability insurance—was made by the Carnegie Council on Children as a way to help families absorb the extra costs of caring for handicapped children.[30]

Mary Jo Bane laid out what an insurance plan designed specifically for child care might look like. She noted: "There are a number of periods in people's lives when they are unable to support themselves by work. Two of these periods, old age and temporary unemployment, are recognized as times when social insurance is necessary to tide people over."[31] Most Americans accept the notion of Social Security not only because it is "billed as insurance and not relief," but also because so many have received benefits that they trust the program to work. Given the popular acceptance of the theory of Social Security, Bane continued, "another period during which people cannot support themselves is childhood; this period, too, might be sensibly covered by social insurance programs."[32]

The way Bane's child care insurance proposal would work is that current workers (aged 20–65) would contribute more of their earnings to the Social Security pot. Payments could be made to children who need child care (or other necessary services). The payments could be seen as "loans," which children would "pay back" when they became productive workers by contributing to the overall Social Security fund.

On its face, all families who had children would benefit since they could use the funds for needed services. The poor would benefit disproportionately since the sum they would receive for child care in all probability would exceed the amount they could spend for such a service (due to the risk-sharing component of insurance, where all families contribute but the payments are equal to all those who use child care). As Bane noted, "The risk of being rich or poor as adults would be spread evenly among children. The scheme could thus have a fairly powerful effect on equalizing the resources available to children and providing all children with an environment conducive to survival and growth."[33]

Child care insurance has several advantages. It would remove once and for all any stigma attaching to child care from its relation to pathological, poor, or incompetent families. It would acknowledge the need for the service as a normal family support widely used by rich and poor alike. It would help even out a family's income over its life cycle. Most families experience the high costs of raising young children when they can least afford it—when one wage earner stops out to have a baby, when both wage earners are young and have not yet reached their peak salaries, and when other expenses (such as a mortgage) are high, as well. Having a loan available when a family needs it—paying it back when they can afford to—may relieve considerable economic stress on families. And although the federal government would administer it, an insurance program is based on a series of private decisions and actions.

Unfortunately, the plan's disadvantages are many. Foremost is cost. As Bane noted, "The scheme would involve the transfer of an enormous amount of money, if the payments to children were set high enough to actually affect their environments. The sum is so large that the program is unlikely even to be considered a possibility for national legislation."[34] Especially now when the Social Security fund is already in jeopardy, an additional burden would have little chance of passage.

Insurance would also not address child care service issues which are insensitive to or inappropriate for control by the free market. Provision of start-up funds, monitoring of quality, training for caregivers, information and referral systems to help families identify and choose care, planning and evaluations of programs—all of these would not automatically happen with child care insurance. Its large cost would make it less likely for additional federal funds to be allocated for these important parts of a child care system.

Unregulated insurance also would not prevent the segregation of poor children in inferior quality programs. If each family got $1,000 per child per year for child care, for example, the inflationary impact would drive child care costs up. Families at the upper end of the income scale could supplement their insurance payments with their own funds and purchase better quality care, whereas the poor would have to depend on whatever program $1,000 could buy.

In addition, as Bane herself noted, there may be cash-flow problems, since "the scheme would work best when the population was stable, since at any given time the number of dependents would be less than the number of working-age people and the number of young children would be relatively small."[35] Population growth is not terribly stable, however. The post–World War II baby boom produced many young children; in its aftermath in the 1960s and early 1970s, fertility dropped dramatically. But births are increasing again. The cycle of peaks and valleys in fertility rates would continually upset the balance of an insurance fund.

Policy Option 6: A Federal Family Policy. There are those who have argued that the fundamental problem with public support for child care is that by proposing programs for *children*, families' strength, power, and integrity are threatened. Some abhor the notion of treating children as a separate group requiring special services, for they see children as inextricably embedded in the family unit. Others, while not in philosophical disagreement with an attempt to help children, note that many services help children best when they work directly through families.

Thus, the need for "a family policy" gained popularity during the second half of the last decade. There was a spate of articles, studies, and conferences calling for consideration of a family policy. In 1979 President Carter appointed a director who began planning a White House Conference on Families (preempting in 1980 the traditional decennial White House Conference on Children, which was postponed to 1981). Also in October, 1979, an Office for Families, lodged in the Department of Health and Human Services, was created.

These were largely political and symbolic actions. Specific policy or programmatic dimensions have not been defined. Several analysts, however, have put together principles and components for a proposed federal family policy, and while they are not precise enough for enactment, they lend some shape to the discussion. They have argued that a family policy must look beyond child care to include a wide range of problems and their solutions for all family members: children, parents, and grandparents who, in their later years, may become dependent on families for financial and emotional support. They have proposed an inclusive agenda with such recommendations as: tax credits for the care of frail parents by their children; mandated quotas of specialized and subsidized housing for the aged; policies allowing relatives to be paid for providing services such as rehabilitation, homemaking, foster care, child care, care for the aged; tax credits replacing the dependent deduction, so that low-income families benefit; subsidized facilities and travel for working-class family vacations; income maintenance for the working poor, the able-bodied unemployed, the disabled and unemployables, and parents rearing infants; policies prohibiting discrimination in and subsidizing housing for families with children.[36]

Specfically regarding the need for child care services, a broad family policy could include:

- Paid maternity or parental leaves, enabling employed parents to care for their newborns for six months or more.
- Credit toward social security entitlements for mothers who leave the labor force for one or more years to care for newborns.
- Paid leaves for a specified number of days each year for care of children when they are ill.
- Comprehensive, preventive maternal and child health services.
- A family allowance in the form of a monthly cash payment toward childrearing costs, but one that is taxable to allow recovery from the more affluent.
- Available, voluntary preschool programs.
- Adequate child care programs to cover after-school, evening, weekend and holiday child care needs.[37]

Still others have urged businesses and the government to ease the need for child care by promoting such family policies as flexible job schedules, shared jobs, and part-time positions.[38]

Thus, child care fits into a family support system as one of a number of services all families need from time to time in raising their children. Whatever the names used—homemakers or maids, counseling or therapy, job training or continuing education, parent education or professional advice, AFDC or children's allowances, day care or babysitting—there is a range of services that strengthens families' ability to raise their own children, improve the quality of family life, and prevent family dissolution or out-of-home placements for children. The recommendation from many is to recognize the diversity of family needs and devise a system capable of responding to them —with child care as one of a number of possible services families could choose to use.

Given the wide range of hypothetical services and policy changes proposed above, it is impossible to estimate federal and other public and private costs. It should be noted, however, that the federal government already spends a considerable sum on family-related services.[39] A family policy might better coordinate and use these funds more effectively. Furthermore, many services proposed are preventive (for example, counseling enabling families to stay together); relatively low-cost (for example, homemakers compared to foster care); and cost-saving (for example, worker absenteeism rates decline and productivity increases when child care needs are addressed satisfactorily). A careful cost-benefit analysis taking these and other factors into account should accompany more specific proposals if and when they are advanced.

What are the major advantages and disadvantages of a national family policy? The major advantges are two: one rhetorical, the other substantive. First, talking about strengthening "families" is more appealing than picking out only one piece of their needs— children—and addressing it separately. Second, since families' needs are not only diverse *among* families, but change over time *within* families, a policy offering many varied services better fits their changing needs. A family needing child care one year, homemaker services the next, and flexible work hours for two years after that could be able to make those decisions for itself if a range of equally available, affordable, and acceptable options were part of national policy. There would be less inappropriate use of some services (for example, institutional or foster care) because of federal and state laws, policies, fiscal incentives, and practices that now distort the array from which families must choose.

The disadvantages of a national family policy are also both rhetorical and substantive. Although it would be difficult to find an individual or group opposed to strengthening families or changing the antifamily policies and practices that now exist, it is misleading to believe that therefore there is cohesion on how best to accomplish these ends. The problem is acute. As one observer wrote about the 1980 White House Conference on Families, "The planners can't even agree on the definition of 'family,' and delegate-selection conventions in several states have become nasty confrontations between interest groups, mainly pro- and anti-abortion advocates."[40] If analysts thought the child care debate was muddy and suffered from lack of clarity of purpose, policy details, and plans, they would shudder at the vagueness of family policy proposals.

But politics and rhetoric aside for a moment, the substantive difficulties of envisioning, planning, coordinating, legislating, and implementing such a comprehensive notion as a family policy are staggering. Writing about the feasibility of a comprehensive childrens' policy, analyst Gilbert Steiner doubted that a broad one could ever marshal the support needed to enact it. Instead, he concluded that "the children's policy most feasible—and most desirable—is one targeted on poor children, handicapped children, and children without permanent homes: unlucky children whose parents cannot provide them with a start equal to that provided most children."[41] The same may be said of a family policy. Without a specific focus, purpose and well-defined goals, the task of general coordination of services and policies affecting families is a hopelessly diffuse and intangible aim. Amid the resulting confusion, policies and support for child care may get lost.

References

1. Divoky, Diane. 1976. "The Making of a Prestigious Research Report or If The Data Aren't There, Dream Awhile," *Learning* (December), 10.
2. Crawford, Alan. 1980. *Thunder on the Right* (New York: Pantheon Books) 5–6.
3. For demographic projections for the 1980s affecting the use and availability of child care services see Ralph E. Smith, "Women in the Labor Force in 1990" (Washington, D.C.: The Urban Institute, March 1979); *Current Population Reports*, Series P-25, No. 601, "Projections of the Population of the United States: 1975–2050," Table 8 (October 1975); and George Masnick and Mary Jo Bane, *The Nation's Families: 1960–1990* (Boston, Mass.: Auburn House Publishing Company), 11–12.
4. Several states have made some efforts to upgrade their child care systems. Pennsylvania, for example, worked on its own standards for quality and has supported a unique coordinating system between child care and child health services. California advocates were successful in getting the state

legislature in 1980 to pass a bill allocating new funds for child care services and mandating levels of quality similar to those in the revised federal day care standards. California, too, is continuing to support its network of resource and referral programs which help families across the state find care and help providers with training, information and advocacy services. These selected efforts, while important, however, still do not meet the level of need expressed across the country for child care services nor the demand predicted in the upcoming decade.

5. Beck, Rochelle. 1974. "The White House Conference on Children: An Historical Perspective," *The Rights of Children* (Cambridge, Mass.: *Harvard Educational Review*, Reprint Series No. 9), 103.

6. For a more extensive discussion of the inadequacies of the numerous studies of child supply and demand see Rochelle Beck, "The Child Care Policy Stalemate" (Cambridge, Mass.: Harvard University Graduate School of Education, doctoral dissertation, 1980), especially Chapter 2.

7. Many social scientists have acknowledged the difficulty of measuring effects of interventions in children's programs. For an overview of the state of the art, see, *Report of the Panel on Outcome Measurement in Early Childhood Demonstration Programs* (Washington, D.C.: National Academy of Sciences, 1981).

8. See, for example, discussion of the difficulty of linking childhood outcomes to adult behavior in Sheldon White, *et al.*, *Federal Programs for Young Children* (Washington, D.C.: U.S. Government Printing Office, 1973), Vol. I.

9. For example, information about Title XX-funded child care reports recipients by quarter. Some of those recipients are the same from one quarter to the next, some are dropped and new ones added. Simply adding quarters to find out how many recipients each year receive child care is not possible. Furthermore, some states report the recipients of child care funded by Title XX as numbers of children. But some define the recipient as the current or potential welfare dependent, i.e., the mother. In those states, an adult is counted as a recipient for child care, and one adult per family may be reported even though child care is provided for more than one child per family. When the data are compiled across states, it is impossible to known precisely how many children are covered by Title XX funds.

10. Opening statement of John Calhoun, Commissioner, Administration for Children, Youth, and Families, to the Child Care Group, June 2, 1980.

11. Interview with Judith Heintz, Director, "The Shoe" (a child care program for school-aged children) and Debby Genz, researcher, Children's Defense Fund, Washington, D.C., November 11, 1980.

12. This is so because the largest increase in women entering the labor force and increasing their participation from part- to full-time is among the middle- and upper-class families. These women will also be more likely to get higher paying, professional jobs. Black and poor women have always worked in greater proportions than white and middle-class women, gone back to work sooner after their babies were born and more often worked full-time. And Black women's prospects for increased salary or promotion are not expected to grow over the next decade. The result is that Black and

poor families will earn about what they do now, but White and upper-middle-class families" income will increase greatly.

13. U.S. Congress, Congressional Budget Office, *Childcare and Preschool: Options for Federal Support* (September 1978), Table 9. Other estimates place the figure at somewhat over $2.5 billion.

14. U.S. Department of Commerce, Bureau of the Census, *Statistical Abstract of the United States: 1979,* Table 7-14.

15. Statistics on federal expenditures for child nutrition and education come from *Statistical Abstracts of the United States: 1979* (Table 522); child health federal expenditures come from Robert M. Gibson and Charles R. Fisher, "Age Differences in Health Care Spending, Fiscal Year 1977," *Social Security Bulletin,* Vol. 42, No. 1 (January, 1979), 8.

16. *Statistical Abstract of the United States: 1979,* Table 723.

17. Interview with Judith Heintz, November 11, 1980.

18. U.S. Department of Labor, Bureau of Labor Statistics, unpublished data from the *March 1979 Current Population Survey.*

19. Title XX has current authorization levels of $2.9 billion for FY 1981, $3.0 billion for FY 1982, $3.1 billion for FY 1983, $3.2 billion for FY 1984 and $3.5 billion for FY 1985.

20. See Zigler, E. and Valentine, J., eds. *Project Head Start: A Legacy of the War on Poverty* (New York: Free Press, 1979).

21. H.R. 8109.

22. See *The National Day Care Campaign Legislative Initiatives* (Washington, D.C.: National Association for Child Development and Education, May 15, 1980).

23. See, for example, the description of the Pilot Project in Family Day Care initiated by Cornell University in the *Carnegie Quarterly,* Volume XXV, No. 3 (Summer 1977), 7.

24. "Day Care: Why federalize?" editorial in *The Washington Star* (March 6, 1979).

25. For further discussion of the ways in which public policy can recognize mediating structures, see Peter L. Berger and Richard John Neuhaus, *To Empower People: The Role of Mediating Structures in Public Policy* (Washington, D.C.: American Enterprise Institute for Public Policy Research, 1977); and Brigitte Berger and Sidney Callahan, eds., *Child Care and Mediating Structures* (Washington, D.C.: American Enterprise Institute for Public Policy Research, 1979), particularly 1–16.

26. Interview with Ken Jaffe, Director, Contra Costa County Children's Services, Contra Costa County, California, December 10, 1980.

27. In 1979 comparable figures were a poverty level of $7,450 and a BLS lower living standard of $12,585 for a family of four. See U.S. Department of Labor, Bureau of Labor Statistics, press release U.S.D.L. 80–278, April 30, 1980, "Autumn 1979 Urban Family Budgets and Comparative Indexes for Selected Urban Areas"; and Community Services Administration, "General Characteristics of Community Action Programs; Income Poverty Guidelines (Revised)," *Federal Register,* Vol. 45, No. 78 (April 21, 1980), 26712–26713.

28. U.S. Congress, Senate, Committee on Labor and Public Welfare, *Compre-*

hensive Child Development Act of 1971, Joint Hearings before Subcommittee on Employment, Manpower, and Poverty and the Subcommittee on Children and Youth on S. 1512. 92d Cong., 1st sess., Part 1, May 13 and 20, 1971, 3–55; and House, Committee on Education and Labor, *Comprehensive Child Development Act of 1971, Hearings before the Select Subcommittee on Education on H.R. 6748 and Related Bills.* 92d Cong., 1st sess., May 17, 21 and June 3, 1971, 2–60.

29. U.S. Congress, Senate, Committee on Labor and Human Resources, *Child Care Act of 1979, Hearings Before the Subcommittee on Child and Human Development on S.4.* 96th Cong., 1st sess., February 6 and 21, 1979, 6–31; and U.S. Congress, House, Committee on Education and Labor, *H.R. 1121, A Bill to provide assistance and coordination on the provision of child-care services for children living in homes with working parents, and for other purposes,* 1–26. There was also S. 676, the Child and Family Services Act, introduced in 1975. It, however, was virtually identical to the 1971 bill and so does not represent another model to be contrasted in this discussion.

30. Keniston, Kenneth *et al.* 1977. *All Our Children* (New York: Harcourt, Brace-Jovanovich.)

31. Bane, Mary Jo. 1976. *Here to Stay* (New York: Basic Books), 129.

32. Ibid.

33. Ibid., 130.

34. Ibid., 131.

35. Ibid.

36. Kahn, Alfred J. and Kamerman, Sheila B. 1976. "What *Is* a Family Policy Agenda?" Unpublished paper, 1–3.

37. Ibid.

38. Brozan, Nadine. "Conference on Families Produces a 57-point Plan," *The New York Times*, June 9, 1980.

39. For example, 34 different programs provide funds for children needing out-of-home placement. See *Children Without Homes*, (Washington, D.C.: Children's Defense Fund, 1977), particularly Chapter 5 and Appendix P.

40. Schellhardt, Timothy D. "Mr. Carter's Family Plans," *The Wall Street Journal*, May 1, 1980.

41. Steiner, Gilbert Y. 1976. *The Children's Cause* (Washington, D.C.: The Brookings Institution), 255.

Chapter 17

THE BATTLE FOR DAY CARE IN AMERICA: A VIEW FROM THE TRENCHES

by Edward F. Zigler and Jody Goodman

Day care is not just for children, it's for working mothers. It's for fathers, so their wives can help support the family. It's for families, so their children can grow up in a healthy environment. And it's for people who don't have children, so the economy can run smoothly. Because of changes taking place in the American family, day care is no longer simply a service that enables poor women to work, nor is it a luxury for wealthy women who want more time to themselves. It has become an essential part of a much broader national picture, and it must be reckoned with as an important social issue.

The need for day care grows as more and more women enter the work force. Most women take jobs because their families need the additional income. Other women who are divorced or widowed are the sole supporters of their children. Fewer and fewer families are made up of the traditional father, housewife-mother, and children.[1] It is estimated that by 1990, only 25 percent of married women will be full-time housewives and mothers. The number of children under six with working mothers is expected to increase from 7.1 million to 10.5 million.[12] Existing day care facilities are unable to meet the growing need for their services.

Day care does not necessarily take place in a traditional day care center. In fact, most day care takes place in private homes.[21] A child may be cared for by a relative, a paid caregiver, or a neighbor who tends several children during the day. But even with many alternative types of service, parents currently have a very difficult time finding someone to take care of their children while they work.

Some parents who are unable to obtain day care leave their children to fend for themselves. There "latch-key" children, so-called because they wear their house keys on strings around their necks, may suffer neglect when left to their own resources. In *Windows on Day Care,*[7] Mary Keyserling cites a typical case:

> *Peter, age three, gets his own lunch every day. He has to. No one else is home. . . . He eats what he can reach and what his still uncoordinated hands can concoct if he can get the refrigerator or cabinet doors open. Some day it might be poison. . . . (p. 13)*

Simply providing more day care will not solve the problem of children like Peter. Not only do we need more day care facilities, but we must ensure that those facilities provide adequate services. In 1970 the White House Conference on Children named quality day care as the number one need of American families and children.[19] Despite this declaration, there are still virtually no federal standards for day care quality.

The absence of federal regulation of day care leaves states on their own to establish criteria for licensing day care facilities. Some states, such as New York and Connecticut, have fairly strict, reasonable standards. Other states, like Florida, Mississippi, and New Mexico, permit one adult to care for ten infants. This high a staff/child ratio is very dangerous. How could one adult get ten infants out of the building if there were a fire?

Windows on Day Care, the 1972 study by Mary Keyserling, documented terrible conditions in many day care centers. Untrained teenagers were often solely responsible for young children. Settings were filthy and unsafe. Keyserling saw centers where children did not play or learn, but sat mesmerized in front of a television all day. She saw centers where toddlers were tied to their chairs. While there have been no more recent systematic studies like Keyserling's, other observers have noted similar conditions in day care settings. In *Every Child's Birthright*, Selma Fraiberg[5] describes the Merry Mites preschool nursery, a fictional place based on personal observations of actual centers across the country:

> *Twenty children between the ages of three and six are milling as we enter. The equipment and toys are battered and ill-chosen by educational standards. A scratchy record player is booming with a rock record. The sound of unearthly laughter is coming from a TV, where a cartoon animal chase is performed before the glazed eyes of five children. (p. 111–112)*

A recent article in *The Miami Herald*[8] described the Small Fry day care center in West Hialeah, Florida:

> *When a reporter opened the door, the first sensation that greeted her was the smell—an acrid mixture of urine, dirty diapers, and unwashed mattresses. In the center of the room, about eight babies were sprawled on the floor. Another four were sleeping in their cribs. A single adult was diapering another wailing baby in one corner. There was only one toy in sight. (8/3/80)*

The Federal Interagency Day Care Requirements (FIDCR) were adopted in 1968 to prevent abuses such as these, but they are unspecific and inadequate. They do not include provisions for children under two years old; they do not deal with noncenter day care; they do not clearly define the responsibilities of day care providers, caregivers, and administering agencies; and they do not cover care for handicapped children.[3] Because of these problems, the standards have been virtually unenforced since their inception. To make matters worse, Congress imposed a moratorium on the enforcement of the prescribed staff/child ratios, the most important element of the standards.

Child care advocates and liberals in Congress have tried for the past decade to expedite the passage of new standards. They have met with tremendous opposition from conservatives in Congress and in the Office of Management and Budget. Finally, Secretary of Health and Human Services Patricia Harris had the courage to approve new requirements in March, 1980. The new standards required day care facilities to provide nutritious meals, protection from fires, trained staff, and safe staff/child ratios. Two months before they were to take effect, the Senate voted to postpone their implementation, allegedly to save money. Actually, the savings will be minimal —an estimated $25 million, which is less than one percent of the yearly federal day care budget.[4f]

The Senate vote against day care standards is symptomatic of a broader problem in this country. Throughout history, government has been averse to enacting any wide-reaching child care legislation. What the United States needs is a national commitment to provide for the daily needs of its children and families. Instead, policymakers have found it easier to turn their backs on the problem. Meanwhile, American children—and consequently, all Americans—suffer the consequences.

Child care in this country is put to shame by the comprehensive systems in many other nations. In the United States, only eight states offer kindergarten to all their children.[18] Of the more than 7 million children under six whose mothers work, only 2½ million— 35 percent—are in federally funded day care.[23] In contrast, the

Israeli government provides kindergarten for all five-year-olds, and child care is provided for 50 percent of all 3–4 year olds. Sweden provides child development centers for 85 percent of its preschoolers, and Hungary provides nurseries for 50 percent of its 3–6 year olds, and crèches for others.[10] In China, nurseries are available for virtually all children from the age of 56 days on.[11] Cuba offers care for children as young as 45 days old as part of a national child care system; the goal for the next decade is to provide day care for all mothers who want it.[18] Many of these countries also routinely provide children with health care as part of a comprehensive child care system.

In *Child Care—Who Cares?*, Pamela Roby[10] describes the difference between the American system and some foreign child care systems:

> *Americans entering Scandinavian or Israeli children's centers are immediately struck by their hominess. . . . American visitors to these nations are also struck by the seriousness with which their hosts explain that child-care center policies should be considered only in the context of a comprehensive social policy for the promotion of the children's well-being and development and the well-being of their parents. Many nations' provision of comprehensive children's services stands in marked contrast to the American practice of attempting to assist low-income children by providing one isolated service after another rather than a comprehensive program of services. (p. 6)*

In a hearing on a comprehensive child care bill that would have bridged part of this gap, had it not been vetoed by President Nixon, Representative Bella Abzug declared:[15]

> *We're terrorized that [other countries] might beat us in building a supersonic transport—but when it comes to child care, that's something else again. You know and I know that we are the richest nation in the world, that we need these services desperately, and that we have the capacity to pay for them if we only would.*

The problem is, "we" won't. Time after time, women's groups and child advocates have lobbied for legislative reform for child care. The Department of Health and Human Services (formerly HEW) has formally attested to the need for such reform.[4f] Yet, during the past 12 years, virtually no progress has been made. Policy makers with control of federal purse strings have refused to acknowledge day care as an urgent social need.

Proponents of child care reform are as aware as anyone that federal money does not grow on trees, and that programs cannot always be implemented just because they are needed. Priorities must be established, and some plans must take precedence over others. Day care should be a top priority concern. It affects not only the work force

of today, but the citizens—workers, voters, and parents—of tomorrow. The day care problem will not eventually disappear like an
unwelcome guest; it will grow just as surely as children grow. And
it will only worsen and become more entrenched unless tackled
head-on.

Legislative Milestones

Lanham Act

Although day care has existed in this country since the 19th century,
it was virtually ignored by government until the 1930s. During the
Depression, nursery schools were funded by the Works Progress
Administration (WPA) to provide jobs for unemployed teachers
and staff, and to assist children from needy, unemployed families.[10]
Day care became a critical issue during World War II, because so
many mothers went to work for national defense. Women were
needed in the war effort, but there was no one to care for their children while they worked. Children were left in locked cars, while
others roamed the streets. Congress responded to this dire situation
by passing the Lanham Act of 1941. The bill provided matched federal funds for states to establish day care centers and nursery schools.
By the peak of the program in 1945, between 105,000 and 130,000
children were enrolled in Lanham centers.[13,2]

The Kaiser shipyards in Portland, Oregon opened two day care
centers for their employees as part of the wartime program. Located
at the shipyards, the Kaiser centers were open twenty-four hours a
day, six days a week. They provided health care for the children,
with additional services for parents, including the low-cost sale of
prepared meals that could be heated up at home after work.[14,6]

After the war, women were expected to return home to their children. Lanham centers closed, as did the Kaiser shipyards and their
centers. Many women who wanted to continue working protested,
but their cries fell on deaf ears. In New York, women demonstrated
in protest outside Governor Thomas E. Dewey's home. He called
them "Communists" and refused to see them. As Gilbert Steiner
states in *The Children's Cause*,[13] the Lanham Act was "a win-the-war
program, not a save-the-children program."

Closing the Lanham centers was probably the gravest error the
federal government has made in the history of child care in this
country. Women did not simply return to their roles as housewives
after World War II as predicted. The number of working mothers
has increased steadily over the years. Lanham centers could have
been used as the foundation for a broad, national child care system

that would have met the needs of both children and working mothers. It would have aided our present-day economy, which desperately needs a productive working population to fulfill the needs of a changing society. If policy makers had had the foresight to build on the Lanham system in 1946, we would not be faced with such a tremendous day care dilemma in 1980.

1950s and '60s

In the years following World War II, public sentiment ran strongly against working mothers. There was next to no government involvement in day care, and working mothers sought private centers, babysitters, and relatives to care for their children. The first major change occurred in 1964, when the Head Start program was instituted to provide compensatory education for disadvantaged children. Soon afterwards, child care professionals redefined day care as including child development and education, rather than existing purely as a custodial service.

Even with this advance, day care was still inextricably associated with poverty throughout the 1960s. Most Americans saw it as a service for welfare mothers, so it did not carry much political weight. That view began to change as the women's movement gained momentum. Feminists argued that all mothers, regardless of their economic status or their reasons for working, were entitled to day care. This shift gave mothers the new freedom of choosing between homemaking and working, and it helped foster a political climate more favorable to child care legislation.

Comprehensive Child Development Act

The year 1971 marked the closest this nation has ever come to enacting a comprehensive program for child care. A bipartisan coalition in Congress united with a coalition of child care advocates to support the Comprehensive Child Development Act of 1971. President Nixon dealt a devastating blow by vetoing the bill. Since then, there have been attempts at passing other child development legislation, but to no avail. The favorable circumstances surrounding the 1971 bill are not likely to be replicated, and the prospects for a broad system of child care in America remain bleak. The story behind the 1971 bill explains why.

The Nixon Administration originally supported the idea of child care legislation. In 1969 the president had expressed his dedication to improving "the first five years of life" of American children. Child care reform also fit in well with Nixon's plans for welfare reform. Democrats responded to his receptive attitude by drafting a child care bill in each House of Congress. Walter Mondale, with 23 other Democratic senators, sponsored the Senate bill, while the House effort was led by John Brademas.

Nixon, though endorsing the bills in theory, balked at supporting legislation controlled by liberal Democrats. The Administration responded with the stalling tactic of proposing an HEW study of the child care problem.[13] In the meantime, Congress held hearings on the bill. After months of study and deliberation, legislators, child care professionals, and HEW staff all reached the same conclusion: this legislation was important, and urgently needed.

The Child Development Act provided $700 million for federal funding of child care for welfare recipients during the first year of its operation. The bill also authorized $50 million for the creation of new child care facilities. It increased income tax deductions for child care services, and increased from $6,000 to $12,000 the maximum income of families permitted to use the child care deduction. It expanded the Head Start program, and provided for health care, adequate nutrition, and educational enrichment for preschool children.[16]

Obviously, supporters of the legislation differed on certain issues. The main source of contention was prime sponsorship: how large a population should be represented by each local administrator of the new programs. Ultimately, 100,000 was established as the population limitation for prime sponsorship; that is, administrative agencies would be set up for every 100,000 people.

Elliot Richardson, secretary of HEW, and Edward Zigler, director of the Office of Child Development, met regularly with Senator Mondale and Congressman Brademas to iron out disagreements over the bill. Finally, it seemed that all were satisfied, and the bill went to a vote. In September, 1971, it passed the Senate by 49–12. It squeaked by on the House side in November by a close 186–183.

By the time the Comprehensive Child Development Act reached President Nixon's desk, a political wind from across the country reached Washington that may have prompted the narrow victory margin in the House, and definitely influenced the fate of the bill. Right-wing activists, from fundamentalist church groups to the John Birch Society, formed a giant coalition to stop the bill. They wrote thousands of letters to their representatives and the president protesting that the bill was an "invasion of the family." Child care advocates and citizens' groups in favor of the legislation were caught off guard, and failed to mount a countercampaign.

Democrats in the Senate still believed that they had administration support until November 18. On that date, Secretary Richardson wrote a letter to Senator Gaylord Nelson, chairman of the House-

Senate conference, indicating that he was no longer supporting the bill, regardless of the agreement that had been reached. Unbeknownst to Congress, Richardson had spent hours at the White House defending the bill. But Nixon had changed his mind, and Richardson had no choice but to back off from his original position. Richardson was in an embarrassing position with his hands tied; all he could do was sit and watch months of effort go down the drain.

On December 9, Nixon vetoed the bill. The veto message was inflammatory and extremely controversial; it sent Washington into an uproar. Had the message been written by a political moderate, it could have raised objections to specific problems—such as prime sponsorship, which many believed should have been given to the states—without destroying the future of other child development legislation. Instead, Nixon attacked the very foundation of the bill.

Echoing the right-wing groups, Nixon declared that the bill, "the most radical piece of legislation to emerge from the 92nd Congress," would lead to the breakdown of the American family. The president stated that "for the federal government to plunge headlong financially into supporting child development would commit the vast moral authority of the national government to the side of communal approaches to child rearing over against the family-centered approach."[4e] This reference to the right-wing argument that a child development program would "Sovietize" America's children was, according to Elliot Richardson, a "fish" thrown to opponents of Nixon's China policy.[13] It was a means of appeasing his most conservative critics.

Nixon's veto virtually destroyed the movement for child development legislation. Had Nixon just attacked specific problems with the bill, other systems could have been developed later on. But with such a strong presidential antipathy, coupled with vociferous opposition from their conservative constituents, even moderate senators were reluctant to continue supporting child development legislation.

After the veto of the 1971 bill, the child development coalition all but fell apart, and the drive for legislative reform lost momentum. The Senate passed a weaker child development bill in 1972, but it failed to get through the House. An even more scaled-down version of the original bill did pass both Houses in 1975, only to be vetoed by President Ford. One last attempt was made in 1979, when Senator Alan Cranston introduced a new child development bill. After months of hearings, the bill died. Richard Nixon was gone from office, but he and right-wing groups evidently instilled a political aversion to child development legislation that lingers on in Washington. In this type of atmosphere, it seems unlikely that similar legislation will pass in the near future.

The Carter Administration

When Jimmy Carter became president, child care advocates renewed their hopes for legislative action and federal support for a child development program. Carter made two campaign speeches promising change in the child care system and endorsing a program of federal subsidies for day care centers operated by state and local groups. Good intentions took the form of legislation in 1979, when Senator Alan Cranston sponsored a new child care bill. But major obstacles confronted this new effort: child care advocates had lost their primary spokesman in the Senate when Walter Mondale became vice president; the child care coalition had fragmented, and was not nearly as strong as it had been in 1971; and the administration suddenly changed its position from support to opposition. The administration testimony against the bill was unexpected and devastating. In fact, it was probably the *coup de grâce* that destined the bill for failure.

Arabella Martinez, assistant secretary of HEW for Human Development Services, gave the administration testimony at the hearings on the 1979 Child Care Act. Martinez declared that although the administration shared the concern of child advocates for improved standards and licensing procedures for day care centers, "we do not believe that another categorical program for child care is warranted at this time." She explained that working mothers do not necessarily "want or need center-based or formal, governmentally supported care," and that mothers actually prefer to have their children cared for by relatives in their homes. The proposed program was therefore deemed unnecessary.

Martinez's testimony was inconsistent with the testimony of virtually every other witness during six hearings on this bill. Dozens of witnesses from across the country had unanimously decried the lack of child care services in their communities. Martinez's statement confounded Senator Cranston, who declared:[17]

> I must say that it is indeed ironic that we have a Carter-Mondale administration appearing before this subcommittee in opposition to child care legislation. As you know, the subcommittee was created through the effort of Senator Mondale, who for years worked hard for child care legislation. President Carter, in his campaign, made a specific commitment to join in the development of child care legislation. . . . (p. 238)

Martinez responded by reiterating the administration's commitment to improved standards for day care, but she said they were wary of creating a fragmented system of services through excessive categorization and bureaucratization. Despite this rationale, the motivation behind the testimony remains unclear. What caused the sudden shift in the policy of an administration so openly dedicated to child development reform? One possible explanation lies in the process of preparing testimony.

Administration testimony is often written by the Office of Management and Budget (OMB). Suzanne Woolsey, associate director of Human and Community Affairs in Carter's OMB, wrote an article in *Daedalus* that closely resembles much of Martinez's testimony. Woolsey wrote that parents do not need or want center-based day care; that mothers usually manage to make arrangements for child care without federal assistance; and that day care should actually be categorized as a secondary political issue.[19] It is quite conceivable that Woolsey was involved in preparing the HEW testimony on the Child Care Act. That would explain the intent and the wording of the testimony. Martinez's statement also had to pass White House approval, however, and the question remains as to how it became the official administration position. Whatever the explanation, it stands until the administration makes another statement to the contrary.

The Carter administration did purge itself somewhat of its betrayal of the child development cause when it defended the revised day care standards of 1980. Arabella Martinez had emphasized the administration's support of new standards when she testified before Cranston's subcommittee, and the administration remained true to her words. In the face of considerable opposition from conservatives in Congress and special interest groups, Secretary of Health and Human Services Patricia Harris approved new standards in March, 1980. Unfortunately, the Senate later delayed their implementation for one year as an alleged money-saving measure. The result is that little or no progress has been made in child care services during the Carter administration.

Conclusion

Contrary to Arabella Martinez's testimony on the Child Care Act of 1979, the need for day care most certainly does exist. Virtually every professional in the child development field has attested to this fact. In 1970, the White House Conference on Children voted quality day care the number one need of American children and families. This year, regional meetings for the White House Conference on Families emphasized that a solution is needed to this nation's day care problem. Laura Lee Simon, chairwoman of the Connecticut delegation to the conference, declared that her group's recommendations "came down very strongly in favor of day care; the need is really keen."[9]

The need for day care is broad as well as acute. It involves not only traditional day care centers, but alternative types of care as well. Martinez was correct when she said that many parents prefer not to place their children in center-based care. Alternatives should be made available to those parents, since they cannot always locate needed services on their own. Not everyone has an "Aunt Jane" ready and willing to mind her children. It is up to us to establish a broad system of child care that can meet the diverse wants and needs of all members of our society.

The Carter administration's position on the 1979 Cranston bill is indicative, not necessarily of unconcern for this issue, but of a pervasive reluctance in government to invest more federal dollars in sweeping social programs. In this time of inflation and economic instability, that attitude is understandable, albeit unfortunate. Federal involvement is essential to a comprehensive, national child care system, but if federal programs are not forthcoming, there can still be improvement. State and local governments, community and church groups, and private industry can all effect change without federal assistance. Such action is imperative.

Child care services could be improved by training high school students and senior citizens in child development. They would provide a valuable resource as regular child care workers and for emergency care, such as when a child or parent becomes ill.[22] Local agencies could establish communication networks between day care centers and home care providers. This would expand the materials and information available to each caregiver. Churches could contribute by providing extra space at little or no cost for child care programs.[2]

Private industry holds the greatest potential for child care improvement. Companies could help working mothers either by establishing day care centers for employees or reimbursing them for child care costs. Companies could also extend maternity leaves and grant paternity leaves. At present, American companies provide much shorter leaves than foreign companies. Finally, industry could channel support dollars into child care through their corporate funding program. Corporations can legally donate as much as five percent of their net profits for charitable causes, but most actually contribute less than one percent.[22]

Clearly, there is room for a great deal of improvement in child care services, and the resources for change are available. Political progress may be slow in coming, but with a concerted, consolidated effort, the American people can overcome the obstacle of governmental sluggishness. But we must act now. We cannot let the child care crises worsen. Otherwise, the legacy of the International Year of the Child, a year devoted to championing the rights of children, will be simple maintenance of the status quo. Children—and their parents—deserve better. And if children had a say in the matter, they would probably agree.

References

1. Advisory Committee on Child Development. 1976. *Toward a National Policy for Children and Families.* National Academy of Sciences, Washington, D.C.
2. Auerbach, S. 1979. *Confronting the Child Care Crisis.* Beacon Press, Boston.
3. Cohen, D.J. and Zigler, E. 1977. "Federal day care standards: rationale and recommendations." *American Journal of Orthopsychiatry* 47:456–465.
4. Congressional Record. January 15, 1979, S76–77 (a); September 9, 1971, S14010 (b); November 12, 1971, E12165 (c); December 2, 1971, E12897 (d); December 10, 1971, S21129 (e); June 30, 1980, S8927 (f).
5. Fraiberg, S. 1977. *Every Child's Birthright: In Defense of Mothering.* Basic Books, New York.
6. Hymes, J. 1944. "Child care problems of the night shift mother." *Journal of Consulting Psychology*, November: 225–228.
7. Keyserling, M.D. 1972. *Windows on Day Care.* National Council of Jewish Women, New York:
8. *Miami Herald*, August 3, 1980.
9. *New York Times*, June 1, 1980. Connecticut weekly, p. 1.
10. Roby, P. 1973. *Child Care—Who Cares?* Basic Books, New York.
11. Sidel, R. 1972. *Women and Child Care in China.* Hill & Wang, New York.
12. Smith, R.E., ed. 1979. *The Subtle Revolution: Women at Work.* The Urban Institute, Washington, D.C.
13. Steiner, G.Y. 1976. *The Children's Cause.* The Brookings Institution, Washington, D.C.
14. Stolz, L.M. 1943. "The nursery comes to the shipyard." *New York Times*, November 7:20, 39.
15. U.S. Congress. 1971. House committee on education and labor, select subcommittee on education. Comprehensive Child Development Act of 1971, 92nd Congress. May 17–June 3.
16. U.S. Congress. 1971. Senate committee on finance. Child Care. 92nd Congress. September 22–24.
17. U.S. Congress. 1979. Senate committee on labor and human resources, subcommittee on child and human development. Child Care Act of 1979. 96th Congress. February 21.
18. Walk, K. 1978. *Children of Che: Child Care and Education in Cuba.* Ramparts Press, Palo Alto, California.
19. White House Conference on Children.. 1970. *Report to the President.* U.S. Government Printing Office, Washington, D.C.
20. Woolsey, S.H. 1977. "Pied piper politics and the child care debate." *Daedalus*, Spring: 127–145.

21. Young, D.R. and Nelson, R.R. 1973. *Public Policy for Day Care of Young Children.* D.C. Heath and Co., Lexington, Massachusetts.
22. Zigler, E. and Finn, M. 1981. "A vision of child care in the 1980s." In *Facilitating Infant and Early Child Development*, L.A. Bond and J.M. Jaffe, eds. University Press of New England, Hanover, N.H.
23. Zigler, E. and Heller, K.A. 1980. "Day care standards approach critical juncture." *Day Care and Early Education* 7(3):7–8, 47.

Chapter 18

THE DILEMMA OF AFFORDABLE CHILD CARE

W. Gary Winget

The question is not whether there is a child care problem but rather, what can be done about it. This is the dilemma confronting federal policymakers and thwarting new initiatives. This chapter addresses the central problems of affordable child care for working families* and concludes that there is an effective, reasonable, and economical approach for making child care affordable—an amendment to Section 44A of the Internal Revenue Code creating a "sliding" tax credit for child and dependent care expenses.

Child care is now and will continue to be a necessity for America's

---

* A working family is one with children under the age of 14 years and in which the parent or parents are employed, enrolled in a training or educational program leading to employment, or actively seeking employment.

In August Congress adopted and the President signed the Economic Recovery Tax Act of 1981 which amended the child and dependent care tax credit effective January 1982. The amendment created a 30/20% sliding tax credit. If a family's income is $10,000 or less, the credit will equal 30% of the expense; if a family's income is more than $10,000 but $28,000 or less, the maximum credit of 30% will be reduced by 1 percentage point for each $2,000 of income (or fraction thereof) over $10,000; if a family's income is more than $28,000, the credit will equal 20%. The estimated increase in benefit will be $250 million annually. References to the "current" child and dependent care tax credit in the text refer to the 20% flat credit. Similarly, references to estimated 1982 Title XX child care expenditures are those in the proposed budget and do not reflect the 22% reduction in actual Title XX funds as adopted by Congress in the final budget. The above changes are not reflected in the text of the chapter because they occurred too close to the date of publication.

economy, its families, and its children. However, many working families cannot afford to purchase the care they need and want, and this is resulting in immediate and long-range human and financial costs. The proposed amendment in the child and dependent care tax credit would provide a benefit for lower- and middle-income working families sufficient for them to afford quality child care services; however, it would not result in an unreasonable or unnecessary federal cost.

After describing the context in which the problem exists, the analysis defines the affordability problem, constructs an analytical framework, and analyzes three approaches currently being discussed in the child care field.

Setting of the Problem

Before proceeding, it is necessary to review social realities, trends, and attitudes which establish the context in which the child-care affordability problem exists. These circumstances help in emphasizing the importance, magnitude, and priority of the problem.

Demographic, Social, and Economic Realities

It is a demographic reality that America is an aging society with relatively few children and an increasing number of elderly persons. Whereas there were 100 children to every 30 senior citizens in 1950, by 2010 there will be only 48 children for every 30 persons over the age of 65.[29] As we pass the year 2000, continually increasing economic and social demands will fall on a relatively small work force composed of children growing up now. The very well-being of our future (for example, our standard of living, retirement systems, national defense) depends upon their abilities as parents, workers, and leaders in the next century.[12] Given this reality, the care and nurturing of today's children must be considered critical to the long-range future of the nation.

An equally significant reality is the dramatic change in the composition of the American work force; women have become a significant, growing, and permanent part of the nation's labor force. However, the large-scale movement of women, and particularly mothers, into the out-of-home work place is having immense consequences on our economy as well as on family life, and frequently results in hardship and inequities for working women and their families.[11] Because the nation has not been fully supportive of mothers and fathers as they seek to accommodate their dual roles as workers and parents, there is concern as to whether all children are growing up in environments which are conducive to their optimal growth and development.

A third reality is that the vast majority of working parents are in the labor force because their incomes are necessary for economic survival.[15] This assertion is supported by the fact that over half of all working families would either have no income or be classified as lower-income families if they did not work. *Specifically, 25% of all working families are maintained by single parents who would have no earned income if they did not work, and 30% are maintained by two earner parents who would have an income below $13,000 (1978) if the mother did not work.*[6] Thus, many working families who must use child care arrangements while they are away from the home may have difficulty in purchasing the care they want and need.

Child Care Trends

The structure of the child care market and changes that may be expected to occur during the coming decade will have an influence on the magnitude of the affordability problem.

Need for Care. More than half of all children under the age of 14 now live in families with working parents* (see Table 18-1). Despite a declining birth rate throughout most of the seventies, there was a significant increase in the number of children needing care during the decade (for example, 33% for children under the age of six).

The need will grow even more dramatically during the next two decades because not only will the rate at which mothers enter the labor force continue to increase but more children will be born, a reversal of the seventies' trend of decreasing births. Based upon projections of population and labor force participation rates, one may expect the need for preschool care to rise by as much as 70% in the eighties and then level off in the nineties. The need for school-age care will rise at a much slower, but steady, rate during the same period.

The need for care among single-parent families, maintained by either mothers or fathers, has become significant. Two-thirds of the children in single-parent families need care, and approximately one of every four children needing care lives in a single-parent family. By comparison, half of the children in two-parent families need care.

Use of Care. The patterns of child care usage vary. However, while there is no "main" method of care which dominates, there are

---

* The numbers data in this section do not include parents enrolled on a full-time basis in training or educational programs leading to employment.

Table 18-1   Percentage of Families and Number of Children with Parents in Labor Force by Family Status and Age of Youngest Child

Family Status and Age of Youngest Child	Percentage of Families			Number of Children (in millions)		
	1970[a]	1980[b]	1990[c]	1970[d]	1980[b]	1990[e]
All Families						
Under 14	41%	56%	64%	18.4	22.4	31.3
6–13	53	65	71	12.7	14.8	18.3
Under 6	32	47	57	5.7	7.6	13.0
Single-Parent Families						
Under 14	62	67	71	2.8	5.0	—
6–13	71	75	74	2.1	3.6	—
Under 6	53	56	64	0.7	1.4	—
Two-Parent Families						
Under 14	38	53	62	15.6	17.4	—
6–13	49	62	70	10.6	11.2	—
Under 6	30	45	55	5.0	6.2	—

NOTE: "Own" children in family. Percentage of families for 6–13 age groups for 1970 estimated to be the same as 6–17 age groups. Number of children in the 6–13 age group for 1970 calculated from 6–17 age group using distribution from Johnson.[6]
[a] Johnson[6] and USBC.[24]
[b] Grossman[4] and USDOL.[35]
[c] Smith.[18] Estimated number of single-parent fathers and added to projected numbers.
[d] Johnson.[6]
[e] Moore & Hofferth,[9] Smith,[18] and USBC.[21,22] Based upon mid-range projection of population (that is, 2.1 birth rate); linear projection of percentage of parents in the labor force; and estimated percentage of children with parents in the labor force.

different patterns of usage between preschool and school-age and between single- and two-parent families (see Table 18-2).

While it is difficult to compare data over time, various studies have shown that there were no dramatic shifts in patterns of usage between the mid-sixties and mid-seventies.[10,20] While there will be a dramatic increase in total child care usage during the eighties resulting from the projected increase in need, it is anticipated that usage patterns will remain essentially the same within age groups.

Expenditures for Care. Half of all working families pay for their child care arrangements.[15,41] The average child care expenditure among those who pay for care is about $1,100 a year,[39,41] and the average expenditure for full-time care for one child ranges from about $1,000 for care in the parents' home by a relative to $2,000 for care in a center.[8,15,17] However, the age of the child, location, and other factors cause these expenditures to vary greatly. Total expenditures for care among working families (excluding nonparent expenditures) were in excess of $6 billion in 1978,[41] and the largest portion was for the purchase of out-of-home care by a nonrelative

Table 18-2 Percentage of Employed Households Using Main Method of Care, by Age of Child and Household Status

Age of Child and Household Status	In-Home Rela-tive	In-Home Nonrela-tive	Other-Home Rela-tive	Other-Home Nonrela-tive	Center	Other	Parent or Self-Care
6–13	13%	9%	15%	14%	5%	0%	44%
Single-Parent	17	12	17	20	3	0	31
Two-Parent	11	7	14	12	5	0	51
Under 6	13	16	18	22	18	1	12
Single-Parent	20	9	13	20	30	1	7
Two-Parent	11	18	20	22	15	1	13

SOURCE: Rodes & Moore.[15]

(36%), followed by center care (24%) and in-home care by a nonrelative (22%).[15]

In the absence of any information to the contrary, one may expect that the ratio of paid and nonpaid arrangements will continue to remain roughly equal. Average annual expenditures can be expected to continue increasing at a 7% rate if the cost of providing care follows past trends.[37,40] However, total expenditures for care should increase significantly because of the increase in the number of children needing care.

Public Attitudes

Child care has become a priority on the nation's agenda of issues, and there are clear indications that the public supports helping working families solve their child care problems. With regard to the affordability problem, four recent expressions of public support are noted:

1. A Gallup survey of "American Families—1980" found 70% of the people favored tax credits for families to meet part of child care costs incurred by working parents.[44]
2. The 1980 White House Conference on Families adopted recommendations for child/dependent care tax credits, increased child care funding, promotion and support for a variety of child care choices, and personnel policies that recognize, among other things, the need for child care services.[44]
3. The *National Childcare Consumer Study* found that 82% of all parents with children under the age of 14 felt that the cost of child care should be adjusted according to a parent's ability to pay, and another 9% favored free care.[16]

4. *Better Homes and Gardens* found that 60% of its readers responding to a questionnaire agreed that the current tax credit should either be increased or adjusted for inflation.[7]

Thus, there is a growing public recognition of child care problems confronting working families as well as support for specific types of action that would help make care more affordable.

Statement of the Problem

The central child care problem confronting policymakers is that many working families who want and need to purchase child care services cannot afford these services; and when working families cannot afford to purchase such services there are both immediate and long-range costs borne by the economy as well as by families and children.

Costs of Unaffordable Care

The following statement by a parent summarizes some of these costs borne by families when they cannot afford child care:[27]

> To decrease the expenses for child care, I work a p.m. shift and my husband works a day shift. I drop the children off at 2:30 p.m. and he picks them up at 5:30 p.m. I am half asleep when he leaves before seven in the morning and he is asleep when I return a little past midnight. This is a terrible way to live, but we cannot afford to spend $400 per month for child care.

The human and financial costs caused by parents who cannot afford child care can also be significant and have both short and long-range impacts.

The most striking and direct cost to government results when parents who cannot afford care either quit work or do not go to work in the first place. For example, among families below the poverty line, 56% said that it did not pay to work if they had to pay someone to take care of their children.[16] Thus, unaffordable care has a direct impact upon welfare costs as well as on the family's ability to support government through the payment of sales, property, income, and social security taxes which could significantly offset the cost of their child care subsidies.[3,5,13] A more subtle cost to government occurs when parents who benefit from a fully subsidized child care program are not offered a sliding fee program once they become ineligible for the full subsidy. Faced with the full cost of care because of a relatively small increase in salary, parents have strong economic incentives to limit their incomes and maintain the full subsidy even when they could afford to pay part of their child care costs.

To the extent that parents place their children in inadequate arrangements, various financial and human costs are imposed upon employers and families. Employers absorb costs such as work interruptions, absenteeism, and employee turnover. Parents live and work under increased levels of stress and guilt, and children are exposed to increased risks to their health, saftey, and development.

However, the ultimate cost of unaffordable child care will be borne by our aging society three and four decades into the future; the failure to meet the needs of today's children will limit the potential of tomorrow's adults to support the social and economic institutions upon which larger and larger numbers of older Americans will be dependent.

Extent of the Affordability Problem

One-quarter of the working families in the nation have incomes which would indicate that they cannot afford anything more than a nominal payment for child care *if they have to purchase their care.* Of the 14.3 million working families, 24% have incomes below the U.S. Bureau of Labor Statistics' lower family budget.[35,36,41] The BLS's lower budget is chosen as a threshold below which families cannot afford substantial payments for child care since it represents an income level (a) requiring "frugal and careful management, leaving little room for choice in achieving what Americans regard as an acceptable standard of living,"[43] and (b) assumes no expenditures for child care. The BLS budget shows the cost of a hypothetical list of goods and services which describe a "lower standard of living" for an urban family of four: a husband employed full time, a nonworking wife, and two schoolage children. In 1979, 90% of the budget went for food ($75 per week), housing ($201 per month), transportation, clothing, medical care, and taxes; all other family expenses had to be paid from the remaining 10% of the budget.[36] In comparing the incomes of working families at various levels before and after a hypothetical $4,000 child care expenditure, the impact on child care expense can be better understood (see Table 18-3).

As the incomes of working families increase over the threshold level of the BLS's lower family budget, they can afford to make more substantial payments toward the cost of purchased child care. However, depending upon the cost, the point at which a family can afford the full cost of child care will vary; for example, a family with $1,200 in expenses for the part-time care of a school-age child can afford the full cost at a lesser income level than can a family with

Table 18-3   Effect of Child Care Expense Upon the Income of Working
             Families at Different Income Levels

Income Levels	Before Expense	After Expense	Percentage Reduction
At Median Incomes[a]			
Single-Parent, Mother	$ 8,500	$ 4,500	47%
Single-Parent, Father	16,000	12,000	25
Two-Parent	21,800	17,800	18
At BLS Family Budget Incomes[b]			
Lower	12,600	8,600	32
Intermediate	20,600	16,500	19
Higher	30,300	26,300	13
At Poverty Income[c]	6,700	2,700	60

NOTE: Child care expense of $4,000 represents average cost of full-time center care
for two children between the ages of 3 and 5 years old.[17]
[a] Johnson.[6] 1978 incomes for working families.
[b] USDL.[36] Autumn 1979 incomes for an urban family of four with the husband
working.
[c] 1979 income for an urban family of four persons.

$4,000 in expenses for the full-time care of two preschool children.
Thus at income levels over the BLS threshold, some families still
cannot afford the full cost of care.

Federal Programs and Their Shortcomings

Federal child care policies have been based on the general assumption that working families should arrange and pay for the care their
children need. However, during the past fifty years the federal government has also recognized that specific types of child care supports were necessary. For example, the Work Project Administration
(WPA) sponsored day nurseries in the thirties to provide both child
care for working parents and jobs for the unemployed; during World
War II the Lanham Act was used to fund child care services for
children because their mothers were needed in the labor force; and
more recently the Social Security Act was used to provide child
care in order that welfare families could participate in job training
and seek employment.[17]

   While there are several programs that currently address the issue
of child care, only four major programs focus on working families
and provide substantial benefits. These programs are reviewed here,
with detailed attention to the tax credit and Title XX programs
which provide four-fifths of the child care benefits to working
families.

   Child and Dependent Care Tax Credit.   Section 214 of the Internal Revenue Code of 1954 authorized a very limited child and

disabled dependent care deduction for gainful employment. The provisions included an itemized deduction for the care of (a) children under the age of 12 years if the working parent was a widow, widower, divorcee, or in a two-parent working household with an income of $4,500 or less where the deduction was phased out at $5,100, (b) the incapacitated spouse of a working mother, and (c) dependents who were unable to care for themselves because of a mental or physical incapacity.[19] A major revision of the deduction took place in the Revenue Act of 1971 when the income limit was increased to $18,000 and the maximum deduction was phased out at $27,600. Single and married working parents were treated the same with regard to eligibility and income limit, and household as well as dependent care expenses were allowable. The code was amended again in 1975 to increase the income limit to $35,000 and the maximum deduction was phased out at $44,600.[19]

Although there were various attempts made to amend the deduction and make it a refundable credit during the 1974–76 period, the end result was to include in the Tax Reform Act of 1976 a new Section 44A of the Internal Revenue Code which provided a non-refundable credit equal to 20% of dependent care expenses. The bill set the expense limits at $2,000 for one and $4,000 for two or more children, removed the income limit, included married couples where one was a full-time student, and included other specific provisions.[19] Benefits provided under the tax credit equaled $792 million and went to 3.8 million families in 1979.[40] Projected benefits for 1982 are $1,175 million.[2]

The tax credit has historically served dual purposes: (a) recognition of child care expenses as a "cost of earning income" and, therefore, comparable to an employee's business expense[24,25] and (b) recognition of the "financial problems" faced by certain families (for example, widows and divorced mothers, low-income families) who must provide care for dependents if they are to work.[24] While the 1976 amendments intended to address both purposes, the benefit has greatly favored families using the provision as a credit for employment expenses over those using it to make child care more affordable. For example, 83% of the 1978 benefits went to families earning over $12,000; but only 75% of working families earn more than $12,000, and most of these families can afford child care.[39,41] In order for the tax credit to provide more benefits for those who cannot afford child care, the credit would have to be adjusted to provide lower-income families with increased benefits, provide those benefits on a timely basis, and phase the benefits down as income increases.

Title XX Social Services Program. Since the fifties, the federal government has made matching grants to states for social services under the Social Security Act, but the grants did not become a major source of social service funding until after 1968 when the Congress required the states to offer child care to welfare clients in work and training programs. By 1972 state expenditures had increased so dramatically that Congress placed a $2.5 billion ceiling on social service expenditures under Titles IVA and VI of the Social Security Act.[30]

The Social Services Amendment of 1974 amended the Social Security Act by adding a new Title XX which authorized 75% matching grants (with certain exceptions) to states for social services, including child care. Services could be provided without charge to lower-income persons and certain eligible groups and on a sliding fee basis to moderate-income persons. States were given the authority to decide which services would be provided and in what amounts. If child care was provided, facilities had to meet standards established by the Secretary of Health and Human Services (currently delayed by legislation), and care could be provided by the state or individually purchased.

Child care benefits for working parents (that is, those employed or in job training) under Title XX amounted to $596 million and reached an average of 464 thousand children in 357 thousand families in 1978; benefits for working and nonworking families equaled $709 million.[33] In 1982 it is estimated that the working and nonworking benefits will amount to $916 million and serve 467 thousand families.[1] (Legislation has been proposed to include Title XX in a larger social service block grant and reduce the funding by 25%.)

While it is possible that the benefit from Title XX can make child care affordable for lower-income as well as middle-income families who cannot afford to pay the full cost of care, the availability and adequacy of the benefit varies widely from state to state and even within individual states. For example, in 1979 one state provided no Title XX child care benefit, and expenditures in other states ranged from 5% to 50% of the Title XX funds; two states excluded the working poor, non-AFDC families; the cut-off points for services ranged from 40% (poverty level) to 115% of state median income; half the states had cut-off points below the U.S. Bureau of Labor Statistics' lower family budget level; many states did not have any sliding fee provision.[31,32,33] Furthermore, one of the major limitations of the program results from the federal ceiling on Title XX expenditures. The number of families served has not increased as need and demand have increased, and is actually expected to decrease between 1978 and 1982.[1,33]

Other Programs.   Under Title IV A and C of the Social Security Act, child care benefits are provided for Work Incentive (WIN) program participants and employed recipients of Aid to Families with Dependent Children (AFDC) who receive a child care expense deduction from actual earned income before determining benefits, thus paying for child care with AFDC funds. Estimated 1977 expenditures under Title IV A and C were $140 million for 230 thousand recipients.[28]

The Child Care Food Program authorized by the National School Lunch and Child Nutrition Act of 1966 provided reimbursement for meals which are served to eligible children and which meet U.S. Department of Agriculture nutritional requirements. The program provided $120 million in benefits and served 580 thousand children in 1977.[28] The projected 1982 benefit is $336 million.[1]

Framework for Analysis

The objective of this analysis is to identify effective, reasonable, and economical approaches that will make child care affordable for all working families. Specifically, the analysis is concerned with working families who want and need to purchase child care services but cannot afford the full cost of care.

Three approaches will be examined to determine their impacts upon the affordability objective in 1982. The analytic framework includes a working definition of needed benefit, criteria against which each approach can be evaluated, and impact models for use in describing the results of the analysis.

Needed Benefit

The first element of the analytic framework is a working definition of needed benefit—the child care benefit needed to make care affordable for working families. As discussed earlier the BLS's lower family budget is an income below which a family needs 90% of its income for basic necessities excluding child care, and this income is estimated to be about $15,000 in 1982. As income rises above this threshold a family can pay an increasing portion of its child care expense; however it is recognized that this expense is similar to an employee's business expense and, therefore, should continue to be discounted as in the current 20% tax credit.

For purposes of this analysis, then, needed benefit is defined as follows:

1. If a family's income is $15,000 or below, the needed benefit equals 100% of the expense for care.

2. If a family's income is over $15,000, the needed benefit equals the larger of either (a) 100% of the expense for care reduced by an amount equal to half the added, net income over $15,000 (that

is, income over $15,000 less federal income and social security taxes on the income over $15,000) and represented by the equation: $N = E - \{[(Y - y) - (T - t)]/2\}$, where N is the needed benefit, Y is the adjusted gross income, y is $15,000, T is the federal income and social security taxes on Y, and t is the taxes on y; or (b) 20% of the expense for care.

Criteria

The following criteria will be used to evaluate the alternative approaches for making child care affordable for working families.

1. The benefit should equal that needed by a lower-income family.
2. The benefit should equal that needed by a middle- or higher-income family.
3. The benefit should be available to every working family needing it.
4. The benefit should be easily accessible.
5. The benefit should be provided when it is needed.
6. The program should be simple and inexpensive to administer.
7. The program cost should be reasonable in relation to projected budget expenditures for current programs.
8. The spillover costs (costs resulting from the program but not reflected in the program cost) should be minimal.

Impact Models

The analysis will be implemented using two impact models. These models provide a method for examining the results from each approach in relation to an individual family and in the aggregate.

Family Impact Model. The family impact model examines the results of each approach in relation to the impacts of affordability criteria items 1 through 5 on individual families in 1982.

For purposes of analysis, a hypothetical family composed of two working parents and two children is examined at two different child care costs (the average annual expense of $1,300 in 1982 and a full-time annual cost of $4,000) and at various annual adjusted gross income levels (the lower-income threshold of $15,000 and selected levels up to $45,000). For each situation the benefit needed by the family is computed, and the percentage of needed benefit provided by each approach is determined. Needed benefit is computed using the 1982 social security tax rate on the total family income and the 1980 income tax provisions, assuming a joint return, no itemized deductions, and no credits other than child care.[38] This model provides a microview of the degree to which each approach achieves certain criteria.

Aggregate Impact Model. The aggregate impact model examines the results of each approach in relation to impacts of affordability criteria items 6 through 8 on all families in 1982.

The cost results are categorized and reported by three annual adjusted gross income ranges: lower-income (under $15,000), middle-income ($15,000 through $35,000), and higher-income (over $35,000). The data base for the model is as follows: the number of participating families (before considering elasticity) is the same as those projected for the 20% tax credit (4.6 million; calculated from the forecasted cost[1] divided by the average family expense) and work-related Title XX program (0.3 million; calculated from projected work and nonwork-related costs[2] and the 1978 ratio of such costs[34]); the average family child care expense is the average for the 20% tax credit (the 1978 average expense increased by 7% per year) or work-related Title XX program (the projected cost divided by the projected participants). The distribution of incomes of participating families (before considering elasticity) for the 20% tax credit is assumed to be the same as in 1978,[39] using $12,000 as the lower-income threshold level. The elasticity of demand for each of the alternative approaches is estimated from two studies which identified effective demand curves.[16,41] (A third study[14] of elasticity of demand was found, but its results were not considered useful for the ranges found in this analysis.) No information on the elasticity of supply was identified; however, an estimated elasticity is used based upon judgements about how the supply would respond to increased demand. It is assumed that each approach is fully implemented; therefore, no allowance is made for reduced costs usually experienced during the start-up phase of an expanded program.

Analysis of Approaches

In selecting approaches for analysis, consideration was limited to those being actively discussed in the child care field. Three approaches have been selected: first, a targeted Title XX child care program supplemented by the current tax credit; second, a 50/20% tax credit supplemented by the current Title XX program; and third, a 90/20% tax credit supplemented by the current Title XX program. The first approach alters the current Title XX program and structures, while the second and third approaches alter the current child and dependent care tax credit. All three approaches can be described as creating a "sliding" benefit.

Each approach is examined and compared in relation to the affordability criteria at the one-family and aggregate levels in order to assess the relative desirability of the approach.

Description of Approaches: Alternative 1

The first approach incorporates a targeted Title XX child care program supplemented by the current 20% child and dependent care tax credit.

Targeted Title XX Child Care Program. This program, which would require an amendment to the Social Security Act, provides child care benefits for working families under the following circumstances:

1. If a family's income is $15,000 or below, the benefit equals 100% of the expense for care.
2. If a family's income is between $15,000 and $25,000, the benefit equals 100% of the expense for care reduced at a rate equal to $600 for each $1,000 of income over $15,000 and represented by the equation $B_1 = E - [(Y - y)/1,000 \times \$600]$, where B_1 is the benefit from the program.
2. If a family's income is over $25,000, there is no benefit.

20% Child and Dependent Care Tax Credit. The current credit, equal to 20% of the expense for child care, supplements the targeted Title XX program by providing a benefit when the credit's benefit equals or is more than the targeted Title XX benefit.

Alternative 1 has been selected because the targeted Title XX program represents a direct benefit mode that can be implemented through existing structures, and the combination of the two programs offers the possibility of a comprehensive program designed to meet the affordability criteria. The $15,000 and $25,000 Title XX limits are equivalent to 65% and 115% of the 1982 national median income level established for Title XX by the U.S. Department of Health and Human Services. The approach assumes that the targeted Title XX child care grants will be equal to 100% of the cost and that the program will be fully funded.

Description of Approaches: Alternative 2

The second approach uses a 50/20% tax credit supplemented by the current Title XX program.

50/20% Child and Dependent Care Tax Credit. This credit would require an amendment to the Internal Revenue Code in order to create a maximum/minimum, refundable credit toward child care expenses as follows:

1. If a family's income is $15,000 or below, the benefit equals 50% of the expense for care.
2. If a family's income is between $15,000 and $45,000, the benefit equals a percentage equal to 50%, reduced at a rate of 1 percentage point for each $1,000 of income over $15,000, of the expense for child care. This provision is represented by the equation $B_2 = \{.5 - [(Y - y)/1{,}000 \times .01]\} \times E$, where B_2 is the benefit from the credit.
3. If a family's income is over $45,000, the benefit equals 20% of the expense for child care.

Title XX Social Services Program. The current Title XX program supplements the 50/20% tax credit. It is used when the credit provides a benefit less than the Title XX benefits but only to the extent the Title XX program is available in the states.

Alternative 2 has been selected because the 50/20% tax credit component is similar to a bill (H.R. 1894) introduced into the 97th Congress; the tax credit and Title XX programs are considered a comprehensive program. The alternative assumes that there will be no change in budgeted Title XX funds and expected state child care expenditure levels.

Description of Approaches: Alternative 3

The third approach includes a 90/20% tax credit supplemented by the current Title XX program.

90/20% Child and Dependent Care Tax Credit. This credit, through an amendment in the Internal Revenue Code, provides a maximum/minimum, refundable credit toward child care expenses as well as an advance payment of the refundable portion of the credit. Its provisions are as follows:

1. If a family's income is $15,000 or below, the benefit equals 90% of the expense for care.
2. If a family's income is over $15,000, the benefit equals the larger of either (a) 90% of the expense for care reduced at a rate equal to $200 for each $1,000 of income over $15,000 and represented by the equation $B_3 = (.9 \times E) - [(Y - y)/1{,}000 \times \$200]$, where B_3 is the benefit from the credit; or (b) 20% of the expense for care.

Title XX Social Services Program. The current Title XX program supplements the 90/20% tax credit by providing a benefit when the credit is less than the Title XX benefit in the state, recognizing that Title XX child care benefits and availability of funds are different in each state.

Alternative 3 has been selected because the 90/20% tax credit is similar to a mode being considered for introduction in the U.S. Senate. It is assumed that the Title XX program will continue as budgeted and that states will continue to spend the same portion of their funds for child care.

Comparison of Approaches

Using the one-family and aggregate impact models, the three approaches, in addition to the current 20% tax credit and Title XX program, are examined and compared to the affordability criteria. The results are summarized in Tables 18-4 and 18-5.

The current programs, the 20% tax credit and Title XX program, are used as a base for purposes of this comparison. With regard to the three approaches, the results of the analysis are as follows:

Alternative 1, which proposes a targeted Title XX child care program supplemented by the current 20% tax credit, makes child care affordable to lower- and higher-income families. However, the approach only makes care more affordable for most middle-income families, involves numerous barriers to participation, is the most complex and expensive to administer, and is the most costly approach.

Alternative 2, which proposes a 50/20% child and dependent care tax credit supplemented by the current Title XX program, makes child care affordable for most middle- and higher-income families and the cost of the approach is reasonable. However, the approach only makes care more affordable for lower-income families and those families at the bottom of the middle-income range and provides a very large over-benefit to most middle- and some higher-income families.

Alternative 3, which proposes a 90/20% child and dependent care tax credit supplemented by the current Title XX program, makes care substantially affordable for lower-income families and affordable for middle- and higher-income families and the cost of the approach is reasonable. However, the approach provides a large over-benefit to a limited number of middle-income families and involves a somewhat more complex administrative process in that employers are required to make an advance payment of the refundable portion of the credit.

A summary observation is that Alternative 3 is the most desirable of the three approaches because it is the most effective approach given its relatively simple administrative procedures and moderate cost. However, each of the approaches could be improved in terms of the affordability criteria used in the analysis. For example, the targeted Title XX child care program could use a smaller marginal rate of reduction, although this would result in a sudden drop in benefit at the end of the phase-down range if the expense for child care was relatively high; it could use a voucher system which may reduce the administrative complexity and place more reliance upon competitive market forces to control costs. The 50/20% tax credit could increase its maximum credit to 90% or 100% of the expense for care and increase its marginal rate of reduction; or it could be coordinated with a fully funded but altered Title XX program which assumes that a working family would claim a portion of its benefit under the 50/20% tax credit and the remainder under the altered Title XX program, although this would be very difficult to administer and would leave many gaps in benefits. The 90/20% tax credit could be revised to increase the marginal rate of reduction to $300 per $1,000 of additional income and to exclude smaller employers from the complex advance payment procedures.

It should also be observed that the 50/20% tax credit costs the same as the 90/20% tax credit even though the 50/20% tax credit provides a benefit substantially less than that needed by lower-income families and those families at the bottom of the middle-income range. This result is a function of the amount selected for the lower-income threshold and the methods used to reduce the credits from their maximum to the minimum of 20%. If the lower-income threshold is reduced, the number of families claiming the maximum benefit will be fewer and the 90/20% tax credit will cost less than the 50/20% tax credit; for example, at a $10,000 level, the cost of the 50/20% tax credit will be $2.7 billion compared to $2.1 billion for the 90/20% tax credit. If the lower-income threshold is increased, the 50/20% tax credit will cost less than the 90/20% tax credit. The marginal rate of reduction in the two tax credits, at the average child care expense level of $1,300 a year, is $13 per $1,000 of additional income for the 50/20% tax credit and $200 per $1,000 of additional income for the 90/20% credit. While both reduction methods decrease the maximum credit at a rate lower than the $369 per $1,000 of additional income used in computing the needed benefit for the hypothetical family of four, the 50/20% tax credit's reduction method is at such a low rate that it provides an extremely high over-benefit to an extremely large number of middle- and higher-income families. This over-benefit is so large that it, in effect, cancels the under-benefit the 50/20% tax credit provides to lower-income families and those families at the bottom of the middle-income range.

While the analysis does not explicitly address the political feasibility of the three alternatives, it is apparent that the 50/20% tax credit in Alternative 2 will be the most attractive of the three approaches even though it does not effectively target its benefit or achieve the affordability objective. The attractiveness of the 50/20%

Table 18-4 Comparison of Benefit Needed by a Hypothetical Family and Provided by Approaches at Different Family Income and Child Care Expense Levels

Family Income Level	Amount Needed by Expense Level		Percentage Provided								
			Current[a] by Expense Level		Alternative 1[b] by Expense Level		Alternative 2[a] by Expense Level		Alternative 3[a] by Expense Level	
	$1300	$4000	$1300	$4000	$1300	$4000	$1300	$4000	$1300	$4000
≤$15,000	$1300	$4000	20%[c,e]	20%[c,e]	100%	100%	50%[d]	50%[d]	90%	90%
$16,000	924	3624	28	22	76	94	69	54[d]	105	94
$17,000	563	3263	46	25	46[e]	86	111	59[d]	137	98
$18,000	260[e]	2901	100	28	100	76	235	65[d]	219	103
$19,000	260	2539	100	32	100	63	230	72	142	110
$20,000	260	2177	100	37	100	46	225	83	100[e]	119
$21,000	260	1830	100	44	100	44[e]	220	96	100	131
$22,000	260	1483	100	54	100	54	215	116	100	148
$23,000	260	1137	100	70	100	70	210	148	100	176
$24,000	260	800[e]	100	100	100	100	205	205	100	225
$25,000	260	800	100	100	100	100	200	200	100	200
$30,000	260	800	100	100	100	100	175	175	100	100[e]
$35,000	260	800	100	100	100	100	150	150	100	100
$40,000	260	800	100	100	100	100	125	125	100	100
≥$45,000	260	800	100	100	100	100	100[e]	100[e]	100	100
Marginal Rate of Reduction[f]	$369	$358	$0	$0	$600	$600	$13	$40	$200	$200

[a] The benefit equaled that provided by the tax credit. Some families would have been eligible for a higher benefit under the Title XX program; however, because the Title XX benefit was different in each state and there was a general shortage of funds, the Title XX benefit was not used.

[b] The benefit equaled that provided by the targeted Title XX program until the benefits fell below 20% of the expense; then, the 20% tax credit was used.

^c The benefit was less than shown when the tax credit exceeded the income tax liability because the credit was nonrefundable. At the $1300 expense level, a family with an income below $9600 received less than the full benefit; at the $4000 expense level, a family with an income below $12,600 received less than a full benefit.

^d A portion of the benefit was not available until the annual income tax return was filed because the portion of the credit which exceeded the income taxes liability withheld by the employer was not paid in advance.

^e The minimum of 20% of expense was reached at this level of income.

^f The marginal rate of reduction was the reduction in the benefit for each $1000 of additional income in the range preceeding the income level (e) at which the minimum benefit was reached. (The rate for the needed benefit ranged from $376 to $346 due to changes in the income tax rate.)

Table 18-5 Comparison of Approaches by Criteria

Criteria	Current	Alternative 1	Alternative 2	Alternative 3
1. Benefit equals benefit needed by lower-income family.	*Credit*: only 20% of need; less if credit exceeds tax liability.	*Credit*: only 20% of need.	*Credit*: only 50% of need.	*Credit*: only 90% of need.
2. Benefit equals benefit needed by middle- and higher-income family.	*XX*: varying % of need. *Credit*: only 20% of need at bottom of income range; but increases to 100% of need at higher incomes.	*XX*: 100% of need. *Credit*: (same as Current Program).	*XX*: varying % of need. *Credit*: only 50% of need at bottom of income range; 200% of need at $25,000; but decreases to 100% of need at $45,000, the end of the phase-down range.	*XX*: varying % of need. *Credit*: averages about 140% of need over phase-down range; but 100% of need after phase-down.
	XX: usually 0%.	*XX*: 100% of need at bottom of income range; but less than half as benefit phases down; 0% of need after phase down.	*XX*: usually 0%.	*XX*: usually 0%.
3. Benefit available to every working family needing it.	*Credit*: all; except single parents enrolled in an education program leading to employment and working parents without a net earned income.	*Credit*: (see Current Program).	*Credit*: (see Current Program).	*Credit*: (see Current Program).

Table 18-5 Comparison of Approaches by Criteria (continued)

Criteria	Current	Alternative 1	Alternative 2	Alternative 3
4. Benefit easily accessible.	XX: only some; generally inadequate funding and varying eligibility standards.	XX: all.	XX: (see Current Program).	XX: (see Current Program).
	Credit: requires only filing new W-4 form with employer and/or 1040 tax return with 2441 form.	*Credit*: (see Current Program).	*Credit*: (see Current Program).	*Credit*: (see Current Program) and filing advance payment form with employer if advance requested.
	XX: barriers vary but generally include inadequate notice, complex application procedures, loss of privacy, welfare stigma, and limited choice of provider.	XX: (see Current Program).	XX: (see Current Program).	XX: (see Current Program).
5. Benefit provided when needed.	*Credit*: yes; except for some lower-income families.	*Credit*: (see Current Program).	*Credit*: yes; except for most lower-income and some middle-income families at bottom of range:	*Credit*: yes.
	XX: yes.	XX: yes.	XX: yes.	XX: yes.

Table 18-5 Comparison of Approaches by Criteria (continued)

Criteria	Current	Alternative 1	Alternative 2	Alternative 3
		Aggregate Impact		
6. Program simple and inexpensive to administer.	*Credit:* involves one federal agency and employers; utilizes IRS regulations, instructions, and forms; requires adjustment of withheld taxes and processing of forms with tax returns. XX: involves one federal agency, one or more state and local agencies, and providers; utilizes HHS, state and local regulations, procedures, standards for service, and forms; requires plans, reports, evaluations, intake, monitoring payments, collections, etc.	*Credit:* (see Current Program). XX: (see Current Program).	*Credit:* (see Current Program). XX: (see Current Program).	*Credit:* (see Current Program) and processing and payment of advance payments. XX: (see Current Program).
7. Cost reasonable in relation to projected expenditures for cur-	*Credit:* base cost;[a] $0.2 = Lower $0.8 = Middle	*Credit:* 8% decrease;[b] $0.0 = Lower $0.8 = Middle	*Credit:* 158% increase;[e] $0.6 = Lower $2.2 = Middle	*Credit:* 158% increase;[d] $1.2 = Lower $1.6 = Middle

Table 18-5 Comparison of Approaches by Criteria (continued)

Criteria	Current	Alternative 1	Alternative 2	Alternative 3
rent programs (amounts in billions by income ranges; number of families in millions).	$0.2 = Higher $1.2 = 4.6 Families.	$0.3 = Higher $1.1 = 3.5 Families.	$0.3 = Higher $3.1 = 5.2 Families.	$0.3 = Higher $3.1 = 5.0 Families.
	XX: base cost;[a] $0.7 = Lower $0.1 = Middle $0.0 = Higher $0.8 = 0.3 Families. *Total:* base cost; $2.0 = 4.9 Families.	XX: 413% increase;[b] $3.3 = Lower $0.9 = Middle $0.0 = Higher $4.1 = 1.8 Families. *Total:* 160% increase; $5.2 = 5.3 Families.	XX: 0% change;[c] $0.7 = Lower $0.1 = Middle $0.0 = Higher $0.8 = 0.3 Families. *Total:* 95% increase; $3.9 = 5.5 Families.	XX: 0% change;[d] $0.7 = Lower $0.1 = Middle $0.0 = Higher $0.8 = 0.3 Families. *Total:* 95% increase; $3.9 = 5.3 Families.
	Credit: none.	*Credit:* none.	*Credit:* none.	*Credit:* employers will have to process advance payments of credit.
8. Spillover cost minimal.	XX: none.	XX: states will have increased need for developing approved services.	XX: none.	XX: none.

[a] EOP [1,2] and USDHHS.[33]

[b] EOP[1] Rodes and Moore,[16] UM,[41] USDHHS,[33] and USIRS.[39] The 20% tax credit is less than the budget projection because those families benefiting more from the targeted Title XX program will use that program. The targeted Title XX program has been calculated using an estimated elasticity of demand ranging between .36 and .41. The elasticity of supply is assumed to be .94.

[c] Ibid. The credit has been calculated using an estimated elasticity of demand ranging from .50 to .63 and an assumed elasticity of supply of .86. The Title XX program is as projected in the budget.

[d] Ibid. The credit has been calculated using an estimated elasticity of demand ranging from .38 to .52 and an assumed elasticity of supply of .94; the cost for the middle-income range has been adjusted upward by 22% to account for an estimated understatement of cost resulting from the use of the average expense.

tax credit results from its reasonable cost and lack of objectionable features. On the other hand the 90/20% tax credit, which has an equal cost but largely achieves the affordability objective, breaks the psychological barrier of a 50% maximum tax credit; and the targeted Title XX child care program is out of step with the current philosophy of reducing social service spending and eliminating national priority services programs. However, it still appears appropriate to focus on Alternative 3 and the 90/20% tax credit as the cornerstone of a federal policy for making child care affordable since its overall desirability is significantly greater than the other approaches.

Summary

When the three approaches for making child care affordable are examined and compared in relation to the eight criteria, the analysis concludes that the 90/20% child and dependent care tax credit, supplemented by the current Title XX program, is the most effective, reasonable, and economical approach for making child care affordable for all working families.

The 90/20% tax credit approach should be revised in light of this analysis. In its revised form it should propose an amended Section 44A of the Internal Revenue Code that will provide a 90% credit against the child care expenses of lower-income families, reduce that credit by a rate equal to $300 for each $1,000 of income over the lower-income level, retain the current 20% credit against expenses as a minimum, make the credit refundable, and provide an advance payment of the refundable portion of the credit. This tax credit should serve as the cornerstone for federal initiatives making child and dependent care affordable for all working families.

However, it must be recognized that the 90/20% tax credit will not solve all child care problems. The Title XX program will still be needed for certain working (for example, families in transition to employment) and nonworking families, and state and private funding will be needed to fill the inevitable gaps resulting from emergency, hardship, and other similar circumstances. Continued state, private, and limited federal resources will be needed to stimulate an increase in the supply of child care, improve information and referral services, maintain consumer protection services, train caregivers, etc.

In the final analysis one must conclude that child care is a necessity in an aging society that will become increasingly more dependent upon a relatively smaller labor force and in an economy that finds most of its mothers entering the out-of-home labor force as a matter of financial survival—it is a necessity for America's economy, its families, and its children. The 90/20% child and dependent care tax credit, supplemented by the existing Title XX social services program, is the most effective, reasonable, and economical approach for resolving the dilemma of how to make child care affordable for all working families during the decade of the eighties and thereafter.

References

1. Executive Office of The President. 1981. *Budget of the United States, Fiscal Year 1982. Appendix.* U.S. Government Printing Office, Washington, D.C.
2. Executive Office of The President. 1981. *Special Analysis. Budget of the United States Government, Fiscal Year 1982.* U.S. Government Printing Office, Washington, D.C.
3. Freis, R. and Miller, M. 1980. *The Economic Impact of Subsidized Child Care: An Economic Analysis of Valley Child Care from November, 1976 to June, 1979.* Freis and Miller Associates, Livermore, California. (ERIC Document Reproduction Service No. ED 188 787). (Abstract).
4. Grossman, A.S. 1981. "Working mothers and their children." *Monthly Labor Review* 104(5):49–54.
5. Hosni, D. 1979. *An Economic Analysis of Child Care Support to Low-Income Mothers.* University of Central Florida, Orlando, Florida.
6. Johnson, B. 1981. *Marital and Family Characteristics of the Labor Force, March 1979.* Special Labor Force Report, 237. U.S. Government Printing Office, Washington, D.C.
7. Keating, K. 1980. "Is government helping or hurting American families?" *Better Homes and Gardens* (Sept.): 24.
8. Minnesota Department of Public Welfare. 1980. *Trends in Day Care Services: October 1979.* Author, St. Paul, Minnesota.
9. Moore, K. and Hofferth, S. 1979. "Women and their children." In *The Subtle Revolution: Women at Work*, R. Smith, ed. The Urban Institute, Washington, D.C.
10. Moore, J. 1980. "Parent Decisions on the Use of Day Care and Early Education Services: An Analysis of Amount Used and Type Chosen." Doctoral dissertation, The Catholic University of America.
11. Pifer, A. 1976. *Women Working: Toward a New Society.* Carnegie Corporation of New York, New York.
12. Pifer, A. 1978. *Perceptions of Childhood and Youth.* Carnegie Corporation of New York, New York.
13. Ramsey County Child Care Council. 1978. *An Evaluation of the Pilot Child Care Sliding Fee Program in Ramsey County.* Author, St. Paul, Minnesota. (ERIC Document Reproduction Service No. ED 157–609).
14. Robin, P. and Spiegelman, R. 1978. "An econometric model of the demand for child care." *Economic Inquiry* XVI(1):83–94.
15. Rodes, T. and Moore, J. 1976. *National Childcare Consumer Study: 1975*, Volume II. Unco, Incorporated, Washington, D.C.

16. Rodes, T. and Moore, J. 1976. *National Childcare Consumer Study: 1975*, Volume III. Unco, Incorporated, Washington, D.C.

17. Ruopp, R. et al. 1979. *Children at the Center.* Abt Associates, Cambridge, Massachusetts.

18. Smith, R. 1979. "The movement of women into the labor force." In *The Subtle Revolution: Women at Work*, R. Smith, ed. The Urban Institute, Washington, D.C.

19. Talley, L. 1980. *Income Tax Treatment of Dependent-Care Expenses: A Legislative History.* The Library of Congress, Congressional Research Service, Washington, D.C.

20. U.S. Bureau of The Census. 1976. *Daytime Care of Children: October 1974 and February 1975.* Current Population Series, P-20(298). U.S. Government Printing Office, Washington, D.C.

21. U.S. Bureau of The Census. 1979. *Illustrative Projection of State Populations by Age, Race, and Sex: 1975 to 2000.* Current Population Reports, Series P-25(796). U.S. Government Printing Office, Washington, D.C.

22. U.S. Bureau of The Census. 1980. *A Statistical Portrait of Women in the United States: 1978.* Current Population Reports, Series P-23(100). U.S. Government Printing Office, Washington, D.C.

23. U.S. Bureau of The Census. 1980. *Household and Family Characteristics: March 1979.* Current Population Reports, Series P-20(352). U.S. Government Printing Office, Washington, D.C.

24. U.S. Bureau of The Census. 1980. *Population Profile of the United States: 1979.* Current Population Reports, Series P-20(350). U.S. Government Printing Office, Washington, D.C.

25. U.S. Congress, House, Committee on Ways and Means. 1954. *Internal Revenue Code of 1954, Report to Accompany H.R.8300* (83rd Congress, 2nd Session, House, Report No. 1337). U.S. Government Printing Office, Washington, D.C.

26. U.S. Congress, Joint Committee on Taxation. 1976. *General Explanation of the Tax Reform Act of 1976.* (H.R.10612, 94th Congress, P.L.94–455). U.S. Government Printing Office, Washington, D.C.

27. U.S. Congress, Senate. 1978. *Congressional Record* 124(135):S14388.

28. U.S. Congressional Budget Office. 1978. *Childcare and Preschool: Options for Federal Support.* U.S. Government Printing Office, Washington, D.C.

29. U.S. Department of Commerce. 1980. *Social Indicators III.* U.S. Government Printing Office, Washington, D.C.

30. U.S. Department of Health, Education, and Welfare. 1977. *First Annual Report to Congress on the Title XX Social Service Act.* U.S. Government Printing Office, Washington, D.C.

31. U.S. Department of Health, Education, and Welfare. 1979. *Technical Notes: Summaries and Characteristics of States' Title XX Social Services Plans for Fiscal Year 1979.* Author, Washington, D.C.

32. U.S. Department of Health, Education, and Welfare. 1979. *Title XX National Comprehensive Annual Services Program (CASP) Information.* U.S. Government Printing Office, Washington, D.C.

33. U.S. Department of Health and Human Services. 1980. *Annual Report to*

the Congress on Title XX of the Social Security Act Fiscal Year 1979. U.S. Government Printing Office, Washington, D.C.

34. U.S. Department of Health and Human Services. 1980. *Social Services U.S.A.* U.S. Government Printing Office, Washington, D.C.
35. U.S. Department of Labor. 1980. "Marital and family characteristics of workers, March 1980." *News.* (USDL 80–767). Author, Washington, D.C.
36. U.S. Department of Labor. 1980. "Rise in autumn 1979 family budget marked by transportation and taxes." *Monthly Labor Review* 103(8):29.
37. U.S. Internal Revenue Service. 1979. *Statistics of Income—1976, Individual Income Tax Returns.* U.S. Government Printing Office, Washington, D.C.
38. U.S. Internal Revenue Service. 1980. *Federal Income Tax Forms, 1980.* U.S. Government Printing Office, Washington, D.C.
39. U.S. Internal Revenue Service. 1980. *Statistics on Income, Preliminary—1978, Individual Income Tax Returns.* U.S. Government Printing Office, Washington, D.C.
40. U.S. Internal Revenue Service. 1981. "Individual income tax returns for 1979." (Uncorrected, unpublished data). Author, Washington, D.C.
41. University of Michigan, Institute for Social Research. 1980. Panel study of income dynamics, 1978 total family income by child care expense. (Unpublished data). U.S. Department of Health and Human Services, Washington, D.C.
42. Waldman, E. et al. 1979. "Working mothers in the 1970's: a look at the statistics." *Monthly Labor Review* 102(10):39–49.
43. Watt, H. 1980. "Family budget studies." *Monthly Labor Review* 103(12): 3–9.
44. White House Conference on Families. 1980. *Listening to Families.* U.S. Government Printing Office, Washington, D.C.

Chapter 19

THE PROSPECTS AND DILEMMAS OF CHILD CARE INFORMATION AND REFERRAL

by James A. Levine

At the beginning of the 1970s, a convergence of forces made the establishment of a national day care program seem imminent. To both Democrats and Republicans concerned about "the welfare problem," day care seemed a promising piece of social engineering, an acceptable way to get poor women out to work. To scientists investigating the early years of learning, developmental day care augured—along with Head Start and other early intervention programs—a way to compensate for the effects of what has been broadly termed "disadvantage." And to the rapidly accelerating number of parents with young children who simply had to or wanted to work, some form of day care was essential. Given the commitment of a newly-elected President Nixon to "providing all American children [with] an opportunity for healthful and stimulating development during the first five years of life," and Congressional passage in 1971 of the Comprehensive Child Development Act, the first major federal support of day care services during a peacetime or nondepression economy was literally a presidential penstroke away.

It will probably be a long time before such a scenario is played out again. At the beginning of the 1980s, in a climate of increasing

The research for this article was supported by grants from the Robert Sterling Clark Foundation and the Ford Foundation. For consultation or review, the author thanks Patti Siegel, Gwen Morgan, Mary Rowe, Mary Jo Bane, Sheila Kamerman, Alfred Kahn, and Susan Berresford.

fiscal restraint, a convergence of forces makes the establishment of a national day care program seem remote: right-wing opposition to day care as an intrusion of the state into the family, disagreement among academics about the effects—and even the purposes—of day care, disagreement among policy makers about the need for day care, and disagreement among the child care advocates who helped push legislation through Congress in 1971. As a sign of the times, in January, 1979, Senator Alan Cranston (D-California) introduced a new child care bill (S.4)[31] and withdrew it three weeks later, citing opposition from around the country, opposition from the Carter administration, and, not the least of it, the failure of the child care advocacy community to rally support.

Despite the dim prospects for a national program, day care in America has not spent the past ten years in a Sleeping Beauty state awaiting the kiss of legislation to bring it to life. There has been a substantial expansion of day care during the last decade, and a substantial increase in public funds being spent for that purpose. Between 1970 and 1976, for example, the number of day care centers serving three-to-five-year-olds jumped from 14,000 to 18,300, a thirty percent increase.[7] Under Title XX, federally funded day care for the poor has expanded. The child care tax credit, a mechanism more responsive to middle income families, has been written into law. And both Head Start and kindergarten programs—which many families use in combination with other arrangements for day care purposes—have grown. In effect, the United States has witnessed the expansion over the last decade of what policy analyst Gwen Morgan of Wheelock College refers to as a "purchase-of-service delivery system for day care." It is not the type of federally sponsored system envisioned by proponents of the 1971 legislation, it is not sufficient, and it does not work particularly well. However, it is what we have to build on in the years ahead.

As we head into the 1980s, the challenge for those who would improve day care is to recognize and understand how the current system works—in all its complexity and diversity—and to make it work better. As Harvard's Mary Jo Bane has put it, the policy question of moment is not "whether government should begin to 'interfere' in child-rearing, but whether government should extend or change its participation." (p. 2)[2] For Bane, and for a diverse array of students around the country, that means determining what "mechanism" of government participation is most appropriate and politically feasible.

A number of mechanisms have significant potential, when considered alone or in combination, for making the system work better while preserving its diversity: vouchers, extension of the tax credit, implementation of sliding fee scales, or extension of the Title XX eligibility requirements. This article focuses on one of the most interesting, and least examined in any depth: child care information and referral (I&R).

Put simply, child care information and referral services act as a "broker" to put parents in need of child care in touch with those who provide child care. These services began emerging as a distinct type in the early 1970s when President Nixon's veto of the Child Development Act, limitations on Title IV-A, and state cutbacks in social services dimmed any prospects for rapid expansion of center-based care and made it necessary, in many communities, to explore new approaches to locating and supporting child care. Parent organizers of these new I&R services—such as San Francisco's Childcare Switchboard or the Child Care Resource Center in Cambridge, Massachusetts—were often users of family day care (licensed and unlicensed), playgroups, or other cooperative child care arrangements; many were not eligible for public subsidy, though they worked towards facilitating child care arrangements for all parents. Aside from helping parents find child care, these services typically engage in a wide variety of related activities: they offer technical assistance to start, sustain, or improve child care programs within their communities; they gather data for planning and advocacy purposes; they offer support groups for single parents; and they offer clearinghouses for people seeking jobs in the child care field.

While there are now about sixty of these specialized services in the country, some forty are concentrated in California where they were encouraged by 1976 legislation designed to foster "innovative approaches" to child care.[26,27,28] Another stream of I&R, quite distinct from these specialized services, offers information on a broad range of social or community services, sometimes including child care. These "general" information and referral services often operate from welfare departments, United Way agencies, and other community agencies. Though specialized and general approaches may not be mutually exclusive and often address different policy issues, they are often in competition at the local level, a point that will be taken up later.

From a policy perspective, child care information and referral is interesting because it may improve the functioning of the child care market in a number of ways: matching supply and demand; maximizing consumer choice; and providing data about patterns of supply and demand that can be used for planning at the community level and aggregated for state or national purposes.

This chapter explores the current interest in child care information and referral (in the context of the larger debate about child care), examines earlier interest in this type of service by policymakers, and points both to its promise and to some of the practical problems that will have to be resolved in order for it to become a central element in American day care policy.

Background: The Changing Day Care Climate

As a background for discussing child care information and referral as a specific instrument of social policy, it may be useful to look, albeit briefly and broadly, at how thinking about child care emerged over the last decade. If the 1970s did not give rise to the "national debate" that President Nixon called for in vetoing the Child Development Act, it was a decade of reassessment. More money was spent than ever before to study the effects of day care on children, to examine federal licensing requirements, to create national advisory panels and commissions that would rethink the day care problem and, we hoped, give us a new sense of direction. At the risk of oversimplifying, three aspects of that reassessment—and trends of political life—help explain why I&R is likely to increase in importance during the 1980s: (1) the waning of support for a national program and the new emphasis on "making the system work better;" (2) an expanded notion of what the child care system includes, of its diversity; and (3) an increasing emphasis on family and parental choice.

Making the System Work

Despite Jimmy Carter's campaign pledge to "recommend legislation" to support a "national child care program," the interest of the federal government shifted under his administration from the development of a comprehensive national program to what might be called "tuning up" the existing system, making it work somewhat better. Whatever one calls this perspective—minimalist intervention, neoconservatism, political realism—it is increasingly shared, for a variety of reasons, by Democrats and Republicans alike. Under the Carter administration it was the harbinger of things to come.

Ironically, it was HEW Secretary Joseph Califano, one of the principal architects of the Great Society of the 1960s, who sounded the Carter administration's retreat on child care. Addressing the 1978 annual meeting of the Day Care and Child Development Council of America, and pointing to the "more austere landscape" of the 1970's, Califano said:[5]

> *It is every bit as important that we tend to existing programs sufficiently as it is to break new ground. . . . We must demonstrate that*

*we can manage effectively the programs that already exist if we are
to earn the confidence of the Congress and taxpayer. (p. 2)*

Six months later, when Califano's Assistant Secretary for Human
Development Services, Arabella Martinez, was forced into the embarrassing position of presenting the Carter administration's opposition to Senator Cranston's proposed child care initiative, she took the
same line:[25]

*Given the size and nature of [the federal government's existing]
commitment, we do not believe that another categorical program for
child care is warranted at this time. We do agree that more coordination would be helpful, that more information on a number of issues
would be useful, and that efforts should be improved in a number of
key areas.*

In these times of fiscal restraint, and well before the Reagan
victory, even some of the staunchest supporters of a national program have argued for a more limited approach. For example,
Edward Zigler, former director of the Office of Child Development,
has recommended that private foundations adopt a more "piecemeal approach" to day care:[38]

*While social scientists fantasize about wiping the slate clean and
writing national policy from scratch, the knowledge and services
produced by a more piecemeal strategy are far more likely to win
public support and be implemented, while building slowly towards
the same goal. (p. 34)*

Family Choice

In the face of widespread and widely publicized changes in the
structure of American families, family choice has surfaced as a key
phrase in recent political campaigns, its invocation strengthened and
justified by a long-standing tradition of sanctifying and romanti-
cizing the virtues of the family. Perhaps, too, it is a reflection of our
interest in finding private solutions to problems that a little more
than a decade ago seemed to require massive public interventions.

In the case of day care, the assertion of parental choice has become a politically necessary response to right-wing attacks that day
care would undermine the family. Senator Cranston's 1979 bill, for
example, emphasized that it did not "authorize any public agency
or private organization . . . to interfere with, or to intervene in,
any childrearing decision of parents."[31]

The importance of family choice has been buttressed by the
conclusions—or lack of conclusions—from a decade's worth of research in child development. Recent publication of findings by the
High/Scope Educational Research Foundation[30] and by the Con-

sortium for Longitudinal Studies[21] about the positive long-term effects of early intervention programs have clearly begun to influence policy in substantial ways, particularly the reauthorization of funding for Head Start. However, in the absence of information about the effects of different programs on child development, several prominent researchers suggested that we begin to develop services that meet one elementary requirement. According to Urie Bronfenbrenner and colleagues, services should be responsive to "the expressed needs of parents as they perceive them." (p. 18)[4] Or, as Alison Clarke-Stewart puts it in her review of child development research, "a variety of programs is called for to meet the needs of different families and different children, in different circumstances, with different cultural values." (p. 76)[6]

An Expanded Notion of Day Care

One of the most important "discoveries" of the last decade of research and debate about child care in America has been the recognition of its diversity, especially the widespread use of "family day care," the arrangement whereby a child is cared for during the day in someone else's home.

Contrary to persisting popular belief, or at least to the media image of American day care, most children are cared for not in centers but in homes. As the Congressional Budget Office noted in its 1978 report on child care:[10]

> *Only about 9 percent of all children who use some form of care for more than 10 hours a week are enrolled in either a day care center or a nursery school, while almost all of the remainder are cared for in a family- or home-based setting. . . . [However] the preferences of those administering the governmental programs have often led to an emphasis on day care centers rather than family-based care. About 55 percent of federally subsidized children are enrolled in centers, while 25 percent are in family or group day care home (the remainder are provided care in their own homes). (pp. 19–20)*

To those critical of federal involvement in day care—and especially to those opposed to the establishment of a national day care program—no point has been seized on with so much passion and persistence as this apparent disparity between the types of child care arrangements that most people use and/or want and those that federal policy promotes. It constituted the backbone of mid-70s policy analyses by Meredith Larson and Suzanne Woolsey that raised the ire of the child care advocacy community, and it now underpins the position of the increasingly influential neoconservative thinkers, who argue that child care is not really a major problem in this country, that most people get along fine with relatives or neighbors.[20,37] As neoconservative writer Peter Skerry puts it, if the government is to be involved, it should not be to establish a new program, which would be intrusive, but to "preserve and reinforce the present 'system' that allows for a great deal of diversity and choice." (p. 102)[32]

Actually, the call for recognition of the diversity of the American child care system, and for the use of family day care in particular, was sounded early in the 1970s by Arthur Emlen, who warned that[13]

> *day care has been conceived in such a way that it cannot be funded, nor delivered, nor used on a large scale. At the same time, very little effort has been spent to strengthen the kinds of child care arrangements that most families use and prefer. (p. 106)*

According to Emlen,

> *America was asking the wrong question. It was asking "How many day care facilities should be created?" when it should have been asking, "How can we expand and improve the patterns of child care that families are already using?" (p. 106)*

Emlen's question may have been ahead of its time in the early 1970s. Now, however, a spurt of research activity in different parts of the country is trying to answer it. Lein[22] and Malson[24] at Wellesley, Powell[29] at Merrill-Palmer, and Hill-Scott[15] at UCLA are using a variety of techniques to learn about "natural networks" or "informal systems" of child care that families use. In the 1980s Emlen's question is likely to be the one of most interest to policy makers; if emerging trends are at all predictive, its answer is likely to include a call for child care information and referral.

Proposals for Information and Referral

The notion of child care information and referral services has been gathering support over the last decade from an impressive array of experts who do not necessarily agree on many aspects of policy. Indeed, a consensus has been building over the last decade—from a far-ranging and unlikely set of bedfellows—about the desirability of child care information and referral services as an instrument of federal child care policy.

According to Edward Zigler, former director of the Office of Child Development and one of the most ardent backers of comprehensive legislation, "a major problem with day care is the lack of centralized information to help parents locate existing day care services." He recommends the establishment of "community referral agencies

. . . separate from welfare and other social services, that could help refer families to reliable day care providers of various types." (p. 9)[39]

Similar recommendations have been made by the National Academy of Sciences and the Carnegie Council on Children in their sweeping analyses of American policies for children and families. According to the Academy's 1976 report, *Toward a National Policy for Children and Families*,[1] "Parents should have sufficient information regarding available alternatives in child care services to enable them to make reasonable choices and to shift from one alternative to another as their needs and preferences change." (p. 78) In *All Our Children: The American Family Under Pressure*,[19] the Council calls even more specifically for "referral-and-appointment center[s] . . . where families can go find out about the available services they may need, to get proper referrals to the correct services, to make appointments and so forth." (p. 143)

It is not just experts and social policy analysts who perceive the need for child care information and referral. When the most comprehensive national survey to date asked parents to rank-order those programs for which they would most like to see government funds allocated, they chose, above all others, "a referral system where parents could get information about screened and qualified people and agencies to provide child care." (p. 21)[34]

Even those who oppose increased federal involvement in the expansion of day care on the grounds that there is no evidence of unmet need or that it is prohibitively expensive are sympathetic to the development of child care information and referral as a mechanism for making the existing system work better, making it more responsive to parental choice. In her controversial 1975 report for the Stanford Research Institute, *Federal Policy for Preschool Services: Assumptions and Evidence*, which claimed that there was no evidence of need for new services, Meredith Larson stated that "the most pressing problem for individual families may be the lack of thorough and realistic information at the local level about both formal and informal facilities."[20] Two years later Suzanne Woolsey, then of the Urban Institute, raised the ire of the day care community with a *Daedalus* article that made a similar point, though in more acerbic terms:[37]

(P)olicy makers are importuned by ideological and interest group pied pipers, promising to rid us of various forms of pestilence: oppression of women, a thoroughly unworkable welfare system, emotional disturbance, and school failure. . . . The data do not, however, support the contention that a heavy federal subsidization of institutional care is desired by parents or would significantly promote other broad social goals. . . .What we need is closer concentration on what people need and want to help them cope with their child-

care problems. . . . A focus on the parents and children might simply produce some modest tinkering at the margins of the system. Information services to enable parents more efficiently to make their own arrangements would be welcomed. (p. 129, p. 143)

What Woolsey so offhandedly referred to as "tinkering at the margins" is likely to become the centerpiece of policies for child care recommended by the American Enterprise Institute, one of the leading bastions of the neoconservative thinkers. One of the most intriguing propositions generated by neoconservatives Peter Berger and Richard John Neuhas is that the need to rely on as well as limit the welfare state be accomplished by diverting more attention—and dollar resources—to so-called "mediating structures," i.e., "institutions standing between the individual in his private life and the large institutions of public life." (p. 2)[3] Berger and Neuhaus argue that mediating structures such as the neighborhood, family, church, and voluntary association need to be "more imaginatively recognized in public policy." (p. 3)[3] The problem with this elusive concept is translating it into specific measures of public policy, something that the government can actually do. In this regard, child care information and referral may be one of the only measures that the neoconservatives can latch onto, as they seem to have done. In a working paper entitled "Mediating Structures and Public Policy,"[32] Peter Skerry singles out information and referral as "one of the most exciting possibilities for dealing with child care without imposing a monolithic public program on a nation with diverse needs and tastes." (p. 108)

At the present time there is no specific or explicit federal policy regarding child care information and referral. Although Title XX of the 1967 Social Security Amendments encourages states to provide I&R for all human services without regard to income or eligibility criteria, planning for and implementation of I&R under Title XX has not focused on day care.

However, child care information and referral is beginning to figure more prominently in federal consideration of policy options. The Congressional Budget Office, for example, outlining five alternatives to current policy in its 1978 report, *Child Care and Preschool: Options for Federal Support*, included child care information and referral as a necessary adjunct to any type of child care voucher program. And, in its proposed revisions of the Federal Interagency Day Care Requirements (FIDCR), which apply to all HEW funded day care services provided to children outside their homes, HEW (now HHS) recommends that state agencies administering day care provide "information and referral services."[35]

More important to I&R's currency in Washington than these acknowledgements from the federal bureaucracy may be California's establishment in 1976 of the nation's most extensive experiment with child care information and referral. Where child care policy is concerned, California has always tended to be an anomaly, the only state that, following World War II, voted state funding to maintain the system of Children's Centers set up under the Lanham Act. However, the way in which and reasons for which California got involved in information and referral are of significance, and worth a digression. For undergirding the development of I&R in California is the philosophy of Governor Jerry Brown who, perhaps more than any other politician in the country, has become adept at turning the liability of scarce resources into a political asset; as E.F. Shumacher, a Buddhist priest, or Jerry Brown might put it, "less is more."

After a 1976 campaign pledge to increase child care, Brown promptly and somewhat shockingly vetoed the appropriation of ten million dollars to expand the statewide system of Children's Centers administered by the state Department of Education. But, at the same time, he pledged to spend the ten million on more innovative and cost-effective approaches to child care. As staffers close to the governor relate, he had no particular plan in mind but did not want to extend the power of the state Department of Education; and, despite his professed sympathy for the women's movement, he couldn't quite understand why children couldn't be taken care of at home as he had once been. Whatever the motives, Brown's political instincts caught the temper of the time: antigovernment spending (though still wanting government to provide some services), pro–day care, and pro–family choice.

With the help of a small internal planning group which brought in several operators of community-based child care information and referral services, the Brown administration offered up what is without doubt the most interesting combination of policies and programs that any state has seen, a package deal designed to test the cost-reducing features of a variety of mechanisms including vouchers and child care information and referral (called "resources and referral" in California). So far, it is a program that has met with enormous success. In the wake of Proposition 13, when other services were being cut, the experimental child care program was expanded, and the budget for information and referral services—approximately 40 of which are now spread through the state—increased from 1.5 to 2.5 million dollars. Moreover, even before an evaluation of the experimental program was completed, the State Department of Education's Commission to Formulate a State Plan for Child Care (popularly referred to as the Riles' Commission, after Wilson Riles, the Superintendant of Public Instruction) recommended the expansion of resource and referral as one of its top priorities for ensuring that all families have access to child care.[8]

Pointing to the success of child care information and referral in his own state, Senator Alan Cranston made it a prominent feature of the child care bill he introduced in 1979. Even though Cranston's proposed legislation was shortlived, the diversity of support for I&R suggests that its political viability is likely to increase in the 1980s— in California, in other states, and in the federal arena. But before examining either the promise or the dilemmas that I&R may pose, it may be useful to take a brief look at the historical record, at the forerunners of current interest in I&R.

Déjà Vu: A Brief History of I&R

Actually, the idea of using information and referral services to make the social services system work better is not exactly new. When looked at in some historical perspective, the recent flurry of interest in I&R for child care can produce a sobering sense of déjà vu.

The concept of information and referral has been a presence on the social services scene since the 1870s, when the charity organization movement gave birth to the social service exchange, a type of coordinating body designed to increase access to and reduce duplication of human services. However, major government involvement in I&R did not come until World War II. Just as the United States geared up during wartime to provide day care in a way never since duplicated, so it geared up to provide information and referral. Not for child care, but for veterans.

Toward the end of World War II, the Retraining and Rehabilitation Administration of the Department of Labor sponsored the development of community advisory centers, modeled after the Community Advice Bureaus that were established in Great Britain during the war and which continue to this day; 3000 were in place by 1946, operating with local financing and community support. The centers were set up to be "the single place where every organization of the community combines and coordinates their efforts to serve those who seek help in taking up their lives in the community." (pp. 55–73)[23] The national plan was to serve a variety of groups in transition from wartime to peacetime. In practice, however, the local focus narrowed to veterans, and the centers became popularly known as Veterans Information Centers. By 1949 most of them had disbanded; as with day care, the United States had demonstrated its ability to meet a national crisis, but not to integrate the services it developed into national planning and delivery.[23]

As with day care, national attention to information and referral sparked again in the mid-1960s, the era of the Great Society and the War on Poverty, when there was an upswing of concern for new approaches to making the social services system work better. Within a very short time, a wide variety of agencies, including the Department of Housing and Urban Development, the Bureau of Employment Security (Labor), National Institute of Mental Health (Community Mental Health Centers), Social Security Administration, and Office of Economic Opportunity, to name a few, began developing plans for information and referral functions. President Johnson established an Interagency Advisory Group of top level officials from each department and charged them with making "the government more accessible to the people it serves." And still another high-level task force made up of representatives from HEW, HUD, Labor and OEO recommended the establishment of a national network of 500 "one-stop neighborhood centers" that would help people find the services they need."[17] Meanwhile, the Ford Foundation commissioned Columbia University's Alfred Kahn to investigate the British system of Citizen's Advice Bureaus and see how transferable it might be to the United States. Reviewing a well-documented "need for new approaches to information, advice, referral, advocacy, community education, accountability, service coordination and the like," (p. 60)[17] Kahn and his associates called for a national experiment with Neighborhood Information Centers, and laid out a very thoughtful and comprehensive plan for both research and demonstration.

By the end of the 1960s Kahn's work had spurred the development of the Alliance of Information and Referral Services, a national membership group of professionals involved in the delivery of I&R through United Way and other organizations. But federal support for the development of community-based information and referral in child care or other areas never fully materialized; it was bogged down in the competing claims of different agencies and by arguments, which persist to this day, that available funds should be used for direct service, not for information which provides access to services.

Of the federal initiatives for child care in the late 1960s, the only one designed to provide information and referral was the Community Coordinated Child Care Program (4–C), a twenty-four pilot project effort which might well have succeeded—if its mandate and resources had been greater, and if it had not been terminated just as it got going. In its 1972 assessment of the short-lived program, the National Research Council–National Academy of Sciences concluded that the concept had great potential and "attributed the failure of the 4-C program primarily to the lack of federal legislative mandate and to the inadequate administrative mandate, staff, and funding allocated to the program." (p. 68)[18] (Some of the 4–C's, it should be noted, continued to be viable in their communities after the withdrawal of federal endorsement. Indeed, their viability seemed to increase in the 1970s, as limitations on Title IV-A and cutbacks in social services spending made it necessary to explore new approaches to locating and supporting child care.)

At the end of the 1970s, federal interest in information and referral reemerged, accompanied once again by federal interagency panels, task forces, and reports which decry the lack of access to the "increasingly complex" social services system. Save for the change in acronyms as new federal agencies and bodies got into the act, much of the substance could simply have been recycled from the 1960s. In March, 1978, for example, the General Accounting Office issued a report to the Congress calling for the Office of Management and Budget, along with the heads of other federal agencies funding information and referral activities, to "establish a task force to develop, for consideration by the Congress, a national policy and plan to consolidate such activities and promote the establishment of comprehensive information and referral centers." (Title Page)[9] Little recognition was given in the report to the fact that just such a body—an Interdepartmental Task Force on Information and Referral consisting of no less than 17 agencies—had been established three years earlier by the Interdepartmental Working Group of the Cabinet Committee on Aging. Perhaps that is just as well. After three years of activity, the Task Force—which had as its primary concern the assessment of existing federal sources of information and referral and the development of a plan of action to improve I&R services to the elderly—published an incredibly simplistic "I&R Guide" that outlines the "five essential components" of any viable I&R service: Staff, Resource Inventory, Communications, Linkages, and Funding. Presumably this was to provide "a uniform definition and criteria [which] will promote a clearer understanding and will facilitate a more consistent approach in the provision of I&R services."[16]

Meanwhile, other groups in both the public and private sector were investing in the potential of information and referral. The Administration for Public Services commissioned a study of social services administration in three states—New York, Florida, and Maine—with examination of information and referral as one of its main features. President Carter's Task Force on the Reorganization of Social Services, staffed out of the Office of Management and Budget, cited "access" as the key problem with the social services system, and recommended I&R as the first of three necessary elements for effective reorganization. (Unfortunately, the Task Force never released its report; its recommendations for reform were tied to the development of an overall plan for welfare reform.) And in the child care arena, the Ford Foundation and the federal Administration for Children, Youth, and Families committed some 2.5 million dollars to a national research and demonstration project on child care I&R.[28]

Almost simultaneously, the National United Way was gearing up to promote information and referral with all of its local affiliates. As a December, 1978, position paper entitled "Information and Referral: Challenge to United Way" puts it:[36]

> *More than any other program, Information and Referral provides the critical linkage between people and services. Possibly no other type of program can play so important a role in reducing the alienation endemic to our times, restoring faith in our basic institutions, and demonstrating in real and practical ways that our voluntary and public people serving agencies work—for all of us.*
>
> *Information and Referral is a must in every place where people live and work. The need is clear. . . . People need an effective point of entry into the increasingly complex human services system.*
>
> *United Ways have a special responsibility to ensure a unified system of Information and Referral encompassing direct service and technical assistance. In the future, United Way of America will develop additional tools to assist local United Ways in meeting their information and referral responsibility.*

At the end of the 1970s, then, it appeared that information and referral would once again be very much on the federal agenda, as well as on the agenda of the private social service agencies and the nation's biggest and most influential foundation. Will it still be on the agenda by the middle or end of the 1980s? What will come of it all? Much of this, especially in the area of child care, depends on how well we really allow for a testing out of the possibilities that I&R does offer, and on how well we resolve the dilemmas that it presents.

Prospects and Dilemmas

Put most simply, the greatest potential advantage that child care information and referral offers is the ability to make the child care market work better, linking supply with demand and maximizing consumer choice. But neither the child care market nor the role of I&R in it are quite that simple when one takes into account the interest of government in spending tax dollars effectively and in protecting children from harm. In many ways, I&R represents a shift from professional and governmental regulation to consumer choice. However, there are probably significant limits inherent in such a shift. How far can (and will) the encouragement of consumer choice go? What can (or should) be the role of governmental agencies and their professional advisors in maintaining standards of quality? Serious consideration of information and referral as an instrument of federal child care policy must, sooner or later, confront a number of dilemmas, the most important of which have to do with the regulation of child care and of I&R. (There is obviously a broader problem of the lack of an adequate overall supply of child care. This chapter deals only indirectly with this broader problem, and does not mean to suggest that resolving the dilemmas of I&R will solve the broader supply problem.)

Consumer Choice vs. the Regulation of Family Day Care

One of the strongest arguments made for child care information and referral is that it would make more visible—and accessible—the home-based or family day care that most families currently rely on and that they seem to prefer as much as any center-based programs. By identifying family day care homes to consumers eligible for federal subsidy, information and referral services might effect a substantial shift towards the government purchase of family day care, thereby counteracting the marked tendency of federal policy to favor center-based care.

However, as the experience of several operating child care information and referral services indicates, the promotion of family day care and consumer choice may conflict at some point with federal or state regulatory policies which make it a misdemeanor to make a referral to an unlicensed family day care home. San Francisco's Childcare Switchboard, one of the nation's pioneers in the delivery of child care information and referral, is a case in point. When it began providing services in 1973, operating with several small grants from private foundations, the Switchboard routinely made referrals to unlicensed family day care; in effect, one of its goals was to identify the underground or informal care that people didn't know about and to extend the community's informal networks of child care, making them more visible so that they could be used. Aside from running the risk of a criminal conviction, the Switchboard's practice made it ineligible to receive much-needed federal funds; in 1974, in order to stabilize its finances, the Switchboard stopped making referrals to unlicensed homes.

Since 1974 the Switchboard has been relatively tenacious in trying to bring illegal unlicensed homes into the licensed legal market. However, there are considerable resistances to licensure. Aside from the fact that some people don't want to be licensed—either as a matter of principle, or because they don't want to report the income they are earning from family day care—the system of licensing in

California, as in other parts of the country, is discouragingly capricious and slow. It usually takes from three to sixteen months to get a family day care home licensed in California, and often, because of inadequate staffing in licensing offices, it can take over two years. While they are waiting to be licensed, homes are not eligible for referral; many simply drop by the wayside, even though they would have been well qualified to care for children. (In order to avoid such constraints, at least one New York-based information and referral group has decided to run the risk of prosecution, and continues to refer to unlicensed homes while doing its own "screening.")

Unless information and referral services refer to unlicensed homes or unless they are able to bring a substantial number of such homes into the licensed market, their ability to increase consumer choice may be severely limited. However, if they refer to unlicensed homes, albeit safeguarding for quality by screening, they then have appropriated a quasi-regulatory authority and committed a misdemeanor.

What role, then, should information and referral agencies take on? How can they position themselves with regard to the large family day care market? A number of suggestions have been made for resolving this dilemma.

For one, it has been suggested in California and other states that the "regulatory issue" could be obviated if information and referral services were to simply take on the licensing responsibility. Few information and referral agencies, it appears, would jump at such an opportunity. As a report of the California Governor's Advisory Committee on Child Care states,[14]

> *It is impossible to mix the roles of advisor/confidante to parents and programs with the role of policeman/regulator which would be inevitable if R&R [Resource and Referrals] were called upon to regulate FDC [family day care] or any type of child care. Distrust would undoubtedly emerge from such a fusion of roles and would greatly inhibit R&Rs from providing their most basic and mandated services.* (p. 12)

A seemingly different approach would be to allow information and referral services to refer to all homes, telling parents whether a particular home was licensed or unlicensed, and explaining the difference. Legalities aside, this might be practicable because parents are often more concerned with the characteristics of a home care arrangement—especially the number of children being cared for at one time—than with its licensing status. However, the experience of existing information and referral groups suggests that parents usually want some external sanction of a home; a policy of "open referrals" might put information and referral services under pressure —even more than they feel now—to evaluate and recommend particular programs. In effect, they would be forced into the quasi-regulatory role that they are trying to minimize.

An alternate and more practicable approach would be to change family day care licensing practices. Systems of family day care registration, such as Massachusetts's, may provide a level of checks and balances among all parties concerned—parents, family day care providers, I&R services, and the state—that allows for optimum functioning of I&R in the family day care market. Because it requires minimal proof of competence, registration can be accomplished quickly, drastically reducing involvement of the bureaucracy necessary for licensing. It presumes, in effect, until proved otherwise, that a home is capable of providing family day care. At the same time, however, it preserves a role for the state—the ability to close down a home. And it reduces the pressure on information and referral services to help get homes licensed, to take on the official licensing capacity, or to play an unofficial quasi-regulatory role.

Child care information and referral does appear to offer great potential for increasing consumer choice and for increasing utilization of the family day care market. But unless we recognize the dilemma that licensing creates for I&R, unless we develop new approaches to licensing in conjunction with I&R, we may miss the opportunity that it offers. (Aside from replacing licensing with the more feasible registration procedure, the solution requires finding ways to eliminate separate problems with the zoning, sanitation, fire, and building safety systems.)

I&R as a Quasi Regulator

What is doubtless a matter of common sense may be quite problematic for any public policy regarding child care information and referral: people seeking information want that information evaluated; in seeking referrals, they really want recommendations.

According to Brenda Dervin, a communications specialist who has studied information needs of the average citizen in order to help design information and referral services: "The most used sources of information on most topics for most people . . . are peer-kin network contacts (friends, family, and relatives). People meet, talk, and ask advice from people essentially like themselves." (p. 30)[11] That is, people turn to sources that are familiar and trustworthy because they want more than objective information; they want specific and subjective recommendations. In one of Dervin's studies:[11]

> 66 percent of a group of general population respondents wanted to know specifically "where" to buy a product and 33 percent wanted to know where to get the "best" buy. . . . Such results suggest that

*information counselors who want to deal solely with information may
have a difficult task ahead of them . . . advocacy may be a necessary
component of an information program. (pp. 28–29)*

Recent research on patterns of child care preference and utilization bears out Dervin's point. Both the large-scale survey work for
the National Child Care Consumer Study[34] and ongoing small-scale
small-scale ethnographic work by Lein and Malson suggest that
choice of child care involves a complex "calculus of costs and
benefits," in which cost, convenience, and geographic factors are
mediated by concerns about reliability, physical well-being, cognitive development, warmth and love, discipline, and overall values.[22]
In effect, parents want to find caregivers they can trust. And in
seeking information about day care, parents want to know—as do
Dervin's "average citizens"—where they can find all the qualities of
caregiving they seek for their child. They want not a list but a
specific referral; they want to know if a program is good or bad or
right for their child.

For child care information and referral services, the problem is
how to respond, and it is more complicated than it might seem at
first glance. If the effectiveness of I&R depends, as the research
suggests it might, on the ability to give either recommendations or
evaluated referrals, then current regulations may restrict that effectiveness. In Nashville, Tennessee, to cite but one example, the
Division of Day Care Licensing receives more calls for information
about child care than any other organization. According to the
director of the licensing unit:

*Everybody wants to know who I would recommend, or whether I
know anybody who has used a particular child care arrangement and
what they thought about it. But I can't tell them, even if I really do
think a certain provider would be better for them than another.
Many of the programs which this division licenses are terrible, but
it would be against the law for me to tell them one way or the other.
The best I can do is give a parent several names in her area and tell
her to be sure and look carefully at them before enrolling her child.
I guess that's some help, but it's not as much as I know I could give.*

If information and referral services make referrals that are subjective and evaluative in nature, they may, in effect, take on quasi-
regulatory functions, steering parents towards some and away from
other providers, and controlling access to the child care market. In
Nashville, the Director of Licensing reports that she has "providers
calling in to check on me, pretending that they're a parent needing
child care, to see if I'll say something nasty about their program—or
if I won't mention them at all." And in San Francisco there has
already been one challenge to the quasi-regulatory function of an

information and referral service, in the form of a lawsuit brought against the Childcare Switchboard. A licensed family day care provider charged that the Switchboard refused to make referrals to her home, discriminating against her because she was a self-proclaimed lesbian. In fact, the Switchboard did make referrals to other gay providers, but did not make referrals to this particular home because it had visited and was concerned about the quality of care offered. Arguing that she was licensed and that the Switchboard was her main link to the community's child care market, this provider charged that the Switchboard was restraining free trade. Although the judge found no grounds for sexual discrimination, and upheld the Switchboard's "responsibility to the community" to be concerned with quality, he pushed the Switchboard towards developing more standardized procedures for collecting information about the providers to which it makes referrals. More objective records were needed than the impressions of staff members.

Once again, the question is what role I&R should take with regard to the child care market. Should it be allowed to pass on qualitative information, collected in a more standardized manner, as the judge in San Francisco allowed? If so, how should the information and its collection be standardized—and by whom? Or should it only be allowed to make "objective" referrals, providing parents with a minimal amount of information, as in Nashville? If child care information and referral services are ever to receive substantial amounts of public funding, this question takes on particular importance: how will they maintain their unique role as sources of the sort of information that people seek from kith and kin and, at the same time, fulfill their public responsibility?

At this early stage in the development of child care information and referral, a variety of practices are being proposed and tried out, each with significant implications for the daily operation and regulation of I&R. Organizations such as the United Way and the Alliance of Information and Referral Services are developing uniform standards for all information and referral services; presumably these could be self-imposed or monitored by governmental agencies. In California, meanwhile, two very different approaches have materialized, and could lead to a clash among child care I&R agencies regarding any statewide standards for the evaluation of information. The majority of agencies have stopped making visits to child care providers; they argue that by collecting less information, they can be more "objective" and devote more attention to educating parents as to what they should look for. While they also do such parent education, a few other agencies persist in making visits as the only way of gathering the type of information that parents need. The Childcare Switchboard, for example, makes "welcome wagon visits," an approach which minimizes the evaluative or quasi-regulatory aspects of collecting information. To standardize such visits and make them more efficient, the Switchboard is also considering adaptation of the work of Pacific Oaks College researcher Elizabeth Prescott, whose day care observation instruments have been used throughout the country in day care training and in several major federal studies of day care.

Just as registration may be essential if I&R is to work effectively in the family day care market, so we will no doubt have to test and find the right mixture of procedures that allows I&R to be both formal and informal, objective and subjective, at the same time; that guarantees providers access to the market; that gives consumers the type of detailed or evaluated information that they want and that they seek from kith and kin; and that meets some acceptable standards of public responsibility.

Competing Delivery Systems of I&R

The question of what operating standards—if any—might be developed for I&R—and by whom—is closely related to another important dilemma: who will deliver child care information and referral? Already there are different streams of I&R service delivery. If federal dollars should become available, there is likely to be significant competition among different agencies and different approaches to child care information and referral.

A number of national organizations—with the General Accounting Office leading the way—have argued that the most efficient approach is the consolidation of all information and referral—and not just that for child care—into "comprehensive information and referral centers;" i.e., depending on the size of the community, one center might well service the entire population and all of its needs.[9] With its member agencies located in most major communities in the country, the United Way of America has more or less agreed with the GAO position; according to its national Director, local United Ways are in a[36]

> unique position to help in restructuring, developing, or expanding an Information and Referral Service. They have extensive volunteer involvement, professional expertise and liaison with human service organizations and other resources. They are a natural vehicle for carrying out Information and Referral.

So, as they see it, are state and local welfare departments and a number of other organizations, including the nation's public libraries. Since the early 1970s, there has been a slowly burgeoning movement

to use libraries as a central resource for all community information—
including the social services information that many libraries provided during World War II. In 1972, for example, the Kansas State
Library initiated the Kansas Community Information Center Project;
in 1973, New York City received a 4.5 million dollar grant to establish Citizen Urban Information Centers at 55 branch libraries in
Brooklyn (the City's fiscal crisis prevented the project from being
implemented); in 1976, the American Library Association published
Information for the Community, the only useful anthology on the
design, implementation, and evaluation of comprehensive I&R services to date.[12] And in 1979, looking ahead to the future, *Library
Journal* published a special issue which staked out the potential of
libraries for playing a central I&R role in their communities.[33]

As might be expected, organizations with some specialized knowledge of or interest in child care have different visions for the future,
and would argue for an entirely different approach to I&R. For the
most part, they oppose the comprehensive approach—whether carried out by United Way, welfare departments, libraries, or any other
agency—and favor a categorical approach, in which I&R is specifically oriented to child care. Once again, however, there are potentially competing approaches. For the national Head Start program
—and for those politically aware of Head Start's popularity—the
Head Start Child and Family Resource Program has been seen as a
natural way to deliver information and referral to the rest of the
community. But the 60 or so groups scattered around the country
who specialize in information and referral for child care would argue
that effectiveness vis-à-vis the entire child care system is incompati-
ble with provision of a specific child care service, and that it requires
instead the provision of a range of services that go far beyond I&R,
including technical assistance, parent counseling, legislative advocacy, and child advocacy.

For all the competing, or potentially competing, approaches to
I&R, there has been surprisingly little attempt to evaluate effectiveness. The General Accounting Office, for all its touting of the desirability of consolidating I&R functions into "comprehensive centers," refers to no evaluation to substantiate its position. The national office of United Way, which boasts of its unique capability for
I&R, is unable to point to a single study of its effectiveness at the
local level; nor can state welfare departments which have budgeted
Title XX funds specifically for I&R. Only a handful of the community-based groups providing child care information and referral
have taken systematic steps to see if what they are doing works, and
how it works.

At this point it is unlikely that the dilemma of competition will be
resolved, nor should it be, lest we become locked into supposing

that there is one best model which will fit all communities. Indeed, we have not come very far in learning about different models of information and referral since Alfred Kahn's mid-sixties monograph, *Neighborhood Information Centers*,[17] concluded that "because several major federal programs are in transition and offer important possibilities for location and funding, we propose a series of experiments and comparative analyses." (p. 120)

Conclusion

Perhaps the worst dilemma we face with I&R will be the tendency to expect too much of it. I&R was largely ignored at the beginning of the 1970s. As we now enter a decade where evershrinking resources are likely to mix with an increasing demand for consumer choice and for deregulation, I&R is likely to be seized upon as *the* solution for breaking the day care stalemate. Signs of that already appear in the work of the neoconservative axis; they may be pushed ahead if other politicians latch on to Jerry Brown's "less is more" philosophy; and they may be furthered by a federal government very eager to find a way to make the system work better.

I&R does appear to have enormous potential: if we don't look to it for an instant success and are willing to work through some of the dilemmas it poses; if we recognize that it may work only in combination with the redesign of our regulatory system, or with a mix of procedures that allows it to give parents the type of evaluated information that they want.

Fifteen years ago, Alfred Kahn laid out a plan for a wide-ranging national experiment with information and referral; fifteen years later I&R may indeed work—especially if we learn some lessons from the past, recognize its complexity, and provide the funding that will give it a chance.

References

1. Advisory Committee on Child Development, National Research Council. 1976. *Toward a National Policy for Children and Families.* National Academy of Sciences, Washington, D.C.
2. Bane, M.J. et al. 1978. "Child care in the United States." Unpublished working paper, Wellesley College Center for Research on Women. Wellesley, Ma.
3. Berger, P. and Neuhaus, R.J. 1977. *To Empower People: The Role of Mediating Structures in Public Policy.* American Enterprise Institute, Washington, D.C.

4. Bronfenbrenner, U. et al. 1976. "Day care in context: an ecological perspective on research and public policy." Background paper submitted to the Department of Health, Education, and Welfare. Washington, D.C.

5. Califano, J. Cited in *Day Care and Child Development Reports*. Vol. 7, no. 13. Plus Publications, Washington, D.C.

6. Clarke-Stewart, A. 1977. *Child Care in the Family*. Academic Press, New York.

7. Coelen, Craig *et al.* 1978. *Child Care Centers in the United States*. Abt Associates, Cambridge, Ma.

8. Commission to Formulate a State Plan For Child Care and Development Services. 1979. State Department of Education, Sacramento, Ca.

9. Comptroller General of the United States. March 20, 1978. Report to the Congress: *Information and Referral for People Needing Human Services— A Complex System that Should be Improved*. HRD-77–134, Title Page. General Accounting Office, Washington, D.C.

10. Congressional Budget Office, Congress of the United States. Sept. 1978. *Child Care and Preschool: Options for Federal Support*. U.S. Government Printing Office, Washington, D.C.

11. Dervin, B. 1976. "The everyday information needs of the average citizen: a taxonomy for analysis." In *Information for the Community*. M. Kochen and C. Donohue, eds. American Library Association, Chicago, Ill.

12. Donohue, C. and Kochen, M. 1976. "Community information centers: concepts for analysis and planning." In *Information for the Community*. M. Kochen and C. Donohue, eds. American Library Association, Chicago, Ill.

13. Emlen, A.C. 1974. "Day care for whom?" In *Children and Decent People*. A.L. Schorr, ed. Basic Books, N.Y.

14. Governor's Advisory Committee on Child Development Programs. April 1979. AB 3059, *Alternative Child Care Programs: Policy Implications of a Three-Year Experiment*. Governor's Advisory Committee, Sacramento, Ca.

15. Hill-Scott, A. 1979. "Assessing the status of child care. Working paper." School of Architecture and Urban Planning, University of California, Los Angeles, Ca.

16. Interdepartmental Task Force on Information and Referral. 1978. *I and R Guide*. National Clearinghouse on Aging, DHEW, Washington, D.C.

17. Kahn, A.J. et al. 1966. *Neighborhood Information Centers: A Study and Some Proposals*. Columbia School of Social Work, N.Y.

18. Kamerman, S. and Kahn, A.J. 1976. *Social Services in the United States: Policies and Programs*. Temple University Press, Philadelphia, Pa.

19. Keniston, K. and The Carnegie Council on Children. 1977. *All Our Children: The American Family Under Pressure*. Harcourt Brace Jovanovich, New York.

20. Larson, M. 1975. *Federal Policy for Preschool: Assumptions and Evidence*. Stanford Research Institute, Palo Alto, Ca.

21. Lazar, I. and Darlington, R. 1979. *Summary Report: Lasting Effects After Preschool*. A report by the central staff of the Consortium for Longitudinal Studies. Publication No. OHDS 79–30179. DHEW, Washington, D.C.

22. Lein, L. et al. *Families and communities project funded by National Science*

Foundation. Wellesley College Center for Research on Women, Wellesley, Ma.

23. Long, N. 1976. "Information and referral services: a short history and some recommendations." In *Information for the Community.* M. Kochen and J.C. Donohue, eds. American Library Association, Chicago, Ill.

24. Malson, M.R. February 1977. "Parental needs, parental choices: day care from a parental perspective." Unpublished qualifying paper submitted to the Harvard Graduate School of Education. Cambridge, Ma.

25. Martinez, A., Assistant Secretary for Human Development Services. February 21, 1979. Statement on S.4, The Child Care Act of 1979. Senate Subcommittee on Child and Human Development, Washington, D.C.

26. *McCall's Working Mother Child Care Directory.* January 1981. In *McCall's Working Mother*, volume 4, number 1.

27. Northern California Child Care Resource and Referral Network. 320 Judah Street, San Francisco, Ca.

28. O'Hara, J. et al. 1979. *Phase I Results: A National Profile of Child Care Information and Referral Services.* Project Connections, American Institutes for Research, Cambridge, Ma. Contract no. 105-78-1301/Ford Foundation Grant No. 780-0192.

29. Powell, D. with Eisenstadt, J.W. 1980. *Funding Child Care: A Study of Parents' Search Processes.* A report prepared for the Ford Foundation. The Merrill-Palmer Institute, Detroit, Mi.

30. Schweinart, L. 1980. *High Quality Early Childhood Programs for Low Income Families Pay for Themselves.* Center for the Study of Public Policies for Young Children. High/Scope Educational Research Foundation, Ypsilanti, Mi.

31. S.4. January 15, 1979. The Child Care Act of 1979. 96th Congress, first session. Washington, D.C.

32. Skerry, P. 1978. "Mediating structures and child care policy." Unpublished draft for the Mediating Structures Project. American Enterprise Institute, Washington, D.C.

33. Turick, D. 1978. "Community Information Services in Libraries," *Library Journal*, Special Report Number 5, N.Y.

34. U.S. Department of Health, Education and Welfare. 1976. *Statistical highlights from the national child care consumer study.* DHEW Publication number OHD 76-31096. Office of Human Development, Washington, D.C.

35. U.S. Department of Health, Education and Welfare. June 15, 1979. "HEW day care requirements—proposed rules; public meetings." In *Federal Register*, Volume 44, number 117, book 2. Washington, D.C.

36. United Way of America. 1978. "Information and referral: challenge to United Way." Draft number 10. United Way, Services Outreach Division, Alexandria, Va.

37. Woolsey, S. 1977. "Pied piper politics and the child care debate." *Daedalus.*

38. Zigler, E. and Anderson, K. May/June 1979. "Foundation support in the child and family life field." In *Foundation News*, volume 20, number 3.

39. Zigler, E. and Hunsinger, S. March, 1977. "Bringing up day care." In *American Psychological Association Monitor*, volume 8, number 43.

Chapter 20

CONSIDERING PROPRIETARY CHILD CARE

by Sharon L. Kagan and Theresa Glennon

Recent trends in American society have signaled major changes in the status of women, particularly with regard to their participation in the labor force. As women surged back to work and single-parent families became more common, parents urgently needed more day care for their children. Both government and private entrepreneurs responded. Business magazines encouraged businessmen to take advantage of this wide-open market, while child development experts pleaded with the government to both regulate day care conditions and assume primary responsibility for providing child care for low-income families. Many feared that without government intervention the nation's children might fall victim to profiteers.

Experience has soothed some fears. While cases of real neglect appeared, state licensing requirements have worked to ensure a minimum degree of quality in centers of all kinds. The fear that large chains of profit-making centers would produce a generation of "Kentucky fried children" has been allayed to some extent. Many early opponents of proprietary day care, like Alice Lake, have modified their views. In the September 1980 issue of McCall's *Working Mother* she conceded "that the quality of a child care center is not primarily a result of corporate size or profit orientation."[3]

While popular business and women's magazines reported on the growth and increasing acceptability of proprietary child care, academic and bureaucratic debate concerning federal child care policies primarily addressed nonprofit child care. Discussions centered on public responsibility for meeting the child care needs of families with low incomes, whether or not there was enough child care available to meet the nation's need for child care, for whom federal (and state) government should meet child care needs, and what standards of safety and quality should be imposed on centers that receive government funds.

Researchers, seeing large amounts of government funds distributed to nonprofit centers, and the centers' concurrent growth, often focused their studies on children cared for by nonprofit centers. They researched, among other topics, the minimum standards of quality needed by children and the longitudinal effects on children of full-time day care.

While research remained concentrated on nonprofit child care, the federal government gradually opened up four important federal subsidy programs to owners and clients of proprietary day care. An amendment to Title IV-A of the Social Security Act permitted child care to be deducted as a work-related expense. Title XX of the Social Security Act permitted states to subsidize child care for low-income families. The states have the option of opening both these funds to proprietary centers and their users. The Child Care Tax Credits allow parents to deduct up to 20% of their child care expenses from their income tax.[12] In addition, a legislative change in the Child Care Food Program has expanded eligibility to Title XX children in proprietary centers.[10]

These efforts, coupled with recent congressional debates concerning revisions of the Child Care Tax Credit System and the general economic push toward increased corporate involvement in child care, have led researchers to begin to investigate proprietary child care. One recent national study, the National Day Care Study conducted by Abt Associates in 1977, explored demographic questions. Abt Associates found that there were 18,310 day care centers in the United States. The majority, 59% were nonprofit, while an astonishing 41%, close to 7,500, were profit-making centers.[4] As these figures indicate, the for-profit sector is large and, according to many experts, growing. Richard Ruopp, President of the Bank Street College of Education, believes that the need for child care will grow most for middle-class families, traditionally the largest group of consumers of for-profit day care.[3]

Clearly, then, as Congress considers shifting child care funds away from direct subsidies of public centers to "demand subsidies" in the form of increased tax credits, it is time to look more carefully at the profit sector. This chapter, using the scarce information now available, will address the following questions: What are the characteristics of proprietary centers? What are some differences between proprietary and nonprofit centers? What are important issues for parents, practitioners, and policymakers as they consider the future of child care in the United States?

The Characteristics of Proprietary Centers

The for-profit sector of the day care industry is divided into three types of ownership. While the first two types, chains and franchise operations, make the headlines, most for-profit day care centers (approximately 86%) are independently owned and managed, often by a husband and wife team.[4] Consideration of the differences among these ownership structures is crucial to developing government child care policies and understanding how they will affect proprietary centers.

Chains

There are many child care chains in the United States; here we shall discuss Kinder-Care, the largest of the chains.[*] Mainly through the acquisition of smaller chains, Kinder-Care Center's founder, Perry Mendel, now has more than 700 centers in 36 states and Canada. His centers serve a clientele that ranges from infants to twelve-year olds, with the largest concentration among three- to five-year-old children. The centers provide before- and after-school care, operating from 7 a.m. to 6 p.m. By most accounts, children who attend Kinder-Care centers receive adequate care.[13] While Perry Mendel tries to assure uniform quality in all his centers, one observer found that "the personalities of teachers had more to do with the care children received than the eclectic and generally platitudinous guidance in the teacher's manual that's distributed from Montgomery."[7] Mendel guarantees that children will be given colorful toys instead of junk food and T.V. Parents are assured of a 1-to-10 staff/child ratio.[13]

The standardization of a large chain like Kinder-Care has both advantages and disadvantages. Bulk buying and central production reduce costs considerably. Kinder-Care produces many of the goods used by its centers and takes advantage of scale economies, presumably leaving more money for better services. Yet, because the chain must satisfy its investors, money saved is plowed back into capital for new centers. Like several other major chains, Kinder-Care has sought to "diversify." In addition to child care service, the centers may sell T-shirts, tote bags, and even children's life in-

---

[*] Our focus on Kinder-Care does not imply endorsement or disapproval; it was selected because of its prominence in the field.

surance. Perry Mendel sees Kinder-Care "eventually as a great mail-order business whereby Kinder-Care will publish a unique catalog for parents to take home and browse through at their leisure. It has tremendous potential. I envision it as a big, big business some day."[13]

Funded by eager investors and meeting the growing day care needs of middle-class families, the national chains are expected to remain the fastest growing sector in the child care business. Unlike the owners of independent centers, national chains can accumulate the capital needed to buy new centers and to advertise. Often faced with limited options, parents entrust their children to an advertised name that they recognize and consider dependable.

Franchise Operations

Many of the national chains, including Kinder-Care, began as franchise operations. Through this structure an investor buys the use of the name and any instructional or play materials offered by the company. The investor also pays an annual percentage, often around 6%, to the parent company.[1] While a few franchise companies still exist, most businesses discovered that, without tight control, owners of the franchises were not successful. Many managers loved children but didn't understand how to run the business aspects of the centers and couldn't meet their financial obligations to the company. The number of franchises has been decreasing and new growth is not expected.[8]

Independent Centers

Independent centers are by far the most numerous type of center within the for-profit structure. They are also the most diverse, and to date little research has focused directly on them. The quality of care provided by independent owners varies greatly—some is merely custodial, while other care includes a rich and diversified experience for children.

Often, independent centers are managed by a husband and wife team and are distinguishable from nonprofit centers in the same towns only by their legal designation. They may also become an endangered species, for they have been especially hard hit by inflation and the mandatory minimum wage. Unable to take advantage of scale economies available to chains, many centers are faced with four options: conversion to nonprofit status; raising parent fees at the risk of losing some clients; selling out to a chain and recouping their real estate investment; or bankruptcy—a sad but growing phenomenon.[3]

Differences between Proprietary and Nonprofit Centers

Quality of care offered by the sectors is one area of difference that is frequently debated. Both for-profit and nonprofit center operators claim that they provide high-quality child care. Proprietary operators maintain that efficient managerial skills make their centers profitable without any reduction in the quality of care provided. Supporters of nonprofit child care assert that even if managerial efficiency does produce a profit, the extra money should be used to improve either the quality of care or the wages of the child care providers and not for outside investment. Nonprofit operators point to the greater amount of money they spend per child, the more stable personnel force, and often more comprehensive services provided to their clients as indicators of the higher-quality service they provide.

Clearly, the quality question is an important one, one that warrants deeper investigation. Narrower in focus, this chapter will explore differences between nonprofit and for-profit centers on several other important issues: staff wages, expenditure per child, and source of income and clientele served.

In some cases, it is helpful to refine the comparisons so that they are not solely determined by legal status (that is, profit vs. nonprofit) but include federal funding as a criteria. Thus, on certain issues, we follow Abt Associates in looking at four categories of centers: (1) for-profit, non-federally funded centers (31% of all centers); (2) for-profit, federally funded centers (10%), (3) nonprofit, non-federally funded centers (25%); and (4) nonprofit, federally funded centers (34%).[12] Given these distinctions, what do the data show about child care centers?

Staff Wages

The percentage of a center's annual operating budget spent on staff wages varies quite clearly by the nonprofit/for-profit distinction. For-profit centers fairly consistently spend 10% less of their budget on wages—only 63% compared with the 73% spent by nonprofit centers. Average weekly salaries range from $89 to $124 in for-profit centers, and from $94 to $160 in nonprofit centers. Whether or not the center receives federal funding is not a decisive factor here. Government funding in each type of center seems to lead to slightly higher weekly wages, but it does not close the gap between them.[4]

Due to the pressure both to provide quality care and to yield a profit, many proprietary centers pay their staffs the minimum wage allowed by federal law. In fact, the January 1981 issue of *Child Care Information Exchange* carried a warning to operators of all child care centers that they must, by law, pay their staffs at least minimum wage.[9] The recent surplus of teachers has enabled centers to attract well-qualified individuals despite the low pay: the average educational attainment of day care providers in all types of centers is two years of college. Well-qualified day care providers do not, however, seem to remain for long periods of time where they earn such wages. Staff turnover in both sectors is high, although it is slightly higher in proprietary centers than in nonprofit centers. For-profit centers replace 17% to 20% of their staff every year, while nonprofit centers replace 13% to 15%.[4]

Expenditure Per Child

Proprietary centers are often criticized for spending far less on each child than nonprofit centers. In fact, the data is more complex. While for-profit centers that do not receive federal funds spend the least ($1,230 per year per child), two categories—nonprofit non-federally funded and for-profit federally funded—spend the same, $1,430 per year per child. The big spenders were the nonprofit federally funded centers, spending $2,190 per year per child.[12] When looking at expenditure per child data, it is critical also to consider what services are offered to each child. Nonprofit federally funded centers usually provide more support services than the other centers, which may account for some of the cost differential.

Sources of Income and Clientele

The geographic and income distribution of the consumers of child care across the United States creates an interesting picture. Most proprietary day care centers have arisen in suburban areas; almost none are in rural or inner-city areas. Individuals who want to open for-profit centers seek "prime market" areas. They look for lenient licensing and zoning requirements, inexpensive land or rent, and areas with a high employment rate and a high percentage of children under six years old.[8] This has led to an uneven distribution of for-profit centers across the country. Consideration of these factors has encouraged a disproportionate number of for-profit centers to locate in the South and Southwest.

While both government sponsored and privately funded nonprofit centers often receive outside donations, for-profit centers rely mainly on parent fees for their support. They are not likely to receive volunteer staff or donated space and equipment.[12] This reliance on parental support leads proprietary centers to focus on a certain type of clientele. Bob Benson of Children's World, Inc., the nation's third largest child care chain, states, "We're looking for middle Americans

with incomes 10 to 15% above the median."⁸ The study by Abt
Associates confirmed this, showing that 42% of the families using
proprietary day care had incomes over $15,000. Non-profit centers
care for 84% of the children in centers from families with incomes
under $6,000.¹²

While the number of proprietary centers receiving federal funds
is still low, some states have made Title XX funds available to profit
and nonprofit centers. Many states allow Title XX reimbursement to
proprietary centers only after all available spaces in nonprofit centers
are filled, but a few states now leave the choice of center to parental
discretion and will reimburse any licensed center. Not all proprietary
centers are interested in receiving Title XX money. Acceptance of
government funds may mean endless paperwork and fiscal review
by state auditors, requirements which increase a center's operating
costs.

Controversies

Proprietary owners claim that they have been subjected to unfair
criticism, at times, by scholars and child development experts. The
criticisms are based on the belief that the profit motive and concern
for child welfare are ultimately irreconcilable. Critics of proprietary
centers point to their low staff wages and low expenditures per child.
A study conducted by the Women's Research Action Project, published in 1974, found that cost-cutting methods used by the proprietary centers that were owned by chains went beyond efficiency
into areas that seriously affected the quality of care provided to the
children at those centers. The report stated that while all centers
met licensing requirements, none exceeded minimum standards.
Centers were clean and bright, but unimaginative. Ratios were 1
staff person for every 10 children, as required by law, but the staff
received no paid breaks and in the afternoon may have had little
energy left to be divided among ten children. Low-paid and vulnerable to sudden layoffs when enrollment declined, the staff often
suffered from low morale, which in turn led to a serious discontinuity in staffing, even from month to month. The report further
indicated that instead of using income to improve quality, funds not
required for operations were generally funneled into other in-
vestments.¹

Proprietary owners counter these criticisms by asserting that not
only do they meet licensing requirements but that these requirements are often more stringently enforced against for-profit than
nonprofit centers. Many licensing officers, they claim, are too lenient
with nonprofit centers, and they point to a recent fatal fire in a

nonprofit Atlanta day care center that had not met all licensing requirements as proof of the dangers of this official lenience toward nonprofit centers.

Whether or not for-profit centers are discriminated against is debatable, and the situation probably varies from town to town. A recent study indicates that for-profit centers would be required to spend much more than nonprofit centers in order to comply with the Federal Interagency Day Care Requirements (FIDCR). Samuel Weiner's 1977 study in Seattle and Denver showed that while non-profit centers would have to increase their labor expenditures by 4% to 20%, for-profit centers would have to spend 25% to 51% more to meet the federal standards. These figures are predicated on implementation of the 1968 FIDCR.[15]

These FIDCR standards, however, have themselves become the focus of controversy. Day care centers must meet federal standards in order to receive Title XX and Child Care Food Program funding. For-profit centers have unified in their opposition to these regula-tions, claiming that the required staff-child ratios are overprotective and prohibitively expensive.[11] While FIDCR are generally endorsed within the nonprofit sector, directors of nonprofit centers express the concern that government funds be allocated at levels sufficient to implement and maintain any new federal standards.

Future Issues

Participants

Child care in the United States involves and must meet the needs of diverse populations. The critical element in securing quality day care that meets these many needs is active participation by all those concerned. Both parents and day care providers must identify areas in which they can improve day care conditions.

The primary issue is quality. Child development experts can dis-seminate information to parents concerning variables that are as-sociated with quality care. Armed with this information and their own knowledge, parents can observe carefully the care their chil-dren receive. This can be accomplished through direct observation or volunteer work at centers, through communication with other parents, and, if necessary, through organizing for change. Day care providers can encourage parent involvement through advisory boards, parent-teacher conferences concerning each child, and evening get-togethers where issues of concern to all can be discussed informally.

Parents should also become aware of their own purchasing power. They can ask careful questions of the center directors and staff. Keys to quality can be found in a number of observable variables: staff/child ratio, classroom size, group size, and staff turnover. If parents refuse to patronize centers of low quality, market pressures will either force these centers to improve or cause new ones to develop.

Parents can also press for day care where they work. Employers with a large percentage of female workers—such as hospitals and garment factories—have already realized the importance of child care to keeping their employees both at work and productive. Other businesses can also be encouraged to provide child care facilities; energetic employees in Minneapolis and St. Louis have even managed to persuade groups of small businesses to sponsor day care facilities in the downtown area.[5] The Connecticut State Legislature recently passed a bill allowing a 25% tax credit for expenses incurred by corporations for planning, constructing, renovating, or establishing child care facilities that are used primarily by the children of the corporation's employees. Clearly, as the number of single parents and two-income families continues to increase within the work force, vociferous workers and unions can make employers understand the benefits of meeting the child care needs of their employees.

Parents and day care providers must join to exercise their political power in favor of quality day care. Organizations on both the state and federal levels will awaken legislators and policymakers to the nation's concern for quality child care. One such organization is the National Association for the Education of Young Children (NAEYC). With a membership of 30,000, NAEYC speaks out on child development and curriculum issues. Concerned with management issues, the National Association of Child Care Management (NACCM) is comprised of proprietary day care center owners and managers. NACCM has become a strong lobby on Capitol Hill. Those interested in day care must take the time to find areas of agreement and express their opinions as Congress and the states consider future government involvement in child care.

Efforts to improve the quality of day care often suffer from a lack of public awareness. For example, through both government and private efforts a new credential has been instituted in the day care field. The Child Development Associate (CDA) credential assures that a provider is well trained, yet few parents even recognize its name. Greater public awareness can make the CDA credential an indicator that will assist parents in making their child care decisions. CDAs can also organize among themselves as effective spokesmen for children in centers.

Policymakers

As the voices of those with conflicting opinions on day care issues grow louder, policymakers will find themselves faced with many difficult decisions. Often they will find that the available research does not meet their needs. For example, in deciding national policy toward both the nonprofit and for-profit sectors, policymakers will need research data describing the differences between the two, especially concerning matters of quality. Researchers will need to consider what types of centers provide what kinds of care, and under what conditions. In considering policies that favor either non-profit centers or for-profit centers, policymakers will need to know precisely how legislative support will affect the stability and growth of both types of centers.

Ultimately, government policies should allow parents to make their own child care decisions. Policies that increase the options open to all parents should be explored, and such policies must go arm-in-arm with public information and awareness efforts so that parents will be able to make informed choices. Given the power to choose and the necessary information, parents can then select what is best for their children.

References

1. Avrin, C. and Sassen, G. 1974. *Corporations and child care: profitmaking day care; workplace day care; and a look at alternatives.* Women's Research Action Project, Cambridge, Massachusetts.
2. Canon, B. 1978. "Child care where you work." *Ms.* 6(10):83–87.
3. "Child care in the 80's—status report on for profit child care." 1981. *Child Care Information Exchange* (January) 17:19–26.
4. Coelen, C., Glantz, F. and Calore, D. *Day Care Centers in the U.S.: A National Profile 1976–1977.* Abt Books, Cambridge, Massachusetts.
5. Corrigan, P. 1979. "Where day care is everybody's business." *Ms.* 8(2):25.
6. "Job and family: the walls come down." 1980. *U.S. News & World Report* 88(23):57–58.
7. Lelyveld, J. 1977. "Drive-in day care." *New York Times Magazine* (June 5): 110.
8. Ling, F. 1978. "Babysitting is big business." *Forbes* 122(2):80–84.
9. "Minimum wage alert." 1981. *Child Care Information Exchange* 17:30.
10. *National Association of Child Care Management News* (January, 1981): 2–3.
11. *National Association of Child Development and Education Chalk Talk* (December, 1980):1.
12. Ruopp, R. et al. 1979. *Children at the Center: Summary Findings and Their Implications.* Abt Books, Cambridge, Massachusetts.

13. Smith, G. 1979. "Perry Mendel's golden diapers." *Forbes* 123(13):67–69.
14. "Taking care of the kids." 1976. *The Economist* 259(6922):36.
15. Weiner, S. 1978. "The child care market in Seattle and Denver." In *Child Care and Public Policy*, P. Robin and S. Weiner, eds. D.C. Heath & Co., Lexington, Massachusetts.

Chapter 21

DAY CARE: A BLACK PERSPECTIVE

by Evelyn Moore

Despite the past decade and a half of heightened public sensitivity toward family needs, many Black families continue to suffer disproportionately from the twin hardships of discrimination and economic deprivation. Government programs are far too meager to answer the most basic needs of the indigent, let alone to begin assisting the thousands of Black families whose marginal incomes place them below governmental standards for "acceptable" living. Even more worrisome, existing economic trends and emerging government policies are likely only to exacerbate the disparities further. For young children, many of whom experience the harshest burdens of economic stress, the dearth of quality child care programs compounds the inequities they may face later in school and the job market. Many parents who need child care to meet their employment needs similarly suffer from the inadequate supply and exorbitant cost of care. Thus, as a service which combines early educational programs for children with relieving parents for employment, child care holds a particular importance and promise for Black families, especially those living on the margin of economic sufficiency. For them, it is an issue whose urgency has never been more critical.

The Black Perspective on Day Care— Why Is There One?

The need for a Black voice on child care stems from much more than purely demographic considerations. For a variety of reasons that range from the high participation rate of Black mothers in the

413

labor force to the lasting benefits that child care can give to all children, day care touches upon many Black families in a unique and complex fashion. When pieced together, these diverse factors argue persuasively for a distinct platform of child care priorities.

Child care simultaneously addresses the needs of Black children and their parents. Unlike most other services and programs, child care offers the unique—and sometimes confusing—attribute of enhancing educational and social growth among children while promoting economic self-sufficiency for parents. Inasmuch as each generation has its own respective reasons for needing child care, its value for Black families rests upon two extremely different, but quite complementary perspectives.

Ever since research in the early sixties first began to show direct relationships between cognitive development and early childhood education, reformers have seen child care as a key vehicle for social progress. By placing young children in an educational environment that emphasizes interaction with trained caregivers, other children, and their environment, child care can teach a multitude of skills that are becoming increasingly useful as urban schools and environments grow more complex. For many Black children, particularly those who will face a wall of discrimination and disadvantage throughout their early adulthood, child care can offer an initial positive boost towards overcoming society's most pathological and subtle roadblocks. Ultimately, the potential value that day care holds for improving the lives of children still stands as its most essential function for Black families.

Apart from its inherent value for their children, child care has for generations also provided Black families with the means to combat poverty and discrimination by allowing both parents to work simultaneously. Although child care itself usually does not make a critical difference in bringing a family up from poverty to middle-income levels, it does play a vital role in helping parents establish their self-sufficiency and/or finish their education. Many Black families (39%)[32] live under or perilously near poverty levels, even though most such parents, mothers and fathers alike, participate in the labor force. For them, assistance with child care is an essential component of any strategy for economic growth and development.

Conditions for many Black families are steadily worsening at a time when the demand for child care is growing more competitive. The economic deceleration of the last decade has caused particular hardships for Black families, many more of whom now live in poverty than did in 1970.[11] Even "working poor" families, whose incomes exceed eligibility limits for child care subsidies, simply cannot afford quality child care without extraordinary sacrifices. At the same time, the progressive contraction of government resources is beginning to cause a decrease in the supply of subsidized centers as well as reductions in subsidy eligibility standards that will leave an increasing number of parents unable to afford the care they prefer.

As the economy weakens, however, the need and demand for expanded child care services has, ironically, risen. Nearly 40% of all Black families are headed by single women,[31] most of whom bring home substantially lower earnings than their White counterparts. White mothers, too, are entering the work force at a record pace, in fact so rapidly that by 1990 three-fourths of all mothers are expected to be employed or seeking work.[28] Unless a new source of assistance becomes available, it is quite unlikely that Black families with low disposable incomes will be able to compete with an influx of new families who can afford quality care without any government assistance.

Growing restrictions on welfare and public assistance recipients may force more parents into the full-time work force without accounting for their children's needs. Child care, along with vocational training, counseling, and other employment-related services, has proven to be a critical component of any program that effectively reduces welfare caseloads. Contrary to popular stereotypes, a majority of Black families that receive AFDC payments already work, even though a lack of adequate support services, such as child care, impedes their access to full-time jobs and financial independence. If, as many policy-makers now advocate, welfare is to be turned into a massive "workfare" project, quality child care must be available to any parent(s) compelled to work, seek vocational training, or pursue an education at institutions of higher learning.

Since child care is a vehicle that socializes Black children at their most impressionable age, Black families and communities have a particular stake in the conception, organization, and administration of child care services. Such issues as curriculum, training, integration, and parent involvement all directly contribute to the quality and the sensitivity of any child care program. To those Black families who use child care for much more than the temporary care of their children, the content of day care programs is an especially relevant concern. If child care programs are indeed intended to prepare Black children to achieve their potential later in life, then the structure and substance of the entire child care system must incorporate an active Black perspective at every level of decision-making, be it national or local.

Many Black communities, especially those with the low- and moderate-income families most in need of child care assistance, have unique features and preferences. Although no current data adequately breaks down parent preferences according to race, income, and child's age, utilization patterns clearly show that these Black communities rely on care in centers or from relatives much more than do White or other higher-income areas. Similarly, both the very presence of various supportive institutions throughout such communities and the relative absence of others—well-funded schools or industry—will directly affect the viability of a particular child care program for those communities. In short, any wholesale solution to the growing child care crisis must specifically accommodate the desires and resources of certain Black communities if it is to amply address their needs.

The necessity for a Black perspective on child care does not, therefore, rest merely upon the universal need of poor and near-poor working families for child care. Rather, the combination of a variety of factors—the relative degree of its importance for lower income Black families; its potential for overcoming social inequities, worsening demographic and economic factors; plus the unique concerns of Black families and communities about the type, content, and delivery of programs to their children—contributes to a specific Black perspective. Indeed, the proper question is not so much "Why is a Black perspective necessary?" as it is "Why not?"

What Is the Black Perspective on Child Care?

The following platform does not attempt to speak for all Blacks, nor does it purport to address the child care concerns of all Black families. Instead, it focuses particularly on the needs of Black families who either live in poverty or else barely manage to stay above a subsistence level through a marginal income ($10,000 or less for a family of four). Faced with a child care policy that simultaneously subsidizes the very poor without allowing them to raise their incomes, ignores the working poor, and provides tax relief to the middle and upper classes, poor and near-poor families experience problems overwhelmingly greater than those of other groups. Our agenda, then, is primarily directed to answering their difficulties.

The child care system should guarantee a diversity of options with equity of access. Underlying the entire child care delivery system is an extraordinary diversity in types and purposes that ranges from informal family day care to comprehensive preschool or even nursery school. This patchwork partly derives from parent preferences, which similarly vary across a wide spectrum of tastes, and partly from the inconsistent supply of certain providers and the high costs of still others. Since, however, parents do differ in their preferences, they should have the right to obtain the care of their choice, regardless of their own income or the cost of the service.

Diversity has always been a considerable factor for child care in Black communities, who have traditionally utilized relatives and the extended family for child care long before it came into vogue. Currently, Black preferences appear to vary somewhat from White ones, in that relatives and centers are both utilized at higher rates by Blacks.[29] Any effective child care policy must therefore respect the clear desire of many lower income Black communities to keep a wider range of options available.

By itself, however, the mere availability of child care does not make it a practical option for all parents, especially those whose incomes exceed subsidy levels but remain far too insufficient to afford the inordinate costs of comprehensive care. Hence, a progressive child care policy must address itself toward making all options economically accessible to all parents, even when their incomes might be high enough to pay for inexpensive forms of care. All families should have the *right* to choose and obtain quality care without extending their own resources past the relative level that middle and higher incomes must pay. In other words, working Black families must not suffer any greater economic dislocation from merely using quality care than do families with "comfortable" incomes.

For many Black families, the principle of equity of access stems much more from a genuinely sincere and real need than it does from a vaguely socialist philosophy. Quality child care is seen by many such parents as a necessary element in providing their children with a sound education, but its prohibitive price keeps them from offering skills to their children comparable to those the "well-to-do" receive in nursery school. That the preschool years are seen by most academicians to be the formative ones in a child's development only buttresses the critical importance of making quality care accessible to all parents. To deny many poor and working families access to such an education or any other child care of their choice is, ultimately, to deny them the right to invest in their own children's futures.

The Federal government must take an active role in making these options available and accessible to all parents, not just to the destitute. Considering the tremendous costs associated with child care, no viable solution can succeed without government cooperation and participation. Since all families, irrespective of their state or locality, have a right of access to child care, it is as proper that the federal government underwrite child care expenses as it is correct that the government support urban education programs. No matter what form the resolution of the child care crisis might eventually take, a strong federal role is both desirable and unavoidable.

The federal role should not be limited, as it currently is, to addressing only the needs of the indigent. Of the majority of Black families who do not live in poverty, few can afford quality care, yet existing programs and policies are all targeted at the poor. Indeed, just as Head Start, Title XX, and Title I all have stringent income standards that prohibit much assistance for the working poor, so too, government-funded research has almost exclusively focused on the positive effects that day care holds for the most disadvantaged child, ignoring its potentially great value for other children in need of services. Through its narrow concentration on the problems of the "deprived," government has reinforced the stereotypes that federal programs can only help those who cannot help themselves; that most Black families live on welfare; and that by accepting government aid, a family proves its weakness and pathology.

Federal participation must go far beyond a mere dispensation of money to states without any voice in policy or quality control. Sadly, not all states have lifted their own standards to the level mandated in the 1968 Federal Interagency Day Care Requirements, and many successfully opposed implementation of the even more minimal 1980 HHS Day Care Requirements. To prevent the future abuse of children and the misuse of federal dollars, it is imperative that Washington complement its funding of day care with an expansion of its right to regulate, monitor, and coordinate day care programs and policies.

Finally, for any program that cares for children, and, more critically, for any program that utilizes federal or state funds, a minimum floor of quality must be mandated and enforced. While child care programs funded either privately or by states should be licensed and monitored by states, those programs which in turn receive federal funds should then comply with federal expectations (that is, regulations) for acceptable care. Since children all have the same needs for development, no matter what state they live in, it is both possible and advisable for the federal government to develop national minimum standards of care.

The private sector must become more involved with child care. Since neither the mood nor the economy of the country makes it likely that government will by itself answer all of the most pressing needs in child care or other services, the private sector—industry, businesses, and unions—must actively work to relieve the child care burdens of parents. Considering that many of its employees face serious child care difficulties, industry must recognize its obligation to involve itself with their child care needs.

By assisting child care programs, businesses would constructively contribute to the economic well-being of parents, and ultimately, to the revitalization of their own communities. Child care programs, even nonprofit centers or homes, are essentially businesses, but often they lack the administrative acumen to provide quality services without incurring financial troubles. A partnership between businesses and individual providers would help to expand and stabilize day care programs, benefiting employees, children, and the community alike.

Child care policy should emphasize the provision of quality care to all families who want it, regardless of their social class or income. Numerous studies have repeatedly demonstrated that quality care is directly linked to progress in several areas of a child's development, whether the care is a comprehensive preschool[7] or an ordinary Title XX day care center where even minimal protections can have documentable results.[25] Others have documented the long-term positive effects of preschool upon supposedly "disadvantaged" children by discovering reductions in special education referrals, teenage unemployment, and "delinquent" behavior.[26] In light of the distressing facts that 8.5% of all Black students are enrolled in special education programs (41% of all students placed in classes for the Educable Mentally Retarded are Black);[35] that the youth unemployment rate for Blacks straddles the 40% threshold;[32] and that in some states as many Black youth are in prison as attend college, the potential value of quality care for many Black communities is inestimable. Yet the need for quality care does not result entirely from its potential contribution to Black progress, as some states that provide center-based care do permit harmful conditions to flourish in programs that serve predominantly poor children.[9] Since for many Blacks the provision of quality care is necessary to both protect their children from harm and to enhance their development, it is essential that sufficient funds be made available to afford such quality, with enough left over to ensure its regulation. Training of caregivers, an integral component of improving the quality of care, should similarly be considered an indispensable item in the overall child care budget.

Child care programs that serve lower income Black communities should be designed to reflect their special needs and draw on their unique strengths. Since day care is usually the first socializing experience a child encounters outside the home, programs must be especially sensitive to ensure that the socialization process will enhance the child's self-esteem, emphasize the parents' values, and reflect the heritage of the Black community. Curricula, training, and activities must therefore be carefully developed to both incorporate a Black perspective in programs and to encourage as much parent participation as possible. Also, since many Black families face a bewildering puzzle of bureaucracy and programs, social and health services should be linked to child care centers to minimize difficulties in negotiating through the maze of services.

Blacks must play a decisive role in designing and administering

the programs and policies that will affect their families and children.
As a family service, child care can constructively complement the
efforts of parents to socialize their children and to prepare them for
school, but the success of a program is predicated on its attitude
toward the children. For at least the past two decades, many Black
families have learned that some well-intentioned programs, like
foster care or AFDC, can, if not administered correctly, be much
more destructive than supportive, largely because the original researchers and the subsequent planners did not have a positive,
objective view of the families they were trying to assist. In child
care, the same perspective holds true; to be effective, the program
must actively recognize that neither the family nor the child is
inherently deficient. Unfortunately, while some individual programs
may be able to project this perspective onto their staffs, rooting out
the pathological outlook and instilling a positive one throughout
the entire research, policy, and program system will require the full
participation of Blacks in every stage of policy-making and every
level of administration. Such a goal is fundamental for any long-
term policy intended to address the needs of Black families.

If, then, these principles frame a Black perspective on child care,
the natural question is, how does this view differ from other approaches? For the most part, the distinctions derive from a varying
emphasis on the importance of each issue for the respective communities, rather than from a strong disagreement over the appropriate solutions. Many White families experience economic difficulties
similar to those faced by poor and near-poor Black families, but each
group may approach child care from somewhat different vantage
points. Specifically, the Black perspective is shaped by the value of
child care for promoting the healthy development of children and
their families; the traditional need of working Black two-parent
families for child care; the accelerating number of low-income Black
single mothers; the presence of an active kinship system in many
Black communities; the persistence of the myth that Blacks lack a
strong work ethic; the need for an ethnically sensitive curriculum;
and the importance of eliminating the pathological, "deficit" perspective that dominates much child care policy. Taken collectively,
these concerns add up to a unique and cohesive policy.

While the differences between perspectives may be significant,
they have a complementary effect on each other. Many families need
child care, and of these, most need some form of financial assistance
to defray the expenses. Although lower income Black communities
do, by virtue of their overwhelming needs, have a stronger cause to
stress the expansion of quality day care, the issue stands as an important concern to all families, Black or White. Variations in emphasis and degree should not be mistaken for divisiveness among child

care advocates; if anything, such mild differences only prove that resolving the child care crisis will assist both a wide variety and a large number of American families.

The History of Day Care for Blacks

Child care played an important role in helping Black families meet their most essential economic needs long before the recent trend of White families to seek out-of-home-care. Due to the need to supplement their husband's low incomes, Black wives have traditionally worked regardless of the presence of young children. As far back as 1890, 36% of all Black women were gainfully employed, compared with 14% of all White women.[31] The disparity did not close in subsequent years; in 1930, for instance, Black women were still twice as likely as their White counterparts to participate in the labor force (39% vs. 20%).[31] Nevertheless, within the past thirty years, the margin has dropped from a 46% to 31% differential in 1948 to virtual parity (52% and 51% for Black and White women, respectively) in 1980.[34] The critical point is that since child care has recently become a significant concern for White families, the public now openly acknowledges the problem, in sharp contrast to America's earlier indifference when the problem primarily involved Black families.

Working Black mothers rarely had the luxury of placing their children in centers or nursery schools. Instead, most day care was provided informally, through an extended family system that still exists to some extent today. (According to one estimate, even as late as 1973, the extended family assisted 40% of all working Black women who needed child care.[10]) In addition to the thousands of Black grandmothers, aunts, and elder neighbors who cared for most of the children, a few day care centers also existed at Black colleges, churches, neighborhoods, and settlement houses in scattered cities across the country. While these programs were definitely conscious of quality, they differed from White "day nurseries" by providing and emphasizing day-long care to meet the employment needs of working Black parents. Their roots in the Black community were deep, as even before the Civil War informal field nurseries had served Black slave children.[8]

This pattern was not disturbed by the Lanham Act of 1942, which provided day care for working mothers as part of the World War II industrial effort but discriminated against Black families, nor did it change much when many White parents in the fifties began to use half-day nursery schools.[8] Of the few publicly supported centers that served Black children during this period, nearly all had a "welfare orientation," and little emphasis was given to the types of educational benefits that White children received in nursery school. A gradual exodus of Black school teachers from the South into northern day care centers helped introduce or upgrade the educational component, but the change did not affect public attitudes.[8]

The first substantive move towards addressing Black child care needs came in the early sixties, when "interventionist" research projects tried to determine if early childhood education could "save" disadvantaged (that is, Black) children from their pathological environment. While these programs did indeed prove that preschool can help a child's intellectual development, they also unintentionally enhanced the stereotype that Black children are cognitively deficient. Despite that drawback, however, their strong proof of the definite need for an educational component in day care has allowed countless child advocates to subsequently press for quality care for all poor children.

The enactment of Project Head Start by the Economic Opportunity Act of 1965 marked a watershed for Blacks. Although the comprehensive preschool program was targeted at "disadvantaged" children, by combining novel elements of community control and parent involvement with quality educational programming and access to social services, it successfully overcame any "deficit" mentality in its conception. Once policy-makers and evaluators stopped looking at Head Start as a panacea against poverty (as an infamous Westinghouse study did in 1969), few experts have doubted its worth or effectiveness.

One important byproduct of Head Start was the impetus it gave to efforts to organize community-based child care efforts for Blacks. By 1970, community groups were actively seeking AFDC funds from Title IV-A of the Social Security Act to support Black administered and designed child development programs for Black youngsters. In several states, particularly in the South, organizations like the Black Child Development Institute helped establish day care federations to coordinate funding efforts for minority-oriented child development programs. Most of these federations are still working in their states on behalf of poor families and minority programs.

The broad expansion of Title IV-A funds in the 1969–72 period encouraged a rapid growth in federally supported day care centers for parents either receiving or in danger of needing welfare assistance. Black children were substantially assisted by both the growth in Title IV-A funding and the enactment of Title I of the Elementary and Secondary Education Act, which devotes approximately 8% of its funding towards preschool education.[6] Other new federal programs similarly buttressed day care programming, especially the Child Care Food Service Program of the Department of

Agriculture, the Work Incentive (WIN) program, the Community Development Block Grants program, and various pilot projects of the Department of Labor. Most importantly, with the creation of Title XX of the Social Security Act in early 1975, the old Title IV-A program lost its categorical nature, as total control over social service and client selection was given to states through the creation of a large block grant. On the other hand, Title XX did shift the emphasis away from a "welfare" mentality toward a more positive objective of lifting family incomes above poverty levels, though it has yet to begin fulfilling this promise.

The Current Child Care Panorama for Black Families

The present system of publicly supported child care for Blacks is largely an uncoordinated smörgasbord, ranging from informal care paid through the AFDC income disregard to Title XX-funded centers and homes to comprehensive Head Start preschools. Subsidies are generally available only for the poorest families, who often find that rigid income standards and the lack of sliding fee scales impede their efforts to overcome their poverty status. For the near-poor, practically no relief is available, leaving informal family care as their only option.

Beyond such general impressions, it is impossible to precisely quantify the utilization of different types of child care by Black families, let alone to numerically demonstrate their preferences. Unfortunately, due to both a paucity of hard current data on Black child care choices and serious flaws with earlier studies, most information is less often scientifically documentable than it is inferred or conjectured. The following description will, nevertheless, give whatever data is available to provide an overview on child care utilization by Black families.

Centers

According to the most recent data available (1978), approximately 900,000 children each year receive either part-time or full day care in centers.[25] Of these, 28% (over 250,000) are Black; approximately half come from families with incomes below the national median (nearly $17,000), and an estimated 30% have families living at or below the poverty level.[25] More significantly, among those children who attend nonprofit centers that receive federal subsidies (the most common and heavily frequented type of center), Black children comprise 44% of the total enrollment,[25] more than double their national proportion of all children (17%). Well over 60% of the Black children who are enrolled in centers attend programs that receive some federal (presumably Title XX) subsidy.

Apart from the sheer number of Black children attending centers, little else is documentable. According to a 1971 survey, less than 20% of Black children under six years old with working mothers were enrolled in centers,[5] still a substantially higher percentage than that for White children then, and one which has probably risen since. Although Black families still utilize centers with a much higher frequency than White families, it is not exactly clear whether that disproportion stems from the availability of subsidies or from a sincere preference for that type of care.

Head Start/Preschools/Nursery Schools

Preschools differ from centers by virtue of their heavy emphasis on educational components, although for Black children the distinction is somewhat obscured by the fact that their preschool usually lasts for most of the day, unlike most nursery schools.[29] Hence, the estimate that 21% of the national preschool population is Black[29] may be no better than a rough estimate, despite the availability of Head Start and Title I subsidies for poor children. Head Start remains the paragon of preschool programs serving poor families, and it now provides mostly half-day care to approximately 375,000 children, 40% of whom are Black. Over the years, longitudinal evaluations have been conducted on many of the early intervention projects begun around 1960; all of them demonstrate marked and apparently permanent benefits for both students and their families.[7] In Black communities, Head Start centers have become invaluable resources, as they provide employment services for parents, social services to the family if needed, and a nutritional component for children. Nevertheless, despite an abundance of qualitative and quantitative evidence which together argue persuasively and convincingly for the broad expansion of quality care as a resource for children, Head Start still serves only 25% of its eligible population even after several boosts from the last Administration.

Family Day Care/Informal Care

Here, data is even scarcer, as a mammoth three-year HHS study has been delayed in publication. Nevertheless, even if the lack of figures prevents a precise estimate of the number and proportion of Black children using full-day family care, preliminary data and other statistics do paint a general picture. As is true for all economic, social, and ethnic groups, Blacks rely on family care much more than on any other form of child care. Nationally, well over three million children utilize full-time family care, and almost two million more receive it part-time; the greatest proportion of these children are younger than three years old.[1] Only 6% of all day care homes have been licensed by their state, thus leaving few homes eligible for governmental subsidies and most not subject to any quality controls.

Although Black families probably choose this mode of care with the same pattern and frequency as other families, 1975 evidence indicates that Black parents are more prone to utilize relatives for family day care,[29] perhaps a clue to the continued vitality of Black extended families. Also, corroborating evidence soon to be released by HHS will show that Black family day care providers are, on the average, at least twelve to fifteen years older than comparable White providers and much more likely to care for at least one of their relatives' children, often a grandchild.[1] When coupled with a recent Urban League survey that found approximately 85% of urban Black families to have relatives living in their city,[21] it is clear that a kinship network has survived to some extent, though it is unlikely that its present role in day care rivals that of previous generations.

Parental Preferences

Despite the availability of some survey and poll data, pinning down the child care tastes of any group of parents remains an elusive goal. By themselves, utilization patterns do not resolve the picture, since the availability and feasibility of different types of care varies with each individual case. Conceivably, the disproportionate numbers of Black children in centers can be explained by the much greater availability of subsidized care in centers than in the few licensed family day care homes. By the same logic, the extremely high rate of infant and toddler care supplied by family day care could be attributed to both the higher cost of center-based care for this age group and a widespread scarcity of center slots, rather than a common parental sentiment in favor of a family-like environment for infants.

While 1975 survey data showed an overall contentment with these child care arrangements, subsequent experiences belie this premise. As the "welfare" stigma attached to centers fades away, more parents, including Blacks, are increasingly attracted to centers and preschools but are discouraged by the inadequate supply and prohibitive costs. Waiting lists at many centers are now longer than a year, regardless of the availability of subsidies. In Los Angeles,

one recent study of a moderate-to-low-income Black community
found that over 45% of all Black parents who sought care outside
their home wanted center care, but many had severe troubles finding
programs with vacancies, let alone any they could afford.[12] For the
large portion of the families who actually sought center care for
their infants, Los Angeles proved no different from most of the
country, which faces a profound shortage of infant care slots in
every region except the South.[25] Even more surprising, the study
found that day care homes were filled only to 55% of their capacity
despite the community's huge demand for day care, perhaps reflecting both a distinct preference for center-based care and a glaring
absence of a coordinating mechanism for parents. That a recent
survey of predominantly white middle-class mothers found a similar
growth in the desire for center or preschool care[36] only corroborates
a general perception of the accelerating popularity of day care
centers.

Deciphering why parents favor a certain type of care is even more
enigmatic. Apparently all parents, Black and White, weigh heavily
such factors as cost, distance, quality, and safety, but the actual
prioritization varies from family to family. So far, no poll of parent
attitudes has determined that any of the considerations stands out
decisively.

Child Care Problems for Black Families

The major child care problems facing many Black parents do not
differ substantially from those of comparable White parents, but
the relative severity of the crisis in Black communities accentuates
their urgency. First, as stated above, the supply of center-based care
is far too insufficient to meet the high demand in many Black communities. Between tortuous waiting lists for centers and few licensed
day care homes, many Black families simply cannot find the type
of care they prefer with the subsidies they need or at a cost they can
afford. While these problems are already acute for parents seeking
care for three- to five-year olds, they are particularly insurmountable
for families that want center care for either infants or school-aged
children.

Part of the problem stems from inadequate public funding, which
either limits Title XX subsidies to only the poor who can find
vacancies in licensed care, or else provides minimal AFDC payments
that are far too low to help parents obtain quality care. No incentives
or mechanisms are present to help parents raise their income standards, presumably an objective of Title XX and AFDC alike. Finally,
without a coordinating body to help parents know what options

are available to best suit their needs, child care in most Black communities remains a fractured, unconnected system that leaves parents without the resources they need to negotiate their child's care.

Worsening Child Care Problems for Black Families

Upon an already inadequate and rather chaotic foundation of child care in Black communities, a sudden coincidence of demographic and economic trends promises to exacerbate the problems even further. Although the changes taking place in Black and White families may differ, the cumulative effect of these changes on an already-saturated child care market does not bode well for those on the lower rungs of the economic ladder, especially Black families.

Probably the most dramatic—and pervasive—development in Black families has been the meteoric rise in the number of Black single mothers. Between 1970 and 1978, the proportion of Black families headed by single mothers rose 40%, so that 39% of all Black families are now headed by single women, accounting for 44% of all Black children.[31] Even though they earn a median income of less than $6000 per year, less than half of such mothers use public assistance and almost 60% participate in the labor force.[34] For these families, to balance their marginal incomes with paying child care costs is a hopelessly impossible task; their rapid growth, more than any other factor, accounts for the urgent need for massive child care assistance. Conceivably, some critics might argue that even if a husband were present, single mothers would still probably work and need some form of child care. As the only source of income for their families, however, they are more likely to need full-day care and require federal subsidies; any continued growth of Black families headed by single mothers will therefore only stretch thin federal dollars even thinner.

The declining economy of the seventies has substantially arrested Black progress; since 1970, the income gap between comparable Black and White families has risen, more Black families are impoverished, and inflation has made quality care an increasingly unaffordable item in the budget of most moderate-income Black families. Unlike many White families, whose wives are entering the labor force for extra income, most Black two-parent families lack this simple option because 59% of the wives in these families already work,[34] usually even when young children are present. In 1978, for instance, as many as 57% of all Black mothers with children younger than six worked or sought jobs,[33] but for many of these families, even

428 Social Policy Issues

this "extra" income still did not bring quality child care within their reach.

If existing conditions in child care are already approaching a precipice, then the unprecedented surge of White mothers into the labor force may very well push the system over the edge. By 1990, three-fourths of all mothers will be in the labor force, as will two-thirds of all mothers with children younger than six.[28] Approximately three million extra preschoolers will need some form of care outside their homes, presumably provided by a currently overloaded child care market. Where will they go? At present, only 15% of all preschool-aged children can obtain licensed care; the rest rely on diverse combinations of parental, informal or unlicensed care.[19] If one also considers that these very mothers are growing more and more inclined to choose quality center-based care (44% according to the survey mentioned earlier),[36] and that many of them will have sufficient incomes to afford it, it is not too farfetched to imagine to all but the poorest subsidized families being squeezed out of licensed care in a competitive market.

To round out this gloomy picture, the federal government, heretofore the mainstay of the child care system for many families, is slowly abrogating its responsibility to subsidize the child care needs of the poor. Every year, states spend a slightly lower percentage of the total Title XX allocation on day care; last year a temporary decrease of the Title XX ceiling saw wholesale dislocations for the entire social services community, but nowhere so frequently nor so violently as for child care. Even without the new Administration's budget-cut proposals, the expiration in 1982 of a special $200 million Title XX allocation for child care will significantly accelerate the gradual shift of Title XX funds from day care into more crisis-oriented social services. Already presaging the inevitable squeeze, day providers across the country are now facing severe budget cuts that have closed or threatened to close many government-sponsored or administered programs. Finally, with passage of the budget proposals, the pace of the withdrawal would speed up from a canter to a gallop, leaving many Black families suddenly very alone and very wanting. Taken collectively, then, the emerging child care trends are hardly auspicious for those Black families—poor, near-poor, and moderate—who need child care the most.

Black Perspectives on Existing Programs and Issues

Before weighing possible solutions to resolve the child care shortage, it is important to first discuss existing measures—both funding and programmatic—to ascertain their effects on Black children and families. From that base, it should then be much easier to judge the relative merits of various proposals to determine if they really hold genuine promise for helping Black families along the guidelines espoused earlier.

Title XX

As the principal funding mechanism for low-income day care, Title XX has played a critical role in helping poor children receive center-based care. In 1979, approximately 860,000 children were estimated to receive day care services under Title XX,[15] a substantial jump from 1976 levels that mostly reflects the special $200 million appropriated for day care every year since fiscal 1977. Child care still ranks as the leading service funded by Title XX, although its share of the annual appropriation has slowly slipped down to 22%. Title XX subsidizes more than twice as many children in centers as it does in day care homes, so that 25% of all children enrolled in centers receive some Title XX assistance, in sharp contrast to the 97% of family day care children who do not.[22] Most likely, over 40% of these children are Black.

In spite of day care's prominent role in Title XX, the relationship between the two has not been exactly harmonious. While it is understandable that as Title XX's largest service, day care would eventually face some relative cuts due to inflation (the Title XX ceiling has risen only 16% in nine years), many procedural problems also persist. Perhaps the best example of the drawbacks of lumping day care into a noncategorical block grant program is the fate of the special $200 million annual appropriation for day care (P.L. 96–401) in most states. Originally authorized in late 1976 to compensate states and day care programs for higher costs likely under new federal regulations, much of the P.L. 96–401 appropriation has never gone to day care, even though states received the dollars free, without any matching requirements. Instead, at least twenty states, accounting for 60% of the allocation, switched their ordinary Title XX funds from day care to other programs and then substituted most of the new appropriation to support already existing day care services.[4] It was not surprising, therefore, that when HHS finally issued minimal regulations for Title XX day care in 1980, many states pleaded poverty and scuttled the rules.

While Title XX has certainly not proven to be a bonanza for day care providers, it has disappointed even more day care consumers. Although the hope behind the original legislation was clearly that Title XX would become a graduated service that would help families reach self-sufficiency via phased-in fee scales, few states have implemented effective procedures. As of 1979, only two-thirds of all states imposed fees for Title XX day care for families earning less than 80% of their state's median income, only 28 states had any sliding fee schedules, and very few of those states had effective scales.[15] Instead, most states simply provide subsidies to parents up to a certain income level (often 60% of the state's median income) and automatically cut off assistance as soon as it is reached. Such a policy cruelly leaves countless families trapped in a helpless dilemma: if they already have gone off welfare but still receive Title XX subsidies, any raise in income will usually push them above the eligibility limit, remove their child care support, and drive them back to public assistance. Equally as disgraceful, for the vast majority (67%) of Title XX subsidized families who receive AFDC, the Title XX income restrictions in many states will prevent them from accepting a second or higher-paying job that would eliminate their need for welfare, but would also keep them from using licensed quality care. It is no less than a national tragedy that so many poor *working* families should face conditions like those in Montana, where eligibility limits were found to inhibit many AFDC families from raising their incomes by as little as $1,000.[17] Surely we cannot afford to continue leaving families with such an impossibly convoluted choice as that between independence from welfare and child care, yet as Title XX eligibility limits creep downward, we are forcing this unfortunate quandary on to more and more working parents.

AFDC Income Disregard

Aside from Title XX, the federal government also substantially contributes to child care for the poor by allowing AFDC recipients to deduct their child care costs from their reported income as a work-related expense. In 1977, this mechanism served 145,000 children, and with the heightening competition for, and the decreasing supply of, Title XX subsidies, this number can only have risen. The Income Disregard provides states with an expedient mechanism for cutting their child care costs, since every family that switches from Title XX to AFDC saves the state Title XX dollars that are then plugged into other financially strapped social services. Families, who are left with insufficient funds to pay for center care, and the federal government, which shoulders most of the AFDC bill, bear the major burden of the state's savings. Unfortunately, a study of the problem found that for working families forced on to the disregard, to continue Title XX-type care would require individual income losses as high as $125 a month, obviously an impossible sum for poor families.[24]

Widespread use of the income disregard would pose a direct

threat to poor Black families who want center care for their children. Not only would it reduce the federal stake in Title XX day care, but, more critically, it would also allow states to circumvent the federal responsibility for providing and ensuring a minimum floor of quality care to working parents in need across the country. To exploit a program intended to supplement Title XX day care by using it to shrink that resource is more than distressing—it signifies a callous indifference to the need of children for stimulating care, not to mention the right of parents to choose and receive that care. For Black children and their families, it looms as a growing affront to their very right to social justice and progress.

Child Care Tax Credit

For the vast numbers of families whose incomes make them ineligible for subsidies, the federal government does attempt to provide some sort of child care assistance. Any family may receive at the end of the year a tax "credit" of 20% of their annual child care expenses of $2,000 or less for one child, $4,000 or less for more. No family may receive credit for more than $400 for one child and $800 for two or more children, and the amount a family receives is ultimately contingent upon whether the family pays enough taxes to offset the credit at the end of the year. Nearly four million Americans now use the credit for child care expenses, drawing down the largest single federal expenditure for child care, approximately $1 billion in fiscal 1981.

Whom does the credit benefit the most? In 1977, two-thirds went to families above the national median income (now $17,000), and less than 15% went to families earning under $10,000.[6] Lower-income families, who do not have high enough tax liabilities to match against the credit, whose salaries are so low that any nominal payment still would not bring them close to affording quality care, and who need cash up front, not at the end of the year, have little stake in the credit. For the 50% of Black families who earn less than their median income of almost $11,000, the credit does not even begin to help meet their expenses, let alone provide coverage equal to that gained by higher income families. Who benefits from the credit? Ironically, those families who need it the least.

Unfortunately, the failure of the present credit to help the working poor is not its only drawback. By spending such a large sum of money on child care without specifying any directions or applications, the federal government surrenders much of its prerogative and concern for the quality, safety, and licensing of all child care that receives federal support. Without any stipulation that federal dollars must be used only in care that at least meets some standards, government only encourages the patronage of care which does not; again, the needs of children are sacrificed for the supposedly free choice of parents. Secondly, while Black and other advocates do not begrudge the middle class their child care relief, they are justifiably fearful that when policy-makers assess the need for further federal support of child care, all federal child care dollars will be lumped into one aggregate sum without considering how and to whom those dollars are distributed. In such an event, the various child care constituencies would necessarily be pitted against each other, so that whatever disproportionate degree of federal largesse the middle class gets—or has—would, in the long run, be taken from the pockets of marginal-income families.

Regulations

Federal regulations are absolutely essential for a sound infrastructure of any child care system that receives federal support. Last December's Congressionally-imposed delay of implementation of the HHS Day Care Requirements was therefore as painful a blow to child care as it was to children. Indeed, any statement that the federal government should have no voice in determining the minimum quality of federally sponsored child care utimately implies that the federal government has no prerogative to concern itself with the quality of life for children—even when federal dollars may be hurting, not helping, those children. Is this a statement that the lives of the poor children who would be protected by the regulations are not worth saving? If the children were not predominantly minority, 40% Black, and extremely poor, if they were almost exclusively White, mostly middle class, but equally as vulnerable to deplorable care, would the Congressional furor against the regulations have been any less ardent? A close examination of the supposedly "expensive", "unnecessary", and "bureaucratic" regulations makes one wonder.

The suspended regulations are actually quite minimal and far less demanding than their 1968 FIDCR predecessors that had attracted an even greater controversy. According to HHS estimates, 75% of all centers currently receiving federal subsidies (and 80% of all nonprofits) already comply with or exceed the staffing ratios and group sizes, the two most expensive requirements.[23] More importantly, at least three different provisions of the regulations make available temporary extensions, waivers, and various compromises for any provider or state that justifiably needs to gradually phase in the standards. In short, only the most regressive states and the most lenient providers had reason to fear the regulations—precisely the targets the regulations aimed at, and precisely the opponents who skillfully capitalized on the growing antiregulatory and defederalizing mood across the country. They do not speak for the vast majority of day care providers, parents, and advocates who appreciate the incontestible need and value of the requirements.

Just as the burdens imposed by the regulations are minimal, the benefits from implementation would be extremely significant and vital. Children, especially infants and preschoolers, are very impressionable and vulnerable to any of a variety of negative environments. Unless enough trained adults are on hand, for instance, a fire could have disastrous consequences for any group of young children, whether they are at home or in a center. The same principle applies to child development, where the relative quality of child care—that is, the group size and the ratio of caregivers to children —can determine whether the care will have positive or negative long-term effects on children. If true, then the policy of a few states to permit low-quality care to flourish with federal sponsorship demands immediate remedial action to protect the children, if nothing else. Even a partial listing of the most glaring faults in many state licensing codes—one third of all states do not require health evaluations or tuberculosis tests; ten states do not mandate a minimum ratio of caregivers to infants despite their defenselessness against fire; less than half of all states meet minimum staffing requirements recommended in national fire safety codes—indicates a clear dereliction of state responsibility which invites and obligates federal intervention. When Louisiana can allow voluntary licensing for non-subsidized centers, when Idaho can permit voluntary compliance with its licensing code, when many states do not even try to effectively monitor their programs, the inability of all states to control quality by themselves can no longer be at question.

Yet beyond protecting children from the worst horrors of unregulated care, the requirements also impose a series of significant and positive measures for children. Caregiver training, a cost-effective and developmentally sound emphasis on group sizes rather than costly staff-child ratios, minimum health and safety requirements, state monitoring, social service referrals, and parent involvement are all mandated, but in a flexible and reasonable context. For each of the 900,000 low-income children directly affected by the regulations, implementation would assure that a minimum quality of care with potential long-term benefits is guaranteed. Equally as important, however, implementation would also cause a ripple effect that would encourage states to raise their licensing codes up to federal levels, thereby improving the quality of care for even those children untouched by the federal rules. Surely these benefits, precautions, and protections are sufficient to warrant a federal role in child care regulation.

Most critically, though, the vulnerabilities and needs of young children do not vary across state lines any more than they do for socioeconomic classes. If state promises and state codes cannot enforce a minimum floor of quality care for low-income children whose parents depend on day care to meet their most essential economic needs, how, then, can Washington not be responsible for protecting such children from the harm it sponsors? Most Americans would demand no less for their own children.

Licensing

In addition to the numerous deficiencies within individual state licensing standards described above, the very process and scope of state licensing has growing implications for Black children. The vast majority of all children who receive out-of-home care utilize family day care homes, 94% of which have not been licensed by their states. To license and monitor all homes and centers is a monumental task that far exceeds the current capabilities of state agencies, especially since most states have not made licensing a high enough priority to even warrant adequate funds for present licensing activities.[27] Furthermore, in some states, the very idea of family day care appears so close to a form of state regulation of grandparents and relatives that the concept is politically untenable. This inherent problem has led to the growing preference of states like Louisiana and Idaho to permit voluntary licensing and of others, such as Iowa, North Carolina, and Texas, to allow homes to simply register with the state and then monitor themselves.[27] This attitude, combined with the prohibitive cost of licensing, has left the vast majority of children in child care without any government protections.

Nevertheless, even if the popularity of licensing has diminished, the need has never been stronger. Once licensed, family care providers have greater access to training, social services, and technical assistance that can help improve the quality of care and lessen the incidence of custodial ("care by television") programs.[27] Also, due to a frequent lack of knowledge of safety and health procedures, unlicensed homes are particularly susceptible to accidents or fires that can and do kill children. Finally, as more mothers, especially those with infants, enter the work force, the demand for family care will rise so significantly that, according to one projection, one million more day care homes may be needed by 1990.[13] If this figure is correct, then states must begin immediately to upgrade their licensing programs to prepare for, and hopefully prevent, a massive utilization of unsafe and unregulated care of children. Certainly, for once in our nation's history, we should not wait for a rash of fires and child fatalities before we are willing to invest in safety precautions.

Inspections, Monitoring, and Enforcement

Of course, no licensing or regulatory system is worth implementing unless the standards and rules will be enforced. Unfortunately, as last year's tragic and preventable explosion in an Atlanta Head Start center profoundly emphasized, inspections and monitoring often rank at the bottom of a state's or local agency's priorities. The threat to human life, especially a child's, must not be overshadowed or obscured by any other concern; so long as government has received the responsibility for preventing such accidents, it cannot defer that charge for any extraneous reason, be it staff limitations, inadequate funding, or excessive caseloads. Our children cannot afford to wait for yet another version of Atlanta's "accident" until we learn that even if child care funds are so limited that some services must be sacrificed, no activity should preempt the monitoring and inspection of vital health and safety procedures. Are children any less important than the customers of restaurants, hotels, or any other government inspected facility?

Caregiver Training

One of the most striking, though not surprising, findings of HEW's massive National Day Care Study was that caregiver training had extremely positive developmental benefits for all children.[25] Yet training does more than merely upgrade the quality of a provider's service; it also helps caregivers, many of whom are young CETA or AFDC recipients themselves, to develop a career with the potential for an official credential. Nevertheless, despite both its overall value and its particular importance to minority children, who need care from adults sensitized to minority concerns, training has been available to caregivers only on a sporadic and inconsistent basis. Over the past year, previously open-ended Title XX training funds have been capped, cut dramaticaly, and all but castigated by Congress for misuse and ineffectiveness. Most likely, training funds will face a severe, if not complete, cut this year, thereby forcing the cost of a critically vital, but equally as expensive, need onto states which may well prefer to ignore that need. For low-income children in day care, the prospect of receiving care from nontrained caregivers only makes the possibility of custodial care that much more likely.

Information and Referral

If the parental right to freely choose from a diversity of options is to actually become a guiding principle for the child care delivery system, that latitude will serve parents only to the extent that they already know what choices are available and practical. It is ironic, therefore, that a system that prides itself on its diversity and its versatility in fact funds only fifty to sixty information and referral (I & R) agencies across the nation,[2] despite I and R's citation by parents in 1975 as a child care resource they most needed but did not have.[29] That these agencies are most useful for low-income and minority families,[2] but are unavailable in many communities, implies, perhaps, that low-income and minority families suffer most from the bewildering array of child care types, choices, and problems. For a fractured patchwork system to work, then, some coordinating mechanism like I and R must become an integral part of whatever structure does exist in the system.

Infant and Afterschool Care

As difficult as arranging day care for the "traditional" age group (three- to five-year-olds) may be, parents who need out-of-home care for their older or younger children often face notoriously frustrating searches. Only 4.5% of center-based care is devoted to infants,[25] and even with family homes, the supply and the organization is inadequate to meet the demand. Since center-based infant care is almost exclusively concentrated in the South, many northern states are besieged by requests for infant care; during a one-month study, the state of Maryland fielded one hundred inquiries a day for assistance with infant care.[27] The problems of infant care are most acute for young single mothers, many of whom must work or finish school but increasingly do not have a third-generation relative who will care for their child. In light of the accelerating teenage pregnancy rate in Black communities, which is now seven times higher for Black unmarried adolescents than it is for their White counterparts,[20] the situation can only deteriorate further.

Parents with infants at least have a chance of finding center-based care; working parents with school-aged children, on the other hand, have practically none at all. Whatever after-school care exists for the 18 million children aged between 6 and 14 with working mothers is given almost exclusively by in-home or family day care providers, but even those sources, plus the rare after-school programs that do exist, are not sufficient to accommodate the one million school aged children who do not have supervised care.[3] For low-income Black communities, whose streets are saturated with negative role-models and intense peer-group pressures, after-school care offers a promise of greater adult supervision with less exposure to unknown influences and pressures. Such communities cannot afford to continue letting the streets raise their children; sooner or later, policy-makers must be convinced of the same conclusion.

Possible Long-Range Solutions

Given both a steadily worsening child care situation for many Black families and the inadequacy of existing programs to solve even their present problems, some large-scale, long-range measures must eventually be taken. A variety of proposals have been recently suggested by policy-makers and advocates, each with its own relevance to the problems of Black children and families. The following analysis will briefly discuss each scheme to determine whether it genuinely addresses the issues and criteria laid out in the introduction.

An employment-related comprehensive child care bill. Over the last several years, some child care advocates have gradually shifted their emphasis away from universally available comprehensive child care to a measure comparable in scope but limited in eligibility. By addressing child care as an employment service for parents, rather than as an educational medium for children, the bill would make quality care available and affordable for any parent both in the labor force and willing to pay a liberal fee set according to income. Despite the proposal's focus on employment, it need not lessen any of the quality inherent in a more traditional approach in order to make it palatable to policy-makers. Arguing for parents does not require sacrifice from children.

The impetus for employment-related care cannot be construed to imply that a purely comprehensive child care bill has lost its constituency. Rather, many child advocates still have a deep concern that, ideally, child care should promote the free educational development of all children whose parents want quality care, but they also recognize the political realities of the times. Employment is a burgeoning national concern, and if capitalizing on that trend can get better child care for more children, with equity of access and choice for parents, then we are obligated to promote that concept.

Would such a bill promote equity of access and diversity of options? So long as parents can choose the type of care and can easily afford its price, the essential requirements would be met. To ensure that a sufficient supply of quality options are available for parents to select from freely, both federal regulations and a reasonable reimbursement scale would also be necessary. Within such parameters, the bill could still answer the developmental needs of Black children; assist the employment needs of struggling Black families, particularly those of Black single mothers; and solve the moral needs of American society for a more equitable treatment of its children. At this point in time, that would be quite an accomplishment indeed.

An expansion of the federal child care tax credit. Other child care advocates have sought to exploit the current tax credit fever by expanding the child care tax credit to the point that it can provide substantial relief to working families. While several proposals have been suggested, one in particular deserves close examination. Starting with families at the lower end of the spectrum ($10,000 per year or less), the proposal would raise the credit from 20% to 50%) of their total child care expenses, and make the credit refundable at the end of the year to compensate if the family's tax liability is too low to offset the credit. Up from that bracket, the credit would decrease by 1% for every $1,000 earned by the family, so that by $40,000, a family would receive only its previous 20% credit.

Could establishing such a "sliding credit" and making it refundable solve the problems of distribution of funds, equity of access, and quality control inherent in the credit's present form? From a Black perspective, probably not. First, by weighting the credit toward the bottom of the scale, the present disproportionate distribution of dollars in favor of the middle class would lessen, but since the total of dollars ultimately depends on the individual's child care expenses, which will still be much *lower* for the working poor, a decided tilt in distribution will remain. Secondly, even if allowing the working poor a higher credit would distribute more money to them than to the middle class, an extremely dubious supposition, that amount would still not be sufficient to allow families with marginal incomes to afford the same quality care which suddenly would be within reach of the middle class. That many working poor families would also need to wait until the end of the year to collect their refunds would only ignore their basic lack of disposable income, in contrast to the middle class, which would receive its entire benefit immediately. In other words, giving a few extra dollars to the lower brackets will not by itself achieve equity of access. Lastly, an intrinsic problem with the tax credit remains—namely, how can quality controls be established to ensure that federal funds are spent on quality care? Conceivably, if the credit were either limited to licensed care, or, perhaps, restricted to federally regulated care, quality care would be utilized, but in pragmatic terms, neither one is enforceable, practical, or even desirable to the tax credit advocates. Most likely, enactment of the tax credit proposal would see children of the working poor increasingly served by a low-quality, inexpensive market that may well be dominated by proprietary chains with little interest in children except profits. Regrettably, that frightening trend has already begun to infiltrate low-income Black communities.

Sliding fee scales for Title XX. If answering the most desperate child care problems—those of the poor and near-poor—stands as the foremost priority in child care, it might prove more effective to simply focus on those concerns rather than address the overall child care issue head-on. Many proponents of this strategy favor widespread expansion of Title XX sliding fee scales, since they provide both continuity of care for the poor when their income rises as well as quality care for the near-poor who would otherwise not qualify.

The best application of sliding fees clearly lies with parents who are already receiving Title XX subsidies and, most likely, AFDC support. By allowing these families the opportunity to leave welfare without disrupting the quality or location of care for their children, sliding fees have been demonstrated to actually reduce AFDC caseloads by as much as 50%, generate substantial federal and state tax revenue, and keep many families from ever turning to AFDC.[14] For the poor, expansion of quality Title XX sliding fee scales to all states would certainly constitute a major triumph.

The benefits of sliding fees do not, however, necessarily extend so completely to the working poor, who also need assistance to afford quality care. Since these families may have incomes over $10,000, to provide them with an equitable access to quality care would require either such a gradual sliding subsidy scale that it would lose its effectiveness for poor families, or some other funding mechanism, perhaps tax credits or vouchers, to compensate. The scale therefore can help only those poor working families just earning beyond the "margin." Even then, by making more families eligible for Title XX, assistance might, under present supply conditions, only increase the competition for slots, possibly conflicting with Title XX's policy that 50% of all service recipients must receive welfare. Clearly, to implement a truly national policy to support sliding fees, Title XX payments for day care would need to be substantially increased. Yet, as the P.L. 94–401 experience vividly testifies, any new money injected into Title XX without a maintenance of effort provision to prevent the "supplantation" of existing funds will not meet its objective, even if the allocation were specifically targeted for day care. In sum, then, sliding fees clearly and constructively resolve the major child care dilemma for poor families, but to assist those families with somewhat higher incomes, a much larger and more diverse package will be necessary.

Industrial Participation. As the emphasis on work-related child care has risen in the past few years, industry has been increasingly viewed as an appropriate resource for assistance. Throughout the past decade, much attention has been devoted to on-site (at the factory) care for the children of employees. A considerable number of programs were established at the beginning of the seventies, many of them in southern textile factories, but the 1974 recession, an unsatisfactory rate of utilization, and the lack of data to indicate cost-effectiveness led to the closing of most programs. Some on-site centers do exist, but, for the most part, it is improbable that even the availability of many such centers can overcome the apparent preference of parents to patronize neighborhood-oriented child care that does not require so much transportation of the children.

Nevertheless, aside from centers, industry can still make valuable contributions toward easing the child care pressures in many communities, without requiring burdensome investments. In upper New York State, for instance, Welch Foods and Chappequa Opportunities, Inc. provide a subsidy and administrative services to a nearby center, much as Control Data Corporation has made bookkeeping and other services available to the Northside Child Development Center in Minneapolis. Another approach which worked quite successfully for Illinois Bell Telephone involved the establishment of a child care information and referral service which helped employees find appropriate care, recruited family day care providers, and promoted their licensing. Over a two-year period, the program saved an estimated $97,000 per year through reduced turnover, and it also served many more employees than could an on-site program. In short, industries can engage in a wide variety of activities, none of which are so extensive that the businesses would be compelled to justify them on a cost-effective basis, yet which would still promote child care in their communities by applying business expertise and dollars as seed investments.

Finally, even beyond supporting child care organizations and agencies, businesses could introduce more progressive policies to help their employees either care for their children themselves or seek alternative arrangements outside their homes. In the first instance, flexitime, maternity leave, paternity leave, and part-time personnel policies must be introduced to at least offer parents the opportunity to care for their children through whatever adjustments are possible. To help those parents who prefer or require child care, a business could also provide child care "allowances" or vouchers as part of their regular benefits package. These and other innovations must be forthcoming in the near future if business is to successfully adapt to the sudden transformation of America's workforce.

Conclusion: Ultimate Objectives and Results

If the United States should ever implement a child care policy along these guidelines, existing data already hints at the benefits that would fall on both the entire society and the children themselves. After comparing the cumulative costs and the aggregate benefits, it will become much clearer why America should place such a stake in child care and in its children.

In and of itself, better child care would enhance the development of children. Regardless of whether the benefits throughout the lifetime of a child can or cannot be demonstrated, study after study has documented that quality child care *does* benefit children in their immediate social, cognitive, emotional, and physical growth.[22] Education does not need to justify that on a cost-benefit basis, a cost-effective basis, or even a longitudinal basis, its services are worth society's investment; child care, too, should have a similar latitude to let its intrinsic benefits to children suffice without further debates on its profitability for society. Black and all other children deserve the investment on their own merits.

A properly constructed child care system would promote the self-sufficiency of America's poor families. Most AFDC families who utilize publicly funded child care do so in order to work, seek work or receive job training.[16] While the availability of center care would not by itself determine whether a parent does enter the labor force and eventually leave welfare, evidence is beginning to accumulate that child care can make a substantial difference. Studies of sliding fee programs in both Florida and Montana have shown both dramatic reductions in AFDC assistance among families who entered their programs and, even more importantly, a sharp rise in the number of families who used child care to deliberately avoid receiving AFDC.[14,17] No reason exists why, given sufficient time, resources, and funds, such results cannot be replicated across the country.

Child care gives long-term benefits to children. Within the past few years, longitudinal studies of early education programs established in the 1960s have uniformly demonstrated that such programs can substantially improve the subsequent school performance of low-income children.[7] Over a length of time lasting at least into high school, graduates of these programs are markedly less likely to be placed into special education classrooms, to be held back in their grades, to have low I.Q. and achievement test ratings, and to have "negative" attitudes aboout their education. Considering the pathology of problems that society inflicts on low-income Black children, such positive results offer real hope for combating some of the most discouraging and discriminatory conditions present in our nation today.

Child care is a cost-effective use of taxpayers' dollars. Using the longitudinal data as evidence, it can now be demonstrated that an investment in early childhood development would eventually save the government subsequent costs from supporting remedial health and education programs for children, welfare and unemployment assistance for parents, and even the juvenile and criminal justice system. A longitudinal study conducted in an Ypsilanti, Michigan, preschool just recently found that public school costs sharply declined, juvenile justice costs associated with delinquency decreased, while projected lifetime earnings sharply rose.[26] Government, society, and the children all earned a hefty profit on an initial investment which, within this context, was minimal.

Child care's employment assistance to parents similarly results in directly measurable net benefits to government and society. According to the Florida study mentioned above, child care for newly working parents more than amply paid back both its federal and its state investments through increased income tax, Social Security, and sales tax revenues, without even considering a 45% cut in state and federal AFDC costs.[14] Colorado has similarly found that more than 3% of the state's entire tax base was generated entirely by higher taxes paid by both parents who utilize child care to work and by child care staff.[18] If the incalculable social and economic benefits of strengthening America's work-force are also considered, child care clearly can serve as a very cheap investment in national productivity. An ounce of prevention *is* worth the trouble.

Providing all families access to quality care is a necessary step toward social equity. If child care indeed has a lasting effect on a child's life, then its provision is as much a component of equal opportunity as is any other aspect of education. Families should no more have to be poor to receive day care than they should have to be rich to attend nursery school. Early childhood is, educators now know, a critical period in which a child develops and masters many of the skills needed throughout his/her adult life. Surely, then, no families should be compelled to accept anything other than the care and the quality their children need.

Child care therefore uniquely benefits children, parents, government, and the society alike. For many Black children and their families, it offers an effective start to overcome even the most subtle obstacles society has placed in the way of their progress. It is, ultimately, a fundamental service to families who cannot afford to wait any more than can a new generation of children who face the same inequities their parents faced. They, their families, and their country deserve no less.

References

1. Administration for Children, Youth, and Families. 1981. *National Day Care Home Study.* U.S. Department of Health and Human Services, Washington, D.C.
2. American Institutes for Research in the Behavioral Sciences. 1980. *Project Connections: A Study of Child Care Information and Referral Services, Phase I Results.* American Institutes for Research, Cambridge, Mass.

3. Advisory Committee on Child Development. 1976. *Toward A National Policy for Children and Families.* National Academy of Sciences, Washington, D.C.

4. Benton, B., Field, T., and Millar, R. 1978. *Social Services: Federal Legislation vs. State Implementation.* The Urban Institute, Washington, D.C.

5. Brito, P. and Shortlidge, R. 1977. *How Women Arrange for the Care of Their Children While They Work: A Study of Child Care Arrangements, Costs, and Preferences in 1971.* Ohio State University Center for Human Resource Research, Columbus, Ohio.

6. Congressional Budget Office. 1978. *Childcare and Preschool: Options for Federal Support.* U.S. Government Printing Office, Washington, D.C.

7. Consortium for Longitudinal Studies. 1979. *Lasting Effects After Preschool.* U.S. Department of Health, Education, and Welfare, Washington, D.C.

8. Dill, J. 1973. "The Black child and child care issues." In *Child Care— Who Cares?*, P. Roby, ed. Basic Books, New York, N.Y.

9. Gross, B., and Rayson, R. 1979. "The laws don't protect your children." In *The Fort Lauderdale News and Sun Sentinel*, July 29, 1979, Vol. 17, No. 61, Fort Lauderdale, Fla.

10. Hill, R. 1977. *Informal Adoptions Among Black Families.* National Urban League Research Department, Washington, D.C.

11. Hill, R. 1980. "Black families in the 70's" In *The State of Black America: 1980.* National Urban League, Inc., New York, New York.

12. Hill-Scott, K. 1979. "Child care in the Black community." *Journal of Black Studies* 10(1):78–97.

13. Hofferth, S. 1979. "The implications for child care." In *Women in the Labor Force in 1990.* R. Smith, ed. The Urban Institute, Washington, D.C.

14. Hosni, D. 1979. *An Economic Analysis of Child Care Support to Low-Income Mothers.* University of Central Florida.

15. Kilgore, G. and Salmon, G. 1979. *Technical Notes.* U.S. Department of Health, Education, and Welfare, Washington, D.C.

16. Massachusetts Department of Social Services. 1981. *Day Care Consumer Profile Study.* Massachusetts Department of Social Services, Boston, Mass.

17. Montana Department of Social and Rehabilitation Services. 1978. *Sliding Scale Day Care, and Analysis of the Region V Demonstration Project.* Montana Department of Social and Rehabilitation Services, Helena, Montana.

18. Morgan, G. and Redmann, S. 1979. *Day Care Returns Tax Dollars.* Massachusetts' Children's Lobby, Brookline, Mass.

19. National Black Child Development Institute. 1980. *The Status of Black Children in 1990.* The National Black Child Development Institute, Inc., Washington, D.C.

20. National Center for Health Statistics. 1979. *Health, United States 1978.* U.S. Government Printing Office, Washington, D.C.

21. National Urban League Research Department. 1980. *Black Pulse.* National Urban League, Inc., New York, N.Y.

22. Office of the Assistant Secretary for Planning and Evaluation. 1978. *The Appropriateness of the Federal Interagency Day Care Requirements.* U.S. Department of Health, Education, and Welfare, Washington, D.C.

23. Office of the Assistant Secretary for Planning and Evaluation. 1980. *Addendum to Draft Regulatory Analysis—Proposed HEW Day Care Requirements*. U.S. Department of Health, Education, and Welfare, Washington, D.C.
24. Reap Associates. 1978. *Policy Implications of Alternative Child Care Funding Mechanisms*. U.S. Department of Health, Education, and Welfare, Washington, D.C.
25. Ruopp, R. et al. 1979. *Children at the Center*. Abt Associates, Cambridge, Mass.
26. Schweinhart, L. and Weikart, D. 1981. *Young Children Grow Up: The Effects of the Perry Preschool Program on Youths through Age 15*. High/Scope Educational Research Foundation, Ypsilanti, Mich.
27. Sheenan, P. 1980. "State survey of day care licensing procedures—part I". *Day Care and Child Development Reports* 9(10):7–10.
28. Smith, R. 1979. *Women in the Labor Force in 1990*. The Urban Institute, Washington, D.C.
29. Unco, Inc. 1975. *National Childcare Consumer Study: 1975*. U.S. Department of Health, Education, and Welfare, Washington, D.C.
30. U.S. Bureau of the Census. 1979. *The Social and Economic Status of the Black Population of the United States, An Historical View: 1790–1978*. U.S. Government Printing Office, Washington, D.C.
31. U.S. Bureau of the Census. 1980. *Current Population Reports*, Series P-60, No. 125. U.S. Government Printing Office, Washington, D.C.
32. U.S. Bureau of Labor Statistics. *Special Labor Force Report No. 218*. U.S. Department of Labor, Washington, D.C.
33. U.S. Bureau of Labor Statistics. 1979. *Special Labor Force Report No. 219*. U.S. Department of Labor, Washington, D.C.
34. U.S. Bureau of Labor Statistics. 1980. *Special Labor Force Report No. 233*. U.S. Department of Labor, Washington, D.C.
35. U.S. Office of Civil Rights. 1979. *Statistical Report: Enrollment in Special Education Programs*. U.S. Department of Health, Education, and Welfare, Washington, D.C.
36. U.S. Women's Bureau. 1979. *Community Solutions for Child Care*. U.S. Department of Labor, Washington, D.C.

Chapter 22

HEALTH CARE SERVICES FOR CHILDREN IN DAY CARE PROGRAMS

by Julius B. Richmond and Juel M. Janis

> On every level of behavior, the psychological, the sensory-motor and the physical [the preschool child] is acquiring both healthful and unhealthful habits of activity. Although he may not learn to read in the preschool years, he is mastering the alphabet of life.
> It is because the alphabet of life is so much more important than the alphabet of the primer that the health education of the kindergarten is of such great consequence. (p. 10)

> Arnold Gesell, *The Kindergarten and Health*, 1923

Recognition of the importance of both health education and health services for the preschool child is clearly nothing new. Educators and health professionals have long acknowledged the value of including a health component in programs for young children.[12,13] Early efforts in this area[12] concentrated on *health education* and emphasized the formation of healthy habits of "personal hygiene" promoted by teachers who believed that " 'Clean hands and a pure heart count more than academic achievements." (p. 16) The actual provision of *health services* for children in day care centers is a relatively recent phenomenon which accompanied the growth of day care centers in this country.

Today when we speak of health and day care the reference is to both health services and health education. In particular, the optimal health program would be one which includes: (1) preventive health care services by the center's staff, including training for day care staff regarding detection of problems, appropriate referral services, and emergency and safety prevention procedures; (2) referral and follow-up treatment by health professionals in the community; and (3) health education programs for children, teachers and parents.

The rationale for including these services in day care is based on the premise that the goal of a good day care program[13] is to help "each child attain his fullest growth potentialities physically, mentally, emotionally and socially." (p. 3) Accordingly, the protection of physical health is basic to the development of a sound program for preschool children.

While acknowledgement of this point has been a basic tenet of those concerned with trying to assure quality preschool programs, it was not until 1965, with the advent of the Head Start program, that this principle was given recognition at the national level. In particular, "health and socio-emotional development" were listed as the first two of seven major objectives outlined for the Head Start program.[24]

Up to that time, with relatively few exceptions, the provision of any type of health services for children in day care programs was quite limited. According to several surveys conducted in the late 1950s and early 1960s, day care centers offered few health services of any kind.[8,18,20] Following the success of the Head Start experience, a few years later the Child Welfare League of America,[9] and the United States Children's Bureau[10] published comprehensive guidelines for health services in day care.

In 1970, Edward Zigler, who was then serving as Director of the Office of Child Development in the Department of Health, Education, and Welfare, identified the provision of health care to low-income preschool children as a high priority and recommended extending health services to a larger number of children than those served in Head Start. This proposal resulted in the establishment in 1971 of Health Start, a program which attempted to encourage innovative ways to provide health screening and treatment for preschool children from low-income families.[28]

In 1973 the American Academy of Pediatrics published health recommendations for day care centers, along with a policy statement endorsing the value of day care and encouraging the participation of pediatricians and other health professionals in working with day care programs.[1,2,3] Yet, despite this recognition of the importance of health services for preschool-age children, and the efforts to encourage the use of health services and the incorporation of health education into day care centers, a recent survey of day care centers in Berkeley, California, indicated that many of the centers surveyed had only a minimal level of health services or health education included in their programs.[7] According to this survey: "Over one-third of the centers lacked a designated health coordinator; one-fourth of the centers lacked written health guidelines and/or emergency guidelines; almost one-half lacked nutrition education services; and over two-thirds lacked a dental health education program." (p. 373)

Interestingly, in the Berkeley study there was a significant difference in the types of health care services provided between day care centers that received federal and/or state funds and those that did not receive such funds. Centers receiving federal and/or state funds were almost three times as likely to have a health coordinator and almost twice as likely to have written emergency procedures and a dental health education program.[7] Since the presence of a designated health coordinator has been shown to be closely related to a greater number of health program activities and participation by health personnel, the overall quality of health services in centers receiving federal and/or state funds, with a health coordinator, was considerably higher.

What is of concern here is that if the Berkeley survey of health care services for preschoolers is an accurate reflection of day care centers throughout the country, and there is evidence to suggest that this is the case,[21] then surely some action must be taken to address this situation. In particular, our concern is primarily with the need to assure the availability of comprehensive health services and health education programs in those day care centers that serve children from low-income families, for it is these children who are most in need of such services, most likely to benefit from them, and least likely to have them.

Studies of both the Head Start and the Health Start programs have provided documentation of the health care needs of the children in these programs.[16,17,25,28] For example, in the Health Start program, of the approximately 10,000 preschool-age children enrolled in 1972–73, 39 percent had no medical care and 50 percent had no dental care in the 12 months prior to entering, and only 19 percent had an up-to-date immunization status.[29] (p. 6) Upon entering the program it was determined that more than 25 percent of the children had medical conditions classified as "severe" (defined as "likely to interfere with future health or performance if not treated").[28] (p. VIII–3) More than 52 percent of these children had dental problems that required some type of treatment.[29] (p. 7) Further, of those children with identifiable health problems detected in the Health Start program, less than one percent were under care before entering this program.[28] (p. IV–4)

The findings from the Health Start and Head Start program are based on studies of a selected group of preschool-age children from low income families. However, a comprehensive report on the status of child health in the United States, issued in 1980 by the Select Panel for the Promotion of Child Health,[27] provides further verification of the need for health care services for preschool-age children in day care. This report noted that preschool children are much more likely to live in low-income families than older children. Only 6.8 percent of all children under six years of age were in families with an income of $25,000 or more. (p. 23)

According to this report, "children in low income families are less likely to have a regular source of medical care, less likely to have received any medical care during the year, and much less likely to have received care from a private physician. They are, however, more likely to have been hospitalized and, if hospitalized, to have remained in the hospital longer." (p. 24)

Children in low-income families are more likely to live in inadequate, overcrowded housing, with incomplete plumbing (pp. 25–26), all of which contribute to the spread of contagious diseases and infection. In this case, while there was remarkable progress made in the late 1970s in immunizing children entering school (nine out of ten children who entered kindergarten or first grade in 1978 had been immunized for measles, rubella, mumps, diphtheria, and tetanus), comparable progress for preschool children has not been achieved: "In 1978, of the 12.2 million children one to four years of age, only about six out of ten had received full protection for measles, rubella, and polio. . . ."[27] (p. 31) Here again it is the preschool minority children who are the least likely to be immunized. Significantly, while the lack of access to health care providers for immunizations is believed to partially account for these low immunization levels, parental beliefs also contributed to this problem. That is, in 1978–79, "22 percent of . . . minority parents in contrast with 12 percent of all parents, believed that most children's diseases had been conquered and there was no need to immunize against them; 44 percent of the minority parents in contrast with 28 percent of all parents believed that it was the responsibility of the government and the schools—as opposed to the parents—to immunize children against childhood diseases."[27] (p. 31)

With respect to the problem of obtaining care, the findings of the Select Panel's Report supported those identified in the Health Start program: "Forty-five percent of the black children and youths and 39 percent of children and youths in families with incomes under $5,000 did not have a regular physician. . . ." (p. 63)

In light of findings such as those noted above, the need to include both health services and a health education program in day care programs serving children from low-income families is apparent. Unfortunately, however, inclusion of a health component in day care is too often seen as an unnecessary "frill." Perhaps the most persuasive documentation on the need for a health component in day care is the recent monograph by Pizzo and Aronson[21] dealing with health and safety issues in day care. This report examines the major health and safety risks for children in day care, reviews program characteristics that can help to prevent or minimize these risks, analyzes current health and safety practices in day care, and makes recommendations for future actions.

The research for the Pizzo-Aronson monograph was initiated in 1976, as a part of a congressionally mandated study to examine the "appropriateness of the 1968 Federal Interagency Day Care Requirements." As a result its focus is on the special problem of low-income children since "most of the children currently in day care purchased by federal funds are low income children." (p. 22)

In this chapter the authors consider the distinction that is sometimes made between "custodial" care and "developmental" care. "Custodial" care is seen as an unskilled function involving menial activity which nearly any person can perform. "Developmental" care is described as care which "focuses on cognitive and socio-emotional development," with some attention to good nutrition, health and safety.

It is their thesis that this distinction has "negatively influenced general awareness of health and safety risks in day care" insofar as it can lead to a situation in which so-called "custodial" care can result in what they describe as the "sometimes incredibly hazardous conditions which have been found in federally funded day care." (p. 17) That is, where caregivers are not aware of the health and safety risks to children as a result of either the physical environment or the caregivers' health practices, there is a considerable risk to the children of accidents and the spread of infectious diseases.

According to Pizzo and Aronson, children in federally funded day care centers are "at risk of iron and vitamin deficiencies, hearing loss, dental disease and lead absorption," all constituting health problems and conditions that they have labeled as "quiet conditions" which can "go undetected for long periods of time with negative consequences for the child's healthy development." (p. 80) Yet, day care programs which have included screening or health assessment measures have been quite effective in both detecting and treating these conditions.[19,28]

With respect to the present status of health and safety conditions in day care, based on a review of nine major studies by Pizzo and Aronson, there appears to be more than ample documentation of their assertion that "in the areas of emergency preparedness, accident prevention, fire and burn prevention, detection of lead paint, sanitation, (and) staff health care" that day care centers are woefully inadequate. Further, in a review of other studies of "both the content and the process of regulation by individual states" of health and safety risks in day care, it appears that the existing standards are not sufficient to protect children from health and safety risks. In addition, according to a Day Care Management study of 50 states, there is virtually no state training and technical assistance for licensing day care center staff and providers about health or about the safety features of the physical plant of day care programs.[12] (p. 4)

While certainly a major concern of any effort to upgrade the health and safety aspects of day care is to ensure the health of the center's children, a recent problem with hepatitis that has been linked to day care centers suggests that improved health standards in day care are of considerable importance to adults' health as well. Specifically, several recent studies on hepatitis show that there is a high incidence of viral A hepatitis (VAH) associated with centers that care for children under the age of three. While the young children who act as carriers of the disease often manifest no symptoms, the disease has severe effects on the adults who come in contact with these children. According to unofficial estimates based on Center for Disease Control data, "20 percent of all serious VAH cases in the country can be linked to day care centers."[15]

It appears that the magnitude of day-care-center-related hepatitis is directly associated with the size of the center, the hours of the center's operation, and the age of the children. In Maricopa County, Arizona, for example, where day care centers were large and served a high proportion of children under two years of age, the day care associated incidence of VAH was 45 percent.[6]

The transmission of this disease from the children to the adults seems to be directly related to the sanitary practices followed by the center staff for food preparation, feeding, and toileting. Requiring caregivers in day care centers to take a short training course in basic health practices would be a reasonably inexpensive and effective means of preventing the occurrence not only of hepatitis but of other communicable diseases as well.

With respect to the cost of such training, this cost could well be measured against the cost of the disease itself. In one survey of the cost of illness of adults who had contracted hepatitis through a day care contact, "the mean expense paid out-of-pocket was $444; an additional mean of $400 was paid by third parties. The mean lost wages not covered by sick leave was $725. . . . The [total] estimated cost was $1,952. . . ."[26] (p. 1517) While costs such as these basically add to the overall burden of the nation's total health care costs, they represent costs that are avoidable through preventive actions on the part of day care center staff.

The cost issue is one which is often used as a justification for not including health services in day care. Yet, a 1975 national survey of parents of children under 14 using some form of child care indicated a majority (80%) would be willing to pay extra for immunizations and medical and dental check-ups. Further, 89 percent of the parents queried concurred with the need for specific standards relating to the health conditions of staff and children, and 94 percent felt there should be standards relating to the cleanliness and sanitation of the facilities, as well as for fire and safety.[23]

Evaluations of the effectiveness of some type of health component in day care unanimously support its value. Although a large scale, longitudinal evaluation of the health component of the Head Start program is now under way, the findings from this study will not be available until 1982. In the Health Start program, however, project performance data has been collected. It has revealed significant increases in the number of children receiving immunizations and medical and dental care as a result of participation in this program:

- *In the year prior to Health Start, 37 percent of the children had no medical care. In Health Start 75 percent of the children received a medical screening or examination.*[29] *(p. 14)*
- *Upon entering the program, 81 percent of the Health Start children needed immunizations. In Health Start 35 percent of these children were immunized.*[29] *(p. 14)*
- *In the year prior to Health Start, only four percent of the children had received some dental care.*[29] *(p. 6) In Health Start 60 percent of the children received dental exams in the first year of the program.*[29] *(p. 14)*

In addition to the preceding accomplishments of the Health Start program, even more encouraging was the fact that Health Start "linked 28 percent of the children to the same medical services used during the program year and 31 percent to the same dental services."[29] (p. 29)

Other studies of day care centers, that include a health component in the South and in Appalachia, cite successful detection and treatment of disease, improved immunizations and identification of handicapping conditions and of undernutrition.[21] (p. II) Moreover, findings such as these which indicate positive health benefits to children in these programs are paralleled by positive findings relating to both the parents and the communities that have been associated with day care center programs. In a national survey of the impact of Head Start Centers on community institutions, the authors reported that the Head Start programs "were *highly* involved in 53 percent of the health changes in their communities" and that "there was *some* Head Start involvement in at least 73 percent of the health changes in those communities."[21] (p. III)

In looking at both the health care needs of preschool children from low-income families and at the clear advantages provided by attending to these needs in day care center programs, it is clear that federal standards for children in day care must be set and must include health and safety standards. Joan Z. Bernstein, who was general counsel of the Department of HEW in 1979–80 when the issue of setting federal standards for day care was being considered, expressed this position particularly well when she noted:[5]

> *Children in HEW-funded care are low-income children and are especially vulnerable in terms of their basic developmental needs. Many suffer from the well-documented effects of poverty—poor nutrition, poor health, and inadequate intellectual stimulation. Numerous studies show that positive day care experiences, including adequate nutrition, health care, and adult attention, can enhance a child's development and prevent problems which may be more costly and difficult to remedy later in a child's life.*

The final day care regulations[14] signed by Secretary Harris in 1980 reflect an important effort to translate the concerns expressed by Ms. Bernstein into action. In particular, the rules relating to the health and safety of children in day care represent the essential minimum requirements needed in any quality day care program. These rules state:

1. Day care centers must have on record for each enrolled child a statement from a licensed health practitioner that the child has received a health assessment and all appropriate immunizations. (Note: this statement is not required for children whose parents object to the receipt of immunizations and health assessments on religious grounds.)
2. The standards to be used for health services are those set by Medicaid's EPSDT[11] program since the majority of children eligible for HEW funded day care are also eligible for this program. The standards of the American Academy of Pediatricians (AAP)[4] are also referenced for the immunization and health assessments provided to children who are not eligible for Medicaid.
3. The statement for each child must be on record within 60 days of enrollment, and must be updated according to the recommended schedule for routine health supervision of the AAP or the EPSDT National Recommended Health Assessment Plan.
4. Day care centers are required to provide information to parents, as needed, concerning child health services available in the community.
5. Day care centers are also required to assist parents in obtaining needed services.

6. State agencies are required to provide information to each day care center about the availability of child health services in the community and about how the services may be obtained.
7. State agencies are required to make arrangements to allow children in HEW funded health services, such as those provided under Medicaid's EPSDT program or the Title V Maternal and Child Health Program, to receive those services when needed.

In the discussion that took place prior to the signing of these rules it was noted that the Department of HEW had determined that "any burdens associated with requiring state agencies to inform day care centers about the availability of community health services and to make arrangements for providing the services are outweighed by the health benefits of such a requirement."[5] This discussion also noted that state agencies were not expected to "create new health resources for day care children" but simply to "make use of already existing publicly funded child health programs for the children in HEW-assisted care who are already eligible for the programs."

To understand how minimal the actual rules are, it should be noted that these rules do not include any of the recommendations set forth in the appendix attached to these rules. These recommendations include such items as "having on hand first aid materials," "displaying emergency numbers by the telephone," "insuring that facilities are free of lead-based paint," "assuring that all toys, playground equipment, and other materials are safe for children," and "having an adequate number of adults to supervise children during swimming activities." Further, the requirements relating to the physical environment of the center are equally minimal insofar as they simply direct state agencies in states without adequate sanitation in child care facilities to establish child care facility santitation requirements and stipulate that day care centers caring for HEW-funded children adhere to these standards.

As noted earlier, the regulations establishing standards for federally funded day care programs were signed by Secretary Harris in the closing months of the Carter administration. Nevertheless, there still seems to be some question as to whether or not they will be implemented, and according to what timetable. In particular, there continues to be some controversy regarding the health component of these regulations. Yet, considering how minimal these standards are it is difficult to understand that there could be resistance to them.

From past personal involvement in child care and in child development programs, from the medical literature, and from recent studies and evaluations of day care programs, we believe that the rules relating to the health and safety of children in day care do provide certain basic protections. Certainly with respect to the immunization and health assessment component of these day care regulations, to accept anything less that that which has been proposed would be medically and developmentally unsound. Further, we are assuming that the requirements for a health assessment include the provision of treatment for identified problems and a continuity of health care to all of the children receiving these assessments.

Preventive health services, such as immunizations and health and safety practices, can greatly reduce the problem of infectious diseases. The detection of health problems in young children that occurs in a health assessment can result in the elimination of a health problem at a time when it can be easily corrected, prevent the greater cost in time and money that is associated with late identification of a child health problem, and prevent the problems that can occur in a child's academic development if such problems are not detected early enough. Further, insuring health services to preschool children has the added advantage of linking siblings and other family members to an on-going source of health care. And lastly, providing health education for children, parents, and day centers' staff can have a geometric effect, extending its benefits throughout the entire community.

In the future it is hoped that all day care programs, regardless of whether they are supported by federal, state, or private funds, will work toward the inclusion of comprehensive health care services and health education programs. Surely the advantage of doing so will, in the long run, far outweigh any expenses that may be incurred.

References

1. American Academy of Pediatrics. 1973. "Policy statement on day care." *Pediatrics* 51:947.
2. American Academy of Pediatrics. 1973. *The health professional as a health and mental health consultant: How to be an effective consultant to a child care program.* Evanston, Illinois.
3. American Academy of Pediatrics. 1973. *Committee on Infant and Preschool Child: Recommendations for day care centers for infants and children.* Evanston, Illinois.
4. American Academy of Pediatrics. 1977. *Standards of child health care.* American Academy of Pediatrics. Evanston, Illinois.
5. Bernstein, J. February 1980. Memorandum to the Secretary: Final day care rules, Department of Health, Education and Welfare, Washington, D.C.
6. Center for Disease Control. 1979. "Report of fact-finding survey concerning outbreaks of hepatitis in Maricopa County, Phoenix, Arizona, Day Care Centers." Atlanta, Georgia, Department of Health, Education and Welfare.

7. Chang, A., Zuckerman, S. and Wallace, H. 1978. "Health services needs of children in day care centers." *American Journal of Public Health* 68(4): 373–377.

8. Chaplin, H. and Jacobziner, H. 1964. "A health program for children in day care services." *Public Health Reports* 74:567–572.

9. Child Welfare League of America. 1969. *Standards for day care services* (revised), New York, New York.

10. Dittman, L. 1967. "Children in day care—with focus on health." *Children's Bureau Publication* No. 444. Department of Health, Education and Welfare, Washington, D.C.

11. Frankenburg, W. and North, A. 1974. *A guide to screening for the early and periodic screening, diagnosis and treatment program*. Prepared for Social and Rehabilitation Service, U.S. Department of Health, Education and Welfare, Washington, D.C.

12. Gesell, H. and Abbot, J. 1923. "The kindergarten and health." *Health Education* No. 14. Department of the Interior, Bureau of Education, Washington, D.C.

13. Hartenstein, H. and Richmond, J. 1965. *A health program for the nursery school*. National Association for Nursery Education, University of Rhode Island, Kingston, Rhode Island.

14. HEW Day Care Regulations. 1980. (45 CFR Part 71) Office of the Secretary, Department of Health, Education and Welfare, Washington, D.C.

15. McCorry, J. November 16, 1979. Information memorandum to Secretary of Health, Education and Welfare. Hepatitis and center-based day care, Washington, D.C.

16. Mickelson, O. et al. 1970. "The prevalence of anemia in Head Start children." *Michigan Medicine* 69(13):569–575.

17. Mico, P. 1968. "Head Start health: The Boston experience of 1965." In *Disadvantaged Children, Vol. 2, Head Start and Early Intervention*, J. Hellmuth, ed. Bruner/Mazel, New York.

18. Morris, N. et al. 1964. "Children in day care: A health-focused look at current practice in a community." *American Journal of Public Health* 54: 44–52.

19. North, A. 1979. "Health Services in Head Start." In *Project Head Start*. E. Zigler and J. Valentine, eds. The Free Press, MacMillan Publishing Company, New York.

20. Peters, A. 1964. "Day care—A summary report." *American Journal Public Health* 54:1905–1913.

21. Pizzo, P. and Aronson, S. 1977. Concept paper on health and safety issues in day care. Submitted to Office Assistant Secretary Planning, U.S. Department of Health, Education and Welfare, Washington, D.C.

22. Richmond, J. 1964. "Paediatric aspects of day and institutional care." In *Care of children in day centers*. World Health Organization, Geneva, pp. 102–111.

23. Rodes, T. and Moore, J. 1975. *National Child Care Consumer Study*, Vol. 1. Basic tabulations. Unpublished report to the Office of Child Development, Department of Health, Education and Welfare, Washington, D.C.

24. Stebbins, L. et al. 1978. *Evaluation design and implementation plan for Head Start health evaluation.* Prepared for Department of Health, Education and Welfare, Office of Human Development, Contract No. HEW-105-77-1042. Abt Associates, Inc., Cambridge, Massachusetts.
25. Stone, D. and Kudla, K. 1967. "An analysis of health needs and problems as revealed by a selected sample of Project Head Start children." *Journal of School Health* 37(9):470–476.
26. Storch, G. et al. 1979. "Viral hepatitis associated with day-care centers." *Journal American Medical Association* 242(14):1514–1518.
27. The Report of The Select Panel for the Promotion of Child Health: 1980. *Better Health For Our Children.* Vol. III, A statistical profile. Public Health Service, Office of the Assistant Secretary for Health and Surgeon General, U.S. Department of Health and Human Services, Washington, D.C.
28. Vogt, L. et al. 1973. *Health Start: Final report of the evaluation of the second year program.* The Urban Institute, Washington, D.C.
29. Vogt, L. et al. 1973. *Health Start: Summary of the evaluation of the second year program.* The Urban Institute, Washington, D.C.

Chapter 23

SCHOOL-AGE CHILD CARE

School-Age Child Care Project

Day Care for the young school-age child—before school, after school, during school holidays and vacations when parents must work—is a national problem, affecting more and more families every year. For the increasing number of two-paycheck, dual-career, and single-parent households in America, three hours of kindergarten or six hours of elementary school cover only part of the working day and leave much room for anxiety.

Signals of need are coming not just from parents, but from many different sources. School principals express concern about children who arrive at unsupervised playgrounds an hour before school officially opens and who also hang around, under the same circumstances, into the late afternoon. Child care information and referral services, which collect data on local needs, typically find infant and school-age care to be the services for which supply is least adequate to demand. And community service agencies—Y's, boys' and girls' clubs, and recreation centers—realize that although not officially in the child care business, their facilities and programs are, in fact, being used more frequently for that purpose.

Although what some describe as the "latch key child" phenomenon —because children often wear house keys around their necks—is on

Staff members of the School-Age Child Care Project, all of whom participated in the preparation of this chapter, are: James A. Levine and Michelle Seligson Seltzer, co-Directors; Wendy Gray, Ruth Kramer Baden, and Andrea Genser, research associates; Judy Pacquette, administrative assistant; and Joan Johnson, secretary. The research on which this article is based was supported by grants from the Ford Foundation, William T. Grant Foundation, Carnegie Corporation, Levi Strauss Foundation, General Mills Foundation, and the National Institute of Education.

457

the rise, a number of communities throughout the United States are developing programs to meet the growing need. The variety of models being used includes the use or modification of services available through park and recreation departments, churches, Y's, day care centers, and family day care homes. However, one of the most interesting and significant movements is the use of public school facilities for before- and after-school child care.

This chapter offers an overview of school-age child care, with particular emphasis on the use of the public schools. It examines five areas: (1) the historical emergence of school-age child care as an issue of policy concern; (2) the current need for school-age child care; (3) the existing delivery system for school-age child care, with particular attention to the delivery of services in school facilities by schools *and* by nonprofit groups; (4) current and potential problems with the use of the schools for the delivery of school-age child care; and (5) future directions.

The information presented here is based on the work of the School-Age Child Care Project, an "action research" project initiated in May 1979 at the Wellesley College Center for Research on Women to meet the growing need expressed by communities throughout the country for information and technical assistance in designing and implementing programs for the young school-age child. This chapter draws upon technical assistance with programs in some 30 states, on field research at 25 program sites, and on research for the Project's forthcoming policy report on school-age child care.

Historical Perspective

Social concern with day care for the school-age child can be traced to the late nineteenth and early twentieth centuries, when a confluence of forces—industrialization, urbanization, and the rise of the public school—changed patterns of childrearing within the family.

In an agrarian and home-based economy, the "care" of children was not readily distinguishable from other family functions. Children as young as 5 or 6 years old could make an economic contribution to the family by doing farm tasks or household chores, helping out with home manufacturing activities, or helping to care for their younger siblings. However, the transfer of traditional forms of home manufacture—such as sewing, baking, canning, and preserving food —to the factories, and the enforcement of child labor laws to prevent the exploitation of children in factories, led to more separation between parents and children and made some form of child care necessary.

Attendance at public school, made compulsory in all states by

1918, served that purpose for at least part of the day. However, many working parents still needed their school-age youngsters at home to care for younger siblings. In order to combat the resulting school absenteeism, the Los Angeles Board of Education established day nurseries in 1917 so that children ages 6 to 14 could attend public school while their younger siblings were cared for in the day nursery. By 1929, the Board of Education had opened over 20 day nurseries caring for about 1400 children in Los Angeles. In fact, such programs were continued even into the late 1930s.[37,39,53]

To meet child care needs during the hours when school was not in session, some turn-of-the-century day nurseries extended their preschool programs. For example, in 1894, children could attend the crèche of the Buffalo Charity Organization Society after school, where their activities included washing the clothes of the younger children, wiping dishes, or paring the potatoes. (p. 333–340)[32] In 1899, the Cleveland Day Nursery Association began its first summer "vacation school" for children ages 5 to 10, organizing special programs for some 400 children on school playgrounds.

By 1912, "organized activities" on the playground were being touted as an important educational innovation having "intimate connection with the school."[25] In effect, however, along with the recreation programs offered after school and during the summer by Y's and neighborhood settlement houses, they provided a form of child care for working parents.

During the 1920s and 1930s, another educational innovation, the play school, had an impact on the care of children after school and during the summer. Under the leadership of John Dewey and other progressive educators, a new philosophy of education evolved, viewing children as individual, creative human beings who needed flexibility to nurture their learning processes. The concept of dramatic play was developed—arts and crafts as well as recreational activities —and implemented in progressive schools, which were generally private. Many educators felt that this innovation should be provided in the public schools for "underprivileged" children. As a result, the idea of the play school was developed and promoted throughout New York City—in settlement houses, community centers, and public schools—by the Child Study Association of America.[22] As Clara Lambert stated,[22]

> The play schools parallel, during the summer, the program offered by progressive schools, with emphasis upon knowing children and their individual differences, age-level interests, and potentialities for "learning by doing." (p. 4)

Although most playschools were viewed as an innovation in education, operated during the summer, and were not targeted to children with employed parents, some did provide an early model of public school–based school-age child care. The Chelsea Recreation Center, for example, located in P.S. 33 in New York City's lower west side, first offered after school care and then expanded to include summer care and a special "after kindergarten program." (Kindergartners went to the Hudson Guild Settlement House between noon and 3 p.m. and returned to the school after that to attend the play school.) Serving nearly 300 children from an ethnic neighborhood, P.S. 33 was chosen because of its large number of working mothers and its sympathetic school principal. Partial funding for the program, which opened in the 1930s, was obtained through the Works Progress Administration, with in-kind contributions from volunteer staff and an advisory committee of parents, educators, and social work professionals to ensure quality programming. (p. 2)[14] By 1942, the Chelsea Recreation Center had become a part of the New York City school budget. A second program was started in Harlem, and both programs were renamed "All-Day Neighborhood Schools." (p. 5)[14]

As a result of the various experiments in New York City, the play school idea spread to other cities, continuing to flourish during the 1920s and '30s and becoming increasingly popular with the onset of World War II, as more mothers entered the labor force. (Whereas the play schools were originally designed for low-income children, more programs were developed for middle-income children with employed mothers.)

The demand for female labor during World War II brought unprecedented national commitment to—and funding for—day care, including a wide variety of school-age programs. Play schools were a natural to receive funds under the Community Facilities Act, commonly known as the Lanham Act. The public schools in suburban Detroit, for example, opened 17 "after school canteens" for children ages five to eight, and the Dallas Board of Education opened 20 "school age centers," in housing projects as well as in the schools. (p. 162–163)[23] Day nurseries, too, were pushed to include school-age children by social workers and teachers[30,36] who [4]

> . . . Were discovering that youngsters often came to school with house keys tied to their necks so that they could let themselves into empty houses after school and sometimes were responsible for the care of even smaller children at that time. (p. 10)

Since school-age children were to be cared for in the day nursery, a new term was coined—the "day care center"—to reflect the provision of care for both preschool and school-age children.[27] (p. 4)

At the federal level, responsibility for the development of day care centers in the public schools was given to the Office of Education, while the Children's Bureau was assigned responsibility for their development through local social service agencies and settlement houses. For a variety of reasons, 95 percent of all centers ended up under school auspices. For one, school buildings, so many of which were constructed during the Works Progress Administration in the 1930s, were available.[17] Schools were seen as the most viable place to locate programs because they minimized transportation problems for parents. And, compared to the day nurseries, which for so many years had been stigmatized as a form of charity, schools had "status" as community institutions, especially to the middle class.[16,23] Regardless of the location, many school-age child care programs were implemented during World War II. Nearly 3000 "extended school programs" served over 100,000 children, and 835 "school-age child care centers" served nearly 30,000 children. In addition, there were several hundred combined nursery school/ school-age child care programs.[47]

After World War II, when federal funds for day care were no longer available, some cities and states (New York City, Philadelphia, and the states of Washington and California) continued to maintain school-age child care programs for limited and varying periods of time.[48] However, interest in day care as a matter of national social policy did not really return until the late 1960s and 1970s. When it did, care for the school-age child was treated as a somewhat marginal issue. It was included implicitly in the Mondale-Brademas Comprehensive Child Development Act,[41] vetoed by President Nixon in 1971, but then excluded from the Child and Family Services Act,[42] which Mondale and Brademas introduced in 1974. Moreover, while the federal government mounted study after study of day care in the 1970s, the greatest share of attention was given to care for the preschool child, not the school-age child. The marginal level of concern with school-age child care was reflected, perhaps, in the fate of a special federal interagency School Age Day Care Task Force, established in 1972 by the Office of Child Development, with representatives from both the Department of Health, Education, and Welfare and the Department of Labor. Although the Task Force identified school-age care as a growing need, requiring more programs and research, its report was never publicly released.[34]

It was not really until the end of the 1970s that school-age child care began to surface again in discussions of federal policy. The Child Care Act of 1979,[40] introduced by Senator Alan Cranston (D.-California), called specifically for school-age child care, noting that "the lack of available child care services results in many children being left—some all day—without adequate supervision" and that such children were at risk for "school vandalism, juvenile alcoholism, and serious juvenile crimes."[40] Although the Cranston bill never made it out of committee, and although the prospects for any type

of comprehensive child care legislation under the Reagan administration look extremely bleak, the demographics of need at the
beginning of the 1980s have made school-age child care very much
a national issue—a concern of communities throughout the country,
if not of the federal government.

Current and Projected Need

A variety of demographic indicators—including the number of
working mothers, number of children in single-parent families, and
projections of fertility—suggest that the need for day care services
for school-age children is pervasive, and that it will increase; however, none of these indicators allows for a precise determination of
national need. As Sheila Kamerman explained to the Select Committee on Population Regarding Projected Needs for Child Care
Services in the 1980s, "we can assume that there is both need and
significant demand for child care services among parents of the
under-threes and parents of school-age children, at least through age
eight and nine. But thus far an accurate quantitative assessment is
impossible." (p. 620)[21] This section reviews some of the difficulties
with the interpretation of national need.

For one, in most official tabulations, the young school-age population is defined to include children between the ages of 6 and 13,
which coincides roughly with the elementary and junior high school
years. What these figures do not include, significantly, is the population of 5-year-olds, who, given the prevalence of half-day kindergartens, may well be the age group with the greatest need for some
form of before- and/or after-school care in the United States.

According to the most recently available figures from the U.S. Department of Labor, for example, 62 percent of mothers with children
ages 6 to 13 are employed; most (75 percent) are employed full-
time.[49] Unfortunately, the Department of Labor blurs the figures for
5-year-olds by combining the data on all children under the age of 6.
However, data from the National Center for Education Statistics
indicate that well over 1.5 million 5-year-olds have mothers who are
employed full time.[12] To leave out this age cohort is to greatly under-
represent the population in potential need.

A second difficulty with the assessment of need is the failure of
national data to discriminate among the types of child care arrangements that families use and, therefore, to overestimate the adequacy
of those arrangements. In its September 1978 monograph, *Childcare
and Preschool: Options for Federal Support*, for example, the Congressional Budget Office reports that of approximately 23.0 million
school-age children (ages 6–17) with working mothers, "1.7 million

. . . participate in some form of organized before- or after-school program" and most of the remaining 13 million "are cared for in much the same way as younger children—for example, by relatives or in family day care homes."[9] Aside from its exclusion of 5-year-olds, this analysis fails to consider how many children in the 6-to-13-year-old range care for themselves with no supervision or access to an adult or how many 6-year-olds are in the care of "relatives" who are no more than 7 or 8.

A third complication of national data, this one leading to over-estimations, is the failure to discriminate for significantly different needs among younger and older school-age children. At the upper end of the 6-to-13-year-old range, children usually have a much greater capacity and desire for self-sufficiency than those at the younger end. Staff in after-school programs throughout the country report that the greatest demand for services is from families with children in the 5-to-9-year-old range (roughly kindergarten through third grade). However, depending on the maturity of their children or on where they live—inner city vs. suburb, for example—parents may vary greatly in how comfortable they feel about having their 10-or-11-year-olds unsupervised before or after school.

Reviews of the literature on school-age children by Siedman[35] and Bergstrom[3] agree that when these children are left alone they are at significantly increased exposure to risk from household or automobile accidents, overexposure to television, exposure to drugs or alcohol, improper nutrition leading to obesity, and peer pressure leading to juvenile delinquency. According to James Garbarino, a nationally recognized expert on child abuse and neglect from Pennsylvania State University, there are both risks and opportunities associated with children being on their own. While some children benefit from the responsibility of being "independent," "It is the premature granting of responsibility that seems to be damaging."[15]

While accurate determination of need is difficult, data from several sources suggest that significant numbers of young school-age children do care for themselves prematurely and that parents are not satisfied with this arrangement. The Census Bureau's 1976 report, *Daytime Care of Children: October 1974 and February 1975*, indicated that among the population of children aged 7 to 13, 1.6 million out of 12.2 million, i.e. 13 percent, were taking care of themselves.[44] In a more recent survey, conducted in February 1979, based on the analysis of a nationally representative sample of reader responses, *Family Circle Magazine* found that 28.5 percent of children aged 6 to 13 took care of themselves, that parents were not satisfied with this arrangement, and that 33 percent of parents—whether their children were in self-care or not—felt that they had inadequate arrangements.[54]

The *Family Circle* survey was nationally representative of the U.S. population in all respects except income, in which it was slightly higher. However, data from the Children's Time Study, in which University of California sociologists Victor Rubin and Elliot A. Medrich are examining how 11- and 12-year-olds in Oakland, California, use their time after school, suggests that families with lower incomes have even greater needs. In the wake of California's Proposition 13, Rubin and Medrich have paid particular attention to "the consequences of diminished local government commitment to after-school services."[33] Given the number of 11- and 12-year-olds who care for themselves after school, Rubin and Medrich conclude:[33]

> . . . *either that parents believe their sixth-graders do not need direct supervision after school and that they are old enough to care for themselves, or that child care arrangements simply cannot be made, or both of these things. . . . With more and more mothers in the labor force—and fewer able to be home after school hours—the need for organized child care settings is increasing . . . reductions in after-school programs will not affect children randomly. Rather, those who are from lower-income homes and can least afford private sector alternatives will . . . be left with the fewest opportunities. (p. 23–25)*

A confluence of demographic factors suggests that the need for school-age child care will increase during the next decade.[24] By 1990 there will be a 10 percent increase in the number of children between the ages of 6 and 13, attributable primarily to the coming of parental age of the post-World War II "baby boom" generation. While there were 27.8 million children between the ages of 6 and 13 in 1979, there will be 30.6 million in 1990.[43]

Continuing a trend of several decades, the mothers of these school-age children are almost twice as likely to be employed—and employed full time—as mothers of preschoolers.[24] Using conservative estimates of working mothers (60 percent, as opposed to a more probable 80 percent for this age group), about 18 million children between the ages of 6 and 13 may need some form of school-age child care by 1990.[2] In addition, at least 1.6 million 5-year-olds will have a mother working full time, and may need some form of child care if kindergartens still operate for a half day.[12]

While the need for school-age child care is increasing, the resources to meet that need within families and within neighborhoods are likely to become less available. Continuing a trend already apparent, by 1990 families are expected to have fewer children and to have them more closely spaced—that is, it will be less likely for families to have adolescent children present to care for young school-age children.[38,26] And, since more and more women will be employed outside the home, families will find it more difficult to turn to aunts, grandmothers, or family day care providers to take care of their children.[18] To care for their children before school, after school, and during school vacations, more and more families will need alternative arrangements.

The Delivery System

Accurate quantitative assessment of the manner in which school-age children are cared for is no less problematic than accurate quantitative assessment of need. We do know, however, that most families use a mixture or "package"[1] of arrangements, combining care by parents with regular formal arrangements (including day care centers, licensed family day care homes, and after-school programs), informal arrangements (including care by relatives, babysitters, and unlicensed family day care), and, in what may be almost 30 percent of instances, self-care by children.[54]

For purposes of simplification, three broad streams of formal service delivery can be identified. The first, and perhaps most well-established throughout the country, consists of the youth-serving agencies—the Y's, boys' and girls' clubs, and park and recreation programs—which have traditionally offered activities to children at the end of the school day and during vacations when school was not in session. Though not usually designed to provide day care, interviews throughout the country indicate that these programs are more and more being used for that purpose, and are therefore being pressed to shift the way they think about their programming.

The second major stream is comprised of day care centers which, though typically focused on the preschool population, do sometimes serve young school-age children. In 1977 the National Day Care Supply study conducted by Abt Associates, Inc., estimated that there were 18,300 day care centers in the United States serving approximately 900,000 children..[7] Slightly more than one-third of that enrollment was comprised of children aged 5 and over, with 5-year-olds representing 21 percent of the total enrollment and children age 6 and over representing 14 percent.[7] However, a substudy of this large national sample found that about four-fifths of the kindergarten-age children (5- and 6-year-olds) were enrolled in these centers full time, and one-fifth on a part-time basis.[7] This suggests that many parents are using day care centers as a full-day alternative to the half day of public kindergarten, but that when their children enter the first-grade, parents do not very often rely on day care centers as an adjunct to the school day. (No more than 6 percent of children in center enrollment is for after-school care.)

Indeed, from a center's point of view, the inclusion of school-age children on a part-day basis is usually not a very cost-effective procedure. Assuming that it is serving its maximum allowable number of preschool children, a center can take in an 8-year-old at 3:00 p.m. *only if* one of the preschoolers goes home at the same time. During school vacations, when both the preschooler and the 8-year-old may need full-time care, the center can care only for one, unless another space opens up. The expansion of the national capacity to provide care for the young school-age child via integration in the traditional day care setting is problematic and limited.

Possibilities for expansion may be greater in the use of the third stream of service delivery, the public schools, which, as we have seen, have been used in the past—especially during World War II—for school-age child care. Using school space to care for children before and after school can solve several problems simultaneously. For parents, it eliminates the need to arrange for end-of-the-day transportation to a new program, as well as the worry about whether or not a babysitter will really be there. For school administrators and taxpayers faced with declining enrollments, the use of empty class-rooms and gymnasiums represents an effective utilization of resources. And for existing providers of school-age services, such as community youth agencies and day care centers who are hard-pressed to find space to meet the new demand, the prospect of working in partnership with the schools opens up totally new programming opportunities.

From a child's point of view, going to a school-based child care program, if it is done properly, can be a very enriching experience, not just a longer school day, and far better than staying home alone in front of the television set. With one staff member for every 10 or 15 children, most good programs try to provide a relaxed and diversified recreational setting in which children can do arts and crafts or cooking projects, catch up on homework, play team sports or individual games, take field trips to local parks, libraries, or museums, and—transportation and resources permitting—keep up with Scouts, 4-H, or music lessons.

At least 100 of the nation's school systems are now involved in the provision of before- and/or after-school child care. In most cases the schools are *not* directly responsible for the day-to-day operation of programs or for their financing, though in a few instances they are. In Arlington, Virginia, and Minneapolis, Minnesota, for example, the schools administer extensive programs, hiring separate child care staff who do not need teaching credentials and who earn about half as much as classroom teachers. Parents pay for these services on a sliding-fee basis. In Lawton, Oklahoma, Raleigh, North Carolina, and other communities where the addition of day care services to the regular elementary school program is being used as a "magnet" to effect voluntary racial desegregation, the school budget carries most if not all of the costs of the program. In Lawton, for example, families from any section of town do not pay any fees to send their children to a specially designated "school for working parents," open from 7:00 a.m. until 6:00 p.m.

To offer more variety to children, the Orange County Public Schools in Orlando, Florida, are developing what they call a Home Base Child Care program. Before school, but after their parent(s) have left for work, children will go to a participating neighborhood home. After school, children will return to the home base until their parent(s) arrive home from work. Home Base parents, employed by the public schools, will be available to transport children to and from Scout meetings, lessons, or sports activities.

In most communities the new programs are being offered as a result of what might best be described as partnerships between public schools and other organizations. The programs are housed in the schools but they are administered—and have been spearheaded —by a variety of local parent groups, civic organizations, and non-profit agencies; for example, the YWCA in El Paso, Texas, the state office of Child Day Care in Hartford, Connecticut, the Camp Fire Girls in Sparks, Nevada, the Chinatown Planning Council in New York City, and a parent group called the School-Age Task Force in Nashville, Tennessee.

In Denver, Colorado, for example, where the public schools have approximately 300 empty classrooms scattered among 84 elementary school buildings, the Mile High Child Care Association, a nonprofit agency with 11 other day care centers, operates programs in five elementary schools. Mile High leases the empty classroom space, at $2 per square foot, and runs its program year-round, including summer, Christmas, and Easter vacations, from 6:30 a.m. to 6:00 p.m.

In the Boston suburb of Brookline, after-school care (not before-school) is available in each of the town's eight elementary schools. Although each program is administered by a separate parent group organized as a nonprofit corporation, all programs operate as part of the Brookline Public Schools in accordance with a highly formalized set of guidelines adopted by the Brookline school committee. Brookline's Extended Day Program has been so successful that the school committee has voted to include "specific space designated for Extended Day" in all future building plans.

Other communities are having equally positive experiences. Legislation in Connecticut now encourages the use of available public school space for day care—especially under "parent controlled, non-profit cooperative arrangements"[10]—and has made funds available for the renovation of empty classrooms so that community groups can use them. The Nashville, Tennessee, public schools have developed guidelines to make it easier for groups wishing to use their space for school-age child care programs.

Public School Partnerships: Issues in Service Delivery

Despite the promise that the new public school partnerships hold, the establishment of alliances that can provide stable and high-quality services to children and parents is fraught with a number of complications. Attempts to use the schools for day care often meet with resistance, for a variety of reasons, from school boards and administrators, private-for-profit day care operators, and taxpayers at large.

The Day Care Stigma

Public schools are one of the nation's most established—some would say entrenched—institutions; day care, no matter how widely used, is one of the newest, and has been improperly stigmatized as a service used mainly by the poor or as a place where careless parents simply park their children.

Even as they make their schools more responsive to the needs of working parents, not all communities like to admit that they have a need for day care—at least not in those terms. In Jacksonville, Florida, where the parent-teacher association did not want the schools to be seen as running a day care center, the new program is called Extended Day Enrichment. And Brookline, Massachusetts, calls its program The Extended Day Program of the Brookline Public Schools, even though, as one parent says, "everybody who uses the program or who works for it knows it's day care. That's the reality, but people don't like to admit it publicly."

Limits of School Responsibility

Distinctions between day care and extended day are not necessarily just quibbles about nomenclature. Instead, they may reflect deep-seated concerns about the limits of school responsibility. In Arlington, Virginia, both the school board and superintendent strongly support Extended Day, but stand firm against letting it operate on days when school is not in session, such as vacations, snow days, or parent-teacher conference days. The program is literally an extension of the school day, not an extension on days when school is not in session. According to Superintendent of Schools Larry Cuban,

"Extending the program to vacations and so forth would be taking the program to a philosophical position further than I'm comfortable with. Our current policy avoids the charge that we are providing day care that competes with the private sector."

Legal Limitations

Self-imposed limits aside, questions have been raised in Virginia and other states about the legality of using school space to offer before- and after-school care. Virginia law allows public institutions to "exercise only those powers conferred expressly or by necessary implication."[8] According to the December, 1978, opinion of Virginia Attorney General Marshall Coleman,[8] this means that public schools are not legally authorized to operate day care centers, though they could allow programs operated by other groups to use school property. This opinion was affirmed by the Virginia legislature in 1981 with a law which, while prohibiting schools from direct provision of day care services, enables Arlington to continue its program through 1984, pending a special study of the "educational effectiveness of its programs."[52] Other Virginia communities with after-school child care programs, such as Fairfax County, have avoided the legal issue by transferring administrative responsibility for its program from the school to the county, even though the program continues to operate in the schools.

Such arrangements are, however, being challenged in other states. A bill introduced in the Arizona legislature in 1981 (H.B. 2147) would allow school districts to operate their own day care programs, but would prohibit the operation of such programs in school facilities by outside groups except during the summer.

Costs and Financing

One of the most attractive features of public school partnership models is their effective utilization of existing resources. By combining three resources—available school space, federal funding through Title XX and CETA, and parent fees—partnerships optimize the ability to achieve a balance between keeping parent fees down and keeping staff salaries up.

Since they have the space available, most school systems have been willing to donate it—or rent it on a nominal basis— to non-profit organizations operating before- and after-school programs. Likewise, schools have often waived fees for utilities or custodial services, especially if maintenance for the school-age child care program can be managed within the normal routine of the custodial staff.

Now, however, unprecedented rises in energy costs are forcing schools to take a second look at what they make available for day care or any other community service. In Atlanta, Georgia, and Madison, Wisconsin, rental charges for the use of school space have put a squeeze on parental ability to pay for services. In Newton, Massachusetts, the school board is considering a charge for janitorial services that would raise the average cost of after-school care from $25 to $35 per week, a 40 percent increase.

When combined with cutbacks in both Title XX and CETA under the Reagan administration, similar changes throughout the country are likely to force parent fees up even further, prevent program expansion, and restrict the participation of low-income families.

Licensing

School-age child care is like an adolescent whose growth is so rapid and unexpected that the "authorities" aren't sure which rules to apply. There are no uniform regulatory standards at the federal level; the revision of the 1968 Federal Interagency Day Care Requirements have not, as of this writing, been approved by Congress, nor is it likely that they will be under the Reagan administration. On a state-by-state basis, licensing standards vary greatly. In states such as Arizona, Florida, South Carolina, and Rhode Island, staff-child ratios are set at 1:25; in New York, Maine, South Dakota, and others, by contrast, they are 1:10.

Regulations regarding the use of public school facilities for school-age child care are also varied. In some states—for example, Utah, Wisconsin, Connecticut, and Illinois—school-based programs may automatically operate without licensing; it is assumed that if schools are safe enough for the education of children from 9 a.m. to 3 p.m., they are safe enough to care for them for a few hours before or after that. In other states, however, most notably Colorado, day care licensing requirements do not make that assumption at all. For example, while they are in the morning kindergarten program in one of Denver's public schools, children take their lunch in a spacious, well-lit, and brightly colored cafeteria, which happens to be in the basement level of the school building. When the kindergarten program is over, many of these children remain in the same building, simply switching over to the after-school program run by the Mile High Child Care Association. Once they are officially in child care, however, these children would not be allowed into the same basement cafeteria. To avoid this type of situation, Denver's school-age child care programs are officially licensed not as day care but as day camp, a more lenient regulatory category.

The development of high quality school-based programs in the future will require a reexamination of licensing for school-age child care, with both a tightening of staff-child ratios in many states and the loosening of requirements for the use of school facilities.

Role Ambiguity of Staff

Relative to other professionals who work with children, the staff of school-age child care programs often lack a clear definition of role or status.

They may work in a school building, but they are not teachers; indeed, in some school-based programs, regular classroom teachers make it quite clear that school-age staff are second-class citizens. However, many school-age staff have been trained as teachers and approach their work as professionals. They are often called upon to help children with homework or to act as a liaison between the child or family and the school. Furthermore, children often refer to them, quite naturally, as teachers.

Similarly, though they provide child care, school-age staff do not usually have an identity as child care workers, as staff working with preschoolers do. Though they supervise recreation, they are not really recreation leaders either.

To reduce the role ambiguity of staff, which can greatly undermine morale, a variety of different steps have been taken. Some sensitive school principals formally recognize school-age staff as part of the total school community, including them in all faculty meetings, coordinating their work with classroom teachers, and generally supporting their work. In Fairfax, Virginia, where the program is run in the schools by the county's Office for Children, staff training is a continuous and well-supervised process, which, in encouraging staff to provide feedback to one another, also helps to define their role. One of Brookline's Extended Day programs now offers "tenure" to staff; although this is not really a financial guarantee, it distinguishes the importance of the role, comparable to teacher. And, in another effort to give the role more professional status, Wheelock College in Boston is now offering a degree with emphasis in school-age child care.

Future Directions

Serious attention to both the potential and the complexities of the public school partnership model of school age child care—and others —is just beginning.

Even though significant efforts have been made to define and describe quality programs,[5,13,19,29] and even though individual programs may unilaterally agree on basic criteria, there really is no generally shared understanding of what makes a good program. This is not the case, by contrast, with child care programs for preschoolers, where there is general agreement about the kinds of experiences and basic types of materials (for example, sand, water table) that should be provided.

To provide stable high-quality care that balances the needs of children, parents, staff, and community, work will have to be done on many fronts: elimination of the stigma attached to day care, training of staff members (and school personnel) for new roles; reexamination of existing licensing codes; reworking of ways to finance this form of child care.

Obstacles notwithstanding, a combination of factors is likely to bring a considerable expansion over the next ten years in the use of schools for before- and after-school day care. Growing parental need will increase pressure for the use of empty classrooms; even if not free, such space will be available at a lower cost than most other community facilities. Moreover, the part-day care of 5-, 6-, and 7-year-olds largely avoids the debate that continues to plague discussion of care for younger children, the disagreements about whether programs should be educational, or developmental, or custodial—and about just what any of those terms really mean. The idea that public schools be used for the care of infants and preschoolers has, predictably, met with strong opposition, even from those who strongly favor the extended day idea. But entry to kindergarten or first grade acts as a threshold for many parents; once they have begun sharing the care of their children with the schools, it is not so difficult to extend that sharing for a few more hours during the day.

Impetus for these programs comes, it is important to realize, not from school administrators or from unemployed teachers eager to find jobs, but from families, from the community. And where programs are working successfully, they are working not because school systems want to take over family responsibility or because parents want to relinquish it, but because they have truly formed a partnership to meet the needs of a changing society.

References

1. Bane, M. et al. 1979. "Child care arrangements of working parents." *Monthly Labor Review* 102(10):52.
2. Beck, R. 1980. "The child care policy stalemate: an analysis of federal policies and an examination of options for the 1980s." A paper presented at the Aspen Conference on Child Care in the 1980s, Washington, D.C.

3. Bergstrom, J. and Dreher, D. 1977. *The Evaluation of the Existing Federal Interagency Day Care Requirements: Day Care for the School-Aged Child.* Contract No. HEW 100-76-0143. U.S. Department of Health, Education, and Welfare, Washington, D.C.
4. Bragdon, E. 1943. "A day care project." In *The Impact of War on Children's Services: Nine Monographs.* Child Welfare League of America, New York.
5. California State Department of Education. 1979. *Child Care and Development Services: Report of the Commission to Formulate a State Plan for Child Care and Development Services in California.* State Department of Education, Sacramento, California.
6. Cohen, D. et al. 1972. *Serving School-Aged Children.* Publication No. (OHDS) 78-31058. U.S. Department of Health, Education, and Welfare, Administration for Children, Youth and Families, Washington, D.C.
7. Coelen, C., Glantz, F. and Calore, F. 1978. *Day Care Centers in the United States: A National Profile, 1976–1977.* Abt Associates, Cambridge, Massachusetts.
8. Coleman, M. 1978. Memorandum to Vincent Callahan, Virginia House of Delegates, on the legality of schools operating day care programs. Richmond, Virginia.
9. Congressional Budget Office. 1978. *Childcare and Preschool: Options for Federal Support.* U.S. Government Printing Office, Washington, D.C.
10. Connecticut General Statutes. (1979) Section 10-88, Public Act 78-78.
11. Day Nursery Association of Cleveland. 1957. *Giant Steps. 1882–1957.* Cleveland, Ohio.
12. Dearman, N. and Plisko, V. 1980. *The Condition of Education, 1980 Edition.* National Center for Education Statistics, Washington, D.C.
13. Diffendal, E. 1974. *Day Care for School-Age Children.* Day Care and Child Development Council, Washington, D.C.
14. Franklin, A. and Benedict, A. 1943. *Play Centers for School Children: A Guide to Their Establishment and Operation.* William Morrow and Company, New York.
15. Garbarino, J. 1980. "Latchkey Children." *Vital Issues* 30(3):1–4.
16. Gray, W. 1981. *Day care as a social service strategy, 1890–1946.* ERIC Clearinghouse on Elementary and Early Childhood Education, Document No. PS 011918, Urbana, Illinois.
17. Greenblatt, B. 1977. *Responsibility for Child Care.* Jossey-Bass, San Francisco.
18. Hofferth, S. 1979. *Day Care in the Next Decade.* Urban Institute, Washington, D.C.
19. Hoffman, G. 1972. *School-Age Child Care: A Primer for Building Comprehensive Child Care Services.* Publication No. (SRS) 73-23006. U.S. Department of Health, Education, and Welfare, Washington, D.C.
20. Johnson, B. 1980. "Marital and family characteristics of the labor force, March 1979." *Monthly Labor Review* 103(4):48–52.
21. Kamerman, S. 1978. "Testimony Regarding Projected Needs for Child Care Services in the 1980's." In *Consequences of Changing U.S. Population: Baby Boom or Bust.* Hearings before the Select Committee on Population. U.S. House of Representatives. 95th Congress, 1st & 2nd sessions.

22. Lambert, C. 1939. *From the Records: An Adventure in Teacher Training.* Child Study Association of America, New York.

23. Lambert, C. 1944. *School's Out: Child Care Through Play Schools.* Harper and Brothers, New York.

24. Masnick, G. and Bane, M. 1980. *The Nation's Families: 1960–1990.* The Joint Center for Urban Studies of MIT and Harvard. Auburn House, Boston, Massachusetts.

25. Miller, W. 1912. "A plan for organized play in a city school." *Education* 32(7):409–412.

26. Moore, K. and Hofferth, S. 1979. "Women and their children." In *The Subtle Revolution,* R. Smith, ed. Urban Institute, Washington, D.C.

27. Morton, D. 1943. "Planning with mothers for the care of their children." *Child Welfare League of America Bulletin* 23(6):4–6, 20.

28. Prescott, E. and Milich, C. 1975. *School's Out! Family Day Care for the School-Age Child.* Pacific Oaks College, Pasadena, California.

29. Prescott, E. 1975. *School's Out! Group Care for School-Age Children.* Pacific Oaks College, Pasadena, California.

30. Reeder, G. 1942. "Community planning for the care of children of employed mothers." *Child Welfare League of America Bulletin* 21(7):1–3, 9–10.

31. Rodman, H. 1980. "How children take care of themselves." *Working Mother* (July): 61–3.

32. Rosenau, N. 1894. "Day Nurseries." In *Proceedings of the National Conference of Charities and Corrections.* George Ellis, Boston.

33. Rubin, V. and Medrich, E. 1979. "Child care, recreation, and the fiscal crisis." *The Urban and Social Change Review* 12(1):22–26.

34. School-Age Day Care Task Force. 1972. "Report of the School-Age Day Care Task Force." Unpublished draft. U.S. Department of Health, Education, and Welfare, Office of Child Development, Washington, D.C.

35. Seidman, E. 1973. "School Age Day Care: A Review of the Literature." Unpublished draft. U.S. Department of Health, Education, and Welfare, Office of Child Development, Washington, D.C.

36. Sherman, D. 1943. "Central intake bureau of a day care program." *Child Welfare League of America Bulletin* 22(5):5–7.

37. Smith, F. 1936. "Day Nurseries in Los Angeles." *Child Welfare League of America Bulletin* 15(4):3, 7.

38. Smith, R. 1979. *Women in the Labor Force in 1990.* Urban Institute, Washington, D.C.

39. Tyson, H. 1935. "Day Nurseries." In *Social Work Yearbook.* Russell Sage Foundation, New York.

40. U.S. Congress, Senate, Committee on Labor and Human Resources. 1979. Child Care Act of 1979, 96th Congress, 1st session. U.S. Government Printing Office, Washington, D.C.

41. U.S. Congress, Senate, Committee on Labor and Public Welfare. 1971. Comprehensive Child Development Act of 1971, 92nd Congress, 1st session. U.S. Government Printing Office, Washington, D.C.

42. U.S. Congress, Senate, Committee on Labor and Public Welfare. House Committee on Education and Labor. 1974. Child and Family Services Act

of 1974, 94th Congress, 1st session. U.S. Government Printing Office, Washington, D.C.

43. U.S. Department of Commerce, Bureau of The Census. 1975. "Projections of the Population of the United States: 1975 to 2050." In *Current Population Reports*, Series P-25, No. 601, Table 8. U.S. Government Printing Office, Washington, D.C.

44. U.S. Department of Commerce, Bureau of The Census. 1976. "Daytime Care of Children: October 1974 and February 1975." In *Current Population Reports*, Series P-20, No. 298. U.S. Government Printing Office, Washington, D.C.

45. U.S. Department of Commerce, Bureau of The Census. 1980. "Marital status and living arrangements: March 1979." In *Current Population Reports*, Series P-20, No. 349, Table 4. U.S. Government Printing Office, Washington, D.C.

46. U.S. Department of Health and Human Services, Administration for Children, Youth and Families. 1980. Day care demonstration and research activities. Day Care Division, U.S. Department of Health and Human Services, Washington, D.C.

47. U.S. Department of Labor, Women's Bureau. 1953. *Handbook of Facts on Women Workers*. U.S. Government Printing Office, Washington, D.C.

48. U.S. Department of Labor, Women's Bureau. 1953. *Planning services for children of employed mothers: a report prepared by a subcommittee of the interdepartmental committee on children and youth*. U.S. Government Printing Office, Washington, D.C.

49. U.S. Department of Labor, Bureau of Labor Statistics. 1980. *Perspectives on Working Women: A Databook*. Bulletin 2080. U.S. Department of Labor, Washington, D.C.

50. U.S. Office of Education, Federal Security Agency. 1943. *School Services for Children of Working Mothers*. School Children and the War Series, Leaflet No. 1. U.S. Government Printing Office, Washington, D.C.

51. Virginia Delegate Assembly. 1980. A bill authorizing the school boards of Arlington County and Falls Church City to provide certain programs and directing the Division for Children to conduct a study of such programs, House Bill. No. 1726. Richmond, Virginia.

52. Virginia Delegate Assembly. 1981. An act to authorize the school boards of Arlington and Falls Church to provide certain programs outside regular school hours, S. 602. Richmond, Virginia.

53. Whipple, G. 1929. "Day nurseries." In *Twenty-eighth Yearbook of the National Society for the Study of Education*. Public School Publishing Company, Bloomington, Illinis.

54. Whitbread, J. 1979. "Who's Taking Care of the Children?" *Family Circle* (February): 88, 92, 102–3.

Chapter 24

DAY CARE AND EARLY CHILDHOOD EDUCATION

by Millie Almy

Some years ago Bettye Caldwell described day care as a "timid giant" that was growing bolder.[5] Today the giant continues to grow, although estimates of the extent of growth, and of the demand for further growth, depend somewhat on the age of the children being considered. Whether the growth is healthy and the day care giant strong and thriving is another question.

An important factor in the giant's present state is the contribution made by the field of early childhood education. The material that follows examines that contribution, looking at it first in the perspective of certain events of the last half-century, a period of increasing amalgamation of the two fields. In general, early childhood education has responded to the challenge of changing circumstances in day care with an attitude akin to that of the little engine in the well-known story for children, "I think I can," and, as the years have gone on, "I knew I could." While this inclination to tackle difficult problems with zest has often benefitted day care, there are at least a few instances where early childhood education's optimism may have exceeded its effectiveness. Eventually some historian will review this history more objectively, weighing the evidence to be found in the records of various associations and in contemporary journalism, as well as in the recollections of those who participated in the events. Although I have drawn on some historical appraisals, personal recollection guides much of my description.

Coming closer to the present, some issues that surround early childhood education and day care are discussed. These have to do with the promotion of child development in day care programs, the role of parents in such programs and the professionalization of the teachers. Finally, I consider how the resolution of these issues may influence early childhood education's ability to serve as a powerful engine for the day-care giant.

Problems of Definition

The relationships between day care and early childhood education cannot be adequately examined without giving some attention to problems of definition. Both terms have parallel antecedents in the nineteenth century's kindergartens—initially private and middle class, later specifically directed to the children of the poor, and only gradually incorporated into the system of public education—and in the day nurseries, philanthropic agencies intended to assist poor working mothers.

Over the years, day nurseries have become "day care," or, perhaps more often, "child care" centers. Such centers, however, currently provide care for only one out of every ten children who need care. The remaining nine are in "family day care," care in the homes of relatives, or neighbors, or others.[15] Some of these homes are licensed or registered, but many are not.

Day care is not always defined broadly enough to include all the children who receive it. For example, an extensive study of day care by Keyserling, conducted in the early 1970s, defined it as "direct care and protection of preschool children outside of their homes on a full-day, year round basis."[14] This definition permitted consideration of infants and toddlers but ruled out school-age children who may need care after school and during vacations. It excluded "foster homes where children are cared for day and night" and nursery schools which operate for part of the day and part of the year.[14]

Many people prefer the term "child care" to "day care," believing that the emphasis should be on the child rather than on the time at which the care is offered. As child care workers, teachers in day care can affiliate with either or both the National Association of Child Care Workers and the National Association for the Education of Young Children.*

Fuzziness in the definition of day care, and particularly the frequent failure to document adequately the demand for out-of-home care for school-age youngsters and infants and to overlook the day care function of nursery schools and other preschool programs,

---

* The Conference Research Sequence in Child Care Education, Pittsburgh, Pa. November 6–9, 1980, brought together educators and trainers from both day care and residential care.

complicates planning on the part of policy makers. Kamerman and Kahn note, for example, that there is clearly a demand for out-of-home child care programs for 3-to-5-year-olds that cover, at a minimum, the normal school day. They suggest that there is little need to make distinctions between educational programs and day care programs since neither parents nor providers distinguish among such terms as "child care center," "child development center," "playschool," "preschool," or "nursery school."[12]

If distinctions cannot be made, perhaps it can be said that the early childhood education engine has supplied the day care giant so generously that day care and early childhood education programs are, for all practical purposes, identical. Unfortunately, as the history of their relationship shows, day care has sometimes received less than the best of early childhood education, and the question of whether day care can afford to include early childhood education is still raised.

Like day care, "early childhood education" has a multitude of meanings. According to the *Encyclopedia of Education*, it encompasses the age range from two or three years to eight years.[6] Increasingly, however, the age range is extended downward to birth. In the minds of many, early childhood education is equated with nursery schools, preschools and prekindergartens, or with preprimary education. Some see the focus of these programs as the promotion of the children's development, while others focus more on readying the children for academic learning. For some, the curriculum of early childhood education is unique, set apart from that of the elementary school, while for others it is an extension downward of the elementary school.

For the purposes of this chapter, I give primary consideration to the nursery school or preschool aspects of early childhood education, and my definition of day care corresponds to that of Keyserling, cited earlier.

Events in the Transformation of Nursery Education to Early Childhood Education

Early childhood education in this country had its origin in the nineteenth-century development of kindergartens. The idea that some form of education outside the home might be appropriate for children before they entered the first grade paved the way for the later development of nursery schools.

The first nursery schools appeared in the early 1900s. Their development was facilitated by the concern for mental hygiene and the burgeoning interest in the science of child development that followed World War I. By that time kindergartens had increasing acceptance in public education, and were caught up in curriculum issues. Nursery schools developed rather separately from them and in close affiliation with the beginning science of child development. As noted in the *28th Yearbook of the National Society for the Study of Education*, "professional training in child development with a center of interest in the preschool* child" was just beginning.[22] In the various research institutes, many of them supported by the Laura Spelman Rockefeller Fund, preschool teachers, along with students from nutrition, sociology, psychology and other disciplines, learned an interdisciplinary approach.† In these early days, according to Forest, preschool teachers accrued more advanced degrees than teachers in any other segment of the educational enterprise, except, of course, the university.[7] The new movement grew rapidly, increasing from 3 nursery schools to 262 in the decade between 1920 and 1930.[19] With some notable exceptions, such as the Ruggles Street Nursery, transformed from a day nursery by Abigail Eliot in 1922, most of these early nursery schools served middle-class families.

The 1930s presented the early nursery school teachers with their first large-scale opportunity to demonstrate that the nursery school was also good for children and parents who were poor and came from diverse backgrounds. Under the aegis of the Federal Emergency Relief Administration and later the Work Projects Administration, the number of nursery schools grew to 1900 by 1934–35.[10]

Responsibility for this accomplishment lay with a National Advisory Committee of professional educators and that small circle of nursery school teachers who had been trained in child development. The WPA programs were designed primarily to give work to unemployed teachers, few, if any, of whom had had preparation for teaching children under the age of five. The programs also had other goals, including improving the morale of the parents, improving the nutritional status of children and teachers, and raising health standards for the children. These programs were designed as nursery schools and did not operate for the "full day" required by Keyserling's definition of day care. On the other hand, they did provide lunch and nap, as day care does.

To locate facilities for the nursery schools, equip them, and train teachers who had taught high school or elementary school or nurses

---

* "Nursery school" and "preschool" are used interchangeably here. My impression is that the experts of the early days made certain subtle distinctions that are not currently very important.
† Updegraff, R. The early child research centers, unpublished interview with James L. Hymes, Jr. December 1977; Jones, M.C. Personal communication, 1979.

who were accustomed to the sick room to become sensitive to the developmental nuances of 2-, 3-, and 4-year-olds and to deal sympathetically with their parents was no small challenge to that pioneer nursery school group. And all of that, in the early days of the program, with no staff other than the unemployed.

Meanwhile, the existence of the WPA nursery schools and the need for more advanced training gave impetus to the development of college programs focused on child development and preschool education. Some of these graduates moved into positions as teachers in philanthropic day nurseries. These nurseries still served the children of working mothers, but the experience of the children changed drastically as educational programs were introduced. In one nursery, for example, the nursery school teacher, with an array of blocks, housekeeping toys, and art materials, took over supervision of the children from a cleaning woman who made the children sit quietly on benches while she mopped and a cook who threatened to use her knife on any children who were obstreperous.

Not everyone approved an educational component for day care. Beer maintained for years that nursery school teachers failed to understand that the primary need of the children was not education, but care.[4] In the light of the continuing problems teachers in day care centers have in programming for naps and the long afternoons, one wonders whether Beer received the hearing she deserved.

Some of the concern about an overemphasis on education came from social work. Day nurseries were usually affiliated with social work agencies, and their directors—when they had training—were usually social workers.

The ultimate test of the nursery school teacher's ability to adapt to the demands of day care came with World War II. By then the WPA nursery schools had been considerably transformed. Improved employment conditions led to the departure of many teachers from the program. In some instances not only assistant teachers, but cooks and clerical workers were pressed into service as teachers. Accordingly, those WPA nursery schools that shifted to a day care function under the Lanham Act often did so with minimally prepared staff. In all instances, Lanham Act Centers competed with war industry for staff and confronted wartime mobility. Well-qualified teachers were hard to find and keep.

The Kaiser Child Service Centers, supported by and based in the ship-building industry in Oregon during the war years 1943–54 provide a superb example of what nursery school teachers could do in day care. Open 24 hours a day, 364 days a year, the centers at their peak served over a thousand children. Facilities included infirmaries to care for mildly ill children and various services for parents, such as take-home food. The teachers were paid salaries equivalent to the shipyard workers and well above those paid their colleagues in Lanham Act Centers, but they worked 48 hours a week, 50 weeks a year, with only a two-week paid vacation.[11] As Dowley has noted, the Kaiser experience led to considerable rethinking of nursery school techniques, with a revision of child care objectives and greater insight into the emotional and social needs of children.[7]

According to some critics, a concern for the emotional and social development of children, even to the exclusion of concern for their intellects, permeated nursery education for the next 20 years. Whether this is an accurate view, or whether postwar changes increased the incidence of emotional disturbance among young children, it appears that many experienced nursery school teachers were unprepared for what was called the "rediscovery of early childhood education" in the 1960s, and its heavy emphasis on cognition.

When had nursery or preschool education become early childhood education? Probably as nursery schools became more widely known and states that had not had kindergartens began to consider expanding downward. Also, increasing child development knowledge pointed to the continuity between nursery school and kindergarten. In 1947, for example, the National Society for the Study of Education devoted its 46th yearbook to early childhood education. This content contrasts with both the 6th and 7th yearbooks, concerned with kindergarten, and the 28th, dealing with preschool and parental education.

The academic "rediscovery" of early childhood education in the '60s was precipitated in part by Benjamin Bloom's analysis of longitudinal data from the various institutes of child development research, by the increasing interest in and availability of the studies of Jean Piaget, and by the writings of Jerome Bruner and J. McV. Hunt. The focus on poor children seemed quite appropriate to the many nursery school teachers who had taught in the WPA nursery schools, in settlement house nursery schools or in day care. However, many of them found distressing the emphasis on academics that characterized many of the "early intervention" projects. They noted, too, that the teachers chosen for the projects were often elementary school teachers, or sometimes educational psychologists, with minimal background in early childhood development. On the other hand, many nursery school teachers found some of the new ideas stimulating and began modifying their curricula to take account of them.

Nineteen sixty-five and the rediscovery of poverty brought a new and continuing challenge to nursery school teachers when the federal government also rediscovered early childhood education. At that time a multidisciplinary planning group for the Office of Economic

Opportunity laid the groundwork for Head Start. As in the case of the WPA nursery schools 30 years before, well-qualified early childhood personnel were in short supply. Hymes, a member of the planning committee, describes the situation: "This huge program for young children was actually getting underway without a single soul who was an expert in Early Childhood Education in on any of the operating decisions."[11] Eventually, however, 170 early childhood educators, based in a variety of colleges and agencies, came on as consultants. They helped in planning, and in organizing training and many have continued to serve Head Start.[11]

The vast majority of Head Start teachers have been drawn from poor communities and have been trained as they work. Several thousand have received training through college courses that may lead to A.A. or B.A. degrees. Current Head Start policy is directed toward having every teacher hold either a B.A. degree in early childhood education or the Child Development Associate credential.[21] This credential is based on individualized, flexible, competency-based training emphasizing field work.

Head Start has not featured day care. The majority of mothers are not employed and most programs operate for less than a full day. Nevertheless, it has many aspects, such as the emphasis on collaboration with parents and on health and nutrition, that should enable its teachers to move effectively into day care. Recent recommendations also call for Head Start to explore options for full day care.*

This catalog of events to which early childhood education has responded in its first half century shows how often challenges have been met and at what odds. A major impetus for the expansion of early childhood education has been programs funded by the federal government (WPA, Lanham, Head Start). Yet, the establishment of all these programs has been primarily motivated by concerns other than child development. In all of them, the major responsibility for the children has rested with individuals who received training as they worked.

Emphasis on the federal government should not obscure the fact that preschool programs have also been sponsored by state and local schools, by churches and social agencies, and that many are privately operated as either nonprofit or for-profit ventures. Kamerman and Kahn note that from 1967 to 1977 nursery school enrollment for 3- and 4-year-olds jumped from 14 to 31 percent. About 64 percent of the 3-to-5-year age cohort participated in some form of school or out-of-home program. Only half of these children were from families

---

* Head Start in the 1980's: A report requested by the President of the United States, September, 1980.

with working mothers, indicating a considerable demand for pre-school programs, aside from their day care function.[12]

In the light of this picture of gradually increasing acceptance of early childhood education programs, especially for 3- and 4-year-olds, we can turn to the question of the continuing relationship of early childhood education to day care. Will it be a relationship in which the child development knowledge of the early childhood teacher, together with skill in applying that knowledge in working with young children as individuals or in groups, is brought to bear systematically in day care settings? Or will matters be left more to chance, with some day care teachers and providers having access to as much support as they need, and others struggling along with minimal assistance? Consideration of these questions demands attention to the possibility that federal government involvement is likely to decrease, necessitating search for other kinds of support. Resources will need to be found or developed within families and their neighborhoods, in churches, private agencies and foundations, unions and industry.

The experienced early childhood educator can only contemplate these possibilities with a sense of *déjà vu*. Nursery schools would never have gained their present acceptance had not directors and teachers found a place in their neighborhoods, scrounged for materials and equipment, sought advice from the visiting nurse, arranged for parents to seek counsel at the mental health agency, and persuaded local industry to establish scholarship funds. Over the years, as social service agencies have become more specialized and as bureaucratic structures have become more rigid, this aspect of the early childhood educator's work has become more difficult, but it still goes on. It still seems appropriate that a teacher whose primary goal is the promotion of the child's development should be concerned with all the factors that may affect that development. Scarce resources and continuing, if not increasing, needs for day care constitute yet another challenge to the realization of that goal.

Promoting Child Development

While the "promotion of development" is a phrase that comes easily to the tongue, explanation of what the teacher means and does is more difficult. Over thirty years ago, with reference to educational programs for young children, John Anderson wrote that the teacher must "recognize and encourage specific abilities and interests and is adaptable and acute in developing an educational program to utilize them for individual development and group purposes." He adds, "If the teacher is able to set the stage so that the child can acquire competence through his own efforts, she will do well . . ." and the "teaching function is conceived in terms of setting the stage in such a way that she is part of the situation without seeming to be."[3]

We know considerably more about early development, particularly in the areas of intellectual and language development but increasingly also in social development, than was the case then. Accordingly, teachers can be much more explicit in identifying the abilities and interests they are promoting. On the other hand, to make such identification accurately requires a level of knowledge that is not likely to be reached with minimal education and training.

That some training makes some difference in the effectiveness of day care teachers has been demonstrated in the National Day Care Study. Observations in several hundred classrooms indicated that in classes supervised by teachers who had had "child-related education/training, the children show more cooperation, attend longer to tasks and activities and are less often noninvolved than is the case where teachers lack such preparation. The children also do better on a measure of early achievement—The Preschool Inventory."[8] These are important findings and underscore the importance of training for the teacher in day care. But they should not be taken as sufficient evidence that the development of each child has been enhanced in the way John Anderson had in mind.

At issue here is not the documentation of development. That can be done, although the procedures are time-consuming and difficult to accomplish effectively outside the research center. The problem lies rather with the lack of fit between what many early childhood teachers assert goes on in programs and the actuality as seen by informed observers. As Eveline Omwake states in her analysis of Head Start programs, the "experience of many children on a day-to-day basis may not be all it's cracked up to be."[17] Omwake notes that many factors contribute to the gap between what is said to happen and what does happen. Among these are philosophical differences among early childhood educators, the confusion of preschool goals and curriculum with that of the elementary school, and various political struggles within and relating to the organization.[17] Perhaps the "I think I can" philosophy of early childhood teachers also deserves consideration.

Effective work with small children requires self-confidence and a certain optimism. The child's behavior today may leave much to be desired. The teacher's belief that the child can improve, can develop into a more socialized, more mature individual, and that he or she can help in the process, is an essential feature in changing that behavior. Small wonder that early childhood teachers come to wear their rose-colored glasses so much of the time, or that they develop a certain sentimentality about children and their own ways of teaching them.

A tendency for early childhood teachers to be less than realistic about the limitations of their own knowledge and skills when it comes to various aspects of day care is also sometimes evident. Thus one sees programs for infants and toddlers, or school age children, that mimic the usual program for 3- and 4-year-olds rather than adapting appropriately to the specific ages and developmental abilities of the children. On a positive note, the teachers who have coped most effectively with the long day in day care are those who have been able to think about the afternoon program as something other than that of a typical nursery school. Some teachers have also come to realize the special advantages family day care has for some children, particularly the very young.

The promotion of children's development is more than a matter of knowing the activities, the materials and equipment that are likely to be appropriate for a particular age group. It also includes knowing the special characteristics and the unique background of each of the children so that the day care experience can be adapted to their special needs, interests and capabilities. The teacher cannot promote the child's development without also taking into account the parental and family influences on the child.

Working with Families

Recognition that the family is the primary influence on the child's development was built into the conception of the nursery school. However, as the title of the 28th yearbook of the National Society of Education, *Preschool and Parental Education*, suggests, the emphasis was perhaps more on teaching parents what was then known about child development and "scientific" child rearing than on collaboration with them. Books for teachers with titles like "Parents as Partners" seem to have come later.

It is not clear whether parents in the early days felt patronized. In retrospect it seems to me that distinctions between the parental role and the teacher role were more clearly understood then and that mutual respect more often characterized the parent-teacher relationship in the nursery school than has been the case since the expansion of early childhood education beginning in the 1960s.

Teacher Role vs. Parent Role

The roles of the teacher of the young child and those of the parents clearly overlap. The parent takes care, guides, instructs, and facilitates learning. So does the teacher. The important differences rest not so much in what either one does for or with the child as in the dimensions of their roles.

As Katz notes, the mother's function is comparatively diffuse and unlimited, whereas the teacher's role is specific and limited. The intensity of affect is high for the mother, lower for the teacher. The mother tends to be biased and partial to her own child, the teacher more impartial. Finally, the responsibility of the mother is limited to the individual child while the teacher's responsibility extends to the whole group of children.[14] Somewhat similar dimensions may also apply to the father's role.

In the early days of the nursery school, the teacher's role was seen to be one of supplementing and complementing the parental role. Day care, with its longer hours, necessitates the teacher's taking on more of the caretaking functions but it does not mean that the teacher role supplants that of the parent. The teacher role and the parental role cannot be equated.

Uncertainity About Parent Involvement

That many teachers feel unsure about how their prerogatives as teachers mesh with the prerogatives of the parents is highlighted in a recent study by Sponseller and Fink. Early childhood teachers in 46 states in response to a questionnaire asserted their belief in the benefits children can gain from scientifically based child development programs. They also indicated a commitment to parents' rights and to the family as a focus for child rearing. However, they displayed a lot of uncertainty about how the goals of educational programs, on the one hand, and of child rearing in the family, on the other, are best made available to children. Significantly, given an opportunity to express their concerns, most of them mentioned parent involvement and participation,[19] suggesting that they do not find collaboration with parents easy.

A number of factors seem to have contributed to this concern. Despite the emphasis on parent involvement in the last 15 years, it is probably the case that teacher education and training for early childhood focuses much more on techniques and skills for working with children than on those for working with adults, especially parents. In addition, teachers, and perhaps parents as well, may be getting mixed messages about their own roles.

The attempt to empower poor parents, making them responsible for policy decisions in Head Start and other poverty programs, has benefitted many parents. At the same time it has left many teachers uncertain about their own rights. What are the areas where they can exercise their "professional judgment"?

The teachers may feel supported, although no less confused, when they consider how many of their skills and techniques have been emphasized in programs that have attempted to teach parenting to mothers while their children are still infants and toddlers. Alison Clarke-Stewart, after completing a survey of 200 such programs, reported to a recent conference of educational researchers that parents who participate in them come to play parental roles that closely resemble the role of the teacher. Teachers may agree that parents are the child's first teachers but they may also wonder whether emphasis on the teaching aspects of the parental role may not somehow diminish the importance of their own role.

Teachers who recognize and accept the differences in the parental and teacher roles seem more likely to be able to collaborate with parents effectively and to engender mutual respect than teachers who are confused about their relationship to the child and to the parent. Such recognition and acceptance seems essential if teachers are to maintain a warm and open relationship with parents.

Unfortunately, evidence suggests that some teachers do not communicate effectively with parents or realize their own supplementary, complementary functions very well. The result is a day care experience for the children that has little, if any, connection to their experience at home. Powell studied 212 parents and caregivers in 12 group child care centers in Detroit. He comments: "The image of the social worlds of the children that emerges from the study is one of fragmentation and discontinuity. For many children the boundaries of the center and family are sharply defined, with the child's family, other childrens' families, and the day care center functioning as independent, detached systems."[18]

Young children often demonstrate surprising resiliency, quickly learning the behaviors that are acceptable in one setting but not in another. Nevertheless, great disparities between home and center call into question the concept that day care can promote and need not disrupt development. Even if the child is undisturbed by differences, the parents may feel diminished in competence when the center demonstrates certain accomplishments with the children that the parents have been unable to achieve. Just as teachers need to understand the parental role, parents need to know how the day care setting differs from the home and how it facilitates certain kinds of behavior.

One reason that parents are said to prefer family day care to center care, other than its greater availability, is that they believe the family provider is more likely to have similar child-rearing values. Even when this is true, however, good communication must be established between provider and parent. Since providers report that they, like teachers, often have difficulty with communication, it appears that, at least in our highly individualized society, shared rearing of young children has certain inherent problems even when those involved come from the same social setting. When one of the partners has a degree of "professional" or "expert" status, the relationship becomes even more tenuous.

Professionalizing Early Childhood Education and Day Care

In the days when nursery schools were first being established it seems likely that the teachers thought of themselves as "professionals." They met one of the criteria, as set by sociological analysis, for a profession in that they based their practice on the body of knowledge subsumed under "child development." They had, however, no overly protective feelings toward that knowledge, they formed no exclusive associations, and set forth no code of ethics for themselves. All of this, plus the ambiguity of the client (to whom is the teacher responsible—the children? the parents? the agency that employs him or her?) places early childhood education as, at best, a semiprofession. In this it parallels nursing and social work.

The Low Status of Early Childhood Education and Day Care

For a number of reasons the status of early childhood education as an occupation has important implications for day care. As an occupation that, in one sense, represents work traditionally done in the home, and by women, early childhood education, at present, tends to have low status. Day care, where long hours and the necessity for maintaining a safe ratio of adults to children often involves employing staff members with no specific preparation, also ranks low.

With a few exceptions—where childhood teachers hold credentials that encompass "nursery through sixth (or ninth) grade" and where they are employed in school systems with single salary schedules—early childhood teachers receive wages considerably less than those of their elementary school colleagues. For example, a recent study of 95 staff members in 32 San Francisco child care centers, including public and private nonprofit and proprietary, placed them in the lower 10% of adult wage earners.* These results are compatible with the 1978 findings in the National Day Care Study,[8] although the San Francisco earnings are somewhat higher

---

* Whitebook, M. and others, 1980. "Who's Minding the Child Care Workers: A look at staff burnout." Unpublished report.

than those reported in the national study. The San Francisco study also found that length of day did not make a significant difference in earnings. Individuals who worked in short-day public programs, such as those in community colleges, earned as much as those working eight hours in day care programs. The only teachers earning over $800 a month were those employed in public school centers.

In the San Francisco study, many of the staff members held credentials as early childhood teachers. It should be noted, however, that teachers in charge of groups of children in day care often have only minimal background in child development and early childhood education. Furthermore, assistants and aides, although they often lack such qualifications, are usually also identified as teachers.

The improvement of the occupational status of teachers in day care can be viewed from different perspectives, not necessarily mutually exclusive. One, concerned with the improvement of the quality of the teaching and the programs, looks toward professionalization. Another, concerned with wages and working conditions may look toward unionization.

Improving the Quality of Teaching

Head Start, and its Child Development Associate credential, provides an example of an attempt to upgrade teaching performance. It has been described as a program producing "indigenous paraprofessionals." Since the CDA credential has gained considerable acceptance and has been adopted by at least 12 states as a licensing requirement for child care workers,[17] it deserves mention here. It is awarded after one to two years of individualized, field-based, flexible training, when the trainee can demonstrate the accomplishment of a set of competencies deemed necessary to promote the development of young children in a group setting.

Steiner contends that the CDA credential is ill-conceived, partly on the basis that child development is not a sufficiently exact science to permit the development of specific requirements, and partly from skepticism about securing adequate evidence that the requirements have been met.[20] Trickett maintains that in the years since Steiner made this criticism the CDA competencies have been made more specific, and that assessments do agree on whether or not the CDA candidate possesses them. She adds, however, that evidence has not yet accumulated to show whether or not teachers with the CDA credential function better on the job than those without them.[21]

The CDA, it should be noted, does not constitute professional training. It has no general education requirements, is not dependent on any specified number of credit hours, nor on any degree. On the other hand, it may be combined with degree work, and eventually lead to the meeting of "professional" requirements for public school teaching, or supervision and administration in early childhood education.

A critical factor in the further acceptance of the CDA, particularly for use in day care, will be the extent to which day care expands or contracts, related to the general state of the economy. As long as other jobs are not plentiful, day care seems likely to go along much as at present, using the seemingly endless supply of young people, many with college degrees and some with specific preparation in child development and early education, who are willing to work for minimum wages. Such individuals may not stay very long (a high turnover rate is one of the problems in day care) but they enable centers to keep going.

Those teachers who stay on in day care, even at minimal wages, according to Whitebook and others, do so because of the reward they get from working with young children. When the problems they encounter in a center—differences in educational philosophy, other difficulties in staff relationships, working beyond the hours paid—become unbearable, they seek another center. Even so, 20 percent of those interviewed expected to leave the field in the next year and only 24 percent expected to make a lifetime commitment to it.

Circumstances such as these make it difficult to envision early childhood education as related to day care becoming more professional in orientation. Unionization seems a more likely direction, although one not yet pursued very widely. On the other hand, the fact that the relationships between teachers, children and parents are often quite intimate in nature impels one to wish for professional attitudes, in the best sense.

The Importance of Professional Attitudes

Lilian Katz calls attention to the fact that early childhood teachers, especially in day care centers, have "virtually total power over the psychological goods and resources of value to the young in their care."[13] She also comments on the low status of day care teachers and the problems of ambiguity in the knowledge base and in the definitions of roles. Katz emphasizes that teachers in day care especially need a code of ethics to help them to act on what is right rather than simply practical. Such a code resembles those that at least theoretically guide the behavior of those who are truly professional.

Katz outlines the kinds of problems that cannot be settled on the basis of scientific evidence that can come between the teacher and parent. Among these are conflicts that may arise from differences in experience and values, such as those surrounding informal vs. structured curriculum, emphasis on academics, and punishment for behaviors that the parent sees as "wrong" and the teacher regards as "normal" at a particular stage of development. Other problems relate to the confidentiality of information the parent shares with the teacher. What does the teacher do when it appears that the child (or the parent) is at grave psychological risk? Another set of problems arises in the relations between employers and teachers. What, for example, is the responsibility of the teacher when the employer tries to circumvent licensing procedures by enrolling more children than regulations permit? Or when the employer misrepresents the program to a parent?[13]

Not all these problems seem to be as much matters of life and death as the professional issues that the physician and lawyer encounter. But they do show that the early childhood teacher, especially in day care, confronts problems that need to be dealt with in a professional way.

Alternatives to Professionalization

If, as seems likely, it is not feasible to attempt to professionalize the majority of early childhood teachers, are there alternative possibilities? Some would argue that more is to be gained by avoiding any professionalization, trying to build instead an organization in which parents and teachers share and share alike in responsibilities. Head Start, in its conception, seems to have been designed in this way. Zigler describes its beginning: "Disadvantaged families were no longer seen as passive recipients of services dispensed by professionals. Instead they were viewed as active, respected participants and decision makers, roles they assumed with an unexpected degree of success."[21]

Other examples of deemphasis of professionalism in early childhood education can be found. Cooperative nursery schools, originating in the 1920s, place policy decisions in the hands of the parents. They may employ a qualified early childhood teacher, but the parents also share in the teaching. In some communities, day care has also been organized on such a cooperative or collective basis. However, many parents apparently feel that they do not have sufficient time and energy to add extensive participation in day care center affairs to their already full schedule of employment, homemaking, and child rearing. (This statement reflects the usual complaint of day care teachers. The question of parent involvement in day care, as suggested above, deserves much more study. Parents' "lack of time" may be an excuse that reflects a feeling of being excluded.)

Professionalization at the Director Level

A different approach to the problems of professionalization in early education and day care is to emphasize the role of the person who serves as administrator, director, supervisor, trainer, or consultant. This is the person whose role I have described as an "early childhood educator" in contrast to the role of "early childhood teacher."[1] This person has the skills of the early childhood teacher plus, at a minimum, a thorough and current knowledge of child development and skills in working with adults. He or she might also have additional specialization in administration and management, or assessment and evaluation, or research. Such a person could bring to a large center, or several smaller centers, or a system of day care homes, or some combination of homes and centers, the depth of knowledge that is needed if day care is to reflect the "quality" that early childhood teachers often talk about but less often realize.

The need for more personnel who can function at this level was underscored in a recent informal survey of education and training for day care.* The respondents involved in day care training in various states stressed the need for on-site training for those working directly with the children. They indicated that such work is currently too often done by individuals who are already overcommitted. They stressed the paucity of advanced work in supervision, administration, and management appropriate for day care. While each respondent could describe some bright spots in day care, the general picture was that of a "bootstrap" approach. A relatively small contingent of well-prepared early childhood educators with less than adequate resources is struggling again to improve programs.

It has become increasingly clear that adequate preparation for the role I describe as "early childhood educator" involves more than courses in education and psychology. Several universities have been experimenting with interdisciplinary approaches. In some respects these go back to the early days when preschool education was often tied to the child development research institutes. The present conviction behind these programs is that increasing specialization in the various disciplines that relate to early education and child development necessitates greater effort to insure adequate communication among them. Early childhood educators need to develop an ability to see the child and its family from the viewpoints of anthropologist, sociologist and social worker, pediatrician, nurse, nutritionist, econ-

---

* Almy, M. "Current Structure of Education and Training for Day Care: Implications for child care education." Prepared for the initial conference, Conference Research Sequence in Child Care Education, Pittsburgh, Pa. November 6–9, 1980.

omist, political scientist, and legislator, as well as educator and psychologist. Rather than having the early childhood educator confront these specialties as they are interpreted by other early childhood specialists, as has usually been the case in advanced study, these programs try to bring them into more direct contact, often through field work tackling problems in the "real world."[2]

The proposal that some solution to the problems inherent in providing good quality day care lies in providing advanced education and training at levels beyond that of the teacher will meet with a variety of objections.

Objections to Professionalization for "Early Childhood Educators"

In these days of inflation and budget constraint, cost is a prime consideration. Unfortunately, those interested in early childhood education and child development programs have not distinguished themselves as very accurate estimators of either the possible expansion of the need for day care or the costs of credentialing entry-level workers, as with the CDA. Nevertheless, it seems that the costs of bolstering a particular day care system with a specific number of early childhood educators, as here described, could be figured.

A second objection relates to the increased differentiation of staffing. While a close examination of both nursery schools and day care centers often reveals tension between the teachers in charge of the group and their aides or assistants, the early childhood tradition is that "we are a team, we all work together and everyone does everything." When this is a fact about which all members of the team feel equally good, and not just a cliché, the interjection of an individual with specific responsibility for such matters as training, curriculum evaluation and revision, developmental assessment of children, and certain kinds of counseling with parents could create problems. One hopes, however, that the early childhood educator's skills in working with other adults would be sufficient to preclude the arousal of ill feeling. Furthermore, there is evidence in Whitebook's survey cited earlier, that under present circumstances, aides, assistants, and sometimes teachers resentfully participate in tasks they feel rightfully belong to those who receive more pay.

A third objection lies in current and pervasive dissatisfaction with the "helping professionals." Caught between the needs of their clients, children and parents, on the one hand, and the procedural demands of the organizational structure, they opt to meet the latter, often at the expense of the former. This is an important objection. A tendency on the part of some professionals (and semiprofessionals) to prefer to do what has become routine rather than risking greater involvement is very real. Such a tendency is evident in the Massachusetts human service workers who are reported to have refused to take a competency-based test designed to reveal among other things, "faith in people"—the ability to stick with a difficult case. It can also be illustrated by the child care center directors in a large city who resented being given assistants to take over their clerical work so that they might be freed to give more direct supervision in the classroom.

Problems of these sorts are common across all professions today. Some argue, and particularly in reference to day care, that they will be eliminated only as the complex structures of government are replaced by the simpler ones of neighborhood and small community. Perhaps so. It may be equally realistic, however, to accept the need for professionals to build into their preparation an understanding of the hazards of professionalization and into the structures of day care devices such as sabbaticals and recurrent opportunities to serve at different levels of the structure, designed to prevent burnout.

As I see it, the position of early childhood educator should be reserved for those who combine advanced academic and practical preparation with the personal characteristics of interest in adults as well as children, an open and inquiring mind, and maturity of perspective. It would represent a major step up on what to date has been a career ladder largely limited to aide, assistant teacher, and teacher. As such it might provide career opportunities so that those who have been described as "indigenous nonprofessionals" could, with experience and study and certain personal characteristics become "indigenous professionals."

Summary

This paper has examined some of the ways early childhood education has contributed to day care and examines some of the possibilities for the future. It shows how early childhood education, always with a "can-do" attitude, has tackled some seemingly insurmountable problems. It suggests that the times, and the needs of the day care field, call for a more limited and realistic approach to the promotion of children's development and a continuing and more informed partnership with parents. Also called for is the creation of what is, in some respects, a new role, that of early childhood educator. Such a person would have a deep knowledge of child development and special skills and personal characteristics for working with adults. Early childhood education is still an engine that thinks it can, but it must find new sources of power and new ways of distributing that power if it is to support the growing giant of day care effectively.

References

1. Almy, M. 1975. *The early childhood educator at work.* McGraw-Hill, New York.
2. Almy, M. 1981. "Interdisciplinary preparation for leaders in early education and child development." In *Advances in Early Education and Day Care*, Vol. II. S. Kilmer, ed. JAI Press, Greenwich, Conn. (in press).
3. Anderson, J.E. 1947. "Theory in early childhood education." In the *Forty-sixth Yearbook of the National Society for the Study of Education, Part II: Early Childhood Education.* N.B. Henry, ed. University of Chicago Press, Chicago, Ill.
4. Beer, E.S. 1938. *The Day Nursery.* Dutton, New York.
5. Caldwell, B. 1971. "Day Care: a timid giant grows bolder." *National Elementary Principal* 51:74-8.
6. Deighton, L., ed. 1970. *Encyclopedia of Education*, Vol. III. Macmillan, New York.
7. Dowley, E. 1971. "Perspectives on early childhood education." In Anderson, B.H. & Shane, H.J. *As the Twig is Bent.* Houghton-Mifflin, Boston.
8. Final report of the National Day Care Study: *Children at the Center, 1979.* Abt Associates, Cambridge, Mass.
9. Forest, I. 1927. *Preschool Education: A historical and critical study.* Macmillan, New York.
10. Hymes, J.L. Jr., Living History Interviews, Book 2: *Care of the Children of Working Mothers.* Hacienda Press, Carmel, CA.
11. Hymes, J.L. Jr., Living History Interviews, Book 3: *Reaching Large Numbers of Children.* Hacienda Press, Carmel, CA.
12. Kamerman, S.B. and Kahn, A.J. 1977. "The day care debate: a wider view." *The Public Interest.* 54:74-86.
13. Katz, L.G. and Ward, E.H. 1978. *Ethical behavior in early childhood education.* National Association for the Education of Young Children, Washington, D.C.
14. Katz, L.G. 1980. "Mothering and teaching: some significant distinctions." In *Current Topics in Early Childhood Education*, Vol. III, L.G. Katz, ed. Ablex Publishing Corporation, Norwood, N.J.
15. Keyserling, M.D. 1979. "Overview—day care standards, past, present and future." Paper presented at the seminar on day care standards: What's Ahead, Washington, D.C. ERIC Document Reproduction Service, No. ED 172 937.
16. Keyserling, M.D. 1972. *Windows on day care.* National Council of Jewish Women, New York.
17. Omwake, E. 1979. "Assessment of the Head Start preschool education

effort." In *Project Head Start: A Legacy of the War on Poverty*, E. Zigler and J. Valentine, eds. Free Press, New York.

18. Powell, D.R. 1980. "Toward a sociological perspective of relations between parents and child care programs." In *Advances in Early Education and Day Care*, Vol. I, JAI Press, Greenwich, Conn.

19. Sponseller, D.B. and Fink, J.S. 1980. "Early childhood education: a national profile of early childhood educator's views." *Education and Urban Society.* 12:163–173.

20. Steiner, G.Y. 1976. *The Children's Cause.* The Brookings Institution, Washington, D.C.

21. Trickett, P.E. 1979. "Career development in Head Start." In *Project Head Start: A Legacy of the War on Poverty*, Free Press, New York.

INDEX

and quality of day care, 147

Lanham Act (1941), 74, 342–343, 358, 421, 460

Lanham Act Centers, 480

Larson, M., 383, 385

"Latch-key" children, 339, 457–458

Laura Spelman Rockefeller Fund, 479

Learning, as factor in adaptation, 46

Legislation, child care, 342–347 (*see also* Comprehensive Child Development Act)

    Cranston bill, 346–347, 461–462

    employment-related, 437

    Lanham Act, 74, 342–343, 358, 421, 460

    Long-Mondale bill, 287–289

    Mondale-Packwood bill, 289–291

Lein, L., 384, 395

Lewin, K., 50

Lewis, M., 37

Libassi, F. Peter, 297, 301, 302

Licensed day care centers, numbers of, 76

Licensing

    and Black children, 434

    and health services, 450

    and information and retrieval, 394

    and public school partnership, 470

Life events inventory, in developmental study, 112

Lipton, R., 47

Locus of Control scale, 206

Loewenstein, R.M., 38, 46

Long, Sen. Russell, 278, 284, 287, 288

Long-Mondale bill

    vs. administration position, 288–289

    provisions of, 287, 288

    as response to Title XX, 287–289

    veto of, 289

Louisiana, Voluntary licensing in, 433

Low-income families (*see also* Income, family)

    day care arrangements of, 122

day care programs for, 94

Lustman, S., 37

McCutcheon, B., 11

McGovern, Sen. George, 286

Maccoby, E., 169

Macrae, J., 10, 230

Main, M., 7, 105

Maladjustment, and quality of day care, 147–148 (*see also* Adjustment)

Maladjustment score, 145

Malson, M.R., 384, 395

Marble-in-the Hole task, 159

Marketplace, day care, 94

Martinez, Asst. Sec. Arabella, 297, 346, 348, 382

Massachusetts, day care regulation in, 394

Matas, L., 113

Maternal assessments, in developmental study, 112

Maternal Attitude Scale, 119

Matthews, F. David, 286

Maturation (*see also* Adjustment; Developmental study)

    of child, 36–37

    as day care issue, 38

Mayall, B., 14

Medrich, E.A., 464

Mendel, Perry, 404, 405

Mental phenomena, Prugh's functional approach to, 64–65

Methodology

    continuous nature of, 249

    randomization, 245–247

Mills, J., 231

Mills, Wilbur, 278

Milwaukee Project, 202

Mondale, Sen. Walter, 278, 284, 286, 287, 288, 289, 326, 344, 346

Mondale-Packwood bill

    passage of, 290–291

    provisions of, 289–290

    as response to Title XX, 289–290

Monitoring, and Black perspective on day care, 435

Moore, T., 11, 16, 17, 20, 110, 154

National Day Care Study on, 484
and professional attitudes, 490–491
Temperament, and response to day
care, 21
Tennessee, Division of Day Care
Licensing in, 395
Tester ratings, in Yale study, 213
Thomas, A., 37
Three-year-olds
and issue of attachment and day
care, 105
studies of, 7
Title I, ESEA, preschool, 318
Title IV-A program
for Black-administered day care, 442
and FIDCR, 276
Title IV-B program
enrollment in, 318
expenditures in, 318
Title XX program, 359–360
background of, 282–283
capping of, 310
Congressional action on, 284
cost analysis of, 364
current status of, 304
and day care for Black families,
423, 429–430
development of, 283–284
as direct child care provider, 317
enrollment in, 318
expenditures for, 318
and FIDCR standards, 409
and inflation, 262
on information and referral, 386
limitations of, 426
and Long-Mondale bill, 287–290
low-income focus of, 317
and Mondale-Packwood bill,
289–290
and proprietary child care, 403
provisions of, 283–285
reaction to, 285–291
reporting under, 311
sliding fee scales for, 438
and spending trends, 428
standards in, 282
supplemented by tax credit,
365–366

Toys, child's developing interest in, 44
Tradeoff analysis, 88, 90
Treasury Department, on Title XX,
284
Trickett, P., 184, 196, 489
Turnover, staff, in determining quality,
410
Two-year-olds
day care adjustment of, 26
and issue of attachment and day
care, 105

Unionization, 489–490
United Way, I&R activities of, 391,
396, 398
Upbringing, polymatric vs. monomatric, 15–17

"Vacation school," 459
Vandell, D., 10, 11
Vaughn, B.E., 106, 107, 111, 231
Veneman, John, 281
Verbal attention-seeking score, 159

Waelder, R., 48
Wages, in proprietary vs. nonprofit
centers, 406–407
Wandersman, L.P., 185, 197
Waters, E., 104
Weikart, D.P., 184
Weil, A., 38
Weinberger, Casper, 284, 285
Weiner, S., 409
Welfare reform
and affordability of child care, 357
and child care, 415
and Nixon administration, 343–344
Wellesley College Center for Re-
search on Women, School Age
Child Care Project of, 458
Werner, 50
Wertheimer, 50
Westinghouse Study, 277
Wheelock College, 471
White, Burton, L., 47, 200

DATE DUE